A HISTORY OF
SURINAME

sidestonepress

.

A HISTORY OF
SURINAME

HANS BUDDINGH'

Published by Sidestone Press, Leiden
www.sidestone.com

Lay-out & cover design: Sidestone Press
Photograph cover: Railway station in Paramaribo, 1925-1927. Unknown
photographer. Rijksmuseum, Amsterdam, public domain via Wikimedia
Commons.

ISBN 978-94-6426-139-4 (softcover)
ISBN 978-94-6426-140-0 (hardcover)
ISBN 978-94-6426-141-7 (PDF e-book)

CONTENTS

New Amsterdam

Nieuw
Nickerie

Skeldon

Totness

Paramaribo

Nieuw Amsterdam

Galibi Nature
Reserve

Groningen

Wageningen

Lelydorp

Paranam

Moengo

Albina

Saint-Laurent
du Maroni

GUYANA

Bitagron

Jodensavanne

Apoera

Brownsweg

Brokopondo

FRENCH
GUIANA

Raleighvallen
Nature Reserve

Brownsberg
Nature Park

(FRANCE)

Pokigron

Brokopondo
Reservoir

Benzdorp

Demerara

Courantyne

Nickerie

Coppename

Saramacca

Suriname

Commewijne

Maroni

Mana

Berbice

Kabalebo

Lucie

Suriname

Tapanahony

Lawa

Essequibo

Courantyne

New

Paloemeu

Oelemari

Litani

(disputed territory)

(disputed
territory)

Kutari

Sipaliwini

Paru do Oeste

Maroni

Cafuini

BRAZIL

Paru

N

50 Kilometers

50 Miles

Suriname

Via Wikimedia Commons.

PREFACE

'One sees amidst the verdure the golden glimmer of the fruit of a lemon tree, while birds feathered in a thousand different colours show an overwhelming richness of plumage. And add to this all that man has created to further enhance the charms of this enchanting coast. Buildings whose graceful appearance rivals that of European dwellings rise up on the banks of the rivers. Creeks irrigate the land in all directions.'[1]

Such was the way the Belgian painter, commercial agent, ship's captain-*cum*-globetrotter P.J. Benoit described his first impressions when visiting Suriname in circa 1830. The account presented in his *Voyage à Surinam; description des possessions néerlandaises dans la Guyane* (Brussels, 1839) does not differ a great deal from all I encountered in 1979, when visiting Suriname as a tourist for the first time and having already become acquainted in the Netherlands with migrants from the former Dutch colony. It was indeed a rather strange experience to be able to converse in the Dutch language while staying at fringes of the Amazon rainforest. Did not Naipaul correctly state in his book *The Middle Passage: Impression of Five Colonial Societies - British, French and Dutch in the West Indies and South America* that 'Suriname feels only as a tropical, tulip-less extension of Holland'?[2] Often reality does turn out to be more complicated.

In 1981 I was given the opportunity, as a budding journalist, to gain a better understanding of Suriname. The desire to fathom this country was indeed reinforced by a series of dramatic developments I witnessed from that moment on, to wit, military coups, political assassinations, an internal war and the state's top leaders being involved in drug related crimes. And, all this within a multi-ethnic society experiencing the outcome of centuries of colonial domination and all its ramifications.

The present publication is the result of my journalistic curiosity, historical interest and an attempt at interpretation. It consists of the English translation (plus a modest extension) of the 8th edition of *De geschiedenis van Suriname*, first published in 1995.

Leo Morpurgo, the late editor-in-chief of the daily newspaper *De Ware Tijd* and the pioneer of independent journalism in Suriname, was the first to patiently explain the kaleidoscopic Surinamese reality to me. Without realizing it himself, he thus provided the initial impetus for *De geschiedenis van Suriname* and now its English rendition. Furthermore, my late colleague at the daily newspaper *NRC Handelsblad* Frans van Klaveren must surely be mentioned here as a source of inspiration, too. I am also grateful to Vincent Mentzel not only for kindly providing a number of photographs to be included in the present publication but also for his much valued companionship experienced during our trips to and across Suriname.

In addition, I would like to thank Marcel Haenen, Rosemarijn Hoefte, Sjoerd de Jong, Humphrey E. Lamur, Peter Meel and Gert Oostindie who since the publication of the first Dutch edition onwards have carefully read (parts of) the text. Fokke

---

1   Benoit 1980 [1839], 27.
2   Naipaul 1962, 164.

Gerritsma, Willum Morsch and Anita Slagter skillfully produced graphics as well as maps. Erlan Sleur, Edward Troon and George Findlay kindly provided several photographs. I am also indebted to Carl Haarnack who kindly offered me a valuable picture included in his remarkable private antiquarian collection titled Buku-Bibliotheca Surinamica. I must also mention Henk ter Borg, publisher at Uitgeverij Nieuw Amsterdam, for encouraging me to continuously update *De geschiedenis van Suriname*. Last but not least, I express my gratitude to Peter Richardus, who with his wide-ranging expertise contributed more to *A History of Suriname* than merely a translation into English.

Antwerp, December 2022.

CHAPTER 1
Original inhabitants and the first colonisation

In 1529, the Portuguese cartographer Diogo Ribeiro (died 1533) drew one of the first maps of Suriname. This Spanish sea map only shows the shoreline and the estuaries.[1] The Marowijne River is named Rio Baxo (Low River), the Suriname River is referred to as Rio Salado (Salt River), the Coppename as Rio Verde (Green River) and the Corantijn as Rio del Places (River of the Sandbank).

The European discovery of Guiana, the coastal area located between the Orinoco and Amazone Rivers, is attributed to the Spanish explorer Alonso de Ojeda (1465-1515). In 1499, this companion of Christopher Columbus (1451-1506) sailed past Guiana towards the Northwest. The name Guiana has native roots and probably means: land of currents. Ribeiro's map indicates that nothing of value had been found here. Seafarers therefore took little interest in the 'Wild Coast'.

All this changed when a city of gold was presumed to be discovered in Guiana. Amerindians had handed down the legend of Lake Parime and the wealthy capital of Manoa, the seat of a king dressed in gold robes. The roofs of houses were made of gold, too. The Spaniards, who had already discovered goldmines elsewhere on the South American continent during the early 16th century, initially searched for El Dorado (The Golden One) in the Orinoco River region. Sir Walter Raleigh (1552-1618), the English nobleman, writer, courtier-*cum*-explorer, who during a voyage of exploration had navigated the Orinoco River, sent Capt. Lawrence Keymis (died 1618) to Guiana in 1596. The Amsterdam cartographer Jodocus Hondius (1563-1612) utilised their reports for his *Nieuwe Caerte van het wonderbaer ende goudrijcke landt Guiana* (New Map of the wonderful land Guiana abounding in gold).[2]

On this map Hondius also included Lake Parime, which would never be found. Rivers are given Amerindian names, very similar to their present ones.[3] Raleigh's account entitled *The Discoverie of the Large, Rich, and Bewtiful Empire of Guiana* [...] (London 1596) was to entice many to sail from Western Europe for the Wild Coast.[4]

The government official Abraham Cabeliau (1571-1645) wrote the earliest Dutch travelogue on Guiana.[5] His report dated 1598 is addressed to the States General, the parliament of the Dutch Republic, and deals with the exploration of several rivers. Sailors from the provinces of Holland and Zeeland as well as from France and England established contacts with the Amerindian population. Many trading posts were founded on river banks. Europeans offered to exchange axes, knives, nails, needles, shirts, mirrors, beads and guns. In return they received gold, resin, dyes, hammocks, species of wood, such as the much sought-after snakewood (aka letterwood). Towards the end of the 16th century, Dutch merchants had already founded trading posts on the Essequibo and Pomeroon Rivers.

---

1   For this and other maps of Suriname, see: Koeman 1973.
2   Ibid.
3   Wekker 1990, 7-24.
4   Harlow 1971 (repr. 1932); Parker 2015, 9-64.
5   Lichtveld & Voorhoeve 1980, 29-33.

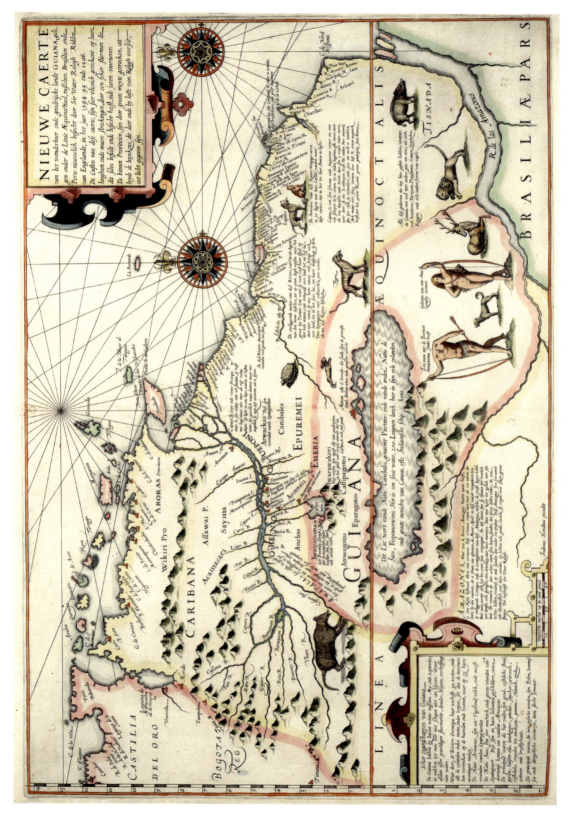

Figure 1.1. A hand-coloured map of Guiana drawn by Jodocus Hondius in 1598. Public domain, via Wikimedia Commons.

A History of Suriname

In 1613 such a post had been established at the present site of Paramaribo, the capital of Suriname. This trading post, founded by the merchants Dirck Claasz van Saenen (1560-1653) and Nicolaas Baliestel is mentioned in a notary's act dated 31 January 1617. On that day a steersman named Cornelis Jansz. Scheur appeared before the notary Frederick van Banchem to state he had sailed up the Surrenant River in 1613 to go ashore near a village named Parmurbo. Scheur had come to testify, on behalf of these two merchants, with regard to a certain Christoffel Albertsz. (1588-1612) who had assassinated an Amerindian. This event had provoked retaliation, in the course of which the ship cook was murdered.[6]

The majority of trading posts consisted of not more than a few wooden houses surrounded by fields producing food crops for immediate consumption. Wooden palisades had often been constructed in order to protect against possible attackers, be it Amerindians or Europeans. At that time no colonisation had taken place, although attempts to do so were witnessed in Suriname during the first half of the 17th century. These efforts failed due to either infectious diseases among settlers, attacks by Amerindians or other misfortunes.[7]

In 1621, establishing the Dutch West India Company (WIC) led to a shift of interest within the Republic of the Seven United Provinces towards Caribbean islands, Brazil and North America.[8] The politics behind that development were: the States General had granted the monopoly of the transatlantic trade to the WIC, which initially served as an instrument of war against the Spaniards. The plan to strike out at Spain in the Americas was initiated by Willem Usselincx (1567-1647). This Flemish Dutch merchant had fled from the Spaniards, after the fall of Antwerp in 1585, to move to Amsterdam. After all, King Philip II of Spain (1527-1598) applied resources from the Americas in order to finance the war waged against the Republic.

Much to Usselincx's disappointment the WIC was engaged in privateering, not in colonisation. In the eyes of the directors, who governed the WIC on behalf of the participating towns and provinces, privateering was much more profitable thanks to the quick gains. Piet Pietersz Hein's (1577-1629) conquest of the Spanish treasure fleet in 1628 was undoubtedly the WIC's largest trophy.

After several years the WIC's policy changed somewhat. By order of the board of directors, referred to as *De Heeren XIX* (the Nineteen Gentlemen) a title based on their number, the WIC conquered Pernambuco (Northeastern Brazil) in 1629.[9] This region had formally been Spanish territory since 1580, after Portugal had been subjected to the Spanish crown. In the course of Count Johan Maurits van Nassau Siegen's (1604-1679) governance this Brazilian colony prospered greatly, particularly thanks to sugar cultivation. A shortage of labour however became acute after many Black slaves ran away from the plantations. The WIC therefore decided to take up trading in slaves. To this end a flotilla, which had been equipped in Pernambuco, conquered the São Jorge da Mina Castle (in present-day Elmina, Ghana), which served as the

---

6   Van Brakel 1914, 83-86.
7   For an overview of the initial period of the Dutch on the Wild Coast, see: Goslinga 1971.
8   Den Heijer 2013, 13-33; Emmer 1981, 71-97; Fatah-Black 2015, 16-40.
9   For an in-depth survey on the Dutch in Brazil, see: Boxer 1957; Den Heijer 2013, 33-51.

main Portuguese depot for slaves on the African coast.[10] Johan Maurits however resigned in 1644, as the WIC was not prepared to provide sufficient financial means in order to maintain the military defence of Pernambuco which eventually again fell into Portuguese hands in 1654.

Following the expansion of its activity, *De Heeren XIX* had placed the WIC under the supervision of chambers where the interests of Dutch towns and provinces would be better represented. The majority of the properties located in Guiana were granted to the province of Zeeland. After all, Zeelanders had already established trading posts here, the most important of which were located on the Essequibo and Pomeroon Rivers. Several properties had been declared a *patroonskolonie*. They were modelled on the Portuguese *capitanias* whereby a wealthy family became the patron and was allowed to run the colony on its own account. From 1627 on, Berbice had been a *patroonskolonie* privately governed by Abraham van Pere, a merchant from Zeeland.

After the loss of Northeast Brazil, the WIC wished to limit its activities to (slave) trade. Investments in costly colonisations were considered too great a risk. The English were thus the first to establish a colony in Suriname to which, in 1651, the then Governor of Barbados Sir Francis Willoughby (1605-1666) dispatched, on his own account, a ship carrying 100 colonists as well as a number of slaves originating from this Caribbean island.[11] The shortage of land on Barbados, where colonists mainly cultivated sugar, had already encouraged Sir Francis to examine opportunities for setting up plantations across Suriname which, thanks to experienced settlers, soon became a flourishing colony. The then capital Thorarica was situated *c.*75 km upstream on the Suriname River. Further northwards, the then Governor of Suriname William Byam (died 1672) had built Fort Willoughby in order to protect the colony against invaders.

The Zeelanders must have observed these developments with a certain degree of jealousy. Next, during the Second Anglo-Dutch War (1665-1667), the States of Zeeland (i.e., the provincial government) equipped a fleet comprising seven ships under command of Abraham Crijnssen (died 1669). In 1667, he conquered the colony of Suriname during a surprise attack, hereby retaliating the demolishing of those settlements Zeelanders had founded on the Essequibo and Pomeroon Rivers.[12] These acts of destruction had been carried out on Sir Francis Willoughby's order given during the First Anglo-Dutch War (1652-1654). Built on a location already known as Paramaribo, Fort Willoughby was renamed Fort Zeelandia.

Abraham Crijnssen had received the order from Zeeland to not only occupy the Wild Coast but also to attack other English properties located in the West Indies and along the Eastern coast of North America. After a triumphant mission, during which the isle of Tobago had been conquered, too, Crijnssen returned to Zeeland with around ten confiscated English merchant ships. They were laden with tobacco, the most successful cash crop grown in the Colony of Virginia (North America).[13]

---

10 For details on Portugal's deep, gold-driven involvement with Africa and its local rulers, evident as early as during the 15th century, see: French 2021, 66-101.

11 Parker 2015, 69-88; for further details on Anglo-Dutch relationships during the colonization of Suriname, see: Zijlstra 2015, 25-34,

12 Warnsinck 1936, 10-40; Parker 2015, 219-232.

13 Warnsinck 1936, 68,74.

A History of Suriname

On 31 July 1667 France, Denmark-Norway, England and the United Provinces (i.e., the Dutch Republic) signed the Treaty of Breda, which marked the fact that the English lost Suriname as well as their other assets on the Wild Coast but that they did acquire Nieuw-Amsterdam, the future New York.[14]

According to an English nobleman named George Warren, a resident of Suriname for 3 years, c.500 families populated this colony in 1667. Between 40 and 50 of these families possessed sugar-works described as 'yielding no small profit to the owners'.[15] In total, white colonists and slaves numbered c.4,000 souls.[16] At that time the number of Amerindians must have been much higher. The estimates most frequently applied here derive from mid-17th-century reports on Guiana forwarded by an Englishman, Major John Scott (1634?-1696).[17] According to Scott, c.800 Carib and 1,400 Paracutto families were living in the vicinity of the Marowijne River, whereas in access of 5,000 Carib families populated the banks of the Suriname, Commewijne, Saramacca, Coppename and Corantijn Rivers. Moreover, 1,400 Tuuromak resided on the banks of the Saramacca and Upper Suriname Rivers whereas more than 1,200 Sapayo populated the Upper Corantijn region. Approximately 8,000 Arawak families populated an area west of the Corantijn as well as the Berbice and Essequibo regions. According to maps dating from that era, the Arawak were also located east of the Marowijne River. Numerous names can be encountered in time-honoured records pertaining to these diverse Indigenous communities, the majority of which can probably be traced back to the Caribs and Arawak. Scott's data reveal that Suriname was mainly inhabited by Caribs.

Based on prehistoric finds one assumes that the first Amerindians arrived in southern Suriname between 9,000 and 10,000 years ago.[18] Migration from Alaska to Central and South America by these Palaeolithic hunter gatherers, who had crossed the Bering Strait, began c.12,000 years ago. Amerindian arrowheads and other artefacts have been excavated at sites spread across the Sipaliwini savannah. After Amerindians arrived here this savannah expanded rapidly across southern Suriname, possibly because they set fire to the savannah forest in order to facilitate hunts after which they may have left.

The definitive settlement of Amerindians in Suriname took place when the Arawak people arrived in c.500 CE. They had travelled from the West, to enter the coastal plain of Guiana, hereby presumably displacing other ethnic groups.

The migration of the Arawak, a gradual and prolonged process, had begun much earlier in the Amazon region. In c.3,000 BCE, Amerindian ethnic groups located in the Central Amazon Basin had succeeded in establishing a stable existence by means of sedentary agriculture, manioc being the main crop. Thanks to these favourable conditions the population increased rapidly thus requiring fresh agricultural land. The Arawak now moved upstream because other Indigenous peoples occupied the lower reaches of the Amazon River. Via the Rio Negro and the Orinoco River, they

---

14   Parker 2015, 233-245.
15   Warren 1667, 17.
16   Wolbers 1861, 34; Zijlstra 2014, 90.
17   Abbenhuis 1943a, 93-94; Van der Linde 1966, 37.
18   For the source of these figures and further details, see: Bubberman 1974, 1-9; Janssen 1974, 10-20; Bruijning & Voorhoeve 1977, 506-515.

Figure 1.2. Drawing by
J.G. Stedman (orig. 1790)
portraying an Arawak
woman with a parrot,
which she had stunned by
means of a blunt arrow.
J.G. Stedman 1987.

eventually reached the Caribbean Sea to then transmigrate to islands. Pottery finds reveal that Arawak inhabited self-constructed mounds of clay located in the swampy coastal zone of West Suriname where elevated farmland was created near Hertenrits.

In *c.*1100 CE, the Arawak were not only forced to leave their habitat but also to give up their sedentary agricultural system following an invasion by Caribs whose migration had also begun in the Amazon Basin. This resettling had indeed taken on the nature of a conquest, as the Arawak did already occupy the best farmland. After a number of Caribs had set off towards the North along the Orinoco River, those who eventually reached Suriname had travelled via the lower reaches of the Amazon River and next along the Atlantic Coast towards the Northwest. Fights between Caribs and Arawak were on-going when the Europeans arrived in the Western Hemisphere.

Sir Francis's colonisation of Suriname had not encountered any resistance from Amerindians.[19] English settlers, in accordance with all the colonists inhabiting other parts of this continent, took astute advantage of hostilities rising between Indigenous peoples. Caribs acted as intermediaries when trading 'red' slaves, while exempt from becoming slaves themselves. They sold Arawak prisoners of war in exchange for European goods. Furthermore, Caribs assisted colonists by either capturing or killing runaway slaves, other Black people and Amerindians. Steady streams of immigrating

---

19   Parker 2015, 96-102.

A History of Suriname

colonists led to a military advantage for the white population, thus further reducing a risk of being attacked by Amerindians. Not only did English colonists settle down in Suriname, a small group of Jewish settlers arrived here from Cayenne (French Guiana) in 1664.[20] This favourable demographic development came to an end after an epidemic of an unknown nature had struck.

Naval commander Abraham Crijnssen gained control over a colony not only weakened by this epidemic. Two months after the Treaty of Breda had been signed, an English fleet had once again arrived at Fort Zeelandia.[21] Governor William Willoughby of Barbados (c.1616-1673) had equipped these ships. This brother of the now deceased Sir Francis was perhaps unaware of the existence of the Peace of Breda. It is more probable however that he wished to recuperate his family property.[22] After all, King Charles II of England (1630-1685) had placed Suriname in the hands of a 'patron', to wit, the Willoughby brothers. A garrison of 120 soldiers which Crijnssen had left behind in Fort Zeelandia proved no match for Willoughby's fleet. English sailors captured Fort Zeelandia while both warring parties were still negotiating the terms of surrender. Colonists had to witness their sugar mills being destroyed or removed. Commander Maurits de Rame along with a number of his troops were transferred to the isle of Barbados. Zeeland-based authorities had meanwhile dispatched a fleet under Capt. Willem Hendricksen's command to Suriname in order to enforce the implementation of the Treaty of Breda. Nevertheless damages to the Dutch colony only increased when William Willoughby's son Henry interrupted his raids executed elsewhere along the Wild Coast in order to sail up the Suriname River. Houses, sugar mills and sugar plantations were destroyed. Cattle, slaves and sugar were transported to Barbados. An instruction forwarded to William Willoughby by Charles II, who felt bound by the Treaty of Breda, to reimburse the inflicted losses was most probably ignored.[23]

In April 1668, Suriname was peacefully returned to Zeelandic hands, be it after Crijnssen himself had set off with a fleet towards Paramaribo. However, even by means of extensive tax concessions, he could not prevent any English colonists from departing with most of their slaves, even after being ransacked by Lieutenant General Henry Willoughby (1640-1669), Sir Francis Willoughby's nephew. In the course of the following years, a majority of the English colonists gradually left together with their slaves, in particular for Jamaica.[24] A vindictive William Willoughby had encouraged those who had stayed behind to relocate as well.

Incoming colonists were not very motivated to settle in Suriname due to all the uncertainty. Moreover, a dispute between the provinces of Zeeland and Holland, in particular Amsterdam, concerning the administrative responsibility for Suriname hampered reinforcing this colony.[25] Zeelanders, having made all these efforts, wished to keep Suriname for themselves. The Republic's parliament (henceforth the States General) however pointed out it had financed the entire endeavour. Moreover, the

---

20   Wolbers 1861, 37; Parker 2015, 132-133.
21   Parker, 2015, 43-44, 237-242.
22   Ibid., 231-232.
23   Kesler 1930, 117-118; Parker 2015, 241-243.
24   Zijlstra 2015, 42, 52-59.
25   Van der Meiden 1987, 23; Wolbers 1861, 46-47.

States of Holland felt the WIC should obtain the authority over Suriname, in which case the province of Holland would also have its say. Zeeland strongly opposed this solution, not least because the WIC was now almost bankrupt due to excessive spending and dividend payments and thus not in a position to resolve a large number of issues. In the end, Zeeland held on to administrative responsibilities for Suriname, thereby allowing ships from Holland to sail for the colony. Needless to say, the supremacy of the States General was recognized.

Crijnssen officiated as acting Governor of Suriname until 1669. In order to keep the peace he implemented a policy of reconciliation towards the Caribs, who enjoyed a large degree of freedom during English rule. Next, when Caribs complained about assaults carried out by Arawak living in the vicinity of the Berbice River (Guyana), Crijnssen not only requested the local commander to terminate these attacks but also did not permit Caribs to continue to aggress any Arawak. His successor Philip Julius Lichtenberg (1637-1678) also understood the need for good relations with Caribs. In a letter, dated 18 March 1669, addressed to the States of Zeeland he wrote:

> '[...] *will as much as possible through all means of civility and politeness that can serve to that end, try to oblige them and do my best to learn the language* [...] *which brings the English great advantage* [...].'[26]

Successive governors were nonetheless unable to stop these hostilities. Caribs in particular acted very independently as the conduct of white traders infuriated them. Disputes on prices and payments occurred on a regular basis. In 1675, after Amerindians had murdered two traders during an argument held near the Coppename River, Governor Pieter Versterre (died 1677) decided to carry out a punitive expedition. The Amerindian chief managed to escape and then threatened to retaliate.[27] In Cayenne, Amerindians had proven that such threats had to be taken seriously. They had once even driven French settlers out of Guiana for a certain period of time.

The departure of even more colonists had further weakened Suriname. Here in 1675, according to Versterre, only 120 English families remained, of which approximately 80 wished to leave.[28] In a letter addressed to the States of Zeeland dated 16 December 1675, he pointed to the danger caused by English colonists when taking their Amerindian slaves with them:

> '[...] *the Amerindians, a people without reason, will immediately believe that their friends or children have been sold as slaves, as the Amerindians also say that the English have spread the word we would have sold them as slaves* [*to the English*].'[29]

---

26 Zeeland Archives, ZA, 2.1., 2035-124. These and other 17th- and 18th-century texts quoted in the present publication were originally written in the Dutch language common to that era. They have been translated in order to acquire the most literal result.

27 Buve 1966, 16.

28 Letter sent to an unknown recipient and dated 4 July 1675, Zeeland Archives, ZA, 2.1., 2035-260.

29 Zeeland Archives, ZA, 2.1., 2035-271.

A History of Suriname

In this letter Versterre suggested that such rumours had caused the murder of the two (English) traders early in 1675. In a previous letter, he had referred to the low number of men left capable of fighting, to wit, 134 Dutch, 57 Jews and a garrison comprising 116 troops and four sailors.[30]

The Caribs must have been well aware of Suriname's limited colonial defence capacity. When during the second half of 1678 Amerindians rather unexpectedly initiated a guerrilla war, this posed a direct threat to the colony's survival. Caribs almost simultaneously launched attacks directed at plantations founded at various locations.[31] Ten colonists were killed near the Perica River and *c*.30 were slain on the banks of the Para Kreek. Casualties were incurred near Thorarica too.[32] This precarious situation forced colonists residing in the vicinity of the Para Kreek to seek refuge in Paramaribo. Elsewhere attempts were made to defend themselves, too. An unnamed Jewish colonist reported that *c*.30 Amerindian 'ringleaders' had been hanged. His letter, dated 18 January 1679, also reports that African slaves participated in the colonial expeditionary force, mentioning '100 negroes'.[33]

Amerindians had also plotted a raid on Paramaribo, but this plan had leaked after the detention of a half-Amerindian spy, named Anthony Barbier, who was hanged after confessing.[34] Initially Amerindians also assaulted Black slaves but soon changed their tactics, now encouraging slaves to run away from the plantations. Slaves increasingly responded to this appeal, not least as a result of a dire food scarcity due to the guerrilla war.

Conditions in Suriname were chaotic when Governor Johannes Heinsius (1625-1680) reached its shores in December 1678. Commander Abel Thisso, having served as interim governor, informed Heinsius upon his arrival by means of a letter. In it he not only described dozens of massacred colonists but also that the objective of Amerindians was to 'totally extirpate the entire Dutch and Jewish Nation here'.[35] As the fear had become great, a number of colonists, including Thisso, had already retreated on to ships moored on the Suriname River. A few months later, on 3 May 1679, Heinsius reported to the States of Zeeland on the Amerindians that

'[...] *it is certain that they have shouted that our people who had come with ships, should leave with ships again, that the land belonged to them* [...].'[36]

Heinsius, the incoming Governor, had no prior information on the condition the colony was in. In a letter to the States General, dated 21 August 1679, he wrote

---

30 Ibid.; for annexes listing names, see: ZA 2035-261 and 2035-262; for the letter sent to the States of Zeeland dated 25 March 1675, see: ZA, 2.1., 2035-249/250; for the annex listing the names of soldiers, see: ZA 2.1. 2035-251.
31 Buve 1966, 14-26; Hira 1982, 38-47; Wekker 1993, 174-186.
32 As stated in a letter sent by commander Abel Thisso to the incoming Governor Johannes Heinsius dated 18 December 1678, Zeeland Archives, ZA, 2.1., 2035-282.
33 Zeeland Archives, ZA, 2.1., 2035-326.
34 As stated in a letter sent by Commander Abel Thisso to the incoming Governor Johannes Heinsius dated 18 December 1678, Zeeland Archives, ZA, 2.1., 2035-282; for more information on Anthony Barbier's trial, see: ZA 2.1.2035-307-309.
35 Ibid., ZA, 2.1., 2035-282.
36 Ibid., ZA, 2.1., 2035-328.

to have 'unexpectedly' found Suriname to be engaged in an 'open war with the Amerindians'.[37] To his surprise only 400 colonists and 30 soldiers were left in the colony. Its economy had almost come to a standstill.

He was nevertheless able to prevent immediate danger. Experience acquired as a government official serving in Brazil (where colonists had to cope with a siege carried out by Portuguese and their Amerindian allies) will have assisted him. Having commissioned the construction of a palisade surrounding Paramaribo, within which growing patches could be created to ensure the food supply, he furthermore decided to close down the Para Kreek in order to prevent Amerindians from reaching Paramaribo. A ban on leaving the colony was also imposed. This necessary step was taken because the Governor of Barbados continued to persuade colonists to migrate to this island. The English were still seeking the collapse of the Dutch colony. It was thus no surprise that Heinsius's request for food to be sent to Suriname from Barbados had been refused.[38] All these measures did by no means suffice to end the guerrilla war. The largest obstacle was a lack of manpower. In the aforementioned letter addressed to the States General, Heinsius petitions for a dispatch of between 300 and 400 troops, adding the implication that Suriname should possibly be abandoned in case the Republic would not be able to provide any help:

'[...] *giving the colony in the hands of a Christian potentate rather than let it be consumed by the bloodthirsty Indians* [...].'[39]

Heinsius wrote that colonists had merely considered this option and also referred to the visit a Jewish colonist had paid to Barbados asking for military assistance, while offering to cede the colony of Suriname to Barbados in case the Republic failed to send troops within 10 months. Underlining he had not ordered to do so, however, by mentioning the possibility of losing Suriname Heinsius apparently wished to put pressure on the States General. In due course a modest force of 150 men, which the Admiralty of Zeeland paid for, arrived in Suriname. Due to a dispute on funding it had taken the Republic as long as 12 months to deal with this issue.[40]

Meanwhile Heinsius had requested the Commander of Berbice named Lucas Caudri to see to it that not only the Arawak once again turned on the Caribs but also that Arawak reinforcements including white soldiers were sent to Paramaribo. Caudri responded positively. Nonetheless the military assistance failed to produce any results due to the unwillingness of the Arawak to fight. No doubt their fear of the Carib Amerindians' combat skills played a role here.[41] Even during the march from the colony of Berbice towards Paramaribo these Arawak reinforcements refused to attack Caribs residing close to the Coppename River. The Arawak chief named Warray had even held a friendly conversation with Priary, the Carib chief. No wonder expeditions to the Para Kreek and Thorarica failed. Heinsius was more successful

---

37   Molendijk-Dijk 1992, 15-17.
38   As stated in a letter sent by Governor Jonathan Atkins of Barbados to Johannes Heinsius dated 28 May 1679, Zeeland Archives, ZA 2.1., 2035-331.
39   Zijlstra 2015, 83.
40   Ibid., 84; Van der Meiden 1987, 28-29.
41   Buve 1966, 19-21; Hira 1982, 42-46.

when establishing relations with Caribs living near the Corantijn and Marowijne Rivers, hereby isolating their fellow tribesmen in Central Suriname. In early 1679, the Carib chief Amasabo, while staying near the Corantijn, had expressed his willingness to set off for Paramaribo accompanied by auxiliaries. Initially several Caribs were opposed to reconciling with colonists, but Amasabo brought this resistance to an end, be it with the help of white colonial forces. In April 1680, after the arrival of military reinforcements from the Republic, a small garrison was positioned along the Corantijn River, thus controlling West Suriname.

Negotiations with Caribs held at the Marowijne River were much tougher, mainly due to unfair practices upheld by certain white tradesmen. It was not without reason that Heinsius wrote to the States of Zeeland, on 24 March 1679, that colonists who demanded the punishment of Amerindian chiefs by means of assassination, were 'not considering that they themselves are the cause' of these attacks.[42] This was not the only frustration Heinsius had felt towards attitudes displayed by planters. Not siding with them (as had been the case with his predecessors), he complained about efforts planters made in order to evade taxes, at a time Suriname was in danger. Planters who did pay their taxes were described as 'crazy to pay the governor'.[43] Heinsius further even suggested that the States of Zeeland should ban a number of unwilling plantation owners from the colony and then sell their property, in order to set an example.[44]

Eventually peace could be achieved during 1680. Moreover, Johannes Heinsius's demise, in April 1680, proved no obstacle to implementing his battle plan. It aimed at exhausting Caribs residing in the Saramacca, Coppename and Suriname River regions by means of the scorched earth strategy. Dozens of white soldiers, escorted by their newly found Amerindian allies, repeatedly carried out expeditions whereby settlements as well as growing patches were destroyed. Captured Amerindians were usually hanged on trees in the forest. Rebellious Caribs now no longer posed a real threat.

It was not until 1686 that Governor Cornelis van Aerssen van Sommelsdijck (1637-1688) was able to make peace with any remaining Amerindian ethnic groups. According to this agreement, Amerindians could no longer be held in slavery, unless they had committed crimes.[45] This measure however did not apply to runaway Black slaves, most of whom had joined up with Amerindians. They were to be of concern to Suriname for a much longer time.

---

42   Letter sent by Johannes Heinsius to the States of Zeeland dated 24 March 1679, Zeeland Archives, ZA 2.1., 2035-317/318; see also: Zijlstra 2015, 80.

43   Zijlstra 2015, 143; as stated in a letter sent by Heinsius to the States of Zeeland dated 1 January 1680, Zeeland Archives, ZA 2.1., 2035-377.

44   Zijlstra 2015, 142; as stated in a letter sent by Johannes Heinsius to the States of Zeeland dated 24 March 1679, Zeeland Archives, Z.A. 2.1., 2035-317/318.

45   Wolbers 1861, 63.

CHAPTER 2
The Society of Suriname

2.1 Introduction

Not much remained of the vision of a 'new Brazil' after Governor Johannes Heinsius passed away in 1680. The exodus of English colonists and the guerrilla war waged by Amerindians had presented Zeeland with serious problems. Little wonder this province was keen to withdraw from the Dutch colony on the Wild Coast. Amsterdam-based merchants, having started a lobby in order to secure their interests, urged the WIC's Amsterdam Chamber to take over Suriname.

A committee appointed by the Governing Council (*Vroedschap*) of Amsterdam had already concluded that, within 5 to 6 years, between 60 and 80 ships could sail for Suriname annually returning with sugar, snakewood and tobacco.[1]

Amsterdam (i.e., its powerful merchants and bankers) did nonetheless forward a number of demands hereby insisting that (a) sailing for Suriname should be available to all residents of the Republic of the United Provinces, (b) tax rates could only be half the level Zeeland was imposing on colonists, (c) taxes could only be raised with the consent of a government of Suriname, which included the governor as well as 'the most honourable colonists' and (d) the States General should furthermore support between 300 and 400 troops stationed in the colony, thus alleviating the WIC's financial burden. All these provisos would become the core of the 1682 charter (*octrooi*), which may be considered Suriname's first constitution.[2]

The WIC was not unreservedly positive about taking over this colony. In 1674, it had been dissolved after it was unable to repay its debts. In that same year, however, because of commercial interests, yet another WIC was founded. As its number of directors had been reduced to ten, its name: *De Heeren X* (the Gentlemen X).[3] It was no surprise that representatives of Holland and Zeeland appointed to serve in this newly-established WIC were concerned about the high costs related to such a takeover. In due course, after pressure from the Grand Pensionary (*Raadpensionaris*) of Holland and Zeeland, the most important official within the United Provinces, an agreement to transfer the colony was reached between *De Heeren X* and the States of Zeeland. In order to address concerns the WIC's representatives of Amsterdam and Zeeland expressed, it was agreed that Suriname's benefitting from this company's cash money would be subject to authorisation by its key participants.[4]

The States of Holland had meanwhile discussed the concept of the 1682 charter. Their precipitation was understandable. Holland had always challenged Zeeland's ownership of Suriname. For, in Holland's view this colony was a matter of the States General, the members of which endorsed the aforementioned charter on 23 September 1682.[5] In its preamble, the States General stressed the WIC should not acquire a trading post but a colony thus implying it should not chase after

---

1   Van der Meiden 1987, 31.
2   Ibid.
3   Den Heijer 2013, 107-118.
4   Van der Meiden 1987, 32.
5   For the entire text of this charter, see: Wolbers 1861, 834-845.

immediate profits, but invest first 'to in the course of many years enjoy the fruits of its advanced funds and labour'.[6]

The States General did in fact not quite fully realise how this endeavour would fare. Until that moment Holland had merely conquered and not founded any trading posts. Brazil had fallen in the hands of the Portuguese. The WIC having traded, hijacked ships and created large profits now suddenly faced the mission to develop a 'considerable Colony'.[7] We also read in the 1682 charter:

'If initially one treats the colonists kindly and even helps them, and gives them total reassurance they will [...] not be exhausted by burdens and duties, when reaching a state of resources and prosperity [...], a Colony [...] starting out small will in no time be turned [...] into an extraordinary and great achievement.'

And, all that of course:

'[...] with the gracious approval and blessing of God Almighty [...]'.[8]

This charter comprised 32 articles and regulated the administrative organisation in Suriname as well as relations with the Republic. It was further designed in order to provide sufficient guarantees to colonists and those trading with the colony. Only the slave trade was fully reserved for the WIC.

To increase the appeal of Suriname to colonists, they were exempted from all taxes during the first decade (1682-1692), with the exception of a charge amounting to 3 guilders for each arriving and departing ship, and 2.5 per cent for all wares sold at the weigh house. In addition, a head tax consisting of 50 pounds of sugar per person was imposed on white colonists as well as on people of colour and Black people. Other charges could only be imposed with consent of the governor and the *Politycqen Raet* (Political Council), which would later be referred to as *Hof van Policie* (Court of Police).[9] The latter formed a representative body of colonists and is to be considered a unique feature within the socio-political landscape of the Guianas. The WIC was (a) obliged to deliver as many slaves as deemed necessary and (b) responsible for ensuring the recruitment of white colonists. It could commission each and every ship sailing for Suriname to transport at the most twelve white people, for a fee of 30 guilders per adult.[10]

At first Suriname could only trade with the Republic. Later, an exception was made for English ships arriving from New England. Imported goods from North America comprised horses and mules (put to work at sugar mills), but also meat, bacon, fish and flour were permitted because of the frequent shortage of European foodstuffs due to the huge distance to the European continent. Hence, it was thus much easier to keep the peace with the powerful English. Suriname in turn was allowed to provide molasses, rum, cut timber and Dutch import wares. From 1678 on, the States of

---

6   Wolbers 1861, 834.
7   Ibid.
8   Ibid., 834-835.
9   Ibid., 836-837; Van der Meiden 1987, 32-33.
10   Wolbers 1861, 837-838.

Zeeland had also facilitated trade with 'Barbados and other American islands' upon request of the colonists - Suriname needed such an intra-American trade relationship in order to become a profitable colony.[11]

A key privilege for colonists, as laid down in the 1682 charter, was their co-determination as to ruling Suriname which fitted in with the liberal view on democracy then held in the Republic. Suriname had albeit briefly witnessed a form of self-government during part of the English rule (1651-1667). However, under Zeelandic rule, the Dutch Provincial States had denied colonists such a privilege 'as this is unusual, not only in the colony of Suriname'.[12]

According to the 1682 charter, the governor, whom the WIC had elected after being approved by the States General, was the highest authority regarding political and military affairs. However, he was obliged to present all 'matters of importance' to the aforementioned Court of Police, which took decisions by majority votes.[13] According to this charter, colonists could designate, by means of a majority vote, two candidates from 'the most considerable, smartest and most moderate among the colonists' for each of the ten seats.[14] The governor then made his choice and appointed the ten members, who were to occupy their seats in this council for life and without any remunerations. Justice was entirely an issue for the colony itself. The governor and the Court of Police were jointly responsible for crime-related matters. Hence, this council's full name, to wit, *Hof van Policie en Crimineele Justitie* (Court of Police and Criminal Justice). It was also referred to as the *Rode Hof* (Red Court) because of the colour of its employees' uniform. Civil justice lay in the hands of the governor and the *Raedt van Civile Justitie* (Court of Civil Justice) also referred to as the *Zwarte Hof* (Black Court) because its members were dressed in black.[15] The six members whom a governor (who also officiated as chairman) appointed served for 2 years. They were selected from pairs proposed by the governor himself and the Court of Police. A member of the Court of Civil Justice and of the Court of Police and Criminal Justice could be the same person.

Responsible for defending the colony, the WIC had to pay all expenses related to fortresses, equipment and troops. In addition, each Dutch province had to cover the costs of one soldier for every company maintained in the Republic. Reason for the States General to impose this measure was the fact that the WIC would benefit little from the colony, whereas residents of the Republic would hugely profit not only from export of wares to Suriname but also from an import of raw materials. Merchants and clergymen also found each other in the 1682 charter, as the WIC had to ensure it provided Dutch Reformed Church ministers.

The degree to which the States General doubted the feasibility of establishing a real settlement in Suriname can be inferred from the 1682 charter's concluding article. It stated that the WIC could give up the colony if it was unable to pay any maintenance costs. The States General would, in that case, take on this responsibility.

---

11   Zijlstra 2015, 151-153; see also: Fatah-Black 2013, 50-71; Fatah-Black 2015, 41-107.
12   Zijlstra 2015, 32-34, 140-141, 153.
13   Wolbers 1861, 841.
14   Ibid.
15   Abbenhuis 1943b, 103.

Figure 2.1. An engraving (c.1796) depicting the Society of Suriname's coat of arms in which both the coat of arms of Amsterdam and of the WIC's fleet are recognisable. In an earlier version, the Van Aerssen van Sommelsdijck family's coat of arms was included. Leiden University Libraries / KITLV.

The transfer of Suriname, however, had not been settled yet. Apparently the WIC could not pay the purchase price of 260,000 guilders. Amsterdam's governing council had suggested that Cornelis van Aerssen van Sommelsdijck (1637-1688) would provide 75 per cent of this sum.[16] This wealthy nobleman would then be authorized to set off for Suriname as a governor, while serving the directorate of Amsterdam. The WIC's Amsterdam chamber, however, held the view that Amsterdam itself should lend funds to the WIC. Not much later the aforementioned governing council forwarded the proposal implying that Van Aerssen van Sommelsdijck, Amsterdam and the WIC would all jointly participate whereby the former would officiate as a governor who could possibly be called back. Amsterdam-based participants in the WIC agreed hereto, whereas the other WIC members opposed. While negotiations were still on-going, the aforementioned council unexpectedly provided funding. This initiative resulted in Suriname officially being transferred to the WIC on 20 February 1683.

Negotiations concerning any participation at all in the colony to be contributed by Van Aerssen van Sommelsdijck and Amsterdam nevertheless continued. The WIC's chamber at Zeeland feared that the two other participants would impair this company's monopoly in the slave trade. However, in due course, a small majority appeared to exist when *De Heeren X* convened. On 21 May 1683 the *Sociëteit van Suriname* was founded. Two weeks later its first meeting took place at the *West-Indisch Huis* (West India House) in Amsterdam. This society was modelled on the dirigiste economic principles developed by Jean-Baptiste Colbert (1619-1683), the renowned French minister of finances.

All three participants in the Society should divide costs and benefits equally, according to the agreed conditions.[17] They could dispose of their share only by means of mutual consent. Slave trade continued to be left to the WIC. A 3-year transitional period was provided in which the Society took over this trade, whilst a fee of 15 guilders had to be paid to the WIC for each slave sold in the colony. Such an

---

16   Van der Meiden 1987, 34-35.
17   Hartsinck 1770, 638-645.

infringement of this company's monopoly probably explains why Amsterdam, with its economic interests, insisted it must participate in the Society.[18]

Once Van Aerssen van Sommelsdijck had sailed for Suriname as the next Governor, his heirs would in principle be favoured to succeed him. According to the aforementioned conditions, he would perform his duties 'out of love and without receiving any financial remuneration'; the Society would only provide him with as much wine and spices as 'in all honesty' deemed necessary.[19]

Historical research has however shed a rather less favourable light on Van Aerssen van Sommelsdijck's selflessness.[20] The Amsterdam-based governing council had lent him the amount necessary to pay his share in the Society. In addition, notably, in order to exploit a sugar mill and a plantation in Suriname, he had set up a joint venture together with Amsterdam-based notables who were either members of the aforementioned governing council or merchants. That deal was supposed to stay confidential. According to the related deed, the men who appeared before the notary on 30 August 1683 were Cornelis van Aerssen van Sommelsdijck, the council members-*cum*-dignitaries Jacob Boreel (1630-1697), Joan Huydecoper van Maarseveen (1625-1704) and Gilles Sautijn (1635-1689) together with two merchants named Willem Sautijn Heer van Stockum (1639-1686) and Philips van Hulten (1627 or 1632-1692). This event clearly presented an intolerable conflict between both private and public interests. Moreover, Van Hulten and Sautijn Heer van Stockum were both directors of the Society, the first serving as a representative of Van Aerssen van Sommelsdijck and the latter officiating on behalf of Amsterdam. In 1684 Jacob Boreel was appointed chairman of the Society. It can now be concluded that Suriname had primarily become a colony run by Amsterdam.

2.2 The government of Suriname, a continuous struggle for power
Suriname's model of governance differed significantly when compared with Dutch colonies established in South and Southeast Asia. Here the *Verenigde Oost-Indische Compagnie* (VOC; Dutch East India Company) had acquired a total monopoly. Trade with Suriname was free for each and every resident of the Republic whereby the co-determination expressed by colonists was unique. From a governance point of view, Suriname was far ahead of other colonies. At the same time, this situation entailed the risk of conflicts.

In addition, the incoming Governor's uncompromising character did not make things easier.[21] Having been raised as a page at the court of Willem II, Prince of Orange and Stadtholder of the United Provinces of the Netherlands (1626-1650), Cornelis van Aerssen van Sommelsdijck officiated as a feudal lord of Sommelsdijck, Plaat, Bommel and Spijk. He had also been awarded with several French titles of nobility, thanks to his grandfather whom the King of France had elevated to the peerage, when serving as the Dutch envoy in Paris. An opportunistic step was taken when Van Aerssen van Sommelsdijck offered his services to Johan de Witt (b. 1625), the then most

18   Van der Meiden 1987, 35.
19   Hartsinck 1770, 639.
20   Van der Meiden 1987, 38-40.
21   Van der Meiden 1987, 36-38; Oudschans Dentz 1938, 33-42.

important official in the United Provinces. This republican had, in a move against Orangists, abolished the office of Stadtholder as soon as Willem II, van Aerssen van Sommeldijck's tutor, had passed away. In 1672, after De Witt's assassination by an Orangist mob, Van Aerssen van Sommelsdijck just as easily attempted to court Willem III, the future king of England. Van Aerssen van Sommelsdijk was, as a result of his conduct, no longer trusted and thus not eligible for a high post in the Republic. Frustration with regard to thwarted ambitions also prompted his decision to sail for Suriname. Moreover, he was undoubtedly sensitive to experiencing the usual pomp and circumstance when serving as a governor.

Van Aerssen van Sommelsdijck was apparently not the right man for Suriname, particularly as he had to flesh out an innovative, more democratic system of government. Contrary to his father and grandfather, he was by no means a diplomat. In the Republic he was considered authoritarian, rude, bold and reckless. According to a then well-known anecdote, Van Aerssen van Sommelsdijck, when returning from his honeymoon in France, had driven his carriage drawn by six horses across the thin, cracking ice of the river named Nieuwe Maas while his French wife was screaming with fear.

Implementing any sound political governance in Suriname was indeed an extremely difficult exercise, considering the conflicts of (private) interests. The States General wished the interests of colonists to be protected. However, in practice, economic interests in the Republic had the upper hand. The 1682 charter proved ambiguous in this respect.

A major bone of contention was the relationship between the governor and the Court of Police and Criminal Justice. Council members deemed themselves to form the government of Suriname and had turned against every governor acting on his own authority. Governors were however, above all, representatives of the Society's interests, which often were contrary to those pursued by colonists, including numerous planters. Either if pertaining to taxation or to military expenditures, agreements could rarely be reached. It was nevertheless clear that funds were required to build the severely neglected colony. In his first letter sent to the Society, dated 16 January 1684, Van Aerssen van Sommelsdijck had already complained about the miserable conditions he had encountered when arriving in Paramaribo:

> '[...] *without resources, without credit, without gunpowder or guns, the commander had to borrow the gun salutes from the ships, and without food supplies. The entirely derelict fortress, not one gun on its carriage [...], all the storage rooms completely dilapidated, without roofs, doors or windows, in short, a desolate property [...].'*[22]

His primary concern was therefore to raise more financial resources. On 7 April 1684, he issued a decree which imposed a weigh house levy as well as a registration fee of 2.5 per cent on all traded movable as well as immovable property, retroactively to 1 January 1683. A head tax and a levy on arable land (comprising 1 pound of sugar for each field) were retroactively imposed, too. He furthermore laid down specific conditions regarding the issuing of land. Not only was authorisation required for

---

22   Bijlsma 1924, 427.

selling plots of land, owners had to pay 10 per cent of selling prices to the Society during the first 12 years and 5 per cent in the years thereafter.[23]

These measures provoked fierce opposition amidst planters which was mainly directed against the weigh house levy. According to the Court of Police and Criminal Justice, this decree violated the 1682 charter. For, it was for example aimed at imposing lower taxes for residents of Suriname than had been the case earlier during the Zeelandic period (1667-1682). The States General, for that reason, did not hesitate to admonish Van Aerssen van Sommelsdijck. A resolution forwarded by the so-called *Hoogmogende Heeren* (Noble Mightinesses) would haunt him for the rest of his tenure as governor.[24] They declared that this decree infringed the 1682 charter because the 2.5 per cent weigh house levy could only be charged for wares encountered at the weigh house. Van Aerssen van Sommelsdijck was also criticised for stalling the appointment of the Court of Police and Criminal Justice for 6 months. This resulted in council members never discussing this controversial decree. Having in due course appointed only eight of the legally required ten members, he wrote on 13 April 1684 to the directors of the Society,

> *'From the twenty nominated, I have chosen only eight, the numbers 1, 2, 3 etc., due to a lack of substance, or contents, the majority even being very meager and poorly [...].'*[25]

In his eyes there were sufficient reasons to take matters in his own hands:

> *'[...] having found the government here so corrupted, and on such an evil footing, that nothing good could be made out of it .'*[26]

Not feeling very positive about certain chosen members, Van Aerssen van Sommelsdijck even omitted appointing members of the Court of Civil Justice. Indeed, it was not the cream of the crop in the Republic that had sought their luck in Suriname. All officials accompanying him on *De Sint Pieter* sailing from the Dutch isle of Texel to Suriname shared a history of failed careers. However, he also had himself to blame as it had been on his request that riffraff released from *rasphuizen* (penitentiaries) housing young male criminals in the Republic had arrived at the colony in order to serve as soldiers. These men could even acquire a plot of land.

After a few years this Governor wrote he was now at loggerheads with everybody to then offer his resignation in 1685 which the directors of the Society refused to accept.[27] He had also enraged colonists by enriching himself. 'On the account of several directors', he had allowed, for example, *De Rijzende Zon* (The Rising Sun) to sail for and arrive at Paramaribo.[28] According to the States General it had taken meat as well as other foodstuffs on board in Ireland. Van Aerssen van Sommelsdijck

---

23   Schiltkamp & De Smidt 1973, vol. 1, 138-139.
24   Van der Meiden 1987, 43-44.
25   Bijlsma 1925, 42.
26   Ibid.
27   Oudschans Dentz 1938, 64.
28   Van der Meiden 1987, 44-45.

and his companion P. van Hulten had no doubt benefitted from this deal. Taking advantage of transporting slaves for personal gain, too, the former had particularly angered poorer colonists, who were not allowed to pay their purchases of slaves in instalments. Not without reason, the directors of the Society were concerned about the Governor's position and advised him to quickly reach an understanding with the council members as to the weigh house levy.

Not only the Governor and the colonists were engaged in a broil with each other. Disputes between him with as well as Zeeland and the WIC were equally heated. Zeelanders had already witnessed that their stakes in the colony had significantly been reduced as a consequence of the Society being established. They felt Van Aerssen van Sommeldijck was harming them. Zeelandic ship captains even accused him of confiscating sugar from planters who still had outstanding debts to the owners of their ships. In doing so this Governor would have not only favoured the Society but also the other ship owners with whom he maintained relations.[29] For his part, he opined that the Zeelanders only sought to evade the obligation to pay their contributions to the colony's defence. Indeed, since his arrival in Suriname, Zeeland had not paid a single penny towards this goal. Both sides continuously observed conspiracies against each other's interests. Whenever complaints reached the States General, this did not result in a clear statement. The directors of the Society, in response, rejected this accusation. Their letter was also signed by Jacob Boreel, the same individual who had clinched a secret deal with Van Aerssen van Sommelsdijck pertaining to the exploitation of a plantation and a sugar mill.

In sum, the relationship between this Governor and Zeeland was doomed. An argument concerning several Roman Catholic priests, who had travelled to Suriname in his company, was notorious.[30] The directors of the Society had asked for a clarification when complaints had been lodged by the Reformed Church in Amsterdam, after receiving grievances voiced from Zeeland. Remarkably, the director of the Society, P. van Hulten, also a fiduciary of the Governor, had sent these clergymen to Suriname. In 1686 however the latter received a request from the States General to send them back. These clerics had by then passed away, but Van Aerssen van Sommelsdijck commissioned their skeletal remains to be exhumed and returned to the States of Zeeland. He wrote, on 5 September 1687, not without sarcasm to the Society:

'Have sent with Captain Johannes Plas to the Gentlemen States of Zeeland the bones, of the here deceased three papists [...] accompanied by a letter of which a copy is enclosed. I believe that such a chest full of ducats would satisfy and please them more. However until now those fruits do not grow here, but I hope that [...] the abundance of sugars will sweeten and soften their screaming throats, and that syrup and julep will cure them from their raging fevers to then acquire a better knowledge of matters occurring here.'[31]

---

29 Van der Meiden 1987, 47-49.
30 Ibid., 49-50; Oudschans Dentz 1938, 129-134; Wolbers 1861, 74-75.
31 Oudschans Dentz 1938, 134.

These Roman Catholic priests were eventually reburied in Suriname after a complaint from the States of Zeeland was lodged.

Van Aerssen van Sommelsdijck was also at odds with the WIC, which in his view was engaged in the smuggling of slaves. On 29 August 1686 he wrote to the Society:

> 'The more I stir up the muck, the more it stinks and the more the Company's wheeling and dealing disgusts me [...].'[32]

The dissent between Van Aerssen van Sommelsdijck and the WIC is easily explained. After its establishment in 1683 the Society of Suriname had controlled the slave trade for 3 years. This Governor had thus obtained a direct interest herein. In 1686 the WIC took over the slave trade, after which he no longer paid any attention to this company's smuggling activities.

In turn, feeling fed up with Van Aerssen van Sommelsdijck, the WIC's directors laid down their complaints in preparation for a meeting with the town of Amsterdam. This document stated that he did not (a) pay his share in the costs, (b) ensure that delivered slaves were paid for and (c) take action against English shipping activities. His letters were described as 'insulting and impertinent'.[33] Moreover, the WIC's directors did not hesitate to denounce his private interests yet again, now pointing out that his mandate was revocable. The Society did however prove to be not at all willing to dismiss him which would have been difficult anyway because of conflicts of interest. Amsterdam held the view that the WIC would do better to ensure a sufficient supply of slaves.

In due course all conflicts came to an end on 19 July 1688 when mutinous soldiers assassinated Van Aerssen van Sommelsdijck.[34] The military, having built fortresses and dug canals in order to facilitate the water management of plantations, had repeatedly complained about meagre rations and heavy labour. The Governor had initially chased them off with a stick. Nonetheless, 2 days later, approximately 20 troops returned to the his residence. He now rushed towards them with a drawn sabre. The mutineers then opened fire to kill him with more than 40 rounds. His military commander Laurens Verboom (1654-1688), whom the rebels trusted and who had tried to mediate, was accidentally wounded and passed away soon afterwards.

Not much later more than 140 men (including young criminals hailing from penitentiaries whom Van Aerssen van Sommelsdijck had taken with him to Suriname) occupied Fort Zeelandia. This mutiny turned into a fully-fledged coup d'etat, after a military council was installed inside his residence. Thomas Swartsenbolt, a German trumpeter and previously sentenced to the gallows for desertion, was chosen to lead the agitators. However, not all the soldiers took part in this rebellion. Feeling mainly disgruntled they included convicted men who had succumbed to the temptation of a rising. Several high-ranking military joined the plantation owners, who realised that these troops posed a threat to their interests. The mutineers surrendered a few days later be it only after being reassured by the Court of Police and Criminal Justice that

---

32 Ibid., 154.
33 Van der Meiden 1987, 52.
34 Pistorius 1763, 100-160; Hartsinck 1770, 651-672; Wolbers 1861, 78-81; Oudschans Dentz 1938, 157-180; Hira 1982, 52-67; Van der Meiden 1987, 52-53.

only those guilty of the Governor's assassination would be punished. Three soldiers were broken on the wheel and eight were hanged. The others were sent back to the Republic in small groups, where they were released.

Nonetheless, Suriname was better off after 5 years under Van Aerssen van Sommeldijck's rule. For, the Amerindians had been pacified and the production of sugar had substantially increased. The number of plantations had risen from 50 in 1684 to almost 100 in 1688.[35] A garrison had now been built, which at least was paid for. A start had been made to construct military fortifications. A fortress named after the then Governor was being founded on the confluence of the Commewijne and the Cottica Rivers. On balance, it is difficult to assess Van Aerssen van Sommelsdijck's personal contributions to the colony's revival. It is equally possible that his controversial conduct did in fact impede developments.

Governing Suriname remained a source of conflict. For example, Van Aerssen van Sommelsdijck's estate immediately led to discord within the Society. His widow had tried to sell her share to one of the other stake-holders. They did however not express any interest because the Society had declared the now deceased Governor to have defaulted, as he had never fulfilled his financial obligations. For that reason his next-of-kin had, during several years, not been represented by the Society's board of directors. Only in 1708 was a settlement reached whereby Van Aerssen van Sommelsdijck's children received a dividend of 40,000 guilders. Moreover, they were forwarded the sum of 100,000 guilders to be entirely spent on as yet unpaid deliveries of slaves and other liabilities.[36]

During the first decades after Van Aerssen van Sommeldijck's demise his successors did not excel at exercising administrative powers. Many resigned ahead of time. In January 1689 Johan van Scharphuysen, a former member of the Court of Police and Criminal Justice and an influential colonist, was appointed Governor. Having never been able to collaborate with Van Aerssen van Sommelsdijck, Van Scharpenhuysen's nomination illustrated the estrangement between the Society of Suriname and his predecessor.

The Society did not wish new problems to arise from conflicts of interest. Van Scharphuijsen had been involved with several slave transports. Officiating as a governor however his share had been confined to a maximum of three ships. In return Van Scharphuijsen received a salary of 5,700 guilders per annum. This incoming Governor quickly reversed his predecessor's tax measures. The head tax as well as levy on arable land collected in violation of the proclaimed tax exemption of 10 years, were both reimbursed. Moreover, he finally not only appointed Members of the Court of Justice who were to be responsible for civil matters but also initiated the Subaltern College. Its task was to settle minor disputes between colonists.[37]

Suriname was severely tested just a few months after Van Scharphuijsen had taken office. On 6 May 1689 a French flotilla consisting of ten warships, led by admiral Jean-Baptiste du Casse, sailed up the Suriname River.[38] The French considered the entire

---

35   Van der Meiden 1987, 54; Van Stipriaan 1993, 29, 33.
36   Van der Meiden 1987, 62-63.
37   Ibid., 58-59.
38   Wolbers 1861, 85-87.

A History of Suriname

territory acquired by the Republic as acting hostile after Stadtholder Willem III had ascended the British throne in 1689. Though Fort Zeelandia was bombarded with 100-pounders, 250 soldiers and 231 civilians nevertheless endured this attack. The French were forced to retreat after a week. Du Casse and his men would later cause much greater damage to Dutch settlements located on the Berbice and Pomeroon Rivers.

Van Scharphuijsen's tenure of office as a governor ended prematurely in 1696. The Society wished to dismiss him but he finally resigned of his own accord. Yet again complaints had been voiced concerning the fact the WIC had not provided sufficient numbers of slaves. The slave trade with Spanish colonies (not subjected to the restrictions described in the 1682 charter) was indeed more profitable for the WIC. In addition, the directors of the Society were outraged after the Governor as well as the council members had turned to the States General with their grievances, an act they considered a subversion of their authority.[39] Apparently, Van Scharphuijsen had identified too closely with the interests of the colonists based in Suriname.

His successor, the unknown Paul van der Veen (c.1660-1733) was far more the Society representative, thus provoking strong counterforces within the colony. A military Captain named Abraham van Vredenburch and the council member Thomas van Beest even held secret meetings with a group of colonists residing at plantations in order to prepare a strategy regarding the Governor. Needless to say, defence costs once again formed a contentious issue which now pertained to who was to fund the upkeep of Fort Sommeldijck.[40] Van der Veen opined the colonists themselves should do so. They, in turn, reproached him for granting the arbitrary authorisation to English ship captains allowing them to trade with Suriname out of New England (Northeast America). A number of competence-based conflicts had risen too. Interestingly, the former Governor, Van Scharphuijsen, together with a former council member, now lodged complaints with the Society against Van der Veen. The latter had investigated, on the Society's request, a number of grievances concerning the former's governorship. Commander Van Vredenburch had sufficient reasons for conspiring, too. For, he had not been appointed as a governor. Apparently personal issues had to be settled first.

Life in Suriname was always filled with jealousy and machinations, partly the outcome of its small social scale. The directors of the Society reminded the opposing party that Thomas van Beest, a former Lieutenant Captain of the States General troops, had been dismissed from all his duties after misbehaving. The Governor should, in their words, better once again confront him with this fact. The problem soon dissolved, after Van Beest had decided to return to the Republic. Captain Van Vredenburch was dismissed as a result of expenditure cuts. The complaints against Van der Veen were never dealt with. He resigned, on 2 March 1707, after the Society had decided, 6 months earlier, to dismiss him.

In spite of these controversies Suriname had developed in relative tranquillity and prosperity during Van der Veen's governorship. Fresh threats nonetheless soon emerged when slaves fled the plantations in ever-growing numbers. The colony was also affected by conflicts in Europe, where the War of the Spanish Succession

---

39   Van der Meiden 1987, 59.
40   Ibid., 71-72.

(1710-1714) had broken out. Although France's main interests focused on North America, Suriname nor the neighbouring settlements named Berbice and Essequibo were able to escape the violence of war.

A French flotilla under the command of the naval officer-*cum*-privateer Jacques Cassard (1679-1740) caused heavy damage to the colony of Suriname.[41] Here, on 8 June 1707, the military garrison and the civil companies had repelled a first attack. Colonists were furious with regents in the Republic, because the military defence was completely inadequate. The Governor as well as the council members tried in vain to impede captains of the civil militia from submitting a petition to the States General, as this would undermine their authority. These civil officers blamed the Society for explaining the 1682 charter to its own advantage. Fortifications were in a poor condition and the number of troops did not suffice. Moreover, they thus considered colonial taxes to be extremely unreasonable. In their view, the colonists contributed everything necessary for the defence not only by maintaining fortifications but also by organizing expeditions in order to deal with runaway slaves. It would thus be appropriate if the States General would compensate them by means of payments. Civil officers also demanded a ban on additional taxes, hereby denouncing the Governor's and council members' authoritarian exercise of power. The States General forwarded the petition to the Society.

Meanwhile, on 8 October 1707, French buccaneers returned to the mouth of the Suriname River. They were now considerably reinforced by means of 3,000 troops equipped with 336 pieces of artillery placed on eight warships and 30 smaller vessels. Needless to say, little could be done in the face of such overwhelming odds. After shelling Paramaribo, Jacques Cassard sailed upstream while looting and pillaging. He ordered colonists to pay 'one year of revenue', which was estimated either at 15,000 hogsheads of sugar or the sum of 731,150 Surinamese guilders (equalling more than 600,000 Dutch guilders).[42] Payments were mainly carried out in the form of sugar, slaves, foodstuffs, cordage, cauldrons, gold- and silverware, cash and credit letters. Each and every colonist had to take stock of their assets, whereby everyone thus contributed proportionately.

Little wonder the mood within the colony now deteriorated significantly. Council members, in turn, forwarded a petition to the States General requesting a postponement of the payment of the head money to the Society, pending an appropriate compensation. High tensions resulted in a spirit of rebellion among colonists. Governor Johan de Goyer (1710-1715) and the then commander F.A. de Rayneval warned the directors of the Society that voices were heard in favour of establishing a separate government in Suriname. After the States General had sent these complaints to the States of Holland, commissioners serving the 'neutral' town of Dordrecht were instructed to look into the matter. As soon as the directors of the Society had been heard, too, they were aggrieved by the attitude the colonists expressed but also unwilling to provide any compensation. The planters had after all never repaid their debts. For example, 25 per cent of 1,350,000 guilders worth

---

41   Hartsinck 1770, 700-722; Wolbers 1861, 89-96; Van der Meiden 1987, 72-75.
42   Hartsinck 1770, 720-722.

A History of Suriname

of delivered slaves was still outstanding.[43] The directors recognized they had to ensure the reinforcement of fortresses, as laid down in the 1682 charter. However, as constructing Fort Sommelsdijck had been arranged without these directors' knowledge, they opined that colonists should therefore pay maintenance costs. Yet again the Society's complaint was lodged with the observation that not all the Dutch provinces had contributed their part to funding Suriname-based troops. Unsurprisingly, colonists were insensitive to this accusation, hereby not only pointing out that in the Republic as many as 600 companies were kept in a state of war but also that Suriname should thus dispose of an equal number of soldiers as laid down by the States General in the 1682 charter. The directors of the Society, in turn, felt that the governor, commander as well as officers should also be funded through the contributions provided by Dutch provinces. The remaining sum would merely suffice for 181 soldiers, whereby colonists should then pay the rest. Considering it a result of cowardice, these directors also blamed colonists for the defeat against the French.

The dissent between Suriname and the Republic had therefore only increased. Influential merchants-regents in the Province of Holland did not care much for a small group of troublemakers active in a faraway colony. Consequently, on 28 July 1713, the States General adopted a resolution in which civil officers were ruled against on all points.[44] Colonists now did indeed have a say in ruling Suriname. Nonetheless the outcome of this conflict once again clarified where the real power was to be found. Officers of the civil militia were banned from organising protest meetings and overdue head money had to be paid anyway. Moreover, the damage Cassard's attack had caused was entirely reclaimed from the colonists.

Sharp disputes confirmed a lack of harmony when governing Suriname. The shortage of slaves became acute for planters, not least as a result of an increasing number of runaways. In 1713, the Society and the Amsterdam-based WIC chamber finally agreed that the latter company should annually transport as many slaves to Suriname as was requested. In the colonists' view, however, this proposal did not suffice. Many plantation owners had run into huge debts, because either irregular or insufficient supplies had substantially increased prices to be paid for slaves.

Hence a mounting pressure to terminate the WIC's monopoly was expressed in particular by planters residing in the Republic. The Amsterdam-based WIC chamber objected because of the importance of these revenues for this town. An arrangement was eventually agreed upon whereby the WIC was committed to delivering 2,500 slaves per annum. If it failed to do so, private entrepreneurs would be allowed to provide the remaining number. In 1738 the Society decided to open up the slave trade with Suriname to other parties, be it only after the WIC had not fulfilled its commitment.[45] From that moment on the *Middelburgsche Commercie Companie*, a mercantile association founded at the town of Middelburg (the capital of Zeeland), obtained a relatively large segment of the slave trade with Dutch territories

---

43   Van der Meiden 1987, 74-75.
44   Wolbers 1861, 95-96; Van der Meiden 1987, 76.
45   Den Heijer 2013, 133-139, 159-161; Van der Meiden 1987, 78-80.

located across the West Indies. This company was already involved in trading for instance with West Africa.[46]

Plantation owners residing in the Republic further positioned themselves as key actors when a fortress was to be built on the confluence of the Suriname and the Commewijne Rivers. Again costs formed a source of dissent.[47] After Cassard's invasion, a need to establish more fortifications was clear to everyone. However, according to planters, the Society had better abandon the colony if it was not willing to pay for the maintenance of fortresses. The concluding article of the 1682 charter had provided for such an option. The governor according to planters now represented the Society. They therefore wanted council members to acquire the right to convene without the governor's and the commander's presence. On 8 December 1733, despite differences of opinion, an agreement was reached as to financing Fort Nieuw Amsterdam.[48] The Society would, based on a treaty ratified by the States General, contribute 20,000 guilders per annum. Moreover, this society should provide for workers and equipment. Colonists were obliged to pay 60,000 guilders annually. The governor and council members had to ensure a sufficient supply of slaves to work on the fortifications. A 7-year time frame had been set for implementing this defence plan. Fort Nieuw Amsterdam was built on a mud bank known as Tijgershol, rendering it invulnerable to enemy vessels. Thanks to this strategic location, further plantations could be founded on the lower reaches of both the Suriname River and the Commewijne River.

This accord concerning the colony's defence had by no means solved governance issues. Affluent plantation owners residing in the Republic, having witnessed an increase of their influence, now not only acted as the colonists' mouthpieces but also urged them to forward complaints. Having observed that the members of the States General were not immune to their appeals, colonists increasingly involved the latter in governance matters. Simultaneously, Suriname-based council members attempted to extend their say, at both the Society's and the governor's expense.

Johan Raye van Breukelerwaard (1699-1737) was dispatched to Suriname to officiate as a Governor from 1735 on, after completing a 12-year career in the service of the Admiralty of Amsterdam. Overly vigorous, it did not take long for him to engage in a conflict with council members concerning the prosecution of a planter who had murdered a young slave. They did not hesitate to lodge a complaint with the States General regarding the 'incoming Governor's despotic conduct'.[49]

The Court of Police persevered in its efforts to reinforce its power.[50] An attempt to dispose of the treasury containing taxes imposed in order to pay for personal and material expenses came to nothing. The same rings true for the Court's request to the Society to install its own agent in the Republic. This society's directors, in turn, considered it their task to represent the interests of the colonists. These directors also refused to accept a request to exclude Jewish colonists from the right to designate two candidates for each of the ten seats in the Court of Police. According to this

---

46   Bruijning & Voorhoeve 1977, 401-402.
47   Wolbers 1861, 97-99; Van der Meiden 1987, 81-83.
48   Van der Meiden 1987, 83.
49   Wolbers 1861, 104-105; Van der Meiden 1987, 86.
50   Van der Meiden 1987, 86-89.

council's members the right for Jews to vote had led to improper behaviour. The misconduct referred to did remain unclear. Governor Raye's words were apparently not far from the truth when he explained that Jewish colonists refused to sell their votes, thus fuelling anti-Semitic sentiments which flared up during the 18th century. The Governor did not win on all points. The Society felt, for example, that colonial ordinances and other regulations could only be issued in consultation with council members. Moreover, Raye's power to appoint officials remained as yet controversial. Feeling overly impeded when carrying out his administrative tasks, he chose to tender his resignation which the Society then refused to accept.

Governor Raye would in due course resign anyway as a consequence of intrigues characteristic of the colony.[51] The direct reason was the arrest of a coppersmith who, having insulted Raye by referring to him as rabble, was next confronted with a public prosecutor named Willem Gerard van Meel. According to the latter, the accusation against this coppersmith was merely based on testimony provided by a free Black woman. Van Meel frequented bars across Paramaribo informing everyone who wished to listen that he did not at all care about Raye. When the latter wished to dismiss him the complaint forwarded to the Society was to no avail. This was no great surprise because Van Meel's brother officiated as this society's secretary. Raye passed away in Paramaribo on 11 August 1737, before receiving the message that the Society had accepted his resignation.

Governor Raye's successor Gerard van de Schepper served as governor between 1737 and 1742. In due course he stepped down, too, yet again a trait of the colony's small-mindedness. Van de Schepper had issued an official order stating that drunken sergeants should discontinue all habitual abuse of soldiers. Learning from the directors of the Society that his warning had only encouraged such wantonness proved the last straw for him.[52] He had served as the ninth governor of Suriname within just 30 years. During his tenure colonists had frequently complained about his alleged abuse of power. Although the colony may not have collapsed due to any political instability, it had seriously been weakened. In the Republic the discontent with the continuous disputes increased rapidly.

2.3 The fight of the cabalists
The Society felt it was time to set things right. Suriname therefore needed a governor who would be able:

'to redress and repair the abuses that crept into the present government'.[53]

Entrusted with this difficult task, Johan Jacob Mauricius (1692-1768) was dispatched to Suriname on 23 July 1742. His arrival marked the beginning of turbulent times.[54] This extraordinary individual was considered a prodigy in his early years and

---

51   Ibid.
52   Ibid., 88.
53   Van der Meiden 1987, 91.
54   Wolbers 1861, 201-225; Van der Meiden 1987, 91-127.

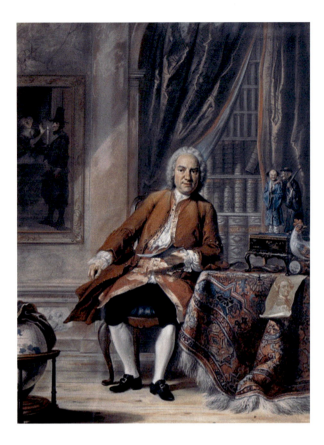

Figure 2.2. A painting (1741) by Cornelius Troost depicting Jan Jacob Mauricius. Rijksmuseum, Amsterdam, public domain via Wikimedia Commons.

in 1708, aged 16, had acquired a doctorate in literature to be followed 3 years later by a doctorate in law. He also became known as a poet.

Lacking required family ties, his political career was rather unimpressive. After initially serving as a pensionary in a Dutch town called Purmerend and later as a representative of the States of Holland, Mauricius was appointed a diplomat in Hamburg (Northern Germany). Here a solid reputation was built as is clear from the fact the Republic asked him for advice on all kinds of issues.

Financial reasons caused Mauricius to accept the post of governor-general in Suriname. Although a salary of 9,000 guilders per annum was not much larger than the 7,200 guilders acquired in Hamburg, he was able to set up his own sugar plantation, La Simplicité. In addition, as a colonial administrator seeing to several plantation accounts, he earned in excess of 10,000 guilders a year. Mauricius had also hoped to suffer less from asthma in the tropics. Intellectually gifted, diplomatic and not as impetuous as Van Aerssen van Sommelsdijck, Mauricius may indeed have paradoxically formed the reason why passions were running high in the colony where now a somewhat arrogant intellectual was confronted with the nouveau riche members of the planter aristocracy.

Defending the colony was yet again a bone of contention. While the threat of war in Europe was increasing, Suriname had as yet no proper military means of defence. Mauricius's fear of a future French attack was not unfounded. The construction of Fort Nieuw Amsterdam, the most important fortification, had still not been completed. Moreover, planters had acquired fortunes thanks to colonial defence efforts, charging 24 *stuivers* a day for each slave they had rented out, twice as much as the normal price.[55] The Court of Police and Criminal Justice had approved this remuneration during an interim period after Raye van Breukelerwaard's demise, when council members took governing in their own hands. Apparently the Society had allowed matters to take their course for years. Its directors now made it clear that this illegal decision should be repealed. Mauricius, in turn, preferred a more cautious approach justifying to a certain degree the way in which plantation owners reasoned. Slaves were working on fortifications at times they were most needed on plantations. Their food had to be transported from afar. Heavy labour made them more rebellious, resulting in higher costs for the planters. Mauricius and the council members therefore put this issue to rest.

Six years later, in 1748, a compromise was reached.[56] The price for hiring a slave was reduced to the original sum of 12 *stuivers* a day. According to this agreement, the Society would send an additional 100 soldiers to Suriname in times of war. Mauricius did not conceal that he considered planters greedy. The colony's taxes were relatively low. Moreover, colonists benefitted from the war in Europe because their wares yielded twice as much as in times of peace. In the meantime Fort Nieuw Amsterdam had been completed and handed over to the Society, whereas Fort Sommelsdijck was abandoned.

The mood across the colony did not improve. Not only did the defence-related costs remain controversial, Mauricius's efforts aimed at improving the quality of justice also increased discontent among influential planters. His predecessors were military servicemen who had left judicial matters to the Public Prosecutor whereas he usually attended sessions held at the Court of Police and Criminal Justice in person. Although the colony's executive and judiciary power were not separated, Mauricius made it absolutely clear that prestige and wealth would no longer licence any breaking of the law. He thus harmed the interests of numerous colonists. From now on, planters seized at every opportunity to cast a negative light on this Governor's activities. A decree obliging residents to once again map their real estate was even explained as an abuse of power. The proviso that petitions addressed to the Court of Police should first be forwarded to the Governor provoked further resentment. Another source of conflict comprised appointing colonial officials, whereby Mauricius did not forget his direct family. His sons Pieter (*c.*1715-1756) and Andreas (1720-1754) both held posts within Suriname's financial administration.[57]

A small number of colonists chose to side with Mauricius. On his birthday (3 May), self-styled Knights of Mauricius (*Mauritsridders*) marched past his residence on horseback in order to demonstrate their support. He however foresaw issues with other colonists, when the 24 knights wished to form a special corps in order to defend the colony in times of crisis. This group was soon to be dismantled.[58]

---

55   Van der Meiden 1987, 95.
56   Hartsinck 1770, 733-734; Van der Meiden 1987, 95-96.
57   Van der Meiden 1987, 94.
58   Wolbers 1861, 216-217.

Mauricius's opponents attempted to position as many of their 'own' men as possible on vacant seats in the Court of Police and Criminal Justice. Governors traditionally chose the eldest members of the Court of Civil Justice (which as mentioned above served as a tribunal for civil cases) in the Court of Police and Criminal Justice. On 4 May 1744, Salomon du Plessis (1705-1785) and Samuel Paulus Pichot (1714-1763) were nominated for a single council seat. Though the former had successfully organized an election campaign, it was not his turn to be appointed. Officiating as a civil captain and as a member of the Court of Civil Justice, Du Plessis was a very influential colonist. In addition, he had acquired a fortune as a planter-*cum*-administrator. Governor Mauricius opined, in his diary, that Du Plessis had been nominated thanks to 18 'jackals' whose votes were on sale for a *rijksdaalder*, hereby not concealing the fact he had Jewish colonists in mind. We read: 'The worst scum of *Hoogduitse* [i.e., Ashkenazi] hustlers' had been influenced by 'intrigues' and certain 'Portuguese Jews of the worst kind' had yielded to pressure.[59]

Elections held in Suriname were indeed not fair. Due to their high debts numerous residents were subjected to threats launched by affluent plantation owners. According to Mauricius, Du Plessis was 'a man of competence and productive, but particularly ambitious and violent, and [...] an antagonist of the Society and those representing it'. He therefore appointed Pichot, 'a moderate and modest man'.[60] When, 6 months later, Du Plessis was once again nominated for a seat, Mauricius did not wish to overlook him again, expecting Du Plessis would continue to behave calmly out of gratitude. This opinion soon proved to be an example of wishful thinking.

Du Plessis positioned himself at the head of a movement aimed at the Governor's dismissal. Mauricius referred to this colonialist coterie as cabal. The campaign to occupy any vacancies in the Court of Police and Criminal Justice was vigorous. Pichot and others emerged as cabalists who did not always succeed in occupying vacant seats. According to Mauricius, in his journal, after a failed attempt Du Plessis while walking outside on a street cursed like a boatman 'biting on a bullet out of anger'.[61] A number of meetings held at the Court of Police and Criminal Justice also witnessed rather undignified scenes. Minutes recorded on 4 May 1744 mention that Mauricius expressed his anger about 'the most impertinent and debauched texts' written on the ballot papers.[62] Wives of prominent colonists also played their part. After a walk with his wife, Mauricius wrote on 14 December 1746 in his journal:

> '*After Scherping's debauched wife had given the example for a year of, seated on her high doorstep, spitting at instead of greeting me and my wife (as we pass by); following that example some other women, too, all living here in a neighbouring street, have since several months agreed not to greet me, my wife and all those who are supposed to be pro-Governor, even when the other greets first [...] but yesterday the point was reached that Pichot's and Brouwer's wives, sitting on the doorstep, booed at my wife with roars of laughter.*'[63]

---

59   Van der Meiden 1987, 97.
60   Ibid.
61   Wolbers 1861, 210.
62   Ibid.
63   Ibid., 211.

Cabalists were more and more intensely heard. The Governor's three fiercest opponents within the Court of Police and Criminal Justice, to wit, Pichot, Du Plessis and Dirk Guldenstede, turned directly to the Society expressing their grievances. They now opposed Mauricius's plan to create a special coffer for the 100 extra troops to be deployed against runaway slaves. Although this Court had already agreed with this measure in 1743, cabalists nonetheless wished it to be reversed.[64]

The directors of the Society felt dismayed that these three council members had turned to them, independently of the Governor. Their initiative was however not without success as, for the time being, a runaway coffer (*wegloperskas*) would not be created. Civil officers also turned against Maurcius and, on 4 May 1746, lodged several complaints with him. This list was also forwarded to the Society. These officers reproached the Governor for having appointed less-well-to-do as members of the Court of Police. The fact he had expressed the wish the colony should pay for costs related to the 100 additional troops in order to control runaways had also stirred up bad blood. Moreover, they criticised him for arbitrarily issuing decrees and imposing taxes.[65]

The cabalists now started to meet on plantations. These events formed a provocation because at that time no freedom of assembly existed in Suriname. The rebellious colonists decided to dispatch Du Plessis to the Republic in order to continue campaigning against the Governor. The latter did not make things better when he decided to expel the civil officers, who had signed the list of complaints. Mauricius apparently wished to prove himself in relation to the directors of the Society, who criticised him for not being sufficiently tough.

From now on, cabalists took their fight to the Republic. In the course of 1747, the States General was bombarded with petitions in which merchants, ship owners and planters asked for reinforcement in the form of two warships. This petition, also signed by Du Plessis, was rather duplicitous as cabalists had never been very prepared to substantially contribute to defending Suriname. Du Plessis himself forwarded the most important petition when he requested, both as a council member and with the authorisation of the cabalists, the withdrawal of Governor Mauricius. One accusation implied that the latter, having pushed things his way when appointing council members, should be held accountable in the Republic for his authoritarian conduct.[66]

The States General forwarded a petition to the States of Holland and to those representing WIC-related issues. The Society was then instructed to report on Suriname's defence's status. In a response this society's directors complained once again not only about the inertia when constructing Fort Nieuw Amsterdam but also about self-enriching planters. They also requested, as cabalists had done, for two warships. At the same time these directors drew the attention of the States General to the fact that the Republic still had to pay the Society for warships sent to Suriname many years ago. Moreover, the Dutch provinces of Utrecht and Overijssel had never complied with the obligation of contributing one soldier for every company they maintained in the Republic. The directors of the Society did not support their own

---

64   Van der Meiden 1987, 98.
65   Ibid., 99.
66   Ibid., 100-101.

cause with such a reply. Hence, after so many petitions, the mood in the Republic had turned against them. The States General, which felt 'highly unsatisfied', immediately returned that letter.[67] The Society's response to Du Plessis essentially implied he was no longer a council member because of his departure to the Republic and thus had to be deemed a slanderer.

Mauricius, infuriated when learning of Du Plessis's complaints, wrote a letter to the directors of the Society in the uncivilised style many colonists often utilised when communicating with one another. Du Plessis was referred to as a 'raging windbag and wigmaker's boy'. Another cabalist was described as 'a real Judas, who in his younger years as a regiment's barber had twice escaped the gallows, and has now made his fortune here'. These directors considered Mauricius's style to be 'somewhat virulent', whereupon he wrote a redacted version to the States General.[68] In it he reported that a number of colonists had been carried off by a small group of related colonists during their rebellion.

Mauricius's response did little to impress. Matters did not improve when the States General yet again received petitions on 16 February 1748. Several plantation owners residing in the Republic had complained about what they referred to as political expulsions. Planters and merchants now also objected to Mauricius's decision to oblige merchant vessels to drop anchor near Fort Nieuw Amsterdam in order to serve as warships in case of an emergency. Du Plessis also forwarded a new petition. Feeling he had waited long enough and wanting to return to Suriname, he also expressed the wish to be recognized as a council member once again.[69]

The States General requested the Society to dispatch representatives to The Hague. Here, on 30 March 1748, a meeting held at the Binnenhof, the seat of the States General, was chaired by the Viscount of Nijmegen, Adriaan van Lynden (c.1710-1785). The Society was able to dismiss the majority of complaints easily. Du Plessis's request to once again be recognized as a member of the Paramaribo-based Court of Police and Criminal Justice proved far more difficult. After all, the 1682 charter stated that vacant seats in that Court should be occupied 'in case of demise or departure'. The Society's representatives further argued that complaints forwarded by Du Plessis were unsubstantiated, as he had never seen to it these had been recorded. They warned that his return to Suriname would even result in murder and mayhem. His supporters might even perhaps mobilize their slaves numbering between 10,000 and 12,000. However, Van Lynden considered this fear to be hugely exaggerated.[70]

Tensions in the Republic increased after the States General had accepted a resolution which was very detrimental to the Society. Most importantly, it stated that Du Plessis was allowed to return to Suriname as a member of the Court of Police. The Society however refused to provide him with a passport. Less than 3 weeks later the States General accepted a secret resolution, hereby suspending the decision on Du Plessis's return. This quite remarkable manoeuvre can only be explained as a result of a personal interference by the Prince of Orange-Nassau,

---

67   Ibid., 101.
68   Ibid., 103.
69   Ibid., 104-105.
70   Ibid., 105-106.

Stadtholder Willem IV (1711-1751). The Society had apparently induced him to apply his influence. In 1749, Du Plessis requested assistance from the Dutch Prince, who thus became more and more involved in this conflict.[71] The former showed no hesitation at all. For, in order to back up his case, another petition addressed to the States General included a series of unsubstantiated accusations against Mauricius. Du Plessis also warned that, as a result of the Governor's actions, the large slave force may 'lead to a general massacre of all Europeans'.[72] He now struck a tender nerve: the fear for Africans felt in the Republic had been stirred up ever since a growing number of slaves had fled the plantations. According to planters, slaves could only be contained by means of harsh discipline, not by peace treaties. Also in 1749 Mauricius had, bearing the divide and rule-principle in mind, declared peace with a group of runaway slaves who had settled on the upper reaches of the Saramacca River. Plantation owners based in Amsterdam thus intensified the campaign against him. The umpteenth petition was now written.

Du Plessis's petition would probably have borne no fruit if, a few months later, news about a slave revolt on the Commewijne River had not yet reached the Republic. Slaves held at the plantation of Bethlehem had killed its owner, Amand Thoma, who was regarded as one of the most prominent cabalists. Mauricius considered this murder, not unjustly, as an outcome of Thoma's cruel treatment of slaves and his fornication with enslaved women. According to planters, this uprising was the outcome of the peace declared with runaway slaves located near the Saramacca River. These planters therefore demanded the Governor Mauricius be removed and the peace treaty annulled. In addition, 1,200 troops should be sent to the colony.[73]

On 3 February 1750, the States General decided to submit all related documents to the High Court of Holland and Zeeland because of 'heated disputes, which have upset the colony of Suriname for some time'.[74] A decision would then be made based on this Court's advice. The Society had now completely lost its grip on events unfolding in the Republic. Fearing that on-going disputes would lead to 'the destruction and collapse of the colony', the States General requested Prince Willem IV to ensure both peace and security.[75] Statements had even been voiced in the Republic to place Suriname under the direct rule of the States General and the Prince. Du Plessis had among others advocated this initiative which would nevertheless not result in an administrative revolution.

Prince Willem IV decided to send a commission to Suriname in order to investigate the grievances against Mauricius. On 20 August 1750 he signed, at Het Loo (a royal palace located at Apeldoorn in the Dutch province of Gelderland), several directives for Major-general Hendrik Ernst Baron von Spörcke and two officials hailing from the towns of Schiedam and Gorinchem.[76] Their task comprised (a) to restore harmony in the colony and (b) to obtain information on conflicts (in particular as to the peace treaty with runaway slaves) and on Amand Thoma's murder. These commissioners

---

71   Ibid., 106-108; J. Wolbers 1861, 222.
72   Van der Meiden 1987, 108.
73   Ibid., 109-113.
74   Ibid., 112.
75   Ibid., 113; Wolbers 1861, 222.
76   Ibid., 115-116; ibid., 222-223.

were authorised to send the Governor back to the Republic, if it would serve the peace. Next, Von Spörcke would officiate as an interim governor. Now once again the States General dispatched more troops to the colony, bringing their total to 300 men. Within the Society, heirs to Van Aerssen van Sommelsdijck's estate initially opposed any financial contributions. By contrast, nonetheless, another participant, to wit, Amsterdam was willing to pay for fear of losing any further influence. In due course it was agreed that the Society, including the WIC, would pay 25 per cent of the costs and the residents of Amsterdam 75 per cent.[77]

The Society's directors, of course, did not appreciate the inquiry the Dutch monarch had ordered. However, their opinion was no longer of much value in the Republic. Strong sentiments in the colony felt against the Governor did indeed impress Von Spörcke and his two commissioners. Although the latter did not object against Mauricius, these three men concluded that peace and order would be best served with his departure. Not delivering comments on the majority of the differences, as the High Court had still to deliver its judgement, Baron von Spörcke c.s. nevertheless did agree with Mauricius on one point, to wit, that the peace treaty declared with slaves at the Saramacca River and the revolt on the plantation of Bethlehem were unrelated. On the other hand, they held the view that Mauricius had (a) prosecuted some of Du Plessis's supporters of rebellion without reason and (b) appointed officials 'who were guilty of misconduct and despised and hated by most and the most eminent residents'.[78]

On 15 May 1751, Mauricius left Suriname as an extremely distraught man. This forced departure aroused his literary genius. In *Gezang op Zee* (Song at Sea) he launched a dramatic appeal to the Prince Willem IV:

'*I was sitting deep in the ship's cabin, embarrassed and defeated*
And deafened by the roar of the sea, musing, how I would best
And the least unpleasantly, with a detailed Petition
Recite my true state to Your Highness [...]
Stunned, dizzy, appalled, defeated and confused,
And deeply affected in the core of my heart
I feel my tongue trapped, and don't know to express,
Which emotions of the soul are hurling and beguiling me.
I see my time-honoured glory clouded and smeared
With thousand lies, even in my hometown;
My honest name downtrodden and violated
By evil slander, and false and fictional tales.
One has shamelessly spit me in the face
Poisoned with a viper, which even Hell abhors. [...]
A noble Prince's heart, that has learned from young age
nothing than virtue and honour, and only knows
dirty deceit and lies by name, is easiest misled,
And can impossibly understand, that the hate

---

77   Ibid., 115; ibid., 222.
78   Van der Meiden 1987, 118.

Of evil people rises till such rage. [...]
Still God knows it, my Prince! I am fully innocent,
Although I bear my cross, gently and patiently,
Don't believe, what one shouts about turmoil and violence,
And revolt by common folk, and what one tells more
With myths, dressed up in all kinds of forms [...].'[79]

The arrival of Mauricius and his personal defence mitigated sentiments across the Republic. Prince Willem IV granted him an audience. The Society now slightly regained its lost position. The suspicion against Du Plessis however increased. At the same time this dispute obtained a greater political significance as its key players now resided in the Republic. Documents pertaining to the complaints forwarded by Du Plessis and his allies even appeared in print. In 1752, Princess regent Anna van Oranje Nassau (1709-1759) was the first to receive this *Recueil van Egte Stukken en Bewyzen* (Collection of Real Documents and Evidence).[80] Prior hereto discussions had been held at The Hague between Society representatives and the aforementioned commissioners. Prince Willem's demise did not influence the course of events because the regent now fulfilled most duties. These commissioners arrived at a clear conclusion: Mauricius was an honest man. However, his return to the colony was, for the time being, out of the question, because the High Court had to deliver its judgement first.

Meanwhile a remarkable development in Suriname had speeded up events. After Baron von Spörcke's demise, on 7 September 1752, cabalists seized the moment to serve their cause. In what could be described as a coup d'etat they transferred the interim governorship to Colonel Otto Christiaan Baron van Verschuer (1720-1753).[81] According to the 1682 charter, Wigbolt Crommelin (1712-1789), commander of the troops, should have been called to that post. The Princess regent Anna made it clear to the Colonel he should resign. He did so without delay. The members of the Court of Police and Criminal Justice apologized for collaborating with this insurrection, stating they 'had acted out of fear for the power, that the man [Verschuer] held in his hands, because the troops were under his command, against which they had not dared to oppose'.[82]

The reality was quite different. The Paramaribo-based Court of Police and Criminal Justice had, based on various pretexts, postponed the succession of the governor to next forward Baron van Verschuer as a candidate. This conflict became even more explosive after Crommelin announced by means of the stroke of a drum that he had taken on the interim governorship. Next, Baron van Verschuer saw to it that the regimental drummers were arrested to then proclaim himself as the interim Governor. Rejecting this obvious explanation which council members had provided, Crommelin wrote in his journal:

---

79   Lichtveld & Voorhoeve 1980, 154-158.
80   Van der Meiden 1987, 122.
81   Wolbers 1861, 237-243.
82   Ibid., 241.

'What a miserable excuse – and at the same time how perfidious – but what are people, who have set aside all honour and shame, capable of doing! The gentleman Colonel would have never thought of taking over the Government, if it had not been placed in his head by the advocates of the Cabale, who have contrived day and night till they had brought things this far.'[83]

The afore-described incident undoubtedly worked in Mauricius's favour. For, on 15 May 1753, the States General acquitted him of all accusations, as per the High Court's judgement.[84] After Mauricius had decided to prosecute him, Du Plessis was imprisoned for a short time. The leader of the *cabale* (conspiracy) was released in due course, benefitting from a general amnesty, but subsequently exiled from the colony forever. To cabalists this outcome meant total defeat. All their requests had been rejected. The Court of Police and Criminal Justice, for example, did not obtain a greater say in colonial affairs. In addition, the peace treaty with the runaway slaves was not condemned either. The High Court had also concluded that both the governor and the Court of Police had every right to proceed with political evictions. The States General, in turn, confirmed the 1713 resolution, stating that the Society had made sufficient efforts towards defending the colony.

The Princess regent Anna appointed an entirely renewed Court of Police and Criminal Justice, excluding all cabalists. Their power had been largely based on the high debts many colonists had incurred. A financial development had equally undermined this position, too, after the Amsterdam banker-*cum*-mayor Willem Gideon Deutz (1697-1757) had started issuing plantation credits. The cabalist movement had cherished the hope Willem IV would finally reckon with regents, who had been most powerful during the Second Stadtholderless Period (1702-1747), once Willem III had passed away in 1702. Their hopes were in vain. Willem IV, by no means a strong character, had chosen to side with regents. The *cabale* had lost its relevance and the Society's authority was now no longer contested.

---

83   Ibid., 241.
84   Ibid., 246-249; Van der Meiden 1987, 123-127.

CHAPTER 3
The white colonial society

3.1 Arrival of the first white colonists
Immediately after Abraham Crijnssen's conquest of Suriname in 1667 the issue had been: how to entice sufficient white colonists to set off for the Wild Coast. In 1667 Suriname counted *c*.1,500 English inhabitants. According to Governor Johannes Heinsius (1678-1680), this number, had dropped to *c*.500 white souls in 1679.[1] In 1669, a group of 55 Jewish and British planters had sent a petition to Governor Philip Julius Lichtenberg (1669-1671), with the request

> *'to provide the colony with whites, be it servants or the like [...] such persons, from whom, with time, workers can be formed. That is the most essential [...]. It is the Seminary from which good and sensible planters must always come forth.'*[2]

The reality was nonetheless different. Though enthusiasm for future colonisation plans had increased during the 17th century, especially after the loss of Dutch Brazil in 1654, those interested in settling in Suriname were mainly financiers or adventurers. Potential colonists often deemed such an undertaking too hazardous. Propagandist pamphlets portraying Suriname as a place where fortunes were for the taking did not reinforce their opinions. Prosperous craftsmen and traders in the Republic simply had little reason to migrate.

In order to populate the newly established colony the authorities thus opted for lawbreakers detained at penitentiaries. After arriving at Suriname as white 'servants', they were to be transformed into 'honest folks', with the prospect of acquiring a plot of land.[3] Soul-sellers lured the destitute to travel to the colony uttering beautiful words and empty promises. These recruiters now and again retained paupers in Amsterdam until contracts were signed. Servants either worked on plantations or cultivated the land as tenants with the help of several slaves. Their numbers in Suriname were however low when compared with indentured labourers active in English colonies.[4]

Complaints about servants were often heard. On 27 May 1687, Governor Cornelis van Aerssen van Sommelsdijck wrote to the Society that the 'soul-sellers were providing bad people, pretended workmen, worth nothing, only as soldiers'.[5] He referred to a court case concerning three carpenters and a tailor who had confessed to the Governor as well as to the Court of Police that they were in fact not craftsmen adding that soul-sellers had instructed them to falsely present themselves as such.[6]

---

1   As stated in a letter sent by Governor Heinsius to the States of Zeeland dated 3 May 1679, see: Zeeland Archives, ZA, 2.1., 2035-328.
2   Van der Linde 1966, 52.
3   As stated in a letter sent by Governor Lichtenberg to the States of Zeeland dated 18 March 1669, see: Zeeland Archives, ZA, 2.1, 2035-124.
4   Van der Linde 1966, 56-57.
5   Ibid., 57.
6   Ibid., 57.

Soldiers often lived in extraordinarily wretched conditions. Together with slaves they frequently carried out heavy labour, for example, when constructing fortifications. This explains why large numbers of troops participated in the 1688 mutiny against Van Aerssen van Sommelsdijck (see p. 29) who served as governor between 1683-1688. His successor Johan van Scharphuijsen (died 1699) wisely requested the Society's directors to discontinue sending such men:

> 'The banned scoundrels are doing so much evil here among the slaves and other craftsmen that the colony does not need them [...].'[7]

In Suriname the concept had also emerged to acquire orphans from overcrowded orphanages located in the Republic. Between 1686 and 1690 dozens of children from the Amsterdam-based orphanage named *Aelmoesseniersweeshuys* travelled to the colony. This initiative aimed at raising the level of its colonists. Before sending them off, board members of this orphanage pronounced the proviso

> '[...] that these children will not be orphaned nor be placed with Jews or non-Christians to be used as slaves, but only with those of the reformed religion to carry out domestic work or their craft.'[8]

Difficulties experienced while building this colony can also be gleaned from the sluggish growth of the number of plantations (see p. 30, 181-182). Interest in settling here stemmed largely from outside the Republic. In 1667, 200 French colonists migrated to Suriname after English troops had conquered Cayenne (French Guiana) only to return 2 years later after its recapture. Two decades later French Huguenots arrived in Suriname via the Republic after Louis XIV had revoked the Edict of Nantes in 1685, hereby heralding the end of religious freedom in France. Prior to 1700, approximately 500 French Huguenots had already settled in Suriname. Hence plantations were given names such as *Peu et Content* and *Mon Plaisir*.[9] These Huguenots soon intermingled with the Dutch population. Several of their descendants officiated as governors of Suriname.

Many migrants originated from the Pfalz (Southwest Germany), fleeing misery and war.[10] They embarked on this adventure not only enticed by stories describing easy money but also encouraged by the Society's German director, Philip Hack (1677-1742). Between 1734 and 1740, more than 100 Pfalzers arrived in Paramaribo with a desire to earn a living in agriculture. Unable to cope with harsh conditions, diseases took a heavy toll. During the aforementioned 6-year period, the Society employed German miners when establishing gold mines. When one of them collapsed forty men perished, causing this colonisation attempt to fail too. In 1749 yet another German settlement was discontinued as a result of attacks carried out by runaway slaves. Governor-general Gerard van de Schepper (1738-1742) had already

---

7   Ibid., 57-58.
8   Ibid., 56.
9   Abbenhuis 1943a, 131-132.
10   Ibid., 133-134; Wolbers 1861, 111-113.

requested to halt the immigration of mainly destitute Pfalzers because they included too much riffraff. Over the years, however, quite a number of German immigrants (e.g., planters, physicians) would settle in Suriname. Of substantial importance were the Moravian Brethren, a pietist movement with socio-cultural influences active in Europe and South America. They had begun to convert Amerindians and runaways to Christianity from the mid-1700s on, as was the case, a century later, with slaves (see p. 66, 144, 163-165, 171-172).

3.2 Jewish immigration

Jews were among the first European colonists to populate Suriname. They also settled on the Caribbean isle of Curaçao, hereby contributing significantly to the economic growth throughout the region. Their sojourn in Suriname had a more permanent character when compared with other colonists.

The Jewish colonisation in the New World had already started during the 16th century. Persecution by the Tribunal of the Holy Office of the Inquisition (aka the Spanish Inquisition) across the Iberian Peninsula formed the key incentive for large numbers of Jews to seek refuge elsewhere, many of whom migrated to Brazil. Here, in the coastal regions of Pernambuco and Bahia, these Marranos could practise their religion once again, partly in secret. Portuguese (i.e., Sephardic) Jews contributed largely to the sugar production. Many made a living for instance by trading in slaves. Their financial success was mainly the outcome of family relationships, which were also business contacts. Marranos residing in Brazil maintained close links with Jews who had moved on either to Amsterdam or Flanders. This immigration reached its peak during Johan Maurits van Nassau-Siegen's (1604-1679) reign over Brazil (1637-1645), where Jews now enjoyed full religious freedom.[11] Their prosperity declined, not coincidentally, with the conclusion of Dutch rule in 1654. In due course, Jews left Brazil when incoming Portuguese not only prohibited them from practising their religion but also from residing on Portuguese territory.

Numerous Jews subsequently travelled across the West Indies. Especially Essequibo (now Guyana), which had been in Dutch hands from 1634 on, proved to be a much valued place of refuge. After all, those immigrants had already experienced liberal Dutch rule in Brazil. After the 1666 English incursion from Barbados, during which all sugar plantations were destroyed, the majority of Jews left for Suriname. Cayenne (French Guiana) was a popular destination, too. In 1664, after French troops had recaptured this town, Jews had also set off for Suriname where they were more than welcome thanks to their expertise both in sugar cultivation and financial matters.[12] The same rings true as to English colonies e.g., Jamaica and Barbados. At around the end of the 17th and the dawn of the 18th century, Jewish communities were founded in North America after Jews hailing from Barbados and Jamaica arrived in New York. On the isle of Curaçao, they were active in the transit trade to South America. When Governor Lord Francis Willoughby (1613-1671) sailed from Barbados

---

11   Boxer 1957, 123-124, 133-134.
12   Wolbers 1861, 37.

to Suriname in 1652, he took many Jews with him.[13] These first Jewish colonists settled in Thorarica, a town located on the Suriname River, north of Paramaribo.

Colonial authorities granted special privileges to Jewish settlers. On 12 September 1659, the WIC had provided the professional colonist named David Cohen Nassy (1612-1685) cum suis with a charter entitled *Vrijheden onder Exemptien* (Liberties under Exemptions).[14] Newcomers had now acquired the right to settle either in Cayenne or at other locations on the Wild Coast. These exclusive rights also allowed for a specific type of autonomy. In later years this charter formed the basis for entitlements presented to Jews. Its Article II stated:

> 'The said David Nassy and his partners shall be allowed jurisdiction over the bays which may be found in the colony, which is to be established and to half of the rivers situated at either side of the colony, of which assignation will be made hereafter, always provided that the Company reserves to themselves or to their assigns, the right of free navigation and trade in those bays and up and down the said rivers.'[15]

Moreover, we read in Article VII:

> 'It shall be permitted to the Jews to have freedom of conscience with public worship, and a synagogue and school, in the same manner as is allowed in the city of Amsterdam, in accordance with the doctrines of their elders, without hindrance, as well in the district of this colony, as in other places of our dominions, and that they shall enjoy all liberties and exemptions of our other colonists as long as they remain there; but the aforesaid patron and his partners shall be bound to preserve the said freedom of conscience to all the other colonists of any nation there and that with the worship and the public rites of the Reformed religion, or any other that may happen to be in the country.'[16]

Jewish colonists were allowed to deal with all disputes or litigations in accordance with their own time-honoured rules and regulations, with the proviso that sentences did not exceed the lump sum of 500 guilders, although an appeal to government bodies remained possible. In 1665, English colonial rulers had granted key privileges to Jewish colonists, too, including the freedom of religion and education.[17]

David Cohen Nassy played a significant role in the Jewish colonisation across the West Indies. Having migrated to Amsterdam after a sojourn in Brazil, where he had acquired a fortune as a trade companion, Nassy was later also engaged in plans concerning Jewish settlements later founded in Essequibo, Curaçao and Suriname. Until the end of the 18th century, his family members continued to occupy a prominent position within the Jewish community. A Jewish colony was called a Nation, a term of no value to international law. Symbolising its rise from the ashes, the Nation of Portuguese Jews was named *De Phoenix*, as was their Amsterdam-based community.

---

13   Parker 2015, 113-115; Oudschans Dentz 1927, 11.
14   Oudschans Dentz 1927, 40-44;
15   Arbell 2002, 55.
16   Ibid., 56.
17   Ibid., 85-86.

A History of Suriname

Figure 3.1. The 'Joode Savanne' on the Suriname River. Drawing by J.G. Stedman (orig. 1790). J.G. Stedman 1987.

In 1685, a synagogue was built south of Paramaribo in a savannah area located on the Suriname River which could be reached only after a 10-hour walk. This *Joode Savanne* comprised a small number of houses and plantations.[18]

The Jewish people residing in Suriname soon achieved relative prosperity. In 1730, they owned 115 of the 400 sugar plantations.[19] After the immigration of Sephardic (Portuguese) Jews, Ashkenazi Jews followed. The latter, however, were less well-off, earning a living either as craftsmen or traders. Differences in status between these two communities caused internal tensions. In due course both denominations were to build their own synagogues.

3.3 Social structure

Plantation owners formed an economic and political elite. The first colonists as yet resided on plantations together with their families and a number of slaves. In later years many planters moved to Paramaribo, mainly for social reasons e.g., not being capable of appreciating loneliness as experienced across the interior of Suriname. The growing danger of suffering attacks by runaway slaves probably played a role, too. A historic report mentions that:

> *'The (lust and) desire to be more with other Europeans, the delectation provided by the town, though hardly sophisticated or noble, attracted them, and now they found, that there were, moreover, important reasons, for example that one could negotiate, thanks to the direct communication with the sea captains, higher*

---

18 See: Cohen 1991, *Jews in another environment, Surinam in the second half of the eighteenth century*; see also: *Essai sur la colonie de Surinam, sa fondation, ses révolutions, ses progrès* [...] 1788, written by leaders of the Nation of Portuguese Jews, including D.C. Nassy; Abbenhuis 1943a, 120-127.

19 Abbenhuis 1943a, 122.

prices for their wares and lower prices for what they needed themselves; and
that one could – this was a weighty argument – have a greater influence on the
administration etc..'[20]

Planters who had acquired sufficient wealth returned to Europa over time, leaving the management of their plantations to administrators after appointing directors, who in turn employed *blankofficieren* (white overseers). In the course of the 18th century, this group of administrators became increasingly important. Their number soared after the 1773 financial market crisis, when numerous plantations passed into the hands of Amsterdam-based creditors. On occasion governors supplemented their salaries when managing plantations. Colonists who administered more than one plantation earned substantial extra incomes. Little wonder mutual envy arose to a degree, whereby one did not hesitate to vilify each other in the Republic, in the hope to seize plantations from rivals. Doctors, lawyers and pharmacists who also formed part of the colonial elite were never able to amass fortunes in the manner planters and administrators had. White overseers, clerks employed in administration offices and low-ranking civil servants led far from prosperous lives. At the dawn of the Colonial Era, civil servants, as yet a small group, did not form a separate social class, as a large number of them either owned land or pursued other commercial interests. However, this all changed in the course of the 19th century, when the public administration expanded.

A genuine class of traders only emerged after the 1863 abolition of slavery. Prior hereto plantation owners and administrators had fulfilled a pivotal role when trading. All colonial wares went through Paramaribo to be taxed and then sent on to the Republic. Administrators and planters personally dealt with purchasing requirements for plantations. In 1798, according to that year's *Surinaamsche Almanach*, Paramaribo counted four wholesalers of American products whereas 32 either large or small traders were dealing in Dutch goods.[21] However, the majority hereof comprised retailers (so-called *vettewariërs*), whom other tradesmen considered to be smugglers.[22]

Initially not many craftsmen were active in Paramaribo, implying that a large quantity of goods had to be imported directly from the Republic. The physician-*cum*-chronicler Philip Fermin (1729-1813) lived in Suriname between 1754 and 1764. Mentioning as little as two tailors, two shoemakers, two bakers, two butchers, two carpenters, one bricklayer and one blacksmith, he adds:

'This at least is sure, that the lack of craftsmen makes everything very expensive;
while one pays for bespoke work on a complete garment 25 or 30 Dutch guilders,
without counting the advance; 25 guilders for a wig; and 4 or 5 guilders for a pair
of shoes.'[23]

---

20   Wolbers 1861, 189.
21   *Surinaamsche Almanach*, 'Naamlyst der kooplieden, winkeliers en neeringdoende ingezeetenen', 1798.
22   Abbenhuis 1944, 106.
23   Fermin 1770, part 1, 95.

Figure 3.2. This drawing by P.J. Benoit (orig. 1839) depicts the fish and timber market located at the Waterkant (Paramaribo). P.J. Benoit 1980.

This shortage became less acute soon after the number of free non-whites in Paramaribo had started to increase (see p. 92ff.). The military garrison also formed a significant part of the white colonial population. Governor Van Aerssen van Sommelsdijck had taken three militias each consisting of 100 men from the Republic with him, thus bringing the total to *c.* 400 troops.[24] That number was further increased in the course of the 18th century in order to cope with the intensifying struggle against runaway slaves (see p. 103ff.).[25] Aside from skilled officers, the quality of the soldiers, hailing from various parts of Europe, was generally poor. A majority had in fact recently been released from prison.

Thanks to the increase of its population and prosperity Paramaribo acquired a certain allure both as an economic and administrative hub. Van Aerssen van Sommelsdijck upon his arrival in 1683 had only come across a fortress and circa 50 houses. At the time of the 1712 attack carried out by French troops, serving under navy Captain J. Cassard, Paramaribo counted around 500 houses. Fifty years later around 800 dwellings had been built.[26] According to a survey carried out in 1787, Paramaribo was home to 2,000 white inhabitants excluding soldiers, but with the inclusion of 615 Sephardic and 430 Ashkenazi Jews. They owned a few thousand slaves, mainly domestic workers.[27] At that time this town housed almost 650 'free

---

24   Van der Meiden 1987, 31, 36.
25   Lohnstein 1987, 67, 72.
26   Wolbers 1861, 178.
27   Nassy 1788, seconde partie, 37.

Mulattos and Negroes', all of them either concubines, manumitted children of white colonists, Black women or those of colour and domestic servants.[28] Now 3,356 whites (excluding troops) and *c.* 50,000 slaves populated the entire colony.[29] One counted here, in 1833 2,045 white inhabitants and thus less than the 4,951 free people of colour and free Black people (see Table 4.2 p. 93). Adriaan François Lammens (1767-1847), who served in Suriname's judiciary between 1816 and 1835, enthusiastically describes the colourful life that could surprise visitors to Paramaribo:

'The observation of the activity, which the trade and shipping generate in certain months, is very pleasant for the philanthropist: - the crowd of porters, barges, dugout canoes, tent boats: - the transportation of the goods with carts: - Whites, coloureds, blacks, Indians coming and going - the markets or wooijwooijen offering foodstuffs in abundance, he can only regard them as evidence of a general prosperity; - for the newcomer, not used to finding himself in one of the most frequented quarters of a mercantile town, it is as if he sees a spiced up story, from the Arabian Nights tales.'[30]

3.4 A society without cohesion

Suriname's colonial society lacked the unity which had been a trait of Spanish colonies across South America where the Roman Catholic Church acted as a binding force. Here, too, a larger number of European immigrants enhanced racial intermingling. At any rate, the Dutch colony's social cohesion was less comprehensive, because of the diverse origins of white colonists. Governor Mauricius clearly noted this fact when writing to the States General:

'[...] and one must always remember, that the majority of the inhabitants of the colony consist of a confluence of various nations, resulting in four natural consequences: (1) That many, being born under a monarchical government and now hearing they are under a free one, jump from one extremity to the other, imagining that the liberty consists of libertinage and anarchy, (2) That at least being alien to most, not having a Dutch heart, and consequently no patriotic sentiments, as they do not consider the Netherlands their fatherland, (3) That between folks of different nations there cannot possibly be such a bond of harmony, that ordinarily exists between uniform countrymen, as in French and English colonies and (4) That they will always retain animum revertendi and thus have no attachment to a country, which they do not consider a domicile for them and their children, but only a country of foreignness and transit.'[31]

A French intendant based at Cayenne named Pierre-Victor, Baron Malouet (1740-1814), having visited neighbouring Suriname in 1777, concluded that a

---

28   Ibid.
29   Ibid., 38-39.
30   Lammens 1816-1822, 63.
31   Wolbers 1861, 172.

specific intermingling of cultures occurred across the board, resulting in what he referred to as 'colonial habits'.[32] The tropical climate, quick earnings and white sense of superiority led to an easy-going, loose lifestyle, which also manifested itself elsewhere in the West Indies. The *animum revertendi* (i.e., an intense desire to return to one's homeland after amassing a fortune), as Governor Mauricius mentions, can be observed in other plantation economies, too. This longing possibly contributed to these 'colonial habits'. In his 1971 social analysis of the history of Suriname, R.A.J. Van Lier aptly spoke of a 'frontier society'.[33] The portraits which contemporaries have painted of colonists are by and large rather negative. Mauricius wrote in a letter addressed to the States General:

> '*One could hereby add remarks, coming from the same source, especially that many are folks either without education, or those who had always been trouble in their fatherland, and (then) have no or very wrong ideas on religion, justice, but especially on what one refers to as order, decency and shame. Such people fall out lightly, and the smallest dispute is bitter and unyielding. But I have to do right to the inhabitants here, that they, as long they stay in a lesser condition, are peaceful and pliable, and even, no matter how much agitated and incited, always showed an aversion to insurrection; but when they climb out of their néant to riches or honour, it usually goes to their heads.*'[34]

Needless to say, the fact that so many governors expressed their sorrows and needs had much to do with an administrative inability to tackle problems which headstrong colonists continuously posed. English colonial authorities often expressed a similar view on the population of their colonies founded in the West Indies and North America. Moreover, those less scarred by frustrations had little sympathy for white colonists residing in Suriname who had in many cases been derailed resulting from the absolute power they were able to wield over Black slaves. Numerous reports describe the cruel treatment they underwent (see p. 79ff.). In his hugely influential publication entitled *The Narrative of a Five Years Expedition against the Revolted Negroes of Surinam* (1790), John Gabriel Stedman (1744-1797), an officer of the Scots Brigade who served in the army of the Dutch Republic, sarcastically portrays an affluent planter thus:

> '*His worship generally begins to yawn about 10 or 11 o'clock - when he withdraws, and being undressed by his sooty pages, he retires to rest, where he passes the night in the arms of one or other of his sable sultanas, for he always keeps a seraglio, till about 6 o'clock in the morning when he again is reparing to his piazza walk, where his pipe and coffee are waiting for his commands, and where / with the rising sun / he begins his round of dicipation like a little king, despotick, absolute and*

---

32   Van Lier 1971, 38-40.
33   Ibid., 7-8.
34   Wolbers 1861, 172-173.

without controlle, and which cannot but have the greater relish to a man, who in
his own country viz. Europe was ten to one a – nothing – which in this colony is too
frequently the case [...].'[35]

The Dutch pastor Gerardus Balthazar Bosch (1794-1837) who visited Suriname during the early 1800s was also by no means measured. We read in his 1842 travelogue a denouncement of those colonists who pursued pleasure 'with a kind of obsession':

'[...] *They are usually also the ones, who, since they have squandered in Europe their belongings in all gaiety, could only choose between suicide, beggary or – leaving for the East or West, where they of course have not filled the purses immediately, but have to carry out activities, which are too heavy for their exhausted nature. Now they seek revenge on the slaves, drink a lot of rum, pursue the pleasure of lovemaking without leaving a trace, and then – they die in despair. Many are struck by this fate.'[36]*

The reality was perhaps slightly more nuanced. For, in the course of the 19th century, the white population's moral standing had improved slightly. Colonists no doubt allowed themselves far more liberties than they ever would have done in Europe. A lack of culture surely played a role in Suriname. Considering its inhabitants' considerable diversity one could hardly speak of a specific tradition. Moreover, Suriname's society was very individualistic. This trait did indeed undermine any local solid socio-cultural developments. The majority of colonists were bereft of strong family ties, as these European fortune hunters had frequently set off for Suriname on their own. Having cohabited with Black concubines and/or those of colour, their offspring was born in slavery. These relations often came to a conclusion when colonists returned to Europe:

'One does not find in the colony that bond of a union, that family relationships have – that requires and obliges parents, to take care of the education of their children, which is so necessary for their life afterwards.'[37]

The lifestyle of the Suriname elite was highly consumptive. As a result of the large cash flow provided by Amsterdam-based creditors, a nouveau riche had emerged during the second half of the 18th century, be it only until the 1773 Amsterdam financial crisis. A large part of their accumulated credits had not been invested but spent on luxury goods and/or trips to Europe. Craftsmen, sailors and soldiers, all without any knowledge of agriculture, suddenly gave the impression they were members of the planter aristocracy. However, their lifestyles would often be more extravagant than those of the 'old' elite, this in contrast to Europe where the lifestyles of wealthy craftsmen would more often be related to their social class than to their

---

35   Stedman 1790, 366.
36   Bosch 1843, 92-93.
37   Lammens 1816-1822, 152.

monetary assets. A traditional social hierarchy was maintained within the colonial society in spite of one's social mobility.

> '*Many people imagine, wrongly for sure, that in Suriname one has a 'depraved' taste, be it in food or clothing. All one can say, is, that a freedom is allowed which is unknown in our large towns.*'[38]

A medical doctor named Philip Fermin (1730-1813) presented the above observation. He was one of the few not to judge the 'ordinary way of living and commerce of the Europeans, living in Paramaribo' in a negative manner:

> '[...] *everyone lives without coercion, except the women, who due to the pleasure of willing to please, are without the same convenience; but, she is forgiven, nobody blames her; they are not the only ones, who are fond of the new fashions, which, almost as soon as they are invented, for the men as well as for the women, are brought from Europe, and which everybody, despite what I have said, uses according to his taste, not without splendour and costs. The multitude of stores and warehouses in the town, which are provided with all sorts of goods, is proof that one dresses at least as well as in Europa, and that splendour reigns as well: broadcloth, velvet, fabric, gold and silver trimming, nothing is lacking; [...] A planter is, to express myself this way, well capable, to have the most delicious and abundant tables, still without taking into account the considerable apparatus, with which one is being served by a crowd of slaves, which makes that the lowest citizens seem like gentlemen; because not only the planters have slaves, but from the highest to the lowest, they have some at their disposal.*'[39]

This grandeur of the planter elite, according to most chroniclers, did not usually testify to a sophisticated taste, but was an outcome of the dissimilar mind set observed across the colony. Hardly any cultural, artistic or spiritual elevation existed, at least not until the conclusion of the 18th century.

> '*One desires everything for the flesh, nothing for the mind.*'[40]

The aforementioned lament was voiced by Marten Douwes Teenstra (1795-1864), a gentleman farmer originally from the Dutch province of Groningen. He had, in *c.*1830, officiated for several years as an agricultural advisor to the government of Suriname. Another source reports that many colonists

> '[...] *consider their books as old clothes, which one stores in a chest or trunk, till they are consumed by moths, cockroaches or woodworms.*'[41]

---

38   Fermin 1770, part 1, 85.
39   Ibid., 86-88.
40   Teenstra 1842, 59.
41   Lammens 1816-1822, 95.

Gaspard Phillipe Charles van Breugel (1798-1888), a planter whose visit (1823-1824) to Suriname lasted 8 months, shared this view on colonists:

> '*The plantation life in this way did not please me at all. Fun! Fun! Always fun, without doing something serious in order to exercise the spirit.*'[42]

To a certain degree, a turning point occurred after the 1773 Amsterdam financial crisis. The large credit flow witnessed during earlier years had enticed enlightened spirits to travel to the colony. *Het Genootschap der Surinaamsche Lettervrinden* (The Society of Surinamese Friends of Literature) was founded in 1785 to later publish several poetry collections and be dissolved 5 years later.[43] Other societies focused on the study of arts, literature, agriculture and nature, e.g., *Docendo Docemur* (We are taught by teaching), initiated by prominent Portuguese Jews, and the *Maatschappij tot Nut van het algemeen* (Society for the benefit of the general public).[44] By and large, these institutes were not destined to exist for a long time.

During the mid-1770s, Freemasons' lodges were established, a number of which disappeared almost immediately. It may be added here that the Lodge Concordia (1761) was the first ever to be inaugurated on the continent of South America.[45] Several governors have been recorded as members of this brethren. Nevertheless all the aforementioned organizations hardly contributed to any form of cultural revival, bar a few newspapers. The below complaint about this absence of cultural life was voiced:

> '[...] *in a country, where one is indifferent to anything, that does not directly make money, or that are not products: - where one asks only for the revenue from sugar, coffee and cotton, the zeal is extinguished.*'[46]

Card games, dice and billiards enjoyed by wealthy white colonists often involved large sums of money, which led to excesses. In 1761 such conduct provided authorities with a reason to ban *hasardspelen* (games of chance) under penalty of a fine of 200 guilders.[47] As to other games, a maximum loss of 50 guilders per evening was imposed. Numerous regularly repeated decrees and ordinances confirm the general impression of a rather uncivilized society. In an ordinance dated 4 February 1761 authorities complained that

> '[...] *arguments occur daily, squabbles and fights, hereby disturbing the common peace and harmony of the good residents here.*'[48]

---

42   Van Breugel 1842, 66.
43   Lichtveld & Voorhoeve 1980, 175; Van Kempen 2002, vol. 3, 90-94.
44   Nassy 1788, seconde partie, 175-185; Cohen 1991, 99-101; Van Kempen 2002, vol. 3, 87-89.
45   Van Kempen 2002, vol. 3, 86.
46   Lammens 1816-1822, 95.
47   Teenstra 1842, 63.
48   Schiltkamp & De Smidt 1973, vol. 2 , 718-719.

After inflicting physical injury a 100 guilder fine had to be paid. Surgeons had to report such events to the prosecutor, also under penalty of a fine. Rules and regulations pertaining to selling alcoholic drams and other spirits were multiple, due to the many disorderly examples of alcohol abuse.

3.5 Sexual relations of whites with people of colour and Black people
Sexual relations between whites, people of colour and Black people were no exception in Suriname. In other colonies, too, this phenomenon was by no means rare, and especially frequent in Portuguese territories. Here, as a result of the shared Roman Catholic faith, the distance between races was relatively small. Indeed, far less intermingling of colonists and slaves took place elsewhere.

According to the first plantation regulation dated 9 May 1686, colonists who 'bond with the negresses or rather with the free female Indians and commit carnal conversation' were to be punished with 'forfeiture of 2 pounds of sugar'.[49] This interdiction was repeated in 1725.[50] And again, on 27 December 1759, when Governor-general Wigbold Crommelin (1757-1768) issued a 'regulation for the plantation servants'; in the case of violations, a penalty of 200 Dutch guilders ensued. This ruling strictly prohibited

> '*explicitly to all inhabitants, plantation servants as well as free craftsmen, without exception, regardless of how or where, to intermingle with female slaves, and even less to associate with several at the same time* [...].'[51]

Colonial authorities regarded sexual intercourse between Black men and white women a mortal sin because it would completely disrupt the social order. Only a few such incidences came to light. A decree dated 28 January 1711 forwarded by Governor Johan de Goyer (1710-1715) stated that unmarried white women who had slept with a Black man should be flogged and then expelled from the colony. A white married woman should also be marked with a branding iron. Black men were to receive the death penalty.[52]

Concubinage became more and more acceptable in the course of the 18th century whereby hardly anyone felt obliged to comply with the official ban. According to an eased plantation rule dated 31 August 1784, a fine of 200 Dutch guilders would only be imposed if 'in the case of any intermingling of white men with female slaves a number of disorders occur on the plantations'.[53] Here, in particular, cohabitation out of wedlock was a frequent phenomenon, being an outcome of demographic trends. At the onset of the Colonial Era, husbands and wives travelled to Suriname together. They both usually worked on small plantations, employing a number of slaves. Following the Amsterdam financial crisis (1773), numerous planters were forced to return to the Republic, as creditors had struck. Generally speaking, unmarried directors and white overseers replaced these plantation owners.

---

49   Schiltkamp & De Smidt 1973, vol. 1, 168.
50   Ibid., 383.
51   Ibid., 669.
52   Ibid., 277.
53   Ibid., vol. 2, 1074.

Indeed the Paramaribo-based administrators did not permit plantation directors to marry, under the threat of being dismissed. This interdiction pertained to the very hierarchical plantation organization whereby the wife of a director could disturb the strict discipline, when entertaining too cordial or close relationships with the wife of an overseer. Overseers did not marry because it could impede a promotion. The surplus of white men was the largest in the districts of Suriname. In 1830, their number was 497 as opposed to only 35 white women; Paramaribo was populated by 766 white males and 545 white females.[54]

White colonists residing on plantations often took in a Black woman, and even better woman of colour. In many cases they paid for manumitting a concubine who often served as a housekeeper as well as a mistress. Interracial marriages were impossible for both legal and social reasons. Colonists could easily find either a Black woman or of colour because entire non-white families were eager to 'catch such a fish'.[55] After all, relations with a white male provided a certain degree of material security and status. In Paramaribo a *Surinaamsch huwelijk* (Surinamese marriage) was often accompanied with a small ceremony underlining its semi-official nature. The consent of one's mother was of great importance. In his travelogue, G.P.C. van Breugel describes such a marital rite thus:

> '*Once the choice has been made, he must declare it; and if this outpouring of love is accepted with delight, then one has to court her for some time. On the day of the union the bride's mother, accompanied by a female neighbour, in black, takes the bride into the groom's bedroom, who is already waiting for his bride; the mother and the neighbour leave, to return to the bedroom the next morning, from where the newly-wed couple has disappeared, in order to next announce to the neighbours that the marriage has taken place; from that moment this is considered legal.*'[56]

The sustainability of these conjugal bonds could vary considerably. For whites hailing from lower social classes and for soldiers, a *Surinaamsch huwelijk* was nothing more than a 'one-month-long marriage'.[57] It has further also been recorded that a male who already had a concubine could again marry a white female. He was blamed the most if taking one more housekeeper, too. Moreover, if not bequeathing a large trousseau to an abandoned concubine, according to the chronicler Van Breugel, such men were considered improper 'although this did not entirely cost him his good name, because the envy and the family of the second housekeeper in turn speaks of the perfidy from her side'.[58]

Abandoned concubines apparently became mistresses (*buitenvrouwen*, lit. outside wives) of men who were either married or already cohabited with a concubine. Now and again wealthy males supported more than one female, with whom they also

---

54   Teenstra 1835, vol. 2, 203.
55   Van Breugel 1842, 30.
56   Ibid.
57   Teenstra 1842, 66.
58   Van Breugel 1842, 31.

had children. In present-day Suriname, concubinage and *buitenvrouwen* are not uncommon phenomena, especially among Creoles.[59]

White husbands did not treat Black women or those of colour as equals. The latter often stayed in the company either of others in similar situations or with members of their own family. These women did not accompany their men on visits and on occasion did not dine with them at the same table. They could not make any claims to their husband's estate, unless recorded otherwise. Aware of the fact such relations were either accepted or at best tolerated, these women realized at the same time that their liaisons would end as soon as their husbands returned to Europe. This notion explains why wives often attempted to acquire certain possessions as a material security for themselves and their children. A number of wives were able to acquire several slaves. Now and again men did indeed designate concubines as heirs. These relations had matriarchal traits whereby mothers were of key importance to the children, especially if their husbands were to leave the colony at some point.[60]

The fact white males maintained sexual relations with Black females or of colour did not lead to any narrowing of social distances between racial groups. In the view of white colonists, this rapprochement was undesirable because hierarchical colonial relationships would otherwise be disturbed.

Quite telling here is the policy outlined by colonial authorities as encountered in the case of a free-born Black woman named Elisabeth Samson (1715-1771) who in 1764 wished to marry a white man. Born into a wealthy family, she was able to increase the value of her assets fourfold to 1,000,000 guilders by means of business acumen, solid management of her plantations and the then benign economy. She had presumably expected authorities to soften their stance because of her wealth to then grant her the coveted status of being a married woman.[61] The marital affairs commissioners to whom the 50-year-old Elisabeth Samson and the 30-year-old Christoph Policarpus Brabandt had applied to register their planned marriage, referred the case to the Court of Police and Criminal Justice. However, its members who did not know how to act either therefore presented the case to the directors of the Society, stating in a letter their pros and cons as follows:

> '*The argument against such a marriage is that it is repugnant and horrible, utterly disgraceful for a white, that he, either out of bad lust or for food, enters into such a marriage, that has always been held in contempt here. It is also for certain, that we are people of a better and nobler nature than they. We must keep our balance in the middle of such a wrong and distorted genus, with our essential might, and what will they even believe of the excellent nature, if they see, that they only have to be free, to have a bond, through a solemn union of marriage with us [...].*'[62]

---

59   Buschkens 1974, 177-185.
60   Lammens 1816-1822, 92-93.
61   In her 1993 publication McLeod established that Elisabeth Samson was an educated woman with business acumen hereby correcting to a certain degree the stereotypical image earlier authors had sketched. The latter all incorrectly suggested Elisabeth Samson had been born into slavery and would have inherited her fortune from her master. McLeod's in-depth research formed the basis for a novel, translated into English entitled *The Free Negress Elisabeth* (2004, 2008).
62   McLeod 1993, 69.

Elisabeth Samson's large wealth presented, according to the aforementioned Court, an argument in favour of this marriage, because her assets would over time end up in the hands of whites,

> 'which is not bad, because having here overly powerful free people among the negroes, from that a lot of evil is to be feared, since it gives already an idea to our slaves, that they can rise high, if we leave the assets of this Elisabeth Samson to her family, it is and remains under [control of] negroes and negresses.'[63]

In due course, Court members aired their opposition against the marriage. For, if they were to condone it, Black men would be able to marry white women, which they deemed to be 'naturally incestuous'.[64] Moreover, Elisabeth Samson had also applied to the directors of the Society who in turn left the decision to the aforementioned Court. Her intended husband having passed away, she wished to marry another white man 3 years later. This Court now consented, be it only after the States General had already stated it saw no legal impediments as Elisabeth Samson was both a Christian and free.[65]

3.6 Education
Even during the economic boom only primary schools could be attended in Suriname. According to the 1682 charter, the governor and council members had the power to levy certain small taxes (*modique lasten*) in order to pay for personal and/or material expenses (e.g., pertaining to government officials, council members, judges, religious services, schoolmasters etc.) 'for as much this would be deemed necessary or useful'.[66] Colonists were not prepared to spend large sums of money on tuition. In Paramaribo, on 5 December 1685, Waltherus van Aernhem after being appointed as the first schoolmaster received a salary of 300 guilders per annum.[67] He was also a precentor, lector and parish clerk in the Reformed Church. A French school founded in 1690 was to be followed much later, in 1766, by a Lutheran school.

At first it was not easy to enroll schoolmasters - no great surprise when realizing considering such paltry salaries. On occasion one even resorted to sailors and laid off soldiers as not that many skills were required. Appointing schoolmasters, who had to be licensed to lead a school, usually lay in the hands of the directors of the Society. In order to exercise the profession of schoolmaster a request had to be submitted to the Court of Police and Criminal Justice, which then authorized the Dutch Reformed Church's council to allow candidates to take exams.

During the 18th century attempts were made to improve the quality of education. In 1740, the cleric Emanuel Vieira, a Jew who had converted to Christianity, proposed to the Reformed Church to send children with 'a witty mind, good comprehension and desire to learn' from the Paramaribo-based orphanage to the Republic for further tuition, at the colony's expense; upon return they would fulfill key tasks,

---

63   Ibid., 68-69.
64   Ibid., 70.
65   Hartsinck 1770, 865.
66   Wolbers 1861, 844.
67   For further information on these and the details given below, see: Oudschans Dentz 1955, 174-182.

for example, serving as a clergyman; in this way 'the foundation could be laid for a higher education in the colony, because a number of these returned young people might be appointed teachers or lecturers in several arts and sciences'.[68] Viera's plan however never materialized because of a lack of able subjects.

The Reformed Church's board (on which two colonial representatives served) had also presented plans to establish a Latin school, whereby children no longer had to be sent to the Republic for their education. This initiative fell through, too. During the mid-1700s however an agreement had been concluded enabling youngsters originating from Suriname to learn a craft at the Amsterdam almshouse named *Aalmoezeniershuis*. This facility created to uplift the destitute and the orphaned received 100 guilders per annum for each pupil. Education levels only began to improve slightly in the course of the 19th century.

3.7 Religion

Once the Society was established, it had become its directors' responsibility to ensure that 'the colonists would at all times be provided with one or more Ministers of the Word of God'.[69] Needless to say, this pertained to 'True Christian Reformed Religion', as it was referred to in the States General's resolutions. The Amsterdam-based classis of the Reformed Church played a key role in appointing clerics to serve in Suriname.

Although the Spanish colonization had been a crusade, too, certainly during the early years, establishing trade posts sufficed the Dutch conquerors. The apostolic imperialism as put in place by the *conquistadores* contrasted with the mercantilist imperialism imposed by Dutch sea captains, merchants and planters.[70] Expressions of religious tolerance encountered in the Republic were reflected in the colony, although here too the Reformed Church was the official state church. In 1741, the Society allowed the Evangelical Lutheran Church to found a community, which initially comprised mainly German immigrants.[71] The fact the Roman Catholic Church had to wait until 1785 before following suit, was no doubt the outcome of anti-Papist sentiments to be observed in the Republic.[72] Both Reformed and Lutheran communities remained almost completely white until the 19th century. Converting slaves to Christianity was as yet a taboo. This may explain why colonial authorities had thwarted the Moravian Brethren (referred to in Suriname as Hernhutters and named after the town of Hernhut in present-day Germany) for so many years (see p. 63).

Puritan persuasions were rarely ascertained amidst colonists in Suriname, this in stark contrast with the religious zeal observed among immigrants across North America. Such a fervor was not in the nature of the former, as a majority hereof only wished to amass as much money as possible. Though Huguenots had fled France for religious reasons, they did over time intermingle with Suriname's white colonial population and/or of colour. Jewish immigrants led their own separate lives. The Labadist sect comprising radical pietists, members of which had reached Suriname in 1683, settled down on a plantation named La Providence to then live in isolation.

---

68   Ibid., 179-180.
69   Wolbers 1861, 844.
70   Van der Linde 1966, 11-13.
71   Bruijning & Voorhoeve 1977, 188.
72   Ibid., 72.

The Labadists, named after the French theologian Jean de Labadie (1610-1674), founded a religious community in Wieuwerd, a small village located in the Dutch province of Friesland.[73] They strived after saving lost souls, but their missionary work remained very modest. Three of Governor Van Aerssen van Sommelsdijck's sisters were Labadists. Having suffered from diseases, attacks by Amerindians and other misfortune this sect decided to abandon its colonization efforts in 1732. Labadists handed down to us a magnificent and to this very day renowned publication entitled *Metamorphosis insectorum Surinamensium* composed by the naturalist-*cum*-scientific illustrator Maria Sibylla Merian (1647-1717).

Clergyman G.B. Bosch expressed his disappointment regarding the spiritual life in Suriname thus:

> '[...] *the passion to be really religiously orthodox is rarely seen in the West Indies. Speaking in Canaan's tongue does not seem to be fashionable here.*'[74]

On more than one occasion, the governor and council members felt obliged to issue ordinances pertaining to the Sunday rest. Governor-general Joan Raye van Breukelerwaard (1735-1737) wrote in an explanatory statement dated 7 May 1736 concerning the ordinance:

> '*that notwithstanding the numerous ordinances issued and pasted here, ordinances requiring the celebration and maintaining of the day of the Lord, this is however defiled and desecrated in many ways* [...].'[75]

Therefore, colonists were once again forbidden to

> '[...] *do any manual labour nor make their slaves do so, be it in the field, in the mill, or elsewhere, to do any trading, retailing and craftwork, buying and selling neither on the streets nor from houses and stores, rowing back and forth with boats, barges and other vessels, to receive, to deliver, or to ship sugar, to serve drinks, to sell meat, bread or any other provisions, to drive with chaises or other carriages or to ride a horse. Everybody should also abstain from getting drunk, fighting, playing dice, games, swearing, on the day of the Lord and the church*[...].'[76]

Only a handful of colonists attended church services. Many, considering Sunday as a day-off, visited nearby plantations in order to enjoy copious meals. Clergyman Jan Willem Kals (1700-1781) complained that his Reformed Church located in the Cottica-Perica district (see map p. 116) remained almost empty, while the planters' tent boats sailed past.[77] Clergymen always complained about the Reformed Church's destitute condition. Adriaen Backer, for example, wrote to the Amsterdam-based classis on 30 August 1681:

---

73   Van der Linde 1966, 30-31, 36-37, 186-187.
74   Bosch 1843, 393.
75   Schiltkamp & De Smidt 1973, vol. 1, 426.
76   Ibid., 427.
77   Van der Linde 1987, 46, 82-83.

'[...] *I have to testify, that the state of God's church, with my arrival here, was rather bad, but has further decayed during my stay here, caused by an odourless unrepentant skill of many, indeed, of the majority of inhabitants, notwithstanding God's harsh judgment by a devastating war with the pagan populations living here, which has already continued for several years, whereby which many plantations are burnt, many Christians battered to death, and a very large number of slaves taken away [...].*'[78]

Moreover, colonists were not willing to contribute a great deal of funds towards their clergymen. Johan Basseliers (1640-1689), the first cleric to serve in the colony, did not even receive his salary of 1,200 guilders per annum.[79] Having to personally ensure which part of the agreed salary one could obtain explains why Adriaen Backer was to leave Suriname. Basseliers, after lodging an unsuccessful complaint with the States of Zeeland, earned a livelihood by means of exploiting not only his own plantation but also his own slaves.

The above description characterizes the colonial church in Suriname as a planters' church. Here, unlike Catholic clerics who could afford to slightly distance themselves from colonial authorities, the cleric of the Dutch Reformed Church strongly depended upon the governor and council members. In the event of disputes, as Kals's ill fate aptly illustrates, the colonial administration drew the longest straw. He was obliged to leave the colony in 1733 after taking his duty (i.e., the conversion of slaves) too seriously.[80] In fact, white protestant churches hardly influenced societal relations in Suriname, where rules as well as regulations and traditions functioned far less as a mechanism of social control when compared with Europe.

---

78   Van der Linde 1966, 225.
79   Ibid., 193.
80   Van der Linde 1987, 84-86.

CHAPTER 4
Slavery

4.1 Introduction

According to law, slaves in Suriname were objects, not individual persons. They were not allowed to own any personal possessions, testify in court cases or marry. The colonial authorities had drawn from Roman legislation in order to create rules and regulations. A reorientation on the time-honoured classical Roman culture had begun in Europe with the Renaissance. It was not by chance that slavery was reintroduced across Southern Europe before the New World was discovered. In general, enslavement comprised a retaliation against Islamic conquerors, who themselves had enslaved captured Christians. The scale of this form of slavery was relatively small. Slave trade was still unknown at the time of the Dutch republics. In 1596, when Middelburg-based merchants wished to sell *c.*100 'Moorish men and women' from the west coast of Africa, they were 'restored to their natural liberty' by order of the States of Zeeland.[1]

The transatlantic slave trade began simultaneously with the development of the plantation economy on the American continent and in the West Indies. A biblical justification had quickly been found. According to the *Book of Genesis*, the nations of the world all descended from the biblical patriarch Noah's sons: Shem, Ham and Japheth. After the curse of Ham, his descendants were doomed to bondage. According to the 'planters theology', Ham was the progenitor of Black people who, as a result of this curse, were therefore predestined to be enslaved. Theological views and the concept of natural law, inspired by Roman and Greek thinkers, had thus easily been integrated.[2] Augustine of Hippo (354-430 CE) also deemed this 'Ham ideology' to be the origin of slavery, but this church father made no reference to the Black race.

During the 17th century, ethical and social issues linked to slavery had already been discussed in the Dutch Republic, be it in small circles. Hugo Grotius (1583-1645) explained in his *De Jure Belli ac Pacis* (1625) that victors in rightful wars should decide on the life and death of their prisoners of war. If those defeated were enslaved, at least their lives had been saved. The Latin term *servus* (slave) is derived from *servare* (to save). According to Grotius, human beings are free by nature, but in a number of cases can fall into slavery. As this outcome does not only concern prisoner of wars, free parents can sell their children as slaves, and a child born to enslaved parents is also a slave.[3]

Not only merchants and planters defended slavery, clergymen considered it to be justified too. In 1660, for example, the theologian Johan Picardt (1600-1670) from the Dutch town of Coevorden published a passionate argument in support of the Ham ideology:

---

1   Vrijman 1937, 17.
2   Jabini 2012, 98-99.
3   Paasman 1984, 99; see also: iep.utm.edu/grotius/

'Paying attention to Ham and his descendants / although they have become mighty nations / how much however slavery has reigned among them! Have most Africans not been slaves of their kings? are many of them not slaves now of the Turks? The inhabitants of Congo, Angola, Guinea, Monomotapa, Bagamidri, & c. are not they nests of slaves / from where so many are dragged hither / sold / and been used for all slave labour?'[4]

In 1638, the Zeeland-based theologian Godefridus Cornelisz. Udemans (1581-1649) formulated a Protestant code of ethics intended for merchants entitled *'t Geestelyck roer van 't Coopmanschip* (The Spiritual rudder of the Merchant ship). His moderate opinion, however, did not contest the admissibility of slavery:

'Regarding the heathens or Turcs, they may be enslaved according to Christians, provided that they are captured in a just war, or bought from their parents or other virtuous masters for a proper price, as is told to usually occur in Angola. Because this is in accordance with Divine Law (Levit. 25, 44-46).'[5]

Udemans drew the line between spiritual and physical slavery. In his view, Black slaves had to be converted to Christianity hereby at least liberating them from spiritual slavery. Once converted slaves had to be physically free as well. Udemans set a 7-year time frame in which to reach this goal. Needless to say, no support from planters was to be expected. They rather referred to the Ghana-born Jacobus Elisa Johannes Capitein *(c.*1717-1747) who had been taken to the Republic as a 10-year-old slave. In his University of Leiden thesis (1742) Capitein defended slavery on biblical grounds. This Latin text was immediately published in Dutch. An inscription added to a printed portrait depicting Jacobus Capitein includes the words 'his skin is black: but white his soul, because JESUS himself as Priest prays for him' (see Figure 4.1). Stakeholders in slavery often also pointed at the fate of serfs across Europe who would not be better off than slaves.

Though numerous slaves had not at all been captured in 'rightful' wars, merchants and planters could not care less. African rulers organized slave hunts among neighbouring tribes hereby acquiring commodities (e.g., textiles, liquor) from European traders. Planters and merchants considered slaves essential for the survival of the colony of Suriname. A Flemish Dutch investor, diplomat and merchant named Willem Usselincx (1567-1647), co-founder of the Dutch West India Company in 1621, therefore did not refer to the permissibility of slavery in his *Octroy of Privilegie* (Charter or Privilege): '[...] leave such to the decision of the Theologians, Legal scholars / whose profession it is.'[6] Along with the transatlantic slave trade also emerged the racial theories, emphasising the inferiority of Black people. Certain people considered Black Africans 'in-between beings', as a link in the chain connecting humankind to apes. Though this viewpoint did not gain any foothold among most colonists, there was no disagreement as to the superiority of the white race. Even the

---

4   Ibid., 101.
5   Van der Linde 1963, 82.
6   Paasman 1984, 99.

Figure 4.1. A portrait (1742) of Jacobus Capitein by J.J. Haid. Rijksmuseum, Amsterdam, via europeana.eu.

abolitionist-*cum*-travel author M.D. Teenstra, who had moved to Suriname to serve as this colony's agricultural adviser for several years, opined:

'*Regarding civilisation, the Ethiopian race has made the least progress and is standing on the lowest step of the existing humanity. To them the negroes, taken to Suriname as slaves, belong too. The negro is coarse of skin and morally as well as physically, less sensitive than a white; his hair is closer to that of the animals, as is*

Figure 4.2. This drawing by P.J. Benoit (orig. 1839) portrays the sale of a mother and her two children, c.1830. P.J. Benoit 1980.

his flat nose with wide holes and his swollen lips. [...] his skull looks more like that of the apes; his mental capacities are more obtuse and his pleasures exclusively bestial.'[7]

A majority of slaves arrived from the coast of Guinea, which included the region located between present-day Ivory Coast and Nigeria, and between Congo and Angola. According to initial estimates, Dutch traders transported more than 300,000 (enslaved) Africans to Suriname. Recent as well as more detailed research indicates this number must have been c.200,000.[8] All in all, the Dutch allegedly transported in excess of 500,000 of the 11,000,000 African men and women who crossed the Atlantic Ocean.[9] Traders would choose, as often as possible, the strongest and healthiest slaves of whom nevertheless, c.15 per cent did not survive the hardships experienced during Atlantic crossings.[10]

After a slave ship had reached its destination a military surgeon would check for contagious diseases such as smallpox. Passengers were allowed to disembark only after the captain and the surgeon had testified under oath that no dangerous diseases had been observed. According to the 1682 charter, slaves had to be publicly

---

7   Teenstra 1842, 115.
8   Postma 2003a, 115-139; Van Stipriaan 1993, 314. The Dutch East India Company was involved in slavery in East Asia and the Cape Colony; see e.g.: Mbeki & Van Rossum 2017.
9   Postma 2003a, 133; see also: slavevoyages.org.
10   Ibid., 137.

auctioned. In order to give owners of small plantations a chance to make a purchase, slaves were sold in pairs. This procedure however did not prevent captains from selling part of their cargo privately to owners of large plantations. Buyers were deceived by means of dubious selling practices, too, whereby captains utilised apparent purchases by accomplices in order to raise prices, leaving planters with the impression they needed to place high bids to acquire the scarce human capital. Penalties for such 'evil practices' were announced in 1754 by way of an ordinance.[11]

Traders and captains usually informed planters on upcoming sales in either a letter or a public announcement. Meanwhile the slaves were revived and fed, rendering them as presentable as possible to potential buyers. Public auctions held in Paramaribo attracted considerable interest, as plantation owners were always in need of slaves. The medical doctor-*cum*-chronicler Philippe Fermin published a sketch of such an event:

'When one brings the slaves to sell, they have to climb, one by one, on a table, where they are scrupulously examined by a surgeon, appointed for this purpose, and when he has assured that the slave, who is auctioned, is healthy and without defects, everybody bids an amount, and one sells them for three to four hundred, yes even till four hundred fifty Dutch guilders, which are usually paid after three weeks; but the buyer has only twenty four hours, to examine if the negro has any defect; if he finds any defect within that time, he can give him back to the Captain, provided he has not marked him, because in that case he has to keep him.'[12]

After the auction, the owner's initials were branded into a slave's oiled skin. Those who had just arrived were described as 'salt water negroes'. Often allowed 2 weeks to grow accustomed to the new environment and to restore their strength, they then started with light work only. Anthony Blom (1744-1807) in his planters manual (1787) delivered the advice to initially treat the enslaved cautiously. After 3 months they would, in his view, be able to carry out the required labour. Nonetheless, Africans experienced huge difficulties while adapting to unfamiliar circumstances. In desperation, several committed suicide. Newcomers were often housed, on the planter's order, with experienced slaves who on occasion would treat them even more harshly than their white-skinned masters. Blom thus recommended his fellow planters to purchase young slaves, who could adapt much more easily to unfamiliar living conditions:

'The most advantageous is to buy slaves, who are not more than twenty or at most twenty five years old: those are reaching the prime of their lives, and can still serve the plantations for many more years [...] but if older, for example, thirty years or more, they rarely grow accustomed to the country and the labour. They always grieve for being away from their fatherland and family, reason why they also start to eat charcoal and soil; decay in withering diseases, and eventually die. When a plantation has its determined number of slaves, it is very advantageous to replace

---

11 Schiltkamp & De Smidt 1973, vol. 1, 615-616.
12 Fermin 1770, part 1, 106.

Year	Sugar	Coffee	Cotton	Other	Paramaribo	Total
1752	19,008	16,029	-	534	2,224	37,835
1774	16,584	37,179	-	3,071	3,089	59,923
1795	12,232	26,710	4,209	2,204	2,800	48,155
1813	10,108	21,968	5,692	3,717	2,559	44,084
1836	17,659	12,942	6,545	2,590	7,143	46,979
1854	17,884	5,584	4,550	4,396	6,401	38,545
1862	19,789	3,892	2,551	4,714	5,538	36,484

Table 4.1. The enslaved population of Suriname per sector (1752-1862); 'other' refers to slaves mainly working in woodlands and vegetable gardens. Van Stipriaan 1993, 311.

the deceased every year, by buying not big negroes, but children, since they rarely grieve for being far from their fatherland and family, but are living happily with each other, and very soon grow accustomed to the country. One lets them gently do light work, suiting their physical strengths, thereby being of great service to the plantation, and they thus become very capable for further labour [...].[13]

The severity of the labour varied according to the kind of work and/or the plantation. Regimes imposed by individual owners also had an impact. Domestic slaves carried out the lightest work. The majority of the white colonists based in Paramaribo, the lower classes included, owned male and female slaves to carry out daily house chores. A wealthy family usually possessed between ten and 30 such slaves, hereby increasing its social status. Slaves fulfilled even the most futile tasks, such as filling their owner's pipe with tobacco and carrying the church book for his wife on Sundays. Now and again children of the well-to-do were provided with personal slaves. Certain owners even forced those they had enslaved to earn money by means of prostitution. Slaves were also sent out onto the streets to peddle. In Paramaribo they could be rented out by their owners to work either as craftsmen or in the fields. On plantations large numbers of slaves worked as domestic servants for either a planter or a director. House slaves were mainly of colour and Creoles (i.e., Black people born in Suriname). Those referred to as 'salt water negroes' almost exclusively worked in the fields.

Labour on sugar plantations was by far the most strenuous. Constructing a plantation with ditches and canals required a huge effort. Cutting sugar cane was exhausting, too. Slaves would gather cane on barges in order to transport it to the sugar mill where its juice was squeezed out. It was then heated in order to produce sugar as well as syrup, part of which served to produce dram. These mills were mainly water power driven, much less by oxen, donkeys or horses. Steam power was utilised occasionally during the 19th century. The fact sugar mills could only be operated at high tide implied that slaves had to work through the night and with full force. If not, the cane would perish. During harvest time, these workers had hardly any sleep. The Commissioner for the Indigenous people G.S. de Veer (1806-1891)

---

13   Blom 1787, 328-329

reports in 1838 that, during a time span of 48 hours, slaves had only a 6-hour time-off to eat and sleep:

'The negroes now, who had continued working all night to bring the cane, carry off the crushed pieces, light the fire (a task to which most of them soon succomb) and boil the sugar, are not allowed to rest the next day, but have to leave the mill immediately for the field in order to cut and transport the cane.[14]

On coffee plantations labour was (slightly) less strenuous. On cotton and cocoa plantations work was less heavy, too, bar the harvest season. Life for slaves in woodlands was by far the most comfortable. For, those carrying out logging work here could not be easily supervised by their owners.

Certain privileged slaves fulfilled supervising tasks as a *bastiaan*. They were allowed to have more than one wife. This favour was aimed at gaining their loyalty. The majority of plantations kept two such slaves who played key roles in maintaining discipline. Domestic slaves also belonged to this privileged group. Those eligible for such tasks were mainly females of colour. They were considered unfit to carry out any heavy labour in the fields.

Over time, slaves included more and more schooled craftsmen (e.g., carpenters, coopers, bricklayers). Here people of colour were over-represented too. Especially skilled carpenters, who were able to build and repair (ware)houses, sluices and barges, were of great value to plantations. Positioned lower in the hierarchy, we see field slaves, including many Black females. Diseased, feeble, elderly and/or disabled slaves are placed at the bottom of this list. On occasion they were able to carry out light chores such as herding cows, pigs and fowl, or seeing to vegetable gardens.

The number of slaves actually at work in the fields was much smaller than the total of those residing on plantations. In his planters manual, Anthony Blom outlined a model of a sugar plantation housing 166 slaves, including 41 children. Young female slaves were generally considered adults when aged 15 and boys when aged approximately 16 years old. Of the remaining 125 adult slaves as many as 71 worked in the fields. The number of supervisors and craftsmen amounted to almost 13 per cent of those 125 adult slaves. Around 10 per cent served either as a domestic slave or as a guard seeing to diseased slaves and cattle. As much as 18 per cent was disabled due to illness and/or old age.[15] The latter were referred to in inventories as *malinkers*. In addition, a number of slaves was rented out to the colonial government.

Based on the small volume of empirical studies on Surinamese plantations one can indeed come across significant deviations from Blom's model, which was aimed at attracting investors. The German-born researcher, naturalist-*cum*-explorer August Kappler (1815-1887) noted that a plantation was 'in a very advantageous situation' if it could dispose of between 75 and 80 field slaves out of a total of 200 enslaved.[16] The percentage of field slaves at work on the sugar

---

14   Oomens 1983, 32.
15   Blom 1787, 92.
16   Kappler 1854, Part 1, 51-52.

plantation named Roosenburg fell far below Blom's norm. In 1801, only 33 per cent of the adult slaves was toiling in the fields.[17]

Skills and physical conditions hugely influenced the assessed value of slaves as the inventory logs kept at the plantation Roosenburg clearly illustrate. Carpenters were considered most valuable. In 1768 their average value had reached 1,106 Dutch guilders. A head carpenter named Trobbel was valued at 1,550 (Dutch) guilders and thus of more worth than a supervisor valued at 1,225 guilders. A Roosenburg-based sugar boiler was worth 840 guilders. Averaging 641 guilders, field slaves were worth far less. The value of female field slaves was 546 guilders. However, in the category of domestic servants, carers and guards the average value of females was not less but in excess of that of males. These male slaves were often either disabled as a result of illness and old age, or employed as guards protecting vegetable gardens, sluices or cattle. Certain disabled guards were valued as low as 96 guilders. The only categories to be appraised considerably higher on balance sheets comprised the traditional healer (*dresneger*) who was referred to in Sranan Tongo as *dresinengre*. He was valued at 1,000 guilders and a cook at 633 guilders.[18]

For their owners, slaves were first and foremost instruments by means of which profits could be maximised. In inventories, disabled and/or elderly slaves were designated as either *aff* (done) or *verrot* (rotten).[19] After all, the enslaved formed one's capital which in due course had to be written off.

4.2 Demographic developments

Across the West Indies the enslaved population could not maintain itself through reproduction. Prior to emancipation, death rates almost always exceeded birth rates. According to one assessment, the pre-1814 excess mortality rate of the slave population in Suriname was 40 per mille; however, between 1848 and 1862, this natural decrease had dropped to 3.1 per mille.[20] Other data do not differ significantly. As to the time frame 1752-1774, it has even been estimated that the excess mortality rate amounted to 47 per mille.[21] During the first half of the 18th century, the excess mortality rate in the British West Indies was estimated at 30 per mille, although 50 and 60 per mille have also been mentioned. Here too improvements could be observed over time. Between 1817 and 1832, the excess mortality rate had dropped to 3.0 per mille.[22]

Suriname's demographics are remarkably less favourable when compared to those recorded on the North American continent. Between 1675 and 1827, *c.*200,000 slaves were sold in Suriname, the average size of the slave population being *c.*50,000 (see p. 70, Table 4.1.). Almost 400,000 slaves had been imported to North America during these 152 years, while the total Black population had reached *c.*2,000,000 in 1825.[23] Climatic differences can only provide a very limited explanation for these developments.

---

17   Oostindie 1989, 103.
18   Ibid., 106-107.
19   Ibid., 110.
20   Lamur 1977, 163.
21   Van Stipriaan 1993, 318.
22   Ward 1988, 121-124, 225.
23   For further detailed information, see: slavevoyages.org; Price 1976, 9.

It has been concluded that the British Caribbean colonies witnessed three phases of demographic development.[24] During the first stage (1650-1700) the number of plantations and slaves was not large as a result of a lack of capital. Thus now not only keen to treat their labourers with compassion, planters also tried to balance the numbers of male and female slaves in order to encourage further reproduction. In the course of the second stage (1700-1800), the large-scale sugar production expanded rapidly, requiring more capital and labour. A growing demand for slaves was dealt with by importing large numbers of Africans. This strategy was less expensive for planters than raising the children of slaves born on plantations. Not only did the planters' demand for female slaves decrease, working conditions, housing, food and medical care of slaves deteriorated too. As a result hereof, the birth rate of the enslaved population declined, while the death rate increased. It is thus no surprise that the quantum of Africans encountered amidst the Surinamese plantation population was high. This quantum was no less than 71 per cent between 1750 and 1769 to then decrease to 52 per cent between 1780 and 1809.[25] However, during the early decades of the 19th century, more than 20,000 Africans set foot in Suriname; hence, at the end of the 1820s this percentage was again higher than in c.1800.[26]

In the course of the 19th century the import of slaves from West Africa decreased as a result of a ban in 1807 by British Parliament and also by U.S. Congress on importing slaves (see p. 159). A shortage of labour now forced planters to encourage the natural growth of the enslaved population. Colonial authorities played an active part here by way of improving legislation aimed a better protection of slaves.

It is difficult to draw any meaningful conclusions from the information presented above. Certain researchers perceive the behaviour of planters to be the main reason for changes within demographic trends pertaining to the enslaved population. Others scholars, however, focus on the age structure and on the numerical ratio observed between male and female slaves. In their view, the on-going creolisation had an impact, too. For, the latter relates to a phenomenon whereby slaves abandoned several African traditions, all the more whenever the relative number of African-born individuals within the enslaved population decreased. In Suriname a similar development could be observed when compared with the British colonies. As previously mentioned, the excess mortality rate significantly declined, at least during the second half of the 19th century. On the sugar plantation named Vossenburg, for example, the birth rate was still 11 per mille between 1790 and 1799, rising to 25 per mille between 1850 and 1859.[27] Here the creolisation of the enslaved population certainly played a role. For, although Creole slaves were not more fertile than African-born slaves, they procreated during a longer time span. This phenomenon is the outcome of lactating for a shorter time, during which mothers were refraining from sexual intercourse. We read on this African tradition:

---

24 Lamur 1987, 24-25.
25 Van Stipriaan 1993, 341.
26 Ibid.; according to the Trans-Atlantic Slave Trade-Database a total of 23,649 slaves disembarked in Suriname between 1801 and 1825, see: slavevoyages.org
27 Lamur 1987, 27-28.

'The mother breastfed the [child] *very carefully, till it reached the age of almost two years; [...] The mother never had intercourse with a man during that time, purporting that the milk in the breast would thereby be spoiled what would be detrimental to the child.'*[28]

The growing stability of family life witnessed among slaves which was influenced by creolisation also resulted in more births. The colonial government contributed to the increase of the birth rate by prohibiting any family separations through sale. Protestant and Roman Catholic missions stimulated the creating of a monogamous family structure too. The Court of Police and Criminal Justice had as early as 1782 prohibited by ordinance the separating of mothers from their children. Apparently such events occurred frequently,

'[...] several complaints and disorders related to the fact that when selling slaves mothers are often separated from their children and sold to different masters.'[29]

The trend pertaining to the mortality rate was far more influenced by means of external factors. After all, hard labour took its toll. On the sugar plantation Vossenburg, for instance, an increasing general physical weakness of the enslaved population formed the main cause of death between 1822 and 1852. Of the 259 deaths among slaves (older than 12 months) as many as 46 could be attributed to this increase.[30]

On plantations across the British West Indies mortality rates varied according to the nature of the labour. This rate among field slaves was much higher than among enslaved craftsmen. Research on data relating to individual plantations in Suriname corroborates this outcome. Significant dissimilarities were observed between mortality rates on sugar and coffee plantations, which are explained by means of the various levels of hard work. Between 1780 and 1810, the excess mortality rate, i.e. the natural decrease of the slave population, on sugar plantations was 29 per mille and on coffee plantations 18.7 per mille.[31] On the sugar plantation Roosenburg, between 1766 and 1789, the mortality rate was reportedly 64.8 per mille among adult men and 41.7 per mille among adult women. Here the fact that males were forced to do heavier work undoubtedly had an impact. On the Roosenburg plantation workloads, measured in acres of cane per adult, clearly decreased during the 19th century. Hence the mortality rate dropped correspondingly.[32]

Comparing the demographic trends of Suriname with those of the island of Curaçao corroborates the assessment that not only the treatment of slaves but also the nature of their labour had a large impact. Research has indicated that data pertaining to Curaçao were much more favourable.[33] This conclusion can partly be explained by the role this Caribbean isle played as a transit port for the slave trade.

---

28   Blom 1787, 336-337.
29   Schiltkamp & De Smidt 1973, vol. 2, 1048.
30   Lamur 1987, 118.
31   Van Stipriaan 1993, 318.
32   Oostindie 1989, 135.
33   Lamur 1981, 87-102. Here Lamur also refers to the high birth rates reported among the U.S. slave population, which can be compared with those pertaining to Curaçao.

It was very important for slave owners to keep their 'merchandise' in good health. Moreover, slaves on Curaçao carried out less strenuous tasks.

After the aforementioned ban on slave trade was imposed, it proved ever more in the best interest of planters to reduce the number of deaths among their 'capital'. Thus, in 1829, the director of plantation Vossenburg, advocated the introduction of steam-driven sugar mills in order to

'relieve the slaves of all night work, thereby substantially preserving and promoting the health of the slave population, in a way it will also affect the propagation, the mortality of the slave population being less and the propagation higher on plantations where now steam powered sugar mills have been placed.'[34]

The on-going creolisation of the slave population probably also resulted in a decrease of mortality rates, as African-born slaves were very susceptible to disease after their passage. Child mortality on plantations, however, was still extremely high. Even between 1848 and 1862, only 12 months prior to the abolition of slavery, 33 per cent of children born on plantation Roosenburg had passed away before the age of 4, an outcome to which poor nutrition as well as the absence of health care had contributed.[35]

Receiving meals which were insufficient and lacked variation resulted in many cases of malnutrition. Slaves consumed almost only low-protein food such as cassava, plantains, maize, the tuber vegetable named *napi*, yams, tayer and sweet potatoes. The staple food comprised plantains. These fruits were abundant as they grew on plantain trees planted on coffee plantations in order to provide shade to young plants. In the course of the 19th century, slaves began to consume rice. Now and again limited quantities of dried fish were handed out. According to a colonial official, slaves at work on the richest sugar plantations received at best 2 pounds of animal-based food weekly. Mainly consisting of salted cod, this handout would often weigh less than 1 pound.[36] Such quantities were not less than was customary in many European countries. Needless to say, due to the extreme slave-related demands, the need for calories was larger.

Slaves cultivated their own produce rendering it difficult to determine how much nutrition was ultimately available. Vegetable gardens did certainly not always yield enough produce. Often planters had to purchase extra food from elsewhere, as these gardens were far too small. As early as in 1685, Governor Van Sommelsdijck had decided that at least 1 acre should be made available to eight slaves, but little had as yet come of this measure. In addition, the colonial government had, by means of a number of consecutive ordinances, imposed requirements pertaining to the quantity of food (and clothing) intended for slaves. A good many planters heeded these mandates. A notification dated 21 December 1775 stated 'still not enough food was given to the slaves on the plantations'.[37]

---

34   Lamur 1987, 47.
35   Oostindie 1989, 135.
36   Lans 1842, 149.
37   Schiltkamp & De Smidt 1973, vol. 2, 889.

Diseases also took their toll among slaves as inadequate nutrition as well as exhausting forms of labour caused them to become susceptible. In addition, physical conditions were not favourable. Plantations as well as the small slave dwellings were located in the marshy coastal region. The warm, humid climate did not help much either. Any health care provided to slaves left a great deal to be desired. Medical knowledge was limited. Exsanguination was a primitive treatment. Midwives as well as male and female traditional healers (*dresinengre* and *dresimamas*, resp.) were practising medicine. Surgeons were Suriname's official physicians, but their number was too low to serve at each and every location. Moreover, plantations and Paramaribo lay far apart. Each individual plantation director was therefore supposed to monitor any health problems experienced by slaves which traditional healers presented to him.

Numerous plantations included a small building where diseased slaves were taken care of.[38] Contagious illnesses could nevertheless spread easily due to poor hygiene. Opinions that colonists held on traditional healers, who mainly prescribed herbs and carrot extracts, were rather negative. A majority of these healers was deemed, rather unjustifiably, to be quacks. Plantation inventories often report *framboesia tropica* aka yaws (*jas*) as a cause of death. This tropical infectious disease is characterised by fungating lesions. Leprosy (referred to in Suriname as *boasi*) was much-feared too.[39] Hence, to prevent any further contamination, leprous slaves were transferred to a location outside Paramaribo. Those who diagnosed a slave with the symptoms of leprosy received a reward of 25 guilders. Planters who did not report a leprous slave were fined 200 guilders.[40] In the course of the 18th and 19th century, smallpox epidemics transmitted from Africa now and again took a heavy toll among the enslaved population.

4.3 Supervising the enslaved workforce

During the second half of the 18th century, the number of slaves was ten times larger than that of white colonists. Their key problem was: how to control the slaves whose fast growing numbers triggered a certain fear. They were now disciplined by means of more and less subtle methods. Severe sanctions were imposed for infringing the many rules and regulations. Certain planters did not hesitate to apply brute force. Colonists demonstrated their superiority to slaves in other ways, too, whereby one was meant to experience white supremacy as being natural. Colonial legislative instruments therefore also aimed at creating distance between slaves and whites. The latter were urged not to become too involved with '*neegers*' (negroes). Respect for their masters would otherwise disappear.

As previously mentioned, white-skinned men cohabiting with Black concubines was accepted whereby practice and doctrine apparently differed (see paragraph 3.5). The government countered other forms of contact, which mainly occurred among colonists belonging to the lower classes. An ordinance dated 9 May 1741, issued by the

---

38 Kuhn 1828, 38-42; Kuhn had served as a surgeon in Suriname.
39 Ibid., 35-37.
40 Van Stipriaan 1993, 366-367.

Court of Police and Criminal Justice and Governor-general Gerard van de Schepper (1738-1742), states:

> '*All those who shall see or hear read, salute; we let you know that from time to time it was brought to our attention that notwithstanding our ban, issued for these indifferent times in our decrees and notifications, many negroes here in Paramaribo caused many disturbances such as stealing and otherwise; many whites, smugglers and other common folk, playing for money and sitting in a café smoking and drinking, cause slaves not only forget due respect for whites and make them mischievous and impertinent, yes make them have such audacity and walk day and night with sticks and clubs, hardly stepping aside for a white and more other disturbances and impertinencies, and also that many white persons do not refrain themselves from buying goods from them that were not goods that negroes had for sale, and buying them for money or other means; and recently that many residents sell lanterns and the like to slaves, without the permission of their masters, thus providing them with more and more opportunities for creating many disturbances, thereby also entailing many disorders and thievery, while these negroes, once fond of playing, search for money by means of forbidden commerce; all these disorders can not only not be endured, but should maximally be punished for the preservation of the colony and the good residents.*'[41]

Colonists could indeed be punished for infringements. Numerous decrees and notifications delivered by the Court of Police and Criminal Justice and the governor concerned courtesies and rules of conduct which slaves had to follow when interacting with white colonists. A notification, dated 6 February 1750, forwarded by Governor-general Joan Jacob Mauricius (1742-1751) and the above Court prescribed:

> '*That no slaves should walk the streets while smoking pipes, whether whites are with them or not, neither pass a white with their heads covered, with hats, or caps or otherwise, without taking it off, but on the contrary, when seeing a white coming down the street, firstly clear the way with all reverence a slave is obligated, deviating with a discreet distance, and keeping it, so that a white can pass amply and unimpeded.*'[42]

It was also instructed, in a notification dated 17 May 1769, that

> '*The slaves, both black and mulatto without distinction, from now shall not wear stockings or shoes in the future.*'[43]

The same notification prohibited slaves from wearing 'cocked hats'. Plantation life was organised according to a strict hierarchy, described as 'a rigour and order which

---

41   Schiltkamp & De Smidt 1973, vol. 1, 481-482.
42   Ibid., 587.
43   Ibid., vol. 2, 820.

one would encounter only on a warship'.[44] Most plantations counted only a handful of whites who had to try to keep a much larger group of slaves in check. Certain sugar plantations housed no less than 400 individuals. The colonial government therefore imposed a minimum number of white-skinned overseers. In 1692 each and every plantation had to see to it that a white colonist older than 15 years supervised ten slaves, on pain of 1,000 pounds of sugar if a white man was not in attendance. Once proven unfeasible for planters, this rule was eased. In 1715, one white male for every 20 slaves was considered an acceptable ratio.[45] In many cases, however, this norm was hardly ever complied with. On plantation Roosenburg, during the 18th century, one colonist had to supervise between 65 and 200 slaves.[46]

Plantation directors appointed white overseers held responsible for surveillance of slave labour and assisted by one or more Black overseers (*bastiaans*). These directors were the absolute rulers of plantations especially when maintaining good relationships with their administrators. A plantation director's daily life was by and large practically identical. He would rise between 5 and 5.30 am, according to Kappler's rosy description.[47] Overseers equipped with whips would wait under the veranda of the planter's house. Having reported on activities and on slaves who deserved punishment, a *bastiaan* would ask for orders regarding the work to be carried out that day. While the director had breakfast, slaves who had deserved a flogging were punished. Next, the traditional healer arrived with unwell slaves. Those seriously ill would receive treatment, others were immediately sent back to work. After reporting to the director, the white overseer set off for the fields in order to inspect the work carried out by slaves. The director then walked along the fields accompanied by his personal servant (*voeteboi*). At around 4 pm, he would enjoy a nap. Two hours later, the Black overseers and the slaves returned to receive a glass of dram. The white overseer drank a glass of jenever.

The social distance between directors and white overseers was large, although both belonged to the group of colonists. Overseers lived in very simple dwellings. Their salary also reflected that discrepancy. In 1727, the director of plantation Vossenburg earned 800 Surinamese guilders per annum, whereas a white overseer was paid only 90 guilders. In 1827, after Dutch currency had been introduced, a director's salary rose to 1,600 (Dutch) guilders whereas that of a white overseer comprised 150 guilders.[48] Many directors also acquired a percentage of the produce. As a number of them rose pigs and poultry, too, considerable extra income was obtained. White overseers hoped to one day become a director. The difference in status between whites sharply highlights the hierarchical relations on plantations. As stated in a revised pre-regulation dated 31 August 1784, the government felt even compelled to urge directors not only to duly support other whites but also not to treat them with contempt 'thus also instilling respect for the lower servants in the slaves'.[49]

---

44   Lans 1842, 37.
45   Schiltkamp & De Smidt 1973, vol. 1, 196.
46   Oostindie 1989, 179.
47   Kappler 1854, part 1, 46-48.
48   Lamur 1987, 99.
49   Schiltkamp & De Smidt, vol. 2, 1071.

In order to ensure the optimal performance of slaves, plantation owners and directors required agricultural know-how as well as understanding, tact and composure. According to Blom's planters manual a good manager should be

'a man who steadily checks and runs the movements and works of the deceitful negroes (who are always negligent in fulfilling their duty).'[50]

Planters applied a policy of division and rule in order to control their slaves. The latter who by no means formed a homogenous group as they hailed from various parts of Africa. Moreover, these 'salt water negroes' differed from Creoles. Several elite slaves, (mainly Creoles) had to create, as it were, buffers between white-skinned plantation owners and field slaves. The privileged group of slaves included overseers, craftsmen and domestic servants. The less harsh nature of their work alone placed them in a better position. Elite slaves also received material benefits such as additional clothes and food. Moreover, they were often allowed to have more than one wife.

Although plantation directors included competent men, most chroniclers portray them in a negative light. In his influential *Narrative of a Five Years Expedition against the Revolted Negroes of Surinam*, the Scottish military John Gabriel Stedman (1744-1797) describes the bad reputation of planters based in Suriname, in the Republic and elsewhere, as expressed in detailed reports on atrocities carried out against those enslaved. During the English period (pre-1667), the image of plantation directors had already been rather belittled. In his *An impartial description of Suriname*, George Warren complained about the appalling treatment of slaves. They were sold 'like dogs', suffered the 'severest usages for the slightest faults' and fled into the forests out of desperation.[51] In *Gezang op Zee* (*Song at See*), published in 1753, the Governor-general J.J. Mauricius held colonists accountable for the rebellious attitude of slaves:

'A slave rebellion, which occurs here year after year
(Mainly by the fault of whites, who by swearing, making a fuss,
Inhumane punishment, and fornication with the women,
Taunt the Negroes, and drive them to fury and despair).'[52]

Stedman also voiced a 'very unfavourable opinion of the humanity of the planters residing in this colony toward theyr negro slaves'.[53] Records kept at the Court of Police and Criminal Justice prove that slave owners were engaged in excesses on more than one occasion. The public prosecutor (*raad fiscaal*), for example, stated on 2 May 1731:

---

50   Blom 1787, 318.
51   Warren 1667, 19.
52   Lichtveld & Voorhoeve 1980, 164.
53   Stedman 1790, 39.

'[...] *several inhabitants treat their slaves very viciously and inhumanely, castigating and punishing them for small faults and offenses in such a way, they die soon or immediately as a result of far too heavy blows.*'[54]

Planters now and again would punish female slaves who refused to satisfy his sexual desires. Stedman describes such an incident as follows

'*The first object that attracted my compassion was / while visiting in a neighbouring estate / tied up with both arms to a tree, a truly beautiful Samboe girl of about 18, as naked as she came to the world, and lacerated in such a shocking condition by the whips of two negro drivers, that she was from her neck to her ancles literally died over with blood – it was after receiving 200 lashes that I perceived her with her head hanging downwards, a most miserable spectacle. Thus turning to the overseer I implored that she might be untied from that moment, which seem'd to give her some relief, but my answer was far from the humane gentleman, that to prevent all strangers from interfearing with his government, he had made it an unalterable rule, in that case always to redouble the punishment, and which he instantaneously began to put in execution – I tried to stop him but in vain, he declaring the delay should not alter his determination but make him take vengeance with interest upon interest – thus I had no other remedy left but to leap in my boat, and leave the detestable rascal like a beast of prey to enjoy his bloody-feast til he was glutted, while from that day I swore to break of*[f] *communication with all overseers, and implored the curse of heaven to be poured down upon the whole relentless fraternity – on my having enquired since for the cause of such barbarity, I was too credibly informed, that her only crime had consisted in her firmly refusing to submit to the loathsome embraces of her despicable executioner, which his jealousy having construed to disobedience, she was thus skinned alive [...].*'[55]

Stedman deemed killing a slave's newly born as the most cruel act:

'*And now what reader shall believe that the above inhumanitys can be exceeded, yet such they certainly were but very lately even by a female when a Mrs. Stolker going to her estate in a tent-barge, a negro woman with her sucking-infant happened to be passengers, and seated on the bow, or fore part of the boat, but were the child crying / without it could possibly be hushd, and Mrs. Stolker not delighting in such musick / she ordered the mother to bring it aft, and deliver it in her own hands, with which forthwith, in the presence of the distracted parent she thrust it out at one of the tilt-windoes, and held it under water, til it was drowned, and while the fond mother / being desperate for the loss of her helpless baby / instantly leaped overboard in the same stream where floated her beloved offspring, and in conjunction with which she was determined to end her miserable existance, -*

---

54   Wolbers 1861, 130-131.
55   Stedman 1790, 264-266.

A History of Suriname

Figure 4.3. Flagellation of a female Samboe slave. Drawing by J.G. Stedman (orig. 1790). J.G. Stedman 1987.

however in this she was prevented by the care of the negro slaves, that rowed the barge, and corrected by her mistress for her unatural temerity – with three or four hundred lashes.'[56]

It may be added here that the historian Julien Wolbers delivered a summary of excesses based on records kept at the Court of Police and Criminal Justice.[57] On 4 July 1733, the below complaint against a certain Hendrik Bisschoff was addressed:

'The Governor reports that 15 negroes, men and women, have come and complained to him about the cruel treatment, inflicted upon them by their master Hendrik Bisschoff; they brought a negro's head that Bisschoff had commissioned to place on a stake; it appeared from an investigation carried out on the spot that their master had shot or beaten several slaves to death, whereby the cut-off heads of three were placed on a stake. Others had been very severely and harshly flogged for futilities, among them a mulatto woman, who was beaten in such a way that pieces of flesh dropped from her body (letter from the Gov. to the Direct. of the Society), furthermore for five years he had hardly given his slaves any food.'[58]

---

56   Ibid., 267-268.
57   Wolbers 1861, 131-132.
58   Ibid., 131.

Bisschoff was arrested only to pass away before being convicted. Records dated 24 October 1743 mention that several slaves from the plantation named Sinabo had come forward to complain about being cruelly treated by the administrator-*cum*-director, Benjamin Pousset. As proof hereof they took with them the heads of a male and female slave, whom Pousset had murdered.[59] The minutes dated 21 November 1742, refer to a barge skipper named P. Hotzz, who had flogged one of his slaves in a such a way the victim shortly afterwards took his own life.[60] On 29 December 1745, Governor-general Mauricius referred in his journal to a search held at the house of a woman named Pieterson who had 'long been known to be crazy and cruel'; having murdered her slaves, she had seen to it they were buried inside her house; not denying these acts, she nevertheless opined 'that she was allowed to destroy her own property, purchased with her money'; Pieterson was allowed sufficient time to flee.[61]

During Van Sommelsdijck's governship, planters had been forbidden to apply the death penalty.[62] Moreover, restrictions had been imposed on corporal punishment as imposed by plantation directors. According to a regulation dated 27 December 1759, the white plantation workforce was not allowed to utilise sticks, only whips. A maximum penalty was set, to wit, between 25 and 50 floggings, and in specific cases 80 'moderate' floggings, only to be aimed at a slave's lower body. More severe punishments could only be handed out either by a planter or an administrator, or with their written consent.[63] A ruling dated 31 August 1784 further explicitly states that slaves should not be lifted from the ground while receiving corporal punishments. The plantation directors - not the planters or administrators - were also prohibited from applying the *Spaanse bok*.[64] This regular form of punishment consisted of tying the slave's hands together, placing his or her raised knees between the arms to insert a stick into the opening created between the arms and knees. Once this stick was secured to the ground, slaves were beaten with a tamarind rod.

Jurisdiction imposed on slave owners thus implied specific limitations. Nevertheless, excesses continued during the 19th century. M.D. Teenstra, the aforementioned agricultural advisor to the colonial government, mentions several cases in which plantation directors had shot male as well as female slaves to death. He further reports on the death by torture of a female slave, named Jansje, at plantation *La Solitude*. We read in the public prosecutor's report dated on 23 February 1823:

'*Certain negress, by order of the often mentioned director, for about 14 days hoisted up a tamarind tree, and punished by flogging; - that she (while the director was absent from the plantation La Solitude) had been left hanging, at his orders, for a considerable time; - that the director, having returned, saw to it she was again*

---

59   Ibid., 131; Beeldsnijder 1994, 244.
60   Wolbers 1861, 131.
61   Ibid., 131-132.
62   Herlein 1718, 52.
63   Schiltkamp & De Smidt 1973, vol. 1, 671.
64   Schiltkamp & De Smidt 1973, vol. 2, 1069-1071.

punished in that position; - next put a peppered herring in her vulva, having then tied her to the drain in the sugar mill, to beat her again, during which crime she died.'[65]

According to the plantation regulation, colonists who had broken the rules concerning sanctions against slaves had to be penalised. The aforementioned ruling dated 31 August 1784 stipulated, for example, that those who had punished a slave either by caning or by applying the *Spaanse bok*, must pay a fine of 300 guilders. Often however colonists were let off with a mere warning. For, on occasion, it proved difficult to establish what had exactly occurred on remote plantations. Slaves were not allowed to testify as witnesses. Moreover, the Court of Police and Criminal Justice, consisted almost only of planters. Independent judgements were therefore not to be expected. As a result of the absence of white witnesses those slaves who complained about cruelties were frequently dismissed empty-handed. It was even reported that complainants received corporal punishment.[66]

Governor-general Crommelin had presented new proposals in order to tighten sanctions against colonists in 1762. He not only expressed the wish that those who had murdered a slave could be sentenced to a form of corporal punishment and even to death but also, in cases of slaves being severely disciplined, that two white witnesses should be present on the plantation. Not surprisingly, representatives serving the aforementioned Court rejected Crommelin's proposals. This Court's members held the view that slaves 'could not be kept under control, if they were aware that their master could receive corporal or capital punishment for beating a slave to death'.[67]

It was only during the 19th century that planters who had engaged in excesses were punished more regularly. The importance of treating slaves in a more civilised manner had increased especially after the prohibition in 1807 of Atlantic slave trade (see p. 159). The government of Suriname had to this goal tightened the rules in order to limit any form of domestic jurisdiction. On 12 June 1824, this measure resulted in the director of plantation La Solitude being sentenced for his association with the death of the female slave Jansje. The Court of Police and Criminal Justice subjected him to being flogged, branded and expelled from the colony.[68] In several cases this Court stripped directors of the authority over their plantations.

Needless to say, the harsh sanctions authorities themselves imposed on slaves did not contribute to any moderation exercised by planters. These penalties were often harsh and cruel. For a minor offense, such as going out while wearing shoes, a slave could be subjected to the *Spaanse bok*. Now and again as in the case of murdering one's master, slaves were hanged alive on hooks inserted between the ribs or into the flesh. The victim was meanwhile tortured with hot pliers. Burning slaves alive also occurred.[69]

Foreigners in particular reported that the regime in Suriname was more relentless than those established elsewhere in the region. Major-general Pinson Bonham

---

65   Teenstra 1842, 151-152.
66   Wolbers 1861, 290-292.
67   Ibid., 294.
68   Teenstra 1842, 152-153.
69   Wolbers 1861., 295.

(1762-1855), the Governor of Suriname (1811-1816) during the British interim rule (1804-1816), wrote on 14 July 1813 in a letter sent to London:

> *'I have yet to visit a colony where slaves are that mistreated, receive such poor food and clothing, but where they are still forced to do such hard labour, exceeding their strength.'*[70]

In a letter dated 9 February 1814, Pinson Bonham again compared Suriname with neighbouring regions:

> *'Having spent 21 years in the West Indies, I have heard in each and every colony that it was a very severe punishment for a negro to be sold to a planter in Surinam, and I can now see for myself this is true.'*[71]

It is difficult to establish if Bonham was right. Other colonies witnessed abuses and excesses too. Rules and regulations aimed at forcing colonists to improve the treatment of slaves were also required elsewhere. Identical conflicts arose among planters pertaining to limitations of their jurisdiction over slaves. For example, after King Carlos IV had proclaimed the 1789 *Código Negro Español*, Cuba-based planters ignored their obligations, while suicide among slaves was no exception.[72] Moreover, negative demographic developments noted among the slave population across Suriname were far from unique.

The legal protection of slaves in Spanish, Portuguese and French colonies was indeed more advanced.[73] Spain adhered to codified laws, whereby slaves were not treated as mere objects. France had composed a specific legislation, the *Code Noire*, for its colonies, though it was not always upheld. In the Roman Catholic colonies, those enslaved had to be converted to Catholicism. Even if such proselytizing was mainly only ostentatious, the resemblance of a certain kind of shared belief evolved which may have resulted in slaves being treated in a more lenient manner.

Across the Dutch and English colonies any direct influence of plantation owners exerted in their colonial governments was larger when compared with Spanish and Portuguese territories, where monarchs held absolute power. It has thus been assumed that in colonies such as Suriname slaves did indeed suffer more than elsewhere. In academia, contrary to earlier opinions, the assessment gained ground that dealing with slaves in Suriname did not differ that much from the way they were treated in other (British) colonies. [74]

70　Ibid.,567.

71　Ibid.

72　Simons 1996, 133.

73　Quintus Bos 1964, 7-8.

74　Within this context, R. and S. Price's revelation is interesting. For, the publisher of the 1796 edition of Stedman's influential *Narrative* [...] added the phrase that slaves in Suriname were treated much worse than in the British West Indies. R. and S. Price having come across this statement when transcribing and editing the original 1790 manuscript however underline that precisely 'because he was no abolitionist, Stedman's accounts of the behaviors and attitudes of Suriname's masters and slaves take on special authority', see: R. & S. Price, 2010 (1988), xv, and see: Oostindie 1993, 1-34. Howard W. French refers to a

　A History of Suriname

Not only a waste of 'capital' prevented a majority of plantation owners from applying any form of excessive physical coercion. Slaves resisted more or less subtly if they felt their master was going too far. The enslaved population was certainly not submissive. The arrival of an incoming director on a plantation could result in open rebellion. In 1759 a strike action occurred at plantation Roosenburg when slaves refused to accept Benjamin Treboulon as their administrator-*cum*-director. This reaction was based on his callous reputation acquired previously when officiating at Roosenburg. In such cases the colonial government would always attempt to intervene in order to avoid any precedents. The Court of Police and Criminal Justice sent two representatives to Roosenburg. Having not been able to succeed in appeasing the slaves, they therefore recommended the appointment of an incoming administrator-*cum*-director. This Court, after dismissing this advice, then instructed the Black supervisors at Roosenburg to accept Treboulon. In addition, they were given the assurance that complaints could be lodged in Paramaribo if 'any improprieties'would occur under the incoming regime. Not much later these two men, after returning to Roosenburg, repeated the above instruction to the black-skinned supervisors who in due course were able to sway the slaves towards accepting Treboulon's appointment.[75]

An almost identical conflict arose in 1799 when a director named P. Mey was assaulted by slaves armed with machetes. He survived thanks to other slaves who came to his rescue. The perpetrators were punished in Paramaribo by means of the *Spaanse bok*.[76] In 1815, problems concerning an incoming administrator arose again on plantation Roosenburg. Now the British interim-government even felt obliged to see to it that armed civilians occupied this plantation. In this instance, too, rebellious slaves were punished by means of the *Spaanse bok*. Several years later, the then director of plantation Roosenburg wrote to its owner in the Low Countries that the slaves were willing to work, partly because 'your honourable Sir took care of them in such a fatherly manner by sending clothes, they have now also been provided with food'.[77]

Conflicts such as those unfolding on Roosenburg befell numerous plantations. Slaves not only often secretly resisted regimes deemed too harsh, they also either sabotaged their tasks or pretended to have fallen ill. As slaves had taken the required knowledge and expertise with them from Africa to Suriname, cases of poisoning their masters have been recorded. Planters were very much afraid of meeting such a fate. E.J. Bartelink (1834-1919), a person of colour who had risen to the post of plantation director before slavery was abolished, wrote:

---

law passed in 1661 in Barbados which was later adopted in other British colonies. It stated that Africans were a 'heathenish, brutish and uncertaine, dangerous kinde of people', hereby giving their white owners almost total control over their lives. French 2021, 187.

75   Oostindie 1989, 79-81, 183.

76   Ibid., 185-186.

77   Ibid., 186.

'Such suspicious directors then took in a five to six year old child removing it from the most influential family among the slaves, as a kind of hostage. The child was the first to taste anything they would eat or drink. They thus believed to be protected against secret attacks.'[78]

A planter could also incur the revenge of a slave if he coerced a female slave into a sexual relationship, a frequent event. If a planter wished to keep at his disposal those slaves who were prepared to carry out the required work, it was appropriate to act discretely. Colonists were hence advised thus:

'In order to govern them well, one should on occasion possess Solomon's wisdom, Samson's powers and Job's patience. Although uncivilised, they know very well how to distinguish good from evil, as well as what their due duty is, and what they have to do. On a plantation, as they receive from their master what is theirs, and those who do not do their duty properly are punished indiscriminately, without exception, the entire slave population will never rebel; or become unruly. One has the least difficulty, everyone carries out their work, and the plantation benefits.'[79]

4.4 Slaves in their own world

The knowledge of the personal world and culture of slaves is limited due to a lack of sources. Slaves in Suriname did not express their thoughts in writing as they were either not able to or not allowed to do so. Nonetheless, memoirs recorded by former slaves hailing from English-speaking colonies do exist (see p. 159). Inventories and archives of plantations mainly included economic information, which was the prime interest of plantation owners. We thus can only learn about the life of slaves in which West African traditions played a key role, when based on observations presented by colonists. Several contemporary novelists have attempted to describe the world through the eyes of a slave.

The language referred to as Sranan Tongo (Surinamese tongue) is perhaps the best illustration of the fact that those enslaved developed their individual culture rapidly. This creole language includes English, African, Dutch and Portuguese elements to become the local *lingua franca* after acquiring a fixed shape at an early stage.

Opportunities for those enslaved to lead individual lives were limited. Urban slaves had more options thanks to the nature of their work, which was lighter in comparison with that carried out by field slaves. Prolonged, strenuous forms of labour almost entirely consumed the majority of slaves. Planters were prohibited, by a decree dating back to 13 June 1669, to 'getting slaves to work before Sunday night at 12 o'clock, under penalty of five hundred pound of sugar'.[80] Sunday rest was however by no means always respected. This ban had to be repeated several times, whereby sanctions were reinforced continuously.

---

78   Bartelink 1914, 17.
79   Blom 1787, 353.
80   Schiltkamp & De Smidt 1973, vol. 1, 45.

Slaves expressed themselves exuberantly when singing, dancing and playing music. A remarkable example hereof was the *doe* (aka *dou*) whereby they gathered not only to sing and dance but also to recite satirical texts on events in daily life as experienced under their white master's rule. Drums, guitars (made of half a gourd, strings and sheep skin) and tambourines (comprising a wooden plank and sticks) served as instruments. A free Black female would lead a *doe*. According to West African tradition, she recited satirical texts, too. Such festivities may be considered the clearest proof of the sophisticated forms of cultural expression the enslaved population of Suriname possessed.

These feasts emerged towards the end of the 18th century, when prosperity in the colony had strongly increased. In 1788, Jewish settlers first mentioned the *doe* in their *Essai historique sur la colonie de Surinam*:

'[...] *having created a certain kind of order, which they name Dou; for example Dou d'or, Bigie dou, Dou de diamant; which means as much as made of gold, of gemstone etc. This extravagance should at least to some extent be restrained, all the more so as one feels already the harmfull effects, relating to thievery, all is necessarily the outcome hereof, and linked to the lower workload the Whites can then impose on them.*'[81]

These dances and singing rituals included styles referred to as *banja, susa, kanga* and *laku*. To date they continue to be part of the *winti* cult, the Afro-Surinamese traditional religion (see p. 142ff.). Songs could pertain to a protest, disguised or not, directed against a slave master's conduct. For example, a *susa* still remembered during the 1970s by elderly people residing in the Para district included the following protest against the limited supply of food:

'*Basja taki pondo doro, ma njannjan no kon.*
Katibo Nengre o [...] *pondo doro ma njannjan no kon.*
O katibo sonde, o katibo sonde.
The basja says that the boat has come, but has not brought food.
Well, negroes in slavery [...] *the boat has come but without food.*
Slavery on Sunday, slavery on Sunday.'[82]

Time and again the authorities attempted to restrict the various cultural traditions followed by slaves. Such manifestations of autonomy were incompatible with a colonial society entirely dominated by whites. In a ruling dated 8 December 1794, *a doe* was strictly forbidden as was 'the wearing of ribbons, slogans or jewelry that have any relation with those meetings'.[83] The 'thievery', which was referred to, was certainly not the only reason for this ban. Although no official reason was given, it had in part been prompted by the fact that, as stated in this regulation, 'even several free coloureds' were members. After all, the colonial authorities imposed as much

---

81 Nassy 1788, seconde partie, 38.
82 Van der Pijl 2007, 73; Wooding 1981, 254.
83 Schiltkamp & De Smidt 1973, vol. 2, 1181.

segregation as possible on the various ethnic groups, for reasons of political control. This measure, moreover, fitted well into the general ban on meetings of slaves as introduced earlier in order to prevent any conspiracy and/or undermining of the colonial authority.

Organizing *baljaren* (dance feasts) was restricted too when in a ruling dated 17 December 1759, Governor-general Crommelin had prohibited such manifestations which included 'drums and other instruments' being held within the boundaries of Paramaribo, under penalty of 500 guilders for colonists on whose properties such events took place.[84] Outside Paramaribo, slaves were allowed to attend a *baljaar*, but only if their masters had granted permission and notified the public prosecutor. Playing either a '*banja* or other soft sounding instrument' was permitted in Paramaribo until 10 pm if the neighbours did not suffer any inconveniences and no slaves owned by other masters were present. The colonial government must have felt rather uncertain about how to deal with dance parties organised by slaves. After 6 months the Court of Police and Criminal Justice stipulated that the prosecutor should authorise a *baljaar* only every 2 months.[85] Crommelin completely withdrew his authorisation as to such feasts on 23 December 1763.[86] This measure did not dissuade planters from turning a blind eye at all, thus allowing a number of dance parties to take place on their plantations each year. Otherwise resentments felt among slaves would only have increased.

Governor Jan Nepveu (1770-1779) introduced, on 15 August 1777, a new regulation, allowing slaves 'to arrange a gaiety or play near or in the region of Paramaribo', after being authorised by the prosecutor and the planter.[87] Nepveu understood that a total ban on *baljaren* would be futile, as he wrote in his personal notes:

'[...] *as they walk at faraway places in the night to enjoy that pleasure, if at all one discovers where it takes place and sends a patrol to raid them, they can rarely be caught because they have placed guards to timely alert them, hence everybody seeks refuge in the hedges or the forests, and if at all in the vicinity of Paramaribo a number of them were detained and severely punished with the Spaanse bok, that would not sufficiently scare them, on the contrary it would cause huge bitterness in their hearts if one never allows them while being enslaved and after their labour a certain diversion (as all people are naturally inclined to that) and that it seems an excess of tyranny to totally ban, especially as it also is a religious ceremony for a deceased, which they surely believe could not be ignored, because otherwise they would in due course take on all the misfortune of their deceased next of kin.*'[88]

Slaves continuously violated the ban on the dance revering their most important water goddess referred to as *watra mama*. This restriction remained in force during the rule of all colonial governors. According to Pierre Jacques Benoit (1782-1854), a Belgian traveller, painter, trade agent and boat captain, such ceremonies were

---

84   Schiltkamp & De Smidt 1973, vol. 1, 663-664.
85   Ibid., 691.
86   Van Lier 1971,145.
87   Schiltkamp & De Smidt 1973, vol. 2, 928.
88   Van Lier 1977, 107-108; Van Lier 1971, 146.

always held on a Saturday at midnight under a kapok tree (*kankantrie*).[89] The dance, music and songs of slaves were closely intertwined with their animistic beliefs. Even to date drums are sounded in order to evoke the supernatural during ceremonies. Across the West Indian colonies, the world of deities imported from West Africa was transformed into an innovated system whereby the Afro-American *winti* cult emerged. In his accounts A.F. Lammens, who officiated as the president of the Court of Civil Justice during the first half of the 19th century, stated on *winti* traditions:

> '*They place, in order to protect their properties, calabashes decorated with leather and other things; - they call this Obiaas, which are often given to them by Lukumans* [i.e. seers]*: - when they arrive at a creek or body of water they have not navigated for a long time, or are not familiar with, they remove their hats off, baptize themselves and offer an egg, a plantain, or something similar to the Watermamma, the Water goddess or the Nymphs of the creek.*'[90]

In recent years, research has disclosed further knowledge regarding religious traditions of the slave population, especially of the Creole (see p. 142ff.). During the 18th century not much more on this topic was reported than

> '*The negroes are not baptized and do not embrace a religion. Their superstition and prejudice are huge and strong: they do believe that nature comprises something grand, which they call a deity or a great gods, and who creates and operates the universe; but they can give no further reason as to what it actually is; while their power of thought about that does not go further. Each of them has a special idol, which they honour such as: a horse, a cow, a sheep, a pig, a deer, a snake, and so on.* [...] *Here at many places in the forests a very high tree (called kankantrie) grows which everyone honours as a god. At certain times they hereby make offerings, while preparing food placed close by; accompanied by great attention and numerous ceremonies.*'[91]

The enslaved concealed their religious activities from white colonists as much as possible. All the more striking was the display of their dance feasts. Time and again chroniclers expressed their surprise at the desire among the Black population for frills, as reflected in their attire and adornments.

According to Jewish colonists, as referred to in their aforementioned 1788 *Essai historique*, the enslaved were so 'unbearably proud' of their splendour that they 'conceived an extreme contempt for the women of the country'.[92] Slaves tried to outshine one another at such events 'in bizarre finery'.[93]

During the 19th century a *doe* could only be held with special permission from the public prosecutor. Teenstra, the then agricultural adviser of the colonial government, was amazed by these festivities and reports:

———————————

89   Benoit 1980 (1839), 64.
90   Lammens 1816-1822, 108.
91   Blom 1787, 345-346.
92   Nassy 1788, seconde partie, 38.
93   Benoit 1980 (1839), 33.

Figure 4.4. This drawing by P.J. Benoit (orig. 1839) depicts slaves on their way to a *doe*.
P.J. Benoit 1980.

> '[...] *on Saturday evening, 28 april 1832, I attended, in the garden of a certain
> Heuvelman, at the Fiotte bridge in Paramaribo, a Doe (dance). Here, amidst the
> multitude of hundreds of negroes and Negresses, I heard to my great surprise very
> ingenious comparisons, recited off-the-cuff by several negresses in front of the large
> crowd, gathered here and belonging to all classes and of all colours.'*[94]

One of the few recited texts on such occasions runs as follows:

> '*The land of the whites is good, / It's like a rabbit hole, / It has many holes; / Suriname
> only has one hole, / That we can't get out of, /We're being held captive.*'[95]

In the course of the 19th century, the social function of *does* changed. Paradoxically
as it may sound, white settlers now organised an event, whereby hostile plantation
owners often stood face to face with officials. Planters not only saw to it that their
slaves set up art circles of which they then became the patron (*jobo*) but also that
renditions of the *doe* were applied to their will in order to denounce people as well as
situations. Governor Reinhardt Frans van Lansberge (1859-1867), for example, served
as patron of a *doe* named *Boenhatti gi ondroefinnie* (Goodness leads to experience).
In that time a *doe* consisted of two groups of art circle members, slaves and wealthy

---

94   Teenstra 1842, 122.
95   Ibid., 123.

A History of Suriname

white colonists. A manumitted woman of colour, whom the art circle's president referred to as *sisie*, maintained contacts between both parties.[96]

Certain slaves had obtained resources in order to acquire a number of possessions. Plantation slaves were allowed to raise poultry (e.g., chicken, duck) and to keep either fully or partly any revenues from sales for themselves. Others earned a living as fishermen. Craftsmen, apparently with their master's consent, personally hired or purchased slaves. Subject to property laws, slaves could not marry. This restriction did not imply they could not enter into a contract, but that their owner's authorisation was required. There was little ceremony of any kind. According to Jan Jacob Hartsinck (1716-1779), a WIC official, only drinking a bottle of brandy (*kilthum*) accompanied a slave marriage.[97] In a report by Anthony Blom we read:

> '*If a man sees a woman, for whom he feels affection, the marriage ceremony is concluded within five or not more than ten minutes; during which the man expresses his fondness to the woman, and also asks, if she loves him too; if the woman answers in the affirmative, the marriage is indeed completed; and they move in together the same evening.*'[98]

A cohabitation relationship and a visitor's relationship were both quite common. At the start of the Colonial Era the latter relationship probably prevailed. For, at that time those enslaved could not easily find partners on their own plantation as a result of the small number of labourers. Moreover, most Black women worked as domestic slaves in Paramaribo. In due course gender ratios on plantations became slightly more balanced. Cohabitation relationships therefore became more frequent whereby creolisation presumably also played a role (see p. 73ff.). In Paramaribo enslaved men and women often maintained a visitor's relationship. Only slaves who worked independently as craftsmen for their owners could be privileged with cohabiting with female slaves. Their dwellings were often built on their master's premises.[99]

Planters preferred their slaves not to maintain any visitor's relationships, as visits they had to pay to other plantations would remove the energy required when carrying out work. Plantation owners did not however prevent this form of relationship. Slaves often maintained several relations. According to Blom, a man in Suriname usually had two or three wives, and a woman more than one husband.[100] In West Africa, too, such partnerships were not uncommon.

Being enslaved did not contribute to the stability of relationships between male and female slaves who, if in a relationship, were not seldom sold separately by their owners. This occurred especially after the 1773 credit crisis in Amsterdam, when many plantations obtained incoming owners. Planters on occasion did not

---

96   Comvalius 1936, 216-220; see also: Fatah-Black 2018, 156-160; the latter notes that the *doe*, originally a cultural expression utilised by those enslaved, now referred to a political organization led by the white elite.
97   Hartsinck 1770, 910.
98   Blom 1787, 335.
99   Buschkens 1974, 55-58.
100 Blom 1787, 335.

hesitate to separate mothers from their children. On 14 August 1782, the colonial government felt obliged to prohibit this practice by means of a notification 'because of the numerous complaints and disorders'.[101] However, a ban on selling men who had fathered children separately remained out of the question, because this would unduly affect ownership issues.

As a result of the shortage of women, female plantation slaves were able to act somewhat independently from their partners. The household of slaves displayed highly matrifocal traits, implying that a female was in fact the head of a family. Another reason for her independent position was: being property of their mother's owner, children would always stay with their mothers after the breakup of a relationship.

4.5 Free people of colour and free Black people

The rise of a class of free Black people and of colour was an anomaly in a society dominated by whites. The colonial authorities therefore attempted to restrict owners manumitting male and female slaves. However, manumission (a term derived from the Roman legal term *manu missio*, meaning sending away from the hand) was inevitable as it directly resulted from sexual relationships white men maintained with Black slaves and/or those of colour. After all, the manumitted slaves were generally either concubines or children born from these mixed-race relations. Now and again domestic slaves were manumitted, as a reward for their faithful service. Other slaves were able to purchase their freedom with hard-earned money. Especially from the 19th century on, chain manumission became more common whereby in turn those who had been manumitted bought slaves free, mainly family members and relatives.[102] This phenomenon led to a strong increase in the number of free Black people and free people of colour (see Table 4.2). As with slave societies elsewhere the perspective of manumission not only contributed to the sustainability of this repressive system but also served as a tool with which to continue repression.[103],

The fact that women of colour initially formed the vast majority among the manumitted slaves resulted from the sexual preference of white colonists. Moreover, manumitted daughters born from relationships between white colonists and Black women were of colour. A manumitted slave was often named after his or her master whereby the prefix '*van*' (from) was added.

Initially the liberating of individual slaves was not impeded, although a decree dated 12 March 1670 did include a provision against vagrancy. This ruling stated: 'all negroes having received freedom from their patrons' must be employed by a slave master.[104] An initial regulation of manumission was issued on 28 July 1733. Henceforth

---

101 Schiltkamp & De Smidt 1973, vol. 2, 1048.

102 Neslo 2015, 177-210, for a comparison of manumission in Suriname with this specific type of manumission as observed elsewhere; see also: Brana-Shute & Sparks 2009 and Brana-Shute 1985.

103 It has been pointed out that Spanish, Portuguese, French and Dutch colonisers, when drafting slave laws, relied on Roman law, on which the legal system in their mother country was also based. Roman legislation included few restrictions on manumission, while freed slaves could also obtain citizenship. British colonizers fell back on common law, which does not provide for manumission, thus placing more restrictions on this practice. For example Watson, in his 1989 standard work, underlines on p. 127-133 that British slave law 'was racist from the start'; see also: Neslo 2016, 85-91.

104 Schiltkamp & De Smidt 1973, vol. 1, 57.

Year	Free population (incl. whites)	Free Black people and of colour	Free Black people and of colour (% of total free population)
1762	2,730	330	12
1781	2,900	821	28
1791	4,260	1,760	41
1805	5,400	2,889	53
1811	5,500	3,075	55
1833	6,996	4,951	70
1861	16,386	14,200	86
1862	17,162	15,000	87
1863 (year of abolition)	49,132	47,000	95

Table 4.2. Free population in Suriname 1762-1863. Hoogbergen & Ten Hove 2001, 312.

authorisation from the Court of Police and Criminal Justice was required. This Court would only give its consent if those manumitted were able 'to earn a living, so that, if this was not the case, they will not burden the colony'; in addition, those requesting a slave to be manumitted must 'commit themselves to having him instructed and educated in the Christian religion'; colonists deemed regulating necessary because of the continuous increase in the number of manumitted slaves and those of colour who '[...] do not save themselves often from mingling with servants by means of inebriation, evil behaviour, debauchery to the great detriment of their owners'.[105]

According to a decree dated 11 February 1788, those enslaved were taxed before receiving a 'letter of manumission'. Males older than 14 years paid 100 guilders, and females and children 50 guilders.[106] The proceeds were placed in a special fund established to finance expeditions aimed at seizing runaway slaves.

In a decree dated 11 July 1804, this tax was raised to 500 guilders for men and women, thus approximately equalling the amount to be paid for a slave. The cost of manumission rose to 250 guilders for children younger than 14 years.[107] Six months earlier, rules concerning this guarantee had already been reinforced because of the 'excessive multiplication' of manumission; before leaving the colony, those who had acted as guarantors for manumitted slaves had to pay a bail either in cash or otherwise, amounting to 2,000 guilders.[108] In 1825, when the supply of Africans stagnated after the ban on slave trade had been imposed, those enslaved in Suriname were no longer allowed to personally purchase their freedom.[109]

---

105   Ibid., 411-412.
106   Schiltkamp & De Smidt 1973, vol. 2, 1117-1118.
107   Ibid., 1237; it may be added here that at that time colonies made manumitting more difficult. This measure was partly a reaction to the successful slave revolt in Haiti, which led to independence here in 1804.
108   Ibid., 1225-1226; Wolbers 1861, 531.
109   Bruyning & Voorhoeve 1977, 393. In Suriname, the number of the free Black people and of colour when presented as a percentage of the entire free population (whites included) was one of the highest in the Caribbean. In 1830, however, the percentage of free Black people and of colour within the entire Black population and those of colour was relatively low, to wit, 9 per cent. Such a low percentage was the case in French and British colonies, too, where, additional restrictions pertained to manumission, partly because of a relatively small number of whites, who always lived in fear of Black masses and those of colour, see: Neslo 2016, 92-93.

The number of free Black people and of colour in Suriname exceeded those of whites in 1805. The fact that, slightly earlier, members of the two former groups had in Paramaribo outnumbered white colonists was in part a result of the founding of the *Neeger Vrijcorps* (Negro Freecorps) in 1772. It comprised *c.*300 slaves whom the colonial government had manumitted in order to act against runaways (see p. 121ff.). Manumission was by and large an urban phenomenon because, in Paramaribo, it was less difficult to acquire the financial means to free either relatives or oneself.[110]

The rapid growth of the group of those manumitted as recorded towards the end of the 18th century can partly be attributed to Governor-general Jan Gerhard Wichers (1784-1790). A rising prosperity had an impact, too. An increase of the number of manumitted Black people and of colour formed a key objective of Wichers' demographic policy. After the 1773 Amsterdam credit crisis, when a major part of the white population left Suriname, such a policy was certainly required. Viewing it as an opportunity to create a middle class, which would be prepared to do their utmost towards the colony on a permanent basis, Wichers proposed to set free those slaves made pregnant by their white masters 'ipso jure with her embryo'.[111] Their offspring would in due course be trained to become either farmers or craftsmen. Wichers expressed his opinions on people of colour in a letter addressed to the Society thus:

> '*They (the mulattoes) are only too necessary in a country, lacking a plebs or lower class, and deserve special encouragement. Attached as they are to this country, and not afflicted with the mania for ostentation in Europe, they make first-rate citizens, but have hitherto been neglected. They have always been regarded as an inferior class, and tainted as it were with a levis notae macula. Admittedly there has been a tendency of late to employ them more and more as private clerks, in secretariats, but they are still persecuted by the infamy of being illegitimate children.*'[112]

Notwithstanding the advancement witnessed among free people of colour, no real social breakthrough occurred at the end of the 18th century. Governor-general Wichers was far ahead of his time. Implementing his ideas would, in the white elite's opinion, have seriously undermined hierarchic colonial relations in Suriname. Here legislation strongly emphasized the subordinate position of free Black people and those of colour. The regulation on manumission dated 28 July 1733 stated that manumitted slaves as well as their offspring should 'pay all honour, respect and reverence' to each patron and his wife; a threat even existed of being enslaved again if manumitted slaves had engaged in 'beating, insulting or any defamation'; the enslaved were, furthermore, obliged to support their former patrons in their livelihoods if the latter should fall into poverty.[113]

Those manumitted had to comply with Suriname's strongly segmented society. Anybody who entered into sexual relationships with slaves risked losing their free

---

110 Slaves were hired out to work as dockworkers, hairdressers or carpenters, while being allowed to keep part of their earnings for themselves; similar practices existed elsewhere. In Brazil for instance, such slaves were referred to as *escravos de ganho*; see: Klein 1986, 129 and Neslo 2015, 186.

111 Van Lier 1971, 108.

112 Ibid., 109.

113 Schiltkamp & De Smidt 1973, vol. 1, 411-412.

status. According to a decree dated 4 February 1761, manumitted slaves who had participated in a dance feast faced the same penalty.[114] The ban prohibiting one to walk on the streets after 9 pm further limited one's freedom of movement. The reason for the latter restraining order (dated 17 May 1769) was, as was the case with slaves, one feared that those manumitted would help runaways.[115] Moreover, the right allowing manumitted Black people to vote was severely restricted in order to prevent them from constituting any political danger. A notification dated 28 February 1775 declared that those manumitted were not allowed to propose candidates for the Court of Police and Criminal Justice. Free-born Black people did however have that right with the proviso they were practising members of the Christian church.[116] Remarkably, the right allowing free people of colour to vote was not restricted.

Those people of colour occupied an ambivalent position in Suriname. According to certain chroniclers, whites and slaves looked upon them with contempt. In 1842, Van Breugel describes how slaves mockingly sing that whites and Black people have a homeland but those of colour do not.[117] Teenstra not only observed that even wealthy people of colour were not tolerated in institutes founded by whites but also that most people of colour were 'arrogant, proud, stubborn and impudent'.[118] Their attitude was perhaps also influenced by the mistrust the whites and slaves held against them. The image contemporaries portrayed when depicting free people of colour and free Black people is rather negative, especially as to the lower classes. According to Teenstra, the former two groups opined 'that the freedom of mankind consists of not working'; he reports that whites regard the well-to-do people of colour as 'dressed dolls' to further note that not a single slave was treated more harshly than by manumitted or free born Black people.[119] Non-whites, for their part, were all too keen on displaying their superiority to Black people. The above assessments can explain the negative attitude slaves felt towards people of colour. Non-white women, whom chroniclers have praised for their hospitality, caring and helpfulness, clearly preferred white men. This choice had not only to do with status. Women wished to give birth to light-skinned offspring.

The aversion free people of colour and free Black people held against work in the fields was the result of the fact they identified it with slave labour. As governmental clerk jobs were scarce, many non-whites had no regular incomes. Those who found livelihoods as craftsmen formed a minority. The opinion voiced by W.H. Lans, a (West Indies) government official, on people of colour who had found employment as either planters or plantation servants was remarkably positive. He held the view that members of these two groups were not only suited for these posts but also that they were less reluctant than Europeans to introduce any innovations.[120] Nevertheless, he endorsed the widespread negative judgement on the conduct of manumitted people of colour and Black people as follows:

---

114   Ibid., vol. 2, 727.
115   Ibid., vol. 2, 820.
116   Ibid., vol. 2, 879.
117   Van Breugel 1842, 32.
118   Teenstra 1842, 48.
119   Ibid., 48.
120   Lans 1842, 40.

'For example: a deacon I no longer know from which community, on his rounds collecting voluntary donations, enters a small house in one of the suburbs to come across two healthy young men stretched in hammocks. 'We are extremely poor, have nothing to donate, and not even plantains to eat.'- 'Why then does this large garden surrounding your house look completely abandoned?'- 'Well, because we do not own any slaves.' - This idea prevails: agriculture and slavery are deemed inseparable.'[121]

The situation that people of colour were by and large born into instable, non-marital relations did not help either. Many white fathers, particularly those belonging to lower social layers, ceased to support their children of colour. A reference to a key cause of their social deprivation, by president of the Court of Civil Justice A.L. Lammens, comprises:

'No father acknowledges his child, if he does not want to: - the mother, raised indifferently, cannot have a keen sense of all that is needed to make her child share in all those social advantages, provided by means of good, regular education, if at all she possesses the required resources and opportunity. - the upbringing is, in general, severely neglected, too: - No families as it were exist (I speak of the largest part of the Society, not of everyone indiscriminately) take to heart each other's interest. [...] This situation, although it may give pleasure, as much as desired, in due course leads more than half of the free, isolated population to become decrepit: - pursues nothing other than sensual pleasures, without the idea of being inspired: - that if belonging to a respectable family, one should behave accordingly, be worthy of that ancestry:- that the parents endeavour, not only by means of thrift but also by providing a better upbringing, to teach their children the true virtue, - to allow them to be prosperous and settled members of the society.'[122]

John Gabriel Stedman expressed his astonishment about such a level of carelessness expressed by white male parents.

Stedman's own son, whose mother was a woman of colour named Joanna, acquired his freedom from the colonial authorities thanks to his father's merits accumulated during the war against the Maroons. Apparently other colonists did not appreciate Stedman's emotions regarding his son. For, we read:

'[...] while the well thinking few highly applauded my sensibility/ many not only blamed me but even publickly derided me from my paternal affection which was call'd a whim, a weakness &c. &c.'[123]

A large part of the people of colour therefore remained enslaved,

---

121   Ibid., 41.
122   Lammens 1816-1822, 152.
123   Stedman 1790, 599.

Figure 4.5. Joanna, the
mother of Stedman's
son. Drawing by J.G.
Stedman (orig. 1790).
J.G. Stedman 1987.

'[...] *near 40 beautiful boys & girls were left to perpetual slavery by theyr parents of
my acquaintance, many of whom without being so much as once enquired after* [...].'[124]

Recent archival research has revealed a more nuanced portrayal of Suriname's free
Black population and of colour as well as of their links to other groups, especially
from the 19th century on. For example, relationships between those manumitted
and slaves was less antagonistic than sketched by contemporary chroniclers. Within
this context, it is interesting to look more closely at the aforementioned 'chain
manumission' whereby those manumitted, in turn, went on to manumit slaves, and
so on. In the course of the 19th century, it became increasingly common for free non-
whites to redeem their Black relatives and/or of colour who were by and large less
affluent than those manumitted by their white owners during the 18th century. After
all, the latter had often not only inherited property owned by whites, they were less
numerous too.[125] Manumission was, as we have seen earlier, not inexpensive. This is
why redeeming slaves, especially by a person who was not their owner, often took
place in phases. The fact that slaves had first to be purchased from their owners
explains why free non-whites also possessed slaves.[126] Next, a statutory tax had to

---

124   Ibid., 599.
125   Hoogbergen & Ten Hove 2001, 317.
126   Neslo 2015, 185.

be paid to the government, a transaction which could continue for years. Free non-whites preferred to see to it that a female was manumitted, because her status would determine the status of her offspring.[127] This form of manumission was, as observed in other colonies, mainly an urban phenomenon. In Paramaribo, slaves destined for freedom could be hired out for all kinds of work enabling them to save money and pay for their freedom later.

Notarial deeds, wills and district registers indicate that free non-whites gladly liberated their relatives from slavery. Phased as well as chain forms of manumission often occurred simultaneously. For example, a carpenter slave called Johannes Figaro was manumitted in 1833 and then named Johannes Zwiep. In turn, he manumitted his son Isaac Massa in 1835 followed 4 years later by another five slaves, to wit, his second partner and his children. One individual manumitted by Zwiep then paid for four slaves to be set free. In 1850, Zwiep freed his future son-in-law, who in turn manumitted another 14 people.[128] The freed Minnie van Gollenstede determined in her will dated 1834 that her two children, Leentje and Daantje, then still enslaved, should be presented with 'the precious treasure of freedom' at the expense of her estate.[129] In district registers, slaves were regularly listed according to their residential addresses and referred to as 'the slaves are owned for freedom'.[130]

The role Jan Houthakker played may be considered remarkable. This slave owner is mentioned as such in the manumission register (introduced in 1832) on no less than 129 occasions. He had been manumitted in 1838 by the aforementioned Johannes Zwiep along with two other slaves. Strong indications exist as to Houthakker later operating within a manumission network and to serving as a representative of abolitionist organisations established in the Low Countries in order to finance manumissions by means of advances.[131] These institutions were named the *Nederlandse Maatschappij ter Bevordering van de Afschaffing van de Slavernij* (Dutch Society for the Promotion of the Abolition of Slavery) and the *Dames-comité* (Ladies committee) (see also p. 175).

The phased and chain manumission can be regarded as another form of agency set up by slaves who hereby also strived for freedom, as they did when creating room for their cultural expressions, aptly termed 'self-emancipation' and 'legal slave resistance'.[132]

---

127 Hoogbergen & Ten Hove 2001, 317. This publication also reports that offspring conceived in legitimate marriages between white men and women of colour were considered white from the 1780s on. In the USA such children would be classified as Black.

128 Neslo 2016, 125.

129 Ibid., 124.

130 Neslo 2015, 185.

131 Meijvogel 2017, 18-20; Fatah-Black 2018, 154-155; Neslo 2015, 192-193; Neslo 2016, 134-135.

132 Van Stipriaan 2006, 76 and Brana-Shute 1990, 119-136. Within this context it is relevant to refer to the stormy discussion on slavery resulting from S.M. Elkins, *Slavery: A Problem in American Institutional and Intellectual Life* (Chicago 1959). In it, Elkins sketches slavery as being an all-encompassing institution which transforms slaves into depersonalized, docile, childlike beings with a so-called Sambo attitude, which would have persisted among many Black Americans. Van Stipriaan, in his ground breaking study entitled *Surinaams contrast. Roofbouw en overleven in een Caraïbische plantagekolonie, 1750-1863* (Leiden 1993), refutes Elkins's static representation. Van Stipriaan follows in the footsteps of E. D. Genovese, *Roll, Jordan, Roll. The World the Slaves Made* (New York 1972) and R. W. Fogel & S.L. Engerman *Time on the cross. The Economics of American Negro Slavery* (New York 1974).

A History of Suriname

Figure 4.6. View of the large fruit-, vegetable- and poultry-market. Drawing by P.J. Benoit (orig. 1839). P.J. Benoit 1980.

An increase in these two manumission-related phenomena also apparently indicates that the cultural distance between those of colour and the Black population was not that comprehensive. Free non-whites and slaves often belonged, as we have seen, to one and the same family, and had mastered the same language, to wit, Sranan Tongo. Occasionally a synthesis of Euro-Christian and Afro-Surinamese elements was encountered. The same rings true for funerary and marital rituals. We can also observe how a number of prominent figures active within the emerging free, non-white elite stood up for the fates of the enslaved (see p. 100ff.). Apparently, in the case of free non-whites, a dualistic identity did exist.

Having become free citizens by means of chain manumission, one was able to contribute to the colony's economic prosperity. Their number included craftsmen (e.g., carpenters, tailors, shoemakers, bakers) as well as accountants, planters and directors or administrators of plantations. Women were mainly active as market vendors, midwives, hairdressers, laundry ironers, domestic servants or seamstresses. The non-white middle class which emerged in the course of the 19th century contributed to Paramaribo's vibrancy, too.

Initially no education was available to free people of colour or free Black people. Both groups were not allowed to attend schools for whites. The first school to open its doors to free 'mulattoes and negroes' was founded in 1776, though it took a considerable effort to accumulate sufficient funds to pay the teacher's salary. According to the Conventus Deputatorum, the board of the Reformed Church, 'a huge persuasive power was required to get those men, who willingly offered premiums of 50 and 100 guilders for killing a runaway negro, to pay a sum of between 200 and 300 guilders for the remuneration of a teacher for the pagan and mulatto children'.[133] The situation of the free people of colour gradually improved in the course of the 19th century. Their demand for education now increased. On 24 May 1794, a weekly focussing on news, culture and science entitled *Saturdagsche Courant van Nieuws, Smaak en Vernunft* (Saturday Weekly of News, Taste and Ingenuity) published an advertisement. In it a government schoolmaster named J.L. van der Tooren announced he would upon request provide tuition 'to coloureds in the evening hours'.[134]

In order to improve the plight of those deprived, initiatives also originated from free people of colour. In 1827, the medical doctor Martinus Mauritz. Alexander Coupijn (1798-1853) and the lawyer Nicolaas Gerrit Vlier (1801-1852) among others founded the *Surinaamsche Maatschappij van Weldadigheid* (Surinamese Society of Benevolence). This institute aimed at not only providing support to the needy but also educating their children.[135] It is reported that Jews joined the organisation, too, because they 'were also cast out by the so-called aristocracy of Suriname'.[136] The suspicion among certain circles now arose that this charitable society harboured secret intentions. After attending one of its board meetings, Governor Paulus Roelof Cantz'laar (1771-1831) and Commissioner-general Johannes van den Bosch (1780-1844) were nevertheless convinced of the opposite.

N.G. Vlier also officiated as a secretary (Paramaribo section) of the *Maatschappij tot Nut van 't Algemeen* (Society for the Common Good). Revived in 1816, it played a key role in intellectual as well as social circles. It counted more than 200 members, both white and free non-white.[137] In 1839, during a speech delivered to the aforementioned society, Vlier extensively praised Petrus Frederik Bijderhand's 'self-sacrificing humanity, which is almost unprecedented';[138] as a slave, the latter had saved five people from drowning for which this society awarded him not only with an 'honorary prize' but also with manumission by the government. Even more risky were Vlier's fiery statements concerning the bitter fate of slaves:

'Even if their conditions were opposed to each other as that of the wolf to the well-fattened dog of Phaedrus, which is far from being the case, still I would prefer for me with the wolf my poverty but freedom, to space and abundance, while hard chains press on me.'[139]

Vlier, who owned several plantations, was not the only person of colour to stand up for slaves. In 1849, Johannes C. Palthe Wesenhagen, a member of the Court of Justice in Paramaribo, published a sharp pamphlet in the Netherlands. In it he advocated the phased abolition of slavery, reproaching the Dutch government of acting with

---

133 Oudschans Dentz 1954, 179.
134 Van Lier 1971, 111.
135 Ibid., 111; Wolbers 1861, 634-635; for further information on the remarkable Nicolaas Vlier, see: Neslo 2015, 194-198.
136 Wolbers 1861, 645.
137 Van Kempen 2002, vol. 3, 188.
138 Vlier 1839, 177.
139 Teenstra 1842, 172.

'indulgence' as a result of which it 'continues to feed the demands which the fighters hold against Emancipation.'[140] We read:

> 'The negro is not completely unworthy of the treasure of freedom, and with more civilisation will not have to give way to the European.'[141]

In 1828, J. van den Bosch was installed as commissioner-general and tasked improving Paramaribo's prosperity as well as the fate of slaves. He soon started appointing meritorious people of colour and Jews to key, until that moment inaccessible, positions. The incoming government's rules and regulations, which Van den Bosch was willing to implement, also aimed at combatting this social disadvantage. Article 116 states:

> 'To all free people, citizens of the colony, no matter which religion or colour, are granted equal civil rights; all public authorities are invited, by their example, to counter the still existing prejudice related to this.'[142]

During the first half of the 19th century several people of colour already excelled at key positions. They included Coupijn and Vlier, founders of the *Surinaamse Maatschappij van Weldadigheid*. Hendrik C. Focke (1802-1856) and J.C. Palthe Wesenhagen, who had both acquired their law degrees in the Netherlands, were apparently 'a jewel for the bar'.[143] Focke later served as a member of the Court of Justice which Palthe Wesenhagen presided during the president's leave in the Netherlands. In 1855, Focke who was active in the literary world, too, composed the first dictionary of Sranan Tongo titled *Neger-Engelsch Woordenboek* (Negro-English dictionary). He is not only the presumed author of the Sranan Tongo poetry collection entitled *Proeve van Neger-Engelsche Poëzie* but also co-founder of a magazine named *West-Indië*.[144] Theatre activities had already begun in the 19th century with companies such as *Oeffening Kweekt Kunst* (Exercise Breeds Art) and *De verreezen Phoenix* (The risen Fenix).[145] In 1840 the mainly Jewish company *Thalia* (of which Vlier was the founding chairman in 1837) opened a theatre with the same name which exists to this very day.[146]

It was not uncommon for well-to-do people of colour to send their children to the Netherlands for further education. In 1809, Johannes Vrolijk having returned to Suriname as a teacher founded a school with educational standards higher than hitherto known. He was probably the first person of colour to take on such a prestigious function.[147] During the years preceding the 1863 abolition of slavery, prejudice against persons of colour had, according to Wolbers, considerably decreased but not yet fully disappeared. He reported that in Paramaribo no person of colour had ever been appointed an elder or deacon, bar by the small Lutheran Church. In

---

140   Palthe Wesenhagen 1849, 42.
141   Ibid., 51.
142   Wolbers 1861, 644.
143   Ibid., 769.
144   Van Kempen 2002, vol. 3, 258.
145   Ibid., 193-196.
146   Ibid., 197-201; Neslo 2015, 196.
147   Van Lier 1971, 111.

Figure 4.7. A daguerrotype (*c*.1846) portraying the married couple Maria Louise de Hart and Johannes Ellis. The former was born into slavery on a sugar plantation, shortly before her father freed her mother and their four children. Johannes Ellis was born into slavery as the son of the highest Dutch official residing in Elmina, the then centre of the Dutch slave trade on the Gold Coast. Abraham de Veer, who in 1822 became governor of Suriname, fathered Johannes to a slave girl named Fanny Ellis. In 1903, after an exemplary military career, the son of the Surinamese couple was appointed Minister of Defence in the Dutch government. Rijksmuseum, Amsterdam, public domain via Wikimedia Commons.

the colonial hierarchy a non-white being nominated a general prosecutor was still impossible as proved to be the case when Palthe Wesenhagen took an interest in this post. Governor Charles P. Schimpf (1812-1886) pondered in a letter addressed to the Minister of Colonies if Palthe Wesenhagen would be able to command any due respect and awe from slaves as well as whites. He was, after all, still related by blood to people of colour 'in the lower class'; it also did not help that, according to Schimpf, Palthe Wesenhagen had in his 1849 pamphlet published a few years earlier included rather positive remarks pertaining to the character of 'negroes'.[148]

---

148   Toes 1992, 65.

CHAPTER 5
Marronage

5.1 Introduction

After peace had been declared with Amerindians and with a small group of runaway slaves at the Coppename River during Cornelis van Aerssen van Sommelsdijck's governorship (1683-1688), the feeling within the colony now prevailed that order had been established, at least for the time being. However, a growing number of slaves and plantations caused the number of runaways to increase too. Suriname was not the only Caribbean colony in which one tried to escape from the yoke of slavery. Such attempts are referred to as 'marronages'. Derived from the Spanish term *cimarron*, which was initially applied on the island of Hispaniola whenever cattle wandered off into the mountains to later describe Amerindians who had escaped from their Spanish colonisers. Since the end of the 16th century, the term 'Maroon' referred to runaway Black slaves across the entire Caribbean and the Americas. In Suriname, Maroons are also known as *bosnegers* (bush negroes), a term they themselves use too.

Scholars have attempted to analyse the factors favouring slave revolts and marronage of which Suriname witnessed the majority of examples.[1] Here the number of slaves, especially on plantations, far exceeded the number of white colonists. Hence, no impressive presence of whites prevented those enslaved from running away. The numerical ratio of slaves and whites was more skewed than in most other colonies. Van Aerssen van Sommelsdijck had already decreed at least one white overseer per ten slaves to be present on plantations.[2] This requirement, however, had to be relaxed more than once. A ruling dated 1 February 1773 stipulated that a single white overseer per 40 'workable slaves' would suffice.[3] However, not everybody complied with this ruling. Refusing to submit hereto was either the result of a shortage of colonists or of the planters' frugality who now and again maliciously dealt with this mandatory declaration as to the number of slaves. In Jamaica, where marronage was also a familiar phenomenon, the numerical ratio was more favourable for colonists.[4]

For a long time, the number of African-born slaves in Suriname was much higher when compared with the number of those born here. In 1740 no less than 90 per cent was African-born. In 1770, this percentage dropped to 70 per cent.[5] These numbers were, of course, the outcome of the high mortality and low birth rate, which required a rapid replenishment of the slave population. Particularly African-born slaves ran off more often than Creoles, who were not only more accustomed to slave labour but also on occasion felt more closely attached to their plantation. The Coromantees (Akan ethnic groups from the Gold Coast, Ghana), the Papas (from the Slave Coast on

---

1   See especially: Hoogbergen's standard work entitled *The Boni Maroon Wars in Suriname*, 1990; Price, 1976, *The Guiana Maroons: A Historical and Bibliographical Introduction*; Price 2013 (1973), *Maroon Societies: Rebel Slave Communities in the Americas*; Campbell 1988, *The Maroons of Jamaica 1655-1796: A History of Resistance, Collaboration and Betrayal.*
2   Schiltkamp & De Smidt 1973, vol. 1, 137.
3   Ibid., vol. 2, 851.
4   Higman 1995, 144.
5   Hoogbergen 1990, 2; Price 1976, 12.

the Bight of Benin) and slaves from Loango-Angola were most rebellious, perhaps a result of the strong political and military tradition upheld in their motherland.[6] In addition, because of the small number of women counted during the first decades after the onset of the slave trade, many slaves did not feel greatly attached to the locations they populated. The geographical conditions in Suriname were, moreover, favourable for runaways. In the dense forest, behind the rapids encountered along the upper reaches of rivers, Maroons could feel more or less safe. Across the coastal plain, along the lower reaches of rivers, treacherous swamps provided protection against pursuers. These natural conditions may explain why Suriname never witnessed any massive slave uprisings. Marronage did indeed present an easier manner to relieve any discontent.

The absenteeism of plantation owners also encouraged the rebellion of slaves. The assumption here is: directors by and large treated slaves less gently and expressed less interest in preserving human capital when compared with slave owners. Atrocities carried out by plantation servants and heavy labour forced numerous slaves to seek refuge in the forest.

The heterogeneous composition of the enslaved population on plantations was, however, a factor which may have inhibited marronage in Suriname. After all, plans to run away were simply betrayed more rapidly in the case of mutual differences. Not only did slaves hail from various parts of the West coast of Africa, those who had arrived on board of the same ship were disseminated as much as possible across various plantations in order to avoid the forming of groups. The high mortality and replenishment by means of newcomers imported from Africa only increased the heterogeneity of the enslaved population.

The uncertain prospect of life as a runaway also prevented attempts to escape. Family and religious ties (e.g., when one's ancestors were buried on the plantation) had the same effect. According to estimates, c.250 slaves (90 per cent males) ran off each year, a third of whom would never return.[7] The entire enslaved population now comprised more than 50,000 souls.

The colonial authorities took various legal measures in order to reduce the risk of conspiracies and marronage. Numerous rules were aimed at restricting the free movement of slaves. According to a decree dated 13 July 1684, for example, the enslaved were no longer allowed to roam the streets of Paramaribo half an hour after sunset.[8] The reason for this measure was that local slaves now and again supplied runaways with victuals. This ruling was slightly relaxed later. A notification dated 12 December 1760 stated that slaves were only permitted to walk around on the streets after the evening drum (later replaced by a cannon shot) had sounded, if they were carrying either a note from their owner or a lantern which could only be purchased with his permission.[9] Gatherings throughout Paramaribo were vetoed too. According to a decree dated 9 May 1741 white colonists even had the right to break up groups of slaves.[10] The Pad van Wanica, a well-known meeting

---

6   Hoogbergen 1990, 2-3; Bruijning & Voorhoeve 1977, 560.
7   Hoogbergen 1990, 5.
8   Schiltkamp & De Smidt 1973, vol. 1, 144.
9   Ibid., 696.
10   Ibid., 484.

place for slaves and runaways located just south of Paramaribo, was declared entirely off limits. Slaves required a note signed by their owners in order to enter this area. White colonists were enjoined to ask passing slaves to present this note. In case of any refusals or 'unmannered' conduct, a slave could be transferred to his 'master'. According to a notification dated 22 May 1745, colonists would then be rewarded with the lump sum of 6 guilders.[11]

More than 20 years later, a notification dated 8 December 1767 stated that free Black people and of colour were also not permitted to enter the Pad van Wanica during evening hours. For, they were seen as potential threats based on possible contacts with runaways. From then on, even a note signed by their masters no longer benefitted slaves.[12] In 1794, their freely moving about in Combé, a part of Paramaribo stretching northwards from Fort Zeelandia along the Suriname River, was prohibited for the same reasons.[13] With not much freedom permitted in the vicinity of the plantations, too, slaves were not allowed to travel on rivers without the supervision of a white man, and only if their masters had given permission. Governor Johannes Heinsius (1678-1680) had already issued such a veto. One was thus entitled to detain Black people and, if necessary, fire at vessels transporting them. A decree, issued on 2 June 1714, was very clear on reasons for such a restriction:

'[...] that moreover as a result of that freedom not only deserting was facilitated, but also the conspiring and seeking of followers to do so, because as a result of the free navigation they have the chance, always and whenever they deem it right and in the numbers that are willing, to come together with others and forge plans in order to reach such a pernicious objective and follow through. That it also often happens, because of that facility to meet up, that negroes, otherwise of sound character, can easily be seduced by those conversations with malevolents and by incitements from them, particularly those residing at plantations upstream, where the slaves often have the opportunity to talk with the runaways and, being debauched by them, to lure others, because of the minor danger they are exposed to, since having those runaways as guides and therefore being assured there is no lack of food or other shortage.'[14]

Slaves constantly committed various acts of resistance directed against their oppressors. Simulating a disease, sabotaging commissioned work, acts of arson such as the fire of Paramaribo (1832) lit by Mentor, Codjo and Present (who were later sentenced to death), or poisoning one's master, could ultimately result in deciding to seek refuge in the forest. Be it now and again a spontaneous reaction caused by dissent, it was more often a carefully prepared plan. It is no coincidence that attempts to escape mainly took place during the rainy season, when pursuers could barely cope with the extreme conditions.

---

11   Ibid., 534.
12   Ibid., vol. 2, 815.
13   Ibid., 1179; Wolbers 1861, 456.
14   Schiltkamp & De Smidt 1973, vol. 1, 302.

Slaves usually left their plantations either in small groups or on their own. Their departure was not merely the outcome of an increasing danger of being betrayed in case of a huge conspiracy. There was simply no need to conspire with large groups as plantations could be left behind easily. However, problems pertaining to the food supply would soon arise in the forest. Therefore, too, runaways initially stayed in the direct vicinity of the plantation. For many, the marronage took place in stages.[15] Once Maroon communities had formed, newly arrived runaways were able to hide in the impenetrable second-growth forest, positioned directly behind plantations. Such a location (*kapuweri*) was created by an overgrowth of the slaves' former gardens. *Kapuweri* men could often only partially keep themselves alive with everything the forest and long-serving gardens provided. They would regularly return to their plantations at night in search of food or sleep with their wives. Now and again befriended slaves would bring food into the forest, too.

In the second stage of marronage, an individual *kapuweri* man would join forces with a group comprising between eight and ten people. Those who had taken shelter (*schuylders*) now moved slightly further away from plantations in order to create their own gardens and grow traditional crops - e.g., cassava, rice, yam (*napi*), peas (*pesi*), bananas, corn and sweet potatoes. Plant materials were acquired from plantations. Fishing and hunting also yielded essentials. These *schuylders* were often forced to steal food from plantations. In order to obtain clothing, tools (e.g., machetes, hoes, axes) and weapons they were even more dependent on theft.

A genuine Maroon community only came about if groups of *schuylders* joined them. On occasion they met by chance, when chased after by patrols set up by plantation owners. In order to deal with a huge shortage of females, Maroons organised raids in order to be reunited with their wives and children, but generally speaking women were taken away from plantations randomly. Slaves could now take advantage of the opportunity to join the raiders and set off for the forests with them. However, fierce fighting could occur especially if the wives of slaves were abducted.

Once the cultivation of sufficient farmland had assured the supply of food, the Maroons settled in villages located further away from plantations. Across the coastal plain they opted for higher land located in marshes and only accessible during the dry season. Villages fortified by means of palisades could often only be accessed via winding underwater paths. Maroon villages were also built on the upper reaches of rivers because colonists deemed confronting rapids very risky.

In 1690, a rebellion on the plantation owned by a Jewish planter named Imanuel Machado, heralded a new era of unrest. Located on the banks of Cassewijne Creek and beyond Jodensavanne, a small group of Maroons had returned here in order to liberate those who had stayed behind. Next, they murdered Machado and went off with all his possessions.[16] These attackers belonged to an ethnic group referred to as Matjáu. Their ancestors formed one of the most important clans of the present-day Saramaka Maroons. Even today this ethnic group inhabits an area located between the Saramacca and Suriname Rivers. In the following years, even more slaves ran away. Their numbers increased in 1712, especially after a raid carried out by the

---

15   Hoogbergen 1990, 6-14.
16   Wolbers 1861, 137.

French navy Captain Jacques Cassard (see p. 32). Prior hereto Paramaribo-based colonists had sent a large number of their slaves off into the forest in order to avoid them falling into the hands of looting French troops. Having taken care of the fugitive white women and children, a majority of these slaves opted not to return to their master after Cassard had left. More runaways joined them later.[17]

An internal enemy thus once again threatened the colony, after the attacks by Amerindians in the 17th century. Plantations were raided and 'slave capital' was lost. In 1698, Governor Paulus van der Veen (1696-1707) raised the reward for catching a single runaway slave to 25 or 50 guilders. This lump sum, which owners of runaway slaves had to pay, depended upon where the capture took place. Eleven years earlier, this reward (consisting of merely 5 guilders since 1685) had already been increased to between 100 and 300 pounds of sugar. The highest reward was paid out in the case of pursuits especially aimed at runaways.[18] From 1717 on, all colonists were allowed to chase after runaways, be it on their own account. This measure illustrates the government's considerable lack of power. For, the Society of Suriname and the planters were not prepared to allocate sufficient funds in order to create a well-equipped task force. If a village that sheltered runaways was detected, the authorities promised to forward 600 guilders; those who discovered the notorious villages of Klaas and Pedro could expect as much as 1,500 guilders as well as extra 10 guilders per individual villager; the slaves who informed their master on the location of Maroon settlements were set free.[19] The same reward was promised to returning runaways if they revealed their former whereabouts. Colonists feared the enticing effect the founding of Maroon villages could have. This apprehension formed a key reason to introduce the death penalty for runaways, as stated in a decree dated 22 July 1721.[20]

Death sentences were often carried out either by means of hanging or the breaking wheel. For runaway slaves however more brutal variants were devised. Eleven Saramakas detained during an 1730 expedition faced a gruesome fate after a ruling by the Court of Police and Criminal Justice. We read:

'To wit the negro Joosie, being hanged from the gallows with an iron hook through the ribs, staying there until death follows, having died the head was cut off, placed on a stake and erected on the Waterkant, the upper body remaining a prey for the birds; and the negroes named Wierai and Manbote, were tied to a pole and burned alive with a small fire, and while burning pinched with red hot pliers. The negresses named Lucretia, Ambira, Aga, Gomba, Marie and Victoria, were placed on a cross to be broken on the wheel, and once executed their heads, once chopped off, were placed on stakes on the Waterkant. The negresses named Diana and Christina, their heads were chopped off with an axe and also placed on stakes on the Waterkant.'[21]

The cruel punishing of runaways occurred more often in the course of the 18th century, but without any noticeable effects. Governor Jan Jacob Mauricius (1692-1768) believed

---

17   Ibid.
18   Ibid., 138-139.
19   Ibid., 139.
20   Ibid.
21   Hartsinck 1770, 764-765.

that slaves had no fear of death. He wrote that, after their passing away, they thought 'they would enter a kind of Turkish paradise, where whites serve them'.[22] In many cases runaways escaped the death penalty because their owners continued to hope for their return and, for that reason, did not report to the authorities. To slave owners, a death sentence formed a pure example of destruction of capital. Mauricius therefore proposed to punish runaways with forced labour after their tongue and genitals had been cut off. Slave owners would then receive compensation if purchasing a new slave. The Court of Police and Criminal Justice rejected this suggestion, although cutting off tongues continued to applied in the case of certain offences.[23]

With the marronage, military actions against runaways also increased. At first, civilian companies were deployed, on occasion supplemented by a small number of soldiers. The Society's troops had been stationed in the colony since 1683. However, in the eyes this society's directors, the fight against domestic enemies first and foremost concerned colonists. It may be added here that financial considerations primarily prompted that stance.

Civil companies had already been founded during English sovereignty (1651-1667). The entire plantation area was divided into sections whereby the directorship was placed in the hands of *heemraden* (administrators), all residing in Paramaribo. The Jewish nation had its own section. The key functionary was the *burgercapiteyn* (civil captain). Serving as head of a civil company, he had protective duties. In practice this position implied that civilian units were to be mobilized in the event of either major unrest occurring at plantations or when Maroons carried out attacks. Members of these civil companies could also be deployed against foreign enemies and, in Paramaribo, acted as permanent night watchmen. All adult colonists had to register for the civil militia and were presented with the ranks of lieutenant, ensign or corporal. The jurisdiction of these civilian captains as well as organising this form of security were both regulated in great detail by means of alarm regulations, which were supplemented from time to time. In case of an emergency, planters were obliged to prepare their 'most capable' slaves.[24] Cannons were positioned at numerous plantations in order to warn their surroundings of any imminent danger when firing a pre-arranged number of round-shots. During major crises, all the white colonists must immediately arrive at the meeting place as agreed upon along with his division and accompanied by between three and six slaves. They had to be equipped with sufficient weapons, ammunition, dry food and beverages to last a fortnight. On each plantation a prescribed quantity of weaponry including muskets, rifles, bullets, gunpowder and flints had to be available at all times. Civilian captains should check the compliance with rules and, if necessary, impose fines.

These civil companies achieved only limited results when combatting marronages. Large numbers of planters were unwilling to make any financial and physical sacrifices in order to defend the colony. Many did not care about any alarm regulations due to the high costs they were confronted with. A proper functioning of civil companies required the cooperation of each and every colonist. Exactly that element

---

22   Wolbers 1861, 134-135.
23   Ibid., 135.
24   See e.g., the alarm regulation dated 1 August 1738: Schiltkamp & De Smidt 1973, vol. 1, 447-451.

was absent in the individualistic colonial society, where the *animum revertendi* and rapid profits were the key incentives. The fact that the Jewish civil company was able to record several military successes was presumably no coincidence. Jewish planters were indeed virtually the only colonists willing to stay in Suriname while having to defend their own nation, too. They were therefore immediately up to the challenge, when Governor Johan van Scharphuysen (1689-1696) stated, after planter Imanuel Machado had been murdered in 1690, he could do nothing thus leaving it to them to avenge his assassination.[25] At the start of the 18th century, the Jewish civilian captain David C. Nassy (1612-1685) distinguished himself by undertaking more than 30 expeditions in search of Maroons.[26] In 1738 the Cormantees, a most formidable Akan ethnic group, killed Manuel Pereyra, a Jewish planter. Next, the Jewish colonist Joseph Arias took on expenditures pertaining to a search-party. His detachment returned after 6 weeks not only with 47 prisoners but also with the six severed hands of slain Maroons, for which a fixed premium was collected.[27]

From a military point of view, colonial units faced an almost hopeless task. For, in the course of the 18th century, members of Maroon communities had become increasingly intimidating opponents, thus incomparable to the first loose groups of runaways. Under no circumstances did Maroons wish to give up their precious freedom. At the same time, civil companies became less effective as, during the 18th century, more and more planters preferred life in Paramaribo to the solitude of the plantation. Those directors who replaced plantation owners expressed little motivation to actually defend their land.

Therefore, after 1730, mainly troops serving the Society were deployed against runaways, although civil companies did remain ready for action in the vicinity of plantations. This society's mercenaries were not very successful as they hailed from various parts of Europe.[28] Their origins did not prove very conducive to any unity or motivation. In 1723, for example, as much as half the recruits were of German descent. The remainder included men from the Dutch Republic, France and Switzerland. In 1753, the strength of the Society's troops was increased from 300 to 600 men. This expansion took place shortly after the State troops, temporarily stationed in Suriname as a result of political difficulties concerning Governor Mauricius, had to return to the Dutch Republic. A large part of this state military then joined the Society. In 1759 the number of its troops was enlarged to 1,200 men. However, the quality of the majority of its soldiers was rather inferior. Amsterdam-based *zielverkopers* (soul sellers), *slaapbazen* (sleep bosses) and *volkhouders* (folkholders) carried out enlisting procedures. Throughout the year these men provided board and lodging to unemployed, who were, on the recruitment days, transferred to the Society or other institutions such as the Dutch East India Company as much as possible. By means of regularly flouting selection criteria, recruiters had already built up dubious reputations during Van Aerssen van Sommelsdijck's governorship.

---

25 Nassy 1788, première partie, 76.
26 Ibid., 90.
27 Ibid., 91-92.
28 For the below-mentioned details on military recruitment etc., see: Lohnstein 1987, 67-84.

Colonial units were hardly prepared for a real guerrilla war against the very mobile Maroon groups. Expeditions usually comprised dozens of white-soldiers. In addition, twice as many slaves participated as gunmen and porters. Returning runaways as well as Amerindians often acted as guides. The logistical problems were immense. For, such large groups, having to carry heavy provisions, could only move with great difficulty due to the inaccessible, treacherous terrain. Many fell ill as a result of hardships encountered during long hikes, the heat and insects. Food (e.g., groats, bread, meat) was lost due to decay or ill luck. Gunpowder became moist when troops waded through swamps. Slaves either sabotaged their tasks or defected to the Maroons. The enemy was lurking everywhere. Captain Lieutenant Carl Otto Creutz (1715-1762), having set off on a major search-party directed against the Saramaka people on 20 September 1749, reported in his journal:

'So when we marched through the second village, through a scrubland, and through a forest to finally arrive at about the middle of a mountain, when climbing we were attacked, the ensign Herge being ten or twelve men ahead of the Capt. Lieut. was shot dead immediately, and a negro was injured in his hand; van Cuijlenburg also shot dead a negro, going between the two cadets, and two soldiers were also hit by grazing shots, one on his chin, the other on his hat, while the negroes were all lying behind trees, so that one could not see them, however having been shooting at them all the time, after which they fled screaming, we only found some blood. Next having had ensign Herge brought back and having continued to march, we walked through the village in good order, and observing nothing anymore, we chased after the enemy with all seriousness, climbing and descending the mountain, and again we were attacked in the same way, they absolutely thought to prevent us from marching, but firing fiercely at them, they fled again behind the trees, nobody of us being injured.'[29]

Among Saramakas this confrontation with colonial troops is to date referred to as the Battle of Bákakúun.[30] The Saramaka version of this event, as Richard Price recorded in his unique research on the oral tradition of this ethnic group, differs hugely from the report presented by Creutz. In 1976, a Saramaka named Peléki stated:

'They were living on the mountain top. And they dug a giant trench running from the very bottom up to the top. It was the only way to get in or out of the village. They cut big logs, just the width of the trench, and many men together rolled them to the top. When the whites came up the path, they did not know that things would come pouring down the trench to kill them. [...] Well, there was no way to run fast enough to avoid them! They were mashed to a pulp. No way to escape alive.'[31]

As is not unusual in the case of warfare, both parties claimed victory. Considering the 'strength of the Saramaka traditions' about the battle, Price opines that the

---

29   De Beet & Price 1982, 61.
30   Price 1983, 135-138.
31   Ibid., 135.

Saramakas must at least have delivered a 'heroic defence' on the hilltop.[32] Maroons increasingly adapted to the difficult forest life, hereby avoiding any direct combat as much as possible, because their weapons were inferior to those carried by colonial troops. Information provided to Maroons by spies on plantations and in Paramaribo often included warnings regarding the arrival of patrols even before their departure. Colonial soldiers would consequently come across empty villages and abandoned farm land. On occasion these men were led astray either by means of specially chopped-out paths that ran aground, or by ambushes. These troops destroyed as many Maroon villages and vegetable gardens as possible. New settlements were usually rebuilt quickly. In addition, extra food supplies were often created, whereby women played key roles. If necessary Maroons could survive for considerable periods of time thanks to the gifts of nature or by stealing food from plantations.

In due course, a number of colonists realised it would be better to declare peace with the Maroon people. During his governorship, K.E.H. de Cheusses (1728-1734) announced the 'total ruin and extermination of that scum' after an attack in 1730 on his own plantation, Berg en Dal.[33] However, even destroying the infamous villages of Klaas and Pedro did not have the desired effect. De Cheusses then offered a letter of pardon to all runaways in order to save them from the death penalty, but only if they reported themselves within 4 months. Not one Maroon responded to this invitation. In 1749 Governor Mauricius finally initiated peace efforts after realising the pointlessness of all those expensive search-parties directed against runaways. On 25 January 1750 he wrote to the directors of the Society:

> '*All one fights for, if the expeditions are very fortunate at all, is that some houses are burned, their produce reduced, and their food in part ruined, because it is impossible to entirely eradicate a vegetable garden, the runaways themselves hide in the inaccessible forests, and as soon as the expedition leaves, they repair their loss very quickly, and fortunately, if they don't outwit some of us on the way back, as it has turned out was the case with Brouwer's expedition, only two means remain in order to take advantage of them, even if one ponders on it for a hundred years, either one makes peace with them, or one hunts them with on-going expeditions, holding posts in the villages which they find, and always goes plus ultra.*'[34]

According to Mauricius, peace was now indeed inevitable for economic reasons alone. In fact, Maroons had threatened to bring the colony's finances to the brink of disaster. Thanks to peace, Mauricius opines, 'the capital of the creditors was safer nowadays'.[35] As that letter clarifies, he wished to achieve his goal by means of the tried, tested colonial strategy of division and rule:

---

32   Ibid., 137.
33   De Groot 1982, 65.
34   De Beet & Price 1982, 38.
35   Ibid.

'Declaring general peace with them all could however become dangerous, if they would then agree together; and for subduing them all, our power is too small. It is therefore possible to incite them against each other. And based on these assumptions I think I can conclude, that of all the plans, which in such a delicate situation can be made with human wisdom (and which plans will then all have their difficulties and objections) the most reasonable and feasible is 1. With those who have now been separated by peace, to keep peace holy, and to cajole them in all ways, and 2. to persecute the others, who are outside this peace, without mercy.'[36]

For Mauricius this initiative comprised peace 'with the sword in the fist'.[37] Captain Lieutenant Creutz was forced to implement a dual strategy in the course of his extensive 1749 expedition in order to, after an 8-week march, achieve what he had been commissioned to carry out. Having destroyed nine Saramaka villages, Creutz then agreed to a ceasefire with the Maroons, which led to signing a final peace treaty in September 1750. Nevertheless, Governor Mauricius' many political opponents, referred to in Suriname as cabalists, did manage to thwart him (see also p. 38ff.). For many revenge on the Governor's person was the main incentive here. Creutz had promised the Saramakas they would receive a large quantity of goods as soon as they signed the peace treaty in Paramaribo. However, the Court of Police and Criminal Justice decided to dispatch a mission to present only a small amount of gifts to the Saramakas in order to probe their feelings once more.

The perception of the events described hereafter varies to this very day. After leaving Paramaribo nothing was ever again heard of this mission comprising three white men and around 20 slaves. Colonists at that time were convinced they had been murdered by a certain Samsam, the head man of the Saramaka village of Papa, who was not involved in this peace process. During subsequent peace negotiations, the Saramakas always denied this course of events. In their view, the three white men had been killed by their own slaves who, once detained, Maroons claim to have punished for their crimes.

Price's aforementioned research into the oral tradition of the Saramakas resulted in a dissimilar viewpoint. Samsam would have wished to protect these three white men and their slaves from disaster. Being the first to observe this mission's boat when it entered the Gaánlio River (a tributary of the Upper Suriname River) Samsam was convinced that these men had arrived to bring peace. He then informed the other Saramakas who were reported to have become enraged because these white men had not kept their promise. Having returned to his village, Samsam urged them to retreat quickly. Their boat presumably sank in the course of its return journey, with fatal consequences.[38] It may be added here that this is but one of the many examples whereby Maroon oral tradition differs from colonial historiography.

---

36   Ibid.
37   Ibid.
38   Price 1983, 140-144; Price learned of this version of events from Saramakas during his fieldwork in the 1960s. However, in 1975, a certain Otjútu informed Price, based on one of his great-grandfather's stories, about events other Saramakas had never dared to recall. In short, Samsam had maliciously warned the white men to flee enabling him to lay his hands on their goods. According to Otjútu, the Saramakas had decided that whites should never hear of this version. Price later received confirmation hereof from other Saramakas.

After the failed peace talks, Suriname remained in the grip of runaways. Expeditions even led to an increase in their number, as many accompanying slaves became familiar with the whereabouts of Maroons. Meanwhile, the sources of conflict spread towards the southeast. In 1757, a spectacular revolt witnessed at six plantations founded on the Tempatie Creek, a tributary of the Commewijne, caused great unrest. It was the only instance whereby hundreds of slaves at as many as six plantations had simultaneously risen. The immediate reason was: the plan forwarded by Jean Martin, a member of the Council of Police and Criminal Justice, to transfer several slaves to one of his other plantations.[39] Slaves worked on woodlands where conditions, thanks to the nature of the labour and the forest lodgings, were better if compared with the strict regime encountered on sugar, coffee or cotton plantations. Slaves at the Tempatie Creek had obtained spacious vegetable gardens as well as cattle and poultry farms. As they were allowed to sell wood waste on their personal accounts in Paramaribo, they became known to be particularly loyal. On several occasions they had even defended plantations against runaways. Now in danger of suddenly losing their privileges, several slaves tried in vain to change their master's mind. Others decided to take action after troops, who had been called to the rescue, forcibly carried slaves off. Those born in Africa were the most embittered and attacked Martin to then cut off his hand. Next, *c.*150 men, women and children left the plantation to seek refuge in the forest.

After losing 30 men, the large military command dispatched to retrieve these fugitives was forced to return to Paramaribo. A second military strike drove them further into the forest, where they teamed up with other runaways. In February 1757, too, uprisings broke out across another six plantations located on the Tempatie Creek. Now several hundred slaves fled into the forest. Runaways from this region joined between 1,500 and 1,600 Maroons living near the Djuka Creek, a tributary of the Marowijne River.

The majority of colonists realized that a peace treaty with Maroons was inevitable. For runaways themselves, the need for quietude had increased as a result of the expanding Maroon communities. When attacking plantations, the Ndyuka, one of the six Maroon peoples, had always left behind letters inviting white men to send a small number of envoys. Boston Band, a Jamaican-born Ndyuka clan head, had written these invitations in English. Any question of peace with the sword in the fist no longer existed now. Governor-general Wigbold Crommelin dispatched two Black men, one of whom had befriended Boston, with letters and gifts to a *granman* (paramount chief) named Arabie.[40] On 10 October 1760 both parties reached a peace agreement in the vicinity of a wood plantation named Auca. Since then, 'the pacified Bush Negroes beyond Auca' have also been referred to as Aukaners.[41]

After the Saramakas had learned of the agreement with the Ndyuka, the former also expressed a desire to make peace with white men. A *granman* named Ajako

---

39   Thoden van Velzen & Hoogbergen 2011, 163-166; Wolbers 1861, 151-154; Hartsinck 1770, 777-779.
40   Wolbers 1861, 154; Hartsinck 1770, 779-780; Thoden van Velzen & Hoogbergen 2011, 167-182. It is emphasized that Boston maintained a long-standing correspondence with high-ranking colonial authorities, a notable feature in the history of slavery, see: Dragtenstein 2009. He includes an appendix containing these letters of which only Dutch translations have been found in archives.
41   Wolbers 1861, 154.

had always offered resistance, but his demise in *c.*1756-1758 cleared the way for peace.[42] The Saramakas had contacted the colonial authorities through the Ndyuka. Ajako's death was to play a remarkable role in this.[43] For, during the latter's funeral ceremony, a Saramaka clan leader named Wíi was found guilty of Ajako's death, after a witch trial had taken place. Ajako's son Dabí had fired his rifle at Wíi in order to determine whether he was a witch or not. Wíi, now wounded, fled via the forest to then reach the Ndyuka. Not much later, Paramaribo-based authorities received a message from Wíi stating the Saramakas wished to sign a peace agreement just like the Ndyuka had done. The Ndyuka, for their part, played an active role when involving these Maroons with the peace process. The Court of Police and Criminal Justice had initially decided to send a head man named Quaku (the then Ndyuka delegate at Paramaribo) to the Saramakas. Having first agreed to take on the mission, Quaku immediately returned to his own territory, for an unclear reason. At the end of 1761, the Ndyuka therefore sent Wíi off on an expedition, for which they later charged colonial authorities with the lump sum of 1,692 guilders. Wíi returned to the Ndyuka in February 1762 with around 40 Saramakas, including six head men. A few days later, the aforementioned Ndyuka clan leader Boston, whom the Ndyuka had named Basiton, requested the Paramaribo-based authorities in a letter to dispatch a small number of white men. An envoy named Louis Nepveu, an experienced soldier who in 1749 had also been involved in Mauricius' peace initiative, arrived less than a month later in order to negotiate with the Saramaka *granman* Abini. On 19 September 1762, after 8 weeks of arduous discussions, a peace treaty with the 'Bush Negroes of Upper Saramacca' was signed.

In 1767, the colonial authorities finally reached a peace agreement with the Matawai. This relatively small ethnic group, led by Saramaka chiefs named Beku and Musinga, had violated the 1762 treaty by attacking three plantations located near the Para River, taking more than 150 slaves with them.[44]

The Maroons, recognised in the peace treaties as 'free folk', were allowed to continue to reside wherever they were at that time, although these treaties lacked precise definitions of their territories.[45] After permission was received from the authorities, these Maroons were also free to settle elsewhere, albeit at 'ten hours distance from the nearest plantation'. They were also given free passage for a limited number of people to trade their goods in Paramaribo against imported foreign products. They would, on a regular basis, furthermore receive a large variety of goods from the authorities. This commitment was not only intended to prevent Maroons from being forced to obtain such goods by means of theft. These supplies could also serve as leverage in order to force them to extradite any runaway slaves. Colonists attached great significance to an agreement as to this issue being included in the peace treaty and paid premiums ranging between 10 and 50 guilders per slave. If threatened by foreign enemies, Maroons had in in turn help defend the colony.

---

42   Wolbers 1861, 158-160, 284; De Beet & Price 1982, 27 ff.
43   See: Price 1983, 167-181; Price relates historical details linking the establishment of peace with the Saramakas to their own oral history..
44   Hartsinck 1770, 812; Wolbers 1861, 285.
45   For texts pertaining to the peace treaties with the Ndyuka and the Saramakas, see: Schiltkamp & De Smidt 1973, vol. 1, 692-694 and vol. 2, 757-762.

Maroons proved to be self-confident as well as intelligent negotiators. In his journal, Governor-general Crommelin marvelled at their 'appropriate answers and healthy judgement'.[46] In no way did Maroons feel to be the lesser party. In their view, white colonists who supplied goods formed an indemnity rather than a favour. The Saramaka *granman* Abini stated, in the course of the peace negotiations, his people would not be content with 'wishy-washy [items], such as puppet bells and other futilities'.[47] Now and again Maroons reprimanded their opponents without hesitation. A Ndyuka head man lectured white negotiators thus:

> '*We beseech you to say, your Governor and the Council, that if they do not want to set up new gangs of runaways, they ensure that the planters themselves keep an eye on their properties, and will not entrust them, as usual, to drunken supervisors, who by unjust and merciless punishment of the slaves, by violating their wives and daughters, by neglecting the ill, prepare the colony's demise, because they deliberately drive good and hardworking people into the forest, people who eat their bread by the sweat of their brow, without whose hands your settlement would soon sink to nothing, with whom you must finally arrive in such an unpleasant manner to seek peace and friendship.*'[48]

A general revelry arose across Suriname after peace had been declared. Thanksgiving services were held in churches in 1760 as well as in 1762.[49] The then Governor welcomed representatives of Maroons who cordially received white men, several of whom got a Maroon woman during their stay.[50] Mistrust did, nevertheless, continue to prevail on both sides. The Maroons were forced to leave behind several hostages in Paramaribo as a guarantee for peace which, in accordance with the treaty signed with the Saramakas, had to comprise children of the chieftains. The Maroons should also tolerate the permanent presence of a resident administrator (*posthouder*) in their midst. This civil servant not only maintained contact with authorities on the behalf of Maroons but also ensured compliance with the peace treaty. In practice these *posthouders* were the eyes and ears of the colonial regime and on occasion even acted as intriguers who pitted groups against each other. From 1835 on, the instruction intended for a *posthouder* even stipulated he should apply all means in order to keep 'the differences' between the various Maroon groups 'alive'.[51]

5.2 The Boni-Maroon Wars (1765-1778 and 1789-1793)

The colonial government assumed that new runaways had virtually no further opportunities to establish any independent livelihoods in the forest. They would come across pacified Maroons (*c.* 6,000 at the time of the peace treaties of 1760 and 1762) who not only wished to protect their own habitats but were also obliged to extradite

---

46   Wolbers 1861, 157-158.
47   De Beet & Price 1982, 140.
48   Wolbers 1861, 155.
49   Ibid., 157, 159.
50   Hartsinck 1770, 798.
51   De Groot 1982, 68.

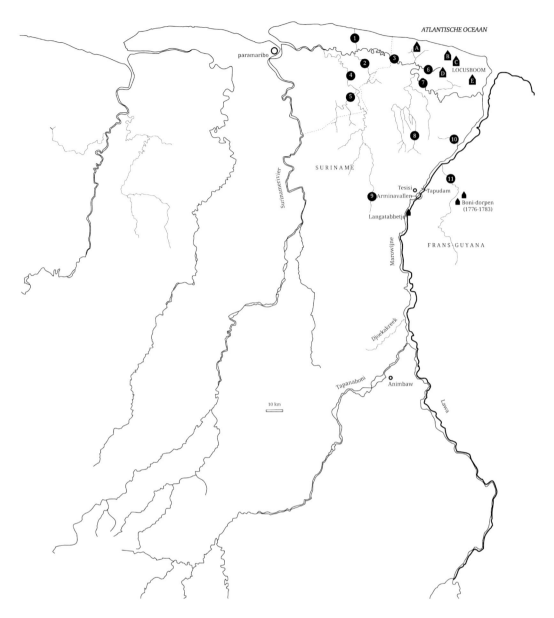

Figure 5.1. A map of the area in eastern Suriname indicating the site of the Boni-Maroon Wars. 1. Mot Creek, 2. Perica, 3. Cottica, 4. Commewijne, 5. Cassewinica, 6. Cassipera, 7. Coermotibo, 8. Paramacca, 9. Tempatie Creek, 10. Boni Creek, 11. Sparouine, --- cordonpad (cordon of defence); A. Buku, B. Holi-mi, C. Kofi-hay, D. Kosay, E. Gado-Sabi. Buddingh' 2021, 139 (after Hoogbergen 1985).

these fugitives.[52] If patrols were to fight these escapees, the Paramaribo-based authorities believed that peace in the colony would return in due course. Moreover, the Caribs had become allies once again after the peace treaty of 1683 to play a key part in the struggle against Maroons, either serving as guides for colonial expeditions

---

52   As to this estimate, see: Thoden van Velzen & Van Wetering 1988, 9.

A History of Suriname

or by carrying out attacks.[53] During the second half of the 18th century, several groups of Amerindians executed armed actions against Maroons. In eastern Suriname however such incidences were relatively few in number, mainly because of the higher numbers of runaways.

The strategy of excluding certain groups of Maroons from peace accords proved counterproductive. Especially runaways who had been sheltering in the forest for decades had hardly any choice but to face confrontation. 'Cottica-negroes' (later referred to as Boni, after their legendary leader named Boni, *c.*1730-1793) residing in eastern Suriname, would fight against planters for decades in a struggle which soon displayed war-like traits.

The Boni originated from three groups that had merged after 1770.[54] The oldest group, from which Boni hailed, had settled down north of the Cottica River, on the Cassipera Creek. Its first chieftain Asikan-Sylvester had fled from a plantation as early as the year 1712, shortly after arriving from Africa. In *c.*1760 his group consisted of around 350 people. A second group, comprising only between 80 and 100 fugitives, was located between the Tempatie Creek and the Marowijne River, and referred to as Tesisi-Maroons, after one of their villages. Their head man was called Fortuyn van Brouwershaven. A third group, led by Kormantin Kodjo, inhabited several villages situated east of Jodensavanne, marshlands positioned between the Suriname and the Upper-Commewijne Rivers. In 1770, Kormantin Kodjo's village was populated by more than 20 mainly African-born men and a small number of women. This group, which hardly carried any weapons, was driven further and further eastwards to finally join forces with Boni in 1773.

Initially the Tesisi-Maroons offered the most resistance. After they had raided two plantations, colonial expeditions set off in search of their villages from 1757 on. The village housing the Tesisi-Maroons was not discovered until 1765. Next, however, having moved on to continue their attacks. Several Tesisi-Maroons teamed up with head man Boni in *c.*1770.[55]

In 1769, a military patrol came across *granman* Asikan Sylvester (1690-1769) and chief of the Cassipera-Maroons who then stayed in an abandoned village located in the Coermotibo Basin. He had been left behind with a female, her husband and child, and another male, because they no longer dared to move their elderly chief because he had fallen ill. Asikan Sylvester stated he was the first Maroon to reside in this area adding that he had officiated as village chief for more than 50 years before transferring leadership to Boni and to Askaan van Marseille several years earlier. The latter (whose name, as with many Maroons, is derived from the plantation he had escaped from) became known as Aluku. Asikan Sylvester passed away in Fort Zeelandia a few days after his statement. The Court of Police and Criminal Justice did not fail to punish him posthumously for desertion. His head was cut off on the gallows field in Paramaribo and placed on a pole.[56]

---

53   Wolbers 1861, 282.
54   Hoogbergen 1990, 23-26, 29-36.
55   Ibid., 33-55.
56   Ibid., 58-62.

In 1768, a civilian patrol discovered the village of Kosay, home to Asikan Sylvester, Boni and Aluku. Here, much to his surprise, ensign B.J.C. Jacot, leader of the patrol, found a complete smithy, 32 houses and a farm with 700 chickens. His report must have again made clear to colonists that Maroons were self-confident, persistent and resourceful opponents. For several days this small expedition (consisting of five armed white men, ten armed Black men, eight porters, two soldiers and an Amerindian guide) marched through now and again difficult terrain. Treacherous marshlands (*birbiri zwampen)*, covered with an overgrown crust through which one can easily fall, were to be encountered in between ridges of sand and shells located across the coastal area.[57] Initially misguided because these Maroons had returned to their village while walking backwards, this patrol after more than a one day journey came across a *c.*25 ha garden. Beyond it lay an abandoned settlement comprising 14 houses. The following day this search party stumbled upon yet another abandoned village, consisting of 11 houses and a plot measuring *c.*20 ha. Ensign Jacot saw to it everything was destroyed and set alight. After setting forth the journey through a savannah, a wide path was discovered. Having spotted a clearance of forest growth on the other side of this savannah, Jacot decided to inspect it, while accompanied by specialist troops. They initiated an assault after one of their men who was unable to control himself fired a shot. This clearing proved to be a mock village composed of felled trees placed on top of each other in a swamp.

Jacot now realized he had been lured into a trap; the noise produced by his specialist soldiers had alerted Maroons, camped a few kilometres away. Before this patrol reached the village of Kosay the next day, the Maroons had long led the women and children to safety via a creek. After an exchange of gunfire, the Maroon men fled too without feeling at all defeated. Their fierce berating did indeed reveal anger, intransigence and pride on which ensign Jacot reported:

> '*You should not think about saying that you will get us so easily, no, we did hear the shot you did yesterday at the biri biri, and we knew you would come here, white dogs, are you not satisfied to have two villages and you think you will get this, No rather destroy us all [...]. If we wanted we would destroy you all, and if you have no powder, come on over here, we will give you & ct..*'[58]

The troops occupied Kosay temporarily in order to prevent Maroons from returning. The runaways (led by Boni and Askaan van Marseille) had fled to the Patamacca region located further south. They merged with part of the Tesisi- Maroons whom Suku headed. This slave who hailed from a plantation named Marseille was therefore also called Lemi or L'Ami van Marseille.[59] Both these groups then moved in a northerly direction. For a short time relative peace had prevailed in the colony. From the end of 1770 on, however, the Maroons stepped up their battle in such a way one would refer to it as the First Boni-Maroon War (1765-1778).

---

57   Ibid., 56-58.
58   De Beet 1984, 78.
59   Hoogbergen 1990, 54.

The leadership of the Boni long remained unclear. Numerous chroniclers deemed a triumvirate consisting of the head men Baron, Boni and Jolicoeur to be the most important.[60] In Paramaribo, during the early years of the First Boni-Maroon War, Baron was thought to occupy the highest position in the hierarchy of the 'Cottica-negroes'. In his widely acclaimed publication of 1790/1796 entitled *Narrative of a Five Years Expedition against the Revolted Negroes of Surinam*, the Dutch-born Scottish colonial soldier John Gabriel Stedman (1744-1797), having fought the Boni-Maroons serving as a Captain in the States army, mentions this triumvirate in one breath.[61] In reality, Baron and Jolicoeur should not be regarded as key leaders.[62] For, Baron was not a chief, not even a clan head. His reputation was based on numerous raids on plantations carried out as a commander, especially in the Patamacca region. Baron was a runaway slave who had been owned and later sold by the Swedish planter Carl Gustaf Dahlberg (a correspondent of the Swedish botanist Carl Linnaeus). Baron must have been headstrong. For, accompanied by a small number of followers, he distanced himself from Boni and Aluku on several occasions to then team up temporarily with them again. In 1774, Baron had fallen in action during an attack which took place on a woodland located in the Patamacca region.[63]

In 1772 Jolicoeur had fled from the plantation named Fauquemberg, established on the banks of the Commewijne River. Only briefly active as a riflemen during the Maroon war, he fell in the course of an armed confrontation with a military patrol in 1773.[64] His fame is probably based on J.G. Stedman's contested version that Jolicoeur, during an attack on the Nieuw-Roosenbeek plantation, murdered its director, the alleged rapist of his mother.[65]

Boni and Aluku were undoubtedly the factual leaders of the 'Cottica-negroes'. Several other men also played key roles, including Kormantin Kodjo and Lemi. Boni was approximately 35 years old when in *c*.1765 Asikan Sylvester appointed him a *granman*. Knowledge concerning Boni's life is mainly based on testimonies forwarded by captured runaways. The most reliable information stems from a Maroon named Jonas van 's-Haagenbosch, who lived among the Boni between 1771 and 1776 and had been captured by colonial troops.[66] In archives Boni is referred to as a bush creole (*boscreool*) as he was born in the forest. According to Van 's-Haagenbosch, Boni had told him that Aluku was his stepfather. His mother had escaped from a plantation named Barbakoeba (aka Anna's Burg), located near the Cottica River. Further information on Boni's father remains vague whereby most testimonies speak of a white man or an Amerindian, implying Boni was either what was then called a 'mulatto' or a so-called *karboeger*. Boni, an excellent blacksmith, fathered several children of whom the best known was Agosu, his son and future successor.

---

60   Ibid., 62-64.
61   Stedman 1790, 400.
62   Hoogbergen 1990, 62-64.
63   Ibid., 64-66, 93.
64   Ibid., 86.
65   Stedman 1790, 271. For a reference to an eyewitness who stated that Boni murdered the director after he had refused to reveal where the gunpowder was located, see: Hoogbergen 1990, 76.
66   Hoogbergen 1990, 63-64; see: De Beet 1984, 52-55, 204-230 for testimonies pertaining to Boni as presented by Van 's Haagenbosch et al..

Boni's great moral authority can be deduced from his nickname *Krutu* (assembly or judiciary). He never engaged in any cutting-edge disputes with Baron, who was considered ambitious. Those who disagreed with Boni were free to leave. Aluku's importance is indicated by the fact that over time Boni named certain places where they resided after him. The village of Kosay, for example, was also known to the Boni as Luku. Labour was divided between the two main leaders. Aluku, who was much older than Boni, was responsible for looking after and protecting the women and children, whereas Boni led the armed struggle. Van 's-Haagenbosch's reports disclose that, in case of any danger, the Boni housed their wives and children in separate villages. In *c*.1774, Aluku was in charge of a village called Holi-mi, an important task because of the scarcity of women among Maroons. It may be added here that colonists were hardly aware of Aluku's existence.[67]

On 8 November 1770, the battle of the Boni was resumed in all its intensity when the Mon Désir plantation located at the Mot Creek was raided. The director and the white overseer were both shot dead. Sixteen slaves and nine guns were seized. This attack was in retaliation of a military patrol which had recently destroyed a large abandoned village known as Kromotibo as well as all its gardens located on the banks of the Cassipera Creek.[68] The Boni made an even greater impression when, in December 1770, they overpowered a military outpost positioned in the village of Tesisi, which Maroons had been forced to abandon years earlier. The assailants not only took the lives of two soldiers, but also seized a large quantity of gunpowder and weapons. On 8 January 1771 the Boni also stormed the military outpost at Kromotibo. Having killed four of the 14 troops, they again seized gunpowder and weapons. When a patrol attempted to drive the Maroons back, they had already left. The slashed bodies of three soldiers had remained in the village.

The strategy of the Boni was mainly aimed at increasing pressure on white colonists in such a way that peace could be enforced. However, the authorities did not wish, under any circumstances, to sign any new peace treaties. For, in their view, this could imply the demise of the colony. The huge determination observed on both sides characterised hostilities. Assaults which the Boni carried out on military outposts were mainly the result of an increased need for weapons and ammunition. Guns and gunpowder were seized on plantations too. Thanks to their contacts with slaves, the Boni were often very well informed as to where the largest booty could be found.

From 1771 on, the Boni stormed plantations almost monthly. Now and again revenge formed an important incentive. A notorious raid on the Capoerica plantation that took place on 13 September 1771, for example, was targeted at its owner Willem Bedloo (1734-1785). This member of the Court of Police and Criminal Justice was also one of the colony's prominent residents. Moreover, this civilian captain who officiated in the Upper Cottica and Perica district was the fiercest adversary of the Maroons. The Boni also took advantage of the aforementioned raid on the Capoerica plantation in order to, for the first time, express to the colonial administration a desire to make peace. This plantation's director was therefore sent to Paramaribo with a special message for the Court of Police and Criminal Justice. Boni made it clear

---

67   Hoogbergen 1990, 200-201 and Hoogbergen 1989, 175-198; De Beet 1984, 207-230.
68   Hoogbergen 1990, 52-55, 66-69.

A History of Suriname

to the colonists that if his peace proposal was to be rejected, he would destroy all the plantations located in Upper Cottica.[69]

During the following months Boni underlined this threat with additional guerrilla actions. Marronage increased strongly in the 1770s. Colonists were especially disturbed by the fact Creole craftsmen now too fled plantations. This category of slaves was always considered most reliable. During the first month of 1772 alone, more than 30 slaves left three plantations.[70] After an attack dated 27 June that same year that took place at the Poelwijk plantation located on the Perica River and carried out by around 20 Boni, including perhaps Boni himself, no fewer than 70 slaves teamed up with them. Several slaves hailing from a nearby plantation joined them.[71] A white plantation servant named Hendrik Müller, whom Maroons had sent to Paramaribo in order to once again express the wish which the Boni had pertaining to peace, declared in front of the Court of Police and Criminal Justice:

'[...] *that the slaves went along voluntarily, most of them showing great joy, especially the dres negro* [traditional healer] *Roij, and the mulatto carpenter of Altena, that more negroes from Altena on the neighbouring coffee ground also went along, that a couple of days earlier the director has sent two negroes with rifles being the abovementioned Roij and Willen to hunt, and see if they could discover traces of runaways, that they also went along, and as he thinks will have spoken with his fugitives, and have prepared the matter, that there was no warning at all before they arrived at the buildings, that he has seen that at first 16 of them had went along, also carrying the muskets of the plantation, that certainly more have followed, in the evening or at night, because the following morning more than 70 were gone.' (Declaration of the White Officer of the plantation Poelwijk because of the events during the raid of the runaways.)*[72]

The military successes of the Maroons had a huge psychological effect on slaves who were increasingly gaining courage to join up with runaways. Civilian patrols proved insufficiently able to cope Maroons. Moreover, slaves who had to participate in such patrols were usually not very inclined to fight. Once familiar with the escape routes fugitives used, these slaves often grasped the chance to desert. Under these conditions, the government was forced to expand its military efforts considerably, although this resulted in a significant increase of the financial burden. In 1770, Governor Jan Nepveu (1719-1779) founded the *Corps van Vrije Neegers en Mulatten* ('Corps of Free Negroes and Mulattoes'). All manumitted and free-born Black people and of colour aged between 14 and 60 were obliged to enlist. As women and children formed the vast majority of the manumitted population, it was only with great difficulty that two detachments each consisting of 50 men could be created. This small, unmotivated corps was not of any great significance. During the war against the Boni, it merely served twice when reinforcing a small number of military outposts.[73]

---

69   Ibid., 71-72.
70   Ibid., 73-74.
71   Ibid., 78.
72   De Beet 1984, 120-121.
73   Wolbers 1861, 319; Hoogbergen 1985, 23-25.

The *Neeger Vrijcorps*, founded in 1772, presented an entirely different case. Captain Stedman, in his aforementioned publication, called them 'Rangers', hereby referring to rangers based in Virginia (North America) who fought against Cherokee Indians.[74] This corps was composed of slaves for whom the government of Suriname had purchased their freedom. Governor Nepveu's plan to create such a corps had been rejected by the Court of Police and Criminal Justice on a number of occasions. However, due to the deteriorated military situation, the councillors conceded over time. The immediate cause to do so formed an assault on the Nieuw Roosenbeek plantation on 28 May 1772, when civilian militias once again proved powerless. Slave owners were obliged to hand over slaves recruited for the *Neeger Vrijcorps* at the assessed value.[75]

As a result of the colony's poor financial status, that value was paid out provisionally in bonds. Following Nepveu's request, the Society found the town of Amsterdam willing to provide a loan consisting of 700,000 guilders, after which these bonds could still be redeemed. On 15 July, 1772 the freedom of 116 slaves was purchased in Fort Nieuw Amsterdam, after holding an inspection, whereby a lump sum of 143,000 guilders was involved. The average purchase price of 1,236 guilders was much higher than the average of around 200 guilders to be paid for newly arrived slaves. This was due to the fact that the two members of the Court of Police and Criminal Justice in charge of recruitment had chosen only craftsmen, mainly Creoles. They were deemed most reliable because of their privileged positions. A few days later the freedom of another 190 field slaves was purchased for a total sum of 227,955 guilders.[76]

Ransomed slaves were given uniforms consisting of duffel trousers and green hats. In addition to clothing and food, they received a salary of 9 guilders per month during actual service. Whenever off-duty, members of the *Neeger Vrijcorps* were allowed to provide for themselves in whatever manner. The colonial government had provided small plots of land in Paramaribo located on the common grassland (*gemeene weyde*) where they were free to build houses.[77] To date this site is referred to as Frimangron (lit.: the ground of the free). The majority of ransomed slaves however preferred to stay together with their wives and children on plantations whenever off-duty. Certain planters were not keen on this, possibly for fear of influencing their slaves. Based on a notification dated 11 November 1772, the government was forced to threaten planters with persecution as their reluctant attitude would harm 'the common good'.[78] In the meantime Governor Nepveu had also requested the army to be reinforced with State troops, to wit, units serving the States General. The first recruitment comprising more than 500 mercenaries under the command of a Swiss Colonel named Louis Henri Fourgeoud (1708-1779) would reach the shores of Suriname in February 1773, having set sail from the Dutch Republic.[79]

---

74   Stedman 1790, 84.
75   Hoogbergen 1990, 52, 76-77.
76   Wolbers 1861, 320-325; Hoogbergen 1985, 25-28; De Groot 1988, 148-149.
77   A special regulation concerning the *Neeger Vrijcorps* came into force on 9 July 1772, see: Schiltkamp & De Smidt 1973, vol. 2, 845-847.
78   Ibid., 847-848.
79   Hoogbergen 1990, 84; Stedman 1790, 27-29, 38-39; Van Gelder 2018, 364.

The government could not wait that long with counteracting. The initial goal was the village of Buku, a name later to become almost legendary across the colony.[80] In September 1771, commando troops had taken Buku, at a time when the majority of the Maroons had left this village in order to participate in an expedition against the Capoerica plantation located in the Perica region. The commandoes, after detaining a number of women and children, had left Buku hastily while failing to destroy it. The Maroons, having regained possession of Buku, further reinforced this village by means of 5-metre high palisades. Small rotating cannons were placed inside this fortress, which was entirely surrounded by swamps. Colonists had heard of Buku from a captive Maroon, who had not only stated that the Boni now considered it their headquarters but also that they no longer intended to leave this fortification. Maroons had not chosen a random name: Buku would 'fall to dust' rather than be handed over to white colonists.

In April 1772, a large army of 150 soldiers and an equal number of porters, led by Captain J.H. Oorsinga, travelled up the Cottica River towards Buku. A patrol had already been dispatched a few months earlier, but it had not been able to reach this village because of strong Maroon opposition. Oorsinga's men were tasked to establish an army outpost from which Buku was to be captured. Even before their arrival, these men had to endure an attack launched by Maroons, in the course of which Oorsinga was wounded by a grazing shot.

The siege of Buku was a humiliating experience for the colonial troops. For months they were stationed right in front of the village, while the Boni shouted abuse at them from behind the palisades. This siege could not prevent Maroons from continuing to attack plantations. During a raid on the plantation Poelwijk, having seized considerable quantities of gunpowder and weapons, they even dared to take by storm the military outpost the besiegers had built. Several dead and wounded were counted on both sides. Baron and Jolicoeur were among the injured Maroons. After this violent confrontation, the colonial troops were almost without ammunition. From the military outpost called 's Lands-Welvaren, located on the Cottica River, fresh supplies were sent under military escort, but they never reached the troops stationed at Buku. A group of Maroons led by Lemi van Marseille intercepted these soldiers and their porters to then defeat them in a devastating manner. A precise report on this assault illustrates how difficult conditions were for colonial troops:

'[...] that Wednesday the 22nd of July being the second day of their march, they had broken up in the morning at the break of day and had almost continuously had rain, having arrived at the large swamp, Major Scholt with Ensign Seweloh and a number of troops together making up 28 men, had formed the vanguard, that he had been required at the ammunition with 10 men, and the rest of the corps had formed the rear guard under Lt. Kraft, that in the swamp the water had reached up to the shoulders, so that the men had to keep their cartouches between their teeth, the rifle with one hand over the head, and in the other a stick to lean on, that when Major Scholt wanted to climb the height, the Bushnegroes posted around them without however being able to see them, have shot a huge number of rounds*

---

80   For a detailed report hereof see: Hoogbergen 1990, 70-82 and Wolbers 1861, 330-332.

at them, so that of the avant-garde soon about 15 men were dead and wounded without resistance, that for our part we also fired as strong as possible, but that the heavy rains prevented us from continuing to shoot, the rain shower being a heavy thunder during the attack above their heads, that [the vanguard] with the third shot was already unable to fire because the gunpowder was flowing off the musket with the rains, that the people who were in the swamp could not shoot and that the rear guard was not able to assist them, due to the vastness of the swamp, as far as he could observe, being 40-50 chains wide; that however much he called that one had to march forward quickly, this has been impossible, that the negroes who fired at them from all sides, shot mainly among the porters, as a result of which some were killed, and the others fled after having thrown away all they carried, that it was thus necessary to take the retreat, in order, being without defence, not to be docked and completely destroyed.' (Examination at and towards Cornelis Wolfvoets, sous Lt. of the Artillery, 29 July 1772.).[81]

The situation was untenable for the troops stationed near the village of Buku as it proved impossible to supply any provisions and ammunition. The siege was thus abandoned. The fiasco would become even more disastrous when the *Neeger Vrijcorps* was sent to Buku during its maiden expedition. The 122 *Zwarte Jagers* (Black Rangers), who could not be timely informed of the Society's troops retreat, now unexpectedly stumbled upon Boni in the abandoned military camp. After Maroons had captured 11 members of the *Neeger Vrijcorps* and escorted them to Boni, he left them the choice of either teaming up with him or to die. All these Black Rangers chose the latter. One of them, Pasop van Clarenbeek, was spared as the gun used to execute him failed twice. Having been tortured, he was then ordered to travel to Paramaribo and tell the whites to agree upon a peace treaty immediately.[82] This renewed request was nonetheless once again rejected.

After the confrontation with the Boni, the Black Rangers received red hats, as many green hats had fallen into the hands of Maroons. From this moment on, members of the *Neeger Vrijcorps* were nicknamed *redimusu*. In Suriname, to this very day, this term is synonymous with 'traitor'. Black Rangers were highly motivated fighters, which can be explained by means of the preferred position they occupied when compared to slaves. Despite being defeated at Buku, the government was very satisfied with their effort, especially after it became public that all 11 prisoners preferred death over defecting to Maroons. Black Rangers were hugely appreciated. Now and again, they built their houses in Paramaribo amidst those of whites. Based on Van Clarenbeek's statements it was clear to colonists that famine prevailed in Buku. The long-term siege had apparently not been without effect. Colonists had destroyed vegetable gardens. Moreover, the village of Buku's population had increased when dozens of slaves teamed up with the Boni after attacks on plantations had taken place. Thus, in August 1772, plantations were raided once again in order to obtain food and clothing.

---

81   De Beet 1984, 131-132.
82   Ibid., 135.

Figure 5.2. A Black Ranger. Drawing by J.G.Stedman (orig. 1790). J.G. Stedman 1987.

In Paramaribo a future assault on Buku was being prepared whereby no further risks were taken. As many as 173 Black Rangers set off on 11 September 1772. In order to boost their morale, a slave declared a freedman named Quassie accompanied them. In Europe, this Afro-Surinamese medicine man (*obiaman*) had acquired a great reputation as a connoisseur of medicines (e.g., *kwasibita*) and had often offered his services. In 1776, because of his merits for the colonial administration, Quassie was even officially received by Willem V Prince of Orange.[83] In addition, a military commando led by Lieutenant Jurriaan François de Friderici (1751-1812), the future Governor of Suriname (1792-1801), along with a further 113 Black Rangers set off towards Buku. Along the way they stumbled upon a lookout manned by Maroons, which was taken after heavy fighting. The dry season had rendered conditions relatively favourable for the commandoes. Both groups met a few days later at Buku. The Boni were initially able to repel the first joint attack in the course of which five Black Rangers lost their lives. On September 20, Buku could be taken by means of a stratagem whereby several troops carried out a mock attack in the early morning, while pretending they were about to cross the swamp.[84] Meanwhile De Friderici and the *conducteur* (commander of the *Neeger Vrijcorps*) sergeant C.G. Mangold, in the

---

83   Dragtenstein 2004, 69-75. For more on Quassie's role, see: Hoogbergen 1990, 36-39.
84   Hoogbergen 1990, 80-82.

company of 180 Black Rangers had already moved to the other side of the village. Here a secret underwater path had been discovered during the failed action carried out a few months earlier. The majority of able-bodied Maroons had already left Buku. Boni himself led the defence with a small group, but their resistance was quickly broken. Black Rangers captured around 50 Maroons, mainly women and children. Evidence of Boni's moderate stance (at least towards his own people, whereas newcomers were severely tested) is: he allowed those who opted to return to their plantations to stay behind in Buku.

The defeat of the Boni had a demoralizing effect on the Maroons and on the slave population. In churches the fall of Buku was celebrated by means of thanksgiving services. More than 100 slaves who had affiliated with runaways either returned to their plantations or were captured, whereby harsh living conditions in forests played a key role.[85] The Boni were nevertheless far from defeated after the village of Buku had fallen. For, under Aluku's leadership precautions had been taken: Boni women and children were moved further to the north-east where in a region referred to as Locusboom, new vegetable gardens were created near the Marowijne River. These plots, of course, did not provide food immediately, causing the Boni to go hungry for a time. Maroons therefore disseminated across various areas. Head man Boni cum suis set off for the Patamacca region (East Suriname).[86]

In February 1773 the arrival of the State army's 530 mercenaries under Colonel Fourgeoud's command initially led to great discord.[87] After the *Neeger Vrijcorps*'s various successes including the fall of Buku, Governor Jan Nepveu (1768-1779), whom the colonists partly supported, no longer considered any extra military power indispensable. For, this would only burden the colony with unnecessary, additional costs. His stance became even more negative as soon as it became known that the Prince of Orange, had ordered his personal friend Colonel Fourgeoud to take command over the entire armed forces, including the Society's troops and the *Neeger Vrijcorps*. In Paramaribo, soldiers hung around idly for months often suffering from venereal diseases due to a dissolute lifestyle.

A few weeks later Colonel Fourgeoud chose to announce his departure. Many colonists however did not wish to see him leave. For, in 1763, he had suppressed a major slave revolt in the neighbouring Dutch colony of Berbice (present-day Guyana).[88] Fourgeoud then chose to first inspect Suriname. Upon his return, the Governor and the Court of Police and Criminal Justice both requested him to stay

---

85   Wolbers 1861, 332.
86   Hoogbergen 1990, 83-85.
87   Van Gelder 2018, 364; in his acclaimed biography on J.G. Stedman, Van Gelder forwards the most reliable and precise figures as to the total number of State troops sent to Suriname in 1773, 1775 and 1776. Based on archival research, these comprise respectively 530, 240 and 350 troops, whereby the latter two numbers tally with those Stedman mentions in his *Narrative* [...], 321, 324, 563). Taking into account the support staff, the total reached *c.*1200 members; it is erroneously stated that the troop reinforcements in 1775 and 1776 amounted to 400 and 750 respectively, see: Hoogbergen 1990, 100, 103-104.
88   The remarkable uprising in Berbice resembled the later Haitian revolution (1791-1804). However, this attempt by rebellious slaves to take over the Dutch colony in its entirety failed. For a detailed and fascinating account hereof, see: Kars 2020. Suriname's colonial administration feared this rebellion would spread amongst slaves populating its territory. Well aware of the events occurring in Berbice slaves even described them in songs, see: Van Lier 1971, 57.

Figure 5.3. This drawing by J. G. Stedman (orig. 1790) portrays the remains of Lieutenant Lepper and six of his soldiers. J.G. Stedman 1987.

on for the time being, as they feared that Saramaka Maroons would violate the peace agreement. The State troops could subsequently act against them if need be. Fourgeoud, however, not only made it clear he had not been dispatched to Suriname for this purpose but also announced again he was about to leave.[89]

Next, a heavy defeat experienced by a patrol forming part of the Society's troops provided a fresh twist. Once it had become known that Lieutenant Lepper along with most of his 30 men had been killed (some executed) by Boni residing in the Patamacca region, angry planters turned fiercely against the colonial administration. In Paramaribo, libellous writings were secretly distributed. They contained a number of sharp accusations against Nepveu. This Governor and the councillors (i.e., members of the Court of Police and Criminal Justice) were once again forced to request Fourgeoud and his men to remain in Suriname. One agreed that the State troops should not leave as yet. Soldiers initially served to reinforce the outposts, as it made little sense to dispatch a military expedition during the rainy season. Meanwhile, the Boni attacked plantations again, having recovered much faster than expected after the fall of Buku.[90]

---

89   Wolbers 1861, 333-336.
90   Ibid., 336-338; Hoogbergen 1990, 87.

Medio 1773 the number of Maroons residing in East Suriname would have totalled *c.*450-500. Boni headed around 250 Maroons. Later *c.*80 Maroons under Kormantin Kodjo's leadership joined him. Baron led 50 Maroons.[91] After the successful attack launched on 29 August 1773 against plantations named Nouvel Esperance, Du Perou and De Suynigheid, all located in the Patamacca region, the Boni retreated with the help of more than 50 slaves further eastwards towards the Locusboom region. Gardens, created under Aluku's supervision, now provided sufficient nutrition.[92]

The feats of Colonel Fourgeoud c.s. have been accurately described by J. G. Stedman in his renowned publication. The latter acquired command over an outpost named 's-Lands-Welvaren, not without reason referring to it as the Devil's Harwar. Here white soldiers could hardly cope with the local natural conditions, as they were completely unprepared. Three of the five officers succumbed during the first months. Thirty-six of the 54 men fell ill, several of whom passed away.[93]

Fourgeoud set off on his first expedition against the Maroons in October 1773. Patrols were carried out during the following 6 months. The entire unit comprising more than 500 men, divided into three sections, took part. He saw to it these troops, according to European tradition, advanced under drum rolls. The chance of coming across any Maroons was therefore rather small. These search parties found only a few gardens and two abandoned villages. In March 1774, Fourgeoud made a futile attempt to find the newly built villages home to Boni and Kormantin Kodjo located near Locusboom.[94] Several such marches through dense forests and across dangerous swamps are described as follows :

'*In short we continued our March till 8 OClock when we arrived at the Society Post Soribo in Pirica, in a most shocking Condition, having waddled through Water and Mire above our hipps, Climb'd over heaps of fallen trees, creep'd underneath them on our bellies – Scratched and tore by the thorns or macas that are here of many kinds. Stung all over by the Patat or Scrapat lice, ants, and wassy-wassy or wild bees, fatigued to death by marching in a burning Sun, and the last 2 hours in hells darkness, holding each other by the hand, and having left 10 Men behind, some with agues, some stung blind, and some with their feet full of Chigoes – being at Sribo in the most Hospitable manner received by the Commanding Officer.*'[95]

Only now and again was it possible to detain a Maroon spy. One of them, Kupido Abo, presented an interesting statement to the Paramaribo-based public prosecutor, illustrating how sound the contacts of the Boni with slaves housed on plantations were. According to Kupido Abo, Boni would pay secret visits to plantations in order to consult Black overseers as well as slaves while gathering information on local situations.[96]

Governor Nepveu hugely objected to Fourgeoud's rather useless combat methods. According to the former, the latter operated along compass lines and without

---

91   Hoogbergen 1990, 87.
92   Ibid., 88.
93   Stedman 1790, 151-153.
94   Hoogbergen 1990, 89-91.
95   Stedman 1790, 157.
96   Hoogbergen 1990, 89-91.

Figure 5.4. Colonel Henri Fourgeoud with behind him Captain John Gabriel Stedman and other soldiers wading through a swamp. Drawing by J.G. Stedman (orig. 1790). J.G. Stedman 1987.

considering any traces left behind by Maroons. The only result hereof, according to Nepveu, was the total exhaustion of the troops.[97] Fourgeoud also refused, much to Nepveu's displeasure, to cooperate with the *Neeger Vrijcorps*, in which he, as a European military, did not have too much confidence. In fact precisely the Black Rangers achieved considerably more success than the troops supervised by the Society and the States General. On 11 July 1774, led by their incoming Commander, a former civilian officer named Philip Samuel Stoelman (1740-1796, or later), they discovered three Boni villages located in Locusboom, which the Maroons had already abandoned. The now militia captain Stoelman saw to it the villages and farms set up by Suku (aka L'Ami van Marseille) and Kormantin Kodjo were destroyed. Having spared Boni's village named Gado Sabi (lit.: God knows) in order to set up a military outpost here, Stoelman left after only a few days because the Black Rangers did not want to stay here. These men not only complained that the stock of salt was exhausted but also claimed they could not do without this essential mineral. One month later Stoelman torched the village of Gado Sabi after discovering that Maroons had been here.[98]

---

97   Ibid., 91; Stedman 1790, 155-156.
98   Hoogbergen 1990, 92-93.

Further fighting was ultimately unsustainable for the Boni. Due to the destruction of garden plots and villages, they were continuously forced to move around. Colonists intensified the battle in the course of 1775 after the arrival of *c.*240 more State troops in March that same year (see p. 126). In August the Boni were hit hard by a large expedition aimed at the newly established villages of Holi-mi and Kofi-hay, built near the Cassipera Creek. Fourgeoud had now transformed his strategy: the *Neeger Vrijcorps* was now also utilised and the drum rolls were omitted. The Boni could do little against this 300-man strong force. A lack of ammunition prompted the Boni to fire small stones and buttons at their opponents. During this battle Boni, Kormantin Kodjo and Aluku had hidden women and children in the villages of Kofi-hay and nearby Busi-krey (lit.: the bush cries). The Maroons set fire to Holi-mi before being forced to flee. Kofi-hay was abandoned too. A few months later Busi-krey, already vacated by the Maroons, fell into the hands of Colonel Fourgeoud's troops.[99]

The Maroons had to disperse again, whereby Boni, Kormantin Kodjo and Suku each went their separate ways. The Boni continued to carry out raids on plantations, but were dealt a decisive blow in April 1776 when Black Rangers were again successful. Assisted by the aforementioned Maroon Jonas van 's-Haagenbosch, they discovered Mokomoko-busi, a village recently built by a group of Boni residing in the same region as Kofi-hay and Holi-mi were located. Due to this rapid attack the Boni were no longer able to reach their villages, although a majority did manage to escape in time.[100]

A few months later, all the Boni crossed the Marowijne River to set foot in French Guiana. After initial reports from the French side, Governor Nepveu dispatched a large patrol comprising more than 300 men enlisted by the Society and supplemented by ten Black Rangers. Having arrived at the border river, these soldiers came across a camp housing 74 huts. The Boni must have stayed here just before crossing the river. The last trace the Maroons had left behind was a number of felled *kwari*-trees, from which dugout canoes had been carved. They had probably started out from a tributary of the Marowijne River, now known as Boni Creek.[101] Fourgeoud nevertheless executed several futile marches through the jungle, where the reinforcement consisting of 350 State troops that had arrived in December 1776 was deployed (see p. 126).

On 1 April 1778, almost 2 years after his delayed departure, Fourgeoud returned to the Republic together with what was left of his troops. The majority had deceased through disease and exhaustion. It is difficult to determine the number of casualties among the Boni. Their survivors almost always managed to escape into the forest and swamp lands. Only rarely did colonial search parties encounter any bodies of fallen Maroons, a result of a combat method the Boni applied whereby three individuals manned a single gun. Hence, they were nearly always able to quickly drag off any dead or injured fellow warriors. Because of their animistic beliefs, Maroons very much wished to prevent a deceased falling into enemy hands. The fact that the Boni wars certainly led to far more victims among Suriname's troops was mainly due

---

99   Ibid., 96-97; for further details on these expeditions, see: Stedman 1790, 389-424.
100   Hoogbergen 1990, 98-101.
101   Ibid., 101-102.

A History of Suriname

to difficult physical conditions. After the return of State troops to Paramaribo, in July 1776, only 366 of the 770 men brought in from the Dutch Republic had survived. Almost half had either fallen ill or were declared unfit.[102]

Governor Nepveu had never placed any faith in Fourgeoud's offensive strategy. He therefore designed a plan to construct a 'cordon of defence' in the East, stretching from the Atlantic Coast to the Suriname River. In his opinion, assaults carried out either by Maroons or by pacified Maroons would now be almost impossible. If any attackers succeeded in breaking through this line at all, they could at least be detained on their way back. It would now also be easier to recapture fugitive slaves. This plan comprised building a series of small military outposts, located within calling distance of each other. Positioned along the entire eastern and southern sides of plantations, these posts were interconnected by means of a more than 90 km long path. At first, the Court of Police and Criminal Justice was not in favour of this strategy. It preferred an immediate nihilation of the enemy. In due course this court's members consented. The Society agreed, too, in December 1775. The defence line was completed 3 years later.[103]

The war waged against the Boni cost the Republic and its colony large sums of money. A jungle march would often require more than 100,000 guilders.[104] Colonists were thus obliged to contribute to the 'till against the runaways'. In 1771 this *hoofdgeld* (head tax) was doubled from 1 to 2 guilders and had to be provided by each individual colonist, slave, free Black person and of colour.[105] Due to the shortage in this till, in 1772, the government could no longer pay rent to those owners, who had made their slaves available to serve as porters in military patrols.[106] The huge financial distress implied, from 1774 on, Dutch and English sea captains also had to forward 4.5 per cent of their profits on sold goods.[107] Two years later Nepveu imposed further financial measures because 'the government is not able to continuously compensate the excessive costs of already such lengthy expeditions against the runaways'; he next not only decided to abolish the head tax, which many considered unjust because of the unfair burden-sharing, but also to instead introduce a 6 per cent tax on profits and incomes amassed by all colonists, a tax which large numbers attempted to evade.[108] Between 1773 and 1775, the arrears at the 'till against the runaways' had almost reached the sum of 500,000 guilders.[109]

With the flight of the Boni, in 1776, the preeminent danger to the colony had vanished. Small groups of so-called '*schuilneegers*' (lit. 'negroes in hiding'), sheltering near plantations, hardly caused its owners any problems. A few remained active but only in the west, near the Saramacca and Coesewijne Rivers. These Kwinti-

---

102 Wolbers 1861, 350. Here Wolbers relied on Governor Nepveu's journal.
103 Hoogbergen 1990, 98-99, 102; Hoogbergen notes that the Boni only attacked in cases of emergency, to wit, if their vegetable gardens were destroyed or if they lacked guns to defend themselves with. However, the Paramaribo-based authorities were not familiar with these underlying motifs, which Maroons took to heart.
104 Wolbers 1861, 147.
105 Schiltkamp 1973, vol. 2, 832.
106 Ibid., 850.
107 Ibid., 868.
108 Ibid., 900-903.
109 Wolbers 1861, 354.

Maroons, never posed any real threats. After crossing into French Guiana, the Boni built villages on the Sparouine River, a branch of the Marowijne River, located several kilometres south of the Boni Creek. A few years later they moved further southwards to settle on the banks of the Marowijne River (see map on p. 140). In a letter sent to Paramaribo, the Governor of Cayenne (French Guiana) had expressed his displeasure at their arrival. Nevertheless he left these Maroons untouched, also because military means required to undertake any action were lacking.[110] In 1782, at the mouth of the Sparouine River, a Catholic priest, while serving as a French envoy, spoke with a Maroon delegation, which included Boni himself. A Maroon ritual confirmed that neither party had any evil intentions when drinking *swerie* (vow), i.e., a beverage which contained a droplet of blood, in this case drawn from that priest and a Boni captain.[111]

Shortly after fleeing, the Boni had on several occasions tried to attack plantations located in Suriname, only to be deterred by the aforementioned cordon of defence. In 1785 however they succeeded in seizing slaves and goods from plantations twice.[112] The colonial government could do little, as patrols were not allowed to take place on French territory. The authorities thus attempted to persuade the Aukaner Maroons (aka Ndyuka), who populated the Tapanahoni region, to take up arms against the Boni. The resident administrator (*posthouder*) had indeed threatened to take military action if the Ndyuka did not discontinue their contacts with the Boni. On behalf of the Court of Police and Criminal Justice, this administrator informed the Ndyuka they were guilty of breaching the peace treaty. For the time being the colonial strategy to set both groups against each other proved unsuccessful.[113]

From as early as 1780 onwards the Boni and the Ndyuka maintained good relationships. In that same year the head man Boni sent a delegation led by his son Agosu to *granman* Pambu demanding the return of two Boni women whom Ndyuka men had abducted from a village located in the Sparouine region (French Guiana), the domicile of a certain Koki, an ally of Boni.[114] The peace was sealed with a *swerie* after the Ndyuka had explained they had not been aware of this alliance. Even marriages between Ndyuka and Boni took place. The fact that the Ndyuka had carried out several patrols against the Boni during the First Boni-Maroon War had apparently been forgotten. From then on both these ethnic groups would support each other. At that time the colonial government exerted pressure on the Ndyuka to break with the Boni. An assistant of the *posthouder* was even sent to them demanding the removal of *granman* Pambu.[115]

In March 1789 Suriname was startled by a raid which Boni-Maroons carried out on plantation Clarenbeek, on the upper reaches of the Commewijne River. They had

---

110 Hoogbergen 1990, 105.
111 Ibid., 118-120; Hurault 1960, 93-101.
112 Hoogbergen 1990, 122-123.
113 Ibid., 114.
114 Ibid., 107-114. A long-standing enmity existed between the Ndyuka and Koki. The Ndyuka had planned to hand Koki along with five others as runaway slaves over to the authorities, an obligation under the peace treaty. When Koki cum suis became aware of this, they fled to then attack the Ndyuka. Their raid on Koki's village was inspired and indeed accompanied by the *posthouder* with the aim of retrieving plantation slaves seized by Koki.
115 Ibid., 114.

A History of Suriname

taken the director hostage either to force peace or to obtain a ransom. The government however informed the Boni via the Ndyuka that it rejected such proposals. Six months later, plantations located on the banks of the Suriname Rivier were attacked, sparking off the Second Boni War (1789-1793).[116] The resumption of assaults by the Boni illustrates how much these Maroons depended on the plantation economy. They probably wished to raise their declining number, especially by removing women and children from the plantation Clarenbeek. Dissatisfaction with the small deliveries of goods by the French may also have played a role. The Boni now also included new runaways, who often still felt strong resentment towards their owners. Boni himself no longer participated in armed actions.

It did not take long for colonists to react. Governor-general Jan Gerhard Wichers (1784-1790) ordered the commander of the *Neeger Vrijcorps*, captain P.S. Stoelman, to establish a military outpost on the Marowijne River. A week after the more than 100 of the Society's troops and Black Rangers had set up camp, they had already experienced several attacks from the Boni whose strategy also comprised psychological warfare. Stoelman reported in his journal on 'many different spectacles', in the course of which Boni performed ritual dances on a sandbank in the river, passed by in their canoes shouting abuse or loudly beating their drums and sounding horns (*tutu*).[117] Only after a few weeks of building the necessary dug-outs did colonial troops take any action. Stoelman first expelled Boni men from their lookouts positioned in the Marowijne River, after which he was able to establish a new military fortification, built further southwards near the Armina rapids. The Boni could not prevent their enemy from advancing any further. As a result of the confusion prevailing in France after the revolution of 1789, soldiers could move around on French territory without any problems. After less than a month, on 30 April 1790, fresh troops under a new command conquered the village of Aroku, where Boni lived. This victory was celebrated in Paramaribo just as exuberantly as when Buku had fallen.[118]

A majority of the inhabitants of the village of Aroku (named after their head man Aluku) had escaped via the Marowijne River towards the south. The condition of the Boni having again moved upstream had become very poor due to lack of food. Moreover, they were now cut off from Amerindians on the coast with whom they traded regularly. Boni thus decided to negotiate the terms of surrender with the colonists, a step apparently motivated by disappointment as to the lack of assistance from the Ndyuka. Three representatives, including Boni's son Profit, travelled to Paramaribo after an intervention by Lieutenant Colonel F.M. Beutler, the incoming commander posted at the Marowijne River. These envoys discussed the plight of the Maroons, asking for a plot of land to live on in peace and quiet. In their view, incited Ndyuka had carried out raids on plantations.[119] Governor-general Jurriaan F. de Friderici informed Lieutenant Colonel Beutler in a letter that negotiations could only be held with the most important Boni leaders. One condition for peace implied that Maroons should

---

116 Ibid., 129-156.
117 Ibid., 133; Hoogbergen 1984, 57.
118 Wolbers 1861, 435-436; Hoogbergen 1990, 137-141; a Ndyuka delegation had visited Aroku at the end of March in order to warn chief Boni, on behalf of *granman* Pambu, that a Boni defector was planning to guide a colonial military expedition directed at Boni villages.
119 Hoogbergen 1990, 141-142.

hand over all the slaves who had joined them since they had resettled to the Marowijne River. Moreover, all friendly contacts with Ndyuka had to be cut off. Furthermore, if the government deemed it necessary, Boni should even declare war on the Ndyuka. Thus the divide and rule-policy remained a key instrument.[120]

De Friderici had no intention of negotiating honestly with the Boni. The issue of cooperating with them, after *granman* Pambu's demise, hugely divided the Ndyuka. De Frederici, aware of this, informed Beutler that fighting the Boni had to be resumed at a favourable moment. Needless to say, their opponent should not notice this initiative at all. Hence tranquillity had to be pretended for the time being.[121] On 19 October 1790 Beutler could report the following to De Friderici:

'The chiefs have asked [...] bitter cassava and bananas, but [I] have placated them continuously [...]. In that manner I keep them out of suspicion while not offending in the slightest. They are already confident that we will no longer act against them, but we have not yet had the opportunity to execute a real coup, because 10 to 12 of them, without one of their chiefs, is not worthwhile. With those negroes one has to work miraculously; on land this is something that can be done, but on water I can assure you, Sir, that it is not possible now, without exposing the people to all kinds of danger, because of the shoals, that are now with this low water unnavigable by canoes carrying small canons. And if a detachment reaches their height in order to establish a station between them and the Aukaners [Ndyuka], *how will I get the provisions to that high position, which, however, must be brought there by covered vessels, so it can only be started after the water rises.'*[122]

The Boni, already severely weakened by a smallpox epidemic, quickly agreed to these conditions. They had not only informed Beutler that the contacts with Ndyuka had been cut off but also that they would do their utmost to return with those slaves they had taken with them, although they considered it difficult because certain clan heads might not cooperate. Within a few weeks the Boni provided 15 slaves, a number the government deemed insufficient. During the following months fresh negotiations, in which Boni himself also participated, took place on a reef in the Marowijne River. Here the Boni handed over several dozens of slaves, thus almost fully meeting the peace terms.[123] However, during a final meeting in April 1791, Beutler demanded the extradition of a few more slaves, setting a 6-week ultimatum. On the very last day Boni showed up to explain to Beutler it was impossible to trace any more slaves. Boni, accompanied by several chiefs, arrived at the agreed location near an outpost known as Nassau. It had been built on Langatabbetje (an isle in the Marowijne River), which the Boni had previously occupied.[124]

---

120 Ibid., 142, 145; Thoden van Velzen & Hoogbergen 2011, 243-247. We read in the latter publication that incitement expressed by Dutch colonial authorities is considered the underlying and main cause of tension between Boni and Ndyuka.

121 Hoogbergen 1990, 148.

122 Hoogbergen 1984, 97-98.

123 Hoogbergen 1990, 153-154.

124 Ibid., 155.

The fight against the Boni was not immediately resumed because the danger still existed that the Ndyuka would turn against colonists. Therefore the government once again attempted to provoke hostilities against the Boni. After the key supporters of cooperating with the Boni, *granman* Pambu and a clan chief named Kwamina Adjubi had passed away, the colonial divide-and-rule policy suddenly proved much more promising. Ndyuka youngsters did not observe any advantages in collaborating with the Boni, who were after all no longer a significant power due to an exhausting warfare. Discontinuing the peace with colonists would be much more damaging. The most important Ndyuka representative was Ma Cato, an influential female ritualist related to the deceased *granman* Pambu.

Posthouder J. Basschal had informed Governor-general De Friderici accurately of the developments. Next, in order to enforce the extradition of a number of Boni, the the latter pressurized the Ndyuka by arresting their envoys, including a chief, while visiting Paramaribo. At the same time he sent a letter to Basschal which included a message for the Ndyuka conveying that Suriname considered itself in a state of war with them because they supported the Boni. Peace could only be restored by means of extraditing certain fellow tribesmen who had collaborated with the Boni. Furthermore, all the Boni still staying in the company of Ndyuka had to be handed over to the colonial government. The aforementioned arrests and letter aroused strong emotions among Ndyuka. After day-long meetings, in the course of which once again mutual dissent arose, they conceded to most issues of content. A military outpost was then positioned at the confluence of the Tapanahoni and the Lawa Rivers in order to prevent the Boni from populating Ndyuka territory located along the Tapanahoni River. After receiving this favourable report pertaining to the Ndyuka people, De Friderici immediately restored peace with them.[125]

In August 1791 an expedition ventured across the Tapanahoni River. It consisted of 120 men enlisted in the *Neeger Vrijcorps* as well as in the Society's troops. Led by Beutler, they soon succeeded in expelling those Boni residing near the Pedrosungu Falls. They did not incur many losses, as a majority had already abandoned their villages. The Boni, after again fleeing southwards, settled down on the banks of the Lawa River. Chief Boni then approached a number of Ndyuka belonging to a matrilineal clan (*lo*) known as Dikan. Having never turned away from him as a result of family ties, these Ndyuka promised to help the Boni if future attacks were to occur. This pact was confirmed by means of a *swerie*, a vow whereby blood of both ethnic groups was mixed and then drunk. Other Ndyuka clans, too, maintained mutual ties with the Boni. [126]

In general, the government's constant pressure incited their enmity. Withholding goods from the Ndyuka also proved effective. The support which the Boni could count on was indeed fragile. For, hardly a year after the aforementioned *swerie*, several Ndyuka (including one of the participants in this ceremony with the Boni) reported to the commander of the colonial troops in order to express their regret. They informed captain P.S. Stoelman, who replaced the diseased Beutler, that they had broken with the Boni. Although certain Ndyuka assisted the Boni by means

---

125   Ibid., 155-157.
126   Ibid., 157-162.

of food and shelter, a majority collaborated with colonists. Ndyuka armed guards stationed at the estuary of the Tapanahoni River (southeast Suriname), for example, captured more than 20 Boni. As agreed, this group was now handed to the *posthouder* for a reward. Forced by increasingly harsh living conditions, Boni would often defect to colonial authorities. Search patrols could discover their villages and garden plots easier with the help of extradited Boni and defectors, some of whom were members of the *Neeger Vrijcorps*. In March 1792, an expedition led by captain Stoelman discovered the village where Kormantin Kodjo lived. Its inhabitants had been alerted by gunshots the enemy troops had fired. The Paramaribo-based government was as yet not satisfied. For, in spite all its efforts, the Boni had remained unconquered. Next, De Friderici commissioned Stoelman to equip a large expedition, even prior to the dry season during which the low water level would render the Lawa River unnavigable. The course of events would however unexpectedly take an entirely different turn.[127]

In July 1792, Boni's son Agosu reported to captain Stoelman in order to renegotiate peace, resulting in a 2-week truce. Each and every Boni had to report to the outpost of Nassau in order to surrender. Stoelman guaranteed they would be allocated a plot of land to settle down permanently. One day before this ultimatum passed, Agosu along with around 15 fellow fighters attacked the Ndyuka village of Animbaw, located on the Tapanahoni River. After a few hours, a chief named Bambi along with a small number of Ndyuka expelled the Boni, who had set this almost deserted village on fire. This raid must have been no surprise to colonists. During negotiations held at Nassau, Agosu announced that the Boni had broken with the Ndyuka and were going to attack them. The fact the Ndyuka were intent on revenge after the assault on Animbaw may well have been welcomed by the colonial government.[128]

Meanwhile Stoelman had moved his military outpost further south, towards an isle strategically positioned in the confluence of the Tapanahoni and Lawa Rivers, which since then is named Stoelmans Island. Under his command, the announced expedition next set off for the Lawa River. Within several days Stoelman managed to find recently built Boni villages situated on an isle which Boni named Sakabanami (meaning.: my brother does not let go any further), which symbolically refers to his *swerie* with the Ndyuka. A few more search patrols were sent upstream from Sakabanami only to come across garden plots and supplies. Thanks to their dugouts the Boni had again escaped governmental troops.[129] The Ndyuka delivered the Boni the final blow. After Ma Cato had made amulets (*obias*) in order to protect the fighters against all dangers, 72 Ndyuka set off for the Lawa River in 22 dugouts on 22 January 1793 under chief Bambi's command. They had received ammunition from a military outpost established on Stoelmans Island. With the help of two Boni captured en route, this expedition found Boni's village built on the banks of the Marouine River, a tributary of the Lawa River which was concealed behind

---

127   Ibid., 161-163.
128   Ibid., 165-168
129   Ibid., 173-174.

many rapids. On February 20 1793, at 3 am, a small patrol led by Bambi arrived at Boni's house.[130]

> *'We learned that we were no longer far from Bonnie, upon which the chieftain Bambie and his patrol went to visit him and found Bonnie in the woods in a hut with his two wives, and two children, where Bambie surrounded him and shot him dead, and cut off his head and right hand. Then his two wives and children were captured. An infant, a bush creole, called Beyman, and a baby named Marietje. Next another negro, called Marquis, was shot dead there. (Travel log of the expedition against Bonnie's gang carried out by a detachment of the satisfied negroes of Auca, seconded on 22 January h.a. from the post located in the Lava region by Major H. Zeegelaar, undersigned by me, 3 March 1793.)'*[131]

On their way back, Ndyuka men came across the village home to Boni's son Agosu, but he had already fled. A few days later they shot Kormantin Kodjo to death in a village built further down the Lawa River.[132] An attempt to find the latter before he too could flee almost resulted in Bambi drowning when his boat capsized in one of the Lawa River's many rapids. The cargo, including Boni's severed head, was lost. His demise led to the creation of myths among Maroons. According to the rich oral Ndyuka tradition, Boni first had to be deprived of his magical protection before he could be killed. Having entered the village in the body of a female monkey, she transmuted into a beautiful women in order to seduce Boni to reveal his secret. Next, after transforming into a monkey again, she fled and returned to the Ndyuka. Boni's head allegedly 'jumped' overboard.[133] The Boni who had fallen into the hands of colonists were treated rather mildly. None received the death penalty. The approximately ten men who had played key roles in raids on plantations were exiled to the Caribbean isle of St. Eustatius and sold as slaves. Others returned to their plantation owners. A number of Boni were even enlisted in the *Neeger Vrijcorps*. Those Boni who were born in the forest were allowed to settle down on the banks of the Saramacca River.

At the beginning of 1790 the Boni counted *c.* 450 souls, whereas in 1793 their number was probably only between 100 and 150. Warfare, hunger and a smallpox epidemic had taken many lives. Moreover, the colonial army had captured another 148 Boni.[134] Agosu was one of the chiefs to remain in office. Aluku had passed away in 1792. The fact that the Boni called themselves Aluku underlines the respect the latter enjoyed. In 1809 the colonial government placed the Boni under the authority of the Ndyuka.

A few years later the Boni returned to again reside on the French bank of the Lawa River, where they presumably lived in poverty. In 1837, while settling down on the banks of the Oyapoc River (West French Guiana), a number of them attempted to escape the surveillance imposed by Ndyuka. The French Governor however dispatched a small army to the Boni for fear of colonists experiencing trouble. This detachment's commander saw to it that four captured Boni were shot dead. This

_____

130   Ibid., 176-177.
131   For this report see: Hoogbergen 1984, 154-160.
132   Hoogbergen 1990, 178.
133   Ibid., 178-183.
134   Ibid., 183.

execution led to such commotion in France that this Governor was called back to Paris and then removed from office. He had nonetheless already been congratulated with the successful action by his Dutch colleague, Governor-general Evert Ludolph baron van Heeckeren (1831-1838).[135] In 1860, under pressure from France (which regarded Boni as its subjects), Governor Reinhart Frans van Lansberge (1804-1873) allowed Boni to settle in Suriname. Moreover, the Ndyuka were no longer permitted to prevent the Boni, now comprising *c.*600 souls, from navigating the Marowijne River.[136]

In 1805, after the final defeat of the Boni, a rebellion in which several dozens of Black Rangers stationed at defence cordon posts participated startled the colony. Having killed several white overseers, these Rangers went on to attack the military post of Armina built on the banks of Marowijne River. The exact circumstances of this raid have never been fully clarified. One presumes this mutiny spiralled out of control.[137] Those rebels sought contact with the Ndyuka who then granted them a plot of land to settle down on. Perhaps these Ndyuka utilised black hunters as a means to exert pressure when obtaining material support from colonists on the pretext it would otherwise be unable to control them. The government took no action. As stated in the renewed peace agreement of 1809, the Ndyuka only had to guarantee that the rebels would not do anything to harm any whites.[138] This group was later thought to be integrated with a certain Ndyuka clan. Large-scale attacks carried out by Maroons no longer took place during the 19th century. Regular patrols, which continued right up to the abolition of slavery (1863), complicated the lives of slaves in hiding considerably. The slave resistance now manifested itself more on plantations. Specific groups of fugitives succeeded in building permanent settlements, but only the runaway Paramaka people could in the end survive.

---

135   Hurault 1960, 116-120.
136   Hoogbergen 1990, 196-198.
137   Wolbers 1861, 547-551; Hoogbergen 1990, 184-185; on this occasion four Black Rangers were arrested (one of whom died while in prison) and the three others were sentenced to death.
138   Hoogbergen 1990, 185.

CHAPTER 6
Inhabitants of the inland

6.1 The formation of Maroon societies

After signing peace treaties, the Surinamese Maroons were able to set up their own societies in the jungle. They were now in unique circumstances thanks to the abundant availability of land - a remarkable difference when compared with Jamaica, for example, where Maroons had integrated much more quickly into the colonial society as a result of a lack of space. In Jamaica, the British colonial government regarded members of this ethnic group as subjects with a special status. Here conflicts with Maroons mainly concerned land ownership, whereas in Suriname the handing over of recently recaptured runaways to the colonial government formed the main issue.[1] Elsewhere, too, Maroons were either absorbed by the other segments of the population or forced to their knees by large armies. Surinamese Maroons did not consider themselves defeated in any way because they had negotiated with white colonists from an equal position.

Estimates of the number of Maroons at the time of these peace treaties vary. The Ndyuka and the Saramaka populations of Suriname must have ranged between 2,500 and 3,000 souls. The number of Matawai did not exceed *c.*300. In addition, several hundred Boni, Kwinti and Paramakas were counted during the 19th century.[2]

Though gardens played a very important role in the Maroons' livelihoods, many men earned money by means of logging. Maroons participated in the colonial economy at an early stage. Many Ndyuka left their village situated on the Tapanahoni River in order to be closer to colonists populating the coastal region, hereby making it easier for them to supply wood to sawmills built on plantations and in Paramaribo. In 1835, according to a reliable census carried out by the *posthouder* (resident administrator) F. Schachtrupp, no less than 900 of the 3,202 Ndyuka inhabited the Cottica region. Moreover, 250 Nyduka had migrated to Sarakreek and 200 to the lower reaches of the Saramacca River. Many Ndyuka women had followed their husbands; according to the peace treaty, Maroons required a special pass to be obtained from the *posthouder* in order to move around, but they did not think much of this measure; in *c.*1850, between 1,000 and 1,500 Ndyuka had settled down permanently in the Cottica and Commewijne regions.[3] August Kappler who for several years had officiated as *posthouder* on the Marowijne River, estimated that a Maroon could easily earn 7.50 guilders a day when cutting 30 cubic feet of wood; Kappler, a timber merchant himself, reported that with those wages a Maroon could purchase enough food on a plantation to last between 3 and 4 weeks.[4]

Suriname-based Maroons had developed their own traditions. Part of their material culture originated from Amerindians, with whom trade relations had been established and who for a long time had known how to survive in the jungle. For

---

1   De Groot 1984, 73-82; McKee 2018, 27-52.
2   Thoden van Velzen & Van Wetering 1988, 9.
3   Ibid., 13.
4   Kappler 1854, part 2, 131.

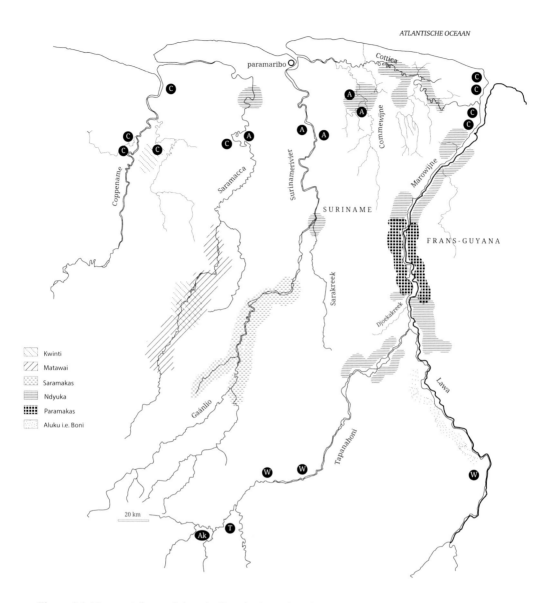

Figure 6.1. Maroon tribes and Amerindians in the 19th and early 20th century. A. Arawaks, C. Caribs, W. Wayana, T. Trio, Ak. Akurio. Since then their habitats have changed little, except for the Boni who largely settled in French Guiana. Buddingh' 2021, 164 (after Thoden van Velzen & Van Wetering 1988).

example, Amerindians poisoned bodies of water to facilitate fishing, a technique observed among Maroons. Although Amerindians had supported white colonists in their struggle against Maroons, in no way did this prevent upholding useful contacts with Maroons. The latter purchased dried fish as well as trained hunting dogs from Amerindians living in southern Suriname.[5] Trade contacts also existed with Amerindians in the coastal region. Mutual influences could be observed. Maroons

---

5   Ibid, part 1, 73.

A History of Suriname

may indeed have taught Amerindians how to best cultivate gardens, a skill acquired as slave labourers on plantations.

The Maroon spiritual culture can best be referred to as being Afro-American. It had largely begun to take shape as early as in the first decades of slavery. After years of debate, a reasonable degree of consensus within scientific circles has been reached regarding this issue.[6] The heterogeneous ethnic origins of Maroons render it difficult to speak of a shared cultural heritage. In spite of its strong West African traits, their legacy did however distinguish itself from expressions of West African culture. As a result of the large number of slaves continuously arriving from overseas, the distance between the plantation society and the West African culture was smaller than it was with Saramakas. Maroons had evolved from early runaways and in due course were largely born on Surinamese soil. Although very aware of their African roots, their oral history only commences with the *loweten* (a Sranan Tongo term meaning: the time when absconding began).

Maroons adhere to a matrilineal kinship structure implying that their genealogy runs along female lines. This ethnic group consists of several *lo*s, which in turn are composed of *bé*s. *Lo*s were formed as early as during the marronage. A *bé* (derived from *bere*, meaning belly) is a matrilineage, the members of which can accurately indicate their mutual relationships. The term *lo* pertains to the term 'clan' as applied by anthropologists. The fact a kinship was often fictitious did not detract from a group's cohesion. Members of a matriclan (*lo*), were often home to the same village as were children who did not directly belong to a matrilineal family, and relatives by marriage. Matrilineal as well as patrilineal forms of kinship occur among West African peoples. The presence of matrilineal kinships among Surinamese Maroons may well be linked to their difficult living conditions.[7] They thus wished to protect themselves against natural as well as supernatural dangers by means of an amulet (*obia*). For this reason several amulets, after proving their usefulness, had to remain within their specific group. A small community then quickly chooses for a unilinear inheritance and opting for the matrilineal form of kinship was obvious. As the survival of the Maroons depended heavily on reproduction it was important to maintain the already very low number of women. Plantation slaves did not yet uphold exclusive matrilineal relationships which once again indicates how the Maroons and their habitat contributed to their choice for matrilineality.

The matrilineal system also played a key role in the administrative and religious relations within Maroon communities. Important administrative duties continued to exist within the matriclan/matrilineage. The *gaanman/granman*, the highest authority of the entire Maroon ethnic group, hailed as much as possible from the clan of his

---

6   In a classical study entitled *The Birth of African-American Culture: An Anthropological Perspective*, 1992, 124 (orig. 1976) Mintz and Price report how enslaved Africans from numerous societies 'began to forge out of common understandings and shared crises a new culture with distinct institutions, religious beliefs, and kinship roles'; In 'The Miracle of Creolization: A Retrospective', in: *The New West Indian Guide* 75. 1-2 (2001), 35-64, Price looks back on the polarized debate his 1976 publication had generated, especially in North America, much less in the Caribbean. Certain scholars have accused both authors of actually denying the existence of an African heritage. Almost 2 decades later, Price mentions in an e-mail sent to the present author (dated May 10, 2018): 'I have seen zero criticism for many years now.'

7   Köbben 1979, 26-76; Price 1983, 314-316, Hoogbergen 1990, 209-219; Van Wetering & Thoden van Velzen 2013, vol. 2, 31-36.

predecessors. The captain (*kapten*), the clan leader, served as village chief. Research carried out among present-day Ndyuka has proven one preferred a member who belonged to a next generation and who should always stem from a different segment than the deceased, whereby all groups were treated equally well. At this point a discrepancy arose pertaining to the matrilineal system as observed among the Akan peoples from West Africa. They not only prefer to choose a member of the same generation but are also not familiar with rotating functions between societal groups.[8] Among Suriname-based Maroons, a *basia*, who assisted the captains, was preferably selected from the same lineage.

Administrative matters were discussed in a *krutu*, i.e., a meeting of male village elders. Depending on the nature of the case, such a gathering could take place at various levels. The intention was to reach a consensus, be it not always possible. According to Kappler, elders and captains visited the chief 'where one argues and shouts the loudest, so that after all, one goes home as wise as one came'.[9]

The traditional religion referred to as *winti* formed the essence of the culture that runaways had taken with them into the forest. Maroons directly linked *winti* to events witnessed in daily life (e.g., disease, death, birth, prosperity, crop failure) and the supernatural.[10] This belief includes the same elements as observed among many West African ethnic groups. Its supreme creator spirit and lower deities are inextricably linked to elements of the surrounding nature, especially air, water, soil and forest. In general, higher deities possess a tutelary effect, but only as long as humankind does not violate divine laws. Lower gods are more likely to harm human beings. The supreme creator spirit is referred to as Masaa Gadu (Lord God). In the sacred African Kumanti language, it is called Anana Kedyaman Kedyampon. It has delegated his power to the pantheons.[11] Ancestral spirits are of great significance to Maroons. Ancestors are seen as intermediaries between humans and gods. Supernatural powers reside in trees, rocks, animals, etc. Witchcraft (*wisi*) plays an equally important role in the lives of Maroons. Individuals suspected of utilising a lesser deity (*bakru*) in order to bewitch other Maroons were either expelled or burned along with all their possessions after being tortured.

Diversity characterises *winti*. Matrilineages could be distinguished by means of specific religious practices performed by separate groups within the Maroon community. Lineages (each with its own ancestral spirits and often its own deity) were frequently housed in separate parts of a village. Here their sacrificial sites were located. The Maroon population lived in great fear of vengeful spirits as they caused diseases or even more ill fate. Such a spirit (*kunu*) could pour itself out over the entire lineage if one of its members either brought evil upon a certain individual belonging to another lineage or had committed some other offence. The often large mutual solidarity within the lineage was considered the outcome of an omnipresent collective threat expressed by vindictive spirits. After providing these spirits with a key position of power within the community, only male and female ritual specialists

---

8   Köbben 1979, 42-49.
9   Kappler 1854, 129.
10 Thoden van Velzen & Van Wetering 1988; Wooding 1981; Wooding 2013 (orig. 1972).
11 Thoden van Velzen & Van Wetering 1988, 31; Wooding 1981, 67, 86.

were capable of contacting supernatural powers through oracles, trance or a medium. For Maroons it was, after all, of vital importance to not only know what supernatural powers had in store for them but also how to appease them.

Now and again certain Maroon clans prevailed over others because the monopoly pertaining to those cults was deemed of 'national' significance, in other words, of importance to all Ndyuka. In *c.*1850, for example, the head man as well as certain (other) ritual specialists belonging to the Oto clan (Ndyuka) were key participants in a cult whereby a Maroon suspected of witchcraft (*wisi*) was taken to Drietabbetje (*Diitabiki*) in order to drink a sacred beverage (*sweli*). Whenever someone subsequently fell ill, he or she would be pronounced guilty of *wisi*.[12] Every few years each clan head set off for Drietabbetje to drink *sweli* together. In this way they renewed their oath of allegiance to the *gaanman* of the Oto clan, who also led the entire Ndyuka people. This ceremony took place in a shrine housing relics of the deceased *gaanman*. The *sweli* cult was thus also associated with the worship of important ancestors to whom every few years, too, various chiefs made libations and presented food offerings, while staying at the village of Puketi (formerly named Animbaw). Later on, people from outside the Oto clan were also involved in this cult.

Generally speaking, relations between clans were nevertheless regarded as equal. This stance was linked to the fact that the majority of cults was only of any significance to a certain clan. The existence of hierarchical relationships within a clan was connected to fulfilling religious tasks. For example, Kumanti-speaking ritualists, who mainly acted as medicine men, were highly revered. When utilising their protective amulets, they had played a key role in the struggle of the Maroons against colonists. As dignified family heads, these ritual specialists could notably influence their clan.[13] The exclusively male Kumanti-speaking practitioners and their assistants were, as indeed all their colleagues, to a certain degree also medical/religious entrepreneurs, who saw to it they were paid for rendering services in kind and money. They were able to increase their influence by being introduced into other Maroon groups who revered Kumanti-related pantheons unknown to them, hereby increasing the value of their amulets. Other ritualists acted either as a seer (*lukuman*) or a healer (*obiaman*), but the Ndyuka deemed the Kumanti-speaking ritual specialists to be the most prominent. In general they were the only masters of the sacred African Kumanti language. These entrepreneurs felt very keen to increase the numbers of followers as this would provide them with even more influence during village discussions, which in turn benefitted those who had joined them. That prevalence explains the on-going disputes between Maroons and the colonial government concerning the extradition of runaways. As a result of their weighty position, ritualists were often able to include these refugees in their kin groups.

Such runaways were even able to occupy key positions within Maroon society. Da Saka (*c.*1825-1914) had once found shelter with the Misidjan *lo* to later become the most important medical/religious entrepreneur of this largest Ndyuka clan. He had actually received support from a female ritual specialist named Ma Djemba (*c.*1790-1880), a member of the Oto clan. She succeeded Ma Cato (see p. 135) and

---

12   Ibid. 1988, 50 ff.
13   Ibid., 21.

presented him with the knowledge of the amulet, in exchange for which Da Saka provided for her maintenance by working as a lumberjack on the coast.[14]

Already during the 18th century, after signing peace treaties, certain colonists attempted to convert Maroons to Christianity. In 1765, the Moravian Brethren founded a missionary post among the Saramaka people. Nonetheless, by and large, such initiatives aimed at converting remained fruitless. All the more remarkable were the results of the missionary work carried out by a converted Maroon named Johannes King (c.1830-1898) during the second half of the 19th century. In 1857, this son of a Matawai mother and a Ndyuka father had turned to Th. C. van Calker, the Paramaribo-based president of the Moravian Church which is referred to in Suriname either as *Broedergemeente* (Congregation of Brethren) or as *Hernhutter*s. God had instructed King in dreams and visions to preach the Christian faith. After being baptized, he learned to read and write. Building a church in the Matawai village of Maripaston, located on the lower reaches of the Saramacca River, was King's first success. A few years earlier in this village, where his family resided, the centre of a Ndyuka snake cult named Papa-Gadu was founded which had caught on indirectly because of King himself. After a number of family deaths, the Ndyuka who was consulted stated that King had created a vengeful spirit. For, as a child he had allegedly killed a snake which the Ndyuka had revered. This malicious spirit had to be reconciled by means of the Papa-Gadu cult.[15] The turnaround in Maripaston came in 1860, after King had freed his brother named Sopo from a *winti* by informing him that the Christian Church would step in and 'devilry' had to cease. King not only liberated other possessed inhabitants of the village of Maripaston from supernatural beings, he also destroyed village shrines and threw amulets into the river. King went on numerous missionary journeys to other Maroon groups.[16]

Having reported extensively in his diaries, he can be considered the first Surinamese (Maroon) author. In descriptions of religious traditions upheld by the Maroons he visited, we see his vision as being unreservedly presented. In his opinion, the religious rituals of all Maroons were similar, whereby however the 'idolatry' of the Ndyuka was the strongest. In *Bekentenisboek uit het land van de heidenen* (Book of Confession from the land of the heathens), originally published in 1864, King reports in Sranan Tongo on the considerable obligations certain rituals could entail. If a Maroon, when creating a garden, accidentally set fire to a *papa*-snake (i.e., a boa constrictor) ritual specialists were needed to ensure that the *winti* would still bury the now lifeless reptile. Family members of the perpetrator had to travel to Paramaribo in order to purchase, for example, two or three boxes containing sweet *sopi*, wine, beer, at least between 20 and 25 jars of rum, five or six jars of liqueur as well as sheep, goats, chickens, geese, large bowls, large plates, many loincloths (*pangi*) and head scarves (*angisa*) as well as several blankets. These goods were mostly divided among the ritual specialist and a *wintiman*. As payment for their services, they also

---

14   Ibid., 50-73; Thoden van Velzen & Van Wetering 2004, 74-77; Van Wetering & Thoden van Velzen 2013, 117-133.

15   De Beet 1981, 1-14; De Beet & Sterman 1981, 173-190; De Ziel 1973, 1-49 (based on a manuscript by J. King); Voorhoeve & Lichtveld 1973, 116-119; see also: Zamuel 1994.

16   De Beet 1981, 7-9; De Beet & Sterman 1981, 184-186; De Ziel 1973, 3-4.

Figure 6.2. Johannes King (left) and his brother Noah Adrai. Unknown photographer. The other persons are, as written in German on the photo, baptised chiefs. Surinaams Museum photo archive.

asked for between 50 and 80 guilders in cash. The people were, as Johannes King reported, 'slaves' (*katibo krinkrin*) of the dead snake.[17]

The success of King's missionary work was mainly limited to the Matawai people. Especially among the Ndyuka he received less support. During a visit to Diitabiki in 1865, the headman named Beiman stated he would not tolerate a church in his village thus: 'I have my magic and when I hear church talk in my ears, then I shall immediately die. My ancestors and my gods will kill me.'[18] Moreover, Beiman did not allow anyone to be baptised in his village. The Ndyuka were however given the opportunity to be baptized in Paramaribo, after which they could return to Diitabiki. A number of mainly senior Maroons were indeed baptized. Fear of being posthumously considered a witch [*wisiman*] proved to be key incentive for many to follow suit.

Johannes King became *granman* of the Matawai in 1895, thus succeeding his deceased brother Noah Adrai. King also met with opposition, resulting from envy whereby his key position certainly played a role. Noah Adrai had once banned Johannes from the village of Maripaston, probably because of the good reputation the latter had established among the Matawai and the colonists.[19] After falling ill, King ascribed this fate to his opponents and then resigned as a *granman*. By now the village church at Maripaston had become less dependent upon King. His assistant Nicolaas Manille, a former slave and African prince, criticised and accused him of relying too

17   De Beet 1981, 76.
18   Voorhoeve & Lichtveld 1973, 123.
19   De Ziel 1973, 14-18.

much on visions when performing his missionary tasks. Hernhutter missionaries interdicted King from proclaiming the Gospel in such a visionary manner.[20] His approach was indeed to some degree comparable to that of traditional ritualists acting as mediums between mankind and the supernatural. This modus operandi may well have contributed to Johannes King's successful missionary work among the Matawai.

The religion of the Maroons was multiform, subject to change and hugely influenced by the socio-economic conditions in which they lived. In *c*.1890, for example, the Gaan Gadu (Great Deity) cult became more and more popular among the Ndyuka to soon reach other ethnic groups. This cult ended in a full-scale persecution, depriving many hundreds of spirit mediums of their status and thus of their income. Even today the Ndyuka people consider it to be a far-reaching episode in their history.[21]

The Gaan Gadu cult originated in Puketi, the ancient Ndyuka capital located on the Tapanahoni River when many dignitaries had gathered here for the funeral of a young woman named Coba. According to a ritual also encountered in West Africa, two gravediggers (*oloman*) first performed a death test, carrying the corpse wrapped in a cloth on a bier above their heads. Each and every movement these two men made was interpreted as a signal of the deceased's spirit. It was a question of certifying the cause of death which, in the eyes of Maroons, is always of a supernatural nature; death tests had to be applied in order to determine if the deceased's spirit could cause any danger. During these tests, such spirits must respond by causing a gravedigger to carry out certain movements. In order to prevent any allegations of deception being levelled, the deceased's family members, having been invited to participate in this test, also served as bearers. By means of a libation the gods and ancestors were requested to provide this test with a successful outcome. In due course the group of gravediggers and assisting family members of the deceased determined the result in a final declaration. According to tradition, the first question forwarded to Coba's spirit was: could it help the *granman* in tracking down a number of missing Maroons? It was also customary for them to have concealed themselves in a hut on the *granman*'s request. The bearers did not move after the first question to then confirm with a nod that the spirit of the deceased could not assist him. This answer was indeed a writing on the wall for many. The fact that the two fresh corpse bearers almost ran into the river not only signalled that the deceased was ashamed to stay in the village but also established that Coba was indeed a witch. The corpses of witches were never buried, but always placed on a special 'witches field' outside the village. Coba's remains were nevertheless kept in Puketi one more night, as it was already late.

The following day, in accordance with instructions given by the deceased's spirit, paraphernalia associated with witchcraft were traced which Coba might have hidden. Not much later this spirit made it clear that a large number of Coba's former assistants were still roaming around in Ndyuka villages. Apparently this spirit would like to assist in tracking down these assistants in order to make up for all the evil Coba caused during her lifetime. The grave diggers decided that each and every adult residing at the village of Puketi had to undergo a witch's test. In order to avoid

---

20   Ibid., 6-7
21   Thoden van Velzen & Van Wetering 1988, 75-120, 387-401; Thoden van Velzen & Van Wetering 2004, 85-92; Van Wetering & Thoden van Velzen 2013, 135-172.

Figure 6.3. *Granman* Oseyse portrayed with top hat and crescent-shaped pectoral, 1891-1894. Unknown photographer. Surinaams Museum photo archive.

being accused of deception in the case of such a sensitive issue, fresh bearers were called upon to verify the deceased's message. They confirmed that Coba wished to reveal a conspiracy against the Ndyuka. In Diitabiki, *granman* Oseyse was consulted in the course of a gathering where this matter was discussed. The aforementioned influential ritualist Da Saka was asked to share his opinion, too.

Both men then gave their permission to conduct a large-scale investigation. Its relevance to the Maroon community was such that within a few days elderly people had arrived from a large number of villages in order to officiate on a special committee of inquiry. All men and women hailing from Puketi had to walk underneath the bier on which Coba's body rested. Investigations among the Maroon population were frequent, for example, if any doubt had risen as to who was responsible for the demise of a fellow villager. However, a method whereby a corpse acted as an oracle had never before been applied by the Ndyuka. If nothing happened, one was considered a decent person. The inquiry committee asked further questions whenever bearers made sudden movements. In due course, it was decided if a suspect should be deemed either a witch or an individual who had inflicted evil upon members of his or her ethnic group. Guilty parties were subjected to purification rituals for which they had to pay compensation to the elderly.

Events suddenly now took an entirely new turn. Not only the Puketi-based Maroons but all the Ndyuka residing on the Tapanahoni River now had to submit to a witch's test. On this occasion practitioners of the *sweli* cult were involved too. Mediums had to endure great suffering. In the course of several months, hundreds were liberated from evil entities, including wrathful and forest spirits. Only the

Kumanti-speaking ritual specialists were kept out of harm's way. This anti-witchcraft campaign, which involved the destruction of altars, amulets and other fetishes, damaged numerous established reputations.

Even Da Saka was instructed to submit to the oracle in Puketi. He did not feel inclined to give up his influence within the Ndyuka community. Especially the fact that *sweli* cult practitioners participated in this test must have alarmed him deeply. For, being the highest ranked *sweli* cultist, witch trials had until that moment always been held under his supervision. As a countermove Da Saka next focused on introducing a new cult. Having realised that the Ndyuka required a portable oracle, which would be consulted in public, he decided to exhume a number of objects located at Santi Goon, the residence of the now deceased female ritual specialist named Ma Djemba. These items had been utilised successfully as amulets during the struggle for freedom against white colonists. In order to enrich the amulets, Da Saka applied a Kumanti bundle of paraphernalia utilised during funeral rites. After all, during the test held at Puketi, Kumanti-speaking deities appeared to be above all suspicion. This bundle was attached to a board, which was placed on the heads of two bearers. The aforementioned movable oracle had to provide clues as to how the time-honoured amulet (i.e. *obia*), referred to as Gaan Tata, could best be composed by means of the unearthed objects. The renewal was symbolized by renaming the *obia* as Gaan Gadu.

Da Saka called on *granman* Oseyse to help see to it the Ndyuka people joined him. The former's grandchildren later described to Thoden van Velzen and Van Wetering how he had succeeded in his goal by means of a mixture of persuasiveness, insight and deception. Da Saka convinced Oseyse to detect a lost bottle of beer by means of this new oracle. The bottle was finally found underneath Da Saka's boat. Oseyse who did not realize that Da Saka had placed it there himself was very impressed. The oracle however made it quite clear to Da Saka and Oseyse that they must both be fined for being mistrustful. Such an atonement is not unusual when introducing an amulet. Oseyse had to forward 12 loincloths worn by females, and one demijohn of rum. Da Saka's fine was: providing 30 loincloths and 6 demijohns of rum.[22] The latter heavier sanction was not uncommon. For, in order to dispel any doubt, the individual who was to benefit most from an amulet had to undergo the most severe punishment.

The Ndyuka accepted this new oracle after a large meeting had taken place in Puketi, presided by Oseyse and Da Saka. The inquiry committee in Puketi was then dissolved. Coba's mortal remains were enterred in a shallow grave, hereby expressing a respectful compromise towards Sweli Gadu, who was after all involved with this oracle. Da Saka, having placed Sweli Gadu in the sacred bundle of Gaan Gadu, thus considerably reinforced his position, as he was the only person familiar with secrets kept by this oracle. A radical religious reform nevertheless did occur. After all, the incoming Gaan Gadu cult displayed similar traits when compared with Coba's oracle. This new, portable oracle would now be publicly consulted, too, hereby not only ending to secrecy but also allowing everyone to convince themselves no further deception existed.

---

22 Thoden van Velzen & Van Wetering 1988, 99-106.; Thoden van Velzen & Van Wetering 2004, 96-111; Van Wetering & Thoden van Velzen 2013, 144-150.

A History of Suriname

Figure 6.4. A Maroon *koelaman* (*c*.1975) seated at the bough of a corjal with a stick in order to fathom shallows and underwater hazards of the Tapahoni River. Photo by Vincent Mentzel.

Opposing a number of spirit medium-related cults remained a major task of the Gaan Gadu ritualists. The Ndyuka adhered to four important cults, each linked to a pantheon. Kumanti-speaking deities had occupied bodies of carrion birds, birds of prey and other predators. Spirits residing in reptiles were referred to as Papa or Vodu, ancestral spirits to Jooka and forest spirits to Ampuku. The anti-witchcraft campaign targeted cults associated with these three pantheons. Spirit mediums active within these cults were mainly women as they had to endure the most. Especially Ndyuka boatmen, who had become rich thanks to gold fever, had asserted themselves in the struggle against spirit-medium cults. These men were simply no longer prepared to give up their acquired prosperity. A witch-hunt aimed at economically weaker groups, in this case comprising mediums, was entirely in their interest.[23] Discovering gold both in the eastern interior of Suriname and in French Guiana had resulted in huge transmutations throughout the post-1880 Maroon society. Thanks to knowledge of rivers and their difficult navigability, Maroons were the only ones, along with a much smaller number of Amerindians, capable of transporting thousands of gold diggers and their freight, shipped in from across the globe. This activity soon replaced logging as a main source of income. As a result of their monopoly, corjal-owning Maroons could charge high freight rates, allowing their annual income to easily exceed a total of 3,000 guilders.[24] In 1921, they walked out for 3 months in

---

23   Thoden van Velzen & Van Wetering 1988, 136-158; Thoden van Velzen & Van Wetering 2004, 44-46.
24   Van Wetering & Thoden van Velzen 2013, 89.

order to voice their protest against high retail prices and low rates, the consequence of the declining gold sector. Here again the Gaan Gadu cult played a role.[25]

The rise of the Gaan Gadu cult can therefore not be considered as being separated from the rapid economic developments. In this context it is noteworthy that in the same period in the western forest area inhabited by Saramakas a completely different cult emerged, propagated by the spirit medium Anake, in the village Sofibuka on the Suriname River.[26] The villages in this area could, due to a greater distance from the gold fields, benefit much less from any incoming wealth. Men who had left for the border region often stayed away for years, leaving their wives and children behind in poverty. Anake had initially prophesied in a messianic vision not only that richly laden ships would steam up the river to reach Sofibuka (hence the term cargo cult), but also that Saramakas would live like Europeans do. When this predicted prosperity was not forthcoming, Anake began to preach on shared property, which would put an end to poverty. Visitors to Anake's territory spoke of 'primitive communism'.[27] It may be added here that material incentives have always strongly affected the collective fantasies in which Maroons believed.

At around the end of the 20th century and the dawn of the 21st century, time-honoured religious practices had continued to be part of Maroon daily life. An in-depth study has revealed that 'the past is compellingly present in the present'.[28] In 1972, for example, a renewed anti-witch campaign was launched under the leadership of a prophet and anti-witch hunter named Akalali, from which the more affluent ('with their yellow-red bag from the Tax Free Shop of Schiphol Airport') were able to escape.[29] In addition, towards the final years of the 1980s, the Jungle Command led by Ronnie Brunswijk adopted various cults in order to protect him and his troops during the Internal War (see p. 326).

A notorious affair arose in 2006 and 2007 pertaining to a witch hunter named Gangáa who ordered thugs inhabiting villages in the Tapanahoni region to target those more affluent. When the Paramaribo judge sentenced him to jail, young Maroons contested the judiciary's competence to rule on such an issue.[30] Cults were now and again also directed against Brazilian gold diggers whenever they arrived at undesired locations. For, certain Ndyuka men, led by ritualists adhering to a deity named Agedeonsu, the protector of man and nature, chased as many as 2,000 Brazilians away from the Sela Kreek and into the Tapanahoni region. In 2009 the same fate befell Brazilian gold diggers as well as several of their Ndyuka co-workers in a sacred forest located at the Djuka Kreek.[31] Cults thus played a role in the Maroon struggle for land rights which notably flared up after the turn of the 21st century (see p. 385ff.).

---

25   Thoden van Velzen & Van Wetering 1988, 233-237; Van Wetering & Thoden van Velzen 2013, 201-223; the latter publication also describes *posthouder* W.F. van Lier's intriguing role hereby treating *granman* Amaketi, the strike leader, in a humiliating manner. During a visit to Paramaribo, for example, Amaketi was denied being welcomed by the then governor. Ndyuka men sabotaged Van Lier's operations from then on; for further information on the Nyudka boatmen's strike, see: H.U.E. Thoden van Velzen 2003.

26   Thoden van Velzen & Van Wetering 1988, 121-135, 387-389.

27   Ibid., 129.

28   Thoden van Velzen & Hoogbergen 2011, 315.

29   Thoden van Velzen 1990 (lecture); see also: Thoden van Velzen & Van Wetering 1988, 331-386.

30   Van Wetering & Thoden van Velzen 2013, 313-315.

31   Van Wetering & Thoden van Velzen 2013, 330; Thoden van Velzen & Hoogbergen 2011, 145-146, 295-296.

Disruptive developments within the Ndyuka society resulting from a 'boom in demon belief' (as expressed by Gangá's performance) have been observed since the end of the 20th century by Thoden van Velzen (and co-authors).[32] Values its members traditionally embraced now disappeared. They had comprised cultural consultation, civilized manners and rituals pertaining to time-honoured tutelary spirits, including those revered by Kumanti-speaking religious practitioners. This heritage was replaced by a belief in demons, whereby differences in wealth played a key role and also directed against gerontocracy. Ndyuka entrepreneurs were threatened as well as vilified. Thoden van Velzen however opined that traditional mourning and burial rituals did continue to form an interconnecting force.

6.2 Amerindians in the colonial society

After the pacification of 1686, specific Indigenous groups gradually receded towards the periphery of the society of Suriname although they did continue to assist white colonists in their struggle against fugitive slaves. After peace treaties had been signed with the Maroons, Indigenous people were no longer of great importance to colonists. An assistant commissioner serving the domestic population merely states on these Amerindians in one of his annual reports:

> 'They are located at a few places in the colony. Not the slightest news came to my attention about them in the course of 1871.'[33]

In Suriname no official information was at that time available pertaining to the exact number of Amerindians. Contacts through trade, Protestant and the later founded Roman Catholic missions did exist. During the mid-18th century, the Hernhutters had started interacting with Amerindians, to wit, Caribs and Arawak populating the coastal plain, located at the lower reaches of rivers. In *c*.1760 several hundred Amerindians were converted by Hernhutters, but in 1808 such activities were terminated. A large group of converts had several years earlier fled the important missionary post of Saron, established on the Saramacca River, in order to seek refuge in the forest. They chose to do so after suffering from reprisals carried out by Maroons in revenge for the help offered to colonists during the struggle against runaways.[34] Only in 1866 did Roman Catholic missionaries become active among Amerindians. The Redemptorist Petrus Norbertus Donders (1809-1877), who was beatified in 1982 for his work amid lepers, had laid the foundation for this Indigenous Catholic mission.

Very early chroniclers did describe Amerindians and their way of life, but their knowledge did not reach far. On occasion myths were created. In his *Nieuwe Caerte van het wonderbaer ende goudrijcke landt Guiana* [...] (1599), for instance, the Amsterdam cartographer Jodocus Hondius portrayed an Amerindian as a headless human creature (see p. 10). Moreover, in a 28-page report entitled *An Impartial Description of Surinam* [...] (London 1667), George Warren included a 5-page description of

---

32   Thoden van Velzen & Hoogbergen 2011, 305-313; Van Wetering & Thoden van Velzen 2013, 311-329.
33   Wekker 1992, 109-110.
34   Ibid., 103-105.

the ´Indians´.[35] He describes their 'Bread and Drink' made from cassava and their boats 'made of one entire piece, being Trees cut hollow like a Trough'. Warren also addressed other aspects of the Indigenous way of life. The grace of the Amerindian women proved especially eye-catching:

> '*The women are generally lascivious, and some so truly handsom, as to Features and Proportion, that if the most Curious Symetrian had been there, he could not but subscribe to my opinion: and their pretty Bashfulness (especially while Virgins) in the presence of a Stranger, adds such a Charming grace to their perfections (too nakedly expos'd to every wanton Eye) that who ever lives among them had need be owner of no less than Joseph's Continency, not at least to Cover their embraces: They have been yet so unfortunately ignorant, not to enrich their amorous Caresses with that innocent and warm delight of Kissing, but Conversing so frequently with Christians, and being naturally docile and ingenious, we have Reason to believe they will in time be taught it.*'[36]

Sexual relations between colonists and Amerindian women already existed at the dawn of colonisation. After the 1686 treaty was signed, Governor Van Aerssen van Sommelsdijck chose a native woman as his wife, a commitment partly intended to underline his desire for peace with Amerindians; in addition, he organised visits to the Netherlands in order to improve Dutch-Amerindian relations.[37] Thomas Pistorius, a member of the Court of Police and Criminal Justice, is slightly more elaborate when dealing with ethnic groups. However, he held no high opinion as to their capacities and life styles:

> '[...] *but of whose life and religion due of ignorance thereof, one can not say much; only I have observed this, that they are very disorderly in their way of life and indifferent in all matters, content themselves with everything however unworthy the objects may be; from which I conclude that they should not have much knowledge, and equal the beasts there, which, when they only have their food but for the rest live on, without making the least reflection of any of the natural causes thereon, and even less so any religious.*'[38]

August Kappler was the first colonist to show any genuine interest in Amerindians. After initially being employed as a soldier, he settled down in 1842 near the Marowijne River to found a timber, agricultural and livestock enterprise. Kappler, who also served as a resident administrator (see p. 139), built a small homestead named Albina in honour of his fiancé and future wife. His knowledge of the Maroons was impressive. In his own words, he could get along better with Amerindians whenever they visited or worked for him.

---

35   Warren 1667, 23-28.
36   Ibid., 23-24.
37   Oudschans Dentz 1938, 84-87.
38   Pistorius 1763, 14-15.

A History of Suriname

Only from the beginning of the 20th century onwards did one set off on expeditions upstream into the interior, where Amerindians lived. For instance, the naval officer-*cum*-anthropologist C.H. de Goeje (1879-1955) encountered the Wayana people during his journey to the Tapanahoni and the Paloemeu Rivers.[39] In 1926 and 1938, the redemptorist Willem Ahlbrinck (1885-1966), having maintained numerous contacts with Amerindians, led expeditions into the upper reaches of the Corantijn River and the Oelemari River.[40] At the start of the 20th century, too, the Suriname-born brothers Arthur Philip Penard (1880-1932) and Frederik Paul Penard (1876-1909) significantly contributed to the knowledge of Amerindians.[41]

The Wayana people, having emerged from an intermingling of several ethnic groups, were initially located in the Amazon region. During the 18th century, a number of them crossed the not too wide watershed in order to reach Suriname, thus fleeing Amerindians armed by Portuguese. The Indigenous Wayana settled down in the Litani region, on the upper part of the Marowijne River Basin. Later they travelled a little further in a northerly direction, attracted by the trade with the Ndyuka, who offered them axes and machetes in exchange for hammocks and trained hunting dogs.[42] The fact that Maroons controlled the lower reaches of rivers may explain why the Wayana came into contact with Europeans at a relatively late stage. In 1937, De Goeje estimated the number of Wayana to be *c.*600, spread across 20 villages.[43]

In addition to the Wayana, the Trio had also settled on the upper reaches of the Paloemeu, Tapanahoni and Coeroeni Rivers. The Indigenous Trio, including smaller groups related to Caribs, had been pushed towards the south by Maroons, with whom they traded. In 1937, the nomadic Akurio, a small Trio group, had briefly encountered white people for the first time during an expedition led by Admiral C.C. Kayser, who was commissioned to determine the exact border between Suriname and Brazil.[44] One year later, Father Willem Ahlbrinck was prompted to equip an expedition in order to contact the Akurio. On 25 September 1938, he met a young woman and child at the Oelemari River:

'We know several Wajana words and shout: jèpë, meaning 'friend'. Then in trade language used between Ndyuka and upstream living Indians: Itoto-wa, meaning 'we are no enemies': and in Carib: 'jacono', meaning friend. In vain! The young woman - who later turned out to be a young mother - walks with her child to the other side of the camp. She shouts, she thrusts the high sounds from the throat with force, she throws them far into the forest, against the slope of the nearest mountain: 'Itoto [...] itoto!' [...] the enemy. [...] Then the approaching man finally brings the solution. I still see him appear from behind the bushes, following the path, straight

---

39   De Goeje 1941, 71-125.

40   Ahlbrinck 1956.

41   Penard & Penard 1907/1908; this publication includes many narratives passed on orally.

42   Boven 1992, 145-161; Boven 2006, 59-62.

43   De Goeje 1941, 72.

44   Boven 2006, 83.

Figure 6.5. Young Wayana during the visit (1955) of Juliana Queen of the Netherlands to Albina (East Suriname). Note their various ethnic paraphernalia and adornments, traditional body painting and a hand-held Dutch flag. Photo by Willem van de Poll. National Archives, The Hague.

towards us. A stocky, sturdy stature, completely naked, the eyes feral, the fierce face
completely pale! The right arm raised, in the threatening hand the short stone axe!
The left arm hangs down, bow and thick bundle of arrows in hand.'[45]

After a peaceful encounter, Ahlbrinck cum suis stayed at a camp set up by Akurio who after 2 days disappeared only to be 'rediscovered' 30 years later. A majority hereof was voluntarily transferred to Trio villages, where American missionaries had become very active.[46]

The lives that the members of various Indigenous groups led during the colonial era disclosed great similarities. They were farmers, hunter-gatherers and fishermen; only the Akurio were unfamiliar with agriculture. Cassava was the main crop, followed by sweet potato, tobacco, corn, pumpkin, sugar cane and

---

45   Ahlbrinck 1956, 98.
46   Bruijning & Voorhoeve 1977, 19.

cotton. Amerindians chopped down trees to create fields in the forests and then set fire to the felled wood, resulting in good compost. After a few years they left their villages and the exhausted soil in order to start again elsewhere. Women were especially active as farmers and were also involved either in gathering fruit, ants, palm larvae, crabs and turtle eggs, or in the production of cotton and pottery. Hunting and fishing were tasked to men. For Amerindians living upstream, hunting was of more importance than fishing; for those residing downstream it was the other way round. When hunting large game, poisonous arrowheads were applied. Amerindians living downstream had access to guns, a result of contacts with white colonists. Varied fishing methods were applied, as yet excluding any nets. August Kappler, whose knowledge was limited to the Caribs and the Arawak, mentions their use of fishhooks and angling rods. He also describes how fish were shot with arrows after a creek was first closed off by way of wickerwork. After adding poisonous plants to the water, the stunned fish could be caught by hand.[47]

The life of an Amerindian was generally speaking family-centered. Labour was divided between spouses. Most men had one wife, but village chiefs and shamans, ritual specialists, were often polygamous. Each family occupied a separate hut. Wedding ceremonies were far from elaborate. Boys married at around 19 years of age, girls often 4 or 5 years earlier. Among Caribs, it was customary for boys to inform their parents when they wished to marry a certain girl. The boy's father then visited that girl's father to offer him an Amerindian cigar. If the latter did not wish this boy to become his future son-in-law or if his daughter did not wish to marry him, the cigar was refused. This outcome was less offensive than a direct rejection. Both men discussed fishing and weather conditions for a while before taking leave. If the answer was positive, the boy sent a fish to the girl. If she then cooked it, she indicated her wish to marry. Having sent this fish or some other foodstuff to the boy, his final vows consisted of eating what was presented. A few days later, the girl would move the boy's hammock to her father's house to hang it next to hers. The marital rites were completed when both had slept together. The first stage was considered a 'trial marriage'. In due course the couple built their own house, often adjacent to that of the girl's parents. Divorce procedures were not complicated, but nonetheless exceptions.[48] Rites of passage did not occur among all ethnic groups. The maturation of boys amidst the Indigenous peoples of the Caribs was a gradual process. For example, the Wayana applied the so-called wasp test to boys and girls whereby a mat to which wasps were attached was rubbed on a child's skin, forcing him or her to endure the stings of these insects.[49]

The Amerindian leadership was not well-developed. Only during times of war, before the pacification in 1686, did real leaders emerge. Villages were small and often home to not more than a few dozen souls. Thus, a need for any powerful leaders did not exist.[50] Chiefs, often the founders of settlements, were not even able to impose their will on others. Whenever they tried to, the majority of villagers

---

47 Kloos 1971, 26-73; Kappler 1854, 46-50.
48 Kloos 1971, 74-142.
49 De Goeje 1941, 109-110.
50 Kloos 1971, 154-187.

would leave. Life was generally speaking harmonious. Conflicts usually arose only during festivities, when invariably large quantities of alcohol were consumed. It may be added here that among Caribs a cassava-based alcoholic beverage (*casiri*), to this very day is synonymous with a 'small celebration'.[51] The shaman (*piai*), whom Amerindians deemed an intermediary with the spirit world, continued to uphold a certain authority in the villages. Interrelated groups all included such a ritual practitioner. On occasion his intermediary tasks in part conformed to those which village chiefs fulfilled. The *piai* was first and foremost a healer. His role is therefore linked to the cause of diseases which, according to Amerindians, is to be found in the supernatural world. A shaman performed rites such as exhaling tobacco smoke and seeing to it tobacco juice was consumed. A male could choose to be trained as a *piai*, whereby the key incentive comprised a disease which had struck either him or his children.[52]

From the second half of the 19th century on, the majority of Amerindians residing upstream were converted to Roman Catholicism. These ethnic groups while proving more receptive to Christianity than Maroons, apparently did not see any contradictions between the Western view on faith and their own spirit world.[53] Nevertheless, after many years of intensive contacts, Father Ahlbrinck, a renowned connoisseur of the Surinamese Amerindians, did acknowledge that the feelings of Amerindians were still 'a closed book' to him:

> '*But I do suspect, that - if one wants to paint the Indian faithfully - one must above all keep in mind: the Indian is free. He knows no bonds. Not any kind of bonds. When he bows or bends, it is not out of free choice. Then there is coercion.*'[54]

The number of contacts Amerindians maintained with the outside world only grew, especially from the second half of the 20th century on. In addition, an increasingly intensive struggle for land rights contributed to the emancipation of this Indigenous group (see p. 385-386) of which none turned its back on any form of modernisation. A standard work on the Wayana states that Amerindians, residing in Suriname, French Guiana and Brazil, were not and are not passive but 'actors of social change'. Whenever they are depicted primarily as the 'exotic other', as numerous observers have done, a static image of Indigenous people is wrongly created.[55] Simultaneously, a desire to preserve the Amerindian identity is to be noted. Chief Ricardo Pané, residing at the Carib village of Christiaankondre which, in combination with Langamankondre, forms a settlement named Galibi (located at the mouth of the Marowijne River), stated near the end of the 1900s:

---

51 Ibid., 188.
52 Ibid., 209-237.
53 Ibid., 234-236.
54 Ahlbrinck 1956, 51.
55 Boven 2006, 12-19. Following in the footsteps of present-day anthropologists, Boven distances herself from the concept of structuralism of which C. Levi-Strauss is the most prominent representative. In its often idyllic descriptions of so-called primitive societies which include an emphasis on harmony, she emphasizes (on p. 16) that structuralism ignores 'the presence of internal tensions, conflicts, personal motives, quarrels, separation and division of groups, in other words the space for change from within'.

'We are in a new world. Every people has developed at the expense of a certain piece of themselves. Withdrawing seems to me to be wrong, you try to maintain the core of your culture during each development; it is a treasure you do not want to lose. By introducing all kinds of modern things, the Carib culture is in decline, that is a fact. [...] In French Guiana almost everything has vanished, Suriname is at risk of moving in the same direction. [...] We are working on the preservation of mores and customs. We still have musical instruments such as the maraka and sambura, costumes etc. But in thirty, or forty years? Maybe we can no longer talk about the original inhabitants of Suriname.'[56]

---

56   Van Kempen 2002, vol. 2, 160.

CHAPTER 7
Emancipation of the enslaved

During the second half of the 18th century, British abolitionists had acquired a large following, whereas slavery was hardly discussed in the Netherlands at the beginning of the 19th century. Perhaps the presence of thousands of slaves in Britain, brought in from its colonies by their owners, explains this discrepancy. Moreover, the influence of modern thought, inspired by the Enlightenment and economic liberalism, was not that strong in the Netherlands, where the innovative industrialisation developed much later than in Great Britain and where fears of an economic decline were more prevalent.

In as early as 1772, a British judge determined, in a case pertaining to a runaway London slave, there was no legal basis for slavery in the country. This court ruling hugely boosted the anti-slavery movement, inspired by evangelical and humanist concepts. At that time a majority of the Dutch had not personally observed examples of slavery although certain planters, having returned from Suriname, did employ Black domestic servants. In the Netherlands, one was unfamiliar with an abolitionist with a stature comparable to that of William Wilberforce (1759-1833), the politician-*cum*-philanthropist.[1] Moreover, in 1789, thousands of copies of the autobiography written by the former slave Olaudah Equiano (*c.*1745-1797) had been sold in Great Britain, impressing readers with his unique account of the difficult lives of the enslaved.[2] The British anti-slavery movement achieved an important milestone when the Houses of Parliament approved a ban, in 1807, on trading slaves across the colonial empire. This measure also extended to Suriname, which had fallen under British administration since 1804.[3] The fact that this legislation pertaining to the slave trade gained majority support in the British parliament was also the result of the tactic pursued by for example Wilberforce: to interpret the proposal as a measure directed against France, which was indeed aimed at preventing British traders from selling slaves to foreign powers.[4]

Due to Europe-based conflicts, Suriname had already witnessed turbulent times. The *Sociëteit van Suriname* (henceforth Society) was dissolved as a result of the proclamation in 1795 of the Batavian Republic, now a de facto vassal state of France. From this moment on, all Dutch possessions obtained in Africa as well as in North and South America were subjected to a special committee, which comprised the Patriots, an activist group opposing the House of Orange-Nassau. Suriname looked upon the French Revolution with concern. For, in Paramaribo, the fear rose now that

---

1   Oostindie 1992, 147-170.
2   Equiano 1995 (1789).
3   Wolbers 1861, 547.
4   During the 1780s, William Wilberforce's friend, William Pitt the Younger who served as Prime Minister of Great Britain (1783-1801) had already established that British traders were increasing French sugar production by selling half their slaves to French colonies, including the leading sugar producer Saint-Domingue which, in 1804, was to become the first free Black republic and to be called Haiti after a slave revolt; see: C.L.R. James *The Black Jacobins: Toussaint L'Ouverture and the San Domingo Revolution* 1963, 53-54.

the spirit of 'liberty, equality and fraternity' would spread among those enslaved. The Governor-general of Suriname, J. F. de Friderici (1792-1801), a supporter of the House of Orange-Nassau, had therefore considered placing French Guiana under his authority in 1793. Nevertheless, the Court of Police and Criminal Justice felt a military intervention carried out by Suriname was too great a risk. In August 1794, several planters forwarded the same request to this Court, after it had become known that the French had abolished slavery earlier that same year (as it turned out later, temporarily) in an attempt to suppress the unprecedented slave revolt in Saint-Domingue (1791-1804). However, this Court dismissed a request to intervene again for the same reason.[5] In due course De Friderici decided to resign to the new order as established in patria, despite Willem V, Prince of Orange (who had sought refuge in Great Britain) asking to allow British warships to prevent a possible French invasion.[6]

A revolutionary spirit was never observed in Suriname, probably also because slaves who had tried in vain to reach French Guiana were severely punished after being captured.[7] Attempting to avert any potential dangers in Suriname, De Friderici had interdicted, in 1795, the founding of societies which spoke of 'human rights'.[8] The French revolutionary spirit, on the other hand, did reach the Dutch colony of Curaçao. On this isle, the developments in Saint-Domingue could be closely followed thanks to the close trade connections. The revolt on August 17, 1795 was led by a local slave called Tula. Aware of the French abolition of slavery, he declared that 'Holland has been taken over by the French, hence we too must be free'. Tula, nicknamed Rigaud after one of the insurgents in Saint-Domingue, was arrested on September 19 and publicly tortured to death on October 3.[9]

The alliance with France was, after all, short-lived. After a British fleet had appeared near the mouth of the Suriname River on 13 August 1799, De Friderici and members of the aforementioned Court soon decided to place Suriname 'under the immediate protection of His British Majesty'.[10] Planters here never had much trouble changing their loyalty as long as they were able to continue trading. Their relationships with the French were already disturbed as they constantly prevented American trading vessels from shipping cargo. Having signed the Peace Treaty of Amiens in 1802, hereby ending this Anglo-French war, the Dutch colony was returned to the Batavian Republic, the flag of which had only briefly flown on the Fort Zeelandia. After hostilities in Europe between Great Britain and France had resumed, a large number of British warships were once again spotted off the coast of Suriname on 25 April 1804. Next, less than 600 troops had to fight between 4,000 and 5,000 British soldiers and marines. The latter easily conquered bulwarks named Purmerend, Leijden and Friderici, all located on either bank of the Suriname River. Next, capitulating was inevitable as British troops also threatened to

---

5   Wolbers 1861, 456.
6   Ibid., 459-461.
7   Ibid., 456.
8   Ibid., 463.
9   Fatah-Black 2013b, 35-60; for further details on the abolition of slavery in Saint-Domingue and other French colonies, see: James 1963, 139-144.
10   Wolbers 1861, 484.

capture Fort Nieuw Amsterdam by means of an unexpected attack from the landside. The members of the aforementioned Court had no intention of defending the colony for fear of losing planters' property.[11]

Compared with the Dutch government, the British authorities expressed more compassion towards the fate of the enslaved population. For, in 1814, Pinson Bonham, the last British Governor of Suriname, announced new rules and regulations in order to prevent any form of arbitrary punishment. In Fort Zeelandia, slaves were only allowed to be punished after a written accusation had been forwarded, whereas the sentence imposed could only be executed after 48 hours. Bonham did not hesitate to prosecute those who maltreated slaves.[12]

The British ban on the slave trade was the most drastic measure to be imposed on Suriname. King Willem I adopted this initiative in 1814 when, after the signing of the peace treaty between England and France, Suriname returned into Dutch hands. However, Willem I did not act of his own free will. The British saw to it this ban was included in the treaty dealing with the transfer of Suriname as they were not driven by mere idealistic incentives. For, a fear of entering into an unfair competition at least played an equally important role. British naval vessels already regularly patrolled the African coast in order to intercept any illegal slave shipments.[13]

In 1818, an Anglo-Dutch court was established in Paramaribo. Its specific task comprised the punishing of slave smugglers. During its 27-year existence, this court only intervened on one occasion. Dutch slave traders of old had long since developed other activities (see p. 165).[14] For shrewd captains it was not difficult to ship African slaves to Suriname by way of false documents, as the restrictions did not apply to trade in slaves who had already been in one of the colonies in the year 1818. The colonial government initially did little to prevent this form of deception as the need for labour on the plantations of Suriname remained great. The illegal trafficking of thousands of slaves only ended when, in 1826, Governor Abraham de Veer (1822-1828) forced planters to maintain a better means of registration. A year earlier De Veer had successfully imposed severe sentences on offenders, penalties to the amount of 10,000 guilders, 15-year prison terms and the forfeiture of vessels. He seized the cargo of several ships, thus bringing slaves under governmental control. The aforementioned court was not involved in these interventions, because its jurisdiction only concerned Dutch and British ships.[15] The colonial administration did attempt to promote import from other colonies in the West Indies by means of a premium system.[16] Nonetheless the permanent mortality surplus among those enslaved led to increasing labour shortages. The Dutch government, while closely scrutinizing developments in Great Britain therefore judged improving the conditions for slaves to be the key objective of its policy.

To this goal, major-general Johannes van den Bosch (1780-1844) was appointed, in 1827, to officiate as commissioner-general of the Dutch West Indies with a special

---

11   Ibid., 503-505.
12   Ibid., 568.
13   Ibid., 608.
14   Ibid., 608; Siwpersad 1979, 45-68.
15   Wolbers 1861, 620-622; Siwpersad 1979, 47-50.
16   Wolbers 1861, 651.

responsibility for monitoring the welfare of the enslaved. He had to consider how their 'morality' and intermarrying could be enhanced, as this would promote reproduction. Van den Bosch not only deemed heavy labour and insufficient nutrition to be major causes of a mortality surplus but also opined that 'an animalistic gratification of their desires' was the only bliss known to 'negroes', allowing venereal diseases to spread.[17] Van den Bosch reported it was difficult to transform the lifestyle of slaves because their behaviour included a certain independence. In his view, only a religious education could contribute to this adaptation in the long run. At any rate, the treatment and nutrition of slaves had to be improved. Rules and regulations must be laid down pertaining to labour that could be required from slaves. They should not be transferred from one plantation to the next against their will. Pregnant women and nursing mothers ought to be exempted from heavy work. Planters must not sell husbands and wives separately after a 'slave marriage' had taken place; notably, Van den Bosch's recommendations aimed at transforming the master's ownership of slaves into a right to their labour 'as far as their civilisation allows'; in addition, slaves should be allowed to serve as witnesses.[18] Although the government of Suriname had requested Van den Bosch to investigate a possible alteration in the status of those enslaved, this issue was not considered very urgent and thus nothing changed. Genuine emancipation was out of the question. The Dutch government thus continued to observe opportunities pertaining to Suriname's agriculture, whereby it considered slaves to be indispensable. For, emancipating them would only burden the Dutch treasury, for example, when financially compensating their owners, especially now King Willem I strongly promoted prosperity in the Netherlands.

Key elements aimed at improving the living conditions of slaves were included in a government regulation dated 1828. Considering it a step too far, conservative planters were particularly opposed to article 117, which sought to provide a slave with a better protection against their owner's arbitrary conduct:

'The slaves will, as far as the daily treatment in relation to their owners is concerned, be considered to be immature to their curators or guardians, to whom the right is reserved to exercise paternal disciplinary authority over them, but against whose maltreatment all public authorities are obliged to guard, and to ensure that the law, designed in their interest, is strictly maintained; the unjust principle definitively being abolished that they can only be considered as property and not as persons by law.'[19]

The provision to consider slaves as individual human beings arose from the colonial administration's desire to allow marriages in order to further promote reproduction. By and large, planters strongly opposed such a fundamental change. Fifty colonists turned to King Willem I stating in a petition that, in their view,

---

17   Siwpersad 1979, 79.
18   Ibid., 80-81.
19   Wolbers 1861, 642-643.

'[...] article 117 had caused misunderstanding and agitation among many negroes, since they now thought they were being oppressed and were under the delusion that the king wished to abolish slavery.'[20]

These colonists also raised serious objections against a ban on transporting slaves to other plantations if they did not wish to move. This measure would cause major economic damage, as a decrease in the profitability of growing coffee and cotton plants would lead to a greater focus on sugar cultivation. For the very same reason, colonists opined that banning the separate sale of enslaved families was equally unacceptable. When the authorities conceded quite quickly the article in question was no longer part of the incoming government regulations dated 1832. Instead, a proviso was introduced allowing slave owners to act in full freedom. The colonial administration only had to improve the living conditions of slaves 'as far as this can be done without infringing the rights of the owners, and without jeopardising the peace and safety of the colony'.[21] With a similar success, colonists opposed those changes in government, which threatened to terminate their political dominance. The Court of Police and Criminal Justice, which strongly represented the power of the planters, was no longer mentioned in government rules and regulations dated 1828. This court had been replaced by means of a High Council, which included the four most senior officials ranked immediately below the governor-general. In 1816, after the Kingdom of the Netherlands was founded, the judiciary (having already been separated from legislative and executive powers) was positioned in a separate court. In the government rules and regulations dated 1832, eminent residents continued to be represented in the Colonial Council. [22]

Although the Colonial Council was merely to serve as an advisory body and the governor-general's position had been reinforced, Suriname remained the plantocracy it had always been. Van den Bosch's recommendations upon which the incoming rules and regulations pertaining to slaves should have been based, were of course not to be put in place. A draft composed by the Governor-general Paulus Roelof Cantz'laar (1771-1831) was not acceptable to the then Minister of Colonies, Cornelis Theodorus Elout (1767-1841), because of its 'extraordinary severity', a reference to milder forms of punishment carried out in the British colonies.[23] Further incoming initiatives were not expected, as the Dutch government was already amply burdened by means of the Belgian Revolution of 1830.

Nevertheless Van den Bosch's mission was not without implications. His plea for religious instruction among those enslaved led to the Moravian Brethren gradually gaining more access to plantations. In 1828, five eminent colonists, to wit, the attorney-general, a Lutheran and a Reformed pastor, a Dutch judge of the Anglo-Dutch court and a planter teamed up to establish the *Maatschappij ter bevordering van het Godsdienstig Onderwijs onder de Slaven en verdere Heidensche bevolking in de Kolonie Suriname* (Society for the promotion of Religious Education among the

---

20   Ibid., 664.
21   Ibid., 675.
22   Ibid., 639-641, 672-673.
23   Siwpersad 1979, 82-83.

Slaves and remaining Pagan population in the Colony of Suriname).[24] These five held the view that Moravians were, thanks to their experience, ideally suited to take on a missionary role. Branches of the aforementioned society were established in towns across the Netherlands, too. Its headquarters located at The Hague led to this institute being referred to as the *Haagsche Maatschappij* (Hague Society). Its board members included senior civil servants, ministers and plantation owners. The latter often considered the religious tuition of their slaves an important tool with which peace and order could be maintained. After all, the Moravian Brethren had never fundamentally opposed slavery. Indeed, two contented planters did report to the Amsterdam branch of the *Haagsche Maatschappij* the fact that, at *Rust en Werk* (Rest and Work) as well as several other plantations,

> '[...] *religious education did not cause the slightest disturbance of the good order, but that among the black workers living on these plantations peace and contentment always reigns, and that the esteem and love for their Gentlemen and Directors has increased.*'[25]

However, the Dutch government was not granted much peace and tranquillity. The diligence the British expressed as to the slavery issue affected Suriname where the emancipation experienced in 1833 across all their colonies caused its inhabitants to suffer from terrifying visions. Slaves in Suriname had taken note of the social changes occurring in British Guyana. A rumour concerning emancipation had already reached those enslaved populating the nearby Nickerie district - not a huge surprise as slaves manned schooners which maintained trade contacts with British Guyana, Suriname's neighbour. On 24 December 1831, a local administrator reported to the Governor-general E.L. Baron van Heeckeren (1784-1838) that 'a rebellious spirit prevailed among the slaves'. In Nickerie even 'a conspiracy to revolt' was rumoured.[26]

This rising did not unfold, but the unrest continued. Amsterdam-based merchants considered the danger to be that substantial they requested their monarch to reinforce the garrison in Suriname with 2,000 men. Nevertheless only 200 troops were sent, because the Dutch treasury could not afford the costs.[27] Immediately following the aforementioned emancipation of 1833, the Dutch colonial government had banned all forms of communication between Nickerie (Suriname) and Berbice (British Guiana). A boat was stationed on the Corantijn River in order to prevent those enslaved from absconding. Though their numbers were limited, the threat that a spirit of emancipation was gathering momentum remained, especially whenever slaves from Paramaribo managed to reach Berbice.[28]

In 1836, an extensive conspiracy led by a slave named Colin was revealed in Coronie (Suriname), the final district in which new (cotton) plantations had been established. After 1808, this resulted in the import of many slaves from British-owned islands. They longed for more freedom having realized the outcome of the

---

24   Wolbers 1861, 645-648..
25   Zeefuik 1973, 174.
26   Wolbers 1861, 813-814.
27   Ibid., 814.
28   Ibid.

emancipation in the colonies of their former masters. Colin had locked himself up for years in his hut located on a cotton plantation named Leasowes, after his master had punished him for inciting others to refuse to work.[29] Colin's religious movement is interesting because of its messianic traits. He presented himself to his fellow slaves as God, who had returned to Earth in order to free them from slavery. In secret meetings he stated that a great flood would destroy the white people. The movement, whose followers addressed Colin as *Tata* (father), *Gadu* (God) or King, resembles the 'despair religions' encountered among Maroons since the end of the 19th century (see p. 149-150).[30] After being betrayed, he and nine of his key accomplices were arrested. Having been sentenced to death, Colin passed away prematurely inside a prison cell.

Slavery in Suriname was not only influenced by the situation in British Guyana. The presence in Paramaribo of British judges attached to the Anglo-Dutch court was at least of equal importance. Certain judges expressed a rather specific view on their duties, which reached far beyond their mandate. Claiming to be true abolitionists, they openly denounced the fate of Suriname's enslaved. This stance not only caused tensions to rise between these judges and the then Governor-general, but also between The Hague and London.

These conflicts included the status of several hundred Africans who had by and large illegally disembarked from North American and French ships to then be detained by the colonial administration of Suriname and subsequently added to the government slaves. Much commotion arose regarding these so-called *snownegers* ('snow negroes'), who had been transported from Africa on a slave vessel called *Snow of the Los Nuevos*. In 1823, the Anglo-Dutch court had not only declared they were free but had also seen to it they were to be transferred to the colonial administration. However, it was only in 1843 that *snownegers* obtained their freedom, after the British envoy at The Hague had intervened.[31] Two years later, in excess of 400 government slaves were declared to be 'free negroes'.[32] Several Africans had already secretly fallen into the hands of private slave owners. The reason for the government's prolonged hesitation as to releasing the *snownegers* is revealed in a letter the Governor-general of the West Indies, Julius C. Rijk (1787-1854), wrote on 26 July 1841 to the Minister of Colonies, Jean C. Baud (1789-1859):

'How will those 29 remaining persons be released without causing a severe turmoil among the other government slaves, many of whom being in the same situation, and since it is known that in the English possessions the emancipation has started with the release of government slaves, so this will undeniably be considered by the entire slave population to be a beginning of Emancipation in these regions and the consequences this can have for the colony are difficult to calculate in advance. I consider this matter to be the most thorny of all the difficulties I have already experienced in my administration.'[33]

---

29   Voorhoeve & Van Renselaar 1962, 193-216.
30   Ibid., 200-211.
31   Siwpersad 1979, 47-48, 53-60.
32   Ibid., 59.
33   Ibid., 54.

The fear of unrest had been so immense that the incoming Governor-general Burchard J. Elias (1799-1871) commissioned the *snownegers* to be shipped to British Guyana. The constant pressure the British government imposed on the Netherlands was also motivated by the apprehension as to unfair competition from within Suriname. Moreover, the British government witnessed a great deal of coercion from a growing number of abolitionists active in its own kingdom. They had founded the British and Foreign Anti-Slavery Society in 1839. The British judges of the Anglo-Dutch court had continuously provided their London-based government with information aimed at besetting The Hague with diplomatic notes. Judge E.W.H. Schenley, who resided in Suriname between 1842 and 1845, went the furthest when interfering with the living conditions of slaves. After being informed of cases of abuse, Schenley did not hesitate to turn directly to the then Governor-general. Now and again slaves themselves secretly reported such incidences to him. His stance caused huge resentment amongst planters. J.C. Baud, the Minister of Colonies, saw no other option but to not only formally request London to recall Schenley but also to possibly move the Anglo-Dutch court to Curaçao.[34] Baud was especially upset when the British government commissioned Schenley's letters addressed to the Foreign Office to be published in order to benefit the Houses of Parliament. In a letter dated 13 November 1844 Baud informed King Willem II that he considered Schenley's presence in Suriname to be 'extremely dangerous':

> *'In his letters he acknowledges that he has channels to do research right down to the heart of the colony. Steadily he utters complaints of slaves, for many years according to his say illegally imported, - and that because of the insistence of England investigations have taken place, which would make most titles of ownership [...] uncertain and endanger the peace, without it being possible to come to the knowledge of the truth in all this, after that what happened to most of the slaves in that twenty-year period. - He receives the complaints of slaves who consider themselves to have been abused, and will on those occasions not say much to the praise of the Dutch government, which he continuously accuses of shameful cruelty and deliberate duplicity. Designs to buy en masse all slaves who are present in Suriname, and to bring them to Demerary, are reasoned and praised by him. - He has, with one word, become a foreign protective power which has penetrated between the slaves and their masters, and endangers the peace of the colony. [...] This interference encourages the slaves to resist, - the masters to increased severity, and is therefore most dangerous, and it is particularly harmful because it will frustrate all attempts by Your Majesty's Government to improve the situation of the slaves through calm and gradual measures, by depriving those measures of the indispensable cooperation of their owners.'*[35]

Judge Schenley had however already decided to leave Suriname after two of his horses had been poisoned and a planter had filed a slander charge against him.

---

34   Ibid., 63.
35   Ibid., 63-64.

A History of Suriname

The British government did not appoint a successor after his departure in 1845. The Anglo-Dutch court therefore ceased to exist.[36]

Schenley's actions had further hampered the already tense relationship between Governor-general Elias and the colonists. He had informed Elias of certain slave maltreatment cases. Wishing to confine the domestic jurisdiction of slave owners, Elias provoked a trial against a prominent colonist named G. L. Röpperhof, an administrator and member of the Colonial Council. Elias however underestimated the colonists' resistance. A conservative attorney-general gave them his support. Although a court dismissed the case, this dispute nonetheless escalated further shortly after Röpperhof's membership of the Colonial Council was suspended as a result of an offensive letter sent to Elias. This Governor-general dismissed yet another councillor after ordering one of his slaves to be punished in an atrocious manner. In due course Elias also expelled the other Colonial Council members as well as one member and two substitute members of the Court of Justice after they had violated a Royal Decree disallowing them to sign protest letters directed against authorities.[37] Amsterdam-based stakeholders had often called for Elias's dismissal. Minister Baud however refused to yield to this pressure and initially did not accept Elias's personal request to be removed. In 1845 the latter, tired of bickering with colonists, was allowed to return to the Netherlands. In his opinion, the majority of the colonists were 'unscrupulous people' and merely interested in 'vile self-interest'.[38]

Immediately after the emancipation in the British colonies, Dutch authorities refrained from drawing up innovative rules and regulations resulting in a better treatment of slaves, fearing that any alterations in the status quo would lead to unrest. After a few years, however, concerns about slaves fleeing to British Guyana and into the forests increased again as did the need to take action. Apparently even at The Hague one now realised that releasing slaves would become inevitable. A key indication hereof can be found in a memorandum the Dutch government dispatched to London on 12 November 1841 in order to voice its objections against the 'inflammatory' language with which the written press in British Guiana welcomed slaves who had fled from Suriname.[39] This notice explicated that financial means to follow the example of the British emancipation were lacking. After the armed conflict with Belgium had formally ended in 1839, the Dutch treasury was indeed virtually exhausted. Therefore the British rulers had to grant the Netherlands a little more time.

Minister Baud, having taken office in 1840, realised the inevitability of emancipation which was cautiously alluded to in the Dutch King's speech of the following year. The term 'emancipation' was carefully avoided in order to prevent any dissent. King Willem II stated on 18 October 1841:

'*The reports from Our Overseas Possessions are favourable. Only the prosperity of the West Indian Colonies is hindered by causes of a special nature. The possibility of a provision draws My attention seriously.*'[40]

---

36   Ibid., 64-66.
37   Ibid., 113-115; Wolbers 1861, 690-697.
38   Siwpersad 1979, 124.
39   Ibid., 24.
40   For the King's speech, see: troonredes.nl/troonrede-van-18-oktober-1841

Representatives of the so-called Réveil forced Minister Baud to take a more precise stance.[41] In 1842 they had petitioned the monarch for permission to establish the *Nederlandsche Maatschappij ter Bevordering van de Afschaffing van de Slavernij* (the Dutch Society for the Promotion of the Abolition of Slavery) (see also p. 98).[42] After consulting the monarch, Baud presented a detailed answer, indicating that the Dutch government was in principle prepared to declare that slaves were now free. At the same time however he indicated that the state of the economy prevented any form of rapid emancipation:

'*The goal of the sensible advocates of emancipation (a goal that also emanates in the petition that is now before me) is therefore not to separate the demands of religion and humanity from the perpetuation and increase of general prosperity. - They do not want emancipation that will result in the disintegration of society, but they intend to recommend measures whose moral and religious value is underpinned and insisted upon by material benefits. Between the government and the signatories of the petition there is therefore no difference of principle [...] Suriname must, this is the petitioner's wish, by emancipation increase in prosperity and blossoming [...]. But that goal can certainly not yet be achieved by emancipation. In the first place, because the Surinamese slaves still generally stand on that low step of civilization, from whom no effort beyond the fulfillment of ordinary animal needs can be expected. Secondly, because the fulfillment of those animal needs in the relatively uninhabited Dutch Guiana does not require regular work, but is offered everywhere amply by the mildness of nature, to anyone who wants to seek a place to stay in the woods and at the banks of the rivers and creeks of that fertile land, - and, third, because such a relatively advantageous market in England is ensured for the products of British Guiana, by the protective duty [...] on all sugars not originating from the British West Indian colonies, that the planter of British Guiana can pay daily wages, which will far exceed the ability of the Dutch planter. When one considers these indisputable facts in their consequences, it strikes one that the emancipation of Surinamese slaves would now irresistibly lead to one of these two outcomes, general establishment in the forests for the purpose of leading the independent but animal life that accrues to the bushnegroes, - or, if, contrary to expectations, needs arose that require regular work, a general move to the neighbouring Demerary in order to receive a much higher wage for the same work. Both in one and the other case, the goal of the sensible advocates of emancipation would have been missed; and to emancipation would be sacrificed the interests of agriculture and industry of Suriname and consequential those of Dutch trade and shipping.*'[43]

Representatives of the Réveil could very well agree both with Baud's cautious approach and his paternalistic attitude towards the slave population. They felt it was

---

41   The Réveil comprised an international revival of protestant Reformed thinking and acting as witnessed in part of 19th-century Europe. In Great Britain, the prominent abolitionist and philanthropist William Wilberforce campaigned for this revival.

42   Siwpersad 1979, 76.

43   Ibid., 73-74.

at least as important to liberate those enslaved spiritually by means of evangelization as to provide them with civil freedom. Although the réveillists Guillaume Groen van Prinsterer (1801-1876) and Isaäc da Costa (1798-1860) contacted British members of the Religious Society of Friends (aka Quakers) who, on behalf of the British and Foreign Anti-Slavery Society visited the Netherlands, the concept of emancipation was less deeply rooted amidst réveillists. Even in a 1823 publication entitled *Bezwaren tegen den Geest der Eeuw* (Objections against the Spirit of the Century), Da Costa described the concept of emancipating enslaved as 'that chimerical human wisdom, which wants to precede the Almighty'.[44] Many réveillists deemed the emancipation of slaves to scent too much of revolution. In their petition addressed to the Dutch king they had emphatically distanced themselves from the French concept of equality:

'[...] *by which every distinction of rank and class is removed, no esteem as ordained of God is respected, debauchery is introduced in all relations and which in the times of the French Revolution, with so called philanthropic zeal also transferred to the colonies, for the slaves, like in Europe for the free, has been the slogan of revolt, murder, and multiple kinds of pity.'*[45]

In addition to the Réveil, a group of liberal campaigners for emancipation also turned to their Dutch monarch with a petition. Opting for the same gradual approach, their humanitarian incentives were much more akin to the concepts of the French Revolution. Attempts by Quakers to unite réveillists (who prioritised education) and liberals failed. For, neither group felt any necessity to push the issue of emancipation to the limit. Nor did both groups feel compelled to protest when the required Royal Approval for their society aimed at promoting the abolition of slavery was not forthcoming. Dutch liberals led by the esteemed statesman Johan Rudolph Thorbecke (1798-1872) deemed the constitutional reforms resulting in the constitutional amendment of 1848 to be of greater significance because it had created the basis for a parliamentary democracy.

For many years the fate of those enslaved had changed little. However, a slight improvement could be observed with regard to delivering sentences. The enslaved now received a lower number of punishments. This outcome was credited to the Governor-general B.J. Elias, who usually dispatched criminal records to the Netherlands. This procedure caused slave owners to be more cautious as they did not wish to acquire a bad reputation in the political circles of their motherland. However, nothing had yet come of amending those slave regulations dating back to 1784. In his aforementioned pamphlet of 1849, these rulings were indeed sharply criticised by Johannes C. Palthe Wesenhagen, the non-white member of the Court of Justice, for 'protecting the most cruel perpetrator' (see also p. 100-102).[46] Colonists and Amsterdam-based stakeholders continuously tried to delay decision-making procedures by forwarding all kinds of demands and objections. They even claimed to be entitled to compensation if the Dutch government was to enforce an improvement

---

44   Da Costa 1823, 26-27.
45   Zeefuik 1973, 158.
46   Palthe Wesenhagen 1849, 45.

upon the living conditions of slaves, arguing that their properties would decrease in value. Although bombarded with a large number of requests, Baud maintained it was part of the 'inalienable rights' and 'sacred duties' of the Dutch government to interfere with managing the enslaved.[47]

On 21 February 1845, Amsterdam-based stakeholders therefore presented a detailed request to the lower house of the Dutch parliament, in which they not only launched a frontal attack on the king's autocratic rule but also deliberately played on the criticism of the constitutional system as forwarded by liberals.[48] The complainants also criticised the financial policy, which had led to the depreciation of the Surinamese currency. These stakeholders may indeed have considered utilising these not unfounded arguments to gain the parliamentarians' sympathy. Baud rebutted them harshly explaining, in a speech to the lower house, the real conflict in no uncertain terms:

> 'They shout against the autocracy exercised with the pen, in order to be able to let those, who possess the whip and the Spaanse bok as tools, exist unhindered with the approval of you Noble Mighty Gentlemen! Behold, Noble Mighty Gentlemen, what the complainants actually want, but what they have not expressed openly in their address.'[49]

It was finally decided to install a parliamentary committee of inquiry in order to consider grievances expressed by complainants. This committee did not hesitate to denounce any 'arbitrary action' and 'requisitioning of authority' carried out by various governors.[50] Nevertheless it simultaneously condemned colonists who resisted the introduction of incoming regulations concerning the enslaved. This committee also proposed a request to be forwarded to the Dutch monarch. Baud must have felt very disappointed because this desiderate no longer referred to the conflict pertaining to slave management. Colonists were also compensated with the pledge of being permitted to exchange the hugely depreciated currency of Suriname at advantageous rates into Dutch guilders. This committee's report once again indicated how little interest the issue of emancipation aroused in the Netherlands. The few lines in this request devoted to this subject concluded that emancipation of those enslaved was still a long way off. Not a single liberal in the Dutch lower house felt the urge to take any action. Notably the conservative J.C. Baud was most convinced of a need for emancipation. Obstruction of slave owners had only reinforced his point of view. Having arrived at the conclusion that the colony would be destroyed by means of a permanent death surplus if slavery was to continue, Baud informed King Willem II in a confidential report dated 20 July 1844 as follows:

---

47 Siwpersad 1979, 116.
48 Ibid., 117.
49 Ibid., 118.
50 Ibid., 119.

A History of Suriname

'[...] *so must not be forgotten (and this is a point on which I would like to request if I may draw the attention of Your Majesty in particular) that in Suriname at least the preservation of slavery will reduce production much faster, yes destroy it completely, than the freeing of slaves. - If slavery continues to exist, then after a few years Suriname will change into a shell without life, the possession of which for the mother state will have little value.*'[51]

According to Baud, rules and regulations (e.g., a ban on owning land) should force freed slaves to continue working on plantations. He hereby referred to France, where the government was preparing such a measure, and further opined that in this way one could prevent a decrease of production, as experienced in certain British colonies during the first post-emancipation years. Moreover, Baud thus explicitly linked emancipation with both preserving and reinforcing Suriname as an agricultural colony. Further proposals were worked out at the Ministry of Colonies, in the deepest secrecy. Baud who above all wished to keep the peace, therefore instructed the Governor-general in charge of the West-Indies assets not to allow 'any freedom of action' to abolitionists hailing from the motherland.[52] In 1842, the chronicler Maarten Douwes Teenstra reported that the colony was 'severely censored'; in his view, 'in a land of stupidity and slavery, no concepts of enlightenment and freedom could be developed'.[53] The affair around the Norwegian-born Moravian Church missionary Nils Otto Tank (1800-1864) was a typical case in point. His father, Carsten N. Tank, had served as a Minister of Finance and had been on good terms with the Swedish monarch Charles XIII, who had been crowned king of Norway in 1814 as the result of the Treaty of Kiel. Carsten N. Tank had presented his son to this elderly, childless monarch as a possible successor to the throne. However, after visiting Herrnhut, Nils O. Tank married the daughter of a member of the Moravian Brethren to then devote himself with heart and soul to this church. Having travelled to Suriname in 1842, he became a key advocate of the Moravian mission. The talented Tank was able to witness the living conditions of the slaves during his many inspection trips to plantations.[54]

In 1848, during a visit to the Netherlands, he wrote a circular addressed to slave owners as well as administrators. In it he strongly objected against the numerous obstacles they placed in the way of missionaries. Slaves were not permitted to freely attend either church or school, not even on Sundays. By disallowing slaves to uphold all forms of even homely interaction inside their dwellings, planters utilised missionaries as tools in order to, in Tank's opinion, 'keep the negroes in subservience and restraint, as if one had a premonition that the means of the whip will once be found to be inadequate'.[55] He denounced the living conditions of those enslaved as well as the way they were treated which, in his view, was worse than elsewhere in that region. We read in Tank's circular: 'Where else do you see negroes naked and

---

51   Ibid., 130.
52   Ibid., 67.
53   Teenstra 1842, 40.
54   Zeefuik 1973, 120-137; Wolbers 1861, 718-720.
55   Zeefuik 1973, 122.

wounded by whipping, roaming the streets?'[56] In addition, he dispraised the sexual excesses of which slave owners were guilty when violating female slaves.

The Moravian Brethren had until then remained silent about such matters for fear of being expelled from the colony. Planters responded furiously to Tank's allegations, having often argued not only that living conditions of slaves were much better when compared with those of many free men in Europe. Moreover, they did not hesitate to accuse him of spreading lies. Three prominent colonists called the Moravian Church, personally represented by the incoming chief H.T.W. Pfenninger, to account. He not only distanced himself from Tank's circular but also denied that reports forwarded by missionaries had formed its basis. Pfenninger remained vague as to the truthfulness of Tank's words, which once again clarified how sensitive the Moravian Brethren's presence among planters had continued to be.[57] The *Haagsche Maatschappij* (founded by colonists in order to promote religious education among slaves, as mentioned earlier) opposed Tank's allegations unequivocally.[58] The entire affair resembled the conflict surrounding the Reverend J.W. Kals (see p. 62-63), who had been forced to leave Suriname a century earlier. Being dismissed, too, Tank was able to continue to serve the Moravian mission in North America.

External influences as yet determined the Dutch policy on slavery. In 1848, the French revolutionary regime's sudden release of all slaves caused a shock. Once this initiative had been announced, a large slave force at work on St Maarten set off for the French part of this isle. Slave owners located in the Dutch part had no choice but to declare that their more than 1,000 slaves were now free. The then Governor immediately confirmed their emancipation in a proclamation, after which former slaves received salaries for their labour.[59]

These events prompted the incoming Minister of Colonies, Julius C. Rijk (1787-1854), to issue a circular urging Amsterdam-based stakeholders to improve at pace the treatment of those enslaved, having already forwarded similar recommendations 6 years earlier when serving as a governor-general. It is worth noting that the tone of the stakeholders addressed had changed dramatically. For, their replies stated 'the signs of the times' had been understood; now their instructions aimed at colonists in Suriname mainly concerned the punishment, housing, food, working hours, medical care, religious education and clothing.[60] Minister J.C. Rijk, a conservative as was his predecessor J.C. Baud, had explicated in his circular it was 'highly dangerous to stubbornly cling to the principle of slavery as it continues to exist in Suriname'.[61] Events following the abolition of slavery by the French government had made such an impression on Rijk that he even contemplated immediate emancipation. Having authorised Governor Reinier F. van Raders (1794-1868) in secret to declare slaves to be free if any events were to echo events that had transpired on St. Maarten, Rijk had already started to prepare an emancipation plan. At The Hague, the *Staatsraad* (Council of State) had, as a result of the enforced

---

56   Wolbers 1861, 719.
57   Ibid., 720.
58   Zeefuik 1973, 125-127.
59   Siwpersad 1979, 156; Paula 1993, 137-139.
60   Wolbers 1861, 717-718; Siwpersad 1979, 157-161.
61   Siwpersad 1979, 157.

emancipation experienced on St. Maarten, advised to immediately release slaves in Suriname without their owners being compensated. This was clearly a step too far for Rijk. From his viewpoint, this would not only be unjust, but also herald the colony's economic demise.[62]

Rijk's incentives which aimed at effectuating a rapid emancipation were identical to those pursued by Baud. Deeming it the only manner to preserve Suriname as an agricultural colony, the former, the incoming Minister, also held the view that the French abolition of slavery had increased the risk of runaways and uprisings. Moral as well as humanitarian considerations applied here, too; according to Rijk, slavery conflicted with 'the most precious rights of humanity'.[63] A key element of his initiative comprised the wish to obligate the employers of liberated slaves to reside in the colony. He hereby hoped that the absenteeism which had caused so much damage to the colony could thus be terminated. Rijk had devised a compensating construction derived from a plan the Government Secretary George S. de Veer (1806-1891) had presented. The State would now expropriate plantations as well as those enslaved. As a means of compensation, landowners were presented with transferable rights of lease. For each slave, a lump sum of 250 Dutch guilders was made available. The amount due would be paid in guaranteed bonds with an interest rate of 4 per cent. The State would then pay off the bonds by means of the rent and an interest of 5 per cent as owed by planters. After 11 years, the land was then to become property of the tenant. Other cabinet members however deemed this plan far too hazardous if considering its financial terms. For, plantation owners would no longer be able to pay the rent nor the interest if the peace in the colony was disturbed or if freed slaves refused to cooperate. The State would then be left with 1,000,000 guilders in debt as a result of the guarantee when granted.[64] Presented in a detailed paper, Amsterdam-based stakeholders, including plantation owners and directors of an investment fund (*negotiatiefonds*) rejected the State's emancipation plan because of financial and practical reasons. In addition, these stakeholders demanded immediate, non-deferred compensations as, in their opinion, not one liberated slave would continue to work. They also categorically rejected an 'eleven-year banishment' to Suriname.[65]

Nevertheless, stakeholders felt far less negative towards the principle of emancipation. Defending their business interests simply forced upon them an innovative course under altered circumstances. Though maintaining that slavery was not reprehensible from both Christian and moral points of view, they now recognised the governmental right to expropriate the possession of slaves. Only the height of compensation was relevant to stakeholders. Fresh initiatives however did not materialize once it had become clear that the danger of a slave revolt occurring in Suriname was less obvious than expected. The Dutch lower house remained unperturbed, too, in spite of its increased influence acquired after the 1848 constitutional amendment. As yet the woeful public finances proved to be a much more acute problem for politicians. The only concrete outcome of all

---

62   Ibid., 162-163.
63   Ibid., 163.
64   Siwpersad 1979, 164-166.
65   Ibid., 182-184.

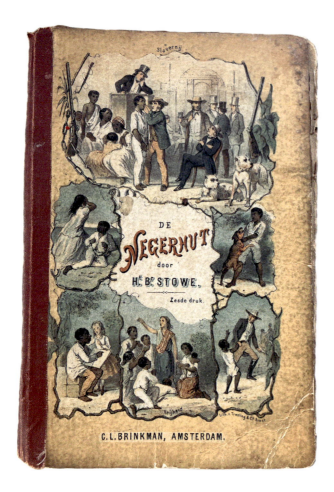

Figure 7.1. The cover of the Dutch translation (6th ed., 1868) of *Uncle Tom's Cabin* (1852). Buku - Bibliotheca Surinamica collection.

this commotion comprised the amendment of 1851 which concerned early slave regulations dating back to 1784. Hence, after almost 70 years, the fate of slaves could in fact be improved.[66]

In due course, emancipation cause was given more priority as the government finances had improved considerably thanks to the increased revenues from the Dutch East Indies, which facilitated compensating slave owners. In addition, abolitionist movements became far more active. Harriet Beecher Stowe's 1852 publication entitled *Uncle Tom's Cabin; or, Life Among the Lowly* also hugely impacted the Netherlands. In 1853, 'Friends' of the Réveil decided to revive the aforementioned Dutch Society for the Promotion of the Abolition of Slavery. Its branches had been founded in The Hague, Amsterdam, Rotterdam and elsewhere. According to its statutes, slavery was 'irreconcilable with the precepts, the spirit and the purport of God's holy Word'.[67] The liberal movement began to manifest itself much more strongly, too, finding a staunch advocate in a member of the Dutch lower house named Wolter R. baron van Hoëvell (1812-1879). His publication entitled *Slaven en vrijen onder de Nederlandse*

---

66 Ibid., 204-209.
67 Van Winter 1952, 72.

wet (Slaves and free under the Dutch law) attracted significant attention. Based on many testimonies he sketched a detailed, realistic portrait of the colony and the harsh lives of slaves. In the Preface we read:

> '*I thought it was my duty to arouse general indignation against slavery if possible; I would like to create a national crusade against its continued existence; I would like to make the Dutch people so horrified of this institution that it will no longer be possible to sustain it.*'[68]

Van Hoëvell fiercely contested the persistent and ubiquitous racial prejudices against Suriname's Black population thus:

> '*In Suriname itself one finds abundant evidence of the high talent of the negroes. But one does not want to see these proofs there, because it the tradition there, to consider everything that concerns them with bias. The slave never hears the free men speak of him or his peers other than with the most contempt. – 'Ugly negro', is now and again addressed to him from the mouth of a female, who is even kind to animals, but harsh and cruel towards slaves. – 'It is only good for a negro' is a very common general expression. – 'He steals like a negro' and he is thus the object of every comparison, which has to express something bad or despicable. [...] Enter the church of the Moravian Brethren on normal days, and you will see the children of the Negroes fruitfully receiving the tuition of these excellent men, who in no way fall behind their white fellow students.*'[69]

In Suriname, too, similar opinions could be heard, as described previously, especially voiced by prominent free non-whites (see p. 100-101). In 1855, the *Dames-comité* (Ladies Committee) was established in Amsterdam in order to not only promote the proclamation of the Gospel but also to abolish slavery in Suriname, hereby raising money in order to manumit slaves there. As mentioned earlier, strong indications exist that this *Dames-comité* and the *Nederlandse Maatschappij ter Bevordering van de Afschaffing van de Slavernij* (Dutch Society for the Promotion of the Abolition of Slavery) worked through a Paramaribo-based manumission network (see p. 98).[70] In order to advocate emancipation other groups simultaneously sent petitions to King Willem III. The number of publications by more and lesser-known authors against slavery increased, too. Nonetheless, supporters of the anti-slavery movement in the Netherlands, remained low in number, even if its impact was considerable.

In 1853, a state commission chaired by the former Minister J.C. Baud was requested to design a plan in order to emancipate each and every slave.[71] Not until a decade later this initiative came to fruition. For, Dutch frugality as well as the narrow-mindedness of conservative governments had impeded reconciliation of the financial interests pursued by colonists and merchants, if pertaining to the

---

68   Van Hoëvell 1854, X.
69   Ibid., part II, 223.
70   Van Winter 1952, 72-74.
71   Siwpersad 1979, 223-226.

right to freedom as desired by several tens of thousands of slaves. In any case, the lower house opined that matters were not proceeding at sufficient pace. Now Liberals and Réveillists were indeed collaborating. In a joint motion, Baron van Hoëvell and the renowned politician-*cum*-historian Guillaume (Willem) Groen van Prinsterer (1801-1876), requested an improvement of the only 4-year-old slave rules and regulations to be installed 'without delay'.[72] This demand was met in 1856 when an amended ruling was introduced. It was aimed not only at improving and ensuring the material condition of slaves but also at further restricting any form of domestic jurisdiction.[73]

Meanwhile, in 1855, a state commission had published its report which included (a) guiding principles whereby emancipation was impossible without any prior compensation and (b) notably, a recommendation that emancipated slaves should, as much as possible, pay costs pertaining to their release back to the state.[74] This commission had therefore also drawn up an extensive plan aimed at guaranteeing Suriname's future as an agricultural colony. Those enslaved as well as plantations were to be expropriated. Former plantation slaves were to be housed in 21 'negro municipalities' home to between 1,500 and 2,000 souls. They had to produce sugar cane for 20 central sugar factories placed under state supervision. Proceeds could then be utilised in order to financially compensate owners of these factories. Being represented in this commission, Amsterdam-based stakeholders were satisfied, as they were to become owners of sugar factories. Nonetheless colonists residing in Suriname deemed their interests threatened. In C.P. Schimpf's view, then Governor of Suriname (1855-1859), almost the entire emancipated population would be sacrificed in this way because agriculture as its sole means of subsistence was stolen from them.[75] In his bill of 1857, the conservative Minister of Colonies, Pieter Mijer (1812-1881), responded to the latter objections by no longer assuming an expropriation of plantations. However, his plan found no mercy amid almost the entire Dutch lower house. The newly established status of emancipated slaves scented too much of slavery due to the introduction of state supervision. The concept of forcing those formerly enslaved to pay personal ransom sums also appalled Dutch parliamentarians. They next forwarded fierce objections against the absence of any provisions pertaining to the supply of immigrants, as required in order to maintain agricultural production.[76] In 1858, P. Mijer's successor Jan Jacob Rochussen (1797-1871) launched a fresh attempt to resolve this long-standing issue. Revealing a lack of statesmanship, the latter submitted three bills across 3 years, which the Dutch lower house rejected on just as many occasions. Key issues continuously concerned the status of former slaves as well as the immigration of contract workers. Colonists and stakeholders residing in the Netherlands who wished to impose costs

---

72   Ibid., 239.
73   Ibid., 239-240.
74   Ibid., 228 ff.
75   Ibid., 228-230.
76   Ibid., 230-232; for an account of the parliamentary debate, see: *Kamerstuk XIII, nr. 6*, 555-571, 1857-1858 (zoek.officielebekendmakingen.nl/uitgebreidzoeken/historisch).

A History of Suriname

Figure 7.2. A daguerrotype (1860) depicting Guillaume Bosch Reitz, a member and future president of the Colonial States (see p. 195), together with his family and two of his slaves. RKD-Nederlands Instituut voor Kunstgeschiedenis, The Hague.

and risks on the government whenever possible, pursued the issue concerning the immigration of contract workers.[77]

Finally, on 9 July 1862, a large majority (47 vs. 11 votes) accepted a new bill which the liberal Minister of Colonies James Loudon (1824-1900) had submitted, be it after a series of amendments.[78] Numerous objections forwarded by parliamentarians against Rochussen's plans had been met with by means of Loudon's draft version. Emancipated slaves would not be obliged to rent themselves out in groups of workers. Former slaves were given the choice as to where they wished to work. The Dutch lower house had now reconciled itself with a form of state supervision, which the government deemed necessary in order to guarantee agricultural production. Nevertheless, several amendments were tabled in order to remove this ruling's sharp edges. A period of supervision was to continue for 'at most' 10 years. The original proposal had been based on a fixed term of 10 years. Former slaves who had behaved exemplarily could be dismissed from being supervised. Loudon's initiative provided for the supply of 25,000 immigrants, for which a lump sum of 3,000,000 guilders was reserved. His plan was also amended after being urged to do so by the lower house. Certain liberals, having lost their faith in the future of the West Indies plantation economy, viewed the financial risks laid upon the government as far too great. Moreover, they considered state subsidies not only as a form of protectionism

---

77   Ibid., 244-255.
78   Ibid., 255-262.

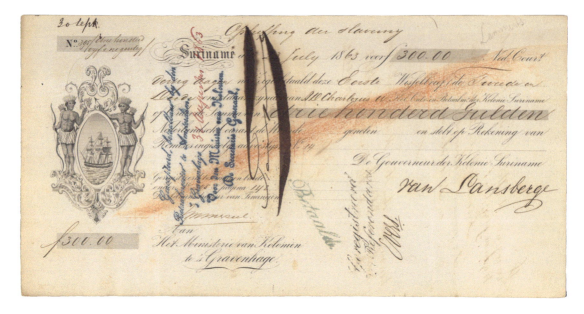

Figure 7.3. This letter of exchange entitled 'Abolition of slavery' was issued in order to compensate a former slave owner. C/o Rijksmuseum, Amsterdam.

but also as opposing their views on laisser-faire economics. Réveillists opined that the evil of immigration had replaced slavery. According to Pieter Jacob Elout van Soeterwoude (1805-1893), the 'import of a colourful and immoral population' could necessitate a surveillance similar to the procedure imposed upon slaves; this assessment caused this parliamentarian to call upon the Dutch government, with eventual success, to not only encourage but also to monitor the establishment of free permanent settlers.[79] The amended proposal implied the supply of workers should be left to private initiatives. The Dutch lower house continued to allow the government to pay a maximum of 1,000, 000 guilders in premiums.

In a proclamation dated 3 October 1862, Governor Reinhart Frans Cornelis van Lansberge (1804-1873) announced to those enslaved that slavery would be abolished, hereby giving the impression that Willem III had provided this special favour:

'It has pleased His Majesty, Our revered King, to determine the day on which slavery in the colony will be abolished forever. [...] But the King, desiring to see happy all those who live under His Majesty's paternal authority, wanted this glad tidings to be made known to you already now. [...] I therefore dare to count on you, through your lust for work, by an irreproachable behaviour and by obedience to your masters, you will prove to be worthy of the beneficence which you are assured against the 1st of July 1863.'[80],

---

79   Ibid., 260-261; see also the account of the parliamentary debate on 5 July 1862, *Tweede Kamer, 1861-1862, XXXV*, 965 (zoek.officielebekendmakingen.nl/uitgebreidzoeken/historisch).

80   *Surinaamsche Courant, Gouvernements Advertentie Blad*, 7 October 1862 (delpher.nl).

The emancipation of the *c.*34,000 Surinamese enslaved was finally realized on 1 July 1863. This outcome had been facilitated by growing colonial revenues extracted from the Dutch East Indies, by means of which compensating slave owners with a lump sum of 300 guilders for each individual was effectuated.[81] During the 20 years prior to emancipation, the income provided by the Dutch East Indies had risen to between 20 and 30 per cent of the government's expenditure. In the course of 1860, these revenues covered even 38 per cent of the total public expenditure, which then amounted to 78,700,000 guilders.[82]

Foreign pressure, economic realism, moral awareness and a guilty conscience had contributed to emancipation. Long before official emancipation, many plantation slaves had gained a certain degree of freedom, a number of which had in a way acquired the status of 'protopeasant'.[83] In Paramaribo, as mentioned earlier, the chain manumission increased strongly during the 19th century when free non-whites paid for the liberation of family members (see p. 98-99) and whereby slavery was undermined from within. When considering the historiography of Caribbean plantation economies, the spectacular slave revolts and the struggle of the Maroons witnessed in the course of the 18th century have slightly overshadowed the much more subtle slave resistance witnessed during the 19th century. Slaves constantly attempted to defend their interests and rights, often with remarkable success.

---

81 Explanatory Memorandum to the draft law on the abolition of slavery, *Tweede Kamer, 1861-1862, XXXV, nr. 4,* 452 (zoek.officielebekendmakingen.nl/uitgebreidzoeken/historisch).
82 Emmer 1989, 83.
83 This apt characterisation originates from Van Stipriaan 1993, 20, 421, 425.

CHAPTER 8
The economy (1651-1863)

In 1651, with the colonization of Suriname by Sir Francis Willoughby, it became part of a rapidly expanding global economy. This development implied that the demand stemming from Western European marketplaces formed the determining factor as to volume and nature of the agricultural production. From 1650 on, Suriname's plantation economy entirely depended on producing sugar. This situation did not change after Abraham Crijnssen's conquest of the colony in 1667. Being such a key commodity, sugar served as a means of payment for a long time. During their colonisation of Northeast Brazil the Dutch had become familiar with both the modus operandi of large-scale sugar production and applying slave labour. Moreover, a large part of this commodity (initially a luxury product) reached the important Amsterdam staple market.

Losing *Braziel*, an event already apparent during the 1640s, increased the demand in Amsterdam for a supply of sugar from elsewhere. This town did indeed possess a number of refineries which processed syrups imported from various foreign colonies in order to provide sugar across Europe.[1] The British colony of Barbados, supported by Amsterdam-based capital providers as well as the West India Company (WIC), was transformed into the main sugar producer of the Caribbean. Sephardic Jews having fled the Inquisition by the returning Portuguese in Brazil, significantly contributed towards revitalising the sugar culture thanks to their huge expertise (see p. 47). Settlers from Brazil played a similar role on the isles of Guadeloupe and Martinique from where raw sugar was transported to Amsterdam, too.

Protectionist measures taken by British authorities (e.g., the Navigation Act of 1651) and the mercantilist policy imposed by Minister Jean-Baptiste Colbert (1619-1683) in France, undermined the Amsterdam-based sugar trade.[2] However, during the 18th century, the number of refineries increased again to around 110.[3] Not only did the Dutch Republic benefit from wars waged either between England and Spain or between France and England, the sugar supplied through the Dutch East India Company also led to an increased activity.[4]

When announcing Crijnssen's conquest of Suriname, the Zeeland-based authorities explained to the population of this Dutch province that settlers disposed of 'suitable and spacious places and fields for growing sugar and other crops'.[5] Planters maintained financial relations with Republic-based merchants They acted as financiers by means of purchasing colonial goods and providing planters for instance with capital. In 1700, around 100 plantations had been established; however, growing tobacco, a remnant of the British era, turned out not to be too profitable; in *c.*1713, the number of sugar plantations had increased to 171, a modest growth rate of less than two newly-founded plantations per annum; in *c.*1750, this number had

---

1   Van de Voort 1973, 89.
2   Reesse 1908, 34-38.
3   Van Stipriaan 1993, 24.
4   Reesse 1908, Appendix, CXIII-CXV.
5   Schiltkamp & De Smidt 1973, 12.

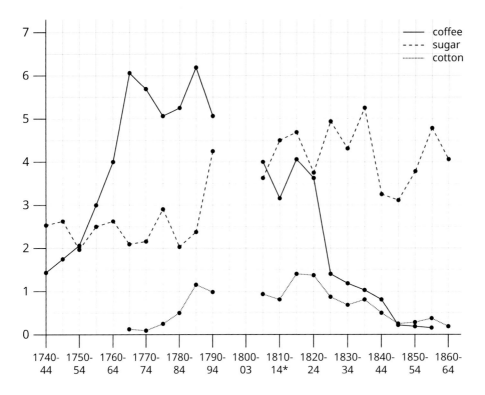

Figure 8.1. Overview of the export value of sugar, coffee and cotton produced in Suriname (1740-1864). Buddingh' 2021, 212 (after Van Stipriaan 1993, annex 3).

dropped to 141, coffee production had in the meantime expanded significantly as the number of 225 plantations proves.[6] During the first part of the 18th century, sugar exports fluctuated at *c.*3,500,000 kg per annum to then reach 6,000,000 kg per annum, occasionally peaking at 10,000,000 kg per annum; its export value during the 1740s amounted to *c.*2,500,000 Hfl; coffee exports did not differ that much when reaching *c.*1,500,000 guilders; during the mid-18th century, the value of coffee exports exceeded sugar exports, now and again reaching 6,000,000 Hfl per annum; during this period of expansion, the coffee production often reached between 6 and 7,000,000 kg per annum to now and again exceed 10,000,000 kg.[7]

Although land was abundant the development of Suriname's plantation culture fell relatively behind if compared with many other West Indian colonies. In 1775, the sugar production in Suriname totalling 6,600,000 kg was almost merely half the produce of the isle of Martinique; Suriname dropped hugely behind Jamaica and Saint-Domingue (which later included Haiti); on these two islands a quantity of sugar was produced exceeding that of Suriname with a factor 6 and 9 respectively.[8] It may be added here that the volume of coffee produced in Suriname amounted to

---

6   Van Stipriaan 1993, 33, 438-439.
7   Ibid., 429-430, 437.
8   Ibid., 29.

between 33 and 50 per cent of that of Saint-Domingue, the largest coffee producer in the Caribbean.[9]

The cause of this underperformance was mainly rooted in the Dutch Republic's policy whereby major interests in trade and transport prevailed. Sugar imported from Suriname thus did not enjoy the level of protection with which Britain and France safeguarded commodities originating from their colonies. British and French consumers contributed to the development of sugar production in the West Indies by paying import duties on foreign sugar. Sugar from Suriname, which had to compete with foreign sugar, played a not insignificant but secondary role in delivering supplies to the Amsterdam staple market. In c.1750, only 33 per cent of the raw materials which Dutch sugar refineries required was sourced from the Dutch West Indies.[10] During the 18th century, the WIC regularly imported foreign sugar to Amsterdam from the isle of St. Eustatius which, especially in wartime, traded clandestinely with surrounding colonies. In 1780, St. Eustatius even supplied Amsterdam with 30,000,000 pounds of sugar.[11]

Meanwhile, a key trade relationship had developed linking Suriname and North American ports, e.g., New York, Boston, Baltimore, Providence (Rhode Island).[12] The Society of Suriname, keen to protect its monopoly position, had initially only made an exception for English trade vessels arriving from New England. They shipped meat, bacon, fish, flour as well as horses and mules (to work at sugar mills) to Suriname in return for liquor, molasses, sawn timber and Dutch wares such as textiles, tools and shoes (see p. 22). Trade with Barbados was also permitted. Governor Paulus van der Veen (1696-1707) had made it clear to the Society that regional trade was 'one of the two legs on which the colony has to walk'.[13] In 1704, his explication resulted in new legislation on British import, hereby liberalising trade, which as yet had not only included restrictions but also imposed both import and export duties.[14] In 1716, holding the widespread view that this law did not suffice, several colonists complained in a pamphlet that their cane molasses was going to waste due to trade barriers imposed on the Caribbean region and on North America.[15]

At this very moment, commercial ties between Suriname and North America were intensified. North American traders circumvented the British duties laid down in the Molasses Act of 1733 in order to facilitate the export of molasses and liquor (dram) from Suriname. This molasses (released when producing sugar) was then purchased by North American distilleries.[16] As much as c.70 per cent hereof was exported to then provide planters with a key additional source of income.[17] As a result, Suriname also benefited from the evolution of the United Colonies into the USA. The number of non-Dutch vessels calling upon Paramaribo at the end of the 18th century did indeed

---

9   Ibid., 29.
10   Van de Voort 1973, 89.
11   Reesse 1908, 205-206.
12   Fatah-Black 2015, 41-62, 167-179; 2013a, 191-218; 2014, 52-71. On the importance of North American-Caribbean trade, see also: French 2021, 189-190, 211-219.
13   Fatah-Black 2015, 52; ibid., 2013a, 62.
14   Ibid., 2015, 53; 2013a, 64.
15   Ibid., 2015, 54; 2013a, 64.
16   Ibid., 2015, 65, 168; 2013a, 87-93.
17   Van Stipriaan 1993, 167.

Figure 8.2. An oil painting (*c.*1752-1758) by John Greenwood entitled *Sea Captains Carousing in Surinam*. It portrays Rhode Island merchants and sea captains enjoying themselves intemperately inside a tavern. Saint Louis Art Museum (Missouri, USA), via Wikimedia Commons.

hugely exceed that of Dutch ships. The fact non-Dutch boats brought in more and more slaves during this time frame was in part the outcome of the Fourth Anglo-Dutch War (1781-1784) which weakened the strong position of the Netherlands as a trading and a seafaring nation.[18]

In addition to trade and transport, financial activities were of huge significance to the Dutch Republic as was certainly the case when, in the course of the 18th century, the British and French began to rule the waves by means of their extensive fleets. Financing provided by the Republic not only displayed a strong international character, it also entirely served provisioning its own staple market. A large part of the money was not invested in the Republic's West Indian colonies but in those of foreign nations. For example, of the almost 70,000,000 guilders the Republic invested in the West Indies between 1753 and 1794, more than 25 per cent reached foreign colonies; especially Danish isles (in casu Saint Thomas, Saint Croix and Saint John) attracted a large sum: in excess of 14,000,000 guilders; nonetheless, during the second half of the 18th century, no less than 36,000,000 guilders were invested in Suriname; plantations located on the Essequibo and the Demerare Rivers received a fair sum comprising 12,000,000 guilders.[19] Establishing sugar plantations required a considerable amount of money. The agronomist Anthony Blom presents a detailed calculation of costs related to a sugar plantation comprising 1,636 'fields', to wit, 208,700 Dutch guilders.[20] In Suriname cost of preparing plantations was higher if compared with other parts of the region. This discrepancy was a result of the

---

18   Fatah-Black 2015, 167-171; 2013a, 230.

19   Van de Voort 1973, 265.

20   Blom 1786, 83.

A History of Suriname

requirement to construct solid drainage systems across low-lying coastal areas utilising techniques applied in polders across the Netherlands. On the other hand, drainage ditches (*trenzen*) created an inexpensive means of transport for products provided by plantations.

From 1753 on, lending money to plantation owners in Suriname had taken off considerably. The first major provider of capital was the five-times mayor of Amsterdam, Willem Gideon Deutz (1697-1757). This trader-*cum*-banker also founded a *negotiatiefonds* which can be compared to an investment fund. He mentions the recovery of the weakened (also referred to as cracked) credit in Suriname.[21] However, an actual credit reduction had never occurred. A recent in-depth study (by Alex van Stipriaan) indicates that a need for capital had indeed increased significantly. Now fresh opportunities for cultivating coffee appeared. Suriname was the first location in the West Indies to grow Coffea arabica, imported from the island of Java, to then profit from it as an export product. Moreover, newly-established plantations proved capable of thriving in close vicinity of the Commewijne and the Matapica Rivers. For, once Fort Nieuw Amsterdam was completed, these plantations were no longer endangered by foreign troops or fortune seekers. Between 1740 and 1750, approximately 150 coffee plantations were established in this part of Suriname alone.[22]

In the Netherlands, merchants were extremely prepared to provide credit. The Amsterdam staple market was in great need of goods imported from Dutch colonies, after British and French fleets had undermined the Republic's key position across the globe. In 1750, the majority of colonial products exported from Bordeaux were no longer shipped through Amsterdam or Rotterdam, but via the Hanseatic town of Hamburg. Moreover, investment opportunities in the Netherlands were limited, while fresh financial resources were released after 1750 as a result of repaying government debts. Merchants could now easily raise funds in order to invest in plantation economies by means of a *negotiatiefonds*. Investors purchased bonds with a nominal value of 1,000 guilders and with a duration of 20 years, upon which they received an interest rate of between 5 and 6 per cent. Bondholders not only appointed merchant-bankers as directors but also a number of supervisory directors, all from their own ranks. Planters were able to borrow money from investment funds against equal interest rates ranging between 5 and 6 per cent up to a maximum of 62.5 per cent of the estimated value of a plantation, which served as collateral for loans. Merchant-directors earned incomes from commissions acquired from planters after carrying out all kinds of tasks for them. Commissions comprising 2 per cent were charged for the sale of plantation products, 0.5 per cent for insuring maritime transports and *c.*1 per cent for purchasing various plantation supplies.[23]

Investors and planters were highly interested in Deutz's fund. Initially the sum of 1,000,000 guilders was to be raised. In due course, bonds even worth 3,756,000 Hfl were issued whereby 89 plantations served as collaterals. A notice circulating in Suriname during 1758 stated that planters owed this fund an additional 900,000 guilders. This notice presumably pertained to overdue interest

---

21   Van de Voort 1973, 93-95.
22   Van Stipriaan 1993, 205-207.
23   Van de Voort 1973, 89-94; Van Stipriaan 1993, 207-208.

receipts, which the now deceased Deutz himself had advanced to bondholders not only to prevent his fund from being discredited but also to avoid a decrease of the bond price. From 1763 on, when repaying planter loans should have commenced, the incoming management of this investment fund saw to it several plantations were either sold or seized.[24]

In spite of the Amsterdam financial crisis of August 1763, money was continuously invested in Suriname. Between 1766 and 1775 almost 30,000,000 guilders flowed into the colony. Rapidly rising coffee prices made investing in newly-founded plantations appealing. Peace treaties with Maroons may also have contributed to a certain degree of confidence. Moreover, the bond rate of between 5 and 6 per cent exceeded the 2.5 to 3 per cent as imposed on sovereign bonds in the Republic, apparently a reflection of the investor risk. However, in the course of the speculative atmosphere witnessed at the Amsterdam stock exchange, many wished to gamble with their surplus cash. Even the dramatic credit crisis of 1773 did not immediately discontinue the flow of capital. Between 1773 and 1776, the investment funds, as aggregated for the entire West Indies, put out 3,400,000 guilders annually.[25]

Investor money now flowed readily in Suriname whereby large numbers of individuals without the necessary knowledge of agriculture were enticed to set off for plantations. Many spent money on personal consumptive excesses, which did not benefit any production. The valuations of plantations were often fraudulent, as a result of which granted loans no longer in any way balanced the collateral's value. In 1764, the Court of Police and Criminal Justice's measures aimed at tightening control, thus preventing any 'tricks' when valuing, proved insufficient.[26] The fact Paramaribo-based agents working for a *negotiatiefonds* did earn substantial commissions for the loans they offered will certainly have contributed to this outcome. The investment funds phenomenon turned out to be an economic bubble as was fully revealed when planters had to start repaying loans in *c.*1775. Now the plantation revenues proved far too small to comply with financial liabilities. Coffee prices had fallen by dozens of per cents. Simultaneously the American Revolutionary War aka the American War of Independence (1775-1783) caused the import of molasses into North America to stall. Bondholders based in the Republic were the main victims. Merchant-bankers had taken no personal risks, but did endanger money owned by others. Always receiving commissions, they often charged plantation owners far too much if supplying plantation accessories. Certain merchant-bankers committed downright fraud, for instance, if secretly paying bondholders lower interest rates than the sums of money received from planters in order to then misappropriate the difference. Merchant-bankers completely controlled plantation owners by means of several agreements. For example, directors of investment funds designated ships to transport colonial goods, enabling him to privately profit from negotiated advantages. In general, switching to another such fund was penalised with a fine comprising 2 per cent of the mortgage sum.[27]

---

24   Van de Voort 1973., 92-100; Van Stipriaan 1993, 208-209.
25   Van de Voort 1973, 94, 103; Van Stipriaan 1993, 218.
26   Wolbers 1861, 261.
27   Van Stipriaan 1993, 220-221.

           A History of Suriname

As a result of the default of the planters, investment funds were frequently forced to reduce the percentage of the interest to be paid out, whereas any debts could by no means be redeemed. Now and again individual bondholders were fortunate enough to retrieve, after drawing lots, the money they had lent if a collateral was sold. In *c.*1780, West Indian bonds had already lost the largest part of their value. Hence, interest payments were often entirely omitted. In a letter dated 10 July 1777, a 'gentleman from Utrecht', on a visit to Amsterdam and accompanied by his son, described to a friend the pitiful state of affairs he had witnessed in Suriname:

> *'Jantje is fine too, but he became very annoyed yesterday during the court hearing and now while I was writing this; [...] Father, he told me straight away, Amsterdam is a beautiful city, but it is sad that court hearings must be held on the affairs of Suriname: he did not hope this would take place every day, and was very surprised when I said to him, that for some time now it is happening weekly: Let Suriname then go, dear father, was his answer; I like coffee and may have a small lump, but I want them both to be omitted if there must be continuous court hearings about it. I do apologize, however, for making this long letter even longer because of the childish language of my boy, but I agreed with him in my heart. Our ancestors were wealthy and healthy, did not drink coffee or chocolate and never witnessed any damage on the colonies. On the contrary, we drink coffee, fall ill and see our capital and interest payments diminish, yes, we may hardly protect our stakes.' (Letter from an Utrecht gentleman, residing in Amsterdam, to his friend in Utrecht, concerning the incident at the court hearing held in the lodgement 't Wapen van Amsterdam, on July 9, 1777, on matters pertaining to the negotiatie of bonds, at the expense of a number of planters in the colony of Suriname, in the years 1765, 1766, 1767, 1768 and 1769, founded under the direction of the honourable Mr. Harman van de Poll; printed in Utrecht.).*[28]

Bondholders, including the aforementioned gentleman, must have lost tens of millions of Dutch guilders. Little wonder that, in the remaining part of the 18th century, a mortgage credit comprising merely *c.*2,000,000 guilders reached Suriname.[29] As a consequence of this debt crisis the ownership of numerous plantations was transferred to overseas creditors. In 1786 as much as 80 per cent of the plantations had already been acquired by these money lenders; in 1786, too, between 80 and 90 planters resided in the colony, whereas in 1813 their number had dropped to 55.[30]

Administrators had now taken over managing plantations, which did not benefit the economy of Suriname at all. Managers of investment funds wished to extract as much as possible from plantations as quickly as possible, resulting in both the land and the slaves becoming exhausted. Such an over-exploitation also implied that investments and maintenance were usually cancelled, resulting in a decline of production. Fraudulent acts carried out by administrators who now and again

---

28   *Brief van eenen Utrechtsen Heer, zich te Amsterdam bevindende, aan zynen vriend te Utrecht* [....], pamphlet, Utrecht 1777, 18-19 (online acces: books.google.com).
29   Van de Voort 1973, 180.
30   Ibid., 201-203.

misrepresented the state of affairs to Netherlands-based owners in order to then benefit themselves, did not contribute to production either. In fact, numerous planters had returned from Suriname to the Republic without much financial resources. Their plight contrasted with British colonists who, thanks to a monopoly on their home markets, had amassed great wealth when trading sugar. In Great Britain, having formed a powerful West India interest group, they acquired considerable political influence. In the Dutch Republic, on the other hand, trade formed the key economic sector.[31]

After losing its monopoly on the slave trade in 1734, the WIC could no longer play such a key political role (see p. 33). Moreover, the WIC had never acquired such a strong position if compared with the Dutch East India Company, which had fulfilled the task of colonizer across Asia. Having lost the aforementioned monopoly in the slave trade, the African fortifications had become a financial burden for the WIC. It was hence forced to impose levies ranging between 4,000 and 5,000 guilders upon vessels transporting slaves out of Africa. This measure resulted in it being less costly to purchase slaves outside these forts through African mediators.[32] The debt crisis also had a negative impact on trade. For, slave traders could now not only no longer count on the acceptance of money orders that planters had drawn on their investment fund in the Republic, they also demanded, in vain, that debts arising from purchasing slaves were prioritised. The Fourth Anglo-Dutch War (1780-1784), a consequence of the British stance that the Republic was not acting in a neutral manner with regard to the American Revolutionary War, inflicted even more damage to the trade across the West Indies, especially after British troops had completely destroyed a depot located on St. Eustatius and relevant to Amsterdam. In 1782, the States General allowed the WIC to borrow 1,000,000 guilders under their guarantee, but only the minimum amount of 63,000 guilders was raised. The States of Holland had to provide the remaining sum. Ultimately, in 1791, the license expired, causing the WIC to face bankruptcy for a second time in its existence.[33]

During the 19th century, Suriname's plantation sector certainly did not as yet belong to the past. For, millions of guilders continued to be invested in the production of both cotton and sugar. Now mainly British and Surinamese capital was invested in agriculture, though precise data are lacking. Administrators who often managed more than one plantation received 10 per cent of the harvest as well as 10 per cent of the revenues generated by means of sales in Suriname. Foreign skippers then purchased these products. Utilising their income, several administrators acquired debt-laden plantations for little money to then transform them into lucrative businesses. Suriname's plantation culture witnessed a boost, especially during the British interim administration. In the districts of Nickerie and Coronie, planters hailing from the British colony of Grenada established new plantations in order to cultivate cotton. During the last quarter of the 18th century, this commodity was

---

31 Van Stipriaan 1993, 44-45; the London West India Society of Planters and Merchants, formed in 1780, increased their representation in Parliament in order to affect legislation on sugar duties and to resist the abolition of slave trade and slavery.
32 Van de Voort 1973, 210-211; Emmer 1981, 79-81; Den Heijer 2013 (1994), 179-181.
33 Van de Voort 1973, 205-207; Den Heijer 2013 (1994), 184-185.

often only a by-product of coffee plantations.[34] The required capital was probably provided by English and Scottish trading houses. At the beginning of the 19th century, cotton production, which had not exceeded a few 100,000 kg for years, had risen to c.1,000,000 kg in 1825.[35] Between 1815 and 1825, the annual export value of cotton reached almost 1,500,000 guilders, totalling c.33 per cent of the sum received for coffee and sugar respectively.[36] In around 1825, of the total number of 346 plantations producing for the export market, 73 had been intended to produce cotton, whereas 178 and 95 plantations produced coffee and sugar respectively.[37] By the time slavery was abolished, cotton production was only a fraction of what it had once been. The American Civil War (1861-1865) triggered a short-lived upturn as to high cotton prices. Nonetheless, as soon as the cotton production in North America had recovered, its production in Suriname collapsed completely.

Following requests from the colony, the Dutch government had tried to revitalise Suriname's plantation economy. To this end and partly initiated by King Willem I, the *Particuliere West-Indische Bank* (Private West Indies Bank) was established in 1829.[38] Its aim was to create a certain degree of order in the chaotic state of the colony's financial affairs - due to the continuous outflow of money from Suriname to the Republic stamped playing cards served as a poorly secured means of payment. Moreover, this bank was to grant loans to planters. The term 'Private' when describing this bank was slightly misleading. The Dutch government failed to secure 3,000,000 guilders for this banking project and thus had to provide a means of funding from its own resources. After the negative experiences with *negotiatiefondsen*, as witnessed decades earlier, it proved very difficult to find any money lenders in the motherland. This private bank was in fact a public institution. Moreover, its most senior colonial officials, to wit, the governor-general, the public prosecutor-general and the controller-general sat on its board. This bank provided more than 1,800,000 guilders in plantation mortgages, in part to purchase steam-driven tools. Without much luck in business, its liquidation followed in 1870.

During the 19th century, plantations located in Suriname continued to witness examples of innovative entrepreneurship. Notably, the coffee sector formed an exception, as a result of a mentality expressed by planters, according to the most plausible explanation.[39] Expecting to accumulate wealth rapidly, mainly newcomers, without any expertise, had pounced on the lucrative coffee cultivation while riding waves of credit forwarded by Amsterdam-based money lenders. These plantation owners deemed long-term investments (e.g., regarding mechanical coffee processing or good fertilisation) merely as attacks on their personal wallets. This state of affairs is apparently the main cause for 19th-century plantations in Suriname being portrayed as poor. Elsewhere, too, as in Saint-Domingue and Brazil, a phenomenon arose whereby recently arrived planters turned to coffee cultivation. This initiative was aimed at making money fast in order to rival the established sugar-aristocracy.

---

34   Van Stipriaan 1993, 231-240.
35   Ibid., 439.
36   Ibid., 437.
37   Ibid., 438.
38   Ibid., 246-252; Wolbers 1861, 624-630, 652-654.
39   Van Stipriaan 1993, 198-199.

The extent to which innovations were implemented across plantations by and large depended on the type of ownership. The absence of owners as well as investment funds had a clear and negative impact. In 1853, for example, 33 per cent of sugar or cotton plantations with owners residing in Suriname and/or British owners utilised steam-driven machines. However, in the case of sugar or cotton plantations with absent owners, this number had fallen to less than 20 per cent.[40] British influence must have been considerable. In 1850, only 10 per cent of the industrial power sources in the Netherlands were steam-driven. However, in 1855 already in excess of 35 per cent of a total 189 plantations producing export goods in Suriname utilised steam engines. This sector's sophistication at that time is rightfully described as 'un-Dutch'.[41] Innovation was the strongest across the sugar sector. A few years after the abolition of slavery, virtually nothing remained of the coffee production, whereas sugar production during the mid-1800s yielded between 16,000 and 17,000 tonnes per annum, amounting to more than double the production level reached in the course of the second half of the 18th century.[42] Although the number of sugar plantations had fallen from 141 to 91, their production levels and size had risen sharply.[43] This phenomenon was partly the outcome of introducing the Otaheite sugar cane, a variety also grown elsewhere across the Caribbean. In Suriname, it was referred to as Moluccan sugar cane. Both names probably refer to the same plant.[44]

Suriname's sugar production per hectare was among the highest witnessed in the region during the 18th and early 19th centuries, only to be surpassed by means of British Guyana's technologically advanced status. The number of kilograms of sugar produced in Suriname per slave was considerably higher than elsewhere, perhaps indicating the strict regime imposed on the enslaved.[45]

Van Stipriaan presented calculations for Suriname concerning the rates of return of its plantations. In the absence of reliable figures on the capital invested he ciphered the profit gained per individual slave, which is then related to the average purchase price of a slave. During the 1800s, returns acquired in the sugar sector were almost always well above the interest rate in the Netherlands (i.e., c.3 per cent), even if the debt burden is taken into account. Between 1840 and 1862, the average annual yield rose from 4.1 to 5.7 per cent.[46] It may be added here that coffee cultivation was in a much worse condition. Needless to say, these figures overestimate reality. After all, those enslaved by no means represented the total sum of the invested capital pumped into the plantations.

In order to appraise Suriname's economic significance to the Netherlands, the value of products imported from the colony as well as the related economic activity in The Netherlands should be taken into account. Paying special attention to this

---

40   Ibid., 199.
41   Ibid., 201.
42   Ibid., 430-432.
43   Ibid., 438.
44   Oostindie 1989, 31.
45   Van Stipriaan 1993, 139-140. Here it is assumed that the higher labour productivity rather resulted from the large-scale application of innovative technology which during the 18th-century included water mills and, during the 19th century, steam power.
46   Ibid., 272-273; the calculations by Van Stipriaan are based on a sample extracted from plantation archives.

assessment, it has been pointed out that (a) the transfer of slaves to the colony of Suriname covered only 15 per cent of shipments carried out between the Netherlands and Suriname and (b) 85 per cent consisted of bilateral trade and thus mainly concerned the export of colonial products.[47] An extensive calculation pertaining to the value of goods mainly comprising sugar (molasses, dram) and coffee exported from Suriname to the Netherlands between 1683 and 1940 reports that the sum of 1.3 billion Hfl was exceeded. This phenomenon was referred to as the 'migration of capital'; according to a valuta conversion table applied in 2006, this would equal more than € 125 billion. [48] The majority of these revenues ended up in Amsterdam.

This calculation seeks to discard the image of Suriname being a 'poor' colony, an impression that had grown over time. Planters here did indeed now and again run into problems. However, the major beneficiaries of the colonial economy were always providers of commercial services whereby more than 66 per cent of the turnover was obtained by merchant bankers, slave traders and administrators, 14 per cent by plantation entrepreneurs and 7 per cent by the government in the form of taxes.[49] Suriname had little to gain from the proceeds of export products, which at that time were processed in the Netherlands.

Of particular interest is the study which for the first time provides us with a methodologically, well-founded calculation of the weight of activities based on Atlantic slavery and contributing to the Dutch economy during the second half of the 18th century. This research includes not only the import, processing and export of slave-produced commodities (e.g., sugar, coffee, tobacco), but also activities such as shipbuilding, shipping, financial services and related domestic production. No less than 5.2 per cent of the Gross Domestic Product (GDP) of the Netherlands and even as much as 10.36 per cent of GDP of Holland, the Republic's most affluent province, was based on slavery in 1770, a year deemed representative for the second half of the 18th century.[50] Previously, contributions to the Dutch GDP had been estimated at merely 0.5 per cent, whereby only the profitability of the slave trade had been taken into account.[51]

The importance of Suriname to the Netherlands did decline during the 19th century when exports dispatched from Java completely surpassed those sent from Suriname. The sugar and coffee production on Java had increased significantly with the introduction of the *Cultuurstelsel* (Cultivation System), which required a certain volume of agricultural products to be devoted to export crops.

---

47   Postma 2003b, 311.
48   Zunder 2010, 206.
49   Ibid., 276-277.
50   Brandon & Bosma 2019, 5-45; see also: Fatah-Black & Van Rossum 2015, 63-83.
51   Eltis, Emmer & Lewis 2016, 724-735. French rightly observes: 'Traditional Dutch histories have placed so much emphasis on the Asian basis of new Dutch wealth in this period that they have discounted, or overlooked altogether, what the Netherlands sought to achieve in the West using African slave labor, shipping power and plantations.' French 2021, 188.

CHAPTER 9
Transforming the colonial society (1863-1942)

9.1 Immigration of indentured labourers from Asia

The emancipation of slaves in Suriname preluded, as in all other West Indian colonies, important social changes. White planters sold their properties before returning to Europe. For, many had lost confidence in the future as a result of crisis-related symptoms observed in the West Indian plantation economy. Between 1 July 1862 and 1 July 1864, a total of 95 plantations and plots of land changed hands of which 54 had formerly belonged to residents of Suriname. Of the new owners, mainly of colour, 82 were based in this colony.[1] They had purchased smaller plantations from owners residing in Europe whose land had been divided into ever smaller plots after being inherited. It may be added here that largest plantations remained in the hands of the original owners.

Pessimism among white plantation owners was prompted, for example, by the imminent threat of a shortage of labour resulting from the abolition of slavery. Moreover, competition from the Far East increased with the opening of the Suez Canal in 1869. This event suddenly caused the huge quantum of labour and land in Asia to be much more relevant to Europe. The rising volume of European beet sugar was a negative factor for planters too.

Due to a lack of income during the final decades prior to emancipation, the state budget of Suriname had run into an annual deficit of several hundred thousand guilders, which the Dutch government cleared.[2] The chronic financial deficits formed a key reason for authorities in The Hague to extend Suriname's autonomy. An incoming government regulation (1865) envisaged encouraging the colonial government to initiate balancing the budget.[3] Any decisions on its preliminary determination should be taken by Suriname, as long as a financial supplement from the Netherlands was not required. The *Koloniale Staten* (henceforth Colonial States) further evolved towards a representative body, though the introduction of selective suffrage limited the electorate to a group comprising only a few hundred colonists. In addition to the nine elected members of this body, the governor appointed four others deemed to defend interests of the vast majority of the population which had no right to vote. The executive power remained with the governor, whom a governing council advised. The restricted right to vote best represented the interests of wealthy planters. Little wonder that, shortly after emancipation, a lobby was established in order to persuade the Dutch government to organise the immigration of indentured labourers. After a period of supervision by the state, which was to end in 1873, planters were by and large reluctant to being forced to employ freed Black people, who may have all kinds of demands.

In 1853, Suriname's colonial government had already imported 18 Chinese indentured labourers from the island of Java (Dutch East Indies) to be employed at a

---

1   Van Lier 1971, 184.
2   Willemsen 1980, 147.
3   Van Lier 1971, 298-302.

government plantation named Catharina Sophia. The arrival of 487 immigrants from mainland China was commissioned in 1858. However, this experimental initiative proved unsuccessful as plantation owners hardly ever employed Chinese as result of the costs, despite state premiums. Next, the then Governor unilaterally changed the terms of the contract in favour of planters. As certain Chinese now refused to work, police flogged them with canes. Finally, the authorities hired several Chinese, in particular at Catharina Sophia.[4]

In 1865 the *Surinaamse Immigratie Maatschappij* (Immigration Society of Suriname) was established in which the *Nederlandsche Handel-Maatschappij* (Dutch Trading Company), the predecessor of the ABN AMRO Bank (founded more than a century later) participated. Aimed at supplying Chinese nationals, this society recruited *c.*2,000 indentured labourers only to be dissolved after 5 years. For, resulting from their own needs Great Britain as well as Portugal closed the ports of Hong Kong and Macao to their foreign competitors.[5] Nearly 500 workers had previously been brought to Suriname from Madeira as was the case with recruits from British colonies in the West Indies. A large number of these labourers returned after their contracts had expired.[6] Between May 1868 and 1873, more than 100 Hindustani immigrants originating from Barbados, St. Lucia, Demerary and Berbice were employed on plantations. The majority hereof had signed contracts pertaining to work in Suriname after their contracts in the British colonies were terminated.[7] Other groups from the West Indies had migrated to Suriname within this time span, too. Between 1863 and 1873, the total number of immigrants from the West Indies amounted to almost 2,500 souls, many former slaves.[8] Towards the end of 1873, almost 1,400 immigrants from the West Indies resided in Suriname.[9] The then Minister of Colonies, I.D. Fransen van de Putte (1822-1902) reported that 'this type of immigrant does not satisfy'.[10] Ultimately the government proved positive about immigrants from China. We read:

'Few of them turn back after accomplished service to their homeland. This class of workers satisfies continuously. In general, it is a sensible and diligent people, capable of withstanding the tropical climate and, when treated well, not difficult to manage.'[11]

Several dozens of immigrants hailing from the Netherlands had also arrived at Suriname in very small groups. Here too, however, 'major disappointments' were experienced.[12] Nonetheless only a few chose to leave the colony. The *Nederlandsche*

---

4   Wolbers 1861, 750-751; *Koloniaal Verslag 1874*, Kamerstuk nr. 5, ondernummer 63, 52. All these reports can be accessed online as presented in the bibliography; see also: Tjon Sie Fat 2009, 67-68.

5   *Koloniaal Verslag 1874*, Kamerstuk nr. 5, ondernummer 63, 52; De Klerk 1953, 37.

6   Ibid. 1874; ibid. 1953, 34, 37.

7   De Klerk 1953, 37; see also: database Hindustani immigrants, (nationaalarchief.nl/onderzoeken/index/nt00345).

8   *Koloniaal Verslag 1874*, Kamerstuk nr. 5, ondernummer 63, 52.

9   *Koloniaal Verslag 1874*, Kamerstuk nr. 5, ondernummer 51, 14.

10   Ibid.

11   *Koloniaal Verslag 1873*, Kamerstuk nr. 5, ondernummer 3, 12,

12   *Koloniaal Verslag 1874*, Kamerstuk nr. 5, ondernummer 51, 14.

Handel-Maatschappij's attempt made to recruit *c.*100 Africans together with their families in West Africa fell through due to the unwillingness of local rulers and those personally involved.[13] Concerns among planters had increased with the impending termination of state supervision in 1873, whereby former slaves were nevertheless forced to continue working albeit now provided with an employment contract. In 1868, the influential G.J.A. Bosch Reitz, a member of the Colonial States, co-wrote a pamphlet together with a small number of colonists. In it he claimed Suriname was able to 'rise from the miserable situation' by means of immigrating contract workers; in particular, the argument that the colony could once again provide all its own resources 'instead of being a continuous burden' must have resonated with the Dutch government which, forced by circumstances, gave up its laisser faire stance.[14]

Recruiting Hindustanis was the most obvious option. In many British and French colonies, after the abolition of slavery, indentured labourers from across the Indian Subcontinent had already been employed. The British had set up a full-scale transport and recruitment system spanning their Indian Empire. Thus, in 1870, the Dutch signed a treaty with the British, giving Suriname the right to import indentured labourers from Northern India. Financing this immigration led, however, to discord between the colony and the government at The Hague. The Colonial States had approved a proposal forwarded by Bosch Reitz and his associates which aimed at creating an immigration fund. All expenditures were to be paid by means of advances, but the Dutch government was reluctant to do so. Escalating tempers in the Colonial States caused certain members to suggest that Suriname should be sold to the British. In 1874, Dutch authorities presented a 'loan to promote immigration' which the colony paid for.[15] An immigration fund was created in 1880, which mainly served to protect the *Nederlandsche Handel-Maatschappij*'s interests. In the end, plantation owners had to pay 60 per cent of the supply costs as well as an annual head money comprising 5 Hfl for a male and 2.50 Hfl for a female immigrant older than 15 years. On balance, each indentured labourer cost each plantation owner *c.*200 Hfl, whereby the Dutch government forwarded the same lump sum. The members of the local population as well as the immigrants personally contributed to these costs by means of a levy comprising import duties on rice.[16] It may be added here that elsewhere in the West Indies it was not unusual for the population to in part cover expenditures incurred.

On June 5, 1873, only a few weeks before the state's supervision was lifted, the first contingent of 399 passengers, to wit, 279 men, 32 boys, 70 women and 18 girls arrived at Paramaribo on the sailing ship Lalla Rookh, to the great relief of many on board. For, in Calcutta (now Kolkata, West Bengal, Northeast India) a total of 410 migrants had embarked of whom 11 passed away en route.[17] During the era of Hindustani immigration, 64 ships transported as many as 34,304 individuals to Suriname.[18] In 1916, the political pressure stemming from nationalists active within the British

---

13   *Koloniaal Verslag 1875*, Kamerstuk nr. 5, ondernummer 52, 258-259.
14   Bosch Reitz 1868, 24.
15   *Koloniaal Verslag 1874*, Kamerstuk nr. 5, ondernummer 51, 13; De Klerk 1953, 127.
16   De Klerk 1953, 126-127; Bruijning & Voorhoeve 1977, 276.
17   De Klerk 1953, 114; *Koloniaal Verslag 1874*, Kamerstuk 5, ondernummer 63, 46; Dalhuisen et al. 2007, 106.
18   Bruijning & Voorhoeve 1977, 277.

Empire put an end to emigration. The majority of Hindustani immigrants hailed from either the Indo-Gangetic Plain or from the state of Bihar (Eastern India). They were born into high and low castes whereby members of the highest caste (from which Brahmins emerged) were strongly underrepresented. Brahmins felt little need to emigrate because of their economically privileged position. They preferred to stay in their country of birth for religious reasons, too. Moreover, the colonial authorities prevented as many Brahmins as possible from migrating based on the fear they could emerge as the leaders of disgruntled labourers.[19] On the other hand, a relatively high quantum of immigrants - De Klerk estimates up to 17.5 per cent - were Muslims and thus presumably felt less religious objections against emigrating; as the followers of Islam were mainly city dwellers, local recruiters could access them easily.[20] The vast majority of male immigrants were either peasants or farmhands. Female immigrants had often been employed as domestic servants. Immigrants were referred to as coolies, a term derived from the Hindi *quli* (day labourer).[21] Indentured labourers initially had no objections against being called coolies, a description later considered humiliating. Next, the term Hindustanis was adopted, as it was common to a language the majority of emigrants from the Northern British East Indies were able to understand.[22]

The aforementioned treaty of 1870, which came into force in 1872, saw to regulating the emigration of Hindustanis in a precise manner.[23] Emigration agents, civil servants appointed by the governor of Suriname supervised the recruiting procedure. In practice always of European stock, these men presided over the main depot located in Calcutta, where emigrants embarked. With the governor's approval, they appointed subagents, physicians, interpreters as well as other staff. Subagents, mainly Hindustanis, were placed in charge of subdepots established in other towns. Their remunerations consisted of premiums for each suitable emigrant registered. Premiums awarded for enlisting women were the highest as they proved more difficult to recruit. After complaints were forwarded concerning these subagents' unreliability, those who excelled when registering now received fixed monthly allowances. Locals who carried out the actual recruitment obtained a premium per emigrant. They required a licence from a Calcutta-based protector of emigrants, the British colonial official in charge of the overall supervision. Recruiters often painted a far too rosy picture of reality. Little wonder the Hindi and Urdu term pertaining to 'making empty promises' became a synonym of 'the mirroring of green gardens by the recruiters of a cooly depot'; in general, an accomplice of official recruiters was not only referred to as an *arkati* (i.e., a sly negotiator or seducer) but also deemed to be of ill repute.[24]

The relatively favourable conditions open to indentured labourers active in Suriname implied that each individual could return to his or her country of birth

---

19   De Klerk 1953, 45-53, 91-113.
20   Ibid., 112-113.
21   The list of castes of Hindustani immigrants in Suriname includes the caste of unskilled workers, referred to as *Kul* or *Kol*, see: De Klerk 1953, 101.
22   Ibid., 43.
23   Ibid., 53-57.
24   Ibid., 56-57.

at the expense of the Dutch government once their 5-year contract had expired. For many, emigration was thus no longer such a huge step. Emigrants were primarily driven by economic motives.[25] Failed harvests, the power of usurers and a decline of the local cottage industry due to the industrialisation across the United Kingdom as well as its Indian Empire deprived many of a chance to create a decent livelihood. Personal incentives also played a role. One often feared one's family members if they were to object against any amorous relationships for reasons of either caste or religion. In Hindustani society, single females were pressured to such a degree that many opted to leave.

According to a colonial report (1874), the arrival of the first migrants from British India, on June 5, 1873, resulted in 'a beneficial effect', as wages could be retained 'within the natural limits'.[26] This report, however, also stated that these groups of contract workers did not meet with expectations due to diseases, poor physical conditions and an unsuitability for plantation labour. Often ten or more immigrants would perish en route from India. On several plantations, as much as between 30 and 40 per cent of workers were hospitalized due to venereal diseases, anaemia or ulcers.[27] The mortality rate among Hindustani immigrants was particularly high. According to the Colonial Report of 1875, their total number had reached 3,085 at the end of 1874, in that same year, no fewer than 652 passed away.[28] The main reason for this dismal outcome was the poor selection procedure. Suriname's government was partly to blame, too. For, the first immigrants had to disembark in Paramaribo at speed, to wit, before the regime of state imposed supervision had ended.

Authorized on the basis of the Anglo-Dutch treaty of 1870 and alarmed by the pitiful living conditions observed among immigrants, the British government decided to suspend all emigration to Suriname in 1875.[29] The Paramaribo-based U.K. consul acted as a protector of immigrants. Moreover, immigrants remained subjects of the British Raj after their arrival in Suriname. Emigration could be resumed only after the Dutch government had promised to improve living conditions.[30] Medical care improved rapidly: employers now contributed financially by means of a medical tax. The legal certainty of the indentured labourers was also reinforced. According to the immigration rules of 1856, any breaches of contract, for example, resulting from laziness or omissions, were subjected to penal sanctions, whereby planters were as yet allowed to act as judges. After the abolition of slavery on 1 July 1863, district commissioners, who were appointed to exercise the state supervision over former slaves, took over this power. From that moment on, employers could be punished, too. Ten years later, shortly before the first Hindustani immigrants arrived in Suriname, a district court was designated to act in case any breaches of contract occurred. Only in 1878 did the nature of possible offences and the level of penalties become clearly defined. Employees were fined and/or detained. In general, employers were merely fined.

---

25   Ibid., 57-62.
26   *Koloniaal Verslag 1874,* Kamerstuk 5, ondernummer 51, 13.
27   Ibid., 14.
28   *Koloniaal Verslag. 1875*, Kamerstuk 5, ondernummer 52, 258.
29   De Klerk 1953, 121.
30   Ibid., 121-126.

Figure 9.1. British Indian women and children, 1895-1898. Photo by Theodore Bernard van Lelyveld. C/o Rijksmuseum, Amsterdam.

A 5-year contract as to toiling 313 days per annum committed immigrants to their employers. The 1870 Anglo-Dutch treaty stipulated that labour was to be carried out during a maximum of 6 days a week, to wit, either 7 hours a day if at work on a field or 10 hours at workplaces. The minimum wage for adult males comprised 60 cents per day. Men, women and boys were paid 40 cents a day if not fully fit. Initially, boys aged 10 and older were allowed to work. This limit was set at 16 years when the Indian Emigration Act was effectuated in 1886.[31]

Immigration did not instantly deliver the expected benefits, although Hindustanis proved to be good workers. The British government's rules and regulations placed heavy financial burdens on employers. Many immigrants utilised their right regarding free return journeys after serving out full contracts. Their savings, on average almost 100 Hfl, were to be paid out in Calcutta. Between 1878 and 1926, *c.*33 per cent of all Hindustanis had returned to their homeland. Nonetheless a number of them set off again to Suriname as they were unable to cope with the British Raj's socio-economic circumstances and rigid caste system.[32] The Dutch colonial government was thus forced to provide newly-arriving immigrants again and again, entailing further costs. Compared with Suriname, expenditures observed across British colonies were much lower as not as many demands were made as to housing and health care. Here the avidity of Hindustani indentured labourers to

31   Ibid., 131-137.
32   Ibid., 157-159.

return to India was much lower. For, this right could only be claimed after a decade had passed. By that time, the majority of labourers employed in British colonies were well-established. Moreover, they had to pay part of the return journey themselves.[33]

High immigration costs and the ongoing British interference prompted Suriname's colonial administration to look for another option. Indeed, frictions between plantation owners and indentured labourers occurred often. The latter were all too well aware of the fact they could always call upon the British consul to intervene. The Colonial Report of 1875 had already mentioned 'a spirit of disorder manifesting itself in the districts'.[34] Indentured labourers, complaining about heavy labour and low wages, had often caused incidents concerning work refusal as well as arson.[35]

In 1884, a serious turn of events took place at plantations named Zoelen and Zorg en Hoop, whereby troops were called in to assist. This year's sugar crisis had not only prompted numerous planters to reduce wages but also to step up the work pace. At Zoelen the district commissioner of Lower Commewijne was attacked with sticks. Having investigated the local working conditions, he had supported this plantation's director. According to the 1885 Colonial Report, it had been established that, although measures pertaining to the control of the sugar cane harvest had tightened, wages 'had not undergone any reduction'.[36] Next, a military detachment occupied the Zoelen plantation in order to remove the ringleaders. Three weeks later an uprising led by a certain Ramjanee broke out at the Zorg en Hoop plantation where workers had started a slowdown action to weigh in on their demands for higher wages. The unrest here was triggered when a so-called 'coolie supervisor', having observed that the sugar cane had not been cut to the agreed measurements, was subsequently mistreated by workers who struck out at him.[37] Troops called to the rescue next shot seven Hindustanis after a request for the extradition of four mutinous workers, who had beaten up this supervisor, had been reciprocated in a rain of stones. In 1891, Hindustani workers hacked directors to death on two other plantations. Earlier that same year, five Hindustanis had been shot dead during incidents at the Zoelen plantation.[38]

The most serious event occurred in 1902 at the Mariënburg sugar plantation, after labourers had in vain demanded an increase in wages. The small pay rise the director James Mavor promised at the very last minute no longer sufficed to meet their needs. When more than 200 irate workers gathered outside the factory, as the 1903 Colonial Report states, they hacked Mavor, an agent employed by the *Nederlandsche Handel-Maatschappij*, to death 'in the most barbaric manner'; it is presumed that his behaviour towards Hindustani women had also fuelled their anger, of which this report makes no mention.[39] When a military detachment intervened the next day, 17 Hindustanis were killed and 39 wounded, seven of whom later succumbed to their injuries. This bloodshed occurred when workers demanded the release of the ten

---

33 Ibid., 150-152.
34 *Koloniaal Verslag 1875*, Kamerstuk 5, ondernummer 55, 265.
35 De Klerk 1953, 139-145; see also: Hira 1982, 199-215.
36 *Koloniaal Verslag 1885*, Kamerstuk 5, ondernummer 10, bijlage (annex) F, 6.
37 Ibid., 7.
38 De Klerk 1953, 140-141.
39 Ibid., 142; a number of elder Hindustanis, who had been involved in this incident, reported this to De Klerk; Hoefte 1987b, 424-427.

men who had been arrested for murdering the director.[40] According to that Colonial Report, a crowd armed with hatchets and the like had assembled near the factory which housed soldiers, civil servants as well as the detainees:

'The attorney general, realizing the precarious situation in which the soldiers and civil servants were in, gave permission to fire. The crowd, ordered up to five times to dissolve and behave calmly, replied with 'boos', a strange cry, which means contempt. The immigrants, probably believing that shooting would not be allowed, increasingly insisted, and then finally the firearms had to be used. [...] This action of the military hugely impressed the rebellious crowd. They immediately broke up and the majority of the labourers resumed work the following morning. The judiciary succeeded in laying hands on several of the main culprits linked to Mr. Mavor's murder and eight of them having been found guilty of manslaughter committed in association were sentenced in this matter to forced labour for the period of twelve years.'[41]

The rebellious workers employed at the Mariënburg plantation included several Javanese. For, in order to no longer depend upon the British with regard to immigration, the Dutch government in The Hague had finally decided to allow the migration of contract labourers from the Dutch East Indies.

As early as in 1873 and 1883 the *Nederlandsche Handel-Maatschappij* (NHM) had attempted to contract labourers from the islands of Java and Madura. However, the Dutch government had imposed a ban fearing a shortage of workers would arise in the Dutch East Indies. In 1890 the NHM was granted a permit to employ, by way of an experiment, 100 Javanese workers on the Mariënburg plantation during a 5-year period; all in all, in 1890, vessels transported 94 immigrants to Suriname.[42] However, in 1894, a second transport consisting of 614 Javanese resulted in a political scandal. Apparently 65 souls had passed away either during or shortly after the voyage.[43] An investigation commissioned by the Minister of Colonies revealed they had been subjected to very poor hygienic conditions for more than 3 months at a depot located in Batavia, the capital of the Dutch East Indies. Not only had the medical facilities been completely inadequate, the provisions had in part become inedible during the 50-day journey. Moreover, these immigrants (the majority of whom were deemed the most destitute inhabitants of Java) had not been provided with warm clothes in order to endure the low temperatures experienced when rounding the Cape of Good Hope. The then Minister of Colonies stated this was all merely a 'confluence of various circumstances'.[44] In 1896, despite these tragic events, the Dutch government permitted the recruiting of labourers from Java on a more regular basis. These emigrants were only allowed to depart from Batavia, Semarang and Surabaya, as depots had been established here. Whenever en route requirements were put in place

---

40   *Koloniaal Verslag 1903*, Kamerstuk 5, ondernummer II, bijlage (annex) M1, 60.
41   Ibid.
42   Ismael 1949, 26-31.
43   Ibid., 32-34.
44   *Koloniaal Verslag 1895*, Kamerstuk 5, ondernummer 1, bijlage (annex) C, 21.

A History of Suriname

Figure 9.2. Javanese contract labourers inside the depot located at the Combé quarter of Paramaribo. Having been medically examined and after a sojourn of several weeks, they were informed which plantation they were to work on. An note on this photograph mentions that these Javanese had arrived in 1894 on the S.S. *Voorwaarts*, a voyage that caused commotion in Paramaribo. For, during this journey and its aftermath, more than 60 Javanese passengers had perished. Photo by Julius Muller. Vink, 1997, nr. 27.

pertaining to medical examinations and provisions, the government only fulfilled a supervisory task, which the labour inspectorate and the police carried out.[45]

The incentives of the majority of Javanese to set off for Suriname were identical to those of Hindustanis. Their employment contracts were more or less the same, too. Recruiting was left to individual entrepreneurs. Implementation lay in the hands of emigration agents, whose assistants carried out the actual work. This form of recruitment led to numerous cases of abuse. Deception and deceit were no exception. On various occasions residents of a village (*kampong*) maltreated unpopular recruiters. When hunting for premiums for each worker, recruiters did not take much care as to the qualifications of the individuals they approached. Financial reasons resulted in mainly unmarried people being sent to Suriname. This phenomenon did not increase the desire among Javanese deemed suitable for emigration. Furthermore, mandatory 5-year contracts held less appeal if compared with 3-year employment contracts common to the Dutch East Indies, which did not encourage more suitable workers to apply either.[46] Between 1890 and 1939, a

---

45   Ismael 1949, 40-41.
46   Ibid., 63-66; Hoefte 1987b, 133-139.

total of 32,956 Javanese men, women and children set off for Suriname of which almost 25 per cent later utilised the right to return to Java.[47]

9.2 Creoles after emancipation

After emancipation a more pluriform society was able to develop. Now a new class of free citizens emerged, whereby differentiation as well as social mobility within the colonial society hugely increased. Feeling attached to their long-term locations and familiar group of residents, many former slaves opted to remain on their former master's plantation during the era of state supervision. The young often preferred to work on plantations closer to Paramaribo. Now and again unwillingness arose among the emancipated, because they considered their wages too low. In the end, however, the imminent prospect of being put to work on government-run plantations did result in a majority signing employment contracts.[48] The Colonial Report of 1875 points to 'the rejoicing circumstance that against all expectations such a quantum of labour was obtained from the Creole population'.[49] Certain former slaves signed contracts with the residents of Paramaribo, for whom services were then provided. They also lived off small plots of land acquired under flexible conditions and located on the outskirts of this town. Artisans did not need to sign plantation contracts. For, in order to be able to continue to express their craftmanship, they often made arrangements with town dwellers. Domestic servants, who were also not obliged to work on plantations, moved to the town. Fraudulent contracts were created especially among women enabling them to sell their goods mainly on the marketplace of Paramaribo.[50] Migration into Paramaribo remained limited after the state's supervision reached a conclusion. Here, between 1872 and 1880, the number of inhabitants increased from 21,191 to 22,552, i.e., from 42 to 46 per cent of the colony's entire population.[51]

Having settled down as smallholder farmers, many Creole workers reclaimed garden plots, only to abandon them after a while. From 1873 on, Governor Cornelis A. van Sypesteyn (1823-1892) initiated the construction of *gouvernementsvestigings-plaatsen* (government settlements), for example, at Fort Nieuw Amsterdam. Here former slaves could rent plot of lands from the government, a measure aimed at providing planters in particular with a labour reservoir. These plots were kept small, forcing tenants to acquire additional means of income on nearby plantations.[52] In order to be assured of sufficient labour during the harvest season certain planters rented land to former slaves. Creole farmers located near Paramaribo, who now and again worked in the capital, hardly prospered at all. Producing mainly for their own benefit, they were unable to take over the supplying of food from plantation owners who, after 1873, entirely focussed on staple products. Creoles residing in the districts prospered much more. They thus belied the view settlers often proclaimed, to wit, that, what they called the 'negro race' was unfit to work in the agricultural sector. The cocoa culture was developing along major rivers e.g., the Saramacca and the

---

47   Bruijning & J. Voorhoeve 1977, 310.
48   Van Lier 1971, 181-188; Klinkers 1997, 121-129.
49   *Koloniaal Verslag 1875*, Kamerstuk 5, ondernummer 69, 290.
50   Van Lier 1971, 181.
51   Ibid., 182, 253.
52   Ibid., 227.

Figure 9.3. Street in Paramaribo, 1891-1894. Unknown photographer. Surinaams Museum photo archive.

Nickerie. As yet familiar to the emancipated and going back to the era of slavery, this culture now flourished thanks to an increasing demand from North America. In 1895, the Witch-broom disease (Moniliophthora perniciosa), a fungal infection, diminished the prosperity of cocoa farmers. They possessed insufficient capital and on occasion knowledge as to applying pesticides, whereas the owners of large plantations did. A lack of cooperation between the emancipated, often originating from slave groups harbouring mutual distrust, also formed an impediment. Former slaves reclaimed their fields at locations as far apart as possible, rendering it difficult to collectively construct irrigation systems.[53]

In Coronie, a district of Suriname, the Creole population succeeded in turning small-scale agriculture into a lasting success. As a result of Coronie's isolated location, Paramaribo could only be reached by sea. These Creoles thus felt little need to move away. After emancipation, former slaves had transformed into landowners because, due to wage arrears, plantation owners were forced to pay their debts by means of land plots. Newly active planters specialised in the coconut culture, which has remained of importance to Coronie to this very day. Even pre-emancipation, small-scale agriculture had been observed. British plantation owners could no longer sell their cotton on the London marketplace because slave labour had been banned in Great Britain. They were not only forced to abandon their cotton plantations but also to free slaves who thus now depended on available plots of land for their livelihoods. Suriname's colonial government accommodated them by establishing the plantation named Totness as a *gouvernementsvestigingsplaats*.[54] In the districts of Para and Boven-Suriname, other conditions favoured forms of small-scale agriculture. Slaves

---

53   Ibid., 228-231; Klinkers 1997, 161-164.
54   Van Lier 1971, 227-232; Klinkers 1997, 164-166.

had always discerned themselves here by means of the independent nature of the work carried out in remote woodlands, therefore creating strong interconnecting social bonds. After emancipation, former slaves became owners of woodlands, which had always been considered common property. Having laid out garden plots, mainly for their own use, they then settled down in villages built on former plantations.[55]

The migrations of the Creoles to Paramaribo really took off at the turn of the century. Issues encountered in small-scale agriculture, particularly cocoa farming, had deprived many of decent livelihoods. Gold mining and the balata manufacturing business now provided alternative employment (see also p. 240-244). In due course these sectors employed between 8,000 and 9,000 labourers.[56] Creoles worked in the forests, while the women and children stayed behind in Paramaribo. Numerous Creole women also worked either at home as seamstresses or laundresses, or elsewhere as domestic servants. Although work in forests was irregular, many families were able to earn reasonable livelihoods. Wages were significantly higher in comparison with those earned on plantations. Gold miners were paid between 2 and 2.50 Hfl per day whereas a balata bleeder's normal daily wage consisted of 1.50 Hfl. Those capable of tapping large quantities of latex earned more. At the start of the 20th century, plantation workers earned an average of 1.14 Hfl a day and women often less than half this amount.[57]

9.3 Tensions within a plural society

Even after emancipation, Suriname experienced great social tensions, inherent to colonial circumstances. Though the sharp dichotomy within the slave society had disappeared, contradictions remained. Both racial and social dividing lines almost coincided, which could lead to unexpected outbursts. Within this context the term 'latent hostility' is applied if referring to various ethnic groups.[58] When an affair involving Governor Maurits Adriaan de Savornin Lohman (1889-1891) escalated, this hidden enmity among the population was exposed.[59] The Dutch government had not been very tactful when appointing De Savornin Lohman to the post of governor in Paramaribo. In the Netherlands he was considered extremely headstrong. A Minister of Justice had reprimanded him for his behaviour while serving as a member of the judiciary. Members of the Jewish community residing in Suriname mistrusted the incoming Governor beforehand because he had published an article in the Netherlands scenting of anti-Semitism. Being the younger brother of an influential politician, De Savornin Lohman's appointment to post of Governor of Suriname savoured of nepotism. In addition, De Savornin Lohman had recently lost all his assets, thus rendering the governor's post all the more appealing. Immediately after his arrival, he fuelled the dissent of civil servants based in Suriname by appointing a Dutch military officer as deputy district commissioner.

Complaints Creole farmers from the Para District launched concerning the level of taxes gave rise to a major conflict, which would lead to a full-scale riot. These

---

55   Ibid., 232-233; ibid., 164-166.
56   Van Lier 1971, 246.
57   Bos 1911, 55-67.
58   Van Lier 1971, 358.
59   Ibid., 339-359; Vink 2010, 89-91; Hira 1982, 215-243.

Figure 9.4. Paramaribo, *c.*1895. In the foreground, we see the Oranjestraat (now Mr. De Mirandastraat). In the background the Suriname River is viewed from the tower of the premises housing the Ministry of Finance. Photo by Julius Muller. Vink, 1997, nr. 1.

farmers refused to pay the head money, which had been increased to 3 Hfl per annum in 1886. When a group of some 40 men and women hailing from the aforementioned district approached De Savornin Lohman shortly after his arrival in May 1889 with a request for exemption, he declared little could be done to assist them. They now set off on a demonstrative march along the Waterkant (Waterfront). Several protesters, referred to as 'Para negroes', were arrested after fighting a police officer. The trial of these protesters, who were sentenced to a 6-day detention, led to new unrest and to the rallying of groups of Creoles from the Para District. The fear grew among Paramaribo-based colonists that the situation would get out of hand. According to a concerned comment published in the newspaper *De West-Indiër*, the opinion threatened to gain ground across the colony that the government 'is incapable of holding its own should the negroes wish it otherwise'.[60] De Savornin Lohman's visit to villages located in the Para District did not bring any changes. In due course he detached 40 troops and ten armed policemen to the Para District, but this initiative ended in failure. For, after being threatened by that district's armed residents, this detachment had to about-turn at the village of Onverwacht. Next, the hard-mouthed De Savornin Lohman instigated the Colonial States' anger by refusing to provide any further information on this issue. He even threatened to dismiss four senior officials, appointees to the Colonial States, from their civil service tasks for supporting an

60   Van Lier 1971, 345.

interpellation request forwarded by the very same Colonial States, which demanded far more forceful action.

Governor De Savornin Lohman attempted to bring the population of the Para District to its knees by positioning a military blockade at the plantation of Onoribo located on the Suriname River, thus cutting off the shipping route to Paramaribo. His only achievement was: those convicted turned themselves in to serve prison sentences. Several Moravian missionaries had mediated in order to prevent this conflict from further escalating, but the inhabitants of this district continued to refuse to pay any taxes. Having realised his lack of means to force a solution, De Savornin Lohman wrote to the Minister of Colonies: 'Apart from the warship, I can only rely on the white garrison troops numbering over one hundred'; though also in charge of Black soldiers and of colour, he questioned in this letter 'whether they can be trusted vis-a-vis negroes'.[61] He had therefore only utilised whites for the failed military expedition to the Para District.

The issue pertaining to this district held the colony within its grasp for 2 years. During this period a group of prominent residents forwarded a petition to the Crown, denouncing De Savornin Lohman's conduct, his governance and his threatening the four appointees to the Colonial States. This stance gradually evolved into a conflict whereby affluent colonists opposed the *petite bourgeoisie* and the lower classes. De Savornin Lohman who sided with the latter layer of society, also realised that members of the Colonial States and their adherents formed the main threat to his position. Moreover, his faithful presence during services held at the Moravian Church, exerted a considerable influence among lower-class Creoles. This conflict was partly fought out in two newspapers, to wit, *De West-Indiër* and *De Volksbode* (The People's Messenger).The former publication chose to side with members of the Colonial States and the well-to-do bourgeoisie. *De Volksbode* was, on the other hand, founded in 1890 in order to give a voice to the emerging middle class and lower class Creoles. A number of carpenters, contractors and teachers serving the Moravian Church were active on the board of the *Vereeniging tot Exploitatie van de Volksbode* (Association for the Exploitation of the Volksbode). Eager to retain a Christian governor for Suriname, members of the Moravian Brethren openly took sides with De Savornin Lohman.

On 14 February 1890, De Savornin Lohman exacerbated contrarieties by submitting a bill to the Colonial States, aimed at extending electoral rights by means of lowering the census from 40 to 20 Hfl, whereby the number of voters would increase from 251 to 413.[62] He now at least gave the impression that his objective merely served to enhance his support within the Colonial States. When this body rejected this proposal the outcome inevitably fuelled anger amidst the lower middle class which now felt excluded by the well-to-do bourgeoisie from governing. Members of this lower middle class turned against the Jewish population in particular, which in their opinion, had far too great an influence. Moreover, lower-

---

61   Hira 1982, 231.
62   Van Lier 1971, 351.

class Creoles held the view that Jews were the descendants of slave owners.[63] *De Volksbode* did not hesitate to stir up anti-Semitism, which had almost always been present in the colony. Jews were time and again referred to as 'the clique of Labad', a term applied when describing *De West-Indiër* as well as its Jewish editor-in-chief W.J. Labad.[64] The Netherlands-based press did indeed participate fully in this polemic. On this issue the Christian government coalition, which needless to say supported De Savornin Lohman, diametrically opposed liberals.[65] *De West-Indiër* and *De Volksbode* often opted to reprint articles extracted from newspapers (e.g., *Het Vaderland, De Standaard*) in order to underline their arguments.

Polarisation came to a head on 12 May 1891 when commemorating the Colonial States' 25th anniversary proved to be the fuse in the powder keg.[66] A few weeks earlier, Governor De Savornin Lohman had filed his resignation in writing after a conflict with the attorney-general J. Kalff. It concerned a futile issue, in which the latter judicial civil servant had refused to prosecute. De Savornin Lohman then demanded Kalff to be recalled immediately, only to receive a negative response from the Dutch government at The Hague. This Governor's supporters increasingly deemed the announced celebration of the Colonial States a provocation. *De Volksbode* called upon the population both in Sranan and in Dutch to not only obstruct him from resigning but also to express their affection for their Governor by demonstrating. Many thousands left their districts to travel to Paramaribo. On the morning of the festive May 12, an enraged crowd demolished all preparations located on the Gouvernementsplein. Homes were damaged, too, whereby the Jewish residents of Paramaribo were particularly targeted. The situation got increasingly out of hand when De Savornin Lohman's initiatives made it almost impossible for the attorney-general Kalff, who also officiated as the Head of Police, to restore order. The former had instructed the military on patrol in lower-class neighbourhoods to return to Fort Zeelandia, after which rioting intensified. De Savornin Lohman threw even more oil on the fire the next day by commissioning a large crowd to welcome him in front of the governor's palace. In his speech, he allowed a dance party to take place in the centre of Paramaribo which demonstrators viewed as a licence to cause further damage. One rioter was shot dead by a police officer. Fear among members of the bourgeoisie and the middle class had reached such a level that the *Vereeniging voor Volksweerbaarheid* (Association for the People's Defensibility) was founded in order to offer protection against attacks.[67] As the uproar continued, the Governor and the attorney-general accused each other in telegrams addressed to the Dutch government of being responsible for allowing matters to escalate. Parliamentarians at The Hague had continuously downplayed any tensions, but now ordered De Savornin Lohman to

---

63   Vink 2010, 102-104, 122-131; here Vink points to the 'latent dissatisfaction' among Christian settlers which resulted from the increased socio-political status of Jews, who now formed more than half the Colonial States' elected members; the Moravian Brethren, in support of De Savornin Lohman, fuelled anti-Semitic sentiment. Competition between this Brethren's flourishing companies and Jewish businessmen played a role, too; see also: Lenders 1996, 340.
64   Lenders 1996, 340.
65   Van Lier 1971, 352-353.
66   Ibid., 355-358.
67   Ibid., 357.

call in the army and the navy to then cooperate with the police. He left the command to Kalff who then, with the help of the navy, managed to restore order within a few days and without further bloodshed. De Savornin Lohman, having lost almost all support in the Dutch lower house, returned to his homeland as a frustrated man.

This affair once again clarified how strenuous relations between Suriname and the Netherlands had become. For, an ambiguous administrative structure now obstructed the greater autonomy which those aforementioned governmental regulations imposed in 1865 had envisaged. The Colonial States and the governor shared the legislative power. In practice however the government in The Hague set the budget because of the continuing deficits. Moreover, the Crown's right to annul decisions severely limited the power which the colonial 'parliament' held. In addition, the Netherlands' economic policy made it virtually impossible for Suriname to stand on its own financial feet. The Hague deemed it a 'reserve colony', which had to remain open for investments in case the Dutch East Indies would be lost. Suriname therefore had accumulated hardly any sources of income of its own with which to finance governmental expenditure. In 1913, in its second report, a committee comprising parliamentarians as well as civil servants presided by the Member of Parliament Dirk Bos, whom the Minister of Colonies had commissioned to report on the economy and the financial position of Suriname, mentioned the 'demoralizing influence' exerted through the administrative system:

'The tendency of the population, and therefore also of the voters, to rely on the government and to expect all salvation, especially that which can be valued in money, from the mother country, had to make us look for an administrative system, that enlivens the awareness of the representatives of the population that, in addition to the Governor, they are primarily responsible for the proper functioning of affairs.[68]

A lack of influence continuously frustrated the Colonial States's members. No collegiate control with the governor existed. Moreover, these appointees were strongly inclined to turn away from Dutch authorities because of their political inability to act. The absence of a political outlet also explains the polemic tone which then characterised the press in Suriname. Amidst the upper classes, a certain anti-Dutch sentiment could be observed, especially among people of colour, who were not eligible for the highest civil service posts which detached expatriate Dutch civil servants occupied. Not the most suited individuals were dispatched to the West. Those who really wished to build careers would rather set off for the Dutch East Indies. Government circles in the Netherlands opined that the people of Suriname were not sufficiently independent to occupy key positions because of their personal relationships within the small-scale colonial society. The Netherlands were not free of racial prejudices either. Pieter Jacob Elout van Soeterwoude, a prominent representative of the (Christian) Réveil, stated in the newspaper *Onze West* published in 1884 not only that the *'kleurling* [person of colour] possesses but few virtues' but that he is also characterised by way of 'laziness, unreliability, lack of energy and

---

68   Bos 1913, 2-3.

A History of Suriname

by excessive conceit', although he 'is not unintelligent and has great aptitude for learning languages and music'.[69] Van Soeterwoude's opinion was that something could evolve from the 'kleurling' if their upbringing improved.

During the mid-1800s, people of colour did indeed hold high official posts, but they were increasingly unseated by Jews. An important reason for this was: having studied in the Netherlands, the non-white were reluctant to return to Suriname. They often felt more attracted to either the Netherlands or the Dutch East Indies, because their social opportunities were greater here. From the turn of the 19th century, Jewish originating from Suriname also increasingly chose to remain in the Netherlands, where living conditions for Jews had improved.[70]

With a decreasing number of white colonists and improved connections which steam ships provided with Europe, certain colonial lifestyles vanished. Concubinage between Europeans and Black women and of colour, a distinct trait of plantation colonies founded in the West Indies, became less common. Many white men married white women, although mixed marriages did as yet take place. The *Surinaamsch huwelijk* (Surinamese marriage) no longer presented women of colour with any great social prestige, as had been the case until well into the 19th century (see p. 58). After all, the non-white population had reinforced its own social positions. Women of colour preferred marrying a male of colour above a concubinage with a white male.[71]

The significance of the non-white and the Black upper and middle classes was able to increase mainly through education. General compulsory schooling of children aged between 7 and 12 years was introduced in Suriname in 1876, i.e., a quarter of a century earlier than in the Netherlands. Compulsory tuition had already been in existence since 1863 for a specific group: children of parents placed under state supervision after the abolishment of slavery, under penalty of a fine. The Creole population initially thus benefited most from schooling. From 1844 on, the Moravian Brethren had educated enslaved children in Paramaribo as well as in districts. Moravian and Roman Catholic missions had received government funding for their schools since 1864. The first public schools were built 3 years later. In 1920, public as well as private forms of education acquired equal financial basis. Between 1878 and 1910, the number of teachers increased from 77 to 261, thus three teachers for every 100 pupils. In *c.*1925 the number of pupils had grown to almost 15.000. Suriname's population now counted almost 120.000 souls.[72]

Compulsory education presented a problem to the children of Hindustani immigrants. For, if aged between 10 and 15, they were contractually obliged to work half the time. A lack of knowledge of the Dutch language amid inhabitants especially in the districts, also placed them in disadvantageous circumstances. In 1890, to accommodate Hindustanis, 'coolie schools' were founded. Here tuition was provided in their mother tongue. These schools were closed in 1907. From then on, unqualified Hindustani teachers were allowed to teach in their mother tongue in ordinary primary schools in preparation of learning how to speak Dutch. Appointing such

---

69   Elout van Soeterwouden 1884, 28-29; Van Lier 1971, 268-269.
70   Van Lier 1971, 256-258.
71   Ibid., 259-260.
72   Ibid., 282-284; Adhin 1973, 99.

non-qualified teachers did not help improve the level of tuition. In 1929, matters deteriorated with the introduction of so-called 'limited primary education' in the districts as well as in the forest whereby qualification standards for school teachers did not apply. From now on, unqualified teachers were allowed to work applying the Dutch language, too, hereby affecting the level even further. Tuition thus increased the social differences between ethnic groups rather than reduce them.

In order to train more teachers, a teachers college was founded in 1877 and, 10 years later the first secondary school. It was named the Hendrikschool to honour Governor Hendrik Jan Smidt (1885-1888). Both forms of secondary tuition played significant roles within the social development of many Creoles, who now had greater access to posts available in the civil service and in education. Hindustanis and Javanese followed these two forms of schooling much later simply because of their deficiencies in the Dutch language. In 1882, a medical school was initiated in order to train government physicians. Its founding was the outcome of an obligation the Netherlands had accepted in order to improve the medical care presented to indentured labourers, after the British had discontinued the immigration of Hindustanis.[73]

The Dutch policy as executed in West Indies aimed at assimilating all the ethnic groups. On the other hand, across the Dutch East Indies, languages of the Indigenous peoples and their time-honoured traditions (*adat*) remained far more untouched. Unlike the East, Suriname was always viewed as a Dutch settlement. According to Governor Abraham A.L. Rutgers (1928-1933) the assimilation policy implied that:

> 'all that was possible (was) being done by the Administration to fuse the entire population, both white and brown, black and yellow, irrespective of whether they are Europeans or Americans, Africans or Asians, into one cohesive language and culture community with a uniform administration of justice right down to matters pertaining to marriage and inheritance. A uniform system of free education with Dutch as the medium of instructions available for all population groups, for whom schooling has been compulsory since 1876 in Suriname.'[74]

The early introduction of compulsory education was therefore a direct consequence of the advocated policy. Initially, Creoles were the only target of assimilation, as long as indentured labourers from Asia were as yet considered temporary workers. Assimilation fell in line with the, usually unspoken, concept which many colonists adhered to: emancipated slaves had no culture of their own. At the beginning of the 20th century, after the introduction in 1895 of a settlement policy for immigrants, enabling them to settle as smallholder farmers, this assimilation policy also served to include Asian migrants whom Christian missionaries attempted to convert with no great success. In 1927, the legal position of the Hindustanis improved as soon as the law on Dutch citizenship, which applied to the Dutch East Indies, came into effect in Suriname.[75] Meanwhile the colonial government had closed all special 'coolie schools'.[76]

---

73   Adhin 1973, 93.
74   Van Lier 1971, 192.
75   Bruijning & Voorhoeve 1977, 278.
76   Van Lier 1971, 192-193.

Figure 9.5. The mosque and the next door synagogue located at the Keizerstraat in Paramaribo. Photo by Vincent Mentzel.

The education policy however was not very consistent. As previously mentioned, in 1929, when the budget expenditure risked getting out of hand due to the equal treatment of funds allocated to private and public education, the government of Suriname again opened the possibility of establishing low-quality schools which provided 'limited primary education' to those living in districts. The Colonial States had twice in vain rejected proposals pertaining to education cuts. Even a petition the population had forwarded at the end of 1924 did not prevent authorities from implementing austerity measures.[77] Governor Aarnoud J.A.A. van Heemstra (1921-1928) defended these incoming rulings after leaving his post by plainly stating that 'there had been an abnormal rise in erudition, and people began to form a class of quasi-intellectuals for whom a place in their proper sphere of destiny could no longer be found'.[78]

Attempts at assimilating Creoles were more successful. Needless to say, tuition was a key factor here. The Moravian Brethren initially taught in the Sranan language, but government policy put an end to this. The Suriname-born education inspector Herman D. Benjamins (1850-1933) was perhaps the fiercest propagandist of the Dutch language. On the basis of his more than 30-year-long career, he must be credited for improving Suriname's education system in a very meritorious manner. Only religious services continued to be held in the Creole language. In fact, the

---

77   Gobardhan-Rambocus 2001, 16-17; in this standard work on education in Suriname the author concludes (see p. 506) that emancipation and the development of population groups 'had never been a policy goal at least until 1950'.
78   Gobardhan-Rambocus 2008, 78.

government aimed at 'de-Africanising' especially the lower class Creoles. In 1878, the Penal Code even included a provision directed against 'idolatry'. Whenever violated, a maximum of 6 months imprisonment and a 1,000 Hfl fine would follow.[79] Moravians and Redemptorists also played a part in the assimilation policy. Almost all lower class Creoles belonged to either the Moravian Brethren or the Roman Catholic Church. However, attempts these religious institutions made aimed at eradicating African cultural elements proved unsuccessful. Utilising Black evangelists and auxiliary missionaries from the end of the 1800s on, did not bring that many changes.

Lower class Creoles continued to consult their ritual practitioners (*lukuman*) and also to present sacrifices to their gods, goddesses and spirits. Views the lower-class Creoles held on marriage and society hardly transformed either. Indeed, at the end of the 19th century, an open conflict concerning these issues rose amidst members of the Moravian Church. From 1850 on, those slaves not allowed to enter into legal marriages had been offered the option to enter into a 'covenant'. After emancipation, the Moravian missionaries wished to put an end to this opportunity. From that moment on, as to those emancipated, the government also stipulated that church weddings were only possible if preceded by civil ceremonies. Those who then opted to not enter into legal marriages were obliged to leave the church. Such a measure was unacceptable to the majority of lower-class Creoles. High costs as well as bureaucracy prevented many from marrying legally. It was possible to obtain a proof of insolvency, but in that case one had to accept the humiliation of having to walk to the Town Hall, while disallowed to wear marriage attire, having to appear barefoot and not permitted to provide a wedding banquet. In *c.*1880, the Moravian Church had already excluded around 5,000 individuals many of whom were converted to Catholicism with its much more flexible traditions and policies.[80] When in 1880 a Moravian missionary named Bernard Heijde turned against church discipline during a service, he received support from almost the entire congregation. Not much later two members of this mission's board travelled from Herrnhut (Saxony, Germany) to Suriname in order to appease tempers. Their consultation resulted in rehabilitating the 'covenant'. In 1893, however, upon the Moravian mission's request, the government removed the financial obstacles impeding civil marriages. Now once again, creating 'covenants' had become impossible. By and large, lower class Creoles continued to prefer concubinage to wedlock.[81]

The traditional plantation colony of Suriname had been transmuted by means of emancipation, a subsequent immigration and an increased social mobility. Rudolf A.J. van Lier, following John S. Furnivall, referred to the outcome of this transformation as a 'plural' society (see also Epilogue). Each population segment differs from the other when looking into races, languages, religions and socio-economic activities. Van Lier states that such a society is 'marked by the absence of unity of race and religion' and furthermore that here 'the different groups live in different economic spheres'.[82] The waning white group, to which Dutch civil servants belonged, formed the upper

---

79   Adhin 1975, 15-21.
80   Buschkens 1974, 128-131; Van Lier 1971, 288-289.
81   Van Lier 1971, 289.
82   Ibid., 9-10; see also: Furnivall 1939, Chapter XIII.

layer. Jews and non-whites, population groups which included the largest number of assimilated individuals, formed a key part of the upper-middle class. Lower-class Black Creoles had also made their way into the middle class when employed as teachers, civil servants or craftsmen. The great mass of those *volkscreolen* formed a lower class to which the majority of Hindustani migrants could also be considered to belong, although their dissimilar language and culture had caused them to live somewhat separated from the rest of society. The Javanese occupied even more marginal positions.

In 1911, A.E. Boers, a minister of the Lutheran Church, was well familiar with the society of Suriname through his work here. Presenting an exceptionally sharp sketch of the difficult mutual relations, he stated in a speech addressed to the *Surinaamsche Volksbond* (People's Union of Suriname):

> '*Because everyone values his interest the most, this country is divided. A population that is not united. One seeks the cause of misery above, outside one's self. The evil lies in the government. The disease lies not in the doctor. But the patient is sick. But he must know he is ill. [...] One hates the government. One hates the Dutch in the government. The Dutchman has done it. He is not tolerated in the colony. Some contradict me, but someone else clearly says yes. [...] I hear it said that the people of Suriname have no part in the government. Only the subordinate position is for them. [...] Remarkably this mass does not want to be ruled by its own men - not by the coloured one and not by the Semites. And the coloured one in these days does not want the Dutchman. The black population does not want the coloured one.*'[83]

This Lutheran minister's words provoked criticism which did not really concern his portrayal of the divisions within this colonial society, but rather pertained to his very condescending words describing the people of Suriname, including members of the upper classes. The lawyers, doctors, teachers and clergymen of Suriname should according to Boers first 'make an effort' in order to become equal to the Dutch; he also mentioned that 'the extraordinary inhabitant of Suriname is only extraordinary in Suriname, outside he is very common', before concluding thus: 'we are more than you are.'[84] John Robert Thomson (1853-1933), the Surinamese publicist-*cum*-school director and later Chairman of the Colonial States, published a razor-sharp open letter. In it he qualified the words spoken by Boers as 'poisonous weeds' because of 'the humiliating way in which you talk about non-white people of Suriname'.[85]

The enmity which had already emerged during Governor De Savornin Lohman's tenure had by no means disappeared. The difficult struggle for life many Creoles experienced in small-scale agriculture, the harsh regime featuring indentured labour which Hindustanis as well as Javanese had to cope with, and the discrimination imposed by white colonists with which non-whites were confronted, could stir up discontent at any moment. These issues must have prompted Frans Pavel Vaclav

---

83   Boers 1911, 7-10.
84   Ibid., 17-18.
85   Thompson 1911, 4, 9.

Killinger (1876-1936) to initiate a coup d'état in 1910.[86] After sojourns in Switzerland and Germany, this police inspector of Hungarian descent joined the Dutch colonial army. In order to carry out this insurgency he mobilised six accomplices, among them police officers, a carpenter and a former Hindustani indentured labourer. Their plans were leaked within 3 weeks after their first meeting. A baker whom one accomplice had offered money to recruit individuals to set out on a risky undertaking reported this initiative to a Roman Catholic clergyman who had in turn informed the attorney-general in person. Killinger was sentenced to death only to later be pardoned and serve his 5-year prison sentence in the Netherlands. During the trial it emerged he had wanted to establish an independent republic in Suriname. Those recruited to carry out this insurrection were especially found among the Hindustani workers who, having taken possession of police weapons, had to apply a stratagem before taking over Fort Zeelandia, which a number of troops protected. According to Killinger, he had wished to put an end to the many forms of abuse, in particular the inferior living conditions of the impoverished. One of the complicit police officers mentioned he had felt disadvantaged as to being promoted to higher positions, for which whites were more likely to be eligible. According to the Roman Catholic newspaper *De Surinamer*, Killinger was a psychopath.[87] Such an assessment was however rather too convenient as part of the lower classes did support him. During his trial hundreds of people, gathered outside the courthouse, would on occasion shout his name. Apparently Killinger voiced widely felt social frustrations. *De Surinaamsche Bode* described him with admiration:

> 'We imagine on the canvas a new country falling from the sky with its government men consisting of a white president who preaches nothing but equality, freedom and fraternity, as well as black and brown judges, Prosec. Generals, Adm. of Finance, Bank directors, etc., etc., in one word those who used to be servants, now become the most prominent. Who is here, dear reader who would not want to cooperate to create such an ideal? Who is here who would not want to give up everything, even his life, to own that land?'[88]

The sympathy Killinger had aroused amidst both the petite bourgeoisie and the working class did reflect an emerging political interest but did not lead to any major political activities. The aforementioned *Surinaamsche Volksbond*, founded after the unsuccessful coup attempt, had sought to extend the right to vote for the petite bourgeoisie, but fell into oblivion after only several meetings. Few saw the point of any political organisations as long as the Colonial States represented only 2 per cent of the population if based on the census right to vote.[89] Needless to say, no leaders could rise under such circumstances.

A few years earlier, however, electoral associations had been established. The incoming electoral regulations of 1905 implied candidates were required to

---

86   Van Lier 1971, 258-261; Hira 1982, 243-261.
87   Hira 1982, 257.
88   Ibid., 258.
89   Van Lier 1971, 334.

stand for election. Hence the need for such associations increased.[90] Newspaper advertisements, be it signed or not, recommended individuals whose concepts had never been discussed. On 9 March 1908, the short-lived *Algemeene Kiesvereeniging* (General Electoral Association) was founded. Soon afterwards, another electoral association named *Eendracht Maakt Macht* (Unity Makes Might) advocated in its statutes to replace the census right to vote with the capacity right to vote. The secondment of Dutch civil servants should be kept to a minimum. In addition, small businesses active in the gold and balata sectors needed to be promoted, resulting here in increased employment opportunities. The initiators included H.J. van Ommeren and P.A. May. Both were members of the Colonial States and served as editors to the newspaper *Suriname*. The association named *Eendracht Maakt Macht* pursued clear social-democratic goals. Several of its leaders were affiliated with the *Sociaal-Democratisch Arbeiderspartij* (Social Democratic Workers' Party) in the Netherlands. Between elections, *Eendracht Maakt Macht* remained rather passive. Several years later further political activities developed, especially after J.J. Leys, the head of agricultural education, expressed in a lecture the desire to establish a political electoral association. As was often the case, the local press continued the debate in all its intensity. According to the newspaper *De West*, nominating candidates should no longer concern the purely influential who in Suriname were referred to as *Statenfabrikanten* ([Colonial] States manufacturers). On September 11, 1918, the *Surinaamsche Kiesvereeniging* (Electoral Association of Suriname) was founded with J.J. Leys officiating as a board member. This electoral association then manifested itself as a party representing plantation owners. In Suriname, however, social relations had now changed to such a degree that this association proved unable to acquire a foothold during elections held in 1922 and 1924.[91]

A growing self-awareness among the Creole population also resulted in the establishment of several trade unions. Teaching staff had already founded the *Christelijke Onderwijzers-vereeniging Broederschap* (Christian Teachers' Association Brotherhood) in 1892, followed 3 years later by the *Surinaamsch Onderwijsgenootschap* (Education Society of Suriname). In 1908 a union for painters was set up. Around 10 years later unions for typographers and porters followed.[92] No real trade union system existed as yet. Activities were thus often limited to one or two strikes. In due course, trade unions began to nominate candidates for the Colonial States.

9.4 The position of Asian populations

At the end of the 19th century, Hindustanis had in part achieved a certain level of prosperity. In 1895 the government transformed land-related policies in order to persuade more immigrants to stay in Suriname. Now, having fulfilled their contracts, they were allowed to either rent or buy a plot of land without losing the right to return to the British Raj. If they chose to later renounce that right, they would receive a premium of 100 Hfl drawn from the colonial budget.[93] The immigration policy had

---

90   Ibid., 332-336; Samson 1947, 161-174.
91   Samson 1947, 166-170.
92   Hira 1982, 279-280.
93   Van Lier 1971, 234; De Klerk 1953, 162-165.

thus in fact become a colonisation policy. These measures had a beneficial effect. In 1895 only 548 Hindustanis were either tenants or owners of land, whereas in c.1913 their number had risen to 5,093.[94] They managed to expand their property rapidly and with great thrift. Farmers who had settled near Paramaribo even became major competitors of the Dutch, who until that moment had always supplied this town with produce such as vegetables and milk. These Dutch farmers descended from a group comprising in excess of 300 immigrants who in 1845 had established an agricultural colony near the Saramacca River. They had set off for Suriname after tempting promises had been made to them by the Dutch government, which had wished to populate its colony with large numbers of white settlers. This measure would at once solve problems linked to unemployment in the Netherlands and labour shortage in Suriname. These Dutch families succumbed to typhoid fever in large numbers. After this attempt at colonization had failed, these immigrants whose descendants are referred to as *boeroes* (farmers) in Suriname, had moved to Paramaribo. Competition from Hindustanis, who as a result of their simpler way of life could ask for less money when trading, forced Dutch farmers to focus more on cattle breeding. Nevertheless rivalry became more and more tangible here.[95]

Hindustanis by and large continued to reside in districts to only gradually become active as retail traders in Paramaribo. The Chinese mainly manifested themselves as retailers. For, as early as in the first decades after their arrival. they succeeded in conquering a place in the distribution of foodstuffs to soon also become active as importers. In 1898 the Chinese had set up 186 grocery stores across Suriname.[96] In Paramaribo, 30 per cent of shops were Chinese-owned and in the districts more than 50 per cent. Family members arrived from China in order to fulfill business tasks. This immigration even led to protests from the established trade elite comprising Jewish, European as well as small numbers of light-skinned Creole merchants. In 1891 they requested, apparently in vain, the then Governor to ban this migration, because 'here as elsewhere trade competition with Asians who have completely different life requirements is not possible'.[97] During this same period, the first of a small group comprising Lebanese migrants, mainly active as tradesmen, had also set foot in Suriname. They formed part of a larger group of Lebanese, often Maronite Christians, who had migrated to the Americas. In Suriname they evolved into a valued be it small group of migrants who, in accordance with the *boeroes*, manifested themselves across all layers of society.[98]

The Hindustani sense of economy and entrepreneurship was striking. In 1904 the teacher-*cum*-trader Jacques Samuels, who at the start of the 20th century was best known as a chronicler contributing to the Paramaribo-based press, wrote a characteristic sketch of his Hindustani 'cartman' Samie:

---

94 De Klerk 1953, 165.
95 Welten 1998, 181-193; see also: Loor & Van Brussel 1995; Verkade-Cartier van Dissel 1937.
96 De Bruijne 1976, 45.
97 Ibid., 46.
98 See: De Bruijne 2006.

A History of Suriname

Figure 9.6. Portrait (1885-1894) of a Chinese immigrant family. After contracts had expired many Chinese, as with the members of this family, prospered as goldsmiths, merchants or shopkeepers. Photo by Julius Muller. Vink, 1997, nr. 31.

'Working on the cocoa plantation did not go quickly in the beginning, but in a relatively short time Samie became familiar with the work, and often he completed one and a half tasks a day, and at the end of week he saw himself paid 5, 6 sometimes even 7 guilders. How it is possible, that with an average income comprising f 6 in the week, from which food, lighting, etc. etc. must be paid, something is left over; someone else may understand this – 'I' do not! But it is certain that one day, after visiting the city, my Samie returned to the plantation with 'something' carefully in his belt - and with a small parcel in his hand. That 'something' was a savings bank book, and the package in his hand was: a pair of shoes no. 12. A few weeks later, Samie had again saved a few guilders and now started his career as a financier! To creoles and others in need of money 2, 3 guilders were borrowed with a weekly interest rate of 1 quarter; - the purchased shoes were rented out at 1 quarter a full day - and they always had renters, because every foot would fit in - so that in a short time the purchase price of the shoes was in the hands of Samie again, who expanded the business by buying another pair, but now accompanied by a pair of striped cotton socks, given to him for free, who paid 50 cents in advance for two days. [...] From a fellow countryman who repatriated because he had gathered enough, Samie now bought a piece of land at Charlesburg, together with a cow and a calf. [...] He also chose himself a companion in life, being one of heart and one of mind, who ran things, if Samie was away from home. [...] Early in the morning, beans, cabbage, milk and eggs, on occasion also fruits, were brought to the market;

a little later Indian bread and cakes were made and sold; at all times kerosene oil was for sale and shoes for rent! And then, despite these several jobs and side jobs, Samie still had time left, he bought himself a donkey and cart and became a cartman. When it goes on like this, Samie even turns into a wealthy man! We should not envy him, for he becomes rich through his own strength and work and through - frugality.'[99]

The caste system in Suriname was only of minor significance and mainly the outcome of the fact that indentured labourers all had to carry out the same work. The now equal conditions observed on plantations resulted in Hindustanis further manifesting themselves as one group. Only Brahmins retained a certain influence and prestige, even when not performing rituals. A key element of Hindu society in Suriname, to wit, marrying within one's own caste soon disappeared. The loss of this tradition was partly caused by a shortage of women during the early part of the migration era. Moreover, lengthy sojourns of large groups of emigrants either in depots or on transport ships had encouraged mixed marriages.[100] The majority of Hindus among immigrants hailing from the British Raj adhered to Orthodox Hinduism. Since the rise during the early 20th century and onwards, of the non-orthodox *Arya Samaj* (Aryan Association) they have referred to their religion as *Sanatan Dharma* (lit.: Eternal Law), which had traditionally existed across India. The *Arya Samaj* was founded in Bombay in 1875 to then expand its influence during the 1920s, also in Suriname. It considered the Vedas, the earliest body of Hindu scriptures, as its only source of knowledge and therefore rejected polytheism, women wearing veils, widow burning (*sati*) and child marriages.[101]

As Hindustanis improved their social status, a need to organize grew. The *Surinaamsche Immigranten-Vereeniging* (Immigrant Association of Suriname), founded in 1910, aimed at promoting their interests 'on moral, intellectual and material level'.[102] Its initiator, the agent-general Corstiaan van Drimmelen (1860-1935), was the highest civil servant in the immigration department. This conservative association with its socio-cultural character not only upheld solid ties with the colonial administration but also tried to urge Hindustanis not to exercise the right of repatriation. This association's main propagandist, the interpreter named Sital Persad (whom Van Drimmelen's predecessor had raised as a foster son) was bestowed with the Order of Oranje-Nassau in Silver, an award for those who had earned special societal merit. Numerous Hindustanis deemed the aforementioned association an instrument of the government and not an advocate of their interests. Their dissent which especially concerned the low level of state funding designated to the agricultural sector resulted in founding an association named *Vrijheid en Recht* (Freedom and Justice) in 1911. Its membership soon rose to 1,700.[103] Though the authorities viewed this organisation with mistrust, its objectives were not very radical. Complaints were lodged pertaining to inferior nutrition, a lack of drinking

---

99   Samuels 1947, 12-14.
100   De Klerk 1953, 167-172.
101   Ibid., 193-195.
102   Ibid., 172-176, 191-193; R. Hoefte 1987a, 25-35.
103   Hoefte 1987a, 26.

	Number	Creole	Jew	Hindustani	Chinese	Dutch	Other
Civil servant	180	58,0	12,1	2,8	2,2	21,0	3,9
Liberal profession (high)	43	46,5	18,6			34,9	
Teacher	135	83,0	3,0	5,9	2,2	5,2	0,7
Cleric [i)]	104	13,5	1,0	3,8		81,7	
Police	145	85,5	0,7	3,4		9,0	1,4
Soldier	165	24,9				73,3	1,8
Merchant / Shop owner	341	12,3	7,9	6,8	60,7	5,0	7,3
Retailer / peddler	106	24,5	2,8	56,6	8,5		7,6
Shop-assistant	290	26,2	0,3	1,4	67,3	0,3	4,5
Cart man	39	21,6		78,4			
Porter	81	95,1		4,9			
Carpenter	195	99,0		0,5			0,5
Shoemaker	75	96,0	1,3			1,3	1,3
Tailor	65	66,2		21,5	9,3	1,5	1,5
Blacksmith	64	98,4		1,6			
Total	2,028						

Table 9.1. Male professionals based in Paramaribo with an income exceeding 500 Sfl listed according to ethnicity in 1930 (percentages); [i)] incl. many Roman Catholic teachers and nurses. Source: *Register Revenue Tax* 1930, De Bruijne 1976, 42.

water and the poor functioning of the immigration department. The prominent planter's daughter Grace Schneiders-Howard (1869-1968), a social democrat and the first female representative in the Colonial States, supported the aforementioned *Vrijheid en Recht*. In 1922, the *Surinaamsche Immigranten-Vereeniging* was renamed *Bharat Oeday* (Upcoming Hindustani). The main reason hereof was: its members no longer wished to refer to themselves as 'immigrants', thus indicating a growing self-awareness among the Hindustani population.[104] *Bharat Oeday* demanded public schools, because Hindustani parents no longer wished to send their children to Christian schools. Nevertheless, no political activities were planned. Eight years later, in 1930, a Christian teacher named Clemens Ramkisun Biswamitre (1897-1980) was the first Hindustani to be elected into the Colonial States; he had served as president of an association named *Nawa Yuga Oeday* (Beginning of a New Age) which young educated Hindustani, including teachers and interpreters, had founded in 1924.[105]

Often treated in a patronizing and depreciating manner, the Javanese were the most disadvantaged. A frequently applied term was *lau-lau Japanesi* (lit.: stupid Javanese). Whereas Hindustanis continued to enjoy the guarantee of being protected by the British consulate, members of the Javanese population proved far more vulnerable. Their living conditions were indeed poor when compared with those of Hindustanis.

---

104   De Klerk 1953, 192.
105   Ibid., 187, 192.

Criticism pertaining to the fate of the Javanese was especially disclosed through the Dutch East Indian press, in which returnees mentioned their negative experiences in The West. Next, planters in Suriname felt their honour had been violated to such a degree they requested the colonial authority to execute an impartial investigation. In his 1909 *Rapport omtrent den toestand der Javanen in Suriname* (Report on the condition of Javanese in Suriname), a Dutch East Indian official named H. van Vleuten, who was responsible for this inquiry, described the condition of Javanese indentured labourers as 'not entirely favourable'.[106] This conclusion was sufficient reason for the Dutch government to keep Van Vleuten's report confidential. In this report he mainly criticized the system of remuneration and tasks, which resulted in a Javanese worker earning no more than 2 Hfl on average per week.[107]

Relatively poor living conditions constituted a reason why the Javanese inferiority feelings towards other population groups were internalized. Their many frustrations resulted, especially during the first part of the immigration era, in fights and theft. Playing dice and drinking were other popular pastimes. The Javanese and Hindustanis both consumed opium.[108] Moreover, a shortage of Javanese women, especially during the first part of immigration era, had led to major social problems within this ethnic group. Javanese men with great physical strength were able to impose their will on others. *Bandols* (a Creole term presumably derived from the Spanish term *bandoleros*, meaning bandits) claimed the most beautiful Javanese women and on occasion their possessions. These women were aware that they, by way of their small numbers, took in dominant positions. Among them, concubinage, promiscuity and prostitution were not uncommon.[109]

Javanese labourers were recruited for plantation work on an individual basis and thus, generally speaking, strangers to each other. The need to establish new social relations had already arisen under the pitiful transport systems. Those who had travelled to Suriname on the same boat considered each other upon arrival in Paramaribo as shipmates (*djadji*). Javanese 'related' in this manner usually worked on the same plantation. These migrants, who had to a certain degree replaced familiar and time-honoured village (*desa*) relationships on Java, were supposed to help each other. At the same time a struggle for leadership was witnessed during which *bandol*s manifested themselves.[110] Only when more women and families were to arrive at Suriname during the late 1920s could the social life of the Javanese improve. Moral order was now restored be it to a certain degree. Hence fewer conflicts between various former shipmates arose pertaining to women. In addition, more Javanese men and women married in accordance with Islamic law and Javanese *adat*. Once again ritualists could fulfil their traditional tasks. In due course Javanese emigrants included those who had passed through an Islamic religious school (*madrassa*) on Java and thus were able to read the Quran. Replacing a *bandol* acting as a leader at

---

106   Hoefte 1990a, 46.
107   Ibid., 24-27.
108   Suparlan 1976, 123-125; Suparlan 1995, 87-88; Hoefte 1990b, 11.
109   Suparlan 1976, 120-123; Suparlan 1995, 85-86; Hoefte 1990b, 8; De Waal Malefijt 1963, 88.
110   Ibid., 117-123; ibid., 85-86.

local levels, these newcomers were often either employed as a foreman (*mandoer*) on plantations or as an interpreter, hereby reinforcing their authority.[111]

The arrival of educated Javanese contributed to maintaining their cultural, especially Islam-related, traditions. Initially, mutual disputes arose not only between orthodox Muslims who, as on the island of Java, wished to continue praying to the West. Those less strict, as a result of a changed geographical situation, deemed praying to the East (thus creating the shortest distance to Mecca) to be the only correct manner. This dissent did not lead to real conflicts. Moreover, it would have been incompatible with mutual harmony (*rukun*) which to this day is of great importance to the Javanese community. Only a minority of Javanese fulfilled religious duties. Muslims who were referred to as *abangans* (fellow travellers) formed the vast majority. To them pre-Islamic rites based upon spirit and ancestor worship were still of huge significance. Rites of passage concerning birth, marriage, the arrival of emigrants and funerals were executed regularly on plantations or in the course of a communal festivity and a ritual meal (*slametan*) in order to honour the spirit world. As had been the case in the Dutch East Indies, plantation directors now and again stimulated cultural as well as religious activities hereby counteracting the widely popular dice games which often led to crimes and social derailment. With this goal in mind the *Nederlandsche Handel-Maatschappij* purchased instruments with which to play *gamelan* music on plantation Mariënburg. Facilities were also created to organize a *slametan* or a shadow puppet (*wayang*) performance. It may be added here that missionary activities had hardly any effect on Javanese who, if baptized, were expelled by their community. An explanation for this lack of success may lie in the puritanical nature of Christianity. The Javanese community distrusted missions considering them an attempt by white colonists aimed at domination.[112] As a result of low levels of education, the Javanese upheld few contacts with other ethnic groups. On occasion economic relationships were established with Hindustanis, who employed Javanese farm workers. Moreover, Hindustani middlemen also purchased products provided by Javanese small farm holders.

9.5 Social struggle during the 1930s

The fierce social struggle, on occasion even of a revolutionary nature, having raged across Europe since World War I, did not touch Suriname. Nonetheless, the severe global economic crisis witnessed during the late 1920s ended this relative tranquillity. In 1930, 20 per cent of plantation workers were laid off. Moreover, planters were allowed to reduce wages. Hence the daily wages earned by men aged 16 and over dropped from 0.8 to 0.6 Hfl, whereas women's wages had decreased from 0.6 to 0.4 Hfl.[113] In practice, newly arrived Javanese immigrants now and again were paid even less. Foreign balata companies folded. Moreover, the number of workers active in the bauxite sector had also been considerably reduced after being established in 1916 thanks to US-based investors. In 1932,

---

111 Ibid., 1976, 127-130; ibid., 1995, 89-91; De Waal Malefijt, 1963, 163-165.
112 Hoefte 1987b, 363-384.
113 Ramsoedh 2018, 52-53.

unemployment among Creole men between 15 and 65 years of age in Paramaribo rose to *c.*25 per cent.[114]

The Moravian Church painted a very unfavourable portrait of conditions in which many town dwellers lived. J.W. Baronesse van Lynden, responsible for the relief of destitute inhabitants of Paramaribo on behalf of the Moravians, mentions in reports dating to 1933 that hundreds of families were starving.[115] Large numbers of Creole women tried to earn livelihoods in Paramaribo either as domestic servants or laundresses, but poverty sadly also forced many into prostitution. The level of personal hygiene was very low. Paramaribo-based lower class Creoles were packed together in small wooden single-room shacks previously occupied by slaves and located in backyards of the large houses on the street side. As the Colonial States- member J.C. de Miranda observed: 'One sees houses, dilapidated and tired, half fallen in, leaky roofs, almost collapsing, three quarters rotten.'[116] He deemed these deplorable living conditions a major cause of the large number of cases of tuberculosis. It does indeed remain difficult to compare living conditions in Suriname with those in the Netherlands where too many experienced extreme poverty during the first decades of the 20th century.

In 1930 and 1931, as a result of the global economic crisis, hundreds of inhabitants of Suriname were forced to leave Curaçao. Here, in the course of the 1920s, they had found well-paid work, especially in the oil industry. Many had become acquainted with contemporary phenomena (e.g., trade unions, socialism, nationalism) for example through contacts with political refugees hailing from Venezuela. The social misery encountered in Suriname sharply contrasted the relative prosperity which these returnees had experienced on Curaçao. It stands to reason that, in those circumstances a number of them developed into leaders of social protest movements. A meeting of around 200 returnees, held on 8 June 1931, resulted in founding the *Surinaamsch Werkloozen Comité* (SWC, Unemployed Committee of Suriname).[117] Louis Doedel (1905-1980) soon emerged as this committee's most prominent leader. Its elaborate set of requirements pertaining to the colonial administration included a labour exchange, rotating the unemployed, providing land to create gold mines, and free meals for malnourished school children.[118] Doedel's reputation, having worked on Curaçao as a tax officer, had preceded him. Aged 25, this flamboyant individual had been expelled to Suriname after publicly criticizing its government in a self-penned article.[119] Doedel had also allegedly incited those originating from Suriname but now residing on Curaçao to turn against the legal authority. A socialist influence on this protest movement was obvious. On 17 June 1931, in the course of a demonstration attended by *c.*3,000 unemployed, signs with texts such as 'Surin. Socialists' was observed. Marinus Lepelblad delivered a speech under the motto 'Word from a socialist worker to his comrades'.[120] However, when accompanied by a

---

114   Ibid., 30, 53; Van Lier 1971, 247-249.
115   Scholtens 1986, 53..
116   Ibid., 54.
117   Ramsoedh 2018, 53-54.
118   De Kom 1981 (1934), 155; Hira 1982, 285-286; Scholtens 1987, 16-18.
119   Hira 1982, 283.
120   Scholtens 1986, 59.

Figure 9.7. Demonstration held by unemployed in Paramaribo on 17 June 1931. Unknown photographer. Surinaams Museum photo archive.

delegation offering a petition to Governor Abraham A.L. Rutgers (1884-1966), Doedel just as easily quoted from the Bible's New Testament, reciting Jesus: 'What you have done to the least of my children, you have done to me.'[121]

A moderate attitude thus marked this movement initiated by unemployed. At first the colonial government reacted favourably. The *Surinaamsche Steun Comité* (Support Committee of Suriname) was set up by around 20 dignitaries. Aimed at not only providing food to malnourished school children but also at helping fight unemployment, it received a grant enabling it to carry out this task. Following a motion forwarded by the Colonial States, Governor Rutgers took several measures in order to combat unemployment e.g., by carrying out public works. In addition, gold mining opportunities would also be made available to small companies, hereby enabling the unemployed. A lottery and import duties were set up in order to finance public works. For the aforementioned SWC, these measures were reason enough to dissolve itself on 5 August 1931.[122] Only a few days later, in order to be able to continue representing the workers' interests, Doedel c.s. revived the *Surinaamsche Volksbond* (SVB, People's Union of Suriname).[123]

It soon became apparent that only a small number of promises the colonial administration had made were fulfilled. Governor Rutgers further ignited the anger of those unemployed by leaving too much influence to the *Surinaamsche Steun Comité*, which was incapable of introducing any real improvements. Criticism voiced by the social protest movement soon became more political. On 26 October 1931,

---

121   De Kom 1981 (1934), 156.
122   Scholtens 1986, 61-62; Scholtens 1987, 18.
123   Ibid., 62; ibid., 18..

Doedel's article entitled 'Stilstand of slakkengang' (Standstill or snail's pace) was printed in the *Werkloozenblad* (Newspaper of Unemployed), a publication of the SVB. In Doedel's view, a 'total failure of capitalism as a social system' had taken place. The government should no longer perform the task of 'guardsman to protect the interests of a certain privileged group'.[124] If unable to provide any employment, rulers should at least support those unemployed in the form of either food or money. Doedel also blamed the Dutch government in The Hague stating:

> *'If the Netherlands does not want to help by uplifting us economically, it can afford to have the luxury of a reserve source, but not at the expense of our heart's blood, our life's existence.'*[125]

Doedel's accusation resembled an echo of the words written by the author (and future politician) Albert Helman (1903-1996). In his 1926 novel entitled *Zuid-zuid-west* (South-south-west) he had accused Dutch 'merchants behaving well on Sundays' of 'being thieves for centuries'.[126] Its epilogue inspired by Multatuli's anti-colonial publication translated into English as *Max Havelaar; or, The Coffee Auctions of the Dutch Trading Company* prevented Helman (pseudonym of Lou Lichtveld) from being appointed a professor at Leiden University a few years later.[127]

During a mass meeting held on 28 October 1931, it became obvious that Doedel's followers could barely be kept under control. The attending Colonial States member D. Simons's promise to discuss all criticisms with the *Surinaamsche Steun Comité* had forced the SVB to cancel the intended demonstration. The gathered crowds of unemployed deemed this outcome far from adequate. The leftist (and also monarchist) newspaper *De Banier* (founded and edited by the Colonial States member P.A. May) described this meeting as follows: 'We trembled when hearing terms such as 'sans culotte'.'[128] Scolding and shouting slogans, the crowd left the hall at the Elize Theatre (later Luxor) without the board even being able to close this meeting. Next, an incident involving a policeman who had drawn his rubber truncheon made things worse. Several hundred men and women now went on a rampage despoiling bakeries. Despite a ban on get-togethers and a curfew, Paramaribo was in the grip of a 2-day 'hunger riot'. In due course police were able restore order after making several dozen arrests. A demonstrator was killed by a police bullet.[129] Frightened by these riots, the authorities took hasty measures enabling gold diggers to be dispatched. The SVB board opened soup kitchens in order to alleviate the greatest needs of the unemployed, but a lack of funds soon terminated this initiative. This people's union soon wasted away.[130]

---

124   Scholtens 1987, 55.
125   Ibid., 56.
126   Helman 1926, 117-118.
127   Ramsoedh 1995, 24; Van Kempen 2016, 118; *Max Havelaar; or, The Coffee Auctions of the Dutch Trading Company*, a novel by Multatuli (the pen name of Eduard Douwes Dekker) was first published in 1860 and subsequently translated into more than 40 languages. Its content delivers a blatant critique on the corrupt colonial system in the Dutch East Indies.
128   Hira 1982, 287.
129   Ibid., 287-289; Ramsoedh 2018, 54.
130   Hira 1982, 291.

Certain board members of this union, including L. Doedel, had already joined the *Surinaamsche Algemeene Werkers Organisatie* (SAWO, Surinamese General Workers Organization). Founded on 4 October 1931, it was officially recognised as a socio-cultural association within several months.[131] In practice it manifested itself as a political party as well as a trade union whereby it not only aimed at sending representatives to the Colonial States but also at persuading the government to introduce social legislation in Suriname. It soon gained a large following. The SAWO's first congress, held on 1 May 1932, immediately drew the attention of the authorities. In his speech, president Theo de Sanders (1893-1976), a returnee from British Guyana, having worked here for several years as a film operator, explained to the almost 500 attendees that the SAWO wished to be part of the international labour movement. De Sanders also denounced churches which he considered to be 'one of the main causes of the deprivation of workers'.[132] Secretary Doedel championed the class struggle which served workers as 'a floating piece of debris for a drowning man'.[133] The SAWO was most akin to the *Sociaal-Democratische Arbeiders Partij* (SDAP, the Dutch Labour Party). In his speech Doedel mentioned the 'fellow party member Albarda', who then chaired representatives of the SDAP elected into the lower house of the Dutch Parliament.[134] The SAWO organised weekly meetings which on occasion 900 people attended. Meetings specially for women attracted several hundreds of attendees. This organisation was also active in districts where Hindustani smallholding farmers received support whenever they risked losing their land due to tax arrears.

The government looked at such political activities with a vigilant eye. In his reports, Governor Rutgers mentioned the looming danger of 'communism' in Suriname.[135] It was not long before countermeasures were imposed. All owners of theatres and other venues received an urgent request to ban the SAWO. On 15 July 1932 this workers organisation was stripped of its legal status with the reproach it had violated its own rules by spreading anticlerical propaganda. Rutgers reported to the Minister of Colonies that Doedel's goal was to 'separate Suriname from Holland'.[136] That claim proved in fact unfounded, as was further based on by means of a letter Doedel had written, dated December 1932, stating 'the Netherlands has a duty to fulfill in The West'.[137] The ban imposed upon the SAWO did not interrupt the social unrest. In addition, discontent with the government was not limited to socialist workers or to unemployed. Even a very moderate trade union named *Rooms-Katholieke Volksbond St. Jozef* (Roman Catholic People's Union St Jozef) also voiced criticism. During a meeting held on 15 January 1933, which *c.*200 people attended, the acting head of the Roman Catholic mission in Suriname, Father H. Ruyter, delivered a speech in which he called upon the government to resolve justified grievances. At his insistence, a

---

131   Ibid., 278-296; Scholtens 1986, 68-74.
132   Scholtens 1986, 69.
133   Scholtens 1987, 79.
134   Ibid.
135   Ramsoedh 1990, 33.
136   Ibid., 34.
137   Boots & Woortman 2009, 106-107.

Figure 9.8. Anton de Kom in 1921. Family archive Anton de Kom, via Wikimedia Commons.

critical motion was accepted, because 'in broad layers of society the measures taken fall short of what is necessary to ensure a living'.[138]

The government of Suriname came under even more pressure after Anton de Kom (1898-1945) had arrived at Paramaribo on 4 January 1933. In a telegram dispatched to the then Governor, the Minister of Colonies had described De Kom as 'a communist agitator for the *Antikoloniale Liga* and *Internationale Roode Hulp*' (respectively the World Anti-Imperialist League and International Red Aid).[139] Having departed for the Netherlands in 1920 aged 22, he had joined the Second Hussar Regiment at The Hague to later work as a salesman in the coffee, tea and tobacco trade.[140] Having been trained as an accountant, he took an interest in politics after contacting the nationalist movement founded by students hailing from the Dutch East Indies. While supporting their opposition to Dutch colonialism, De Kom came in touch with the World Anti-Imperialist League. He also affiliated with a workers'-*cum*-writers' collective named *Links Richten* (Aim at the Left) which published an eponymous magazine. Anton de Kom also wrote articles in the *Communistische Gids* (Communist Guide) and gave lectures on Suriname. During his sojourn in the Netherlands, he acquired material in order to enrich his publication entitled *Wij slaven van Suriname* (We slaves of Suriname) which indicts Dutch colonialism. He has personally ensured never to have been a member of the *Communistische Partij Holland* (CPH).[141] It may be added here that further investigation has never provided any evidence in support of this membership.[142] A key explanation for his relations with communist circles is apparently the fact the CPH was the only party seriously concerned with colonial issues.

While residing in the Netherlands, De Kom had been in touch with foremen of the labour movement of Suriname, among them L. Doedel and T. de Sanders.[143] Just

---

138   Scholtens 1986, 73.
139   Boots & Woortman 2009, 105.
140   Ibid., 37-45.
141   De Kom 1981 (1934), 185.
142   See the excellent biography on De Kom by Boots & Woortman., 63-69, 72-73, 142-144.
143   Boots & Woortman 2009, 106-109; Ramsoedh 1990, 35.

like the latter two, De Kom is committed to improving the pitiful social conditions in which a majority of the people of Suriname live. More than Doedel and De Sanders, however, De Kom realises that the unity of all ethnic groups and confidence in their abilities is required, whereby the 'deeply rooted sense of inferiority of my countrymen' must be fought.[144] In *Wij slaven van Suriname,* De Kom often graphically shares his observations and reflections shortly after arriving in Paramaribo:

'Here in the 'dirty neighborhood' where the proletarians live, it is quiet and dark. In their four-by-four-foot houses resembling lugubrious caves, the coloured families await the morning, vast asleep as a result of fatigue. Not all are happy to find a roof over their head. Many nowadays sleep under the bridges or on the doorsteps of houses. I now also remember how skinny the many faces on the jetty were under the deceptive mask of joy. [...] And perhaps I will succeed in making them feel part of all hope and courage included in that single powerful word I learned abroad: organization. [...] Perhaps it will not be entirely impossible to have negroes and Hindustanis, Javanese and Indians understand how only solidarity can unite all sons of mother Sranan in their struggle for a humane life.'[145]

De Kom's arrival in Suriname created a notable sensation as the extraordinary security measures indicate. The authorities commissioned three specially appointed former police officers to continuously keep track of him. They also prohibited him from holding any meetings. In order to be able to speak with the proletariat, De Kom opened an advisory and information office in Paramaribo located on premises near his father's house, on the corner of Pontewerfstraat and Hofstraat, mainly focussing his attention on Javanese and Hindustanis. A Creole himself, De Kom found much less support among Creoles who may have been deterred after all the problems the SAWO had encountered.[146] The authorities approached various migrant associations in order to exert an influence aimed at keeping Hindustanis and Javanese away from De Kom and his opinions. Hindustanis were most concerned with these warnings. For, being economically more developed, they had a great deal to lose. De Kom did indeed receive more support from Javanese, who worked on plantations often under appalling conditions and for extremely low wages. Many of them looked forward to seeing their native soil again. Responding to this desire and whenever he contacted these immigrants, De Kom acquired an almost messianic status. On plantations located across the Commewijne region rumours spread that, thanks to De Kom's mediation, returning to Java within 4 months was now feasible.[147] It remains unclear if this possibility had been voiced by De Kom or by those surrounding him. According to a Hindustani monthly magazine entitled *Onze Stem* (Our Voice), many indentured labourers hailing from the British Raj considered De Kom the 'representative of

---

144 De Kom 1981, 164; it remains unclear to what extent De Kom was striving for independence. In any case, his first priority was to improve social conditions. In early 1933, a pamphlet circulating across Paramaribo, referred to independence. Its authorship has not been ascertained. De Kom does not mention it in *Wij slaven van Suriname* nor in his speeches, see: Boots & Woortman 2009, 142-144, 191-192; Meel 2009, 260.
145 De Kom 1981 (1934), 163-164.
146 Boots & Woortman 2009, 99-135.
147 Ibid., 120; Scholtens 1986, 79.

Gandhi'.[148] When hundreds of immigrants registered at his office, it turned out that a number of them had sold their belongings while awaiting their departure to either Java or the Raj.

The government of Suriname had apparently fallen victim to a panic brought about by all these developments. Reports forwarded by Governor Rutgers, referred to the possible violent overthrow of the legal authority as a result of De Kom's actions.[149] Although no solid proof for this conclusion were ever found, in the end Rutgers decided to intervene anyway. Next, on 1 February 1933, banning a public meeting in the Pontewerfstraat led to an escalation. De Kom now set off in protest towards the governor's palace, where hundreds of his supporters had gathered. Even before arriving here, he was arrested by the police. In the following days the situation in Paramaribo remained alarming. Now not only immigrants but also Creoles, among them many market women, expressed their presence. On February 4, an angry crowd demanded De Kom's release. Reports appeared in the local press stating he was indeed to be set free within a few days. Although the Governor immediately denied this, several thousand people gathered at the Gouvernementsplein on 7 February. When the crowd pushed further and further forwards in order to hear the good news, the attending attorney-general instructed the police to fire, resulting in two fatal casualties and 22 individuals being injured.[150] In his diary this attorney-general expressed his satisfaction with the result of the shooting and, in particular, with the subsequent preventive effect he believed it would have:

> 'This will continue to work for the future, because the riffraff has now discovered that even the police does not recoil from firing at the masses if need be ... We ourselves are extremely grateful for the process; all things considered, the outcome could not have been better; it had to arrive at a face-off but where and how? The days and nights have been difficult, but suffered pain is soon forgotten.'[151]

Governor Rutgers apparently held the same view. For, he had previously proposed to the Minister of Colonies to create an armed civilian guard in order to 'use force if necessary to counter riotous movements in the colony and to support the legitimate authority in its task of maintaining order'.[152] To this goal he called for the purchase of weapons and equipment which in part had to be acquired by means of private donations, thus delivering an 'insurance premium against the danger of revolution'.[153] Only a few days after the bloodshed had taken place on the Gouvernementsplein, this civilian guard was established. The investigation against De Kom, which lasted more than 3 months, did not reveal any criminal offences. The authorities therefore decided to release him on May 10 and, on that very same day, ship him and his family out to the Netherlands. During World War II, De Kom became actively involved in the

---

148   Ibid. 2009, 120; ibid. 1986, 78.
149   Boots & Woortman 2009, 125.
150   Ibid., 128.
151   Van Hengel 2017, 27.
152   Ramsoedh 2018, 57.
153   Ibid.

resistance. He passed away probably in April 1945, aged 47, in a German prisoner-of-war camp, Sandbostel.[154]

After his demise, De Kom's individuality was for a long time determined by the acclaimed sociologist-*cum*-historian Rudolf A.J. van Lier (1914-1987), professor at the universities of Leiden and Wageningen. For, in his classic publication entitled *Frontier Society. A social analysis of the history of Surinam* (1971; orig. Dutch ed.1949) wrongly dismissed De Kom as a frustrated Creole. According to Van Lier, himself of Surinamese descent, De Kom was 'completely won over to communist ideas'. For, in Van Lier's view, the memory of slavery formed 'part of a pathetic sense of grievance and a rancour which, however much justified by the circumstances in which the lower class found themselves, prejudice a proper insight into the past'.[155] Van Lier incorrectly suggested that De Kom had written *Wij slaven van Suriname* with 'the collaboration of a Dutch man of letters who moved in the same leftist circles as De Kom'.[156] After WW II, De Kom's life and work fell into oblivion. However, during 1960s, certain nationalist students hailing from Suriname and residing in the Netherlands rediscovered him. This renewed interest led to a 1971 edition of *Wij slaven van Suriname*. De Kom's opinions fall in line with those held by nationalists who, in the course of the 1950s and 1960s, laid the foundations of the later independence. Ahead of his time, De Kom had taken a further step in recognising the position of population groups other than merely the Creoles. During the 1980s, a military regime embraced his heritage (see p. 313).

During the unrest of the early 1930s the Paramaribo-based government simply proved incapable of dealing with any opponents denouncing colonial policies. The Dutch government, then presided by Prime Minister Charles Ruijs de Beerenbrouck (1873-1936), mainly focussed on the socio-economic crisis and was thus unable to deal with colonial issues. At that time the easiest way to eliminate opponents was to label them 'communist agitators'. A consequence of the social unrest surrounding De Kom comprised introducing to the Colonial States the 'anti-revolution legislation', which was partly prompted by events unfolding across the Dutch East Indies. Additions and amendments to the Penal Code almost completely corresponded with the rules in force across the Dutch Far Eastern colony, concerning state security, public order, the right of assembly and freedom of the press. Despite objections forwarded by the Colonial States, which spoke of 'muzzle laws', this regulation was enacted by Royal Decree in October 1933.[157] A newspaper named *De Banier van Waarheid en Recht* (The Banner of Truth and Justice), published between 1929 and 1936, was placed on an index composed by the army and police. Moreover, it was repeatedly prosecuted based on incoming legislation. The editor-in-chief was not only sentenced to 4 weeks in jail for publishing insulting articles, but also forced to stop publishing the newspaper due to the repression and subsequent financial problems.[158] Drastic measures were also taken against the comedian and singer Johannes C. Kruisland

---

154 Boots & Woortman 2009, 313-314.
155 Van Lier 1971, 370.
156 Ibid.; Van Lier's claim pertaining to this issue has since been thoroughly debunked, see: Boots & Woortman 2009, 168-192.
157 Ramsoedh 2018, 60-61; Ramsoedh 1990, 84-85.
158 Ramsoedh 2018, 61.

after having criticizing local events for decades while performing at the Bellevue Theatre. It may be added here that military personnel were not allowed to attend these popular evenings. During one of his performances, he referred to the shooting on 7 February 1933 thus: 'To fire on a defenceless people / That's stupid, I find it tough / After all, they had a sprayer, water and / Also hoses plus the staff.'[159] Activist Louis Doedel was incarcerated in a mental institution in 1937, where he remained until his demise in 1980.

9.6 Change in assimilation policy

Significant, too, was the arrival in 1933 of Governor Johannes C. Kielstra (1878-1951). His policy released ethnic sentiments into the colony, hereby pushing class-related conflicts into the background. Applying certain traits of Dutch colonial politics as witnessed in the Dutch East Indies formed the core of Kielstra's strategy, hence the term *verindisching*.[160] Kielstra especially had Hindustanis and Javanese in mind who, in his view, could provide an economic basis thanks to their agricultural activities. His predecessor had been heavily criticised in the lower house as well as in the Dutch press for revealing a lack of vision and determination. In the eyes of those active within The Hague-based political circles Kielstra, having been schooled as a lawyer, did possess these attributes. An authoritarian character was apparently deemed more advantageous than disadvantageous. In a way, Kielstra's appointment implied a turnaround in the Dutch policy towards Suriname.[161] After the abolition of slavery, this colony was almost exclusively viewed an economic problem. As a result of the escalating labour unrest during the 1930s, the enforcement of authority also became a key issue, hereby rendering colonial policies much more political. During the 1920s, the rise of nationalists in the Dutch East Indies caused a shift in thinking about colonial policy towards more conservative views. In the revised constitution of 1922 the terms 'colony' and 'colonial' had indeed vanished. Moreover, the overseas territories became parts of the state.[162] The government of Suriname however moved in a more autocratic than a more liberal direction. In 1935, all political parties were banned whereby the people of Suriname were no longer allowed to belong to parties based in the Netherlands.[163] A newly imposed state regulation of 1937, the outcome of the constitutional amendment dating back to 1922, provided the governor with the liberty to, in 'urgent circumstances', take legal measures on his own authority if the States refused to cooperate.[164] To their huge dissatisfaction, the States (in Suriname called *Staten*; the adjective Colonial had been dropped) realized this 'short conflict regulation' greatly reduced their legislative powers. A former volunteer in military service, Kielstra had spent many years in the Dutch East Indies as a civil servant. He was strongly influenced by the future Prime Minister Hendrik Colijn, whom he had succeeded in 1909 as assistant advisor for administrative affairs in overseas regions. Thanks to his experience in the Dutch East Indies as well as to scholarly studies,

---

159   Van Kempen 2002, vol. 3, 321.
160   Ramsoedh 1990, 91.
161   Ibid., 43-58.
162   Ramsoedh 2018, 22.
163   Ibid., 61.
164   Ibid., 65.

Kielstra had developed ideas on colonial policy at an early stage. In 1918 having been appointed professor of colonial studies and public economics at the now Wageningen University he attained ample authority in these fields.

Policies had initially been highly ethical in nature. Influenced by Christian political parties, they were referred to as such.[165] Western education was viewed a significant contribution to developing the native population. Nevertheless, Kielstra and Colijn, who both had published extensively on their viewpoints, deemed such schooling as a source of national resistance in the Dutch East Indies. According to Kielstra, this type of tuition was to blame for:

'the lack of spiritual harmony, the imbalance of so many of these intellectuals and hence the unscrupulous way in which the knowledge obtained is now and again applied if, through whatever circumstance, a position it desires is not or not immediately obtainable.'[166]

Colijn opined that quality education would alienate the native population from its 'own national psyche'.[167] On the other hand Kielstra had proposed an 'organic' approach to colonial politics.[168] Native peoples must no longer be considered a relatively homogeneous conglomerate, but instead should be fully empowered as independent entities each in its own right. Schooling should be tailored to these needs while applying a far more diverse range of programmes. Kielstra and Colijn deemed enforcing the Dutch colonial authority to be central. Under such impartial authority, the various native groups would, in their opinion, be best served. After Colijn had taken office as Minister of Colonies in 1933, Kielstra's appointment, at the age of 55, as Governor of Suriname was no great surprise.

The most important modification comprised abandoning the assimilation policy as pursued since 1863.[169] Kielstra's policy change which of course Colijn fully supported was partly prompted by the former's vision as to Suriname's economic development. Kielstra deemed small agriculture the only chance to free the colony from an economic swamp. Hindustanis and Javanese, whom he considered the colony's backbone, would have an essential role to play.[170] It was also clear to him that the assimilation policy hardly had any effect on these two Asian groups, both of which continued to cherish their deep-rooted cultural and socio-religious traditions. At any rate indentured labourers led rather isolated lives on plantations, hereby hardly encouraging any forms of acculturation.

Kielstra wished to put an end to this assimilation policy by laying on a number of legal measures. The possibility to appoint five of the fifteen representatives in the Colonial States was introduced in a state regulation of 1937, which had replaced the 1865 state regulation. This initiative allowed the governor to opt for Asians, who could hardly participate because of a limited suffrage based on income. In 1901 such

---

165 Ibid., 22-23.
166 Ramsoedh 1990, 51.
167 Ibid., 51.
168 Ibid., 55.
169 Van Lier 1971, 191-198.
170 Ramsoedh 1990, 91.

a regulation had been abolished whereby the then Governor was able to appoint a number of members in the Colonial States, as the government sought to underline the uniform character of parliamentary representation.[171] With the Javanese village in mind, a key part of Kielstra's policy comprised the formation of village communities.[172] In Hindustani and Javanese population groups respectively, it was thus considered necessary to reinforce any social links based on ethnicity and religion. In his view, too, this policy enabled creating a productive small agriculture, hereby avoiding a considerable migration wave towards Paramaribo. Kielstra had been partly inspired by the report of the Baud Commission that in 1855 had made - never implemented - proposals to promote the establishment of emancipated slaves as small-scale farmers (see p. 176). A genuine administrative decentralisation did not fit in with Kielstra's colonial viewpoints at all. Village chiefs, appointed by the governor, officiated primarily as executors. According to the Village Ordinance, a chief must 'punctually' follow both a governor's and a district commissioner's orders. He also had to keep 'peace and unity' amidst the villagers.[173] In establishing village municipalities Kielstra also intended to facilitate a mass immigration of Javanese to Suriname, to wit 100,000 souls within a decade, in order to thus reinforce the colony's economic base. The then Minister of Colonies, Charles Welter (1880-1972), having considered this proposal financially unfeasible, wished to restrict this number to between 1,000 and 1,200 Javanese immigrants per annum. With the outbreak of World War II, this immigration plan came to nothing.[174]

Predominantly light-skinned Creole members of the Colonial States had strongly opposed 'the East Indies spirit' being imposed on the government administration.[175] Kielstra's self-will also provoked a great deal of resistance. He had already upset representatives when refusing to accept any amendments to the village ordinance. After being reprimanded by Minister Welter, Kielstra was forced to climb down. Relations in Suriname had however been severely disrupted. Kielstra's aim, to wit, to increase the role, as played in the colonial administration, of civil servants who had acquired experience while serving in the Dutch East Indies contributed to this disruption. According to the Governor, only experienced officials were capable of implementing his rural policy with any success. Their knowledge of local language and traditions would enable them to better connect with immigrants from Asia. In 1936, a royal decree thus stipulated that only a graduate in Indology (i.e., a study of Indonesian history and culture carried out while preparing to serve in the Dutch East Indies) could officiate as a district commissioner.[176] Preferring to appoint officials with experience in the Dutch East Indies to other senior positions, Kielstra denied the light-skinned Creoles promotion chances. The aforementioned reintroduction of a limited right of appointment to the Colonial States was also deemed an infringement of acquired rights.

---

171   Van Lier 1971, 197.
172   Ibid., 215; Ramsoedh 1990, 112.
173   Ramsoedh 1990, 113.
174   Ibid., 117.
175   Ibid., 117.
176   Ibid., 120.

Kielstra's plans pertaining to an adapted marriage law for Asians, hereby allowing them to marry according to their time-honoured traditions, also aroused much resentment among the Creole population. Kielstra opined, not without reason, that Hindustanis and Javanese could merely feel all but slightly at home in Suriname as full citizens only after this law had been amended. In his view, that sentiment was of the utmost importance if considering the key economic function he attributed to immigrants from Asia. The Colonial States refused to modify the ruling in question because it would affect the law's uniformity.[177] Members of the light-skinned Creole elite were very committed to the Dutch language and the Dutch cultural community. For, they themselves not only formed part of it, but also derived social advantages from it. It was furthermore pointed out that no separate legislation was introduced regarding concubinage, a frequently observed phenomenon amidst Creoles. After 1940, Kielstra arbitrarily imposed this marriage ordinance by means of dubiously abusing the newly established state of war. In due course his actions generated numerous antagonistic forces through which political developments in Suriname were to gain momentum between 1939 and 1945.

---

177 Van Lier 1971, 195-196.

CHAPTER 10
Transforming the plantation economy

After the turn of the 20th century, the Dutch government based in The Hague regarded Suriname mainly as a helpless colony requiring financial support and having but a few economic perspectives. In 1935, Prime Minister Hendrik Colijn (1869-1944), who also served as Minister of Colonies, delivered a testimonium paupertatis during a discussion on the budget of Suriname held in the upper house of the States General, the legislature of the Netherlands. In it we read:

> *'I have been involved in parliamentary life in one form or another for 25 years now. Among my earliest memories in the political field, as far as Suriname is concerned, is the journey undertaken by the Bos Commission. It was a commission constituted in an all-round manner, led by a truly first class man. That trip did not yield anything [...]. Everything attempted in Suriname [...] it all simply failed [...]. Things are indeed not easy. And that is the reason why I indeed wished someone to, on one occasion, rise in the Netherlands who did know what could be done. I do the possible.'*[1]

Colijn's remark illustrates the level of despondency with regard to Suriname, as was expressed time and again in the States General. In 1930, certain members of the Dutch lower house had even suggested that, by means of the intergovernmental League of Nations, one or more nation states should be searched for in order to take over the responsibility for Suriname.[2] Needless to say, the annual budget subsidies also played a role here. Various expert committees had advised on the policy to be pursued. The prevailing concept here was to rejuvenate the plantation agriculture. In his report of 1926 addressed to the *Vereeniging van Kamers van Koophandel en Fabrieken in Nederland* (Association of Chambers of Commerce and Industry in the Netherlands), a businessman with experience in the Dutch East Indies named Willem de Cock Buning recommended furthering the immigration of Javanese, the costs of which the government should bear. Immigrants would be 'free' settlers. In addition to working on their own plots of land, however, they would also have to labour on plantations during a few days a week.[3] Seven years earlier, in 1919, the *Suriname Studie-Syndicaat,* members of which included representatives of Dutch East Indian culture companies and of plantations established in Suriname had advised to send no less than 100,000 Javanese immigrants to the colony over a period of 10 years.[4] According to this advisory report, it should be deemed a 'reserve'.[5] For, at all times, one had to take into account that the emerging nationalism could endanger assets across the Dutch East Indies. Once proper provisions had been

---

1   *Handelingen Eerste Kamer* (Minutes First Chamber of Parliament), 1934-1935, 9 May 1935, 677; for accessing online, consult the bibliography.
2   Ramsoedh 1990, 7.
3   De Cock Buning 1926, 74-75.
4   *Suriname Studie-Syndicaat* 1919, 205.
5   Ibid., 212.

created in Suriname, especially pertaining to the availability of cheap labour, the indispensable foreign capital could be mobilised. For some time, the colonial government had opined that developing a 'small and medium-sized agriculture' could not be separated from the need to provide plantations with sufficient cheap labour. For this reason, from 1882 on, immigrants from Asia were indeed banned either from harvesting balata or mining gold.[6] The 'government settlements' were largely based on the notion that those who cultivated barely 1 ha of land should always depend on nearby plantations in order to replete their livelihoods (see also p. 202). In addition, according to the government's viewpoint, small farmers could play a modest role in supplying food to Paramaribo. This ambivalent policy limited chances for small farm holders, as the issuing of land most clearly proved. Plots were only rented out at government settlements. Elsewhere, small farmers received land in allodial ownership, i.e., independent of any superior landlord.[7] These pseudo-properties always provided the government with a right to repossess the land, after compensation had been paid, whenever the public interest so demanded. This outcome could indeed be the case if the economic tide affecting large plantations would turn. Allodial ownership hailed from the days of slavery, when land meant for plantations was issued under the strict stipulation that their owners were to cultivate staple products for the Dutch market. For the small farm holders, the absence of a full business title concerning the land proved disadvantageous, because business loans were granted less easily. In 1911, a committee presided by the member of the lower house named Dirk Bos had already pointed this shortcoming out to the then Minister of Colonies in an advisory report entitled *De economische en financieele toestand der kolonie Suriname* (The economic and financial situation of the colony of Suriname). This committee argued in favour of granting land to small farmers in 'normal ownership', while simultaneously ensuring an 'appropriate credit system'.[8] An agricultural bank possessing a capital of between 1,000,000 and 1,500,000 Hfl should, according to Bos and his associates, provide credit to both planters and small farmers.[9]

The lower house rejected creating such a credit institution under heavy pressure from *De Surinaamsche Bank* (founded in 1865) which considered its monopoly position threatened. As from 1907 on, cooperative farmers' credit banks had existed, but the sums of money they could lend were small. Hence, many small farmers were subject to the whims of informal money lenders such as Suriname's richest who were active in, for example, liberal professions and trade. This bank, in which Amsterdam-based financers held stakes, could not properly fulfil its agricultural credit function. Serving as a central bank, it was also responsible for the solidity of banknotes and therefore always had to invest prudently. In 1918, at the insistence of the Dutch government in The Hague, this bank did contribute to founding the *West-Indischen Cultuurbank*, in which the *Nederlandsche Handel-Maatschappij* (now named ABN AMRO) participated. This newly founded bank mainly restricted its

---

6   Heilbron 1982, 214.
7   Ibid., 209.
8   Bos 1911, 121, 125.
9   Ibid., 168-173.

A History of Suriname

activities to financing plantation companies. The absence of a real credit institution serving small farmholders led to protests in the Colonial States, whose members relinquished their mandates after hearing derogatory remarks voiced in the Dutch lower house. Nevertheless, in 1918, the licence of *De Surinaamsche Bank* was simply extended by Royal Decree.[10]

The outbreak of the World War I prompted the colonial government to think more positively about small farming. The import of, especially rice from Java and cornflour from Argentina, had become much more difficult as a result of isolation. Food imports have always been an element of plantation economies which specialise in the production of staple products with low added values. In Suriname, the government itself took an interest in this element because of the import duties that flowed into the colonial coffers. Strong price increases as witnessed after the beginning of WW I resulted in a growth of the domestic production. The government provided small farmers with an extra incentive by means of guaranteeing minimum prices. Between 1910 and 1914, the production of rice (paddy) by small-scale farmers totalled 12,100,000 kg whereas between 1915 and 1919 a total of 36,700,000 kg was yielded. The production of tuber crops (including cassava) grew almost threefold. In 1914 the number of plots meant for small-scale agriculture increased from 9,900 to reach more than 13,000 in 1919. At the same time the built-up area expanded from 12,000 to 19,000 ha. The number of people (including dependent family members) engaged in small-scale farming rose from 29,718 in 1914 to 37,774 in 1918, or from over 30 to almost 36 per cent of the total population.[11] The rapid growth in production implied that Suriname could provide for its own consumption from 1920 on.

Favourable events experienced during WW I led the Dutch government to further increase the production capacity within the small agriculture sector. The Nickerie district in particular developed rapidly thanks to the availability of additional land which was reclaimed and cultivated. An experiment launched by the colonial government allowed farmers to contribute to the infrastructure. In exchange, after a few years, they acquired ownership of the land. Especially the Hindustani immigrants, who possessed the most entrepreneurial spirit according to colonial perceptions, were permitted to draw advantage from these fresh opportunities. Rice cultivation developed to such a level that exports could rise from more than 2,000,000 kg in 1930 to reach almost 6,500,000 kg in 1939.[12] The *Landbouw Proefstation* (Agricultural Test Station), founded in 1903, contributed significantly by developing improved rice varieties, which suffered less from breakage. Governor Kielstra's ruralization policy delivered a further boost during the 1930s (see p. 232). Between 1931 and 1939, the production value in small agriculture (based on coffee, cocoa, paddy, bananas, oranges, maize, legumes, tuber crops, coconuts, peanuts and rice) increased from 1,769,000 to 2,752,000 guilders; the value of the rice production alone had almost doubled, to wit, from 1,093,000 to 2,045,000 guilders.[13]

---

10   Willemsen 1982, 81-86; Bruijning & Voorhoeve 1977, 41.
11   Heilbron 1982, 275-279.
12   Van de Walle 1946, Appendix.
13   Gowricharn 1990, 174.

Between 1930 and 1940, the number of small agricultural plots had increased from 14,832 to 22,852.[14] At that time, the production value of small-scale agriculture was already much larger if compared with that of large-scale agriculture. In 1910, plantations still accounted for as much as 72 per cent of the agricultural production value, whereas the remaining 28 per cent pertained to small-scale agriculture. In 1920, the ratios had completely reversed to 29 and 71 per cent respectively.[15]

Large-scale agriculture had increasingly begun to feel competition from abroad. For, the Suez Canal had shortened the route to the East considerably. Now colonised, Africa no longer supplied slaves but produced staple products. The lack of investor interest formed a key factor in the decline of Suriname's plantation economy. During the 1920s, Governor A.J.A.A. Baron van Heemstra (1871-1957) having returned to Suriname after visiting the Netherlands, reported with great disappointment to the States that, in his home country, one is:

> 'on the one hand still so much interested in the East Indies that the available capital is preferably earmarked for new cultures or for the expansion of existing ones in that part of the world, on the other hand, the prejudice against Suriname is still of such a nature that the courage to take on something new is, generally speaking, lacking.'[16]

The number of plantations had indeed fallen dramatically. Of the 245 counted in 1860, only 42 remained in 1937.[17] Between 1833 and 1926, the number of sugar plantations had dropped from 105 to four.[18] At the start of World War II, only two remained to wit, Mariënburg (owned by the *Nederlandsche Handel-Maatschappij*) and Alliance with British ownership. After expanding and modernizing both plantations, the volume of Suriname's entire sugar production in 1939, now totalling 8,282,814 kg, was only slightly lower than the 10,220,854 kg reached in 1864. However, a sharp fall in prices from 26 to 4 cents per kg implied the production value was far less.[19] Cocoa cultivation had reached its peak in 1895, when almost 4,500,000 kg were exported whereby Suriname remained ahead of Cuba and Haiti; small farmers, including many former slaves, supplied more than 25 per cent of the entire cocoa production. For the first time they were able to achieve a certain prosperity (see p. 203). On plantations, cocoa had replaced coffee beans, the harvesting of which was far too laborious. In 1904, due to Witch's Broom Disease (Moniliophthora perniciosa), cocoa production had fallen to a mere 864,600 kg. A few years later a slight recovery did occur. After a disastrous drought struck in 1925, only smallhold farmers cultivated cocoa trees.[20]

The decline of cocoa created new opportunities for the coffee trade. As early as 1880, Liberian coffee (Coffea liberica) was introduced in Suriname, giving

---

14   Panday 1959, 174.
15   Ibid.
16   Van Lier 1971, 210.
17   Van de Walle 1946, 70.
18   De Cock Buning 1926, 55.
19   Van Stipriaan 1993, 432; Van Lier 1971, 200.
20   Panday 1959, 180-185; De Cock Buning 1926, 58-60.

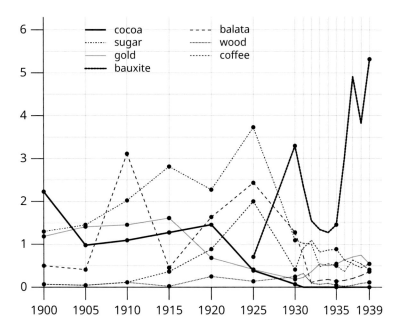

Figure 10.1. Export value of the main Surinamese products (in millions of HFl). Buddingh' 2021, 274 (after Van Traa 1946, 218).

planters as well as the government further expectations. This strong species was preferred over the Coffea arabica plant because it not only ripens all year round and its fruit does not drop to the ground. Hence, harvesting could take place over a longer period of time, requiring far less labour. Coffee plants were once again grown on numerous plantations after the cultivation of cocoa had disappeared. Coffee production during the 1920s was almost 3,000,000 kg, i.e., 50 per cent of the volume it had been during the 18th-century heyday. When the crisis the global economy experienced in 1929 led to a sharp fall in prices, the Dutch government decided to create an aid scheme in order to maintain as many coffee plantations as possible - their number being 58 in 1926 - because at that time coffee was the most important export crop. Planters could now obtain loans on which no interest was due during the first 3 years. This support package was linked to plantation owners being obliged to also grow citrus fruits, hereby for the first time providing this crop with a certain volume.[21] In the end, WW II implied the demise of the majority of coffee plantations, as export markets became inaccessible. Moreover, many workers opted to work in the lucrative bauxite sector.

It was not the first instance that the colonial government had introduced financial support to the plantation agriculture.[22] The outbreak of Witch's Broom Disease at the detriment of the cocoa cultivation inspired the liberal politician and civil engineer Cornelis Lely, the then Governor of Suriname (1902-1905), to seek other export crops. The choice fell on the *bacove* (banana) culture, thanks to good experiences in both Jamaica and Colombia. The perishability of this fruit required triggering the interest

---

21   Ibid., 1959, 185-188; Loor 1992, 81-84.
22   Bos 1911, 139-168, Panday 1959, 189-193.

of the United Fruit Company. This US corporation dominated the marketplace and could provide an insured outlet by means of large refrigerated ships. However, Suriname had to guarantee that delivering large quantities of this fruit was indeed feasible. Its government therefore offered loans to plantation owners in order to facilitate, within 3 years, the planting of 3,000 ha with a banana species imported from Jamaica. In 1906 a 10-year contract with United Fruit Company was signed. Three years later the intended area of 3,000 ha was indeed achieved. However, within a short time span, the Panama disease (aka banana wilt) caused such devastation that exports quickly ended. Hence, this deal with the United Fruit Company was dissolved. A sum in excess of the 2,000,000 Hfl which The Hague had invested in the *bacove* culture had to be considered as lost.[23] This major disaster was largely due to poor preparation. According to a committee named after Dirk Bos, diseases which threatened all the *bacove* species were unknown in Suriname and had thus indeed hardly been investigated. Lely's urge to act quickly had apparently obscured his judgment.

These millions invested in the *bacove* culture was not Lely's only fiasco. The Lawa Railway debacle was even greater. This track aimed at opening up inland areas in order to mine gold.[24] As early as 1873, research conducted into composition of the soil had indicated this precious metal was to be found in the Lawa River region bordering on French Guiana. In 1876, the *Amsterdamse Gouddelving Maatschappij* (Amsterdam Goldmining Company) became the first foreign company to establish itself in Suriname. Within 8 weeks it had built an almost 63 km long road connecting the Suriname River with the Saramacca River hereby enabling further mining.[25] Gold fever had now clearly struck the colony. In order to render the investment climate as attractive as possible, the specific regulation stipulating that 20 per cent of the value of all minerals had to be transferred to the government was withdrawn. In 1880, a 5 per cent export duty was imposed after gold mining proved to be a success. Moreover, a rent comprising 10 cents per ha had to be paid for concessions. It was later decided that a slightly higher amount was to be paid comprising 25 cents per ha from the third year of the concession onwards and 50 cents per ha from the fifth year on. High-ranked officials and members of the Colonial States also benefited fully from the ensuing gold rush, either as concessionaires or as shareholders of gold companies.[26] Each year large quantities were exported. Between 1881 and 1885, 3,199 kg were registered, not to mention the gold smuggled out of the country.[27] The colony's revenues were out of all proportion to what foreign operators amassed. Between 1874 and 1882, at least 4,295,170 Hfl worth of gold was exported; this sum by far transcended the total budget subsidies, to wit, 3,239,292 Hfl provided in the course of the same period.[28] The actual value of the exported gold was in fact even higher. For, in Suriname, 1,50 Hfl was paid for 1 gram of molten gold, while prices to be paid

---

23 Bos 1911, 154.
24 For further details on the gold exploration and exploitation, see: Willemsen 1980 and Heilbron & Willemsen 1982, vol. 1 (1), 66-84 and vol. 1 (2), 87-101.
25 Willemsen 1980, 216-217.
26 Ibid., 216-217, 222-225.
27 Ibid., 331.
28 Ibid., 220, 325.

Figure 10.2. This 1895 photograph is attributed to Julius Muller. It depicts gold mining activities in the Surinamese interior. Surinaams Museum photo archive.

in global markets amounted to c.35 USD per troy ounce; during the aforementioned 8 years, less than 400,000 Hfl pertaining to rent, concession rights and export rights flowed into the colonial coffers; the c.2,000 workers, who were always employed for a maximum of 6 months per annum, received a total of 600,000 Hfl per annum for working 150 days and were thus paid 2 Hfl a day.[29] As a result of the low capital intensity of gold mining, capital costs hardly played a role.

During the closing decades of the 19th century and the first decades of the 20th century, key trading nations applying the gold standard transformed this metal into a highly desirable commodity. Central banks had to acquire vast quantities in order to guarantee the value of the national currency. In 1885, large gold deposits located between the Tapanahoni and Lawa Rivers had thus not only aroused the interest of the Dutch government and of investors, but had also led France to reinforce its claims to this area. In due course, this border dispute was resolved, albeit for the time being, after arbitration by Alexander III of Russia (1845-1894), a decision which was to benefit the Netherlands. Exploitation rights for this location were acquired by a group of investors who called themselves the *Comité De Gelder* in honour of a former member of the Council of the East Indies named J.A. de Gelder. The deal would ultimately turn out to be very disadvantageous for Suriname. A former Minister of Water Management and a future Governor of Suriname (1902-1905), the previously mentioned Cornelis Lely, was also a member of

29   Ibid., 220.

this committee, which renamed itself *Maatschappij Suriname* (Company Suriname). In 1896 it was granted the right of preference for an area of 3,000,000 ha, the best part of which, up to a maximum of 500,000 ha, would be granted under concession for at least 75 years; by way of a derogation from customary arrangements, no tax was payable for 25 years; these very favourable provisos were linked to the investors' obligation to construct a railway line connecting Paramaribo with the Lawa region (east Suriname).[30] When, not much later, a US enterprise inquired after a concession, the Dutch government issued a gold regulation which granted new licences only to (a) Dutch nationals and residents of Suriname or (b) companies established in the Netherlands or in Suriname. The *Maatschappij Suriname* proved incapable of raising a capital of between 10,000,000 and 12,000,000 Hfl in order to construct the railway, upon which the government not only bought off the contract for a sum exceeding 500,000 Hfl, it also decided to finance and build this railway itself.[31] The former Minister Lely played a memorable role, given the obvious conflict of interest resulting from his stakeholdership. After being appointed Governor of Suriname in 1902, he had demanded that the state should build the Lawa Railway.[32] In the Dutch lower house, fears were voiced that Lely, having established a reputation, while officiating as a minister, for commissioning large and expensive public works, would allow subsidies for the colony to flow too profusely. In the end, however, after being permitted to travel to Suriname, Lely himself began negotiations with the *Maatschappij Suriname*. Had he waited a few months, the government would have been free to go its own way by virtue of a clause included in the aforementioned agreement. Lely however made commitments the Minister of Colonies had not approved of. In due course constructing the Lawa Railway was discontinued midway, because a profitable operation had proven impossible. More than 20 years later, Suriname's former Governor-general Gerard J. Staal (1870-1936) lamented:

> 'This is the terminus of the colonial railroad, a sobering aftermath of a dream of the future, acquired for eight million guilders construction costs. What has not been hoped and expected from that railway! Agricultural settlements along the line, villages that would form, lively gold mining, forestry! And what has become of it? Lelydorp, the new establishment at 17 km from Paramaribo, has not become the hoped-for flourishing village, the soil is infertile; The old Para villages further on - Onverwacht, Republiek, Berlijn - have remained what they were, insignificant; Kwakoegron is a police station, nothing more; the gold quarries up to Brownsweg are standing still; up to Republiek (41 km), at the extreme to Berlijn (52 km), there are still some people, but then more than 100 km loneliness; from the sandy savannahs to the wild, unruly forest the train cleaves through the endless, monotonous desolation.'[33]

---

30   Willemsen 1980, 255-256.
31   Ibid., 259-260.
32   Ibid., 261-263.
33   Staal 1927, 92-93.

The financial loss was passed on to Suriname as the interest and repaying the loan of more than 8,000,000 Hfl weighed on the colony's budget. Although the budget subsidy doubled to reach more than 800,000 Hfl (thus in excess of one-sixth of the total expenditure) the large deficits did indeed trigger the austerity rage as displayed by successive governors.[34] It was only in 1950 that the Dutch government cancelled this debt. From the outset of mining activities in 1876 up to the 1930s, c.50,000,000 Hfl worth of gold had been exported; between 1881 and 1890, gold was indeed the key export product amounting to as much as 34 per cent; cocoa followed closely with 32 per cent; however, hardly any profits were reinvested in Suriname.[35] The fact the small business sector was presented with more opportunities after the turn of the century did deliver a positive outcome. Numerous larger gold companies had seen their profitability fall dramatically due either to an improper usage of expensive machines or to the import of inefficient equipment.[36] In addition, sites were often exploited without being sufficiently investigated beforehand as to the presence of gold. Activities of small local gold operators facilitated the development of goldsmithing in Paramaribo, which to date is bound in honour across the Caribbean region.[37] Moreover, being employed in the gold mining sector eased the fate of many Creoles especially when cocoa farmer livelihoods were threatened as a result of the aforementioned plant disease Witch's Broom.

Harvesting the balata tree (Manilkara bidentata) proved most relevant between 1911 and 1920, accounting for c.30 per cent of exports.[38] During its heyday, this sector employed in excess of 7,000 workers, a number of whom hailed from British Guyana.[39] Milky juice (latex) was extracted from the balata tree (Sranan Tongo: bolletrie) after a bleeder had been carved into its bark with a machete. Latex provided the leading insulation material when manufacturing telegraph cables. A rapid global economic development as well as a growing need for means of communication had greatly increased demands for this raw material, which was only produced in the Guianas and Venezuela. Thanks to its elastic properties, latex was also applied when producing transmission belts and rubber soles.

As with gold mining, concession-related provisions presented to foreign companies were extremely favourable. A majority hereof comprised Dutch, British and US enterprises. Despite criticism voiced in the Colonial States, local Surinamese entrepreneurs were only given a chance to request for a concession after the best areas had already been obtained by others. It was not until the unemployment crisis of the 1930s that an individual was given the opportunity to work as self-employed in the balata sector. Due to the competition the rubber production had created, global market prices had now already fallen to such a depth that balata bleeders could hardly earn reasonable incomes. The balata industry was initially very lucrative, although the prerequisites were not as favourable as in French Guiana. For each ha, a concession tax of 10 cents was owed to the colonial government. From 1905 on, a

---

34 Willemsen 1980, 260, 326.
35 Ibid., 245; Gowricharn 1990, 58, 169.
36 Willemsen 1980, 227.
37 Ibid., 244.
38 Gowricharn 1990, 58.
39 Willemsen 1980, 253.

Figure 10.3. This undated photo depicts a balata tree. Its notches serve to tap balata milk (latex) from. In Suriname the labourers are known as balata bleeders. Unknown photographer. Surinaams Museum photo archive.

licence fee of 10 cents for each kg of balata had also to be paid. In 1911, this fee rose to 15 cents. This tax was frequently evaded under the pretext: the balata had been won on old plantation land. Bleeders, who could supply an average of 3 kg of balata per day, earned daily wages of 90 cents. Between 1905 and 1909, at a global market price of just over 3,50 Hfl, profits were estimated to range between *c.*50 and 70 cents per kg. The balata production, which at the beginning of the 20th century fluctuated between *c.*200,000 and 300,000 kg per annum, reached a record high of almost 1,200,000 kg in 1913. In the end, the government obtained 26 per cent of these proceeds.[40]

In the course of 1898, the German geologist G.J. Du Bois, an employee of the gold mining company named *Maatschappij Suriname*, was the first to come across bauxite on the Rac à Rac plantation (aka Rorac) located on the right bank of the Suriname River. His research published in German on the discovery of this aluminium-containing rock, which was applied when paving roads across Suriname, hardly caught any attention. Du Bois opined that these low quantities of ore were not yet exploitable.[41] In 1914, after a new discovery of bauxite thanks to an English mining

---

40   Willemsen 1980, 237-239, 335.
41   Lamur 1983, 4, 108-109.

engineer named William Arthur Pay in the district of Saramacca (North Suriname), various articles published in American business journals aroused interest. Cut off from Europe due to World War I, the US had been feverishly searching for bauxite across the Western Hemisphere.[42]

In December 1915 a delegation of the Aluminium Company of America (Alcoa) arrived in Suriname. Less than 12 months later, this firm had acquired almost all then known bauxite grounds covering an area of nearly 34,000 ha.

In the preceding months Alcoa had already been informed of locations where bauxite could be found. In Suriname, the gold regulation was still in force. It pertained to the exploration as well as the exploitation of minerals as a specific legislation was still lacking. The fact activities were therefore reserved for Dutch and Surinamese residents apparently did not hinder Alcoa.[43] After plots of land had been acquired in Demerara (British Guyana) several years earlier under the pretext of planning to set up citrus plantations here, several intermediaries were deployed in Suriname to purchase valuable land. By means of pointing to the US Surinam Norton Company, which exported small quantities of bauxite for chemical purposes, Alcoa attempted to give the impression to the authorities that there was no question of any monopoly. It did nonetheless subsequently emerge that the US Surinam Norton Company had very close links with Alcoa.[44] Frontmen could easily obtain exploration permits from the government of Suriname. Americans purchased private land after their specialists had carried out research into the bauxite concentrations. These activities also generated the interest of wealthy local speculators. The authorities, with their liberal licensing policy, had themselves encouraged 'bauxite fever'.[45] The fact Alcoa had paid relatively low land prices was the outcome of a lack of information available to Suriname's landowners. Moreover, this company was not hindered by other foreign competitors, as Suriname was isolated due to WW I.

The Governor of Suriname Willem D.H. baron van Asbeck (1858-1935) had played a doubtful role in the bauxite affair. For, on 30 August 1916, he added an article to the gold regulation rendering it possible to transfer permits for the exploration of minerals. Although written permission from Van Asbeck was required for such transfers, he showed great flexibility. This stance can perhaps be explained by a desire to attract as much foreign investment as possible in order to benefit an impoverished colony allowing its coffers, exhausted due to cutbacks, to profit. Personal interests may have played a role here, too. Van Asbeck's leading legal advisors did indeed maintain (family) ties with Alcoa-employed intermediaries.[46] Only several months after taking office, Van Asbeck's successor, Gerard J. Staal (1870-1936), realised that Alcoa was not only utilising a network of intermediaries but also that bauxite mining threatened to fall into the hands of an American monopoly. In 1917, Governor Staal therefore proposed to found a Dutch enterprise, which would be given the right to exploit bauxite deposits located on the Rac à Rac plantation not yet been granted as concessions. This plan nevertheless plan ran

---

42   Ibid., 110.
43   Ibid., 107.
44   Ibid., 40-41.
45   Ibid., 86-89, 109.
46   Ibid., 123-124

into the Dutch government's short-sighted austerity drive executed in The Hague. The then Minister of Colonies Alexander W.F. Idenburg (1861-1935) after an earlier attempt, while serving as Governor of Suriname (1905-1908), to reduce the colony's's chronic budget deficit, refused to set aside 30,000 Hfl for the further exploration of the land. In due course, he saw to it that the rights were awarded to the *Nederlandsche Mijnexploratie- en Exploitatiemaatschappij* (Dutch Mine Exploration and Exploitation Company) established in 1917, of which the Norwegian Aluminium Company (NACO) owned 50 per cent, with the proviso that the latter firm was to pay exploration costs.[47] However, the NACO never took any action and financial problems even forced it to borrow NOK 7.000.000 from Alcoa in 1922. Four years later, Alcoa obtained NACO's shares, hereby acquiring the Rac à Rac plantation.[48]

On 19 December 1916, Alcoa had combined its interests in Suriname into the *Surinaamsche Bauxiet Maatschappij*. Due to a lack of solid legalisation, it took another 6 years before the first large quantities of bauxite were shipped out of Suriname. An ongoing tug-of-war pertaining to concession-related provisos had taken place. In 1918, Governor Staal had offered a draft bauxite decree to the Colonial States in order to 'obtain larger benefits for the colonial coffers', but with a meagre outcome. As a result of the absence of sufficient knowledge and experience, the government of Suriname was hardly able to counteract Alcoa. Once again The Hague's frugality was in play here. For, it was only in 1943 that Suriname created its own government mining services. Provisions were much more favourable than those Alcoa had managed to negotiate with the British in Demerara (British Guiana). An American magazine mentions that 'nothing' had to be paid for Suriname 'because The Netherlands will be glad when released from the annual subsidy'.[49] Nevertheless, legislation pertaining to the bauxite sector did not come into effect. For, the then Minister of Colonies, Alexander W.F. Idenburg, wished to considerably tighten concession-related provisos. Amended rules and regulations, which the Colonial States ratified on 1 January 1920, had been negotiated with Alcoa's Vice President during a visit to the Netherlands.[50] His approval was apparently a tactical manoeuvre in anticipation of better times which did arrive in 1924 with the unfolding of plans for the construction of a processing plant comprising an ore crusher as well as a drying plant installed at Moengo, an isolated site located in Northeast Suriname. This outcome now facilitated a large-scale export of bauxite. The fact a Dutchman presided over the *Surinaamsche Bauxiet Maatschappij* (SBM) improved its relationship with colonial authorities. Moreover, Dutch technicians were to be involved in constructing installations at Moengo.[51]

In 1924, too, Alcoa had requested the reopening of negotiations in order to establish more favourable mining conditions, which should be required to not jeopardise the profitability of the SBM; the Dutch government fully complied with this firm's wishes, to wit, to cut both the concession tax and the bauxite tax into two equal parts; as a friendly gesture Alcoa presented Paramaribo with a wireless station

---

47   Ibid., 185..
48   Ibid., 1983, 8.
49   Smit 1947, 17
50   Lamur 1983, 191.
51   Ibid., 8; Willemsen 1980, 276.

valued at 50,000 Hfl for the symbolic amount of one guilder; needless to say, that sum did not in any way match the benefits Alcoa achieved.[52]

In the Colonial States, critical remarks were voiced, but the incoming provisos were nevertheless unanimously ratified. Unfounded fears Alcoa might completely abandon its activities in Suriname prevailed with a majority of the Colonial States. None of these representees had learned that, from 1922 on, the US government had received an import duty comprising 1 USD per tonne of bauxite. By chance, in 1928, Governor Baron A.J.A.A. van Heemstra (1871-1957) came across this fact when reading Robert J. Anderson's publication entitled *The Metallurgy of Aluminium and Aluminium Alloys*.[53] Van Heemstra's reaction (his term of office had almost ended) was in accordance with his unconventional character. Omitting a consultation with The Hague, he submitted a proposal to the Colonial States in order to increase the bauxite tax as much as twenty-fold to 2.50 Hfl, hereby exactly equalling the US import tax. Moreover, he not only expressed the wish to increase the annual minimum production from 2 to 5.5 tonnes per ha, but also stated in an explanatory memorandum that 'the burden placed on the extraction of this raw material here in this country is by no means in accordance with the commercial value of the product'.[54] Van Heemstra calculated that Alcoa had amassed a gross profit of 480 Hfl per tonne of aluminium at the current market price of 1,250 Hfl. In his proposals, the costs would merely amount to 13 Hfl per tonne of aluminium. After the Colonial States had unanimously approved these regulations, the Crown chose to annul them 6 months later. These rules not only allegedly conflicted with the 'general interest' but were also deemed to derogate the 'legitimate expectations' of entrepreneurs in the bauxite sector. The Royal Decree also referred to a 'deterrent effect' which other potential investors would experience.[55]

How can a much more flexible attitude of the Dutch government towards Alcoa be explained? A. W. Mellon, who officiated as US Secretary of the Treasury (1921-1932) being Alcoa's largest shareholder certainly forms part of the explanation. For years on end, Washington, D.C., had exerted heavy political pressure on The Hague.[56] Furthermore, national oil interests played a key role in this conflict. The Royal Dutch Shell and Standard Oil were fighting over the Djambi oil fields on the island of Sumatra. The fact that both British and French contenders had excluded Standard Oil from the rich oil fields located across the basin of the Euphrates and the Tigris (in present-day Iraq) further added to the appeal of oil reserves found across the Dutch East Indies. Moreover, many US governments had continuously stressed the significance of maintaining an open door policy for foreign investments. A diplomatic clash between Washington, D.C., and The Hague occurred when the exploitation of the Sumatran oil fields was awarded to a Shell subsidiary named *De Bataafsche Oliemaatschappij*. In 1920, the US Congress had adopted the Oil Leasing Act which was mainly directed against France and the United Kingdom in order to prohibit any concessions being given to oil companies run by nations which had

---

52   Lamur 1983, 7-8; Willemsen 1980, 275-276.
53   Smit 1947, 47.
54   Ibid., 47-48.
55   Ibid., 51; Willemsen 1980, 281-282.
56   Willemsen 1980, 282-287.

imposed restrictive stipulations on US competitors. The Dutch government now partly satisfied the US Department of State by allowing Standard Oil to exploit fields, not yet occupied by Shell and located in the Dutch East Indies.[57] This stance was hardly a concession as the Djambi oil fields had already been granted.

Of far more relevance was the Dutch government's concession to Alcoa's subsidiary, the SBM. This event in fact led to an exchange whereby the Netherlands could retain its oil interests in the Dutch East Indies, whereas the USA was able to exploit Suriname's bauxite reserves. After Governor Van Heemstra's departure, the SBM was guaranteed that no fresh attempts would be made aimed at increasing the burden placed on extracting bauxite. In accordance with an incoming bauxite regulation, (a) the existing monetary charges of 50 cents per ha, (b) the fee of 25 cents for each tonne of bauxite (hereby compensating for land now rendered useless) and (c) an export levy of 12.5 cents per tonne of bauxite was to be maintained for a period of 60 years, from 1 January 1929 on. The single concession obtained from Alcoa comprised a minimum production of 150,000 tonnes, with Alcoa paying the income tax.[58]

Alcoa had thus succeeded in acquiring almost all the then known bauxite reserves at a low cost. This company's super profits hugely exceeded the entire government budget of Suriname. In 1927, 176,291 tonnes of raw bauxite were exported with an export value of *c.*2,000,000 Hfl. At that time, 35,000 tonnes of aluminium could be extracted from 176,291 tonnes of bauxite. A cost price of 800 Hfl and a selling price of 1,375 Hfl per tonne resulted in a profit exceeding 20,000,000 Hfl. In 1927, too, only 82,682 Hfl of taxes and levies were transferred into the public treasury, whereas the 623 individuals employed by the SBM received 1,115,598 Hfl in wages and salaries. Investments this firm made between 1916 and 1935 were thus recouped within a single year.[59] During the 1930s, bauxite remittances to the colonial treasury usually amounted to no more than a few per cent of Suriname's entire government budget. All this is in sharp contrast to the Dutch budget subsidy which often exceeded 40 per cent. Only in 1941 when Suriname was briefly listed as the world's largest bauxite producer as a result of the Allied war effort, could it present a balanced budget for the first time.[60]

A boom in bauxite exploitation had in due course also aroused the interest of the Dutch government. Moreover, the Minister of Colonies Charles I.M. Welter (1880-1972) considered it undesirable that Americans were the only ones able to obtain bauxite concessions in Suriname. The uncertain future of the Dutch East Indies, where nationalists were becoming increasingly active, contributed to a slightly larger interest in Suriname. The first shipments followed in 1942 after the *N.V. Billiton Maatschappij*, established in Batavia (Java), had discovered exploitable quantities of bauxite in 1940 on plantation Onverdacht.[61] Continuing to serve as a haven for colonial exploitation pertaining to the expansion of the bauxite sector, the Dutch policy towards Suriname did not seek to provide an independent economic basis. Indeed, developing a middle-class agricultural sector could have offered

---

57   Ibid., 285.
58   Ibid., 281.
59   Ibid., 280, 328.
60   Ibid., 328
61   Bruijning & Voorhoeve 1977, 46-47.

A History of Suriname

good opportunities to reach this goal. For too long a time, attempts had been made to maintain plantation agriculture by means of cheap contract labour. We see here rather a striking difference in comparison with neighbouring British Guyana, where the production on plantations became more capital intensive and therefore more competitive when immigration from foreign shores ended in 1917. The continuous deficit in the government budget as well as in the trade balance reveal the weakness of Suriname's economic base.

A frail, one-sided economic structure implied that tax revenues contrasted sharply with the financial needs of the government which, because of a small population, had to support a relatively costly administrative apparatus. In 1938, when Suriname numbered 174,237 souls, only 5,823 paid taxes based on a total income of just above 8,500,000 Hfl; between 1922 and 1926, the average number of taxpayers was still 9,113; the total of direct and indirect taxes the population of Suriname raised during 1938 exceeded 2,000,000 Hfl, which was 500,000 Hfl less than the budget subsidy; since the abolition of slavery, the trade balance had almost always revealed a deficit of *c*.500,000 Hfl per annum.[62] Suriname thus continued to display the structural traits of a plantation economy, even if bauxite had replaced sugar.

---

62   Van Lier 1971, 203-205; Willemsen 1980, 328.

CHAPTER 11
Towards autonomy and independence

11.1 World War II

Political developments received a new impulse when, on 7 December 1942, the Dutch Queen Wilhelmina (1880-1962) delivered a radio speech from London, where the government was then seated. In it she promised to create a revised post-WW II constellation within the kingdom which would provide its colonies (the Dutch East Indies, the Netherlands Antilles and Suriname) with internal self-government.[1] This statement was mainly (a) a response to the 1941 Atlantic Charter, in which the US President Franklin D. Roosevelt and the British Prime Minister Winston Churchill advocated the right of all nations to self-determination and (b) a signal to Indonesian nationalists who had sided with the Japanese occupier in their struggle for independence. Queen Wilhelmina's speech received a favourable reception in Suriname. This is not a huge surprise considering an increasing resistance directed against Governor Johannes C. Kielstra's autocratism and his policy of *verindisching*, i.e., the application in Suriname of certain elements of Dutch colonial politics applied across the East Indies and focusing on the interests of Asian immigrants (see p. 230ff.).

The Atlantic Charter had been the centre of attention in the Suriname-based press. The light-skinned Creole elite voiced the slogan *Baas in eigen huis* (Boss in our own home).[2] This endeavour was not so much inspired by an anti-colonial attitude as by a desire to take control of administrative tasks, for which Kielstra had recruited Dutch civil servants with experience in the Dutch East Indies. In March 1943, in order to reinforce demands, the *Unie Suriname* was founded. This cultural association had a political slant whereby independence was not an issue. This Creole elite essentially deemed Suriname a Dutch settlement, of which its inhabitants had become culture bearers.

Unlike across the Dutch East Indies, no anti-Dutch sentiments had been observed in Suriname during WW II where a majority expressed compassion for the inhabitants of the Netherlands. The government of Suriname took action in order to detain Germans residents who by and large were either employed in education or served the Moravian Mission. These measures encountered no local opposition. With general agreement, individuals from the Dutch East Indies whenever suspected of sympathizing with members of the pro-German *Nationaal-Socialistische Beweging* (National-Socialist Movement) were later imprisoned in Suriname-based internment camps as were Dutch conscientious objectors originating from South Africa.[3] The launching of the Spitfire Fund, by means of which a war plane for the Allies had to be purchased, proved a huge success. Moreover, the first vessel to sail from Paramaribo to Amsterdam after WW II shipped a donation comprising relief supplies which the population of Suriname had provided.[4] Around 200 volunteers

---

1   See: houseofdavid.ca/queen.htm
2   Dew 1996 (1978), 52.
3   Ramsoedh 1990, 164-166; De Jong 1979, vol. 9 (1), 505-507.
4   Scholtens 1985, 14; Ramsoedh 1990, 161.

Figure 11.1. A US military unit stationed at Paramaribo during WW II. Unknown photographer. Public domain, via National Archives, The Hague.

from this colony served as gunners on Dutch naval and merchant ships hereby protecting them against enemy attacks.[5] In the Dutch East Indies, volunteers from Suriname also fought against Japanese invaders. Harry Voss, a Creole serving in the Royal Dutch East Indies Army, posthumously received the *Militaire Willems-Orde*, the highest and oldest chivalry order of merit to be awarded in the Kingdom of the Netherlands. Voss was executed by the Japanese while shouting '*Leve de koningin*' ('Long live the Queen!'). As an instructor, he had refused to train Indonesians for the Japanese army.[6] More than 400 volunteers hailing from Suriname had enrolled in the Royal Netherlands Motorized Infantry Brigade (later known as the Princess Irene Brigade). The Dutch government however refused to employ them. For, volunteers or conscripts hailing from South Africa might as a result of their racial origins take offence at co-workers from Suriname.[7] The latter felt great affection for the House of Orange, especially the lower-class Creoles who still deemed King Willem III had ended slavery with a single stroke of the pen.

WW II caused Suriname to introduce social changes. This transformation was for the most part the outcome of the arrival in 1941 and 1942 of a more than 2,000 US troops.[8] Deployed to protect bauxite mines, of essence to the war industry, against

---

5   Ibid. 1985, 22; ibid. 1990, 187.
6   See: nl.wikipedia.org
7   De Jong 1979, vol. 9, part 1, 509; Ramsoedh 1990, 187.
8   Scholtens 1985, 17.

A History of Suriname

possible German attacks, their presence generated an unprecedented flow of capital. All in all, the expansion of Zanderij Airport, constructing roads and defence works, intensifying bauxite mining and the consumer spending of the US military personnel resulted in an expenditure of more than 65 million Hfl.[9] This sum exceeded twice the total of the Welfare Fund which the Dutch government was planning to set up after WW II in order to fund Suriname's economic developments. It included in excess of 50 million Hfl spent on wages for local workers and on the supply of local goods. The influx of foreign currencies had for the first time provided many with a certain level of prosperity, although those with fixed incomes (e.g., civil servants), now risked falling into poverty due to a sharp increase of prices. By 1943, c.4,000 employees were actively engaged in defence works; the number of bauxite workers had risen from 500 to more than 2,500.[10] Further economic activities were developed, to wit, producing soft drinks, soap and matches. Hindustanis and Javanese, having abandoned the plantations, now moved to urban environments in order to work for relatively high wages for US employers. Numerous small farm holders found attractive sources providing extra incomes. Mobilizing the militia (schutterij), for which conscription was compulsory, contributed to ending the isolation of districts. The US troops brought the people of Suriname in contact with a Western consumerist lifestyle, which certainly appealed to younger generations. A rapid urbanisation did come with disadvantages. Within urban settings, young people formed gangs after being inspired by omnipresent American crime films. In addition, prostitution, especially of Javanese girls, increased dramatically. A few weeks prior to Princess Juliana of the Netherlands arriving for a visit to Suriname in November 1943, colonial authorities commissioned the internment of dozens of youngsters and prostitutes who were referred to as 'vagabonds'.[11]

Governor Kielstra who had never enthused over the US presence even opined that the negative attitude which the elite of colour expressed towards him was a sign of 'Americanism'.[12] His fear that admiration for the Americans would tip over into an anti-Dutch stance was rather exaggerated as proved especially obvious during Princess Juliana's visit, when the population of Paramaribo thronged the streets to welcome her. The Dutch government had considered the arrival of a US military contingent controversial. In 1940 only 200 professional soldiers and 180 volunteers had been employed across Suriname.[13] Kielstra had prior hereto asked for military reinforcements, a request only supported by the Ministry of Colonies. Paramaribo received no more than 100,000 Hfl and a battery of shore-based artillery dispatched from the Dutch East Indies.[14] The need for military aid only increased after Vichy France (aka Régime de Vichy) was established. For, an attack launched out of French Guiana on bauxite mines located in nearby Moengo (east Suriname) was by no means inconceivable. Kielstra also felt the domestic political motive to improve Suriname's defence: the light-skinned Creole elite would thus have a greater respect for the

---

9   Bosman 1948, 51.
10   Ramsoedh 1990, 155.
11   Ibid., 156-157; Dew 1996 (1978), 48-50; Scholtens 1985, 36-37.
12   Ramsoedh 1990, 162.
13   Ibid., 166-167; Scholtens 1985, 10.
14   Ramsoedh 1990, 167.

Netherlands. In June 1941, during an official visit of the Minister of Colonies Charles J.I.M. Welter (1880-1972) to Suriname, Kielstra put forward yet another argument: if Suriname's armed forces were not reinforced, the USA might well decide to dispatch military personnel to Suriname, which would seriously affect the prestige of the Netherlands. Kielstra's arguments impressed Welter who, during a visit to Washington, D.C., having asked for US naval patrols to be positioned off the coast of Suriname, rejected an offer to deploy US troops in Suriname. Such a deployment by the USA fully fitted in with the American security policy aimed at preventing European colonies located in the Western Hemisphere from falling into the hands of Nazi Germany. Washington-based authorities had agreed, after consulting Central American nation states, upon these states temporarily controlling European colonies in case of any imminent dangers. Suriname had already been included in the strategic defence plan for this hemisphere, as it formed an indispensable bridgehead for the US Air Force when defending North-eastern Brazil. In September 1941, the London-based Dutch government could therefore only respond positively to President Roosevelt's request to station US troops in Suriname. Here the conclusion had been reached that the danger of losing sovereignty over the colony would only increase if this request was denied.[15]

With the arrival of US military personnel, the forming of an army in Suriname was given the highest priority. Here Colonel Johan K. Meijer (1898-1972) of the Royal Dutch East Indian Army had meanwhile been appointed territorial commander. His main task was to create three battalions comprising domestic troops, two of which were to be transferred to Australia and deployed against the Japanese. The third battalion was deemed suited to take over the task imposed on the US garrison located in Suriname. The Surinamese forces, to wit, voluntary town and land guards as well as conscripts of the militia consisted of c.3,000 men. However, all these plans were at risk of collapsing due to the bad relationship between Governor Kielstra and the members of the Staten (the parliament of Suriname). The latter only wished to cooperate with the deployment of conscripts once Kielstra was removed from office. He therefore wanted to commission the dispatching of troops by Royal Decree. However, the then Minister of Colonies Hubertus J. van Mook (1894-1965) considered it unwise to provoke a conflict with the Staten.[16] Commanding officer J.K. Meijer deemed this sufficient reason to do his utmost to bring about Kielstra's dismissal. The infamous affair took on a putsch-like allure as a result of the latter's remarkable behaviour.[17] Having previously played a background role together with several other Dutch officers during the successful 'coup' which US military personnel had staged against the Cayenne-based representatives of pro-German Vichy France, Meijer considered such an intervention, with US support, to also be possible if directed against Kielstra. He then sent the navy pastor to Canada with a file including alleged pro-German sympathies, thus incriminating Kielstra. Wishing to inform Queen Wilhelmina, then on vacation in Canada, this pastor did not get past Minister Van Mook. Previously compromised after being involved in executing two

---

15   Ibid., 168-177.
16   Ibid., 186-187.
17   Ibid., 186-193; De Jong 1979, 509-510.

internees brought from the Dutch East Indies, Meijer was transferred to Australia without much publicity in order to avoid a scandal.[18] This affair clouded relations with the USA. For, one of their Territorial Commanders was involved, having provided a military aeroplane to facilitate the navy pastor's journey to Canada. This US commander was removed from his post, too. At the same time, however, this issue prompted Washington to postpone the departure of troops, as the political situation in Suriname was considered unstable.

Governor Kielstra's resignation had not come any closer. Van Mook felt that the 'foolish action' had made it even more difficult to dismiss him.[19] The degree of resistance levelled against Kielstra has never been entirely clear. At any rate it did include more than 'the always inciting small group' of Creoles as mentioned by the Governor in his correspondence with the Minister of Colonies.[20] After all, the inadequate governance system and the authoritarian stance which the governors displayed had stirred up the ever latent feelings of dissent within the colony on more than one occasion. Kielstra's conduct had also provoked opposition outside the Staten. In July 1943, initiated by a group of citizens, a petition for signature circulated in Paramaribo, demanding Queen Wilhelmina should dismiss him. Its distribution, to which 350 signatures were added within several days, led to the arrest of the initiators. The most prominent detainee, the Staten member Wim Bos Verschuur (1904-1985) was jailed for allegedly endangering the peace and security in the colony. [21] Kielstra explained to Van Mook that the 'Creole group', as a result of the imprisonment, would feel that this reaction had gone too far. On occasion Kielstra's distrust of the Creole population apparently took the form of paranoia. In the night after Bos Verschuur's incarceration Kielstra commissioned Dutch marines to replace Creole guards positioned near the governmental palace.

Moreover, Governor Kielstra sought rapprochement with Hindustani groups in such a demonstrative manner he could never again be considered a neutral arbiter as to sensitive ethnic relations. Presenting its own propaganda, the Government Press Service utilised weekly Hindustani radio broadcasts aimed at fending off pro-German influences. In Kielstra's view, detaining Bos Verschuur should also serve as a warning for Americans that their 'rooting' in Surinamese internal affairs could not be tolerated.[22] He deemed this admonition necessary as investigations had revealed that an English language version of the petition had previously been given to a high-ranking US military official.[23] As a means of protest directed against Bos Verschuur's detention and Kielstra's refusal to provide a full clarification, seven of the ten elected Staten members resigned only to be re-elected by a large majority several months later. Eight of these ten addressed the Crown, hereby reiterating grievances forwarded against Kielstra. Van Mook, having already appointed Kielstra as the Ambassador of

---

18   For more information on this execution, see: De Jong 1979, 507.
19   Ramsoedh 1990, 192.
20   Ibid., 196
21   Ibid., 193-200.
22   Ibid., 196.
23   Ibid., 194-197.

the Netherlands to Mexico, waited several months before announcing this decision in order to avoid the semblance of a link with the 'Surinamese incidents'.[24]

A key incentive for Kielstra's dismissal was: it dispelled Washington's concern about Suriname's political instability, which might accelerate the departure of US troops. Prolonged conflicts here could also have tarnished the international image of the Netherlands as a colonial power. Hence, possible damage could perhaps be inflicted as to policies imposed on the Dutch East Indies. With Kielstra's departure, the obstacle pertaining to the deployment of Surinamese volunteers to the East was removed. Shortly after WW II, in order to improve its international image, Dutch authorities initially supported a plan presented by the Freeland League for Jewish Territorial Colonization. The Staten consented with a small majority after a fierce debate in which fear of a resurgence of anti-Semitism and of a revived white domination played a role. Be it never executed and now long forgotten, this league's goal was to create a refuge in Suriname for thousands of displaced Eastern European Jews.[25]

In fact The Hague did not drop Governor Kielstra. After WW II he was appointed to represent the Kingdom of the Netherlands in the Caribbean Commission.[26] The Dutch government feared the USA would utilise this committee to expand its influence across the Caribbean. Kielstra was par excellence equipped to counter this ambition. For, above all, the Netherlands wished to retain full sovereignty over Suriname. Apparently the apprehension that a precedent for the Dutch East Indies would be created mainly inspired this stance. However, de facto, after all the events unfolding in the course of WW II, an independent Dutch colonial policy could no longer exist.

11.2 Political mobilisation

Relations within Suriname were soon normalized once Kielstra had left. Immediately after WW II, in anticipation of the promised internal autonomy, the political mobilisation started.

The enthusiasm for party formation had never been very strong as a result of (a) the restricted suffrage based on census and capacity whereby the electorate numbered less than 3,000 individuals and (b) the limited power of the Staten.[27] War-time societal changes had led to greater self-awareness among the entire population, as was now expressed politically too. In 1946, both Hindustanis and Javanese united in order to form the *Hindostaans-Javaanse Centrale Raad* (Hindustani-Javanese Central Council). Its main goal was to prevent the *Unie Suriname*, a political vehicle of the light-skinned Creole elite, from separately discussing autonomy with the Dutch government. That same year, the *Moslim Partij* became the first real political party. Not much later the *Hindoe Partij* was

---

24   Ibid., 197-202.
25   Dew 1996 (1978), 64-65; Vink 2010, 36, 124; Heldring 2011.
26   Ramsoedh 1990, 202; the Caribbean Commission, active between 1942 and 1957, began as an American/British cooperative effort to deal with the WW II emergency, e.g., German submarine activity across the Caribbean. It also addressed regional socio-economic issues. The Netherlands (already a member of an auxiliary body since 1943) and France were invited to join this commission in 1946.
27   Dew 1996, 55; Mitrasing 1959, 76.

Figure 11.2. Demonstration in Paramaribo, shortly after WW II, held in order to acquire more autonomy. Unknown photographer. In the background a banner reads 'Baas in eigen huis' ('Boss in our own home'). This slogan was already popular during that war (see p. 251). Surinaams Museum photo archive.

founded.[28] Universal suffrage was the main political catalyst. Representatives of the light-skinned Creole bourgeoisie, having noticed that their comfortable position in the Staten was threatened, declared to oppose all forms of universal suffrage, arguing that the population was not yet ready for it. These Creoles solely strived at 'elite nationalism'.[29] In September 1946, members of the aforementioned Creole middle class founded the *Nationale Partij Suriname* (NPS), the successor of the *Unie Suriname*. Declaring its principles, the NPS presented itself as a national party. However, it did not appeal to the Asian population simply because of its stance on universal suffrage. Creating the NPS formed a response to the *Progressieve Surinaamse Volkspartij* (PSV), established a month earlier. This party was led by the Redemptorist Father L. J. (Jozef) Weidmann (1899-1962) who organised the Roman Catholics among the lower-class Creoles and considered universal suffrage a key objective.[30]

In 1947, Hindustanis and Javanese founded the *Hindostaans-Javaanse Politieke Partij* (HJPP) with the same aforementioned objective. It was led by Jagernath Lachmon (1916-2001), the first Hindustani lawyer in Suriname. An elite group stemming from higher castes favoured the NPS position on universal suffrage and thus formed its own party. Only after 2 years, the HJPP collapsed due to ethnic and religious discord. Next, Hindustani immigrants founded the *Verenigde Hindostaanse*

---

28   Dew 1996, 57, 61.
29   Ibid., 61; Ramsoedh 1990, 185.
30   Dew 1996, 58-61.

Partij (VHP; United Hindustani Party), which was again chaired by J. Lachmon. The *Moslim Partij* and the *Hindoe Partij* merged with the VHP. A small group of Hindustani Muslims joined the NPS.[31] A struggle for independence across the Dutch East Indies had for the first time led to a growing political awareness among Javanese residing in Suriname. For many, the right to return to their motherland formed a major incentive to create a political organization. Hence, Iding Soemita (1908-2001) founded the *Persatuan Indonesia* in 1946 which, 3 years later, became the *Kaum Tani Persatuan Indonesia* (KTPI; Farmers' Association of Indonesia).[32]

Political mobilisation occurred entirely along ethnic lines. Suriname thus displayed all the traits of a 'plural' society, a phenomenon first described by a British-born colonial public servant-*cum*-writer named J.S. Furnivall (1878-1960). Here Siam (now Thailand) inhabited by Chinese, Europeans and various ethnic groups served as an example. Furnivall states that in a plural society, 'distinct social orders live side by side, but separately, within the same political unit' (see also p. 447ff.).[33] In Suriname, other factors reinforced the society's plural character which comprised diverse racial traits, languages and religions. After WW II, Hindustanis and Javanese continued to be predominantly active in agriculture, whereas Creoles were already far more urbanized. A geographical separation of races reinforced not only a social isolation but also communal feelings of identity within each ethnic group. The economic upturn witnessed during WW II had indeed increased the geographical and social mobility of Hindustanis in particular. This phenomenon, however, did result in a pushing between the various racial groups rather than a genuine rapprochement.

Founding their own political parties therefore presented Hindustanis and Javanese with a means of protection against possible Creole domination as well as a powerful instrument to emancipate their ethnic groups. Because the Chinese and Jewish populations had long been assimilated and emancipated, their need to establish parties was less. Moreover, as a result of limited numbers, Chinese and Jews were less capable of making a difference. In Suriname, political parties were established on the initiative of a social upper class, which had to legitimise itself not only in their nation state but also in relationship with the Netherlands. As with political 'entrepreneurs', leaders reacted upon racial sentiments voiced from within their own group in order to mobilise a sufficient number of voters hereby forming the basis of the post-war political system.

In due course, the NPS accepted universal suffrage because the Dutch authorities insisted. Moreover, the other parties did not wish to accept any internal autonomy if this right to vote had not first been settled. In order to consolidate its dominant position, the NPS aimed at introducing a district system. The Netherlands did not withstand the NPS, which had a large majority in the Staten. The boundaries of each of the nine districts were drawn in such a way that Hindustanis and Javanese (whose numbers had risen to more than 50 per cent of the almost 180,000 residents of Suriname) were never capable of obtaining an absolute majority in seats.[34]

---

31   Ibid., 61, 72-74.
32   Ibid., 74.
33   Furnivall 1939, XV.
34   Dew 1996, 69.

Figure 11.3. Politician Wim Bos Verschuur (see also p. 255) during the election campaign for the NPS, where initially light-skinned Creoles occupied the key positions. Undated photo, probably 1948/1949. Unknown photographer. Surinaams Museum photo archive.

However, Hindustani as well as Javanese leaders simply rejoiced in being able to participate at the highest political level. They thus did not oppose an electoral system so disadvantageous to them. In the district of Paramaribo, with its huge Creole majority, a total of 34,234 voters were eligible to vote for ten of the 21 seats available in the Staten. However, in the Hindustani-dominated district of Suriname, 29,877 voters could only elect three delegates. This district was divided into three electoral constituencies, each with a single seat, of which one would always accrue to the NPS in compliance with demographics.[35] The Creoles had strong advantages elsewhere, too.

The result of the first general elections held in 1949 could not have been much of a surprise. The NPS not only won all ten seats in Paramaribo but also the remaining three seats in the Creole districts, securing an absolute majority in the 21-seat Staten. The VHP acquired six seats whereas the KTPI obtained the expected two seats representing the district of Commewijne. Voting percentages per district match almost entirely with the ethnic numerical ratios mentioned in the 1950 Census.[36] The district system, whereby all seats went to the majority parties, reinforced the ethnic factor in politics. It was of no interest to the NPS to mobilise,

---

35   Ibid., 69-70.
36   Ibid., 78-79.

for example, any voters in the Nickerie district and equally not worthwhile for the VHP to campaign in Paramaribo.

Any ideological discord between various parties was difficult to discover. They all wished for an autonomous status for Suriname within the Kingdom of the Netherlands. Autonomy was not realised until 1954. In The Hague, finding a solution for problems encountered across the Dutch East Indies during the early post-WW II years simply had greater priority. When in 1948, a College of General Administration was established, it functioned as a cabinet. In 1950, an interim arrangement had been introduced by means of which the ministers of Suriname could not only arrange internal affairs but also only be held accountable to the Staten.[37]

Negotiations on a final settlement of the incoming constitutional relations with Suriname and the Antilles proved extremely difficult. This arduousness was by and large the result of the Dutch government's intransigence when it refused to respond to a demand by Suriname's parliamentary delegation present at the 1952 Round Table Conference, to wit, lay down the secession right of the overseas territories in the draft Statute. Suriname also sought to create a greater equality between partners within the Kingdom, namely the Netherlands, Suriname and the Netherlands Antilles. Suriname therefore objected to the Dutch requirement that the so-called Kingdom Government, with a decisive say by the Netherlands, could intervene in case of, for example, bad governance.[38] The tough stance observed on Suriname's side was partly the outcome of a power struggle within the NPS, whereby Black lower-class Creoles headed by Johan Adolf ('Jopie') Pengel (1916-1970) had prevailed (see also p. 261-263).[39] After Suriname had threatened to submit the conflict to the United Nations, the newly appointed Minister of Overseas Territories, Willem J.A. Kernkamp (1899-1956) was prepared to comply with Suriname's demand. A majority of both the upper and lower houses however refused to support him. Losing the Dutch East Indies was as yet far too fresh a memory for many parliamentarians. One of Kernkamp's fellow Christian Democratic party members even went so far as to accuse him of 'treason'.[40] A compromise was reached in time without explicitly referring to the secession right described in the legislative text. As parts of the Kingdom were now able to exercise a right to self-determination by amending the Kingdom Statute, this implied that the Netherlands could have a say on this issue. This Statute included the possibility to intervene whenever instances of maladministration occurred. The Hague, which had first threatened to suspend its economic aid plans, rewarded Paramaribo with financial support forwarded under the Ten Year Plan.[41] In Suriname, satisfaction with this Statute was immense. After all, the internal self-government provided a head start over other colonies located in this region. Nevertheless, after only several years, statutory relations were felt as being too constraining.

---

37   Ibid., 65-66, 80-82.
38   Ibid., 95-97.
39   Breeveld 2000, 157-161.
40   Ramsoedh 1993, 47.
41   Dew 97-98; Meel 1999, 48-61.

A History of Suriname

11.3 Fraternization policy and elite-cartel democracy

The aforementioned J.A. Pengel, a young Staten member, had caused light-skinned Creole NPS members to lose their dominant positions within this party after only a few years. In 1950, he had seized upon a conflict surrounding the Minister for Health and Education Lou Lichtveld (venerated author known under the alias Albert Helman) to dismiss his own party's cabinet. Although Pengel's motion was rejected, it did herald the departure of eight light-skinned NPS Staten members. Prior hereto, this discord had resulted in a shift within the party leadership in favour of lower-class Creoles (aka *volkscreolen*). This conflict which went down in history as the *Hospitaalkwestie* (Hospital affair) revolved around Minister Lichtveld dismissing the government-employed physician Hendrik Carel van Ommeren, also a NPS member of parliament and allegedly guilty of 'misconduct and subordination'.[42] Van Ommeren not only represented the voice of Black Creoles but was also loved for on occasion providing medical assistance free of charge. Pengel as well as Van Ommeren mobilised NPS supporters, which not only led to the Paramaribo-based section of this party adopting a sharp motion but also to splitting the NPS fraction in two. It may be added here that this motion accused Lichtveld of nurturing 'dictatorial tendencies' as well as an attitude deemed 'not in keeping with the psyche and mentality of the people'.[43]

This affair, in which elements of race and social status played a part, did render Pengel a powerful factor which nobody involved in Suriname's politics could ignore. Having built up a large constituency prior to being chosen as a MP for the NPS in 1949, Pengel had found employment as a so-called *nengre-oso-afkati* (lit. negro-house-lawyer). Giving advice to the working class brought him great popularity. On the other hand, his activities resulted in a negative image among the elite. Identifying with Black lower-class Creoles was a reason why he, while serving at the registry of the court, could never complete his training as a lawyer.[44] Pengel would literally walk through mud in order to help the underprivileged, for example, by securing their rights to own building plots.[45] His religious background, as with numerous other Surinamese Creoles, played a role as did his membership of the Moravian Brethren. Aversion to the nascent collaboration between Pengel and Lachmon also contributed to the departure of light-skinned prominent figures active within the NPS. Both men were considered second class Staten members by the elite within their own parties; within the VHP those critics were higher-caste Hindus. Pengel's and Lachmon's interests ran parallel. The former required Hindustani support in order to break the power which people of colour active within his own party held in the Staten. By collaborating with Pengel, Lachmon in turn acquired a greater political influence and thus more room to accelerate the emancipation of the Hindustanis he represented.

Prior to the 1955 elections resigned NPS members formed the *Surinaamse Democratische Partij* (SDP). Having established the *Eenheidsfront* (Unity Front), they joined forces with the PSV and the KTPI. Pengel's main opponent within the SDP was David Findlay.[46] This editor-in-chief of the daily newspaper *De West* was also a member

---

42 Breeveld 2000, 134-145; Dew 1996, 83-90; Van Kempen 2016, 395-403.
43 Breeveld 2000, 141-142.
44 Ibid., 69-71.
45 Ibid., 79-90.
46 Dew 1996, 106-107.

Figure 11.4. Children of four ethnic groups (from left to right: Chinese, Creole, Hindustani, Javanese), awaiting the 1955 visit of Juliana, Queen of the Netherlands. Photo by Willem van de Poll. Public domain, via National Archives, The Hague.

of parliament and did not shy away from openly exploiting ethnic sentiments. In an advertisement published in this daily, we read 'Do you wish to be governed by the VHP, do you wish a mass immigration from a certain eastern country?'[47] The electoral system now worked to the NPS's disadvantage. Having obtained 50 per cent of the votes, only eight of the 21 seats in the States were occupied by the NPS and the VHP.[48] After winning all ten seats in the capital, the *Eenheidsfront* formed a cabinet led by Johan Ferrier (1910-2010) who was to officiate as the first President of the Republic of Suriname after gaining independence from the Netherlands in 1975.[49]

Voters did not feel sufficiently confident about Pengel cooperating with Lachmon, considering this, not entirely without reason, to be personal matters for both leaders. Lachmon in particular was emotionally driven to join forces with Pengel. The Creole

47   Mitrasing 1959, 271.
48   Dew 1996, 107.
49   Ibid., 110-111.

lawyer (and ex-Prime Minister) Julius Caesar de Miranda (1906-1956) had tutored Lachmon. Married to a Creole, the latter referred to his goal, to wit, interracial cooperation, as a *verbroederingspolitiek* (fraternization policy).[50] After the elections of 1955, Lachmon even made a VHP seat available to Pengel, whose party had suffered a defeat in the constituency of Paramaribo. Accepting this offer, Pengel was elected thanks to Hindustani votes after a VHP-parliamentarian based in the district of Saramacca had resigned. In order to persuade voters, Pengel and Lachmon had promised to build a major access road leading to the Saramacca district.[51] Looking back on his political gesture which even his own group had resisted, Lachmon stated in 2001:

> *'The [religious organization] Sanatan Dharm has convened at the Koningstraat and the pandits as well as other head priests with their large turbans have called me to account. Then I said if you think I did not have the authority to make that commitment, I did so based on the conviction of my fraternization policy, because otherwise I would be considered a traitor by the Creole group. The NPS has lost so I am going to work with another party. I say I am not going to do that. I acted on my own thoughts [...] I found the partnership with the NPS very important. And without the NPS we would not have been able to defeat the Eenheidsfront. And that is how I said, I am going to show that Jopie Pengel's and my intention is not a wild thought of ours, but a well-considered thought.'*[52]

Time worked to the advantage of both parties. In 1952, Pengel was able to acquire a solid electoral base when founding a trade union federation named *Moederbond* (Mother Union) which he chaired. Moreover, while working as a politician-*cum*-journalist, the newspaper he worked for published opinions which now and again included polemical terms.[53] The NPS also became the representative of an emerging Black middle class. The 1958 elections did indeed bring on the expected political breakthrough. The PSV, whose members gradually felt uncomfortable within the elitist *Eenheidsfront*, had opted to side with the NPS in exchange for a number of the eligible places on the list of candidates. The VHP now for the first time got ministers in a cabinet.[54] The actual rulers, to wit, Lachmon and Pengel remained active in parliament in order to direct political process. This coalition phase, which was to continue until 1967, formed the most prosperous and stable period since the introduction of universal suffrage.

At this stage, Suriname displayed traits which, in his pacification model, the Dutch-American political scientist Arend Lijphart refers to as a 'consociational

---

50 Pengel himself used the term *brede basis politiek* (broad basis politics), see: Breeveld 2000, 174-175. This policy of fraternization was able to flourish in Suriname where in contrast with neighbouring Guyana, class distinctions played a smaller role. In Guyana, Hindustanis had stayed on in order to work on sugar plantations much longer whereas in Suriname they had built up independent existences as farmers, see: Ramsoedh 1997, 155-170.
51 Breeveld 2000, 181-184; Dew 1996, 108-110; Sedney 2017 (1997), 38-39.
52 Khemradj 2002, 43-44.
53 Breeveld 2000, 121-128, 145-150.
54 Dew 1996, 114-119.

democracy'.[55] Governments hereby rest in the hands of a cartel comprising party elites which within the segmented society ensure a stable democracy. Such an 'elite cartel' suited the modus operandi of political parties active in Suriname.[56] The VHP-top comprised a small group of financiers originating from the trade sector as well as parliamentarians. They actually constituted the VHP and assembled the Board from their circle. This set up did not differ much that of the NPS, which upheld slightly superior democratic procedures whenever nominating. As to the 'consociational democracy', parties closely collaborate at the top, while their leaders continue to mobilise their followers based on ethnic sentiments. Political parties in Suriname found support in a cross-section of various social classes. Patronage played an increasingly key role whenever voters were mobilised, as reflected in a steadily expanding civil service. During election campaigns, a sharp rise was always noted in the number of certificates issued by the government entitling underprivileged to obtain free health care. Party propagandists, who formed an effective network in the lower classes, were promised either a position or an improved one. The fact class conflicts hardly played a role in the politics of Suriname does not only pertain to the strong ethnic loyalty inherent to each ethnic group. Patronage relationships not only obscure conflicting interests but also weakened the propensity to social change The small-scaled society also caused class distinctions to lose their sharpness. Within families, all social classes could even be observed.

Lijphart has observed that, as long as elites are aware of the dangers of political fragmentation, a consociational democracy can continue to function. This awareness was certainly present in the minds of Suriname's important political leaders, not least as a result of the horrific ethnic riots in neighbouring Guyana. In addition to behavioural provisos imposed upon the political elite, Lijphart also mentions several 'system conditions' which promote the consociational model's stability.[57] Resulting from a political presence of the smaller group of ethnic Javanese, Suriname maintained a multi-polar rather than a bipolar political system, hereby reducing the danger of ethnic polarization. The fading-out of social dividing lines between groups, especially by means of the emancipation of the Hindustanis, was however a potential source of friction because ethnic groups could crowd out each other in the middle class. Cohesion within separate ethnic groups constitutes a key system proviso, too. An existing albeit dormant rivalry especially among Creoles was the outcome of (a) a greater social differentiation and (b) related dissimilarities pertaining to behaviour patterns within this group. Such a lack of internal cohesion can easily cause leaders originating from their own ethnic group to either 'outbid' each other when defending their group's interests or accuse each other of 'betrayal', a phenomenon for which Suriname was not immune.[58]

The elections of 1963 confirmed the image of a stable elite cartel democracy. As a result of the KTPI (which had replaced the PSV) participating in this coalition government, all major ethnic groups were now represented.[59] At the same time,

---

55   Lijphart 1969, 207-225; Lijphart 1971, 1-14.
56   Hoppe 1975, 145-177.
57   These terms and conditions have been applied to Suriname, see: Dew 1972, 35-56 and Dew 1996, 193-205.
58   Dew 1996, 202-204.
59   Ibid., 129-132.

A History of Suriname

Figure 11.5. The Prime Minister and NPS leader J.A. Pengel (right) and VHP leader J. Lachmon (left) during a press conference held at Schiphol Airport (the Netherlands) in 1963. Photographer Jac. de Nijs. Public domain, via National Archives, The Hague.

counterforces (e.g., a lack of internal group cohesion) as outlined by Lijphart, manifested themselves. Hindustani intellectuals and younger generations held the view that the top positions were left too much to Creoles. In order to stand a chance of winning seats in the Staten during elections, however, this *Actie Groep* (Action Group) was also forced to cooperate with a Creole party.

A serious challenge for the NPS formed the establishing in 1961 of the *Partij Nationalistische Republiek* (PNR), which sought to achieve full independence from the Netherlands. Its founders admired national leaders such as Kwame Nkrumah (Ghana) and Patrice Lumumba (Republic of the Congo). As observed in numerous colonies, academics returning to their motherland proved most active. The PNR, consisting almost entirely of Creoles, not only upheld highly nationalistic principles but also wished 'progressive' men, women and youth to lead the people of Suriname towards a 'nationalist revolution'.[60] Attempts the NPS created in order to portray the PNR as a 'communist danger', impressed Creole supporters to a certain degree. These representations were however not considered very plausible. Nationalist students from Suriname were nonetheless being watched by the Dutch secret service.[61]

The PNR originated from a cultural initiative named *Wi Egi Sani* (Our Own Cause), founded in the mid-1950s. Its inspirer Eddy Bruma (1925-2000) and future PNR leader warmly advocated Sranan Tongo, a Creole language then hardly considered reputable.[62] *Wi Egi Sani* was also inspired by Julius G. Koenders (1886-1957). Shortly after WW II, this black-skinned school teacher played a key role when promoting Sranan Tongo through *Foetoeboi*, a monthly magazine.[63] In 1957, a poetry collection titled *Trotji* (Preamble) was published in Amsterdam by Trefossa, the nom de plume of H.F. de Ziel (1916-1975), hereby establishing a further milestone for Sranan Tongo. Five years earlier, *De Tsjerne*, a Frisian literary magazine, while engaged in a battle between languages, published a special issue on Suriname including work by Koenders. During the mid-1900s, Bruma and other nationalist students became members of the very active *Vereniging Ons Suriname* (Society Our Suriname), based in Amsterdam. Little wonder that cultural emancipation in Suriname was especially popular among Creoles. The most influenced by European-Dutch culture, they were therefore, when compared with other ethnic groups, more engaged in searching for their own specific cultural identity. Moreover, self-consciousness among dark-skinned Creoles had increased. For, while the colonial society was eroding, they had become more and more eligible for occupying higher positions. In 1959, members of *Wi Egi Sani*, led by the poet-*cum*-author Robin Raveles (1935-1983), founded the *Nationalistische Beweging Suriname* (NBS; Nationalist Movement Suriname), in order to present Creole cultural ideals as a means of political expression. This movement immediately launched the concept of complete independence from The Netherlands.

The NPS attempted to deprive the nationalist movement of several of its arguments by means of gestures, a number of which were partly symbolic. Now Suriname acquired its own flag as well as a national anthem which included a verse written in Sranan Tongo by the aforementioned beloved national poet Trefossa. In addition, Pengel underlined once again that the Statute of 1954 was 'not an eternal edict'.[64] By way of a gesture to Hindustanis, July 1, the National Holiday commemorating the emancipation of the enslaved, was given a more neutral name, to wit, Day of the Freedoms. Ideas expressed by the NBS and *Wi Egi Sani* attracted numerous Creole intellectuals, including government members. In any case, the point was reached where the issue of independence was much discussed. The government at The Hague quickly agreed to the NPS leader Pengel's request for a new Round Table Conference. Led by Prime Minister Severinus D. Emanuels (1910-1981), the NPS-VHP coalition had taken office in 1958. Its governmental declaration had called for a change in the Kingdom Statute enabling the pursuit

---

60   Ibid., 127; Marshall 2003, 145.
61   Meel 1999, 238-256; Jansen van Galen 1995, 74-76; Marshall 2003, 81.
62   Dew 1996, 120-129; Marshall 2003, 63-161; Meel 1999, 175-229; on the subject of nationalism in Suriname, see: Meel 1990, 259-290 and Meel 1998, 257-281.
63   For a biographical sketch of J.G. Koenders, see: Reeder, Rijssen & Wijks 2019.
64   Breeveld 2000, 218; Dew 1996, 121.

of more independent foreign and trade policies. Suriname would then more easily be eligible for receiving help from specialized UN organizations. In Paramaribo, the Dutch government's hesitance as to the apartheid regime in South Africa had increased the urgency for more independent action on the global forum. The effect of that stance peaked after Suriname's decision of 1960 to protest against the Sharpville massacre, the turning point in the anti-apartheid movement. This decision which aimed at severing all shipping and trade relations with South Africa had been reversed on the grounds of incompatibility with the Statute.[65]

However, the Dutch government felt no desire to amend this Kingdom Statute. Moreover, it had consistently stated that the Statute was 'a solid basis for harmonious constitutional relations between the parts of the Kingdom'.[66] According to The Hague, Suriname was as yet insufficiently politically or economically mature and thus not yet ready for the next step towards independence. By means of its rapid positive response to the request for a Round Table Conference, The Hague intended to sow discord among the political parties of Suriname in order to solve the problem. Two weeks prior to this conference, the acting Governor Cornelis Nagtegaal (1905-1994) wrote to Prime Minister Jan de Quay (1901-1985) that the Dutch flexibility had 'as expected' caused major problems in Suriname; the then chairman of the *Katholieke Volkspartij* (KVP) Harry van Doorn (1915-1992), expressed his gratitude to Governor Nagtegaal in a letter; for, this tactic applied had provoked 'the hoped-for reaction from the Surinamese side'.[67] The orthodox Hindustanis had especially voiced objections. Supporters of the aforementioned *Actie Groep* warned against a 'negro president' and 'Creole domination'.[68] They therefore wrongly suspected Lachmon of secretly agreeing with Pengel on the issue of independence. The former had contributed to Pengel's Round Table Conference initiative aimed at allowing Pengel to disempower nationalists. In his biography Lachmon stated:

> 'Pengel had to be able to take the wind out of the supra-nationalists' sails to a certain extent so as not to endanger his own political life. And I had to give him that space, because I was convinced that at that time Jopie was the only political leader with whom the policy of fraternization could be further developed.'[69]

In the end, this Round Table Conference came to nothing because the delegation representing Suriname was unable to deliver any concrete proposals. The failure of this conference was the direct reason for founding the PNR which wished independence to be officially declared on July 1, 1963. This was exactly 100 years after slavery had been abolished. However, independence was no urgent issue in Suriname, certainly not after ethnic violence had led to postponing independence in British Guiana. The PNR remained without seats after the elections of 1963, despite an expansion of the proportional electoral system and of parliament.[70]

---

65   Meel 1999, 161-165.
66   Fernandes Mendes 1989, 50.
67   Ibid., 63-64; Meel 1999, 354-355.
68   Dew 1996, 126.
69   Azimullah 1986, 158.
70   Ibid,. 129-132.

Nevertheless, after the 1967 elections, the coalition between the NPS and the VHP was breached. The Hindustanis having increased their number of seats as a result of further changes to the electoral system now demanded an additional ministry.[71] However, Lachmon and Pengel were pressurized by The Hague which felt increasingly less inclined to further finance the enhancement of the civil service. Pengel, after becoming Prime Minister in 1963, could no longer give away a single department under these circumstances.[72] For, it would have deprived him of too many opportunities for patronaging, a phenomenon popularly referred to as *regelen* (to arrange). The VHP's highly racially tinged election campaign held in the district of Nickerie had probably contributed to this break. It was the first time the NPS had put forward a candidate in this predominantly Hindustani region. During a VHP meeting, Hindustani women who had become victims of ethnic conflicts in neighbouring Guyana were brought on stage. The remark 'if the elections are won by negroes, this will happen to you', was the purport of the speeches.[73] The fraternization policy had already felt severe pressure as a result of the economic malaise as experienced after the temporary growth impulse provided by the Brokopondo Dam Project. This phenomenon had especially affected the Creole population in Paramaribo (see p. 289). Moreover, according to the 1964 Census, 60 per cent of the Hindustanis had already been employed outside the agricultural sector, implying they were now directly competing against Creoles in the labour market.[74]

The main bone of contention between the VHP and the NPS comprised the issue of independence. Lachmon deemed the Dutch presence as the best guarantee for a successful emancipation of the Hindustani people, especially as long as Creoles formed the politically dominant ethnic group. In Lachmon's view, Suriname must first become economically more independent, after which independence could possibly be achieved. To this goal he demanded a written guarantee from Pengel stating he would not raise the independence issue again during the next term of office. The NPS leader, having deemed such a claim unacceptable, therefore subsequently rejected any further cooperation.[75]

The break with the VHP did not imply that Pengel had distanced himself from Suriname's characteristic policy of religious tolerance. For example, in 1969, he amended a law which facilitated cremating of the deceased, a key Hindu funeral rite. The immediate cause of this legal adaptation comprised a request from relatives of one of Pengels's Hindustani friends.[76] Having been able to form a coalition with Creoles on the basis of the election results, Pengel nonetheless opted for cooperating with the Hindustani *Actie Groep*. Fear of 'Guyanese situations', as racial riots was termed in Suriname, certainly played a role here. The SDP, with its light-skinned Creole members, also participated in this coalition. Sharp contrasts had always kept these parties divided. However, within the political system of patronage, it was possible to now and again easily establish temporary, occasional coalitions.

---

71   Sedney 2017 (1997), 161.
72   Dew 1996, 142-150.
73   Breeveld 2000, 290.
74   Azimullah 1986, 178.
75   Dew 1996, 148-150; Ramsoedh 2018, 108.
76   Breeveld 2000, 291-293.

After 2 years, strike actions by teaching staff put an end to the second Pengel-led cabinet whereby the Dutch government played a key background role. For, as a result of The Hague's refusal to continue to replenish Suriname's budget, salary increases for school teachers could no longer be met with.[77] No doubt Dutch authorities were keen to see Pengel resign, as he was considered far too stubborn. At the same time public spending in Suriname was getting out of hand due to patronage.

In addition, Pengel had caused great displeasure in The Hague because of his initiatives pertaining to the protracted border conflict with Guyana. Its authorities, at the end of 1967, had established a military post in a disputed area located on the upper reaches of the Corantijne River. Whereas the Dutch had called for restraint in order to utilise diplomatic channels, Pengel not only dispatched a police force in order to establish an armed post here too, but also set up a Special Unit for Defence Police in response to this escalating border conflict. This initiative was at odds with the Kingdom Statute, in which defence and foreign policies were exclusively reserved for and to be executed by the Kingdom of the Netherlands. Its government became even more concerned when, based on intelligence reports, a well-founded suspicion arose inferring that Venezuela had secretly supplied Suriname with heavy weapons in order to reinforce the aforementioned police force. Considering its claims on Guyanese territory, Venezuela had every interest in Suriname being firm.[78]

The PNR, having reinforced its position by means of strikes directed against Pengel, won its first parliamentary seat in 1969. On the other hand, the NPS was weakened as a result of the exodus of disgruntled intellectuals, who had never received a great deal of support from Pengel. They then went on to found the *Progressieve Nationale Partij* (PNP), which joined forces with the KTPI and the PSV. This newly-established party achieved a remarkable electoral success by way of campaigning against corruption, favouritism and Pengel's authoritarianism. However, the VHP, having formed a bloc with the *Actie Groep* and the small Javanese peoples' union named *Sarekat Rakyat Indonesia*, was the overall winner acquiring 19 of the 39 parliamentary seats. When Pengel refused to form a coalition with the VHP, Lachmon teamed up with the PNP.[79] Although Lachmon carefully distributed ministerial posts among ethnic groups and left the position of premier to the PNP leader Jules Sedney (1922-2020), the competing Creole parties described this policy as serving as a façade for a Hindustani government. Meanwhile, the fact the VHP had now renamed itself the *Vatan Hitkari Partij* (Party for the Promotion of National Welfare) did not in any way, shape or form detract from its ethnic orientation. Even renamed the *Vooruitstrevende Hervormings Partij* (Progressive Reform Party) from 1973 on, it did not lose its Hindustani traits. Pengel's demise (June 5, 1970) caused Creoles to further fuel fears of a Hindustani domination. When the coalition government introduced Holi Paghwa and Idul Fitr as national holidays for Hindus and Muslims respectively, this measure caused at least an equal amount of commotion when compared with the appointment of a

---

77 Breeveld 2000, 303-304; here it is also pointed at the Dutch socialist trade union, which gave moral as well as financial support to Surinamese trade union and strike leaders; Dew 1996, 151-153.

78 The supplying of arms from Venezuela was confirmed to the present author by Sjoerd Lapré, the then commander on the ground, in an interview held on 2 June 1993; see also: Meel 2014, 80-84.

79 Dew 1996, 153-157; Breeveld 2000, 305-312.

small number of Hindustanis to the positions of sub-directors of training colleges for school teachers and secondary schools.[80]

The policy of fraternization had in a certain way reached its limits. During the NPS and VHP coalition of the 1960s, many Hindustanis had received scholarships for the first time. Subsequently, seeking to cash in on this societal success, one first had to demolish traditional Creole strongholds positioned at both government and semi-government levels.

Prolonged strike actions taken by all trade unions proved the final blow to the government. As a result of their influence in these unions, the NPS and the PNR formed the driving forces behind these strikes. Eddy Bruma increased the number of his followers by uniting 47 unions into the *Centrale 47* (C47), entirely in accordance with the Surinamese tradition, also found elsewhere in the Caribbean, whereby trade union movements are linked to politics. Government employees joined forces in a sister trade union named *Centrale Landsdienaren Organisatie* (CLO; Civil Service Organization).[81] The consociation model finally stranded when the incoming NPS leader, the 37-year-old Henck A.E. Arron (1936-2000) originating from the banking sector, gained no less than 22 of the 39 seats in the 1973 elections with an almost complete Creole block. It comprised the *Nationale Partij Kombinatie* (NPK) of which the NPS, the PNR, the PSV and the KTPI formed part.[82] For the first time, Hindustanis were not represented in the government. The VHP's defeat was partly due to the electoral system, which did as yet not favour this party. Years later Henck Arron, when speaking with his biographer, analysed these elections which had strongly been dictated along racial lines, as follows:

'[...] *based on what we had learned in the Sedney era, we emphasized the strength of the people, with the Creole element being the binding factor. Because the Creoles thought their position was in danger, they voted en masse for the NPK.*'[83]

11.4 Independence and failed nation-building

The differences were exacerbated when now Prime Minister Arron unexpectedly announced in a government statement dated 15 February 1974 that his cabinet wished to achieve 'the transfer of sovereignty' before the end of 1975.[84] Amidst many Hindustanis a fear of Creole domination was now mounting. In Suriname and also the Netherlands strong forces advocated independence. The PNR had, by means of a combined NPK list, acquired four seats in the Staten, significantly increasing its influence. Within the NPS, more and more young people who strongly opted for independence now came to the fore. Apparently, demographic developments in favour of Hindustanis and the dominant position of the VHP within the Sedney-led cabinet had led to ripened minds. The Creole majority's tone in parliament was: now or never. The fact that the KTPI, as a coalition partner, supported Arron's government

---

80   Dew 1996, 143, 157-159, 165; Ramsoedh 2018, 114-117.
81   Dew 1996, 159-164.
82   Ibid., 165-170.
83   Meel 2014, 132.
84   Dew 1996, 173; Meel 2014, 136.

statement presents further proof of the occasional nature of coalition formation in Suriname. It may be added here that Javanese voters hardly supported becoming independent from the Kingdom of the Netherlands.

Suriname was as yet far from a coherent nation state. The degree of national cultural awareness comprising a shared experience of destinies on common territory as well as a feeling of unity had been quite low. Despite an increasing Western cultural influence, the three largest population groups, to wit, Creoles, Hindustanis and Javanese, had retained their specific identities. The cultural ambivalence amidst many Creoles had resulted in an increased appreciation of their own culture. This phenomenon was most clearly expressed in the more frequent use of Sranan Tongo, the lingua franca of the people of Suriname. Among lower-class Creoles practicing *winti* and traditional healers *obiaman* had never disappeared. Creole family structures continued to feature strong matrifocal traits, in which cultural traditions as well as the weak socio-economic position of lower-class Creoles male played a role.[85] The assimilation policy, certainly in the case of these Creoles had not led to (a) replacing their culture with Dutch culture or (b) merging these two cultures into a new one. Instead a symbiosis of both was created.[86]

Reappraising Creole culture had provoked a defensive reaction among members of the Hindustani population. Their specific cultural heritage now gained more significance. In the course of the 1960s and 1970s we see a revival of cultural manifestations whereby the Hindi language is applied. However, at the same time, Sarnami (a modified Surinamese version of Hindi) became less popular among younger generations.[87] The Javanese were the most close-knit community of whom in 1973 as much as 20 per cent continued to be Indonesian nationals.[88] The older and younger generations both spoke almost exclusively Javanese. Elderly Javanese often compared other ethnic groups with *wajang* puppets. A Creole was deemed a demonic, greedy creature (*buta*); Hindustani males were identified as *anuman*, i.e., a reference to Hanuman, the mischievous anthropomorphic monkey god-king and hero of the Ramayana epic.[89] Christian missionaries had virtually no influence on Muslim Javanese.

Among Hindustanis, *c*.80 per cent continued to adhere to Hinduism. The remaining part of this ethnic group were by and large Muslim, and only a small number had been converted to Christianity.[90] Hindustani religious awareness was further enhanced through social activities carried out by their organisations pertaining to issues such as education, eldercare and looking after orphans.[91] Among Muslims hailing from North India, the messianic revival Ahmadiyya movement had gained much support.

85   Buschkens 1974, 263-270; Brana-Shute 1979.
86   Wooding 1981.
87   Speckman 1966, 60-65.
88   Derveld 1981, 22.
89   Suparlan 1976, 87-89; Suparlan 1995, 62; Derveld 1981, 114.
90   Bruijning & Voorhoeve 1977, 281.
91   Hassankhan 1993, 111-114.

	European	Creole	Hindustani	Javanese	Chinese	Indigenous*	Maroon	Other**
Paramaribo	1,804	53,841	27,841	10,063	3,653	1,395 231	2,542	2,368
Nickerie	203	5,368	22,088	5,721	243	205 539	120	366
Coronie	2	2,710	40	318	242	-	-	18
Saramacca	21	610	7,141	2,868	70	46 413	264	47
Suriname	1,585	46,486	78,250	19,766	1,558	1,510 61	370	2,549
Commewijne	45	1,035	4,983	9,894	92	98 142	393	109
Marowijne	76	3,155	676	2,976	182	346 1,748	16,088	219
Brokopondo	35	297	40	72	5	4 11	15,070	18
Para	228	5,507	1,858	6,008	202	323 976	991	383
Total	**3,999**	**119,009**	**142,917**	**57,688**	**6,029**	**8,050**	**35,838**	**6,077**

Table 11.1. Population groups according to district; *number above refers to 'not living in tribal community'; the number below refers to 'living in tribal community'; ** mainly descendants of Portuguese from Madeira and Lebanese. Source: Bureau 4th General Census (1971-72).

The influence of Christian denominations in Suriname extended far above merely religious aspects, thus opening the floodgates to Western culture. Both Moravians and Roman Catholics had since long been very active in tuition and health care issues. Especially Christian education was of invaluable significance as to elevating large parts of the population. Simultaneously, denominations reinforced social segmentation. As ethno-religious divisions ran more or less parallel, schools based on Christianity in practice evolved into Creole schools. Compartmentalisation and thus a tendency towards segregation had been further enhanced from the beginning of the 1960s. In response to the Christian churches, Hindu and Muslim communities now set up their own schools. Until that moment, children adhering to the latter two religions had mainly attended public schools. Although the number of non-Christian schools remained limited (in part resulting from a lack of professional support from the Netherlands) the *Nationaal Ontwikkelingsplan Suriname* (Suriname National Development Plan) of 1965 delivered the following strong warning: 'a multiracial developing country cannot bear the luxury of too great a compartmentalisation.'[92]

Suriname did favourably distinguish itself from other developing nations thanks to its high attendance level of children in the primary school age group. The fact their numbers exceeded 90 per cent was the outcome of compulsory education and urbanisation. However, the quality of teachers did not match the growing number of pupils. Between 1955 and 1975, the number of primary and secondary school-goers rose from 54,000 to 144,000.[93] Districts were the most disadvantaged, implying

---

92 Mijs 1973, 220.
93 Bruijning & Voorhoeve 1977, 439.

A History of Suriname

that Hindustanis and Javanese were as well. Utilising the Dutch language in schools formed a major problem, too. According to research executed at the University of Amsterdam, only 15 per cent of those Hindustani and Javanese youngsters who attended primary schools conversed in Dutch at home; their number of drop-outs was therefore much higher if compared with Creole primary school-goers, of which more than 80 per cent heard the Dutch language being spoken at home.[94] In terms of its contents, tuition was also strongly oriented towards the Dutch labour market. A UNESCO report published in 1969 rather critically states that:

> *'The educational system of Surinam should therefore be geared to the creation of a worthy and happy Surinamese citizen, prepared to contribute to the progress of the Surinamese community and moulded to its own environment. It is doubtful whether the current educational system is likely to meet this target and to foster the creation of a specific Surinamese cultural and social pattern, because the nature of such a pattern has never been defined by the Surinamese themselves.'*[95]

Therefore, as a result of all these factors, education strongly promoted the identity of the various population groups. A frequently cited study carried out in 1960 reveals that Hindustanis and Creoles held very negative views on one and other.[96] Apparently as much as 63 per cent of the Hindustani held negative opinions on Creoles. More than 83 per cent of the Creoles thought ill of Hindustani. Mainly related to economic and 'discriminatory' conduct, this Creole standpoint pertained to Hindustanis refusing to adapt to the Creoles, whereby the interviewees referred to racial intermingling as well as to behavioural patterns. Regarding economic conduct, accusations were voiced pertaining to 'avarice'. Strikingly, the scarce positive judgments concerned 'thrift' and 'hard work' observed with the Hindustanis. The Hindustanis' negative assessment regarding Creoles was linked to the same category of conduct. Frequently heard reproaches were: Creoles 'play the boss' and have 'little respect' for Hindustanis. One also opined that Creoles made small contributions to the economy. Creoles were accused of both laziness and parasitism. A noteworthy outcome of the aforementioned research was: more than 33 per cent of the Creoles thought ill of their own population group, deeming themselves 'wasteful' and insufficiently prepared to help each other forward. Hindustanis and Creoles delivered extremely favourable judgements on the Javanese, which undoubtedly has to do with the fact that the latter did not pose any economic threats to the other ethnic groups.

The announcement of independence by the NPK-led government caused ethnic contrasts to be more pronounced than ever. Luckily no explosion of any violence occurred, as had been the case in Guyana. Paramaribo was nevertheless startled by incidents of arson, demonstrations, riots and even a brief hostage-taking of the Prime Minister.[97]

---

94 Mijs 1973, 35.
95 Torfs 1969, 2.
96 For the details referred to here, see: Van Renselaar 1963, 93-106 and Speckman 1963, 76-93.
97 Meel 2014, 196-203; apparently, this hostage-taker suffered from personal issues and was not driven by political motives.

Having initially resisted independence, Jagernath Lachmon was forced to change his stance, after the Prime Ministers Joop den Uyl (1919-1987), Juancho Evertsz (1923-2008) and Henck Arron, who respectively served the Kingdom of the Netherlands, the Netherlands Antilles and Suriname, had in May 1974 laid down in a protocol that Suriname would gain independence 'at the latest by the end of 1975'.[98] Having explicated his wish to avoid any racial tension, Lachmon however demanded his party should be included in the Cabinet in order to have a say in the preparations for independence.[99] This proviso was unacceptable to the NPK-led government. Placed under huge pressure by his followers, Lachmon felt embittered about the rejection of the 'outstretched fraternal hand'.[100] He then threatened to grasp each and every means at his disposal in order to prevent Suriname becoming independent. At the start of 1975 Lachmon made it clear his supporters might block the food supply. After several arson attacks, the situation in Paramaribo was so tense that, during Prime Minister Den Uyl's visit in May 1975, a Dutch naval vessel was moored in the Suriname River.

Not much earlier, Lachmon had yet again revealed his willingness to cooperate in acquiring independence 'because the realisation of Suriname's national independence is pre-eminently a national matter'.[101] In a Proclamation of Ten Points, the VHP leader mentioned several provisos such as guaranteeing human rights in the new constitution as well as more ethnically balanced army ranks.[102] He furthermore demanded a proportional electoral system in order to end the electoral advantages the Creole population profited from. In addition, new elections had to be held 6 months after becoming independent. As an extra guarantee, Lachmon had requested the then Governor Johan Ferrier in a confidential conversation to become the first President of Suriname 'because we don't trust anyone else'.[103]

However, a political stalemate arose when three NPK parliamentarians sided with the VHP.[104] In theory, the opposition could count on 20 of the 39 seats, but remarkably this outcome did not result in a motion of no-confidence. One of these three dissidents, Lee Kong Fong, a NPS member, had left the country without a trace. Both the NPK and VHP blocks were now backed by 19 Staten members. In order to control further developments as much as possible, opposition members refused to cooperate in obtaining a quorum in the Staten. They all travelled to The Hague in September 1975 to continue their fight against the NPK-led government there. They returned to Suriname shortly before debates began in the lower house on the law which not only terminated statutory ties with the Kingdom of the Netherlands but would also legally validate Suriname's independence. Events took a remarkable twist when the VHP member George Hindori (1933-1986), who was regarded as Lachmon's crown prince, appeared on television to declare he was prepared, while serving as Suriname's special delegate, to participate in the debate held at the Dutch

---

98   Dew 1996, 171-192; Meel 2014, 149-237.
99   Fernandes Mendes 1989, 98-104.
100   Ibid., 100.
101   Azimullah 1986, 259
102   Ibid., 260-265; Meel 2014, 168-169.
103   Khemradj 2002, 70-71; Jansen van Galen 2005, 88.
104   Dew 1996, 181-182; Meel 2014, 182-193.

Figure 11.6. The ceremony confirming Suriname's independence held
on 25 November 1975 at the national stadium in Paramaribo. From left to right: Prime
Minister Henck Arron, Princess Beatrix of the Netherlands, President Johan Ferrier.
Photographer Bert Verhoeff. Public domain via National Archives, The Hague.

parliament. This statement implied he had publicly distanced himself from his political superior.[105]

Lachmon c.s. then decided to join Suriname's delegation in the Netherlands which Emile Wijntuin (1924-2020), Chairman of the Staten, had assembled. During the debate held in the lower house, in accordance with the Kingdom Statute, delegates from Suriname had the right to speak but no right to vote. Members of Suriname's opposition parties voiced heavy recriminations towards both the Dutch and their own government. The VHP Staten member Alwin Mungra declared: 'Ave Caesar, morituri te salutant. Ave, Den Uyl, rulers, we who are about to die salute you', hereby emotionally expressing the huge frustrations the VHP felt as to this, in his opinion, Dutch government's aloof stance.[106] Among Hindustanis, the opinion not only prevailed that the Den Uyl-led Cabinet had not only more or less imposed independence upon Suriname but also that it had paid insufficient attention to ethno-political sensitivities.

Just a week before gaining independence, scheduled on 25 November, the Staten nevertheless unanimously ratified Suriname's incoming constitution, in which all fundamental rights and principles of a parliamentary system were laid down. After Arron's conciliatory words and the promise that new elections would be held within 8 months, the VHP voted in favour of the draft constitution. As a consequence

---

105   Ibid., 1996, 182-184; ibid. 2014, 203-211.
106   For the account of this parliamentary debate, see: *Handelingen Tweede Kamer* (Minutes Lower House of parliament) *1975-1976*, 22 October 1975, 540; for accessing online, consult the bibliography.

of Hindori's defection, who had announced his support of the draft, the VHP could no longer hold back independence anyway.[107]

11.5 The Dutch stance on independence[108]

In the run-up to independence, the VHP had mainly fired its arrows at social democrats united in the *Partij van de Arbeid* (PvdA; Labour Party), and its leader Prime Minister Joop den Uyl. In its 1972 election programme, this party had preferred to declare independence to overseas territories in *c*.1977. However, less than 10 years earlier, Den Uyl, then a parliamentarian for the PvdA, had denounced the pro-independence party known as PNR, because of its 'ideological background, which is contrary to the notion of democracy'.[109] A decade later, however, social democrats had become sensitive to the stance whereby it was no longer appropriate to hold on to overseas territories. Social democrats were certainly not the only ones. Already during the second half of the 1960s, a change in opinions on political relationships with the territories located in the West was noticeable in more than one Dutch political party. Until that moment The Hague had always emphasized its desire to intensify cooperation within the Statute. In 1967, during a parliamentary debate on the national budget, a 'wait-and-see' stance with regard to the manner in which Suriname sought to apply its right of self-determination was mentioned for the first time. Although the men, women and children hailing from Suriname now residing in the Netherlands numbered only *c*.13,000 souls, the increasing attention the press paid to the influx of immigrants certainly played a role as to the shaping of political opinions.[110] The politico-cultural activities in which many Surinamese students were involved in while studying in the Netherlands and the fact they advocated independence did not remain unnoticed either. The parliamentarian A. de Goede (1928-2016), a member of the leftist liberal *Democraten 66*, was the first who, in early 1969, openly called for an end to the Statute. This suggestion was a reply to the political unrest caused by strikes held against Pengel's government (see p. 269). De Goede nonetheless deemed it unacceptable that, based on the Statute (Article 43), the Netherlands was considered jointly responsible for the situation in Suriname. All major parties opposed his argument.[111]

Things changed in 1969 after riots befell the isle of Curaçao. Under the Statute, the Dutch government was now forced to bring in marines to deal with strikers and looters. The border conflict between Suriname and Guyana as well as strikes directed against the Pengel-led government caused The Hague to fear it would be forced to carry out similar military missions in Suriname. Notably, the Netherlands had indeed insisted on exerting such power in order to intervene at the Round Table Conference of 1952. Suggestions proposed by social democrat party PvdA concerned a need to transform the Statute. Christian-democratic political parties, to wit, KVP, CHU and ARP, as well as the conservative-liberal VVD were more reticent. Their

---

107 Dew 1996, 186-192; Meel 2014, 221-232.
108 For a summary of the evolution of positions in Dutch politics over the years, see: Fernandes Mendes 1989, 48-62; Oostindie & Klinkers 2001, 86-132.
109 Marshall 2003, 159.
110 Van Amersfoort 2011, 4; Van Amersfoort 1987, 478.
111 Fernandes Mendes 1989, 57-58.

A History of Suriname

views on relationships with Suriname were however evolving, too. In 1970, the ARP's advisory council even submitted this radical advice: Suriname should at the latest become independent by 1975. Although this recommendation was a step too far for the ARP, the then Prime Minister B.W. Biesheuvel (1920-2001), an ARP member, declared in the government statement of 1971 that the Netherlands, too, had the right to initiate amending the Kingdom Statute.[112] For this reason, in 1972, a so-called Kingdom Commission embarked upon the warily formulated task of investigating 'feasible alternatives' for the political relations.[113]

Arron's announcement as to a desired independence was only surprising because of its timing, to wit, in 1974. For, the NPK's election programme did refer to independence, but no date was added. In December 1971, however, Arron had already stated in the course of a debate with Lachmon on Dutch television that, if the NPS was to win an election, independence would be realised by the government. Subsequently this debate was repeatedly aired in Suriname.[114] Prime Minister Sedney having already declared his support for independence in 1969 opted for a 'cautious and careful' preparation in collaboration with the VHP, a coalition partner.[115] One year later, a study committee was set up by its coalition partner, the PSV. Including all this party's prominent figures, this group argued in favour of an early independence.[116] In 1973, the Den Uyl-led cabinet had mentioned in its government statement that, following the Kingdom Commission's advice, consultations would be opened with Suriname (as well as with the Netherlands Antilles) in order to 'reach a final decision on the date of independence'.[117] The then Surinamese government as yet led by Prime Minister Sedney had not been informed on this stance in advance nor had Governor Ferrier. The latter had arrived at a personally radical conclusion: Suriname must now 'take the honourable decision' and therefore opt for independence.[118]

After Arron's announcement in 1974, the Dutch government had no choice but to respond positively to the intention of the cabinet he presided over. The Statute, which recognised the right to self-determination, left hardly any room for manoeuvre. In The Hague, the tug-of-war fought out in Paramaribo between the government and the opposition pertaining to the constitution was considered an internal issue. It concerned the question (a) if, based on the aforementioned Statute, could the Netherlands cooperate in the transfer of sovereignty without any solid guarantees for upholding democracy and human rights and (b) if the Staten could accept a Surinamese constitution, should it require a qualified majority. The VHP opposition answered the first question in the negative and the second in the affirmative. The Kingdom Commission, however, be it with the exception of VHP representatives, thought otherwise. According to its advice, the responsibility of the Netherlands

---

112   Ibid., 58-62; Oostindie & Klinkers 2001, 89-90, 97.
113   Fernandes Mendes 1989, 74.
114   Meel 2014, 116-121; Sedney 2017, 104-105.
115   Sedney 2017, 95-96, 99.
116   Ibid., 105.
117   Oostindie & Klinkers 2001, 103.
118   Jansen van Galen 2005, 83.

could not extend beyond the time at which statutory ties were severed. Moreover, a constitution was exclusively a matter to be attended to by Suriname.[119]

The Dutch government which shared this view nevertheless urged Arron and his cabinet to submit a draft constitution in the Staten. It should express the broadest possible support prior to 25 November 1975, the already set date of independence. The Hague's first priority however had always been to achieve Suriname's independence as soon as possible. The minutes of the Den Uyl-led cabinet reveal that all other objectives were to be regarded as less significant.[120] These objectives were discussed during a cabinet meeting held on 19 December 1974, when the strategy for the first summit consultation with the government of Suriname had to be determined. In addition to independence, this issue further concerned (a) restricting the immigration of Surinamese fellow citizens and (b) improving the socio-economic climate in Suriname as well as relationships between ethnic groups. However, the cabinet was aware of the fact virtually nothing could be done in the short term to reach the goals mentioned in (b).

In the course of 1974, attention was largely paid to the increasing number of emigrants from Suriname. The cabinet's minutes disclose great concern about this influx. At the request of Harry van Doorn, the Minister of Culture, Leisure and Social Work (1915-1992) the cabinet paid extensive attention to this issue during deliberations held on 2 and 3 September 1974. It was feared a social disaster would follow, in Amsterdam especially, due to a housing shortage. Certain ministers wished to impose an admission scheme for overseas citizens. Dries van Agt, the Minister of Justice (1971-1977), went the furthest. Pointing to increasing signs of racism and the unwillingness of municipalities to provide housing facilities, he held the view that the Dutch society would not be able to cope with a considerable influx of emigrants from Suriname. Plans to improve socio-economic conditions in Suriname itself could only have a certain long-term effect. Van Agt concluded that an admission system was legally possible and ethically not objectionable, because emigrants would arrive in a situation in the Netherlands whereby they would experience difficulties when adapting. Van Agt also acknowledged, considering the open borders with Belgium and Luxemburg, that the police force and other public services should carry out control measures within Dutch borders, whereby the applied point of reference would inevitably be the colour of the skin. According to Van Agt, this would be an unpleasant development, which did not remove the need for an admission scheme. He received the most support from the Minister of Housing, Hans Gruijters (1931-2005), who had even suggested during a cabinet meeting held on 10 May 1974, that the Netherlands could unilaterally declare itself independent on the basis of the Statute. This initiative would then automatically imply imposing immigration restrictions. Prime Minister Den Uyl, supported by the Minister for Surinamese and Dutch Antillean Affairs, Wilhelm de Gaay Fortman (1911-1997) as well as by a majority of parliamentarians, had always opposed an admission scheme. After all, almost each and every resident of Suriname were holders of Dutch nationality. During a cabinet meeting held on 2 and 3 September 1974, Den Uyl did voice the

---

119   Fernandes Mendes 1989, 95-98; Oostindie & Klinkers 2001, 112-117.
120   National Archives (The Hague), Inv.. nr. 2.02.05.02; Pronk 2020, 83-86.

remarkable suggestion that Suriname's independence could be accelerated in order to curb the flow of immigrants.

Notably, the original reason (i.e., the military intervention executed at Willemstad, Curaçao, in 1969) to question the Kingdom Statute, was not discussed within the cabinet. In addition, the provision in the Statute rendering such an intervention possible was maintained. Concluding that 'Willemstad 1969' no longer played a role in the cabinet's considerations is thus apparently justified. The immigration of fellow citizens from Suriname, on the other hand, was far more a key factor than assumed at the time. The desire the Dutch government felt to establish Suriname's independence rapidly has undoubtedly been at the expense of a careful preparation. A substantial sum of 3.5 billion Hfl (equalling € 1.59 billion) in development aid as promised to Suriname was certainly not only motivated by way of rational economic incentives.[121] As early as 1973, Jan Pronk, the Minister for Development Cooperation (1973-1977) had suggested during a cabinet meeting that Dutch aid to Suriname was one of the few means to exert political pressure in order to bring independence closer.

11.6 The post-1975 malaise

Among many inhabitants of Suriname the hope for a fresh start quickly gave way to a feeling of malaise. Prime Minister Arron broke his promise to organise early elections. Fear of an electoral takeover by Hindustanis, the fastest growing and now the largest population group, was undoubtedly the main advice to be given here. The outcome of Arron's unreliability was a loss of credibility. In addition, the opportunity to become a national leader of an as yet ethnically divided nation was missed. In fact this broken promise fuelled ethnic tensions.[122] In 1977 amidst persistent rumours of an election fraud, the NPK (in which the PNR now no longer participated) again obtained an absolute majority in the Staten. The victory over the VHP-block however was wafer-thin considering the result: 56,176 vs. 54,583 votes.[123]

Frustration regarding both political and economic developments ran high especially among younger generations. Several corruption cases, for which the perpetrators had been convicted, contributed to this discontent. After being sentenced on bribery charges, Willy Soemita (1936-2022), the then Minister of Agriculture, Livestock and Fisheries, and KTPI-founder, was infamously incarcerated.[124] The Dutch development aid had provided a short-term economic impulse whereby an increased level of employment had hardly been achieved (see Ch. 12, p. 294-296). In the course of 1979, the socio-political dissent increased. Young people protested *en masse* in order to accomplish lowering the minimum voting age from 21 down to 18 years of age. Moreover, Paramaribo-based committees took action in order to improve neighbourhood water supplies. Women's organisations protested

---

121   The lump sum was determined in a treaty dated 25 November 1975 (online accessible, see bibliography).

122   In his biography Arron defended himself on the grounds that early elections would have stirred up racial unrest. His biographer did not consider this defence plausible at all, see: Meel 2014, 245-257.

123   Ramsoedh 2018, 145; the PNR's absence in the new government was mainly due to (a) criticism within the NPS concerning this party's uncompromising stance and (b) the malfunctioning of PNR leader Eddy Bruma as a minister. Moreover, the PNR competed with the NPS as both targeted the same Creole voters, see: Marshall 2003, 206-208 and Meel 2014, 267-268.

124   Meel 2014, 260-264.

against the legal incapability of married women. Soldiers organized a military union. Certain left-wing political parties, founded in the course of the 1970s by Suriname's academics (many had graduated in the Netherlands), witnessed how their young adherents increased in number. Especially the *Volkspartij* (People's Party) co-founded and presided by the physician Rubin Lie Pauw Sam (1943-2018) enjoyed sizable popularity while socially active in the lower-class quarters of Paramaribo, where people's committees had been set up. The *Progressieve Arbeiders- en Landbouwers Unie* (PALU; Progressive Workers and Farmers Union), obtained some support, too. Its cadre mainly comprised agricultural engineers educated at what is now Wageningen University. These two parties wished to breach the ethnic political system of clientelism. The result of the 1977 election nevertheless hugely disappointed them, fuelling their dissent once again. Due to polarisation, the loyalty of voters to their own ethnic groups proved strong whereby the left obtained not one seat in parliament. In 1979, ethnic divisions led to the parliament being totally paralysed. Suriname was even threatened by means of a constitutional crisis: the VHP-opposition refused to cooperate when a successor to a deceased NPS member of parliament was to be sworn in. The VHP gave up its resistance only after President Ferrier intervened. Next the NPK's one seat majority was restored.

Almost 30 years after the introduction of universal suffrage, the Hindustani citizens of Suriname were still condemned to playing subordinate roles within the national administration. It is no coincidence that comparable nations (e.g., Trinidad and Tobago, Guyana) faced similar situations.[125] The fact that (a) Hindustanis, with their key positions in trade and agriculture, did hold great economic power and (b) they were the fastest growing population group, made it unacceptable to Creoles for Hindustanis to assume a dominant political role. Moreover, the former group continued to deem Hindustanis as contract labourers being transported to Suriname far more recently than they themselves had been. In other words: Creoles saw themselves as the real Surinamese. An ethnicity-based exclusivity and seclusion of Hindustanis as a group also made it difficult for Creoles to accept them as a legitimate administrative power. Notably Hindustanis were all too aware of these Creole sentiments. This explains why, in 1969, the VHP-leader Jagernath Lachmon appointed the Creole politician Jules Sedney as Prime Minister after the VHP's election victory.

The events leading up to independence had indeed exacerbated ethnic sensitivities. Prior to 25 November 1975, the frustration Hindustanis felt had led to mass emigration to the Netherlands. The number of migrating Creoles was considerable, too. After independence, the failing economic policy and the rising unemployment caused even more immigrants to opt for leaving Suriname. A special agreement ratified with the Dutch government made it relatively easy for them to obtain residence permits in the Netherlands. Just prior to this scheme expiring on 25 November 1980, this exodus reached a new peak. In the Arron-led government's view, emigration served as a safety valve through which social discontent could escape. According to official estimates, *c.*130,000 migrants from Suriname resided in the Netherlands at the end of 1976; at around the time of independence, *c.*50,000 migrants had

---

125 For a comparison of the positions of Hindustanis in Guyana, Suriname as well as Trinidad and Tobago, see: Choenni 1982.

A History of Suriname

left Suriname for the Netherlands; a number of between 25,000 and 30,000 men, women and children emigrated in 1979 and 1980.[126] This sizable migration caused the population of Suriname to drop from 379,607 souls (1972) and arrive at a total of 355,240 souls (1980).[127]

---

126   Bruijning & Voorhoeve 1977, 176; *Central Bank of Suriname, Report 1976-1980*, 6.
127   Numbers taken from the fourth and fifth *Census of the General Population*.

CHAPTER 12
Economic development (1945-1980)[1]

According to the treaty on development cooperation which the Netherlands ratified on the occasion of Suriname's independence in 1975, those pledged billions should contribute to increasing (a) the newly-founded state's economic resilience, (b) employment numbers, hereby improving the population's living conditions, and (c) the regional distribution of wealth.[2] With these terms, the Dutch government implicitly acknowledged that previous aid efforts had not yielded sufficient results.

Immediately after WW II, the government of the Netherlands realised that Suriname would not be able to become economically independent without any assistance. The need for raw materials in order to reconstruct Western Europe-inspired bauxite mining, an activity which had increased sharply as a result of the war effort. Nevertheless, the following structural issues remained unsolved: (a) a one-sided production structure, (b) a low level of employment growth, (c) a looming decline in the national income per capita (in the face of the significant population growth of *c.*3 per cent per annum), and (d) the negative balance of payments, which was only being stabilised by means of Dutch subsidies. The Netherlands' government therefore set up the Welfare Fund in 1947. Within 5 years, 40 million Hfl became available for 'the development of economic sources of prosperity and the improvement of social conditions'.[3] This plan-based approach fell in line with changing views held across the Western world in favour of a more active government role in the economy. Part of this fund thus served to set up governmental institutions e.g., *Stichting Planbureau* (National Planning Bureau), which had to contribute to a long-term programme for the benefit of Suriname's economy. In order to collect the required basic data, this welfare fund financed the 1950 General Census as well as the aerial mapping of North Suriname. In addition, a number of projects were initiated to improve public housing, public credit, agriculture and road construction.

The most important agricultural project comprised the establishment in 1949 of the Stichting Machinale Landbouw (SML; Foundation Mechanized Agriculture), the so-called Wageningen Project for which several new polders were created in the Nickerie district. Conceived shortly after WW II, the original plan to house Dutch farmers here, due to an expected global shortage of cereals, was never implemented. Eventually this project evolved into a mechanized rice farm and, by setting a successful example, contributed greatly to raising the volume of rice tonnage in Suriname.

The aforementioned welfare fund was too modest in size to incite major economic activities. In 1949, its plans had to be drastically revised after the devaluation of the Dutch guilder. Moreover, the spending period had been extended to 7 years. After the Kingdom Statute (officially: the Charter of the Kingdom of the Netherlands) had been realised, in 1954, a Ten-Year Plan was implemented, followed by two Five-Year Plans. In addition to promoting economic growth, the goals of these initiatives were:

---

1   Chapter 12 is largely based on Chin & Buddingh' 1987, 120-140; see also: Buddingh' 2001, 77-88.
2   As stated in article 2 of the treaty dated 25 November 1975.
3   Buddingh' 2001, 77; Chin & Buddingh' 1987, 120.

(a) raising the standards of living among the lowest income groups, (b) reducing structural unemployment, (c) limiting economic dependence and (d) diversifying the economy. In 1954, 127 million Sfl (equal to *c.*244 million Hfl) was earmarked for implementing the Ten-Year Plan; the Netherlands would contribute 33 per cent hereof as a donation and 33 per cent as a loan; next, the Dutch government added 80 million Sfl, while the duration of this plan was extended until 1966; moreover, from 1963 on, bridging loans were regularly granted in order to cover any shortfalls in Suriname's governmental budget.[4] Once this plan had reached a conclusion, 'the foundations would have been laid enabling further economic development on its own'.[5] Now Suriname's government had to finance 33 per cent of this plan. It soon became clear it was unable to do so, mainly due to a rising expenditure pertaining to the growing civil service sector. Paramaribo was therefore entitled to consider projects financed by the European Economic Community (EEC) from 1964 onwards to be self-financed. The provision for the first Five-Year Plan (1967-1971) was to be paid entirely by the Netherlands. It amounted to 240 million Hfl (equal to 125 million Sfl which was then equal to 69.4 million USD); the provision for the second Five-Year Plan amounted to 400 million Hfl; moreover, during the second half of the 1960s, Suriname received a total of 4 million Sfl to reach 5 million Sfl per annum between 1970 and 1975, again funded by the EEC.[6]

Between 1955 and 1975, according to data provided by the General Bureau of Statistics and the Planning Bureau of Suriname, the lion's share of development aid was expended on public works, transport and communication (32 per cent). The agricultural sector obtained 22 per cent, forestry 11 per cent, mining 6 per cent, aerial mapping 6 per cent and industry 2 per cent. The remaining 21 per cent was spent on managing and administrating development aid, public health and housing.[7] Considering the fact that agricultural, forestry and mining related expenditures were predominantly of an infrastructural nature, we may conclude that development funds were expended in a very biased way. The local industry sector benefited the least from this funds. Moreover, the large investments in infrastructure mainly benefited foreign companies (e.g., Alcoa, Bruynzeel, Billiton). The Netherlands supported this so-called policy of industrialisation by invitation, which several Caribbean nations also pursued.

The low priority regarding a Suriname-based industry was not only related to the small domestic market, it also reflected the special position taken in by the local elite. As a result of the traditional dominance of the foreign business community in Suriname - even the energy supply was entirely in the hands of the Dutch *Overzeese Gas- en Electriciteitsmaatschappij* (Overseas Gas and Electricity Company) - this local 'colonial bourgeoisie' had settled mainly in the top of the state apparatus and the (import) trade. This layer of society took every interest in maintaining the status quo as long as foreign companies and their tax payments filled the government treasury in order to pay out the salaries of civil servants. It included businessmen managing

---

4   Ibid. 2001, 78; ibid. 1987, 121-122.
5   Bruijning & Voorhoeve 1977, 606.
6   Buddingh' 2001, 78; Chin & Buddingh' 1987, 121-122; *Central Bank of Suriname. Report 1976-1980*, 56.
7   Chin & Buddingh' 1987, 125.

several large trading houses. A holding named C. Kersten & Co., solely owned by the Moravian Church, imported a wide range of consumer goods. As to the banking and insurance sectors, which were dominated by Dutch interests, the import trade was far more secure than the industrial sector. Large foreign firms and the local trade elite had combined their interests by means of the *Vereniging Surinaams Bedrijfsleven* (Business Association of Suriname), which in turn maintained close ties with the government. Its high-ranking officials often held positions at foreign companies hereby causing a far-reaching conflict of interest which resulted in them being described as *foetoebois* (errand boys).

The structure of the trade union system was not conducive to developing a local small industry either. Trade unions in Suriname have traditionally been organised on a company-by-company basis. To local leaders, they provide a springboard into politics, which increases mutual rivalry. Strong unions active in large foreign companies are trendsetters in wage setting. For, wage costs within this sector are of minor importance. Rivalry between trade union federations, which always attempt to steal trade unions from each other, contributes to raising wages to levels barely affordable for local businesses.

Foreign companies, mainly active within the primary sectors of mining, forestry and agriculture, were able to operate in very favourable conditions.[8] In 1948, a timber factory named Bruynzeel and based in Zaandam (North Holland, the Netherlands) acquired the exploitation rights over 500,000 ha of forest area for a 25-year period. The size of this concession was not only five times larger than usual when compared with most other nations, the *Bruynzeel Suriname Houtmaatschappij* obtained the right to replace inferior forest areas with better ones as long as it did not exceed the maximum concession size. The proviso here was: open a plywood factory. The fee of only 50 cents per log, regardless of its size, species and quality, was equally unique. This agreement did not include any clauses as to reforestation, implying that Bruynzeel was forced to import wood during certain years. Although this company had created 700 new jobs in the course of its first year of existence, a large number of Maroons nonetheless lost their livelihoods in the logging sector. On occasion, members of the Staten of Suriname raised their voices against the favourable conditions presented to foreign entrepreneurs. In 1947, Governor Johannes C. Brons (1884-1964) withdrew his promise to Bruynzeel regarding a concession of 4,200,000 ha of forest land after the parliament had forced him to do so. In 1956, the opposition comprising the NPS and the VHP in the Staten resisted far-reaching promises the *Eenheidsfront* (United Front)-led government had made to the Surinam American Industries Limited (SAIL) owned by E.S. Schweig, a US businessman. They included a 10-year tax-free period as well as a 15-year export monopoly on shrimp and fish. The Staten of Suriname finally agreed to these commitments albeit with a majority of only one vote.[9]

The discussion flared up again when in 1957 the same government, led by aforementioned Prime Minister Johan Ferrier, announced it was to ratify an agreement with Alcoa concerning the construction of the Brokopondo Reservoir in order to

---

8   Van Waesberge 1976, 45-48.
9   Dew 1996, 111-112; Chin & Buddingh' 1987, 122.

Figure 12.1. View of Brokopondo Reservoir and Afobaka Dam including a power station and bridge. Date and photographer unknown. Surinaams Museum photo archive.

generate electricity utilised when producing aluminium.[10] After WW II, the opinion had matured in Suriname that it could be more profitable to process bauxite within its borders. Not only would the export value thus increase, this initiative implied that employment could also grow as a result of the emergence of supply companies and of aluminium-processing industries. In addition, the government's income based upon imposing taxes on profits would increase. In 1950 W.J. van Blommestein (1905-1985), a prominent Dutch hydrological engineer, had presented preliminary recommendations pertaining to constructing a dam on the Suriname River near Brokopondo. Eight years later both the Surinamese government and Alcoa signed the Brokopondo agreement. However, the Dutch government refused to finance this 300 million Sfl project. Because of Suriname's status under international law, any access to international credit institutions (e.g., the World Bank) was impossible, too. Under these circumstances, the government of Suriname was forced to reach an agreement with Alcoa. In accordance herewith, Alcoa's daughter, the *Surinaamsche Bauxiet Maatschappij*, was transmuted into the Suriname Aluminium Company (Suralco). The fact this newly-established venture was based in the US enabled it to benefit from the US legislation which fiscally favoured investments in the Western Hemisphere. Suralco took on the financing of the Brokopondo Dam as well as of the hydroelectric power station (capacity: 180,000 kW) which was to be transferred to the Surinamese government free of charge after 75 years. In addition, Suralco undertook the construction of an aluminium

---

10   Van Waesberge 1976, 40-44; Chin & Buddingh 1987, 122-124; Bruijning & Voorhoeve 1977, 47; for
      Ferrier's discussion on the establishment and importance of the Brokopondo agreement, see: Jansen van
      Galen 2005, 67-68,

smelter and a factory where aluminium oxide (aka alumina) was produced. As was agreed, Suralco could at all times dispose of 90 per cent of the supplied electricity. The remaining 10 per cent was intended for Suriname. Moreover, the government had to ensure the transmigration of between 5,000 and 6,000 Saramaka Maroons, residing in the very location where the W.J. van Blommestein Meer (aka Brokopondo Reservoir) was to be created in the future.

At that time, processing raw materials in a Third World country was not a common phenomenon. With regard to Suralco, this deal included several major advantages. For, it was allowed to carry out exploratory drilling in Eastern Suriname across an area of 500,000 ha, after which the most suitable 20.000 ha would be assigned as a new concession for extracting bauxite. Further, Alcoa was able to enter the European market in a less costly manner as Suriname had been associated with the EEC since 1964.

Inspired by nationalist movements across the Third World, we see how towards the end of the 1960s the notion had gained ground in Suriname, too, that governments should have a greater influence on foreign business ventures. This desire grew once it had become increasingly clear that Suriname's local industry was not taking off adequately. The government which Pengel served as Prime Minister (1963-1969) now launched a strategy of joint ventures whereby it would first participate in foreign companies. Next, shares would be offered to those interested in Suriname-based parties, allowing the use of the term 'surinamisation' of the industry.[11] Due to a shortage of financial means, the government had to call on Dutch aid funds. This cash flow could also serve the acquisition of Dutch firms, which did not make negotiations any easier. Now and again assistance provided by the Netherlands served as disguised operating funds for ailing companies whose machinery was out-dated. This was certainly the case with the aforementioned *Bruynzeel Suriname Houtmaatschappij*, which thus received a credit exceeding 6 million Hfl. The *Handels Vereniging Amsterdam* (Trade Association Amsterdam), which had become active in Suriname during 1969 when it started to produce palm oil, even received millions in loans and donations extracted from development funds which then flowed into its profitable joint ventures called Victoria and Patamacca. Their management remained in hands of the foreign parent company, which received very high remunerations. Although Suriname acquired 60 per cent of the *Overzeese Gas- en Electriciteitsmaatschappij*'s shares in 1971, its Dutch management continued to determine the energy tariffs for Suriname-based consumers. This lucrative procedure saw to it that the price of the remaining 40 per cent of the shares, which Suriname was to take over at a later stage, rose again and again. Their value increased even further when the *Overzeese Gas- en Electriciteitsmaatschappij* received investment loans from Dutch development aid. Although, during the 1960s, the government of Suriname had taken over the banana cultivation, the much more profitable exports and distribution had remained in foreign hands.

The development of national income during the Ten-Year and Five-Year Plans was very unbalanced. Between 1955 and 1963, the annual real growth exceeded 4 per cent, which hardly sufficed to keep pace with a growing population. The exceptionally

---

11   Van Waesberge 1976, 45-50.

	1955	1960	1964	1968	1971	1975	1979
Agriculture and fishery	13	12	11	11	8	10	8
Forestry, wood processing	4	4	4	3	3	2	2
Mining, bauxite processing	34	28	27	32	35	26	19
Industry (incl. water, gas electricity, construction)	8	9	10	10	10	10	15
Commerce, banking	20	22	21	21	20	25	28
Government	17	20	22	19	19	21	23
Other services	4	5	5	4	5	6	5
GDP (Sfl million) current factor cost	112	178	227	445	538	741	1,437

Table 12.1. Gross Domestic Product by sector (in percentages) and in Sfl million; USD = 1.785 Sfl. Source: Planning Bureau of Suriname, General Bureau of Statistics, Central Bank of Suriname, Chin & Buddingh' 1987, 127 and 136.

high average economic growth between 1964 and 1968 reached *c.*13 per cent. It can almost entirely be attributed to a sharp peak in investments within the bauxite sector which was the outcome of the Brokopondo Project. In the course of the 1950s, private investments amounted to *c.*20 million Sfl per annum. During the 1960s they reached an annual average of *c.*70 million Sfl. Most notably, between 1964 and 1966, this average exceeded 100 million Sfl. After the surge of investments in the bauxite sector was over, national income growth declined sharply. Between 1971 and 1975, the real national income increased with only 1 per cent per annum.[12] It was thus only with the help of a considerable emigration surplus that the per capita income did rise continuously. In 1975, with an average annual GDP per capita of 1,296 USD, Suriname could even be ranked among the Middle Income Countries.[13]

The goals of the Ten-Year Plan and the two Five-Year Plans were far from accomplished. The boost which the bauxite sector witnessed during the mid-1960s had only briefly impacted the economic growth. The objective, to wit, reduce the dependency of the economy and enhance its diversification had hardly been achieved. Even more than the composition of GDP (see Table 12.1), the composition of exports indicates Suriname's dependence on the bauxite sector and thus on foreign companies. Between 1955 and 1979, the bauxite sector's share of total goods exports varied between 77 and 91 per cent, whereas the share of agriculture and fisheries fluctuated between 6 and 16 per cent.[14] Moreover, during the early 1970s, more than 33 per cent of government revenue hailed from the bauxite sector.[15] Agricultural exports, too, were largely in the hands of foreign companies whereby the aforementioned SML, United Fruit Company and SAIL provided rice, bananas and shrimps respectively

The one-sided composition of the national income had changed little. A decline in the relative importance of the bauxite sector during 1975 illustrates the influence

---

12   Chin & Buddingh' 1987, 125-126.
13   See: macrotrends.net/countries/SUR/suriname/gdp-per-capita (World Bank).
14   Chin & Buddingh' 1987, 128.
15   *Central Bank of Suriname. Report 1976-1980*, 63.

A History of Suriname

exercised by Alcoa and the BHP Billiton mining company (see Table 12.1). In 1974, Suriname had joined the International Bauxite Association. This group of alumina producing nations had, by means of mutual price agreements, attempted to increase its members' incomes. After negotiating with bauxite producing companies, Suriname introduced a levy comprising 6 per cent of the market price of aluminium, as a result of which an additional 90 million Sfl flowed into the state coffers in 1974.[16] Alcoa responded by increasing its bauxite mining in nations which were not members of the International Bauxite Association.

Moreover, the Brokopondo-push (i.e., extra investments related to both the bauxite sector and the Brokopondo Project) did not provide solutions for (a) the structural unemployment, (b) the mass emigration to the Netherlands and (c) a relentless expansion of the civil service sector. During the 1950s, an annual employment growth of more than 4 per cent proved just enough to keep up with population growth. During the following years, the employment growth dropped to between 1 and 2 per cent only.[17] In 1972, the Planning Bureau of Suriname estimated the unemployment rate to be c.13 per cent.[18] Assessments taking into account the concealed unemployment in the agriculture and in the informal sector reached 30 per cent.[19] Although large foreign companies did indeed produce between 40 and 50 per cent of the domestic production (see Table 12.1), bauxite companies, for example, contributed barely 7 per cent towards employment.[20] Nevertheless, emigration led to a shortage of skilled workers, especially in the construction sector, which in turn led to an influx of immigrants, in particular from Guyana. Suriname's education system could not meet the demand. Here the emphasis had traditionally been on general schooling and not so much on professional or on technical education. It was not until the mid-1970s that Suriname could provide any form of advanced technical tuition.

Notably, employment dropped sharply in the agriculture sector, which mainly comprised a large number of inefficiently producing small farms.[21] This reduction was counterbalanced by means of a growth in the already oversized public sector as well as in commercial services, including import trade (see Table 12.2). Neither sector was able to provide a structural solution to the unemployment problem. The increase observed in the employment level of the industry sector was almost entirely the outcome of a temporary boost in the construction sector.

The structural weakness of Suriname's economy was also reflected in a chronic current account deficit. The balance of trade in goods always revealed a surplus, an outcome of the bauxite companies' substantial exports. However, profit transfers carried out by foreign firms resulted in a negative balance on the current account. It was only through the influx of Dutch financial aid that the balance of payments was restored. Between 1955 and 1975, the sum of profit transfers executed by foreign

---

16   Lamur 1983, 14; Bruijning & Voorhoeve 1977, 47.

17   Van Schaaijk & Van der Straaten 1984, 1044; Chin & Buddingh', 1987, 126.

18   *Central Bank of Suriname. Annual Report 1972*, 56.

19   Rijsdijk 1975, Chapter I, 5.

20   *Central Bank of Suriname. Annual Report 1972*, 56.

21   According to official data, Suriname had 16,078 farms in 1969, 11,901 of which measured between 0.5 and 5 ha, see: Bruijning & Voorhoeve 1977, 363.

	1953	1964	1968	1975	1982
Agriculture, livestock farming, forestry, wood processing	56	35	30	19	17
Mining and bauxite processing	5	7	8	8	5
Industry (incl. utilities and construction)	17	13	19	16	17
Commercial services	9	24	20	25	24
Government	13	21	23	32	37

Table 12.2. Employment per sector (in percentages). Source: Van Schaaijk & Van der Straaten 1984, 1046.

companies amounted to 950 million Sfl, whereas foreign direct investments in the same period amounted to 460 million Sfl.[22]

A Dutch-Surinamese committee, led by the economist H.C. Bos and the Planning Bureau of Suriname's director H.E. Rijsdijk had to prepare for the development cooperation during the post-independence era. They noted that the 'big push' witnessed in the course of the 1960s had led to a considerable increase in income 'but not to the loosening of forces, as a result of which the growth of the economy could continue on its own'.[23] In addition, high unemployment levels as well as an unequal distribution of income had not significantly improved living conditions among large masses of the population. This committee reported on the risk of 'impoverishment' impacting a growing number of unemployed, who were without any form of social security.[24]

The report presented by this committee should have laid the foundations for an integrated multi-annual development plan which never materialised. Due to lack of time prior to the independence date, this report itself served as starting point for the development cooperation. The varied viewpoints of the Surinamese and Dutch experts had however resulted in two scenarios. The first hereof was based on a planning period of 10 years during which the vast sum of 4.5 billion Sfl (equal to 6.7 billion Hfl) would be invested. With an average growth in GDP of 10.5 per cent per annum, unemployment would have been virtually eliminated in 1985. The second Dutch point of view was more cautious. It projected a 15-year planning period and an annual economic growth rate of 7 per cent. Thus, unemployment levels would still reach 17 per cent in 1990, in part due to population growth.[25] After tough negotiations, the Dutch government provided 3.5 billion Hfl (now € 1.6 billion) for a time frame spanning between 10 and 15 years, of which 2.7 billion Hfl could serve to fund projects. 500 million Hfl was designated to provide guarantees for loans on the international capital market. 300 million Hfl would become available, if Suriname raised exactly the same sum of money from its own state savings. In addition, a debt exceeding 500 million Hfl which Suriname owed to the Netherlands

---

22   Chin 1971, 1454; Chin & Buddingh' 1987, 129.
23   Rijsdijk 1975, Chapter V, 1
24   Ibid.
25   Van Schaaijk & Van der Straaten 1984, 1042; Rijsdijk 1975, Chapter VI, 37.

Figure 12.2. A sawmill run by the Bruynzeel timber factory during the 1970s. Bruynzeel produced for example plywood chipboards and prefabricated houses. Having been taken over by the government, this company filed for bankruptcy in 2005. Photo by Vincent Mentzel.

was to be cancelled.[26] Evaluating the projects was entrusted to the *Commissie Ontwikkelingssamenwerking Nederland-Suriname* (CONS; Committee for Development Cooperation the Netherlands-Suriname), which included bilateral experts. According to a distribution key this committee had compiled, 50 per cent of the available funds would be designated to productive projects, whereas the infrastructure and socio-educational projects each received 25 per cent.[27]

The most significant impulse for growth had to originate from the Western Suriname project. It included constructing a large dam on the Kabalebo River which could provide the energy required when processing bauxite extracted from the nearby Bakhuis Mountains with which alumina and aluminium were to be produced. This energy could also be utilised in order to (a) develop an irrigation project creating large rice fields and (b) invest in the timber sector. The former Minister of Development Frank E. Essed (1919-1988) was the main advocate of this project. He had added a document to the CONS report, entitled *De mobilisatie van het eigene: een ruimtelijk-fysieke bijdrage aan de integrale planning* (The mobilization of one's own: a spatial-physical contribution to integrated planning) forwarded on behalf of the Surinamese section of the aforementioned committee. As Suriname's most influential intellectual in matters of economic development, Essed opined that one could not afford to focus only on the development of small-scale production: 'Considering the small domestic market, economic growth will for the most part be determined by the large production for export, which is the carrier of the economic growth.'[28] Essed deemed small businesses to be of huge significance as 'stabilising factors' thanks to their favourable effects on both employment and income distribution. In his view, the agriculture sector required reconstructing. In addition, a negative impact on employment numbers had to be counterbalanced by means of

---

26 As stated in the treaty dated 25 November 1975, see: article 5 and annex 1 (online accessible, see bibliography).

27 *Central Bank of Suriname. Report 1976-1980*, 46.

28 Essed 1975, 10.

land reclamation. In the aforementioned document, Essed developed the so-called growth pole theory, whereby Paramaribo was no longer the nation's only economic hub. For psychological reasons, too, he held the West Suriname project to be of key relevance as it could inspire younger generations to act in a more idealistic and entrepreneurial spirit.

Plans for extracting bauxite in West Suriname had already been made during the early 1960s. In 1968, under a Pengel-led government, an agreement in principle was reached with NV Billiton Maatschappij, Pechiney SA (a French conglomerate producing aluminium in the Netherlands), Alcoa and Ormet Corporation, the latter two US-based. Depending on its profitability, this consortium would later process bauxite into alumina and aluminium on site. In view of the key role NV Billiton Maatschappij was to play here, the Dutch government had agreed upon financing infrastructure facilities. However, for unclear reasons, the Sedney-led cabinet (1969-1973) reached a new agreement in principle with Reynolds Metals Company aka Reynolds Aluminium, which had formed a joint venture with the recently founded Suriname-owned mining company named Grasshopper Aluminium Company aka Grassalco NV. In the presence of between 10 and 50 million tonnes of bauxite, the US-based Reynolds Metal Company would be capable of exporting raw material without any further processing. In the case of much larger bauxite deposits, an alumina and aluminium factory was to be built. As to transporting the bauxite, Suriname was now committed to constructing a railway line leading to Apoera, a village located on the eastern bank of the Corantijne River. The discovery of bauxite in Australia, Guinea and Brazil had already caused the extraction of this sedimentary rock to be less lucrative in Suriname. Therefore, in spite of the proven existence of recoverable quantities of bauxite weighing at least 80 million tonnes across the Bakhuis Mountains, Reynolds Metals Company showed virtually no further interest. The Dutch reluctance to contribute to any infrastructure projects benefitting a US-based firm was one of the reasons why this company withdrew from this project in 1977. The previously mentioned levy which Suriname had introduced as an incoming member of the International Bauxite Association may also have played a role in this decision. The government of Suriname compensated 7 million USD on unclear grounds to then reach a new agreement in principle with Billiton Maatschappij Suriname, at that time a Dutch firm.[29]

After Suriname's independence in 1975, development funds were spent on the West Suriname project with great vigour, although there was still no certainty as to either the economic viability or the genuine interest of private investors. Of the approximately 530 million Sfl forwarded to the Multi-Annual Development Plan at the end of 1980, more than 195 million Sfl had been spent on West Suriname. Of the latter sum, a total of 167.3 million Sfl was designated to the aforementioned railway line, constructed by a US consortium in a joint venture with companies based in Suriname and the Netherlands, whereas 28 million Sfl was expended on preparations pertaining to the Kabalebo Dam project.[30] National prestige and pride both formed key motives for the government of Suriname to realise this project. Thus

---

29   Lamur 1983, 14; Chin & Buddingh' 1987, 132-134; Kagie, 1980, 114; Breeveld 2000, 249-254.
30   *Central Bank of Suriname. Report 1976-1980*, 51 and annexes VI.2 and VI.5.

A History of Suriname

the pressure placed on The Hague to provide funding was substantial. The social democratic Minister for Development Cooperation, Jan Pronk, wrote in retrospect that he occasionally felt 'blackmailed' due to his personal views on colonial relations. For, after all, he did not want to be accused of supporting neo-colonialist principles.[31] This was the first decision Dutch authorities had to take as to concerning the now independent Suriname. In Pronk's view, it was not politically feasible to discontinue the Kabalebo Dam project. When the railway line leading to Apoera was almost completed in 1979, bauxite companies were no longer interested in lower-quality reserves found at the Bakhuis Mountains. A committee which comprised Suriname's government representatives, Billiton Maatschappij Suriname and Alcoa soon arrived at the conclusion that a profitable exploitation or processing of the bauxite in Apoera was impossible.[32]

In addition, the agreed distribution of development funds between the directly productive sectors (50 per cent), socio-educational sectors (25 per cent) and infrastructural projects (25 per cent) had not been realised. Only the social-educational sector (i.e., education, public health, housing, health insurance) came close to the agreed percentage with an outlay totalling 111.9 million Sfl; infrastructure works (expenditure: 259.2 million Sfl) received far too much emphasis as a result of the large amounts spent in West Suriname; as in the past, expenditure regarding the directly productive sphere lagged far behind the target; the sum of 130.4 million Sfl formed less than 25 per cent of the total of which the industrial sector received 21.3 million Sfl.[33] However, this amount was almost entirely forwarded to only three companies, two of which were joint ventures with Dutch firms. They had a strong interest in the allocation of the funds. The *Energie Bedrijf Suriname* (Energy Company of Suriname), a joint venture between the government of Suriname and the Dutch *Overzeese Gas-en Electriciteitsmaatschappij*, received a loan totalling 6 million Sfl; timber firm *Bruynzeel Suriname Houtmaatschappij* was provided with a loan of 7.7 million Sfl; in addition, 5.6 million Sfl was given in loan to the Mariënburg sugar plantation, which the government of Suriname had acquired in 1974 after forwarding a symbolic 1 Hfl to the *Rubber Cultuur Maatschappij Amsterdam*.[34] This loan was to be utilised in order to finance investments in hugely neglected and outdated production facilities.

Activities undertaken by the *Nationale Ontwikkelingsbank* (National Development Bank) as to loans experienced a very difficult start. Financed by Dutch development funds, it had been founded in order to improve opportunities for both small and medium-sized enterprises. This setback was in part caused by a lack of loan requests pertaining to profitable investments. The total amount of loans in 1980 reached a mere 17.1 million Sfl.[35] A significant part hereof went to (a) the lumber and furniture industry or (b) the food, beverage and tobacco industry. These amounts were far too small to provide these sectors with a real boost. Frank E. Essed had calculated in his publication (1973) entitled *Een volk op weg naar zelfstandigheid* (A people on

---

31 Pronk 2020, 218.
32 Chin & Buddingh' 1987, 134.
33 *Central Bank of Suriname. Report 1976-1980*, Annex VI.5.
34 Ibid.
35 Ibid.

the road to independence) that 50 per cent of the imported consumer goods could be produced in Suriname.[36] Seven years later, this situation had not changed much.

The agricultural sector's contribution to the economic development also fell far short of expectations. From 1975 on, the spending of 200 million Sfl on projects had been approved within the framework of development cooperation, but only 37.5 million Sfl had actually been implemented in 1980.[37] Moreover, not much had been done with regard to land reclamation plans.[38] Plans aimed at small dairy farmers increasing their milk production failed too.[39] In addition to a lack of any implementation capacity, the absence of the predominantly Hindustani VHP in the coalition government, which the Creoles dominated, was apparently a key explanation for the large slump in agricultural expenditure. After all, the Hindustani party's electorate included the most farmers. Between 1973 and 1977, during the first NPK-led government in excess of 20,000 ha of farmland located in the Nickerie district was distributed in 5 years to only 30 friendly partners, although more than 1,000 Hindustani smallholder farmers had applied for the allocation of land.[40] The policy applied when issuing plots was a source of corruption. As previously mentioned, the KTPI-leader and Minister of Agriculture, Livestock and Fisheries, Willy Soemita, was sentenced to 12 months in prison for acts of bribery when allocating agricultural land (see p. 279).

According to a multi-annual development scheme, as many as 1,300 jobs would be created annually in the agriculture, livestock and fisheries sectors; in reality, this number dropped from 15,300 in 1975 to 14,200 in 1979.[41] The number of rice farms decreased sharply, especially as to small-scale rice cultivation (i.e., less than 20 ha), from 4,820 in 1976 to 4,180 in 1979.[42] During these 3 years, too, the acreage of the rice fields increased from 48,400 to 58,855 ha. This expansion of large-scale rice cultivation was mainly brought about by private initiative, as *c*.66 per cent of this land was cultivated on a large scale.[43] This increase along with technical improvements resulted in a strong growth of the total rice harvest from 99,240 to 136,320 tonnes; it may be added here that the export volume rose from 67,000 to 102,999 tonnes; at the same time the export value almost doubled from 35.5 million Sfl to 68.4 million Sfl.[44] Due to the EEC levies, rice grains exported to Europe were by and large unpeeled.

Post-1975 economic developments strongly resembled the Brokopondo push of the 1960s. Now, however, an influx of development aid caused government investments to rise sharply and rapidly: from between 40 and 50 million Sfl to *c*.140 million Sfl per annum.[45] Between 1976 and 1978, the growth in investment, also observed across the private sector, resulted in a strong yearly increase in GNP of more than 15 per cent on average; however, stagnation occurred as early as 1979, causing a decrease in GNP of almost 4 per cent; the real per capita income increased

---

36   Essed 1973, 111.
37   *Central Bank of Suriname. Report 1976-1980*, 69.
38   *Central Bank of Suriname. Annual Report 1981*, 82.
39   *Central Bank of Suriname. Report 1976-1980*, 72.
40   Kagie 1980, 165.
41   *Central Bank of Suriname- Annual Report 1976-1980*, 70.
42   Ibid., annex VII c5.
43   Ibid., 70, annex VII c4.
44   Ibid., annexes VII c6 and c7.
45   Ibid., 10; *Central Bank of Suriname. Annual Report 1973*, 36.

with an annual average of 10.2 per cent during the peak years: 1975-1978; in 1979, however, despite a decrease in the size of the population, the real per capita income dropped with almost 4 per cent.[46]

As a result of the nature of development expenditure, from which mainly the infrastructure profited, only a limited quantity of additional production was created. A flow of investment thus not only led to a false sense of well-being but also to structural overspending. The increase in national income was indeed spent almost entirely on consumption, the ratio of which rose sharply, to wit, from 68 per cent in 1975 to 93 per cent in 1982; the total of public as well as private investments dropped from 37 per cent in 1975 to 21 per cent in 1982; although public investment, almost entirely financed by development aid, had risen from 8 per cent to 12 per cent of GNP between 1975 and 1982, the number of private investments had fallen far more dramatically.[47] Data indicate that substitution effects existed on a large scale. Dutch aid had replaced savings accumulated both by Suriname and by private foreign capital. Its government's activities also replaced private initiatives. An intended self-reliance of its national economy had therefore not been brought any closer by means of development aid. As previously stated, the economic structure, in terms of production, export and employment, had not changed much (see also Table 12.1). The increase observed as to the relative significance of the industrial sector was almost entirely the outcome of a brief upturn within the construction sector, which had benefited greatly from the flow of development funds.

The economic cycle was the main cause of the declining importance of mining. In addition, after obtaining independence, Suriname's public sector witnessed the largest employment growth whereby the number of jobs increased from 32,700 in 1976 to 39,600 in 1979; at that time, no less than 38.6 per cent of the 102,600 working population was employed as civil servants; in spite of this growth in the number of posts (almost entirely comprising the public sector) to reach 7,300 during these years, the unemployment figure remained high; according to the ABS (General Bureau of Statistics) and based on the 1980 Census, the unemployment rate in 1980 had reached 18 per cent.[48] This figure is flattered, considering the concealed unemployment in the agricultural and service sectors. Many thousands found livelihoods in the informal sector by means of casual jobs (in Sranan Tongo often referred to as *hosselen*, a term derived from the English verb to hustle).

The distribution of wealth, as formulated in the treaty on development cooperation with the Netherlands in 1975, had proved to be an illusion, too. Figures forwarded by the ABS point to a serious deterioration in the distribution of income between 1968 and 1980. The average monthly income in Paramaribo of the 10 per cent of the most destitute even dropped in absolute terms from 146 Sfl to 109 Sfl per month; their share in the total income dropped from 3.5 to 1.3 per cent whereas average monthly incomes for the 10 per cent most affluent rose from 885 Sfl to 2,616 Sfl; moreover, their contribution to the national total income rose from 21.2 per cent

46   *Central Bank of Suriname. Report 1976-1980*, 13.
47   Van Schaaijk & Van der Straaten 1984, 1047.
48   *Central Bank of Suriname. Report 1976-1980*, 16.

to 31 per cent.[49] According to the ABS, the percentage of the population living below the poverty line had risen from 30 to 40 per cent between 1968 and 1978.[50] Initiatives announced by the government prior to independence as to introducing social security benefits (e.g., a health insurance fund) were put on hold. For those older than 70 years of age, the *Algemene Ouderdomsverzekering* (General Old Age Insurance) now provided for a monthly sum of 25 Sfl. However, authorities soon failed to deliver payments on time.[51]

Both political and economic conditions prevented a proper utilisation of development funds. No integrated development plan was put in place. The aforementioned Committee for Development Cooperation Netherlands-Suriname, with experts from both countries, had not carried out a thorough review of the projects and was hardly equipped for this purpose. In Suriname, a spending rush took place, as the huge amount of financial aid was not indexed to inflation. Hardly any need existed as to scrutinizing the economic returns of projects, because this aid consisted entirely of grants. Suriname's central bank stated in a report that, between 1976 and 1980, in most cases 'the project dossiers did not at all suffice to provide a more than general idea of the contribution that the implementation of these projects would make towards the realisation of the overall development objectives'.[52] For political reasons, The Netherlands had little desire to offer any opposition. According to the 1982 Report of the General Court of Audit (*Verslag van de Algemene Rekenkamer*) of the Netherlands no structured assessment of aid existed on the basis of reports. The Netherlands was also reluctant when auditing expenditures. According to the aforementioned report, a reason therefore was that 'there were indeed no sanctions with regard to Suriname'.[53] Its social elite was in fact given a free hand as to the use of Dutch development aid. Project implementation was indeed entirely delegated to Suriname, making any form of monitoring difficult. Doubtful practices when handling contracts and tenders were no exception. Legal action followed on very few occasions.

---

49   Moerland 1984, 46-47.
50   Woodly-Sobhie 2012, 16.
51   Chin & Buddingh' 1987, 139-140.
52   *Central Bank of Suriname. Report 1976-1980*, 43.
53   Algemene Rekenkamer, *Verslag 1982*, 43.

CHAPTER 13
Military rule (1980-1987)[1]

On 25 February 1980, 16 poorly armed sergeants carried out a by and large well-received coup d'état led by a 34-year-old sports instructor named Desiré Delano 'Desi' Bouterse. The dissent regarding what was called 'old' politics was so widespread that any change meant hope for improvement. This unexpected putsch was by no means unique. After the failed attempt by a police inspector called Pavel Killinger at the beginning of the 20th century (see p. 214), several disgruntled war volunteers, having returned from the Dutch East Indies and led by a certain Simon Sanches, had plotted a coup d'état in 1947.[2]

Conflicts within the army were the direct cause of Bouterse's coup. Part of Suriname's military ranks comprised officers and non-commissioned officers trained in the Netherlands. Having served in the Dutch armed forces, they had returned to Suriname after the 1975 independence. Hence the frustrations which non-commissioned officers in particular experienced, having grown accustomed to better conditions while serving in the Netherlands. They felt dissatisfied with the promotion policy, the inferior military equipment and the archaic concepts pertaining to authority as revealed by Yngwe Elstak, the first commander of the Surinamese Armed Forces (1975-1980). Moreover, these troops had not been transformed into a development army as had been hinted at in c.1975. Such an adaptation would perhaps not only have contributed to Suriname's advancement, but at the same time would have put an end to any idleness observed within the military apparatus. The then Prime Minister Henck A.E. Arron (1936-2000) did not think much of this concept. In his opinion, involving the army in civilian tasks would have all too seriously damaged the possibilities to serve his own political clientele.

In 1979, non-commissioned officers had set up their own trade union in order to represent their interests, hereby following the example set by a military trade union already active in the Netherlands. The government of Suriname refused to recognise this trade union and, in January 1980, saw to it that three members of its board, including Badrissein Sital (1946-2017), were detained. The latter was to play a key role after the military takeover. By means of the insurrection of 25 February 1980, which not only claimed several lives but also destroyed Paramaribo's main police station, the 16 sergeants prevented the court from sentencing these three men. The fact that the police force sided with the government from the very outset would indeed darken its relationship with the armed forces for years to come.

This trade union conflict had been nothing else than the catalyst for the 1980 putsch. The malaise observed among the population formed an important stimulus for the rebellious armed forces. For more than 12 months, plans for a coup d'état had been forged. Desi Bouterse cum suis had made preparations, as had military officers led by Soerendre Rambocus (1953-1982), Badrissein Sital and Chas Mijnals (b. 1947). The latter two were both linked to the leftist *Volkspartij* (People's Party). Shortly after the

---

1   See also: Chin & Buddingh' 1987; Dew 1994.
2   Scheer 1995, 188-194; Meel 1999, 245-249.

coup, Bouterse informed the author-*cum*-journalist Jozef Slagveer (1940-1982) he had started, under the cover of a military trade union, collaborating with Sital and Mijnals as well as Laurens Neede (b.1946) and Roy Horb (1953-1983). A factor contributing to the success of this putsch was the financial assistance provided by several entrepreneurs, who expected a possible advantage to result from a power transition. The troops were supported by the trade union federations with the exception of *Het Algemeen Verbond van Vakverenigingen in Suriname De Moederbond* (The General Alliance of Labour Unions in Suriname The Mother Union), founded in 1951.

The benevolent attitude of the head of the Paramaribo-based Dutch military mission Colonel Hans Valk (1928-2012) certainly played a role, too. His support of non-commissioned officers regarding their complaints about the inefficient military apparatus apparently gave them the impression that the Netherlands would not immediately condemn a coup d'état. According to an official investigation carried out after an article published in the weekly *Vrij Nederland*, Valk had in any case not kept sufficient distance and thus, through his dubious actions, provided non-commissioned officers with moral support.[3] That seemed an understatement. For, when Valk left Paramaribo medio 1981, Bouterse remarked in a speech delivered during the farewell reception held at the Dutch ambassador's official residence: 'Let me now reveal in this audience something only you and I know, Colonel: without you, the coup would not have taken place. We will always be grateful to you for this.' Valk's reaction was equally remarkable: 'As long as I have presided the mission, the mission has supported you and your people' and adding: 'If you continue to act in the spirit I have taught you, you can continue to count on my help. Forever.'[4]

The sergeants' coup was a well-prepared military operation, but from a political viewpoint very badly planned. Power was obtained by a nine-member *Nationale Militaire Raad* (NMR; National Military Council) chaired by Badrissein Sital, a paramedic whose officiating as such was mainly the outcome of his role within the military trade union. Only a minority within the NMR shared his left-wing radical opinions. This council took a very cautious stance, dismissing the name *Nationale Revolutionaire Raad* (National Revolutionary Council) as it was deemed too provocative. In a first communiqué dated 25 February, the putschists called upon the people of Suriname to submit 'regardless of race, religious conviction, political direction and occupation' to the process of 'socio-economic, social and moral reorientation' as well as to the construction of Suriname.[5] In a second statement they explained their wish to present a civil council as soon as possible, which would be charged with executing administrative tasks.[6] Next, Eddy Bruma, already referred to (see chapter 11), member of the *Partij Nationalistische Republiek* (PNR), was appointed

---

3   Commissie van Onderzoek (Committee of Enquiry), *Onderzoek naar de rol van de Nederlandse Militaire Missie in Suriname* [...], 1984); in 2011, the Dutch government decided that the annexes to this report would remain secret until 2060 'because of the interests of the State or its allies', as stated in the *Staatscourant* d.d. 21 February, 2011, see also staatscourant.nl; in De Vries 2021, the author supports, after reading these secret documents, the conclusions of this committee of investigation that Valk did not directly support the coup or help to develop this plan; see also: Verhey & Van Westerloo 1983, where we read that these journalists who worked for *Vrij Nederland* revealed that Valk did indeed play a role in the military coup..

4   Haakmat 1987, 54-55.

5   Chin & Buddingh' 1987, 38; Boom 1982, 139-147.

6   Ibid. 1987, 39.

as a formateur. This lawyer had previously assisted detained leaders of the military trade union. The coup leaders apparently did not wish to proceed on their own, nor were they capable of doing so. Due to their lack of political experience, the military were presumably overwhelmed by a situation they themselves had created. During the first weeks after the putsch, a NMR spokesman asked reporters for handbooks on coups. This coup d'état was quickly, and perhaps justly, renamed an intervention. In the end its leaders had indeed not suspended the constitution. Having installed a civil council, President Johan H.E. Ferrier refused to apply the unconstitutional term 'intervention', stubbornly referring to it as the 'new government' which aimed at 'national reconciliation, national unity and national construction'.[7] Even the parliament of Suriname remained intact, albeit without any real power. By maintaining the constitution, the incoming rulers also succeeded in acquiring the trust of foreign nation states. After only a few weeks, US officials reported to be 'no longer worried by the possibility that the coup would produce a leftist government'.[8]

The civilian government, which took office on 15 March 1980, was led by Henk Chin A Sen (1934-1999), a physician of impeccable behaviour but without any political experience. This incoming Prime Minister was a PNR member. If observed from an ethnic viewpoint, he was considered neutral as a result of his Chinese-Creole descent and thus accepted by Creoles and Hindustanis. His cabinet, which included two military men, consisted partly of technocrats. The PNR was nevertheless able to make the greatest mark on this cabinet.

NMR members visited schools and businesses in order to be informed of all existing problems. They personally checked marketplaces for compliance with price regulations. Officials had to be continuously present at their working places between 7 a.m. and 2 p.m., enabling the determination of whoever was on the payroll in name only. A suggestion box in which citizens could deposit ideas was placed at the entrance of the Paramaribo military headquarters established at the Memre Boekoe barracks. As part of the fight against crime, lawbreakers were publicly caned. Because of their more populist than ideologically inspired policies, the troops were widely praised as *onze jongens* (our boys). Acts of brutality, which several high ranking army officers forced upon against alleged conspirators, did little to detract from this positive image, even after a former Surinamese military man and Dutch national named Fred Ormskerk (1923-1980) was beaten to death in captivity.[9]

On 1 May 1980, the cabinet presented its government statement, in which 25 February was described as a rupture:

'On this day, a system imbued with injustice, corruption, social injustice, bureaucracy and nepotism has gone down ingloriously. [...] To the people of Suriname the 25th of February means a day of liberation, of new hope, a rebirth. The old order has passed, a new era has dawned for our country and people.'[10]

---

7   Boom 1982, 180.
8   Chin & Buddingh' 1987, 40.
9   Kagie, 2012, 164-168, 189-200; here Kagie speaks of 'the first political murder' carried out by the Bouterse regime.
10   Chin & Buddingh' 1987, 40-41.

The Cabinet's programme was very pragmatic whereby the starting point comprised four innovations concerning the political-administrative order, the social order, the educational order and the socio-economic order.[11] In addition, a constitutional committee was requested to amend the constitution. A law on political parties was announced in order to guarantee internal party democracy. The voting age was to be lowered from 21 to 18 years. Democracy would be reinforced both by means of decentralisation of governance and the involvement of civil society organisations in policy-making. The armed forces were as yet to be transformed into a development army. A special court was envisaged in order to try cases of corruption dating to the pre-putsch years. The key announcement was: elections would be held in around October 1982 unless prevented by 'sensitive circumstances'.[12] The incoming government created confidence both at home and abroad. Dutch authorities soon pledged 500 million Hfl hereby facilitating an economic emergency programme which strongly focused on alleviating social needs.[13]

It was, however, impossible to conceal the growing battle of competence between civilian and military factions in Suriname. Both President Ferrier and Prime Minister Chin A Sen (and previously formateur Eddy Bruma) had from the very outset attempted to eliminate the NMR as a factor of power. The NMR's thoughts on the power relationships became apparent immediately after the installation of a Chin A Sen-led cabinet. According to B. Sital, the NMR chairman, administrative tasks were delegated to the civil council, but the policy had to be implemented on the basis of NMR's 'directives'.[14] Prime Minister Chin A Sen attempted to provide a certain degree of clarity in his statement. In his opinion, the government had once again fallen into the hands of civilians. At the same time he did not conceal the fact that the NMR had empowered the government, stating: 'These circumstances, supplemented by the fact that the maintenance of public order and national security continue to demand a high degree of vigilance, prescribe, in the government's view, that this country be governed in close consultation with the military power.'[15]

However, this incantation did not solve the conflict of competence. On the contrary, it would remain a common thread in all further political developments. Traditional constitutional structures were soon deemed far too restrictive. The parliament had already transferred its legislative power to the government by means of an enabling law, shortly after the coup. This procedure, according to the government's declaration, was required 'in order to create the turnaround necessary for the establishment of the new order'.[16] In addition, an amnesty law had been adopted, exempting the key putschists from prosecution. After several months, the constitution also proved to be too large an obstacle. When President Ferrier demanded that parliament should deal with the government's budget, the Prime Minister and the army command opted, on 13 August, to suspend the constitution. Moreover, the military leadership, after discovering a 'conspiracy', led to the declaration of a state of emergency that same

11 Ibid., 41.
12 Ibid.
13 Ibid., 141-142.
14 Ibid., 41.
15 Ibid., 42.
16 Chin A Sen, Regeringsverklaring (Government declaration), 1 May 1980.

A History of Suriname

day. According to decree A, 'subversive tensions' were present in the NMR as well as in army ranks. A 'serious constitutional conflict' now arose with Ferrier, the President.[17]

Another consideration was the judiciary's indulgent approach towards individuals suspected of corruption. In an explanation, Chin A Sen mentioned the fact that 'opposition and stagnation had rendered a radical intervention necessary'.[18] To this end, a Special Court of Justice consisting of civilians and military personnel was established by decree on 8 September 1980.[19] This initiative led to the conviction of several ministers and senior officials. Many cases were however dismissed as there was simply no evidence of corruption. Indeed, nothing could be brought forward in order to incriminate the deposed Prime Minister Arron.[20]

After August 1980, the prime minister also occupied the position of executive president. In addition, André Haakmat, a lawyer who had returned from the Netherlands, was given an influential position in the cabinet as Deputy Prime Minister, Minister of Foreign Affairs, Justice, the Army and the Police. Of a much greater importance to the balance of power, however, formed the fact that the military leadership (now officially referred to as Military Authority) had for the first time been institutionalised as a political factor. According to Decree A-1, the power of the government lay in the hands of the president, the council of ministers and the Military Authority. Hence, the army command had become a co-legislator.[21] A few months later, by decree, it was decided that the Military Authority would provide a substitute for the president if he was incapable of governing.[22]

The intervention of 13 August was in fact an administrative coup carried out by the military commander Bouterse, who had managed to manoeuvre himself and his deputy Roy Horb into the centre of power. Bouterse saw to it that three NMR members (B. Sital, S. Joeman and C. Mijnals) as well as a number of citizens were arrested on suspicion of left-wing putsch plans. The NMR (of which Bouterse had been a member during the first few months of its existence) was thus eliminated as a power factor. It may be added here that this outcome also fitted in with the civilian government's strategy, only to encounter a much stronger opponent in the military leadership. The issue concerning Sital, Joeman and Mijnals took an unexpected turn after their release in March 1981 by order of the military command. Their sentencing to prison terms ranging between 1 and 2 years had provoked strong protests, which were not based on political sympathy but on injustice regarding the punishment; only a small minority of the population of Suriname deemed these accusations credible.[23]

In addition, protests expressed a growing sense of dissent with the curfew, with a ban on gatherings and with other measures restricting freedom. Although no official press censorship existed, intimidating the media had led to self-censorship.[24] During

---

17   Chin & Buddingh' 1987, 44-45; as stated in Decree A dated 13 August 1980, see *Staatsblad* 1980, nr. 59.
18   Chin & Buddingh' 1987, 46.
19   Decree B-9 dated 8 September 1980, see: *Staatsblad* 1980, nr. 72.
20   Meel 2014, 417-418; on p. 399 Meel quotes Arron mentioning a mock execution to which he and several others were subjected which was carried out during his imprisonment in May 1980.
21   *Staatsblad* 1980, nr. 60.
22   Ibid., 1980, nr. 124.
23   Chin & Buddingh' 1987, 45-47.
24   Ramcharan 2008, 173-190;

the putsch, the military had fired grenades at the premises of *De West*, a newspaper which had referred to trade union actions carried out by the military prior to the coup as a mutiny. A few days after 25 February 1980, garrison commander Horb invited representatives of privately-owned media to visit him in the barracks. Here he announced they 'needed to be aware of what is being published and how'.[25] On occasion chief editors had to justify themselves to the military. Certain newspapers were even banned for several days.

Bouterse's opportunistic manoeuvre in March 1981 not only reinforced his position vis-à-vis the overwhelmed President Chin A Sen. Bouterse also paved the way for left-wing radical groups. In a press conference attended by the now released Sital, Joeman and Mijnals, he referred to a 'revolutionary process' stating that

> '*We all aspire to a socialist society, where there is work for all of us, where there is social justice, and where there is no more exploitation, racism or other oppression.*'[26]

Sital spoke of working towards a 'people's democracy, where there will be no place for the old, traditional parties'.[27] In particular for small left-wing parties, the gunshots fired on 25 February 1980 had sounded like blasts of a clarion signalling a genuine revolution. Its members had advocated breaking down of traditional ethnic barriers, but for this very reason had never crossed the electoral threshold. Now, unexpectedly, they not only saw an opportunity to participate in the power of the state but also to transmute their ideas into reality. Iwan Krolis and Rubin Lie Pauw Sam (1943-2018), respective leaders of the *Progressieve Arbeiders- en Landbouwersunie* (PALU; Progressive Workers and Farmers Union) and the *Volkspartij*, sat on the Advisory Council, which the NMR had established in order to serve as a counterweight for the civilian government. The prominent trade union leader and PNR member Fred Derby (1940-2001) and the non-attached lawyer Harvey Naarendorp also participated. Later, a controversy arose within the *Volkspartij* concerning the support for the military. A group of intellectuals oriented towards Cuba split off to then found the *Revolutionaire Volkspartij*. Whereas the latter party wished to continue its support of the military authorities unconditionally, Lie Pauw Sam now retired from the political stage.

The radical groups responded with their ideas regarding the mobilisation of the people to the growing need of a military leadership to build up their own support base. For, on 25 February 1980, putchists had conquered the nation state of Suriname but not its inhabitants. The reversal in favour of left-wing radical groups resulted on 1 May 1981 in publishing a *Manifest van de Revolutie*. This document, drawn up by Krolis, praised the military as 'the brave sons of our people', placing them on a par with Maroons such as Boni and Jolicoeur.[28] For the first time, the radical left, in prose laden with slogans, explicated its wish to take a hard line:

---

25   Ibid., 174.
26   *De Volkskrant*, 7 March 1981.
27   Ibid.
28   Chin & Buddingh' 1987, 47.

'This implies we will fundamentally demolish the untruthful parliamentary democracy of neo-colonialism in order to rebuild a new true democracy from scratch, with the essential influence of specialised mass organisations of our people being guaranteed. [...] Revolution is never based on the lowest common denominator of the interests and views found in the rubble of neo-colonial society, but is based on and guided by the well-chosen interests in society, which are recognized as basic essential facets of the great national interest. In Suriname, the interests of the large sections of our people are disadvantaged by means of colonialism and neo-colonialism. They are therefore the interests of our entire people, with the exception of the kompradores, the profiteers who have built up their empty existence from the crumbs that have fallen from the tables of our exploiters and wish to continue that existence at all costs. [...] Disguised as true revolutionaries, they have pushed themselves to the forefront of the revolution in order to frustrate and endanger the process. Let's expose them, those quasi-revolutionaries who wish to reverse the process.'[29]

A few days after the publication of this manifesto, Krolis and Naarendorp were included in the *Beleidscentrum* (Policy Centre). This unofficial cooperation organ of the president and the military leadership began to function more and more as an alternative government. President Chin A Sen now faced two radical politicians. Their main aim was not only to weaken his position but also to place Bouterse, whose political ambitions were blossoming, in the forefront as their strong man. Naarendorp was already serving as a Minister of Foreign Affairs and Justice, having succeeded the far more moderate Haakmat, who had resigned after an argument with Chin A Sen. A few months after taking office, Naarendorp established diplomatic relations with Cuba.[30] The RVP supporters hereby maintained frequent contact with the Cuban mission, which gave advice on how to develop revolutionary organisations.[31] After the 1980 coup, the NMR founded the *Bureau Volksmobilisatie* (People's Mobilisation Bureau), which set up people's committees both inside and outside Paramaribo. In accordance with the revolutionary view, these institutes were to be given the same task as the Committees for the Defence of the Revolution fulfilled in Cuba.[32] In 1982, an unpublished document entitled *Doel, structuur van de volkscomités* (Purpose, structure of the people's committees) hailing from the *Bureau Volksmobilisatie*, now acting a revolutionary think tank, states:

'Defence includes the timely detection of possible saboteurs [...] and the passing on to the leadership of movements and manoeuvres by the enemies of the revolution and the strict execution of the commands of the leadership with regard to the tactical approach to these enemies.'[33]

---

29   *Manifest van de Revolutie*, 1 May 1987, 12-13.
30   Chin & Buddingh' 1987, 48; the former Prime Minister Arron had previously signed a treaty with Cuba on establishing diplomatic relations, which had never been ratified, see: Janssen 2011, 110.
31   Cardenas 1988, 13-20.
32   Chin & Buddingh' 1987, 48, 51-52.
33   Document included in private archives of the present author.

This document exuded a political culture completely alien to the majority of the population of Suriname. It thus promoted a revolution which was in fact never a revolution. In the course of 1981 a power-political, ideological struggle between the vast majority of the civil sector on the one hand, and the military top and the radical left on the other hand, took on a much more open character.[34] Commander Bouterse, constantly prompted by his radical advisors, stated that the troops would not return to their barracks, not even by a long shot. A draft constitution presented by Chin A Sen and drawn up by a special committee, could find no mercy in Bouterse's eyes. This draft was based on a governance model in which political parties, social groups and popular organisations each had a role to play. Bouterse's objections focused mainly on the position of the military leadership, which only fulfilled an advisory role within a revolutionary council. The military and their radical advisors were mainly interested in a model made up of a democratic style of ruling comprising only social groups and people's structures, thus enabling them to keep a firm grip on political developments. The final parting of ways became manifest on 17 December 1981 when Bouterse in Paramaribo proclaimed a revolutionary front in the presence of delegations from Cuba and Nicaragua, whereas Chin A Sen now in the Coronie district warned against 'evil forces that threaten to take over society'.[35]

The fall of Chin A Sen's government on 4 February 1982 formed the logical conclusion of a process that had already begun immediately after the coup. The direct reason hereof was the President's refusal to deliver a speech written by the PALU foreman Krolis, in which the former distanced himself from his earlier promise to allow free elections to be held in October 1982. On Bouterse's request, Chin A Sen resigned after two PALU ministers had turned against him. A month earlier, thousands of inhabitants of Suriname had shown affection to their leader during a demonstrative anniversary meeting organised in Chin A Sen's presidential palace. After his resignation however no expressions of support were heard. Chin A Sen had little to expect from the old political parties, as they considered him to be a conspirator who, together with the military, had put an end to their rule rather than as an ally in the fight against the advancing dictatorship.[36] In December 1981, the highest echelons at the Dutch Ministry of Defence had already decided to support Bouterse's intelligence service in order to prevent an increase of Cuban influence in Suriname. A month later, the US pledged its support for this stabilisation policy after the Head of the Army Intelligence Service, Colonel A.W. Schulte, had not only explained this Dutch policy in Washington, D.C., but had also complained about the confrontation policy which the US embassy had pursued in Paramaribo.[37]

At the same time little remained of the initial enthusiasm for Bouterse. Indeed, not only among the civilian population of Suriname had the aversion towards those in power grown. Within army ranks, too, Bouterse could no longer count on the undivided support amongst his troops. The attempted putsch on 11 March 1982 carried out by the former Lieutenant Soerendre Rambocus, after stating his wish to restore

---

34   Chin & Buddingh' 1987, 48-50.
35   Ibid., 49-50.
36   Ibid., 50; Dew 1994, 70-75.
37   De Graaf & Wiebes 1998, 363-364.

A History of Suriname

democracy in Suriname, had almost succeeded. The summary execution of a conspirator, sergeant-major Wilfred Hawker (c.1955-1982), one of the coup plotters linked to 25 February 1980, met with general disapproval.[38]

The military leadership left no room for any misunderstandings as to its real intentions. With the Decree A-9 (dated 25 March, 1982) this dictatorship was in fact enacted by law.[39] The highest administrative power fell into the hands of the aforementioned policy centre, which was to further determine 'the direction and policy of the revolutionary process'. Commander Bouterse and his deputy were responsible for the composition of this body, in which they themselves officiated as both chairman and vice-chairman. Moreover, this policy centre proposed ministers whom the president appointed and who then received a purely ceremonial task. Incoming members of government appointed to serve in the cabinet, led by the economist Henry Neijhorst, were merely puppets of the military command. In fact, the same could be said when referring to the then acting President Fred Ramdat Misier (1926-2004), the Court's former Vice President.

As a result of their revolutionary course, the military and their advisors alienated themselves from all major social groups. The radical left considered an independent trade union movement a direct threat to the revolution. In August 1982, members of the *Federatie van Arme Landbouwers* (FAL; Federation of Poor Farmers) which was part of C-47, the trade union confederation, placed blockades in Nickerie District in order to obtain better rice prices from the government. On this occasion a military unit detained several FAL leaders. In September, members of the now established armed people's militia occupied the premises of the trade union named Moederbond. The Revolutionary Front, which initially included C-47 and the Moederbond, had collapsed due to internal dissent. Strikes in the health and education sectors caused matters to deteriorate. Huge unrest was observed at the University of Suriname when the authorities wished to install a 'revolutionary' board.[40]

The concept of thinking in terms of enmity had made its entry into the politics of Suriname.[41] For critics of the military regime, the description of counter-revolutionary worms (based on the Cuban term *gusanos*) became the norm. Supporters of left-wing radical groups had taken over the state media, which were only utilised to spread revolutionary propaganda. Their main target was Cyrill Daal (1936-1982), the Moederbond chairman, who had received advice from former Minister André Haakmat. Daal had organized strikes when Grenada's Prime Minister, Maurice R. Bishop (1944-1983) visited Suriname. It must have been a personal humiliation for Bouterse to be obliged to receive Bishop, a revolutionary leader whom he hugely admired, at a candlelit venue after these strikes had caused the blackout of electricity. After initial successful strike actions, Daal announced an initiative to completely paralyse Suriname in order to force free elections. His popularity was proven by means of a mass meeting held on 31 October 1982, which mobilized 15,000 people. On that very same day Bouterse had barely been able to mobilize 1,500 supporters in

---

38   Chin & Buddingh' 1987, 50-51; Dew 1994, 75-77.
39   *Staatsblad* 1982, nr. 61.
40   Chin & Buddingh' 1987, 52-53; Dew 1994, 77-79.
41   Chin & Buddingh' 1987, 53-59; Dew 1994, 79-86.

honour of Bishop's visit. An enraged Bouterse announced he would pay Daal back in cash.[42] Bishop himself responded with the following, equally fanatical plea.

> *'Revolution is not a tea party. Revolutions worldwide have often been made at the cost of blood. And that is why comrades, we never treat contrarevolution as a joke. They will see us as their sworn enemies, just as we have to see them as our sworn enemies. The Surinamese revolution is too friendly. Reactionary forces are strong. You have to eliminate those who are not with you, otherwise they will eliminate you.'*[43]

Due to dissent within the trade union movement, strike actions did not produce the desired result. C-47 leader Fred Derby feared that Daal was overplaying his hand by demanding the immediate return of the soldiers to the barracks. Explaining his absence on October 31, Derby later stated that he 'will not participate in a play without knowing the endgame'.[44] The Moederbond's leader gave up any further strike actions after Deputy Commander Roy Horb promised, on the Policy Centre's behalf, to present 'new verifiable democratic structures', including 'general and secret elections'.[45] However, this agreement revealed dissent within the military leadership when the Policy Centre, which included radical civilian politicians, refused to confirm Horb's pledge in an official communiqué.[46] Bouterse's role was most remarkable, to say the least. In September, during a secret meeting held on the plantations named Katwijk and Wederzorg, he had on the issue of democratisation in fact fully agreed with André Haakmat, the Moederbond's adviser. Their discussion resulted in an agreement about free elections to be held in July 1983 at the latest.[47]

Tensions rose in a frightening manner early November when Horb was detained in the barracks on Bouterse's order, forcing a televised statement in which Haakmat was portrayed as an unreliable intriguer. This event, not coincidentally, took place shortly after Daal, the Moederbond's leader, had made public how a few days earlier he and his advisor Haakmat had reached an agreement with Horb concerning the restoration of democracy.[48] Accusations the government forwarded suggesting the US embassy had played a role in actions undertaken by the Moederbond at the end of October had contributed to this heated atmosphere. Haakmat fled Suriname after unidentified persons had fired bullets at his residence.[49]

Developments accelerated when the now united trade union movement presented a joint plan aimed at a step-by-step democratization. The core of this proposal was: an assembly comprising representatives of key civil society organisations would within several months adopt a law on political parties and a constitution.[50] While negotiations

---

42   Ramsoedh 2018, 164,.
43   Ibid.
44   Marshall 2010, 161.
45   Haakmat 1987, 181-182; here Haakmat quoted from a statement by the Moederbond, dated 2 november 1982.
46   Ibid., 185; *NRC Handelsblad,* 5 November 1982.
47   Ibid., 159-166.
48   Ibid., 186-187.
49   Ibid., 192-194.
50   Chin & Buddingh' 1987, 54-55; Dew 1994, 81-82.

with the Policy Centre on this so-called 'phased plan' were continuing, Bouterse's sudden televized announcement on 15 November formed a breaking point in the tumultuous developments. Stating not only that 'the leadership of the revolutionary process' would present its democratisation plans towards the end of March 1983 at the latest, he also was to 'announce how the discussion with you will continue'; it was a clear attempt to take back the initiative and to allow only those groups 'who continue to be loyal to the new democratic, people-oriented and patriotic principles' to have their say.[51] This statement provoked the following furious reaction from the trade union movement: 'The announcement of 15 November is a clear demonstration that those in power, and their 'confidential' advisors, have not understood one iota of the common convictions of Suriname's people'.[52] Towards the end of November, the military regime faced not only the trade unions, but almost the entire population of Suriname. Important social groups, including all religious organisations as well as associations of employers, lawyers, editors, publishers, doctors, farmers and women, had united in the *Associatie voor Democratie* (Association for Democracy). It delivered its criticism in a fundamental manner by means of an extensive letter (dated 23 November 1983) addressed to commander Bouterse:

'[...] *You speak of democratic structures and consultation, participation, control and accountability, but the leadership of the state, as united in your person among others, must be accepted by the people as an unshakeable fact. Apparently the people are not yet considered by you to have the insight to choose their own representatives. We understand this to mean that the socio-educational and political-administrative approach you advocate has not yet sufficiently conditioned the people to choose what you stand for. However, this is by no means a democratic, but rather a totalitarian, view of the state. After all, such a vision is characterised by the fact that the leadership's view is decisive and only those who, in broad lines, loyally support that view, are allowed to participate in its further elaboration and implementation. [...] Adult and free citizens regard it as their inalienable right to choose their own leaders and representatives in a state framework, for that is the essence of the set of rights that is referred to as 'political rights and freedoms'. In the 20th century, trying to convince a population such as ours of the opposite seems to us to be an impossible task given her level, her cultural-historical background, her political tradition and her interest in political events. [...].*'[53]

For Bouterse, the time for compromising had passed. A demonstration several thousand pupils and students held early December was dispersed. The real confrontation unfolded even earlier than expected. It displayed a brutality that no resident of Suriname would have considered possible. In the night of 7 to 8 December, the premises of the Moederbond, the daily *De Vrije Stem* and the radio stations *ABC*

---

51   Televised speech by D. Bouterse, 15 November 1982; the full text hereof is included in the present author's private archives.
52   Chin & Buddingh' 1987, 56.
53   Sedney 2017, 137-138; Chin & Buddingh' 1987, 56-57.

Figure 13.1. The then army chief Desi Bouterse flanked by journalist André Kamperveen, shortly before the latter's execution on December 8, 1982 in Fort Zeelandia. This screenshot originates from a VHS recording which includes a 'confession' by Kamperveen (who had served as FIFA's vice-president) concerning a conspiracy as to a coup. This footage was never broadcast on national television, though this had been intended to be the case. For, Kamperveen had been visibly mistreated. However, it was shown during the criminal trial at Paramaribo, that began late 2007. C/o Eddy Wijngaarde.

and *Radika* were set alight. At the same time army units detained 16 prominent opponents who were taken to the army headquarters located inside Fort Zeelandia.

On 8 December, 15 of these 16 men were executed: the lawyers John Baboeram, Kenneth Gonçalves, Eddy Hoost and Harold Riedewald; the journalists Bram Behr, Lesley Rahman, Jozef Slagveer and Frank Wijngaarde; the trade union leader Cyrill Daal; the university lecturers Gerard Leckie and Sugrim Oemrawsingh; the soldiers Soerendre Rambocus and Jiwan Sheombar; the former Minister (and owner of the radio station ABC) André Kamperveen and the businessman Robby Sohansingh. The trade union leader Fred Derby, having been allowed to leave Fort Zeelandia at the very last moment, was the sole survivor of what would have been called the December murders. All victims had been carefully selected. Gonçalves had signed the Association for Democracy's declaration on behalf of the Bar Association, as had Wijngaarde on behalf of the Association of Media Directors. Rambocus and Sheombar, having participated in the March 1982 insurrection, had served a prison sentence. Baboeram and Riedewald had defended putsch leader Rambocus in court. Leckie had inspired student actions. The four journalists had been the most fearless of all their colleagues when criticising the dictatorship.

Shortly after these 16 men had been detained, Bouterse declared they had planned a conspiracy. The only evidence hereof comprised (a) the 'confession' that Slagveer, visibly maltreated, had made on national television that evening and (b) a radio statement given by the heavily molested Kamperveen. The official explanation for the death of the 15 men was: they had been 'shot on the run'.[54] S. Amos Wako, the Special UN Rapporteur, concluded in his investigation presented on 12 February 1985 that 'summary or arbitrary executions' had taken place at Fort Zeelandia; his report also included statements provided by 'at least five eyewitnesses' describing that military commander Bouterse and his deputy Roy Horb had attended these executions (see also p. 377).[55] The murder of their 15 opponents was apparently primarily a matter for the group of sergeants who had carried out the coup d'état in 1980. They had prepared the scenario for this night-time action as was confirmed during the later trial (see p. 411).[56] Critical officers, who no longer wished to identify themselves with the military leadership were soon removed. A majority of these men sought refuge in the Netherlands.

Towards the end of January 1983, the military police arrested Deputy Commander Roy Horb along with several civilians, on conspiracy charges. He passed away 3 days after his arrest and detention after committing suicide, according to the official reading. The bitter joke circulated in Paramaribo he had 'hanged himself on the run'.[57] In the meantime, two US diplomats who had been accused a few months earlier of interfering with trade union actions in 1982 were expelled.[58] Certain democratic forces had considered Horb, whose funeral mobilized thousands, to be the only person capable of ousting Bouterse by means of a counter-coup. Horb's October 1982 visit, which Bouterse had permitted, to the former President Chin A Sen, now exiled in Pittsburgh (PA., USA), had even at this stage led to rumours that a takeover of power was imminent. Horb had frequently explicated he had little in common with the army's leadership's radical advisors.

No serious evidence has ever been presented as to Bouterse's accusation that, in the autumn of 1982, Horb had prepared a coup which the CIA (Central Intelligence Agency) had supported. Plans for a military intervention, as the then US Secretary of State George Shultz mentions in his memoirs, did not emerge until after the December murders. He reports that these plans were not only mainly aimed at reversing the Cuban influence in Suriname but also came up against (a) the Dutch unwillingness to participate and (b) resistance voiced in the US Congress.[59] The American President Ronald Reagan first deals with the events in Suriname in a diary entry (date 26 December 1982) thus:

---

54 *NRC Handelsblad*, 10 December 1982.
55 Wako 1985, 10.
56 Boerboom & Oranje 1992, 53-65.
57 Chin & Buddingh' 1987, 59; Dew 1994, 86. It may be added here that three of Horb's bodyguards later died under suspicious circumstances.
58 Chin & Buddingh' 1987, 176.
59 Shultz 1993, 292-297; Woodward 1987, 265-266; see also: Haakmat 1987, 201-211; here it is mentioned that, in the second half of December 1982, after fleeing Suriname, Haakmat was approached in the Netherlands by US intelligence officers in order to discuss a possible intervention in Suriname.

'I advocate approaching the Dutch about sending in their 4 or 500 marines who are in the Caribbean. We could help legislatively and block out Cuban intervention.'[60]

The sole firm response of The Hague to the December murders comprised the immediate cessation of the extensive development cooperation. With tacit consent of the French authorities based in French Guiana, several Surinamese nationals residing in the Netherlands had started to prepare an armed action. Involving foreign mercenaries, this initiative was directed against the military dictatorship. However, the French authorities had to deport these nationals as soon as this covert operation became generally known.[61] The USA called upon Brazil for assistance in order to increase the military pressure on Paramaribo. After all, the government of Brazil was also gravely concerned about the ever-growing Cuban influence on its northern border. Moreover, Bouterse's visit to the Libyan leader Colonel Muammar Gaddafi (1942-2011), when returning to Suriname from a meeting of the Non-Aligned Movement in New Delhi, had caused concern in Washington, D.C., and in Brasilia.[62]

When describing April 1983, Reagan referred three times to a briefing recorded by the National Security Council (NSC) concerning Suriname.[63] On 4 April, he reports the veto of several plans. Next, it was decided to ask Brazil and Venezuela for help. On 7 April, a 'solid plan' was 'offered' to these two nation states. Both were supposed to provide several hundred combat troops, whereby the USA would provide 'Naval & Air support'. As Venezuela did not agree, a 'different concept' presented by Brazil was discussed during a meeting held in the presence of Reagan and the NSC on 11 April. In his diary it was referred to as 'Operation Guiminish'. The goal, according to Reagan, remained: 'to take Suriname back into the family of Am. States before it becomes a Cuban patsy'.

The unprecedented Brazilian action followed not much later that very same month. The then President of Brazil João Figueiredo (1979-1985) sent his highest national security officer and advisor, General Danilo Venturini (1922-2015), to Paramaribo. While conversing with Bouterse, Venturini made it absolutely clear that Brazil would not allow any Cuban influences to enter its neighbour Suriname. In exchange for concessions, Paramaribo could count on military supplies as well as trade benefits. Venturini's 'diplomatic invasion' and the unveiled threat of military intervention did not miss their goal. The incoming cabinet's draft government statement was immediately stripped of revolutionary rhetoric.[64]

The Surinamese-Brazilian rapprochement, however, led to great divisions within the army and the government. The PALU along with the *Revolutionaire Volkspartij* (RVP) were the only groups still willing to uphold links with military authorities after the December murders and to participate in a cabinet. The incoming PALU Prime Minister Errol Alibux had even praised the military commander Bouterse

---

60   Reagan 2007, 122.
61   Hoogbergen & Kruijt 2005, 101-102.
62   Chin & Buddingh' 1987, 177; Janssen 2011, 127.
63   Reagan 2007, 141-143.
64   Chin & Buddingh' 1987, 177-178; Janssen 2011, 120-121.

as being a 'shining example'.[65] Both parties fought an on-going battle for influence within the military centre of power. The more nationalist-oriented PALU considered curbing Cuban influence as the perfect opportunity to strike out at the RVP. By means of various visits to Brazil, Prime Minister Alibux (1983-1984) rapidly reinforced ties with Brasilia. The Minister of People's Mobilisation B. Sital, an RVP affiliate, considered the Brazilian aid offer to be a 'diktat' and resigned.[66] His temporary exile in Cuba, arranged on Bouterse's request, was intended to pacify Suriname. Foreign pressure nonetheless remained. During a UN General Assembly, in September 1983, US officials made it clear to Paramaribo that Suriname's reaction to the Brazilian step was considered insufficient. Reagan specifically referred to 'the streets of Suriname' in his speech to the UN, demonstrating Washington, D.C.'s concerns.[67] Moreover, Bouterse expelling the Cuban Ambassador Osvaldo Cardenas just after the US invasion of Grenada, on 25 October 1983, was no coincidence. Before and after the expulsion, Suriname's military commander had held lengthy talks with the US Ambassador.[68] This Cuban influence implied that information from the Policy Centre often ended up on Cardenas's desk that very same day. Bouterse must have deemed it a potential threat to his personal position, especially after the events in Grenada during which extremists murdered Prime Minister Maurice Bishop. When Cardenas's expulsion was announced, Bouterse, with a sense of understatement, had mentioned the diplomat's 'somewhat typical' modus operandi.[69]

For Bouterse, after the December murders, the battle to stay in power had also become a struggle for survival. As soon as all civil liberties were resolutely terminated, the fear amongst the population led to a new wave of emigration, especially of skilled personnel. *De Ware Tijd*, the only newspaper to be printed, merely served as the regime's mouthpiece. Only the state-run SRS continued broadcasting. Moreover, the Suriname News Agency (SNA) was placed under military command. The dissemination of information potentially endangering 'peace or national security' was prohibited by decree.[70] A report the Organisation of American States (OAS) published after carrying out a mission to Suriname in 1983, states its population was struck by 'intense fear'.[71] Bouterse's leadership nevertheless was put to the test by means of a mass strike in the bauxite sector. This action taken in December 1983 and January 1984 was initially directed against plans aimed at tax increases. It served an attempt to acquire a USD 100 million loan from the International Monetary Fund (see p. 317). The strike turned political when strikers also demanded secret elections. Not a single trade union dared to support this initiative, which spread to several other sectors. Secondary school students joined in, too. Its leaders remained anonymous for fear of army reprisals. Troops sent to Suralco's bauxite site in order to 'protect those willing to work' had

---

65 This statement was made on 25 February 1983 at the commemoration of the 'revolution' in Paramaribo, see: *Leidse Courant*, 28 February 1983.

66 Chin & Buddingh' 1987, 61.

67 As stated in an address delivered at the U.N. General Assembly (New York, 26 Sept. 1983).

68 Chin & Buddingh' 1987, 177-179.

69 Ibid., 61.

70 As stated in the Decree B-10, see: *Staatsblad* 1983, nr. 55.

71 Inter-American Commission on Human Rights, *Report on the Human Rights Situation in Suriname*, 5 October 1983, doc. 6, rev. 1, ch. II, 12.

returned without having taken any action and after the commander had established it was not, as was suggested, a 'small terror group'.[72] As a result of political complications it would have been difficult to imagine that the army would have gained access to the premises of this US multinational, a fact of which strikers were well aware. Bouterse had already dismissed the Errol Alibux-led cabinet 'because of mistakes'.[73] This outcome was not good enough for the strikers, who wanted the real rulers to step down. In the end they did accept a financial compensation, but only after Alcoa had closed the bauxite company for an indefinite period.

As a result of their political isolation and the growing economic crisis, in part caused by the postponement of Dutch aid, the military rulers of Suriname were forced to seek cooperation with organisations that could count on more support than the left-wing splinter parties had acquired. Once again Bouterse demonstrated his political agility. For, two employers' organisations, to wit, the *Vereniging Surinaams Bedrijfsleven* (VSB; Surinamese Trade and Industry Association) and the *Associatie van Surinaamse Fabrikanten* (ASFA; Association of Surinamese Manufacturers) as well as the trade union confederations now indicated their willingness to participate in a government tasked with creating 'sustainable democratic structures' after an 11-month transition period.[74]

13.1 The 25 February Movement

At the same time, from November 1983 on, the military attempted to establish a political power base with the founding of the 25 February Movement (VFB), named Stanvaste (Gomphrena globosa), a strong plant native to Central and South America.[75] These men had learned from the failure of the Revolutionary Front, of which only organisations were allowed to become members, resulting in major internal conflicts. Thus, only individuals could register for the VFB, at that time the only allowed political organisation. In the eyes of its ideologists, the VFB was to not only become a revolutionary unitary movement following in the best traditions of the people's democracies but also, at the same time, the army's political arm. In the foreword to the VFB programme, which was adopted at its official establishment on May 12, 1984, Commander Bouterse, now referred to as Leader of the Revolution, wrote about

> *the heart of this unity which beats where the military vanguard becomes profoundly involved with the bearers of our direct national production, i.e., our workers and our farmers.'*[76]

It was obvious that the members of the Military Authority who had led Suriname 'in our liberation fight' were chosen in a resolution adopted by its members as the Central Leadership: Desi Bouterse, now a lieutenant-colonel, as the Chairman and Etienne Boerenveen and Paul Bhagwandas, the second and third in command,

---

72 Chin & Buddingh' 1987, 62-63; Dew 1994, 95-97; *NRC Handelsblad*, 14, 16 and 17 January 1984.
73 *NRC Handelsblad*, 9 January 1984; this resignation followed when this company's personnel went on strike.
74 Chin & Buddingh' 1987, 63.
75 Chin & Buddingh' 1987, 81-90.
76 Ibid., 83.

as the Secretary and Treasurer. The most important ideologues of the VFB were Harvey Naarendorp, revolutionary of the first hour, and former NPS member Jules Wijdenbosch. According to them, no free elections could be held for the time being because:

> 'If you hold elections right away, you get the same situation as before. During its initial phase the vanguard rules because they showed the most courage in intervening in a situation which had gone wrong, because they put their lifes on the line [...].'[77]

Even in a booklet for a literacy campaign, entitled the 25th of February 1980, the day that Bouterse et al. carried out their coup, was referred to as a 'great day' on which the 'Revolution for our people' began.[78] According to the authoritative and always critical Committee Christian Churches, the VFB took 'enmity as a basis for action. This is contrary to Christianity and many other religions, and also contrary to the national character and to peace'.[79]

The core of the 25-February Movement consisted of soldiers, radical sympathisers and a number of the *c.*250 members of the people's militia. Board meetings usually did not attract more than a few hundred interested attendees. The ties with the army nevertheless provided the VFB with a key position within the state apparatus. VFB members occupied cabinet seats as well as strategic positions in the civil service and in public enterprises. Moreover, the People's Mobilisation Bureau had links with the Ministry of the Interior and District Administration, which enabled the VFB to obtain public funds for its own political activities. In support of the 'revolution', the movement also annexed Anton de Kom's spiritual legacy (about De Kom see p. 226-229). The University of Suriname, which was closed after the December murders in 1982, was reopened 10 months later and renamed Anton de Kom University in order to symbolize 'the spiritual liberation of the people of Suriname'.[80] All its heads of faculties were now chosen by VFB members.[81] In the same period buttons were distributed with portraits of Bouterse and De Kom. The newly printed banknotes now depicted De Kom. The portrait of the Leader of the Revolution, in military uniform with a bright blue sky in the background, was from then on displayed in all public buildings.

The VFB's support, however, remained small. This movement did not fit in with the Surinamese tradition of political leaders who stemmed from religious, cultural and ethnic groups. Attempts were made to gain influence among Muslim groups, whose members had always been sceptical about the strong Hindu influence in the VHP. The success was limited despite the financial support Libya made available

---

77   Ibid., 84.

78   Ministry of Education, *Suriname voorwaarts!* (campaign Alfa '84), 1984, 117.

79   See p. 5 of a statement published by Comité Christelijke Kerken entitled *Commentaar op concept basisuitgangspunten en hoofdlijnenprogramma van de 25 Februari Beweging* (Comments on draft basic principles and outline programme of the February 25 Movement) which was signed by A. Zichem, Bishop of Paramaribo and Th. A. Darnoud, President of the Moravian Brethren at Paramaribo on 15 November 1983.

80   Boots & Woortman, 2009, 390.

81   Inter-American Commission on Human Rights (IACHR), *Second report on the human rights situation in Suriname*, Washington, 2 October 1985.

for Islamic religious activities. The influence in the trade union movement was minimal, too. Those leaders, who joined the VFB, lost support. The board of the trade union federation Moederbond, whose leader Cyrill Daal had been killed during the December murders, had to pay dearly for its uncritical attitude towards the military when a large number of unions departed to then, a few years later, unite in the *Organisatie van Samenwerkende Autonome Vakbonden* (OSAV; Organisation of Cooperating Autonomous Trade Unions). Neither could one count on the support of the more than 100 people's committees established since 1980. For, it was mainly supporters of the old political parties who had signed up to participate in these committees. They were only interested in material benefits, in accordance with the best traditions of political clientelism. The military regime was however unable to meet these expectations due to the severe economic crisis which not only resulted from the discontinuation of Dutch aid but also from the economic downturn in the bauxite sector. The VFB's largest impediment formed the absolute predominance of the military regime, which after the trauma of the December murders, had lost all sympathy among the population.

13.2 Dialogue with 'old' politicians

Towards the end of 1984 an Assembly was installed in Paramaribo to serve as a legislative body. Its founding was the outcome of a collaboration within the interim cabinet installed 11 months earlier. The concept had been prepared in a so-called think tank with participation of the Revolutionary Leadership, the trade union movement and the business community. The Assembly included members of (a) the VFB (14 seats), (b) the trade union confederations (11 seats) and (c) the employers (6 seats). It thus had a rather corporatist character. The main task to be carried out by the 31 delegates comprised drawing up a new constitution within 27 months.[82] The second interim cabinet of the abovementioned three partners was again led by Wim Udenhout, a former English teacher, more of a pragmatist than an ideologist, and advisor to the military commander Bouterse. Neither of the two cabinets enjoyed any confidence amidst the population. Trade union leaders, having lost a huge part of their authority due to their reluctant stance when bauxite workers went on strike in 1983, were therefore unable to offer the regime a broader base of support within the society of Suriname.

In order to polish its tarnished image, the military regime had relaxed certain restrictions on freedom. These measures were by and large cosmetic. Although privately-owned media were allowed to resume their activities on 1 May 1984, they were as yet not permitted to publish information that could harm the legal authority. Prime Minister Udenhout, totally his masters voice, declared in an explanatory statement, 'one will not pander to those who, under the guise of freedom of expression, wish to prevent the achievement of our national goals by questioning the legitimacy of the revolution'.[83] Another step comprised the lifting of the curfew imposed since the failed coup attempt of March 1982. In January 1985, the National Institute for Human Rights was founded in order to look into complaints. Consisting of government officials, this institute was far from independent. 'It must

---

82   Chin & Buddingh' 1987, 64-65; Dew 1994, 99-102; see also: IACHR, 2 October 1985.
83   *Surinfo* (a bulletin by the Embassy of Suriname in The Hague), July 1984, 12.

be pointed out that its members are appointed by the same authorities whose actions it is to monitor', noted the Inter-American Commission on Human Rights (IACHR) in its report dated 2 October 1985.[84] In its 1986-1987 Report, the IACHR reached the conclusion that the human rights in Suriname were still 'in a precarious state'.[85]

At this stage, Suriname had reached a complete deadlock, both politically and economically. In 1985, Bouterse had no other choice but to start a dialogue with the leaders of Lachmon's VHP and of Arron's NPS, both as yet banned parties. A year earlier secret, but unsuccessful, talks had been held. Bouterse had initially started discussions with Lachmon only who had explicated from the outset he was 'not prepared to talk further about democratisation without the NPS'.[86] This stance was in keeping not only with Lachmon's philosophy of ethnic fraternization, but also with his fundamental understanding of democracy. Bouterse's political opportunism had earned him the nickname *wakaman* ('walking man'), i.e., someone who takes one side, then the other. He now wished to break through the isolation of his regime at home and abroad. With the support of the VHP and the NPS, it would also be easier to implement the necessary economic austerity measures. In addition, the Dutch government could then perhaps be more willing to resume providing development assistance. Conversations were extremely difficult. Lachmon and Arron held on to the democratisation plan they had already forwarded on Bouterse's request a year earlier.[87] They demanded free elections, although they were prepared to accept that the army was to play a supervisory role. The latter wording illustrates the balance of power at the time, to wit, in favour of the military leadership. Bouterse was aiming for a compromise to be as vague as possible, which he would like to present with a certain degree of splendour on the 10th anniversary of independence, on 25 November, 1985.

The parties reached an agreement just in time. Before April 1987, when the incumbent interim cabinet would step down, Suriname was to acquire both a constitution and a people's representative body. This step would be in accordance with the principles of a 'true democracy' whereby 'the dialogue partners guarantee the rule of law'.[88] Lachmon, Arron and Willy Soemita, leader of the Javanese party KTPI, now took part in the so-called *Topberaad* (Supreme Council) in order to discuss political-administrative issues. The participation of the old parties in this important policy-making body placed the Udenhout cabinet in a peculiar position. After the resignation of a few government members on suspicion of corruption, the entire ministerial team eventually stepped down. The VHP, NPS and KTPI then decided to join a new cabinet, which took office in July 1986. The businessman Pertab Radakishun (1934-2001), a VHP member, was the incoming Prime Minister. The political change of direction was especially reflected in foreign policy. The passage in the government's programme on striving to 'strengthen the historical grown ties

---

84   IACHR, 2 October 1985, conclusion 4.
85   IACHR, Annual report 1986-1987, ch. IV, Suriname.
86   Khemradj 2002, 81; also: Meel 2014, 421 and Azimullah 1986, 236-237.,
87   The document, dated 25 May 1984 and titled *Basic Principles and Structures of Democracy*, had been prepared by the VHP but then submitted to the NPS for approval, see: Khemradj 2002, 85; for entire text, see: Azimullah 1986, 288-298.
88   As expressed in a joint statement issued by the political leaders and army chief Bouterse, on 23 November 1985: Azimullah 1986, 299.

with eligible countries' could only mean that the ties with the Netherlands had to be reinforced.[89] However, arrangements for democratisation remained vague. One thing was clear: Bouterse continued to be the most powerful man in Suriname. We see proof hereof when, in February 1987, Bouterse (Chairman of the Supreme Council) announced that Prime Minister Radhakishun had to resign because he no longer had the regime's support. Why? The day before, Radhakishun had forced Henk Herrenberg (the then Minister of Foreign Affairs and an ally of Bouterse) to step down after a number of conflicts had risen.[90] From within the interior of Suriname, members of the Maroon ethnic group led by Ronnie Brunswijk, a former bodyguard of Bouterse, had meanwhile unleashed a guerrilla war, placing the military regime under great pressure (see p. 324ff.).

Attempts by the military to improve the regime's image were severely damaged when, after an undercover operation set up in the USA by the Drugs Enforcement Administration (DEA), Etienne Boerenveen was arrested for allegedly being involved with drug trafficking.[91] In 1986, a Miami (Florida) court sentenced Lieutenant Boerenveen, the then second-in-command of the Surinamese army, to 12 years imprisonment for attempting to establish a cocaine smuggling route into the United States via Suriname to the benefit of South American drug cartels.[92] Laboratories were to be set up in Suriname, too (see also p. 353-357). Such incidents did not really come as a great surprise. For, the President of the Central Bank of Suriname, the former Prime Minister Jules Sedney, resigned and left for the Netherlands in 1983 after the military regime had requested him to become involved with a dubious Colombian loan. In the course of this trial in Miami, strong indications emerged pertaining to the direct involvement of commander Bouterse in the drug trafficking.

These events shed new light on the persistent refusal of the army leadership to relinquish any political influences: only preserving its power would allow the regime to protect its criminal activities. Moreover, the military command had little reason to allow itself to become deprived of monopolising the government apparatus, which had enabled this regime to enrich itself in such a gross manner through the years. In its report on the military rule, the Surinamese Court of Auditors noted on this issue: 'Adherence to established and known official rules, which in normal situations is an official virtue, was often perceived as an attempt to cause 'destabilisation' in the country and was punished.'[93]

13.3 Economic Developments[94]

President Chin A Sen had, in his government statement delivered on 1 May 1980 (indeed, not coincidentally on International Labour Day), announced a 'new socio-economic order' in which differences between the rich and the poor would be smaller. The reinforcement of social policies formed a key element here. The Netherlands

---

89   Ibid., 309.
90   Hoogbergen & Kruijt 2005, 172.
91   *Associated Press*, 25 March 1985 (apnews.com/8c67642423f846d808e01555e9c283d2).
92   *NRC Handelsblad*, 18 November 1986.
93   Rekenkamer van Suriname (Court of Audit of Suriname), *Report 1980-1987*, 21.
94   For an extensive overview of the economic developments witnessed during the military regime, see: Chin
      & Buddingh' 1987, 140-157: majority of the details mentioned here have been sourced from this survey.

was prepared to finance an emergency aid programme comprising 500 million Hfl. Half of this sum had to be spent on the productive sector, 33 per cent on the social sector and 17 per cent on infrastructure. As to social issues, they concerned, inter alia, housing construction, the improvement of old-age benefits and the creation of a state-run health insurance.

Radical members of the PALU and of the RVP, who gradually gained further influence in their role as advisors to the army's leadership, mentioned a desire for greater government influence in order to render the economy of Suriname independent of 'imperialists'.[95] This development nevertheless did not lead to any concrete plans for nationalizations. Future cabinets appointed by military leaders followed a moderate course, too, in spite of the occasionally revolutionary rhetoric. Their main aim was to promote investments across the agriculture, forestry and fishery sectors, as well as to process the products these sectors delivered. The rise in unemployment and urbanisation caused by a disintegration of small-scale agriculture should be reversed in this manner.

However, economic developments took an unexpected turn. After the December murders in 1982, the Netherlands suspended development aid.

The result was an annual reduction in foreign exchange income of almost 200 million Hfl. Simultaneously, developments in the world market also led to a decline in export revenues from the bauxite sector. Alibux and his cabinet, dominated by the PALU and the RVP, which had taken office in 1983, lacked public support for taking appropriate measures. Several large development projects in the housing and agriculture sectors were able to survive thanks to financial resources provided by Suriname itself, causing the foreign exchange reserves to decrease further. In addition, an ambitious state programme provided for a continued high public spending. Military expenditure also rose sharply, although precise figures in support hereof are not available.

The budget deficit reached 312 million Sfl in 1983, to wit, three times as high as in 1982.[96] This deficit was entirely financed by monetary means. Plans to increase taxes failed due to strikes in the bauxite sector (see p. 311). In due course the Alibux-led government collapsed. The government had tried in vain to obtain a loan from the International Monetary Fund (IMF), which, given its radical political colour, was a rather remarkable step.

The incoming interim government continued its policy of monetary financing the public deficit, which in 1985 amounted to 21.5 per cent of GDP; in 1986 and 1987, this percentage, which was probably unparalleled across the globe, was even surpassed by a few percentage points to exceed 26 per cent; the public deficit was almost half of the total expenditure.[97] In April 1984, the government also announced quotas on imports in order to prevent a further reduction in the foreign exchange reserves; these had been so large, partly as a result of the Dutch aid flow, that part of it could be invested abroad. As a result the economy was bound to enter into a negative spiral. The decline in economic activity can be deduced from a sharp drop in the import and export of goods . The value of imports of goods more than halved

---

95   Chin & Buddingh' 1987, 142.
96   Chin & Buddingh' 1987, 148; Central Bank of Suriname, *Report 1982-1985*, 18.
97   IMF Report, *Suriname, A case study of high inflation*, November 1999, 6.

from 921 million Sfl in 1982 to 381 million Sfl in 1987. Exports during this period declined from 765 Sfl to 464 million Sfl.[98] The decline in imports of capital goods and raw materials directly affected the production capacity of companies, which also led to a sharp reduction in export capacity. The real national income per capita therefore fell sharply from 3,680 Sfl in 1983 to 2,970 Sfl in 1987.[99]

Monetary financing, which increased the state's debt to Suriname's central bank from 23 million Sfl in 1981 to 2 billion Sfl in 1987, was no doubt the main cause of the country's economic disruption.[100] The ever-increasing money supply was not matched by a sufficient volume of domestic goods. This led to a strong increase in the demand on the import market which facilitated the creation of a large black market for hard currency. Officially, the fixed exchange rate of 1.80 Sfl against 1 USD was maintained, but in 1987 this rate had already risen to 16 Sfl for 1 USD on the parallel market. The fact that inflation was initially to a certain degree controlled and that it reached 30 per cent only after 1986 was, according to the IMF, mainly a result of strict price controls carried out by the military regime, which imposed severe penalties for infractions.[101] Fear of this regime, moreover, prevented trade unions and workers from striking for higher wages.

Major rice and banana exporters experienced a rise in costs. For, they increasingly had to cover their import requirements by purchasing expensive foreign valuta on the parallel market, while their export earnings had to be deposited into Suriname's central bank's treasury at the official exchange rate. In spite of a postponement of investments, forced by the difficult conditions, production and exports of both sectors remained more or less stable.[102]

Suralco and Billiton, which had formed a joint venture in 1984 to produce alumina, tried to economise as much as possible on their foreign exchange payments. Under the Brokopondo agreement, these two bauxite companies were obliged to pay the local costs (e.g., wages, taxes, material expenses) in USD at the official exchange rate determined at Suriname's central bank. This situation was increasingly unfavourable for companies engaged in the dual exchange rate system. For, when represented in Sfl, the local costs had risen sharply due to over-liquidity. Suralco and Billiton hence remained in the red for consecutive years. Their workforce was therefore almost halved from 5,990 in 1980 to 3,051 in 1987 in addition, less work was outsourced to local companies.[103]

The remaining industrial companies, which produced all, or part of, their output for the local market (comprising food, timber and furniture industries, metal processing, textiles, leather goods) were negatively affected by the decline in consumer purchasing power. Companies depending upon imports of raw materials for their production faced significant expenditure increases in so far as they were

---

98   Central Bank of Suriname, *Report 1982-1985*, 23 and Central Bank of Suriname *Annual Report 1988*, 52.
99   Central Bank of Suriname, *Annual Report 1987*, 10.
100   Ibid., 28-29; Chin & Buddingh' 1987, 155-156; IMF Report, *Suriname, A case study of high inflation*, November 1999, 6; on occasion, according to this report, monetary financing amounted to 20 per cent of GDP.
101   IMF Report, *Suriname, A case study of high inflation*, November 1999, 7-9.
102   Central Bank of Suriname, *Annual Report 1987*, 22-24.
103   Central Bank of Suriname, Report 1982-1985, 41; Central Bank of Suriname, Annual Report 1988, 27.

not allocated foreign exchange at official rates. Several entrepreneurs were forced to close temporarily due to a lack of raw materials. The small-scale of the import substitution industry formed an additional impediment. The price increases on the domestic market positively impacted a company's performance which strict government pricing policies however did strongly mitigate. In addition, a company's room for manoeuvre was limited after a government ban was imposed in 1983 on the dismissal of staff. The total number of official jobs nonetheless, decreased from 98,540 in 1980 to 92,361 in 1987.[104]

From 1983 on, a shortage of hard currency led to an increasingly large shadow economy. In order to spare the official foreign exchange reserves, the so-called EA-system was introduced whereby import licences were granted. The capital letters EA here refer to a decree, but popularly served to abbreviate *Eigen Aanbreng* (Own Provision). EA-importers hereby had to personally obtain foreign currency, without drawing from official reserves. The volume of EA-imports, amounting to only 39 million Sfl in 1985, had already risen to 150 million Sfl in 1987. According to the Central Bank of Suriname, the latter sum represents no less than 30 per cent of total imports (excluding the bauxite sector).[105] These amounts were calculated utilising the official exchange rate, implying that in 1987 EA-imports totalled 81,200,000 USD. Thus, in this year, at the average parallel rate of 1 to 16.2, it must have involved 1.3 billion Sfl. The number of EA-traders was very limited. A majority hereof upheld good relations with military circles. Moreover they had previously hardly been active as traders and often obtained the required import licences after bribing military leaders.

The EA-system thus offered every opportunity to launder black money via the exchange market. The strong growth in EA-imports indicates that illegally acquired funds, for instance, by means of cocaine trafficking had in this manner been laundered. Smuggling goods abroad, where illegal hard currency could be earned, was also an key financial source of EA-imports.

The government considered this form of trade as an opportunity to provide companies with the necessary raw materials and capital goods, despite the scarcity of foreign currency. For the same reason, it established barter trade agreements with a number of countries and foreign firms. For example, cars and agricultural machinery produced by FIAT could now be imported from Italy in exchange for supplies of rice. Moreover, bilateral agreements were concluded on credit lines. As a result of this development, Suriname accumulated a total foreign debt of 154.4 million USD in 1989, a lump sum no longer negligible.[106] For the vast majority of its residents, living standards had dropped significantly after 1982. This outcome can be gauged, *inter alia*, based on a sharp drop in the index of real average labour costs per employee, to wit, from 113 in 1983 to 69 in 1987.[107]

---

104   Ibid. 1982-1985, 41; ibid. 1988, 27.
105   Ibid. 1982-1985, 24; Central Bank of Suriname, *Annual Report 1987*, foreword, 49; Coopers & Lybrand 1990, Statistical Appendix..
106   IMF Staff Country Report No. 95/15, *Recent economic developments*, February 1995, 69.
107   Menke 1998, 199.

CHAPTER 14
Return to civilian rule

14.1 Constitution and elections

The elections held on 25 November 1987 were intended to mark the end of a 7-year military rule. However, Commander-in-chief Bouterse had acquired so many concessions from the 'old' politicians that the military leadership was still able to assert itself. The fragile balance of power was reflected in the incoming constitution drawn up during negotiations at the Supreme Council. Although based on the Western democratic model, this constitution included elements drawn from the Latin American national security doctrine.[1]

Contrary to the 1975 constitution, Suriname now obtained a president with executive powers.[2] He was to be elected by parliament (from now on called *De Nationale Assemblée*) with a two-thirds majority. The vice president is deemed responsible for the cabinet's day-to-day management. At the heart of this new constitution is this assembly, the state's highest body, composed according to general as well as secret elections. However, the National Army, referred to as 'the military vanguard of the people', was charged with 'defending sovereignty and independence as well as protecting the highest rights and freedoms of the country and its people by serving the rule of law, peace and security'; moreover, it had to work on creating 'the national build-up and liberation of the nation'; the military authority's mandate to guarantee conditions under which 'the people of Suriname can achieve and consolidate a peaceful transition to a democratic and socially righteous society' formed a licence for the military leadership to engage with the national government.[3]

The people of Suriname approved this constitution by means of a referendum. However, Bouterse's threat that no elections would take place if the constitution was rejected implied there was no real choice. The electorate was in fact forced to legitimise military power. Nevertheless, these elections evolved into a reckoning with the military regime. The most frequently utilised slogans comprised variations on the 'old shoes' (Sranan Tongo: *owru su*) theme. They had become the electoral symbol of the old parties as large numbers of voters wanted those shoes back. The NPS, VHP and KTPI were united in the *Front voor Democratie en Ontwikkeling* (Front for Democracy and Development) by means of a combined list of candidates to then receive more than 90 per cent of votes. The *Nationale Democratische Partij* (NDP), founded several months earlier under Bouterse's leadership, had to settle for only three of the 51 parliamentary seats.

The Front-led government, presided by Ramsewak Shankar (1937), an agricultural engineer and low profile VHP politician, and the NPS Vice President Henck Arron was extremely cautious when taking action.[4] According to persistent rumours leaders of the old parties had already agreed with the military leadership before the elections,

---

1   See also: Brana-Shute 1990, 213-229; Sedoc-Dahlberg 1990, 173-190; Dew 1994, 139-159.
2   For further details, see: Fernandes Mendes 1989, 224-238 and 309-338.
3   The National Army's role was stipulated in Article 177 of the Constitution, see: Fernandes Mendes 1989, 324.
4   After refusing the post of president, VHP-leader Lachmon had offered it to Arron, who in turn refused as it would have made him a symbol of restoration for many, see: Meel 2014, 458.

Figure 14.1. Party leaders of the United Front portrayed during the election campaign held in 1987: Lachmon (VHP), Soemita (KTPI) and Arron (NPS), from right to left. Collection Arron National Archive Suriname.

Figure 14.2. From right to left: Bouterse congratulates the Front leaders: Arron (NPS), Lachmon (VHP) and Soemita (KTPI) on their election victory, November 1987. Photo by Vincent Mentzel.

A History of Suriname

during a secret meeting held at Leonsberg, which was aimed at preventing the army's influence being further eroded. Officially, this event had always been denied. In 1999, the VHP first published a rendition of the Leonsberg Agreement in a memorial book marking this party's 50th anniversary. According to the text which Arron, Lachmon, Soemita and Bouterse had signed more than 3 months before the elections, all parties would 'look for ways' to eliminate 'the disruption' in their relationships which had arisen after campaign statements by the Politicians. This Agreement referred to a 'joint responsibility' to work on 'stability and national unity' as the basis of 'true democracy', and always 'through dialogue'; according to an explanation added to the VHP's rendition, no further 'secret' agreements occurred.[5] Nevertheless, the promise which the leaders of VHP and NPS had made to alter the constitution after the elections was not fulfilled. The government, having taken office in January 1988, was anxious to avoid almost all confrontations. A small victory was achieved with the adoption in the National Assembly of a law on the *Staatsraad* (Council of State). The military leadership had demanded in vain that this political watchdog should only decide by consensus, which would have enabled it to block any decision.[6]

Much more important was the informal power by and around the military leadership. The government apparatus was not purged. Followers of the former military regime had a major influence on granting import and export licences, foreign exchange allocation, procurement, domestic administration and security services. High-ranking military personnel, sympathisers as well as businessmen were able to continue their corrupt practices without obstructions. Whenever the business elite of the old political parties had not yet become part of the clique, they too were presented with ample opportunity to enrich themselves after power had been passed on. President Shankar described the gravity of the situation in a remarkably frank manner when addressing the National Assembly as follows:

'Corruption cases are often of such a nature that repressive action is not possible, therefore the Public Prosecutor's Office is not in a position to take any action against such persons. The structures in the various departments are such that corruption is facilitated and even encouraged. [...] The existence of a proper system of administrative control of the departments could help to overcome this shortcoming. In practice, it is often the case that people convicted of corruption are retained or even promoted in the same position. It also happens that phone calls from high-ranking persons or politicians are received in order not to remove a particular person from office. It is often the case that those who have given rise to the committing of corrupt acts go unpunished and only the small civil servant is sanctioned; the instigator remains in his post, so that the source of corruption continues to exist.'[7]

It seems highly probable that not only military pressure but also a growing involvement of members of the old parties prevented the Shankar-led government

---

5   *Gedenkboek 50 jaar Vooruitstrevende Hervormings Partij VHP*, Paramaribo 1999, 92-93.
6   Procedural rules for the Council of State, 27 July, 1989, see: *Staatsblad* 1989, nr. 30. (dna.sr).
7   *NRC Handelsblad*, 28 July 1990.

from seriously attempting to tackle the corruption problem. Although this government had, immediately after taking office, reinstated the Court of Auditors, the pressing issues the latter forwarded to ministers usually remained unanswered. Hardly any proper parliamentary control was utilised.

14.2 War in the Interior

Confronted not only with a military shadow force, the civilian government had also lost control of part of Suriname. From 1986 on a guerrilla movement led by a young Ndyuka Maroon, hailing from the Cottica region, named Ronnie Brunswijk (1961) had almost entirely dominated East Suriname. Serving as a member of Bouterse's personal bodyguard, he was dismissed in 1984 because of disciplinary problems after being denied a pay rise. Having initially worked as a warehouse clerk, a kitchen assistant and in gold fields, Brunswijk began purchasing weapons from his military contacts. He then began to commit thefts accompanied by other Maroons whom the army had also dismissed. In an attempt to increase his power base Bouterse had apparently enlisted several hundred Maroons from he Ndyuka people into the army, among them Brunswijk.[8] The latter's popularity grew among the local population based on the distribution, echoing Robin Hood, of goods confiscated during raids on military vehicles. A political dimension arose after a search, in May 1986, was executed at Moengo Tapoe, Brunswijk's home village, during which an army command mistreated local residents and set their dwellings on fire.

Several weeks later Brunswijk held consultations in the Netherlands with representatives of Suriname who had chosen to oppose the military regime, among them former Minister André Haakmat. Brunswijk was encouraged to embark upon a guerrilla war against Bouterse's dictatorship. The former military officer Michel van Rey had fled to the Netherlands, after officiating for several months as the Minister of Defence after the 1980 putsch. He officiated briefly as a military advisor on behalf of Suriname's resistance movement.[9] Its members based in the Netherlands however excelled in mutual dissent. The promised financial and military support thus remained limited. Foreign mercenaries did nevertheless regularly enlist with the so-called Jungle Commando, led by Ronnie Brunswijk.[10]

On 21 July 1986, a small number of armed Maroons raided military posts positioned at the villages of Albina and Stolkertsijver, both located in East Suriname and mainly inhabited by Ndyuka. Here weapons were seized and 12 soldiers detained.[11] This event sparked a protracted domestic war. During the following weeks this small armed group, which first called itself the *Surinaams Nationaal Bevrijdingsleger* (National Liberation Army of Suriname) and later Jungle Commando, carried out several other successful actions. The most important hereof comprised attacking a camp set up by the *Echo Compagnie*, a National Army unit located in East Suriname, whereby an unknown number of fatal casualties befell the latter elite corps. At the same time the town of Moengo was occupied for several weeks, causing the economically relevant

---

8   Hoogbergen & Kruijt 2005, 114; Dew 1994, 120-123; De Vries 2005, 13-18; Van Wetering & Thoden van Velzen 2013, 274-277; Te Dorsthorst 2022, 15-21.
9   Haakmat 1987, 212-220; Hoogbergen & Kruijt 2005, 116-118.
10   For one such mercenary's account, see: Penta 2002.
11   Dew 1994, 123-124; Hoogbergen & Kruijt 2005, 121-125.

Figure 14.3. The Surinamese artist Marcel Pinas designed this memorial to honour the victims of the massacre which took place on November 29, 1986. The central obelisk-shaped column reads *Kibi Wi* (Protect Us). The 38 small surrounding commemorations symbolise the 38 children and adults killed by the National Army. Photo by George Findlay.

local bauxite mining operations to come to a halt.[12] The National Army's response to the Jungle Commando's first actions consisted of a terror campaign. Executed in the vicinity of the Cottica and Marowijne Rivers, it involved deploying the *Delta Force van Inheemsen* (Delta Force of Indigenous Peoples). In the Marowijne, Sipaliwini and Brokopondo districts, a state of emergency had been declared, thereby presenting the military with complete freedom of action. In the Cottica River region almost all the Maroon villages were destroyed. Hostilities reached their darkest hour with the massacre on 29 November 1986 carried out at the village of Moiwana. Here National Army troops murdered in cold blood at least 38 victims mainly women and children.[13] This brutal violence led to a large influx of Maroon refugees into French Guiana. Their number would increase to almost 10,000.[14]

Shortly after the outbreak of this battle, Maroon dignitaries had tried in vain to bring about some form of reconciliation. They did not have any interest in a war in the interior. In addition to the safety of the local population, several other factors played a role. The Paramaribo-based government paid salaries to hundreds of Maroons for officiating either as a captain or as a *basja* (boss, village chief). Many other Maroons residing in the interior carried out paid work for the government,

---

12   Hoogbergen & Kruijt 2005, 123-126, 129-131.

13   Amnesty International, *Suriname, violations of human rights*, 1987; Amos Wako, Special Rapporteur for UN Commission on Human Rights, 44th session, *Summary of arbitrary executions*, 19 January 1988, 36-57; Wako, who visited Suriname (August 1987), estimated the number of civilian deaths during military operations in eastern Suriname at between 150 and 200; he further reported human rights violations and executions of soldiers carried out by the Jungle Commando; Moiwana '86 Human Rights Bureau, *Memre Moiwana*, Paramaribo 1992; see also: The Inter-American Court of Human Rights, *Case of the Moiwana Community v. Suriname, Judgment of February 8, 2006*.

14   The Inter-American Commission on Human Rights (IACHR), *Annual Report 1991*.

too. An armed conflict could cut off this cash flow. A meeting of a delegation led by *granman* (Ndyuka: *gaanma*,) Gazon Matodja (*c.*1904-2011) and accompanied by Jules Wijdenbosch, the Minister of the Interior, proved unsuccessful. For, the latter refused to allow discussions to be held with village chiefs, hailing from the Cottica region, who had been affected by military violence. Gazon Matodja came under increasing pressure from fellow tribesmen who no longer permitted him to travel to Paramaribo again. Bouterse's earlier visit to Gazon Matodja's residence located in Drietabbetje (East Suriname) was of no avail.[15]

Hundreds of people volunteered to participate in this conflict, but many had to be sent home due to a shortage of weapons. Traditional tribal and family relationships created a great sense of solidarity, which was reinforced by the traditional religious cults which members of the Jungle Commando upheld. For example, an amulet (*obia*) served as a means of protection against the enemy. One would often call upon an oracle prior to taking action. Now and again such consults resulted in irresponsible conduct when fighting the National Army. Van Wetering and Thoden van Velzen point to an event on 17 February 1987, which the Jungle Commando refers to as 'the catastrophe', during which five of their men died. A Jungle Commando member described how his fellow combatants stood on one leg in an open field. Each had placed a leaf in his mouth in order to demonstrate their invulnerability after which the National Army 'only had to mow them down'.[16] This event strongly reminds Van Wetering and Thoden van Velzen of the following narrative found in John Gabriel Stedman's report on the war against the Boni:

'*A poor Fellow trusting in his Amulet or Charm, by Which he thought himself invulnerable. Advanced frequently on one of these trees, till very near us, And having Dischar'd his Piece Walk'd off the Way he Came, to Reload With the Greater Confidence and Deliberation, till at Last one of my men - / an intrepid Walloon named Valet / With a Ball Broke the bone of Thigh. [...] Went up to him instantly and Placing the Muzzle of his Musket in his Mouth, blew his Brains & in Which manner Severals of his Countrymen were Knock'd Down – So much for Priest Craft in every Country.*'[17]

The National Army's hostilities, including raids executed among Paramaribo-based Maroons, who were often treated with contempt, only increased the number of the Jungle Commando's supporters, among them Ndyuka and Saramakas. In addition, Brunswijk's men, having established their headquarters on Stoelmans Island, were presented with the required freedom of movement in French Guiana. Here French authorities had always looked at Bouterse's regime with suspicion. Through its contacts with states such as Libya, Suriname could perhaps pose a security risk to the Guiana Space Centre, located northwest of Kourou. In the view of the French, the Jungle Commando provided a means to put pressure on the military regime in

---

15   Hoogbergen & Kruijt 2005, 164-167.
16   Van Wetering & Thoden van Velzen 2013, 306-307.
17   Stedman 1790, 405.

Paramaribo. French, Dutch and US intelligence services kept a close eye on Brunswijk and his commandos.[18]

It is difficult to ascertain if this guerrilla warfare did indeed accelerate the democratisation process. The many dozens of military casualties, whereby the losses amidst Brunswijk's troops were much lower, may have increased the pressure on the Army Command. In December 1986, 6 months after the first clashes, Bouterse announced a new constitution and free elections. The intensity of hostilities waned with the inauguration of President Shankar's government. In Kourou (French Guiana), on 21 July 1989, after difficult negotiations, peace was finally agreed upon by the Jungle Commando and those representing the interior of Suriname.[19] This deal included accordance on releasing prisoners and on alleviating the acute material needs across the interior. Moreover, the government in Paramaribo guaranteed the safe return as well as the sheltering and employing of refugees. The Dutch government had shown its willingness to make development funds available for this goal. According to this agreement, a number of Jungle Commandos were to form part of a special police unit in order to serve in the interior by for example protecting returnees. Next, the National Assembly agreed to establish an amnesty whereby crimes against humanity were explicitly excluded; the state of emergency was lifted.[20]

Shortly after ratifying this peace agreement, Bouterse rejected it as being both a 'betrayal. and 'unconstitutional'.[21] The issue as to integrating part of the Jungle Commando into a special police unit serving the interior met with insurmountable objections raised by military leaders. Bouterse had previously stated that negotiations with 'terrorists' were impossible.[22] In his opinion not only the National Army's honour was at stake. His stance formed a deliberate attempt to weaken the civilian government which he had every interest in undermining, because the NDP's position in the parliament was weak. At that time, this party formed the military command's political arm. Bouterse reinforced his strategy by arming an ethnic group, who attracted attention by means of several violent actions. These Tucajana Amazones, having falsely presented themselves as representatives of all Indigenous groups, were opposed to the Kourou Peace Agreement.[23] Their main complaint was: they were not involved in this accord. Not much later Tucajanas, supported by troops and equipment provided by the National Army, had gained control over a key part of West Suriname. With the support of this army, two more small armed groups of Maroons, to wit, the Mandela (young Matawai) and the Angula (young Saramakas), were formed. They opposed the Kourou Peace Agreement, too. In its 1990-1991 Report, the Inter-

---

18   De Graaff & Wiebes 1998, 368-369.
19   Scholtens 1994, 123-125; , Moiwana 86, *Mensenrechten 1991 Suriname*, Paramaribo 1992, 12-13.
20   Amnesty Law 1989, Staatsblad 1992, nr. 68 (dna.sr/media/136493/Amnestiewet_SB_68_1992.pdf).
21   Moiwana '86, *Mensenrechten 1991 Suriname*, Paramaribo 1992, 13.
22   Hoogbergen & Kruijt, 2005, 197.
23   Dew 1994, 170-173, Hoogbergen & Kruijt 2005, 213-220; according to the latter two authors, the Tucajana included soldiers originating from the Delta Force, who had been involved in the Moiwana massacre and who also held office at Memre Boekoe, a military barracks located in Paramaribo; see also: Te Dorsthorst 2022, 92-107..

American Commission on Human Rights did confirm that members of the Tucajana Amazones and Mandela received military training from the National Army.[24]

The civilian government had lost its grip on developments. Its members now watched how Bouterse profiled himself as a 'peacemaker' when holding a series of meetings with the Jungle Commando, the Tucajanas and Maroon dignitaries. Nevertheless, the violent hostilities which armed groups carried out did as yet not come to a conclusion. The peace negotiations even broke down as a result of a remarkable incident which took place during March 1990 at Moengo, the bauxite centre of Suriname, then occupied by the Jungle Commando. Here a small aeroplane from Colombia carrying 1,000 kg of cocaine had landed. According to its Colombian crew, whom the Jungle Commando had detained, they had lost their way en route to Apoera (West Suriname).[25] Most notably a Cuban exile named Frank Castro, a US resident, had accompanied these Colombians. This former drug dealer who later started working for the CIA, had previously been involved in a failed weapons transport out of Miami and meant for the Jungle Commando.[26]

In the end Brunswijk decided to hand the illicit cargo over to the police. That outcome angered Bouterse hugely as he had requested the transfer of both cargo and crew. This conflict culminated in Brunswijk's arrest inside Bouterse's office, after being set up with an invitation to discuss matters. Two unarmed bodyguards who had accompanied Brunswijk were fatally shot by Bouterse's close associates resembling an event which police refer to as a 'criminal reckoning'.[27] Brunswijk was released by order of the Public Prosecutor's Office and after foreign pressure. Speculations he too was involved in cocaine smuggling would be confirmed in 1999, when a judge officiating in the Dutch town of Haarlem sentenced him in absentia to 8 years in prison for shipping narcotics into the Netherlands.[28]

The peace negotiations, which President Shankar had resumed after Bouterse's preparations, almost came to a standstill. Shankar formally acted as the National Army's commander-in-chief, but his power was nil. On several occasions he openly stated that military operations had not been carried out on the government's behalf. Bouterse did not hesitate to humiliate Shankar during talks held in the palace by sitting opposite him in a neat suit but with bare feet inside dirty shoes, his legs

---

24 Inter-American Commission on Human Rights (IACHR), 1990-1991, Chapter IV); Ronald Karwofodi, the then chief of the Amerindian village named Bernharddorp, informed the present author that high ranking officers had given arms as well as clothing to inhabitants of his village in order to join forces with the Tucajanas, see: *NRC Handelsblad*, 29 November 1997.

25 Dew 1994, 177; Hirschland, *Dossier Moengo '290 uur'*, 1993; here Hirschland, then Brunswijk's secretary, reports on events from hour to hour adding that the crew was able to escape in an as yet unexplained manner.

26 Hirschland 1993, 81, 153-155; Hirschland suggested this cocaine shipment was a trap set by the USA in order to embarrass Bouterse and to keep him under pressure; Douglas Valentine mentions in chapter. 13 of *The CIA as Organized Crime: How Illegal Operations Corrupt America and the World* (2017) that Frank Castro was a former drugs dealer who started working for the CIA. Castro had also joined the Contras in Nicaragua, see: Peter Dale Scott and Jonathan Marshall, *Cocaine Politics: Drugs, Armies, and the CIA in Central America*, Updated Ed., 1998, 30.

27 Hirschland 1993, 130; according to Hirshland, Brunswijk's secretary as based on the latter's testimony, these two were shot by militaries Rupert Christopher and Melvin Linscheer, who were both later associated with drugs for weapons deals with the FARC in Colombia (see p. 354-355); Christopher became Minister of Defence in 1991.

28 *NRC Handelsblad*, 3 March 1999.

crossed demonstratively.[29] Failure of the judiciary to function revealed the weakness of its civilian government in a distressing manner. A report published in 1992 by the international non-governmental organization Human Rights Watch notes that the judicial system had tended to protect soldiers: 'Because military personnel are exempt from the jurisdiction of the civilian police or courts, army [drugs]traffickers, as well as military abusers of human rights, have enjoyed total impunity.'[30] In 1989 a soldier named Orlando Sweedo was released from a police cell, on Bouterse's order. He had been arrested on suspicion of being involved in the Moiwana massacre. In 1989, too, after the failed assassination attempt on Stanley Rensch, director of the independent human rights organisation Moiwana 86, the police only questioned the victim. The Public Prosecutor's attempt to investigate the deaths of Brunswijk's two bodyguards ran out of steam after commander-in-chief Bouterse refused to allow any staff members of his cabinet to be interviewed. The Prosecutor's warrant pertaining to the arrest of Lieutenant Ruben Rozendaal, one of the 16 insurrectionists of February 1980, who was thought to be involved in smuggling 180 kg cocaine, proved fruitless as the Military Police refused to detain him. The file disappeared into a desk drawer after the military had unsuccessfully requested access to witness statements, quite a blatant attempt at intimidation.[31]

The assassination of the police chief Inspector Herman Gooding, on 5 August 1990, caused huge commotion. He was dragged from his vehicle to be liquidated immediately after holding a discussion on an arrested soldier with the deputy commander at the headquarters of the military police. Gooding was not only responsible for a large number of investigations, such as into the Moiwana massacre, but also acted against drug-related crimes in which the military was involved. One month after this murder, Jules R. Ajodhia, the Minister of Justice and Police (1988-1990), declared that the judicial investigation had hit a 'blind wall'.[32] According to the *Comité Christelijke Kerken* (Committee of Christian Churches) Suriname was now 'completely adrift and had degenerated into a battlefield in which the battle for cocaine interests is ruthlessly fought out'.[33]

14.3 The so-called telephone coup

As a result of the National Army's acts of sabotage virtually all vigour had flowed from the government. The way it departed the political scene on Christmas Eve 1990 symbolised its weakness. A telephone request by the *Militair Gezag* (Military Authority) addressed to President Shankar included the words: 'Don't cause any problems. Prevent escalation and go home quietly. The army has taken over the Republic of Suriname's government.' It sufficed to persuade him to resign.[34]

---

29 Ibid., 28 July 1990.

30 Human Rights Watch, *World Report 1992 - Suriname*, 1 January 1992.

31 For further information on these cases, see: Moiwana '86, *Mensenrechten 1991 Suriname*, Paramaribo 1992, 8, 21-24.

32 Moiwana '86 1992, 22; this murder case is documented extensively in a brochure entitled *In memoriam Herman Eddy Gooding*, published at Paramaribo in 1991 by Moiwana '86.

33 The comment was made in a communique issued on 8 August 1990 which the Praeses J. Kent of the Moravian Church and the Bishop of Paramaribo A. Zichem had both signed.

34 For a detailed reconstruction of the coup and its aftermath, see: *NRC Handelsblad* dated 27 December 1990 and the immediately days thereafter; Dew 1994, 180-182.

Bouterse had resigned as commander-in-chief a few days earlier, as he no longer wished to cooperate with a 'joker' such as Shankar. During a meeting held in the army barracks, the military had adopted a motion of no confidence in President Shankar and the members of his government. Moreover, a restoration of the general powers of investigation for the Military Police was demanded, which the Shankar-led government had withdrawn. Acting Commander Iwan Graanoogst was directly responsible for this coup. Undoubtedly Bouterse had carefully orchestrated the entire proceedings. On the morning it took place, Graanoogst, accompanied by Bouterse's cabinet chief Henk Herrenberg, had explained in the army barracks how Dutch authorities had treated Bouterse as a persona non grata at Amsterdam Airport Schiphol, while en route to Switzerland and Ghana a week earlier. His anger was mainly aimed at President Shankar, a passenger on the same flight but with a different destination. Shankar would have compromised Bouterse's dignity by not standing up for him when a visa was refused. The issue was no more than a pretext for the coup. The Military Command had repeatedly proposed to the old political parties as to organising early elections. The military leadership wished that its ally, the NDP, would then participate in an interim government, thus serving its own political interests. In this way, the NDP could position itself well for the upcoming elections, all the more if Bouterse succeeded in bringing peace to the interior of Suriname. Undoubtedly, the military command's interest in trading cocaine also played a role. (see p. 353).

Within the coalition of the the Front, the possibility of early elections had already been considered. This was apparently the only way for the powerless, indecisive government to escape from the politico-economic crisis. In his capacity as chairman of the Military Authority, Bouterse had even discussed the options with the NPS, VHP and KTPI leaders on the afternoon prior to what would become known as the 'telephone coup'. Shankar, however, thwarted the scenarios by recording a radio and television speech on tape, announcing early elections without his government resigning. Although the putschists occupied TV and radio stations that same evening, they could not prevent Radio Apintie from broadcasting this pre-recorded speech.[35] It was suggested within the NDP that Shankar, considered to be Lachmon's puppet, had helped fuel the insurrection by not following Lachmon's instructions.

This so-called telephone coup exposed the constitution's ambivalence, too. Acting commander Graanoogst even claimed there had been no coup d'état. The military had only assumed their constitutional responsibility as they could no longer watch 'the country slipping into the abyss in an exasperating way'.[36]

In Graanoogst's view, the National Assembly should appoint a new president and vice president in accordance with the constitution. There was not much to choose, because the only two candidates had been provided by the military command itself. Little surprise the NDP chairman Jules Wijdenbosch was not only put forward in order to officiate as vice president but also to chair the cabinet. The military command had forwarded the 77-year-old Johan Kraag (1913-1996) as a presidential candidate.

---

35   *NRC Handelsblad*, 28 December 1990.
36   Ibid.

A History of Suriname

The outcome hereof was: this non-active NPS-member had turned himself into an outcast in his own party.

The regime had reached full agreement with the 'old' political leaders on arrangements to be made after the coup and the calling of new elections. In the National Assembly however resistance was greater than expected. Moreover, the Front appeared to be hugely divided. The telephone coup caused the long-standing politico-cultural differences between the VHP and the NPS to resurface. The VHP deemed the agreement with the military command to be a deal which, in any case, did not endanger interests of the Hindustani business elite. Within the NPS, its members were inclined to think more in terms of political principles. VHP parliamentarians had hardly any problems with the compromise, of which their leader Lachmon had been the principal guide. Numerous NPS delegates refused to participate in the 'legalization' of this putsch.[37] Some even accused Lachmon of 'betraying' democratic principles.[38] They could not accept both their party leader also Vice President Henck Arron being 'couped out' for the second time in a decade. A number of delegates ignored his internal appeal to 'accept any humiliation in order to avoid worse'.[39] Lachmon, the then parliamentary speaker, succeeded in saving the compromise reached with the Military Command by means of a procedural trick. He utilised a 1988 law permitting the president and the vice president to be elected by acclamation, whereby the presence of two-thirds of the delegates sufficed. This procedure implied a secret ballot was no longer held, thereby increasing the pressure on the parliamentarians. In the end, Lachmon managed to assemble the required 34 members in the National Assembly.

After the telephone coup, Suriname had become an anomaly in Central and South America. During the 1980s this region had struggled to break away from a lengthy tradition of military dictatorships. In order to quickly repudiate this insurrection, the Organization of American States (OAS) appealed for the 'reinstatement of the democratic institutional order and the avoidance of any act that could aggravate the situation and impair the full enjoyment of human rights'.[40] Moreover, increasingly worrying voices arose from Washington, D.C., pertaining to Suriname's role as a transshipment hub for South American cocaine. On 5 March 1991, assistant Secretary of State Bernard W. Aronson when facing a US congressional subcommittee declared that 'this hemisphere will not accept any new drug dictatorship'.[41] Two months later, he underlined that the USA did not rule out armed intervention if Suriname did not succeed in restoring democracy after the 25 May elections, expecting the Netherlands to support the USA in the event of such an intervention.[42] Comparing Suriname with Panama during general Manuel Noriega's military dictatorship (1983-1989), who had been taken to the USA in 1990 awaiting trial for drug trafficking, Aronson stated in an interview a few months later:

---

37   Ibid., 31 December 1990.
38   Ibid., 29 December 1990.
39   Ibid., 31 December 1990.
40   Inter-American Commission on Human Rights (IACHR), *Annual Report 1990-1991*, chapter IV, Suriname.
41   *The Bulletin of the United States Information Service*, Paramaribo, 3 April 1991.
42   This interview with B.W. Aronson was broadcast on Dutch television and published in *NRC Handelsblad*, 23 May 1991.

'Bouterse and Noriega are both strong military men, a little macho, who use a civilian façade behind which they can do whatever they want. Bouterse is a bit smaller, he doesn't have as big a country, but they're both dangerous men. You have to deal with them.'[43]

The events in Suriname had caused great embarrassment throughout Dutch political circles. For, in The Hague, doubts had risen concerning the validity of its own policy. The military takeover led to a discussion both in the cabinet and the parliament as to whether the Netherlands should not meddle much more intensively in the developments in Suriname. Certain ministers more closely involved even gave orders pertaining to a worst-case scenario including military intervention, in case Desi Bouterse were to carry out yet another coup and the Suriname government, now led by President Ronald Venetiaan, was to ask the Dutch government for assistance.[44] Back in 1986, an invasion plan had already been drawn up. According to intelligence sources, however, The Hague did not take any action, because an alternative to replace commander-in-chief Bouterse could not be found.[45] A quarter of a century later, in 2011, the Dutch Ministers Uri Rosenthal (Foreign Affairs) and Hans Hillen (Defence) did acknowledge in response to questions asked by parliamentarians that 'together with the United States' a plan had been drawn up aimed at restoring 'order and justice' in Suriname and to thus protect 'Dutch and American citizens and interests' with the assistance of Dutch troops; such an initiative would have required 'a temporary elimination of the Suriname armed forces and the Military Command'; contacts related to this plan had been established 'with (prominent) inhabitants of Suriname', whereby 'a request for help' had been discussed.[46]

At least The Hague, for the first time, notably acknowledged having made plans to oust strongman Bouterse. The then US President Ronald Reagan (1981-1989) mentioned, in his diary entry dated 11 December, 1986, a 'request of the Dutch for mil. transport of about 700 of their Marines to Suriname to take over the govt. of the Brutal Dictator who is endangering & taking the lives of the people there, including about 6,000 Dutch citizens'. In his opinion, 'there was no way we could just say no', but more information was needed. Three weeks later, he wrote that 'Holland called off its proposed assault on Suriname in which they'd asked us for transportation'.[47]

Immediately after the telephone coup, Frits Bolkestein now leader of the right-wing liberal VVD launched the concept of composing a new treaty between the Netherlands and Suriname, including agreements on long-lasting assistance regarding issues of domestic governance, and on the judiciary. A few months later, it was leaked that Prime Minister Ruud Lubbers (1939-2018) was contemplating a commonwealth relationship with Suriname. An important objective hereby was

---

43   *NRC Handelsblad*, 27 September 1991.

44   Former Minister of Defence Relus ter Beek dealt with this issue in his memoir entitled *Manoeuvreren. Herinneringen aan Plein 4*, 1996, 119; Janssen 2011, 249-250.

45   De Graaff & Wiebes 1998, 368; on p. 369 the authors also refer to a possible Dutch offer to Bouterse to go into exile in Brazil in exchange for money; see also: Janssen 2011, 198.

46   As stated in a letter sent by the Ministers to the Tweede Kamer (Lower House) dated 7 November 2011, document nr. 1974 (ah-tk-20112012-1974.pdf).

47   Reagan 2007, 458 and 465.

to eliminate the military shadow power, thus facilitating the tackling of problems (e.g., the economic crisis, drug trafficking). These concepts had been formulated in consultation with the most responsible Ministers, to wit, Hans van den Broek (Foreign Affairs), Jan Pronk (Development Cooperation) and Ernst Hirsch Ballin (Justice). There was no concrete plan yet. For Ruud Lubbers, however, this issue was that relevant he fathomed opinions held by the most important nation states in the region, to wit, the US, Brazil, Venezuela and France (because of French Guiana).[48] Their positive reactions, with the exception of Brazil, were hardly surprising. For, through diplomatic channels, they had repeatedly urged the Netherlands to be much more active in Suriname. The US Deputy Assistant Secretary of State for Inter-American Affairs Sally Cowal stated in a committee of the House of Representatives that the Dutch proposals could contribute to a 'constructive change in Suriname' which in her view had been transformed into a 'military-controlled port for drug traffickers'.[49] This Dutch trial balloon was most likely also intended to support those parties which had to compete against the NDP in the elections. After all, voters would by and large opt for parties willing and able to restore relationships with the Netherlands. For a majority of the people of Suriname, a solution to the politico-economic crisis was indeed still to be found at the Binnenhof, in the centre of The Hague, where the heart of the Dutch government resides.

14.4 The Nieuw Front-led government

The NDP, Commander Bouterse's party, completely dominated the Cabinet that took office after the telephone coup. Thus regaining its monopoly on the state apparatus, it utilised the state treasury as an electoral purse, without hesitation. The government imported tens of millions of Surinamese guilders (Sfl) worth of food which entered the marketplace with large subsidies. The salaries of civil servants and provisions for the elderly were substantially increased within the framework of what was called the 'people-oriented policy'. These measures led to an explosion of the government's deficit which, in 1991, had more than tripled to reach 18.2 per cent of GDP.[50] This populist policy was not without results: the NDP not only won 12 seats in the National Assembly but also increased its support mainly among poverty-stricken lower class Creoles who now turned away from the NPS. DA91, with its nine seats, benefited hugely from the dissent many voters felt towards the previous Front-led government.[51] Inspired by D66, the social-liberal Dutch party, several critical intellectuals had founded DA91. D66, founded in 1966, advocated the renewal of politics in the Netherlands. DA91, wishing to discontinue the traditional system of patronage in the politics of Suriname, for electoral reasons chose to collaborate with a Hindustani, a Javanese and a Maroon party.

Including the SPA (Surinamese Labour Party), the Front comprising the NPS, the VHP and the KTPI had been renamed *Nieuw Front* already before the elections. Within this alliance, the SPA could be assured of a number of parliamentary seats.

---

48   *NRC Handelsblad*, 12 February 1991.
49   Ibid., 29 June 1991.
50   IMF, *Suriname: A Case Study of High Inflation*, November 1999, IMF Working Paper WP/99/157, 11.
51   Dew 1994, 185; *NRC Handelsblad*, 27 May 1991.

Next, these social democrats, led by a politician-*cum*-trade unionist named Freddy Derby (1940-2001), formed an attractive partner for the three old parties because of the SPA's close ties with the trade union federations C-47 and the CLO (civil servants). Critical NPS members in particular had insisted on cooperating with the SPA. For, a much-needed restructuring of the economy would be easier if trade union supporters were to participate. Moreover, the SPA, founded in 1987, had from the outset focused on the issue of military political power. The *Nieuw Front* acquired an absolute majority in parliament with 30 seats. This result was nevertheless a major defeat. In 1987, the three old parties, then referred to as the Front, had won 39 seats, although in certain districts they had not even taken part in elections due to the Interior War. On two occasions, the NF failed to obtain the support from two-thirds of the parliamentarians required to get their presidential and vice presidential candidates elected. This result called for a meeting of the *Verenigde Volksvergadering* (United People's Assembly), which includes not only members of the National Assembly but also elected members of regional and local councils. In 1991 they chose with the required simple majority the 55-year-old NPS politician Ronald Venetiaan to serve as President of the Republic. This mathematician-*cum*-physicist, former school director and Minister of Education and Housing (1973-1980; 1987-1990) had built up a reputation of great integrity. Confronted with perhaps the most difficult task a president of Suriname had ever faced, Venetiaan went on to lead a nation with an empty treasury and in which a drug mafia undermined society, armed groups supported by the military as yet dominated large areas and about one in six children suffered from malnutrition.[52]

The incoming government highly prioritised a closer cooperation with the Netherlands, hereby responding energetically to Prime Minister Lubbers' pre-election suggestions (see p. 332-333). In November 1991, during a ministerial conference held on the isle of Bonaire (Netherlands Antilles), talks resulted in the so-called *Raamverdrag* (Framework Treaty). The Bonaire Protocol states that 'the development of democracy and the rule of law in Suriname and accelerated economic development' were the key objectives.[53] Due to the great urgency of this matter, one did not wish to await the realisation of this new treaty. The Hague therefore immediately provided 30 million Hfl for technical assistance as well as material provisions in order to facilitate the public administration and law enforcement. Hereby one utilised resources made available by the treaty which dated back to when Suriname became independent in 1975. The Dutch embassy in Paramaribo was reinforced with a justice and a police mission. The development aid having been suspended after the telephone coup was partially resumed. Hence, 71 million Hfl was released for expenditures, which included 34 million Hfl for further 'bridging aid' and 11 million Hfl for education projects.[54] In addition, a balance of payments support was promised after the government of Suriname had declared its willingness to implement an economic adjustment programme.

---

52   The data were published by the diocese of Paramaribo, see: *NRC Handelsblad*, 26 July 1990.
53   The full text of this Framework Treaty, as published on 18-06-1992, can be accessed online (wetten. overheid.nl/BWBV0001175/1995-05-01)
54   These lump sums were laid down in the Bonaire Protocol, 16 November 1991 which both nations undersigned.

A History of Suriname

On 18 June 1992, Lubbers and Venetiaan signed the *Raamwerkverdrag inzake Vriendschap en Nauwere Samenwerking* (Framework Treaty on Friendship and Enhanced Cooperation) at The Hague. According to its Article 2, cooperation was to now focus on 'maintaining and reinforcing democracy and the rule of law, the structural reinforcing of the public administration and promoting economic development and social justice'. This document broadly outlines agreements on development cooperation, consultations on foreign and security policies, technical assistance pertaining to defence, reinforcing the rule of law, the fight against cross-border organised crime as well as the movements of individuals, language and culture.

President Venetiaan's government had reinforced its formal position by way of amending the constitution. With the National Assembly's full approval, passages upon which the armed forces had based its political role were now deleted.[55] The NDP also agreed with changing the constitution, possibly for tactical reasons. However, tensions in the relations between the government and the army leadership had by no means subsided. Commander Bouterse continued to increasingly profile himself as a politician, treating the government both from the NDP stage and the military barracks in a very critical manner. Through his actions, the NDP developed into the army's political branch. In a speech, he left no room for any misunderstanding: 'Being included in the leadership, we form an integral part of the NDP and if the NDP no longer contains military personnel then the NDP will no longer exist.'[56] Within the party's leadership, this point of view was not without controversy. For, a NDP minority deemed the influence of the armed forces an electoral handicap. This dissent was sufficient reason for two NDP parliamentarians, including the former parliamentary delegation's chairman Frank Playfair, to leave the party.[57]

One of the reasons why Bouterse wished to increase his grip on the NDP was his crumbling influence on developments within army ranks. He was thus capable of maintaining a political platform. The army leadership had always been able to take care of all military matters without being interfered with. The Ministry of Defence was little more than an empty shell. The administrative control over the army was therefore almost entirely absent. The Venetiaan-led government wished to put an end to this situation as soon as possible. Moreover, an austerity measure comprised army personnel being reduced from 4,000 to between 1,500 and 2,000.[58] The staff had especially become far too large as a result of massive promotions. As early as in January 1992, the Dutch Minister of Defence, Relus ter Beek, had promised his colleague in Suriname, the SPA-politician Siegfried Gilds (1939-2020), to provide technical support when restructuring the armed forces. This assistance provided in the Netherlands involved training as well as educating Surinamese soldiers and officials of the Ministry of Defence. Dutch experts would render in the field of

---

55 The relevant passage in the Constitution of 1992 (Article 177) no longer stated that the army was the 'military vanguard of the people' nor that it had to work on the 'national building and liberation of the nation'; the army's task, according to the amended article, was only to 'defend the sovereignty and territorial integrity of Suriname against foreign armed military aggression' (dna.sr).

56 Bouterse made the statement in his New Year's speech, see: *NRC Handelsblad*, 2 January 1992.

57 Dew 1994, 193; Playfair had previously been ousted by Bouterse as leader of the parliamentary group, see: *NRC Handelsblad*, 10 January 1992.

58 Hoogbergen & Kruijt 2005, 246; *NRC Handelsblad*, 21 November and 3 December 1992.

management and legal affairs, too. In addition, a military attaché was to be stationed at the Dutch embassy in Paramaribo.[59] According to both The Hague and Suriname, reinforcing military ties should send a strong signal to the army leadership.

Discussions on the Dutch military aid led to a further deterioration of the relationship between Suriname's government and the army leadership. Bouterse had accused Gilds of not involving the army command in talks held with Dutch authorities. Bouterse buckled after a conversation with President Venetiaan, in which he had to promise to exclude any political statements when delivering speeches, apparently without much effect. Tensions culminated in November 1992, after Bouterse had ignored the veto on meeting his men, as voiced by Venetiaan. On this occasion the former putschist once again accused victims of the December murders of having been involved in a 'CIA-coup'. In a speech Bouterse also intimidated families of the deceased. Now was the first time in Suriname that bereaved family members were able to commemorate their losses, with the President's permission:

'The state is allowing CIA henchmen to organise a demonstration. We will see each other on the streets on 8 December. I am waiting for them.'[60]

The immediate reason for Bouterse's speech was Vice President Jules R. Adjodhia's interview published in the Dutch weekly Vrij Nederland, a week earlier. In it, he stated that Bouterse during his military rule had made himself the 'richest man' in Suriname, by no means an unfounded qualification.[61] Bouterse's statements not only provoked protest from Washington, D.C.[62], In the National Assembly, too, voices were heard calling for the entire army command to be removed from office. A motion to be forwarded by the NF had already been prepared. Minister Gilds, a SPA-member, had previously revealed a lack of confidence when cooperating with army leaders. He had also lectured Bouterse c.s. in no uncertain terms after their refusal to attend a visit by a US military mission. President Venetiaan was more careful, seeking to avoid any form of polarisation. However, Bouterse's position had become untenable. For, shortly after the first incident, he had once again ignored President Venetiaan's orders. The military commander ultimately resigned after being summoned to the presidential palace. Venetiaan had called him by telephone in the middle of his speech, at which point he immediately concluded his presentation.[63]

In the following months a heated conflict erupted between the government and the army command's remaining members, to wit, the acting commander Iwan Graanoogst, the chief of staff Badrissein Sital and the naval commander Chas Mijnals. This dissent pertained to who should succeed Desi Bouterse. All three refused to accept the appointment of Arthy Gorré, an advisor to Minister Gilds at the Department of Defence. Gorré was one of the 16 putschists of 1980 and had left army ranks in 1987 after falling out with Bouterse. The instigators against Gorré's

---

59 Hoogbergen & Kruijt 2005, 237-238.
60 *NRC Handelsblad*, 19 November 1992.
61 For the article published in *Vrij Nederland*, see: Van Westerloo 1993, 47-61.
62 The US ambassador in Paramaribo publicly expressed his support for President Venetiaan, see: *NRC Handelsblad*, 21 November 1992.
63 Details published in *NRC Handelsblad*, 21 November 1992.

appointment precisely included those men who had forged the armed forces into private domains for their personal economic interests, often created by means of either serious abuse of power or criminal, often drug-related, activities.

In the months preceding Gorré's inauguration on 14 May 1993, the situation had become precarious. A few days earlier, armed men had torched the premises of the state-run television. Prior hereto army leaders had accused Gilds of engaging in 'activities endangering the nation'; the resigned commander-in-chief Bouterse had called Gorré 'incompetent' and even warned of a possible coup if the government were to go ahead with its decision; trade union federations referred to Bouterse's statements as an 'insult to the Surinamese people' and threatened a general strike in the event of a new insurrection.[64]

Hence, the Dutch government dispatched a Lockheed P-3 Orion patrol aircraft to Suriname, which had been stationed on the isle of Curaçao. Officially it was announced that its cargo consisted of food parcels. In fact it carried crates of weapons and ammunition meant for troops loyal to the government. A veiled threat of a possible military intervention resonated from The Hague, which did not conceal being in close contact with Washington, D.C., and the Organisation of American States (OAS) [65]

President Venetiaan had already indicated in 1991, when taking office, that he wished for further military backing. The aforementioned framework treaty offered all possibilities. The Netherlands would probably not have been able to reject Suriname's request for intervention without an international loss of face. Gorré had been appointed to the post of incoming commander on 2 April 1993. However, because of a small group of Bouterse's adherents and their continuous opposition, he could only be installed more than a month later. His main task was to transform the military 'to the letter and spirit of the amended constitution'.[66] In due course, the aforementioned Graanoogst, Sital and Mijnals were promoted to advisory positions.

14.5 A more business-like aid relationship and restoring financial stability
After the return of a democratically elected civilian government in 1987, the Dutch government had every reason to adjust its aid policy in order to promote not only productive investments but also economic reforms as soon as the development cooperation resumed. In addition, the economic chaos which the military regime had left behind rendered harsh restructuring measures inevitable. The Hague thus deliberately opted for a more business-like approach, which led to on-going friction with Paramaribo. Of the 3.5 billion Hfl (including guarantees) pledged in the 1975 treaty, more than 1.5 billion in grants were still to be spent in 1988.[67] The Hague and Paramaribo had reached a compromise on the new procedural rules in July 1989. The Dutch government was no longer prepared to deposit treaty funds in the form of hard currency into the account of Suriname's Central Bank. Under the incoming procedure, the Netherlands would directly pay for foreign purchases in order to fulfil projects. From now on, local costs were to be financed by means of the

---

64   *NRC Handelsblad*, 2, 5 April and 11 May 1993.
65   Ter Beek 1996, 117-127; *NRC Handelsblad*, 5 April 1993.
66   *NRC Handelsblad*, 2 April 1993.
67   Brave & Van den Berg 1998, 23.

counter value of project-related goods purchased abroad. The main reason for this procedure was a lack of trust in this Central Bank which had not only been an extension of the military regime for years but was also still chaired by the same president. Next, from now on decisions on the commitment of development funds had to be taken at a high official level and during half-yearly policy consultations. This measure aimed at providing The Hague with slightly more control over the decision-making process. The committee of officials from both countries that previously made the decisions was therefore disbanded. Suriname had to present a restructuring plan before any structural aid could commence. A Dutch proposal requesting assistance from the IMF which pertained to the drafting of such a recovery plan met with firm resistance. The government of the Netherlands thought it would be better for a third party to assess Suriname's economic plans, because of the always sensitive mutual relationship. In due course Paramaribo agreed to request technical support from the European Union (then called European Community). The latter would, as Paramaribo assumed, pay more attention to the social consequences of rigid restructuring measures, such as reducing the government deficit and restoring monetary stability.

In December 1990, the renowned accounting firm Coopers & Lybrand Deloitte presented an initial draft adjustment programme.[68] As the telephone coup occurred in that very same month, no further action could be taken. When, 18 months later, the UK-based Warwick Research Institute released a renewed version of this programme, it took into account the sharp financial deterioration, especially caused by the policy adopted by the NDP after the telephone coup.[69] In November 1992, the Venetiaan-led government had put a structural adjustment programme in place, based in part on the European Commission-funded studies of both aforementioned consultants. The Hague and Paramaribo had both agreed at the time of ratifying the Framework Treaty in 1992 that 1 billion Hfl of the remaining funds would be earmarked for an 'adjustment and development programme'. Money was now earmarked to stimulate private production. This initiative entailed (a) balancing payment support, (b) education, health and public housing, (c) infrastructure, (d) a social programme aimed at reducing the undesirable effects of structural adjustment, (e) reinforcing of the rule of law, (f) public administration and (g) developing the interior.[70]

According to the Structural Adjustment Programme, the main objective pursued during the year 1993 was to end to the monetary financing of the public deficit. Within 18 months, a stable and realistic exchange rate of the Suriname guilder might be reached, facilitating a factual economic growth again in 1993. However, in July 1993, the European Commission felt disgruntled with the lack of progress as to this programme's implementation it was no longer prepared to act as an external monitor. The government of the Netherlands subsequently decided to discontinue the balance-of-payments support. The Dutch demand that Suriname should still request the IMF as well as the World Bank to serve as an external monitor led to a new conflict: Paramaribo regarded this demand as a violation of the bilateral nature of the

---

68 Coopers & Lybrand Deloitte, *A program for adjustment and structural adaptation in Suriname* (Paramaribo 1990).

69 Warwick Research Institute, *A program for structural adjustment* (Paramaribo, 1992).

70 *NRC Handelsblad*, 22 June 1992.

treaty ratified when independence was obtained in 1975. It was also feared that these institutions had insufficient consideration for the social consequences of structural adjustment which would perhaps endanger the already fragile democracy.[71]

A compromise was reached only in the course of 1994. The Dutch government would hence establish its decision on resuming the structural assistance, based on the regular IMF reports, as prepared for each member state. Because of the vagueness of this compromise, the IMF's role continued to be a source of dissent. The VHP had dropped its objections against the IMF's interference. As to the NPS, this step was far more difficult to take considering the huge sensitivity felt pertaining to matters of national sovereignty within this predominantly Creole party, including the President. An inhibiting factor, too, was formed by equally considerable sensitivities experienced in the previous colonial relationship between the Netherlands and Suriname.

Meanwhile postponing the restructuring of Suriname's economy had only caused further expenditures resulting from hyperinflation, increasing poverty and political instability. Inflation, having already reached 224.7 per cent in 1993, increased even further to arrive at 586.4 per cent in 1994.[72] Continuing the monetary financing of budget deficits was the main cause of the severe economic downturn. Especially, in 1993 and 1994, the exchange rate losses of Suriname's Central Bank contributed to the creation of money. These losses, which in 1993 consisted of more than 50 per cent of the general government deficit, were the outcome of the subsidisation of the import of certain goods especially fuel, cooking gas and foodstuffs (e.g., flour, milk powder) by means of a special multiple exchange rate system which benefitted domestic consumers. Hence, the general government deficit (including exchange rate losses) rose to 23.6 per cent of GDP in 1993, compared with 11.1 per cent in 1992. Loss-making state-owned enterprises also contributed to this deficit.[73]

The unification of exchange rates in July 1994 was a major reform which put an end to the Central Bank's exchange losses. Previously, depending on the nature of the transactions, various rates existed at which the foreign currencies were allocated by the authorities. This measure also led to a significant increase in the monthly profit payments by the bauxite companies Suralco and Billiton to the government, forwarded in Surinamese guilders. The mandatory transfers of US dollars to Suriname's Central Bank, comprising the contra value for wage payments as well as local purchases, decreased as a result of the exchange rate adjustment. In exchange for this concession, which resulted in a fall in USD transfers, the bauxite companies pledged over 200 million USD in investments over a 5-year period.[74] In the second half of 1994, the government also saw its revenues multiplying as a result of the free exchange rate which formed the basis of import duties. The Venetiaan-led government had waited a long time for this adjustment, fearing that prices would rise sharply. In 1994, its deficit finally amounted to 11.4 per cent of GDP, less than half of the deficit recorded as to 1993.[75]

---

71 *NRC Handelsblad,* 27 July 1993.
72 IMF, *The IMF Staff Country Report No. 96/34,* April 1996, Suriname – Statistical Annex, 10; see also: Central Bank of Suriname, *Report 1993-1996,* 17.
73 IMF, *Suriname: A Case Study of High Inflation,* November 1999, 11.
74 Central Bank of Suriname, *Report 1993-1996,* 20.
75 IMF, *Suriname: A Case Study of High Inflation,* November 1999, 11.

The introduction of a uniform floating exchange rate for the Surinamese guilder marked a turnaround in the government's economic and financial policies. Immediately after taking office in March 1994, the Central Bank's incoming President, André Telting (1935-2010), a skilled technocrat who would gain a reputation as the silent force behind the financial recovery, had already ended the monetary financing his predecessor Henk Goedschalk had begun. Telting had refused to finance an increase in civil servants' salaries by means of the banknote press. This initiative forced the then Minister of Finance, Humphrey Hildenberg (1945-2017), to make these payments in instalments. At the same time, during the second half of 1994, the Central Bank bought *c*.800 kg of gold from domestic gold miners, hereby increasing the money supply. On the other hand, by adding this gold to the gold reserves, the gold coverage of the Suriname guilder could be raised to the legally prescribed 50 per cent. Stabilization of this guilder was thus within reach.[76]

A weak global marketplace for bauxite products during the early 1990s had contributed to a deficit in Suriname's balance of payments. Towards the end of 1993, the gross foreign exchange reserves amounted to a mere 38.8 million USD which equalled the coverage of the import need for only 1 month.[77]

Introducing a system of multiple exchange rates had proven to be a rather weak attempt to curb the flow of foreign exchange. Moreover, the system encouraged corruption and nepotism. The competitive position of key export sectors did improve with the unification of the exchange rate. Previously, due to the scarcity of foreign exchange, imports necessary for the production process often had to be financed with expensive US dollars purchased on the black market. At the same time export earnings had to flow into the Central Bank's coffers at unfavourable official exchange rates. Hence, the necessary investments were not forthcoming. In 1993, the number of rice fields fell sharply to then gradually increase.[78] Such official production figures must nevertheless be treated with caution, as this unfavourable exchange rate regime led to large-scale smuggling. This situation proved even more difficult for companies which required foreign exchange for their production processes and which only served domestic markets, e.g., the food sector. A shortage of either raw materials or components often resulted in production stoppages.

Prior to 1992, a certain improvement in GDP was observed, partly as a result of the Dutch bridging aid and the balance of payments support, which provided companies with means to carry out necessary replacement investments. According to the IMF, the factual GDP fell by 5.7 per cent in 1993.[79] An improvement in economic and financial policy in 1994 arrived too late to reverse the trend recorded for this year. A sign of the economic decline is indicated by the return to their country of many Guyanese construction workers, who had already arrived in the 1970s to a then relatively prosperous Suriname. The impoverishment of the population, which had continued in 1987 after the return of the civil administration, threatened to take

---

76   Central Bank of Suriname, *Report 1993-1996*, 26; see also: an interview held with André Telting: *NRC Handelsblad*, 28 January 1995; Telting's policy of purchasing gold was also aimed at stimulating the local gold industry and at preventing gold smuggling.

77   *The IMF Staff Country Report* No. 96/34, *Suriname – Statistical Annex*, 28.

78   Central Bank of Suriname, *Report 1993-1996*, 23.

79   *The IMF Staff Country Report No. 96/34*, *Suriname - Statistical Annex*, 5.

A History of Suriname

on dramatic proportions due to the rapidly rising inflation and the depreciation of the Surinamese guilder. In addition, the number of jobs fell steadily. A decline in the public sector employment was not offset by means of private sector job creation. Jack Menke concluded after an in-depth research that 69.5 per cent of Paramaribo-based households may have been living below the poverty line in 1993, while noting that this percentage is high in comparison with elsewhere across Latin America during the crisis years. This actual figure may be slightly lower, as respondents did not always report second and third jobs.[80] Menke also points to the importance of remittances by family members residing in the Netherlands. The majority of the Surinamese people must have indeed lost a considerable amount of purchasing power. A clear indication hereof comprises the development of the index of the mean nominal labour costs and the consumer price index between 1980 and 1993 as calculated by the *Algemeen Bureau voor de Statistiek* (General Bureau of Statistics). Both indices started in 1980 at 100, after which the labour cost index stood at 429 in 1993 and that of the consumer price index at 1,478, which means that in 1993 purchasing power was only 29 per cent of that in 1980.[81] For the trend of the per capita income, see Fig. 16.1. p. 372). The middle class was also affected by poverty and numerous civil servants were forced to take on jobs in the informal sector, such as taxi driving. According to the Suriname's central bank, the informal sector accounted for *c.*20 per cent of GDP during the first half of the 1990s. This low assessment seems to be an underestimation.[82] For many, parcels and money remittances dispatched by family members residing in the Netherlands formed a substantial addition to the incomes of their next of kin in Suriname.

Thanks to its structural adjustment programme, the Venetiaan-led government succeeded, after all the hesitations and delays, in stabilising the economy within 12 months. In addition, based on the participation of the social democratic SPA in the *Nieuw Front*, the coalition had ensured a sufficient level of support in the trade union movement. Notably the aforementioned programme was implemented under its own steam, without any external support. Venetiaan spoke with a mixture of bitterness and pride about the 'zero option'.[83] Due to the lack of progress with this programme, The Hague had decided in 1993, pending further progress, to (a) suspend balance of payments support for the time being and (b) not to approve investments in the productive sphere. Dutch aid to sectors such as education, health and utilities however continued. In 1995, the harmonious cooperation between the Central Bank's President Telting and Minister of Finance Hildenberg resulted in a turnaround.

Medio 1995, Suriname's Central Bank was not only able to intervene in the foreign exchange market by means of its reserves but also to stabilise the exchange rate of

---

80   Menke 1998, 126-127.

81   Ibid., 10.

82   Central Bank of Suriname, *Report 1993-1996*, 19, According to the Inter-American Development Bank, presented in a comparative study on Caribbean economies, Suriname's informal sector averaged between 28.5 and 45.9 per cent of GDP between 1991 and 2012; Suriname was thus the leader in the region which was no surprise considering the importance of illegal gold mining and drug-related crime, see: The Inter-American Development Bank's publication entitled *Estimating the size of the informal economy in Caribbean States*, 2017, 1, 24.

83   *NRC Handelsblad*, 14 November 1994.

the Sfl. At the same time, the upward trend in the global marketplace for bauxite derivatives (i.e., alumina and aluminium) led to a rise in the foreign exchange income. The export earnings of other sectors, like rice and shrimps, increased too.[84] Confidence now restored, the flight capital returned. At the end of 1995, the official gross reserves had already reached a total of 185.8 million USD, almost three times as much as at the end of 1994.[85] After the considerable deficits experienced in previous years, the government budget disclosed a surplus in 1995. Revenues from the income and the profit taxes grew as a result of improving the system of tax collecting procedures, in which Dutch experts were involved. Moreover, a 10 per cent 'solidarity levy' had been introduced. The government tax revenue increased from 20 to 35 per cent of GDP between 1994 and 1996.[86] The IMF, for political reasons not involved with the government of Suriname, now praised this 'major turnaround'.[87] In 1996, the budget balance remained positive, despite a strong expenditure growth. According to the IMF, this increase was entirely a result of the approaching 1996 elections. Financial stabilisation had brought inflation down rapidly. Returning to price stability allowed banks to attract deposits, which facilitated a quick recurrence of lending cash to companies. Simultaneously, the economy began to grow.

---

84   Central Bank of Suriname, *Report 1993-1996*, 21, 23, 25.
85   Ibid., 42.
86   IMF, *Suriname: A Case Study of High Inflation, IMF Working Paper* WP/99/157, November 1999, 11.
87   IMF, *Suriname: Recent Economic Developments, IMF Country Report 97/64*, August 1997, 1.

Chapter 15
Contours of informal power and narcocracy

15.1 The business elite, a divisive force within the Nieuw Front

During its first years, the NF-led government had concentrated on restricting military influence (see chapter 14) to thus, on 8 August 1992, after lengthy negotiations, be able to conclude a so-called national reconciliation and development agreement with Brunswijk's Jungle Commando and the Tucajana Amazones, hereby formally concluding the long-running Interior War. A key part of this peace agreement comprised a law that provided amnesty to the embattled parties, hereby referring to examples of such arrangements made across the globe, but explicitly excluding 'crimes against humanity'.[1] In the end, the government of Suriname also managed to fully stabilise a derailed economy by means of implementing a structural adjustment programme (see p. 337ff.). These tangible successes could not conceal the fact the coalition under President Venetiaan's leadership experienced difficulties when operating. The always fragile ethnic and social balance, if indeed at all the case, had come under severe pressure as a result of various developments.

Economic reforms were the subject of frequent disputes between the NPS and the VHP, the two largest coalition partners. In addition, a large part of the former party's members was well aware of the importance of good governance, fighting corruption and cracking down on drug-related crimes. This awareness applied especially to that part of the middle classes as yet strongly influenced by the European Christian culture. The result of a centuries-long zeal as expressed by both the Moravian Brethren and the Roman Catholic mission indeed could be observed among Creoles. Moreover, it once again became apparent that, across Suriname, economic policies were at the same time very much ethnicity-driven. The NPS and the VHP wished to spare their own constituencies as much as possible. Once elected, President Venetiaan, the NPS leader, had made it unequivocally clear he no longer wished 'a populist display of bread and games', hereby referring to Kraag's and Wijdenbosch's short-lived regime after the 'telephone coup' staged on Christmas Eve 1990.[2] Venetiaan nevertheless resisted restructuring the civil service and state-owned companies, where the majority of the employees were Creoles. The VHP, for its part, saw no point in introducing a property tax. For, such a financial burden would mainly affect the many Hindustani landowners and farmers.

The tensions between the NPS and the VHP had deeper ethnic-political causes, too, arising from changes in the economic power relations. A class of nouveau-riche among civilians and the military had been created after the 'sergeant coup' on 25 February 1980. Its members had amassed great wealth by means of, for example, corruption, drug trafficking and illegal gold mining. The military had taken over the state apparatus to the extent that nepotism as well as criminal practices could flourish more than ever. A budding economic elite was concentrated within the VHP

---

1   For the text of this Amnesty Law, see: *Staatsblad van de Republiek Suriname*, 1992, No. 68 (dna.sr/media/136493/Amnestiewet_SB_68_1992.pdf); see also: Dew 1994, 195-196.
2   *NRC Handelsblad*, 5 December 1992.

and the NDP. The former party was traditionally the political home of the Hindustani trading class, several members of which had further enriched themselves through close links with the military leadership. Predominantly of Creole descent, the NDP's new elite consisted mainly of (former) military leaders and their 'revolutionary' supporters of the past. By and large, the NPS hence deemed its position of power to be under threat.

The economic power shift had to a certain degree side-lined the NPS. In addition, the Creole middle class, which traditionally supported the NPS, had been eroded due to impoverishment. This party had always mainly derived its politico-economic influence from an influx of Dutch development funds, which were distributed through the government. As a result of The Hague's now more stringent requirements, however, this influence had diminished considerably. Moreover, the majority of state-owned companies, the domain of the NPS, were operating very poorly due to both the economic crisis and mismanagement. Venetiaan's public criticism pertaining to the hugely affluent 'tarantulas' aroused anger, especially within the VHP, where it was considered an attack on the Hindustani business elite.[3] In 1993 President Venetiaan exacerbated relations when dismissing the Minister of Trade and Industry, Tjan Gobardhan. The official statement read that the latter had not followed the instructions while negotiating with rice traders. The real reason of his resignation was the fact that Venetiaan considered him a pawn of the influential Hindustani businessman and multimillionaire Dilip Sardjoe.[4] Ever since the military had ruled over Suriname from the 1980s on, Sardjoe had become a symbol of corrupt self-enrichment. The opaque exchange rate system and the extensive licensing procedure offered ample opportunity to earn vast sums of money in no time. For the business elite it was appealing to be well acquainted with the head of the Ministry of Trade and industry because the very lucrative import licences and export transactions were provided right here. After managing to entirely control this ministry, Sardjoe had even obtained official stationery, on which this ministry's head only had to sign. He also officiated as the VHP's treasurer. Hence, the VHP's ministers were expected to serve him. Matters were on occasion dealt with as follows

'A Minister for merely an hour, he says, and he was picked up by Alwin Mungra, the envoy of Lachmon, his party leader. They went for a drive with the car, with the Benz, he states. In due course they stopped in front of Dilip Sardjoe's house. They became acquainted. 'This man', Alwin Mungra mentioned to the incoming Minister, 'has spent a lot of money on our party. Now it's time for you, as a Minister, to return his favours!'[5]

In Suriname everything that initially could euphemistically be referred to as patronage and clientelism had degenerated into gross corruption and outright crime. In 1993 a kickback case involving the Dutch companies named Begro Wagenaar and Insulaire, which became known as the Begro-Insulaire affair, proved revealing.

---

3   Ibid.
4   *NRC Handelsblad.*, 20 September 1993.
5   Van Westerloo 1993, 56.

This case came to light as a result of an investigation executed at The Hague by the Colombia-Paramaribo (CoPa) Team into Suriname's drug cartel. It pertained to a 35 million Hfl contract mainly concerning food deliveries, Its suppliers had to pay 9 million Hfl as a 'commission'. This affair led to the resignation of those who had allegedly received money, including the VHP-treasurer Dilip Sardjoe and Henk Goedschalk, the President of Suriname's Central Bank. The latter eventually reached a settlement with the Dutch judiciary. Bouterse had profited, too, as investigators stated in their report. An involved Dutch businessman reported that in Suriname bribing had 'really run out of control' after the 'telephone coup' in December 1990.[6]

The Begro-Insular affair accelerated investigations executed by the CoPa Team. The result followed in 1999, when a court of law based at The Hague sent Bouterse, kingpin of a drug ring named Suri-cartel, to prison for 16 years in absentia. This sentence was reduced to 11 years on appeal (see p. 355).[7] This CoPa Team's investigation in part revealed activities serving as a cover for cocaine trafficking as well as for laundering drug money, which mostly foreign-registered companies owned by prominent Surinamese (former) military and civilians had carried out. It also became clear how government institutions, for instance, the Suriname's Central Bank as well as state-owned enterprises (e.g., the Suriname American Industries, SAIL, a shrimp exporter) played a role in channelling and laundering of drug money. The CoPa Team reported that those involved included Desi Bouterse, his then deputy military leader Iwan Graanoogst, Henk Goedschalk, the President of Suriname's Central Bank, and a former Minister of Defence, Rupert Christopher (1956-2007) .

Bouterse also maintained close business ties with Dilip Sardjoe. The CoPa Team's report describes how he, commissioned by the government, ordered goods abroad for the *Centraal Inkoopbureau Suriname* (Central Purchasing Office Suriname). Sardjoe secretly sold a number of these goods, which this bureau had paid for, on to Guyana. According to the CoPa Team's report, both Bouterse and Graanoogst shared in the revenues. During the 1980s, the people of Suriname nicknamed the latter 'Mister Ten Percent' because of the 'tariff' he would collect when issuing import licenses.[8] The aforementioned report also mentions 'extremely advantageous' loans which Sardjoe, along with the VHP-member Atta Mungra (1930-2002), would provide to Bouterse and a senior military officer named Marcel Zeeuw (1953-2015) in exchange for business concessions. Since the 1980s, the interests of a large part of the Hindustani business elite had concurred with highest ranked members of the (ex-)military hierarchy. They included many of the still living putschists of 1980 and formed a group of sworn men, who held key shares in the Suri-cartel allegedly led by Desi Bouterse.

The alliance of interests of Hindustani businessmen and (ex-)army leaders in Paramaribo had already led to frequent speculations about a division within the VHP. President Venetiaan's stance against 'tarantulas' apparently rendered such a split inevitable. It was not that difficult for the business elite to respond to

---

6   These and following details are sourced from the COPA-report, see: Haenen 1999, 146-151 and Van den Heuvel 1999, 103-114.
7   *NRC Handelsblad*, 17 July 1999 and 1 July 2000.
8   *NRC Handelsblad*, 15 January 1998.

ethnic sentiments. Certain VHP-members had always mistrusted Venetiaan hugely. For, in the eyes of many Hindustanis, he was all too much an exponent of Creole nationalism. In addition, numerous accusations had been voiced within the VHP as to favouring Creoles in official appointments. Hindustani frustration was so intense that in 1995 the VHP's advisory council recommended the party leadership to start a removal procedure against Venetiaan. This initiative was preceded by an open dispute between the the latter and Pertab Radakishun, a Hindustani businessman who officiated as the advisory council's chairman. The latter having served as Prime Minister (Juli 1986 - April 1987) towards the end of the military regime, accused Venetiaan of 'racist behaviour'.[9] A defamation charge filed by the latter was withdrawn at the last minute.

The Hindustani business elite considered Lachmon to be overly lenient. For him, however, it was of paramount importance that the 'fraternization' policy, launched by the VHP and the NPS during the 1950s, should not be endangered. By means of give and take, Lachmon had made it his life's work to preserve the fragile ethnic balance of power between Hindustanis and Creoles. Nevertheless, in view of the parliamentary elections of May 1996, he could not help but meet his critics to a certain level. Lachmon thus refrained from forwarding Venetiaan as a presidential candidate prior to the parliamentary elections, as he had done in 1991. The VHP was still suffering from the trauma of 1991. At that time, VHP candidates were placed relatively low on the NF's list of the parliamentarians. Some perceived this to be a punishment for the VHP's lenient attitude towards the 'telephone coup'. The NPS, despite a smaller number of followers, was therefore able to acquire more parlementary seats. In order to meet his critics, Lachmon also launched a strategy of preference voting whereby Hindustanis had to vote for Hindustani candidates included on the joint NF list in order to increase the number of seats to be occupied by the VHP candidates. Across Suriname's outer districts this strategy led to a materialistic and ethnically tinged election campaign of which Dilip Sardjoe and a leading rice exporter named George Pahlad were the key financiers. In the important Hindustani districts of Nickerie and Saramacca, the campaign was led by Sardjoe's business partner Atta Mungra, a former director of Surinam Airways, the national carrier, who hailed from a politically influential family. The recently created Hindustani business elite was now able to manifest itself politically more than ever. In Paramaribo, both Sardjoe and Mungra had increased their electoral influence with the establishment of an insurance firm named Parsasco. It was able to attract almost all bus owners and taxi drivers, mainly Hindustani and thus potential voters, as its customers within a small timescale when offering very low premiums. In Saramacca, Sardjoe personally financed the completion of a water supply. This project had been delayed, as the then Minister of Public Works, a NPS-member, did not see any electoral advantage in it.[10] Hence, in Nickerie, roads were refurbished, street lights installed and the water supply improved, all funded by Sardjoe.

However, generally speaking, the election campaigns of the various parties were not markedly ethnic in nature, although at times subtle allusions to ethnic sentiments

---

9   *NRC Handelsblad*, 5 August 1996.
10   *NRC Handelsblad*, 22 May 1996.

A History of Suriname

occurred. In this respect, Suriname still differed from other Caribbean countries comparable in terms of population composition (e.g., neighbouring Guyana, Trinidad and Tobago). For the NF's multi-ethnic coalition, an ethnic campaign would simply have been counterproductive. This also applied to the NDP, which after all also sought support among all ethnic groups. Nevertheless, when drawing up lists of candidates, not one party could escape from taking into account the population's ethnic composition as observed in the various districts.

The NF struggled to find a proper election theme. Although the leaders of this multi-party combination were able to point to the achieved restoration of macro-economic stability, this feat had not yet led to an immediate improvement regarding the fate of the population which in part was impoverished. Creoles, heavily dependent on the government, were experiencing hard times, in spite of an increase in civil servants' salaries and old-age benefits. During the campaign, the NF's leadership did continually denounce the NDP's military past and the responsibility of Bouterse, the NDP's President, for the December murders of 1982. Immediately prior to these elections, Amnesty International produced a documentary about this assassination of 15 opponents of the Bouterse regime inside the military headquarters. It was broadcasted twice on primetime by national television. Moreover, on the very pre-election night, President Venetiaan announced an official investigation into this massacre.[11] An initiative he as yet had not taken, in spite of motions forwarded in parliament. Shortly after his inauguration, Venetiaan had indeed clearly indicated he did not wish to risk a shoot-out. For, in his view, this would be the outcome of prosecuting the perpetrators.[12]

After involuntary resigning as an army leader, Bouterse had been elected to chair the NDP. For certain young Creoles, he served as a role model: an ordinary guy who had made it after years of *hosselen* (hustling). For the time being, the unfolding judicial investigation in the Netherlands into his involvement in drug trafficking did not seem to detract a great deal from this status among certain youngsters. Bouterse conducted an intensive election campaign among Maroons and Indigenous peoples residing in the interior, where the electoral system yielded many seats with relatively few votes. His considerable business interests in the timber and gold sectors had resulted in a good relationship with these ethnic groups. In addition, the NDP had profiled itself as a professionally organised, modern party in spite of its rather anachronistic style of anti-colonialism and nationalism. The ethnic NF parties had slightly less appeal. However, burdened by his past, Bouterse apparently did not feel strong enough to put himself forward as a candidate for the presidency and wisely left the candidacy to Jules Wijdenbosch, who had always proven to be one of his loyal followers from the 1980s on.

15.2 'Old' parties in a minority position for the first time
The elections held on 23 May 1996 produced a historic result. For, since the introduction of universal suffrage in 1949, the three 'old' ethnic parties, the NPS (Creoles), the VHP (Hindustanis) and the KTPI (Javanese) together now for the first time did not obtain

---

11   Ibid., 22 May 1996.
12   This interview with President Venetiaan was published in *NRC Handelsblad*, 22 June 1992.

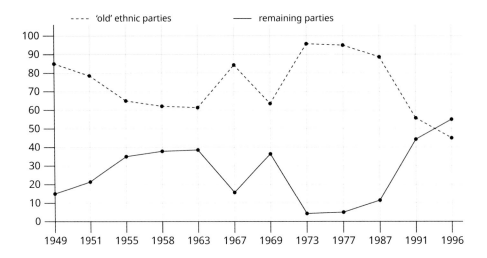

Figure 15.1. The percentage of votes obtained by 'old' ethnic parties and the remaining parties, 1949-1996. Menke 1996, 9.

an absolute majority. Their combination referred to as the NF (which included the SPA) dropped from 54 to 42 per cent, i.e., from 30 to 24 parliamentary seats, when compared to the 1991 elections. The outcome was also a setback for the NDP. Although its support rose from 22 to 26 per cent, i.e., from 12 to 16 parliamentary seats, it had expected much more.[13] On the evening of the elections, the NDP chairman Bouterse hid from his supporters out of sheer disappointment.

The NDP was nonetheless by far the largest party represented in the National Assembly, where the NPS did not occupy more than nine seats. The NF's previously tried and tested strategy of turning the elections into a battle either for or against Bouterse had only resulted in a limited effect on voters. On the other hand, the electorate was not very sensitive to the NDP's populist promise to soon meet the needs of an impoverished population.

Studies into changes as to the role of ethnicity within the society of Suriname indicate that caution is called for when drawing any conclusions (see also p. 391-393).[14] The fact the old ethnic parties lost their majority does not necessarily imply that ethnic factors had become of far less importance as to voting behaviour. The four largest population groups were represented in the National Assembly in virtually the same proportions as after the two previous elections, to wit, Creoles and Hindustanis each with approximately one-third, Javanese with one-fifth and Maroons with one-seventh of the parliamentary seats.[15] The stability in this parliament's ethnic composition was partly a result of the population's one-sided composition as observed in most constituencies. For example, the predominantly Hindustani district of Nickerie had indeed only forwarded Hindustani representatives. However, the ethnic representation of Paramaribo with its multi-racial population also proved

13   Groenfelt & Menke 1996, 71.
14   Menke 1996, 7-13; Schalkwijk 1996, 32-49.
15   Schalkwijk 1996, 42-43.

A History of Suriname

relatively stable. The political parties and the voters apparently took due account of the ethnic identity of the candidates.

The NDP's victory in Paramaribo's popular quarters (e.g., Flora, Tammenga, Latour), where almost 40 per cent of the votes went to Bouterse's party, was remarkable.[16] This outcome was by and large linked to the impoverished Creoles and the deterioration of public facilities in these neighbourhoods. A cultural difference was apparently manifest between lower-class and middle-class Creoles, too. The latter group felt an affinity with the Euro-Christian culture of the Creole political elite, as observed within the NPS. Due to the economic crisis, this elite had less influence on Creoles who inhabited popular neighbourhoods and viewed the NDP as a beckoning prospect.

Initially, the NF seemed to head towards a coalition with the so-called *Middenblok* (Central Block), a partnership of the reform party DA91 and the predominately Javanese party named *Pendawa Lima*. The powerful business elite within the VHP led by the aforementioned Dilip Sardjoe and Atta Mungra had however began to stir again. They deemed the NPS really threatened their business interests. Against the wishes of VHP party leader Lachmon, they thus put forward their own candidate to run for vice president, to wit, Pertab Radakishun, a businessman and a former prime minister. Dissidents accused Lachmon of failing to keep his tacit commitment to personally claim the presidency at Venetiaan's expense. Mungra had now also presented himself as the voice of those within the VHP who had problems coping with Lachmon's autocratic leadership. The conflicts led to a split within the VHP. Now five of the nine VHP members of parliament decided to support a coalition with the NDP. In the past, radical Hindustanis had accused Lachmon on more than one occasion of selling out to the Creoles, for instance, during the 1960s as well as immediately before obtaining independence in 1975 (see p. 274-275). It may be added here that such accusations are not uncommon in either ethnically or religiously diverse countries. However, never before had the now almost 80-year-old Lachmon lost control of his own party members in such a blatant way. The financiers, brought in personally by Lachmon, were now walking out with part of the VHP. These dissidents initially formed a movement within the VHP to, in due course, found the *Basispartij voor Vernieuwing en Democratie* (Basis Party for Renewal and Democracy).

As a result of this internal division, the presidential candidate Venetiaan did not achieve the required two-thirds majority in the National Assembly, not even the second time around. As in 1991, this event necessitated a meeting of the *Verenigde Volksvergadering* (United People's Assembly) which, in addition to the 51 parliamentarians, also included the more than 800 members representing regional as well as local councils. The NF had the prospect of obtaining the required normal majority. Nevertheless, during the run-up to that meeting, the KTPI decided to team up with the NDP. The old Javanese party had often utilised its lucrative 'seesaw' position in order to manoeuvre between the larger parties. At any rate, the KTPI leader Willy Soemita saw little benefit in the coalition of the NF as the *Pendawa Lima*, a rival Javanese party, also participated. The latter had a far more appealing leader in the experienced politician Paul Somohardjo (b. 1943), who was able to

---

16   Groenfelt & Menke 1996, 72.

attract young Javanese voters. However, those five ministerial seats the NDP leader Bouterse had promised formed the key motive for the KTPI to turn around - indeed an unprecedented reward for a party with only five seats in parliament. In due course NDP candidate Jules Wijdenbosch, as previously mentioned, a staunch ally of Bouterse, was elected President by a narrow majority while Pertab Radakishun became Vice President.[17]

15.3 A government of 'a boss and bosses'

The election in the *Verenigde Volksvergadering* entailed persistent rumours that the victory had been 'purchased'. However, the NF did not file an official complaint. Remarkably, an investigation conducted by the Surinamese Court of Auditors later revealed that the NF itself had in fact been guilty of malpractice. According to this court's 1996 report, the Minister of Regional Development had, prior to the session held by the aforementioned assembly, ordered attendance fees to be paid to district representatives as well as to local councils for meetings that had never been held, which thus took on the form of bribes. In an annual report, this court of auditors even referred to 'massive fraud'.[18] In Suriname, anno 1996, it could nonetheless no longer be ruled out that the other party, NDP, as a result of power acquired by means of drug money and other illegally amassed capital, had simply offered more in order to secure an election victory.

In his inaugural speech, President Wijdenbosch referred to the crisis in Suriname stating that an 'all-encompassing' and 'national reconstruction' would now be necessary. He deliberately ignored the previous government's merit, which had restored economic stability. According to Wijdenbosch, the population's living conditions would soon be improved, for which his party had drawn up a '100-day plan'. Having denounced a lack of moral and societal standards, he then announced that 'moral value' would be taught as a part of the school curriculum adding that his cabinet would not only seek to enhance governmental transparency but also reinforce democracy.[19] The governmental declaration which Wijdenbosch delivered in parliament 2 weeks later contained reflections on 'the greatest challenge in our history', thus echoing revolutionary clarion blows that had sounded after the 1980 coup.[20]

Rarely did a Surinamese government deliver so little on its promises. In 1991, Wijdenbosch's short term as Vice President, after the 'telephone coup', had already been an ill omen. A large number of promises soon resulted in the opposite. The few well-trained civil servants who had not yet left for the private sector were often passed over because of political reasons. Hence, rendering a consistent and systematic approach proved almost impossible. It soon became clear that the NDP would occupy a central position within the coalition. In addition to the BVD and the KTPI, several splinter groups participated. Prior to forming a government, the partners agreed as to the NDP not acquiring the sensitive Ministry of Justice. Certain coalition members did not entrust a party led by Wijdenbosch and Bouterse with

---

17   *NRC Handelsblad*, 6 September 1996. On this occastion Wijdenbosch acquired 438 votes and Venetiaan 407.
18   Rekenkamer van Suriname, *Verslag 1996*, Paramaribo 1997, 6-7.
19   *NRC Handelsblad*, 16 and 24 September 1996.
20   Wijdenbosch, *Regeringsverklaring* [Government Declaration] 1 October 1996, Paramaribo 1996, 7.

protecting the rule of law. Ultimately however the NDP acquired the Ministry of Justice as well as the Ministry of Trade and industry, which was of strategic interest to the business elite. The coalition partners had stipulated that Bouterse would not take up a formal government position. Yet this seemed to be mainly a feint to the outside world. As chairman of the largest party, Bouterse did pull the strings behind the scenes.

At the same time, Wijdenbosch reinforced his personal position. Now many departmental tasks were taken over by so-called task forces, which fell directly under the President's responsibility. Numerous ministers were merely extras. This situation created a parallel state structure that escaped democratic control. Moreover, the parliament of Suriname had always been rather weak. After only a few months, the BVD-member Richard Kalloe and also head of the Ministry of Public Works (1996-1997), was the first to resign after a power struggle with Iwan Graanoogst, the former high-ranked military, who was now in charge of a task force. According to the well-informed newspaper *De Ware Tijd*, he had physically threatened Kalloe during a telephone conversation after the latter had indicated he could only receive instructions from the President.[21]

Shortly before the above event, André Telting, President of Suriname's Central Bank had resigned. He refused to accept that his predecessor Henk Goedschalk (b. 1946) whose monetary financing policy he had resolutely terminated, was to be appointed as chairman of this bank's supervisory board. After Telting's departure, Wijdenbosch designated his confidant Goedschalk to take over Telting's position.[22] At that time, the Dutch judicial authorities suspected Goedschalk of carrying out financial activities for the Suri-cartel. In Suriname's political culture it is not uncommon to install one's "own" people in key positions within the governmental bureaucracy, state enterprises and state media. However the speed and thoroughness with which this procedure now unfolded had not even been witnessed during the military dictatorship of the 1980s. Generally speaking, NDP loyalists occupied key positions within the state apparatus. They were often the same individuals who had been active during the military regime. Doubtful or even criminal antecedents proved completely irrelevant.

The NDP's dominance was bound to lead to dissent within the coalition. In August 1997 President Wijdenbosch and the BVD's Chairman-*cum*-Minister of Finance Atta Mungra clashed heavily. In the latter's opinion, this President's financial policies would lead to the fall of the Surinamese guilder as well as to inflation. The BVD was also dissatisfied with its limited influence on diplomatic appointments. This criticism was delivered precisely when the Dutch press leaked that Dutch judicial authorities had issued an international arrest warrant through Interpol, concerning Desi Bouterse who was allegedly involved in transporting cocaine into the Netherlands (see p. 358-359). Atta Mungra probably thought he could enforce concessions from the NDP, now weakened by this drug-related issue. However, Wijdenbosch immediately removed Mungra, whom his own party subsequently abandoned too.[23] Of course,

---

21   *NRC Handelsblad*, 14 January 1997.
22   *NRC Handelsblad*, 28 November 1996 and 1 February 1997.
23   *NRC Handelsblad*, 26 August 1997.

the NDP had no interest in blowing up this coalition, nor did the BVD's business elite. Hence BVD financiers Dilip Sardjoe and George Pahlad, together with the NDP chairman Bouterse, successfully attempted to repair the rift.

Business-based interests in political power were obvious to anyone living in Suriname. In 1997 and 1998, for example, the government's plans to sell oil reserves owned by the state-owned Staatsolie Maatschappij Suriname to Daewoo, a South Korean company, caused huge uproar. For, Staatsolie was doing very well, rendering a quick sale unnecessary, even more so as Sardjoe represented Daewoo in Suriname. The government's secrecy fuelled the suspicion that illicit intermingling of private and state interests was taking place. Apparently these manoeuvres were primarily an attempt to hastily replenish the empty state coffers. The Staatsolie management had carefully been excluded from all plans.[24] Street protests and strikes nevertheless prevented the plans from being implemented.[25] Similarly, because of its key role, the 50 per cent state-owned Hakrinbank risked falling into the hands of the incoming business elite when the government attempted to prematurely, and in vain, replace this bank's supervisory board.[26] An agreement between the privately-owned Suriname Power Generating Company and the state-owned energy company EBS caused a commotion as well. According to contract, the former was to supply electricity to the latter. Here too, Sardjoe, the owner of the former firm, was the key initiator.

The fact the NDP Minister Errol Alibux had transferred hundreds of hectares of publicly-owned land located in the Nickerie district to the rice trader-*cum*-NDP financier Imro Manglie led to an equal level of widespread indignation. Such practices of issuing land were the norm rather the exception. For example, Imro Grep who chaired the pro-government trade union federation Moederbond received a plot of agricultural land located in Saramacca, apparently as a reward for his political support. The political elite, too, served themselves well. Bouterse received land located in the Para district in order to set up tourist facilities. The then Vice President Pertab Radakishun (1934-2001) also acquired a plot of land. Bouterse's right hand man and government advisor Etienne Boerenveen, was gifted a timber concession.[27] Realising they were covered by politicians, a number of businessmen c.q. kleptocrats targeted state-owned companies and other state-owned assets more frequently. The Suriname-based press published information on the collapse of Para Industries, a firm set up under military rule in order to manufacture, e.g., luxury tiles and glass. It was drained out by affiliated trading companies comprising individuals appointed as managers during the military regime. State-owned enterprises such as Bruynzeel, the timber company, and Grassalco N.V. (mining gold, kaolin, natural stone and crushed stone) were apparently neglected on purpose, hereby rendering them easy prey for politically amical business relationships. The ordinary business

---

24 *NRC Handelsblad*, 27 March 1998.

25 Approximately 10,000 people took to the streets on 9 and 24 June 1998 to demonstrate against the government's disastrous financial policy. These initiatives were organised by trade unions, employers' organisations and the opposition also formed a protest against the resignation of the Staatsolie director Eddy Jharap, whom the government had dismissed after his opposition as to selling the company to a Canadian firm, see: *NRC Handelsblad*, 5, 10, 11 and 25 June 1998.

26 *NRC Handelsblad*, 30 August 1997.

27 These land-related issues were revealed in the Surinamese newspaper *De West* on 17 and 24 July 1999.

A History of Suriname

community was constantly complaining about nepotism in public contracts, which were awarded without a public tender. Gold as well as log concessions became an increasingly common reward for services. More than ever before, the contours of an informal power in Suriname had become visible, thus resembling the military civilian oligarchy established by General H.M. Suharto (1921-2008), President of the Republic of Indonesia. Winston Jessurun (b. 1952), an MP of the DA91 opposition party aptly described the NDP as a party of a 'Boss and bosses'.[28]

In Suriname, large-scale cocaine trafficking had transformed the informal power into a narcocracy, whereby the drug mafia had undeniably obtained a grip on political, economic and criminal investigation issues. Even prior to Etienne Boerenveen's 1986 conviction in Miami (see p. 316) - when serving as Desi Bouterse's closest military aide-de-camp - Suriname had obviously become a transit port for cocaine from Colombia and Brazil. Contacts with the Colombian drugs mafia date back to the early 1980s. In February 1983 a report issued by the Netherlands-based *Centrale Recherche Informatiedienst* (Central Criminal Investigation Service) linked Bouterse's name to shipping cocaine from Colombia.[29] In 1983, too, Jules Sedney resigned as President of Suriname's Central Bank as he did not wish to participate in a suspicious Colombian loan. Reliable information describes that, as early as 1983, Bouterse upheld direct relations with Pablo Escobar, founding head of the Medellín Cartel, who had visited Paramaribo in person. Suriname became an attractive transit port when the pressure on Colombian cartels increased. A CoPa Team report states that at this time, 'there was talk of a meeting between the top of the Suri-cartel and the well-known drug baron Pablo Escobar'.[30] Notably, a direct eyewitness stated many years later that Bouterse, in 1983, had even organized a dinner in honour of Pablo Escobar and his entourage in the presidential palace in Paramaribo.[31] This report adds that, in 1988, Bouterse was seen accompanying Escobar, along with other high-ranking officers.[32] According to remarkable information provided by the Brazilian federal police, which is included in this report, the 'telephone coup' of December 1990 had been committed in order to protect Surinamese-Columbian drug interests. According to these Brazilian authorities, Escobar himself was involved in preparing this coup. For, he was reported to have travelled to Paramaribo in August 1990 in order to 'finance the coup, as the deposed President Shankar had banned Colombians from entering the country. One of Bouterse's immediate measures was to allow the re-entry of Colombians into the country.'[33]

Furthermore, significant indications point to the resistance of the military leadership as to the 1989 peace agreement with Brunswijk's Jungle Commando being motivated by an interest in cocaine trafficking. Especially Bouterse objected to plans

---

28 *NRC Handelsblad*, 21 May 1996.
29 Haenen & Buddingh' 1994, 63.
30 Haenen 1999, 44; Van den Heuvel 1999, 53.
31 *NRC Handelsblad*, 15 September 2016; the statement of the eyewitness, Leo Lichtveld, was provided to the present author in an e-mail sent by Michiel van Kempen on 5 September 2016. The latter wrote a biography of the former Surinamese minister-*cum*-author Lou Lichtveld, in the course of which he spoke with his nephew Leo Lichtveld who was in charge of catering during the reception held in honour of Pablo Escobar at the Paramaribo presidential palace in 1983.
32 Haenen 1999, 44; Van den Heuvel 1999, 142-143.
33 Haenen 1999, 46.

to include members of this commando in a special police force to be deployed in the interior of Suriname (see p. 327ff.). Such a force would threaten the control exercised by Bouterse and his troops over large jungle areas. This supervision was vital to the supply of cocaine and cocaine paste on small aircraft. In addition, it has become clear that the National Army provided Indigenous people, in casu, Tucajana Amazones, with weapons. Tasked with sabotaging the peace agreement with violent actions, both groups played an active role when shipping cocaine.[34] They collaborated closely when committing crimes. An illustrative example hereof comprises the notorious assassination, carried out in February 1990 in western Suriname, of a former Tucajana Amazones warrior named Pico Sabajo together with three other Indigenous people. This murder revealed traits of a drug-related criminal reckoning. After fleeing to Guyana, these four men were extradited to Suriname, after which a military aircraft transported them from Paramaribo westwards to the Indigenous village of Washabo, near Apoera, to then be handed over to the Tucajana Amazones commander Thomas Sabajo. Based on various eyewitnesses, the Roman Catholic priest Toon Te Dorsthorst later described these brutal, well-planned murders as follows:

'In Washabo and Apoera the Tucajanas and the National Army operated together as brothers. This was evident from the operation in which the dissident Tucajanas Pico and his companions were brought back to Washabo and then assassinated in a beastly manner by means of motor chainsaws. The murder operation carried out by the Tucajanas under the leadership of Commander Thomas himself was supported and watched by National Army units.'[35]

According to Father Te Dorsthorst, Melvin Linscheer, the then commander of the troops stationed in the interior, played a key role in this operation.[36] It has also been established that the Suri-cartel was involved in an international exchange of weapons for cocaine. In August 1999, the Brazilian police intercepted a Surinamese aircraft transporting automatic weapons, ammunition and a rocket installation. They were packed in Libyan arms boxes and supposedly destined for the Revolutionary Armed Forces of Colombia-People's Army (FARC).[37] A file created by Dutch authorities on Bouterse's activities also mentioned such an exchange. A witness stated it concerned 'brand new automatic weapons' stolen from the Surinamese army. The names of those involved were reportedly: commander Melvin Linscheer and Dino Bouterse, Bouterse's son, who served at the Embassy of Suriname in Brasilia until April 1999. In the Brazilian press, Dino Bouterse and Rupert Christopher, the Ambassador of

---

34   Ibid., 44; *NRC Handelsblad*, 27 July 1991.
35   *Omhoog*, 16 December 2018; Father Te Dorsthorst presented this statement during a service held in Paramaribo on 8 December 2018 to commemorate the victims of the December murders; see also: Te Dorsthorst 2022, 108-111.
36   Hoogbergen & Kruijt 2005, 218-219.
37   *NRC Handelsblad*, 18 August 1999.

A History of Suriname

Suriname in Brasilia, had already been accused of arranging an exchange of weapons for drugs in the Amazon.[38]

On 16 July 1999, the District Court at The Hague sentenced Desi Bouterse to a maximum penalty of 16 years in prison as well as to a 4.6 million Hfl fine for participating in drug transports to the Netherlands. In its verdict, this court referred to the Suri-cartel's considerable power thus:

> 'As the military commander of Suriname, the accused [...] had much power there, also outside the strictly military. For example, those considering to export cocaine, especially to the Netherlands, could not in fact act without the accused's knowledge. In doing so, he stimulated this export, commissioned shipments for his own account and was in charge of the production of cocaine in laboratories located in the interior of Suriname. For this export, an exporter had to possess a 'licence' from the defendant. This pertained to a certain quantity of cocaine and the licence had to be paid to the defendant. [...] The accused ensured through the military apparatus that the Surinamese customs or police did not intercept the cargo or luggage in question. [...] The [...] organisation can be seen as a group of individuals, of whom the accused was the undisputed leader who, for profit, maintained an exclusive market organisation in Suriname for the wholesale trade in cocaine, more specifically the export thereof.'[39],

Finally, on 30 June 2000, the Court of Appeal in The Hague sentenced Bouterse to 11 years in prison for being linked to a transport of 474 kg of cocaine to the Netherlands. Based on lack of evidence he was acquitted of (a) any involvement in five other cocaine transports and (b) participating in a criminal organisation between January 1989 and August 1991. An appeal in cassation did not alter this conviction.[40]

President Wijdenbosch did not see any obstacles to appointing suspects of drug-related crimes in key positions when mentioned in files composed by a Dutch narcotics squad. For example, the Chief Inspector of Police Herman Doorson, whom the CoPa Team deemed one of Bouterse's key accomplices, was installed as head of the *Centrale Inlichtingen Dienst* (Central Intelligence Service). This position enabled him to obtain all the information collected by the police on drug-related investigations.[41] Wijdenbosch designated commander Melvin Linscheer as his personal security advisor. The formerly high-ranked military officer Iwan Graanoogst was awarded the newly-created post of secretary-general of the presidential cabinet. Moreover, the Wijdenbosch-led government appointed Rupert Christopher to officiate as the Ambassador to Brazil. In 1991 the latter, a former military officer, had resigned as

---

38   Van den Heuvel 1999, 183-190; Haenen 1999, 72. Ruben Rozendaal, one of the military putschists in 1980, confirmed on 23 March 2012 (while being interrogated during the trial pertaining to the December murders in which he was a suspect) that he and Bouterse were personally directly involved in arms for cocaine deals with the FARC, see: *Starnieuws*, 23 March 2012.

39   Abridged sentence, 16 July 1999, Case Nr. 09/754087-97.

40   *NRC Handelsblad*, 1 July 2000 and 23 October 2001.

41   *NRC Handelsblad*, 17 May 1997.

Minister of Defence after the Dutch press had reported on his alleged involvement in drug trafficking.[42]

Estimates of the volume of cocaine passing through Suriname vary. Here, in 1997, Humphrey Tjin Liep Shie, head of the narcotics brigade, reported to the local radio station ABC Suriname that per annum an estimated 26,000 kg of cocaine were transported to Europe via Suriname.[43] In Europe the revenues of such a quantity amounted to *c*.1 billion USD. Also, according to Tjin Liep Shie, at least 25 per cent hereof remained in Suriname. This assessment would imply that profits accumulated by means of exporting cocaine was almost as large as the export value of the bauxite industry, Suriname's key export sector.

Exercising informal power was hardly curbed, because the government systematically undermined important state institutions. According to the 1997 report of the *Rekenkamer* (Court of Auditors), Suriname was experiencing a 'constitutional crisis' resulting from the government's refusal to provide this court with documents and information as required under the Constitution. This report also noted that 'government officials have deliberately acted in breach of statutory regulations and by way of defence refer to the orders they have received from above'. According to this court, ministers were guilty of such conduct, too, even if it went against their personal views.[44] In 1997, the National Assembly tabled a no confidence motion pertaining to Hans Prade (1938-2020), then President of the Court of Auditors, because of the 'tendentious manner' this information was shared.[45] At the end of Prade's term of office, President Wijdenbosch appointed a successor considered more flexible.

In a memorandum entitled *Waarachtigheid, Behoorlijk Bestuur en Welzijn* (Truthfulness, Good Governance and Well-being) dated 21 February 1998, the widely respected *Comité Christelijke Kerken* (Committee Christian Churches) outlined a situation of total social degradation. According to these churches, the people of Suriname felt 'misled and betrayed' by their political representatives:

> 'The current socio-cultural and political crisis in our country has reached such proportions rendering the dignity, the good name and the deepest aspirations of the people of Suriname violated. People live in an atmosphere of insecurity, a result of so-called blind walls, untruthfulness and silent threats. [...] The most striking symptom of the decline in recent times can be found in our country's administrative crisis. Numerous institutions set up by the government are hardly functioning, if at all. State bodies, laws and conventions therefore no longer guarantee the order, security and development as proposed by our Constitution. They do exist on paper, but there is no control over their actual functioning nor over the observance of the rules they set. We are thinking of the Court of Auditors and the National Assembly, among others. [...] In the constant political turmoil we have seen in our country, and certainly in recent times, politics seemingly does not serve the development of an administrative order that offers security and well-being to society as a

---

42   His alleged involvement was revealed in *NRC Handelsblad,* 27 July 1991.
43   *NRC Handelsblad,* 8 April 1997.
44   Rekenkamer van Suriname, *Report 1997,* Paramaribo 1998, Preface and 12.
45   Ibid., 3.

whole. Rather, it is at the service of a limited group of people who form centres of power by means of their own culture and structures, also referred to as the culture of patronage. State institutions are subjected to their selfish aspirations, which are aimed at rapid personal enrichment, the creation of excessive wealth and of a culture of excess, waste and material showmanship. [...] The economy of such centres of power also has its own procedures and structures, which are inaccessible to the research bodies of the State and therefore also to democratic control. This encourages the import and transit of drugs, as well as the sale and illegal export of natural resources such as gold, timber and fish.'[46]

A few months after the publication of this memorandum, a huge public outcry arose when, in violation of constitutional rules of procedure, President Wijdenbosch appointed a new president of the Court of Justice as well as a new attorney-general. Next, the members of this court refused to cooperate with their incoming president, the judge Alfred Veldema, because Wijdenbosch had not requested their council as required by the constitution. They also refused to recognise the appointment of the attorney-general Heloise Rozenblad, because the head of state had not awaited their advice. The joint lawyers' organisations expressed their solidarity with the protesting Court of Justice members. The conflict escalated when, a few months later, Wijdenbosch forcibly saw to it the acting president of this court's chamber was vacated, thus allowing the incoming president to take up his task. Wijdenbosch utilised the police force as well as the Central Intelligence Service and even convicted offenders supervised by prison guards. The strategy followed by the presidential 'battle squad' evoked associations with the Haitian Tontons Macoutes at the time of the Duvalier regime (1957-1986).[47] It led to a mass demonstration attended in Paramaribo by *c.*10,000 men, women and children, with the former president Venetiaan in attendance. Now protest was voiced against 'the attack on the judiciary.'[48]

15.4 Crisis in relations with the Netherlands
In The Hague, the regime change of 1996 formed a major setback. The relation with the previous government, led by Venetiaan, had admittedly been somewhat chilly in the early days due to an unyielding Dutch demand to clean up Suriname's economy. Venetiaan's Creole-nationalist reflexes had undoubtedly also contributed to cooling down this relation. However, Hans van Mierlo (1931-2010), the Dutch Minister of Foreign Affairs (1994-1998) had succeeded in improving the atmosphere by means of several informal visits to Paramaribo. Moreover, The Hague's money tap had meanwhile been turned on again, as the economic adjustment policy was starting to bear fruit. The Dutch government had tacitly assumed that the cash flow, partly earmarked for serving as a social safety net for the poorest, would divert the doom scenario comprising a government including Bouterse, who was accused of trafficking narcotics, as its 'shadow president'.

---

46   Comité Christelijke Kerken, Memorandum, Paramaribo, 21 February 1998.
47   *NRC Handelsblad*, 22 July 1998 and 17 March 1999.
48   *NRC Handelsblad*, 22 October 1998.

With President Wijdenbosch taking office, Van Mierlo declared that the Netherlands aimed at achieving a 'constructive and business-like' cooperation. According to the latter, however, cooperation in the spirit and the letter of the Framework Treaty of 1992 would only be possible if the rule of law as well as democracy were reinforced. Van Mierlo considered it 'crucial' to fight drug-related crimes 'at all levels'. He also called for steps to be taken by authorities in Suriname against violations of human rights witnessed in the past (e.g., the December murders).[49] At the end of 1997, Wijdenbosch set up a committee chaired by the lawyer Ludwig Waaldijk in order to prepare an investigation into violations of fundamental human rights.[50] However, a majority of the people of Suriname did not consider this committee credible. In fact Waaldijk's independence was queried after he had acted as Bouterse's legal advisor on more than one occasion.

In his government statement, Wijdenbosch had spoken of the desirability of a 'good and business-like cooperative relationship' with the Netherlands.[51] In December 1996, the positive intentions expressed on both sides led to an initial 'exploratory' discussion between Jan Pronk, Minister for Development Cooperation (1989-1998), and his Surinamese colleague Ernie Brunings, a former NDP member. Pronk indicated that earlier financial commitments would in any case be met.[52] Nevertheless the tone between the Dutch and Surinamese authorities soon became less friendly. In The Hague the irritation especially intensified as to Bouterse's prominent role. This NDP Chairman's mission to Brazil in preparation of President Wijdenbosch's official visit aroused great resentment. The Hague even summoned the Ambassador of Brazil to express 'dissatisfaction' and to also underline that Bouterse was a suspect in an investigation into drug-related crimes.[53] This issue had apparently become an insurmountable obstacle in the Dutch-Surinamese relationship. For, in a letter addressed to the lower house in The Hague dated 17 March 1997, Van Mierlo wrote:

'The relations between Suriname and the Netherlands are reflected in the Framework Treaty for Friendship and Closer Cooperation, in which the promotion and strengthening of democracy and the rule of law are key. Achieving this main objective would not be served by strengthening Mr. Bouterse's position and an official international role for his person who has the status of a suspect in the Netherlands in an on-going judicial investigation into violating the Opium Act and related criminal offences.'[54]

---

49 For an account of the parliamentary debate held on 22 October 1996, see: *Verslag overleg Vaste Kamercommissie voor Buitenlandse Zaken* (Parliamentary Foreign Affairs Commission), vergaderjaar 1996-1997, Kamerstuk 20361, nr. 79 (zoek.officielebekendmakingen.nl/kst-20361-79.html).

50 *NRC Handelsblad*, 6 December 1997.

51 Wijdenbosch, *Regeringsverklaring* (Government Declaration), 1 October 1996, 9.

52 As stated in Minister Pronk's letter sent to Parliament on 16 December 1996, see: Kamerstuk 20361, nr. 80 (zoek.officielebekendmakingen.nl/kst-20361-80.html).

53 *NRC Handelsblad*, 23 January 1997.

54 As stated in a letter to Parliament on 17 March 1997, see: Kamerstuk 20361, nr. 81 (zoek. officielebekendmakingen.nl/kst-20361-81.html).

A History of Suriname

Only a month later, Wijdenbosch decided to appoint Bouterse as *Adviseur van Staat* (Adviser to the State), a post created especially for him.[55] In March 1997, too, attorney general Arthur Docters van Leeuwen had announced, during a TV interview, that the judiciary in the Netherlands would begin to deal with the Bouterse case within a year.[56] The Dutch government had deliberately restrained itself to a distant reaction as it did not wish to be considered responsible for discontinuing sensitive relations. However, dissent escalated even further. For, in early August 1997, it was leaked through the Dutch press that Interpol, on the Netherlands' request, had issued a warrant for Bouterse's arrest a few months earlier.[57] He reacted by stating that his appointment as a state advisor had been a 'political signal' to The Hague.[58] Paramaribo now called back its Ambassador for consultation. The Netherlands did not consider a retaliatory step. In a letter sent to Van Mierlo, President Wijdenbosch requested an immediate revocation of the arrest warrant, which he regarded as a 'political act'.[59] Van Mierlo visited Brazil shortly afterwards in order to meet Wijdenbosch as Paramaribo only wished to talk at a 'neutral' location in order to thus emphasise once again that this arrest warrant was a purely judicial matter, which should not affect relations between the two countries.[60]

It all took a bizarre turn when, not much later, it was again leaked through the Dutch press that Winnie Sorgdrager, the Minister of Justice (1994-1998), had refrained from requesting Brazil to detain Bouterse, in July 1997, when he revisited Suriname's southern neighbour.[61] She took this decision after Minister of Foreign Affairs Van Mierlo, in a telephone conversation from his holiday address, had advised her not to forward this request. His political intervention was indeed remarkable, as he had assured President Wijdenbosch that the Bouterse case was of a judicial and not of a political nature. After allegedly receiving indications that the Brazilian authorities would not cooperate, Van Mierlo explained to the Dutch parliament that he had considered it unwise to submit a request for Bouterse's arrest in Brazil.[62] This explanation raised both widespread and serious doubts. For example, the federal police of Brazil had always collaborated with the CoPa Team in an exemplary way. According to its own statement, this team had even been assured by the Brazilian police authorities that Bouterse would be arrested in the case of an international arrest warrant.[63] The statement the Brazilian embassy in The Hague delivered on the day before the parliamentary debate, mentioning that Van Mierlo had taken 'a wise decision' seemed primarily a gesture of courtesy towards the politically troubled Van Mierlo.[64] Sorgdrager and Van Mierlo barely survived in the Dutch lower house, which

---

55 *NRC Handelsblad*, 29 April 1997.
56 Ibid., 28 April 1997.
57 Ibid., 6 August 1997.
58 Ibid., 7 August 1997.
59 Ibid., 11 August 1997.
60 Haenen 1999, 161.
61 Ibid., 153-162; *NRC Handelsblad*, 21 August 1997.
62 *NRC Handelsblad*, 23 August 1997.
63 Haenen 1999, 158.
64 *NRC Handelsblad*, 26 August 1997.

did not wish to shed any political blood pertaining to this issue only 6 months before elections were due to be held.[65]

The CoPa Team had the impression that Sorgdrager and Van Mierlo had tacitly agreed: in order to allow the legal process to run its course, Bouterse would be prosecuted in absentia. However, he would not be arrested, as this would encumber relations with Suriname. Moreover, issues with Bouterse's adherents in the Netherlands could arise hereby endangering the safety of the Dutch nationals residing in Suriname. Indeed, apparently not an unfounded interpretation if considering Sorgdrager's remarkable initiative in April 1997 when, much to the CoPa Team's amazement, she informed by telephone her Surinamese colleague Paul Ronald Sjak Shie, then Minister of Justice and Police, of the international arrest warrant. The latter was a member of a cabinet dominated by Bouterse's NDP.[66] Paramaribo deemed this message sufficient reason to prepare a state decree aimed at Bouterse being appointed to the post of state adviser, as mentioned earlier, apparently in an attempt to provide him with diplomatic immunity.[67]

The Bouterse case formed a legacy stemming from Ernst M. H. Hirsch Ballin, the Minister of Justice (1989-1994, 2006-2010). Due to an increasing import of cocaine into the Netherlands, he had reached the conclusion that the Surinamese drug mafia chiefs had to be dealt with under criminal law as applied in the Netherlands. During previous years, the Dutch government had apparently kept its eyes closed regarding the Surinamese cocaine trade. Even Lieutenant Boerenveen's conviction (Miami, 1986) for drug-related offences had not led to an extra activity (see p. 316). According to those police officers involved, narcotic-related investigations the Dutch had carried out pertaining to Boerenveen and other high-ranked Surinamese military personnel had indeed been cancelled for 'political and security reasons'.[68] In retrospect, Hirsch Ballin expressed his 'astonishment' about the fact that, when taking office at the Ministry of Justice in 1989, no file on Bouterse existed, despite numerous indications presented by the police pertaining to his involvement in the cocaine trade.[69] The policy change following Hirsch Ballin's appointment ('if they are criminals then the criminals have to be caught') suited the much more active position the cabinet led by Prime Minister Lubbers took with regard to Suriname after the 'telephone coup' of December 1990 (see p. 334ff.).[70] A key expression hereof was the previously mentioned Framework Treaty on Friendship and Closer Cooperation, concluded in 1992. Evidently The Hague finally felt prepared to recognize that Suriname was at risk of degenerating into a narco-state with a military signature. Years later, Relus ter Beek, the former Minister of Defence (1989-1994), revealed that during the autumn

---

65 Many years later, in 2021, former Justice Minister Winnie Sorgdrager mentioned that Van Mierlo, also her party leader, had 'obstructed' the Dutch justice system and that she had been 'angry' and 'frustrated' about that. According to Sorgdrager, it was not Brazil's alleged reluctance to have Bouterse arrested. In fact, the sensitivity of the relationship with Suriname led to the decision to leave Bouterse untouched. She added: 'Van Mierlo said: the relationship with Suriname is already so difficult and we should just not do it. And well, in short, I had my party leader talk me into it', see: *NRC Handelsblad*, 2 December 2021.
66 Haenen 1999, 153-159.
67 *Staatsblad*, nr. 16, 1997; this State Decree was dated 23 April 1997.
68 *NRC Handelsblad*, 31 August 1991; Haenen & Buddingh', 1994, 91.
69 Hirsch Ballin's remarks were broadcast on Dutch television on 14 March 1999.
70 Haenen 1999, 28.

A History of Suriname

of 1991, The Netherlands had prepared plans in order to assist President Venetiaan's government in utilizing military means if army leader Bouterse was to attempt yet another coup. According to Ter Beek, the Dutch military top had for this purpose drawn up a worst-case scenario.[71] Pressure from within this region, particularly by the USA, also forced the Netherlands into becoming further involved. Moreover, The Hague had little choice because of international obligations regarding drug-related crimes. Simultaneously the Dutch government, in close consultation with Washington stepped up the war on drugs in the Netherlands Antilles by setting up a coastguard. The Netherlands now apparently took on a greater responsibility in the Caribbean region thus raising its international profile. Successive cabinets continued this course of action. In March 1997, Van Mierlo confirmed in parliament that the Netherlands was obliged to tighten controls on drugs imported from Suriname, 'also because of its relations with neighbouring countries'.[72] For that reason, one could not abandon prosecuting Bouterse.

The gap between The Hague and Paramaribo seemed unbridgeable as a result of the Bouterse case. Dutch tax experts had already been sent home in June 1997, after Paramaribo deemed them too inquisitive.[73] In November 1997, President Wijdenbosch rather unexpectedly announced the suspension of all ministerial contacts between Suriname and the Netherlands.[74] This temporarily discontinued policy consultations on development cooperation, as a result of which the Netherlands could no longer execute recently established financial commitments to Paramaribo. Wijdenbosch demanded to firstly hold top level consultations pertaining to the relationship between both countries. The Dutch were only willing to agree to this if such a summit was well prepared. For The Hague, it was a matter of ensuring that the summit (i.e., a meeting between President Wijdenbosch and Prime Minister Wim Kok) did not fail, precisely because of the special nature of their mutual relations. Consultations between officials, which had to take place on neutral territory due to great sensitivities felt on the Surinamese side, were fruitless. Wijdenbosch continued to demand a withdrawal of Bouterse's international arrest warrant. The Surinamese government having turned the issue into a state matter, rendered solutions impossible from the very outset.

In due course, however, Wijdenbosch decided to discharge Bouterse of his duty as a state advisor, because he been unable to 'contribute to social peace and a healthy political climate'.[75] This dismissal illustrated the estrangement between these two men as well as the division that had arisen within the NDP (see p. 364). Perhaps Bouterse's prosecution in the Netherlands played a role here too. His forced resignation as an advisor did not conclude the impasse in ties between Suriname and the Netherlands. However, Wijdenbosch did make a remarkable attempt to improve this relationship by, for the first time in years, congratulating the Dutch monarch on Queen's Day, her birthday. In the meantime, Prime Minister Kok's second cabinet had taken office in The Hague, hereby seemingly distancing itself slightly from

---

71   Ter Beek 1996, 119.
72   Report of a parliamentary debate: Kamerstuk 20361, nr. 82 (zoek.officielebekendmakingen.nl/kst-20361-82.html).
73   *NRC Handelsblad,* 23 April 1997.
74   Ibid., 14 November 1997.
75   Ibid., 6 April 1999.

Suriname. The then Minister of Foreign Affairs Jozias van Aartsen (1998-2002) and his colleague the Minister of Development Cooperation Eveline Herfkens (1998-2002) felt less strongly tied to Suriname than Van Mierlo and Pronk, their predecessors, had been. The same stance applies to an incoming generation of parliamentarians. Shortly after taking office, Van Aartsen stated somewhat cynically: 'Suriname is not the centre of Dutch foreign policy'.[76] Moreover, Herfkens publicly denounced the corruption in Paramaribo. In a joint letter addressed to the Dutch lower house and dated 18 June 1999, the latter two ministers sketched an extremely negative, be it accurate, image of the situation in Suriname:

> *'Under the Wijdenbosch government, developments in Suriname have evolved to the point where the country no longer meets internationally accepted criteria of good governance and good policy.'*[77]

15.5 Mass demonstrations against malpractices and corruption

The departure in August 1997 of the BVD politician and Minister of Finance Atta Mungra had made it clear that public finances were again spiralling out of control. The Hindustani HPP and the farmers' party PVF-FAL, which had formed part of the so-called *Alliance* before the elections, also quit the government coalition. President Wijdenbosch's idiosyncratic behaviour had provided very little scope. The coalition of the NDP and the BVD, dominated by financial interests, experienced few difficulties when enticing several members of parliament from small parties in order to secure a parliamentarian majority. However, a stable majority was no longer in place. This coalition often failed to provide the required quorum of 50 per cent plus one in the National Assembly. Hence, parliament could not function properly. In the course of 1997 and 1998, public discontent increased sharply as the effects of economic mismanagement became increasingly apparent. The collapse of several pyramid funds, in which many lost their money, may also have played a role. The NDP coalition attempted to buy off a growing societal dissent by increasing the salaries of civil servants and the pensioner's benefits. A rising inflation and a decrease in value of the Surinamese guilder nonetheless rapidly eroded the purchasing power of citizens. Moreover, the construction of bridges across the Coppename and the Suriname Rivers heavily burdened the state funds (see p. 366). Having become prestige projects for the president and his party, these bridges were also aimed at (a) boosting national self-confidence and (b) yielding electoral benefits in the upcoming elections. The Wijdenbosch-led government was however no longer able to curb social discontent. Due to financial mismanagement important government services (e.g., health care, education) were seriously affected too. The state health insurance fund for example no longer received premiums the government had obtained from civil servants. Hence, this fund could no longer pay hospitals for any provided care forcing them into financial difficulties, whereby patients were obliged to pay for treatments in cash.

---

76 Ibid., 23 July 1999.
77 Kamerstuk 20361, nr. 93 (zoek.officielebekendmakingen.nl/kst-20361-93.html).

Figure 15.2. A demonstration held in protest of the Wijdenbosch-led government (Paramaribo, May 1999). Photo by Edward Troon.

Undermining the independent position of both the Court of Justice and the Court of Auditors had also provoked anger. The accumulation of incompetence, corruption and mismanagement had in the end completely undermined the trust which society had placed in its leaders. The joint opposition teamed up in order to create a broad movement, resembling the *Associatie voor Democratie* which had opposed the military dictatorship at the end of 1982 (see p. 307). The *Gestructureerd Samenwerkingsverband* (Structured Cooperation) proclaimed on 22 October 1998, included opposition parties as well as the trade union movement and the business community. In its proclamation we read:

'*The* [government] *majority is apparently maintained by a limited group of people who form centres of power with their own culture and their own structures, whereby state institutions are subjected to their selfish endeavours aimed at rapid personal enrichment and excessive accumulation of wealth.*'[78]

The opposition to the government gained momentum in May 1999 after the Surinamese guilder had lost 40 per cent of its value on the black market in just a few days (see p. 368). In daily protest demonstrations, the Structured Cooperation demanded President Wijdenbosch's resignation. The streets of Paramaribo witnessed

---

[78] *Gedenkboek 50 jaar Vooruitstrevende Hervomings-Partij VHP* (Memorial book 50 years VHP), Paramaribo 1999, 197.

mass gatherings with tens of thousands present every day.[79] Their orderly and targeted nature, coordinated by the prominent trade unionist-*cum*-politician Fred Derby, was particularly noteworthy.

President Wijdenbosch lost his majority support in the National Assembly when several BVD members of parliament decided to side with the opposition. On 1 June, the parliament seemed to pave the way for dismissing Wijdenbosch when a motion of no confidence was accepted with 27 against 14 votes.[80] His objection hereto: according to the constitution, the parliament could not send him off by means of a simple majority. Although he had even spoken of a parliamentary coup, many refused to take him seriously.[81] A few days earlier, Wijdenbosch had tried in vain to prevent this motion from being carried by dismissing his entire cabinet. Nonetheless, after this discouraging vote in parliament, he allowed his ministers to remain in office and, even in his own party, now drew little support. The same NDP supporters who had shouted 'we want Bosje!' during elections now wrote 'Bosje go home' on their banners. For many years this party's leadership had attempted to establish a power base within the trade union movement by means of a commitment the leadership of the trade union federation Moederbond had provided (see also p. 314). However, those union organisations affiliated with this federation participated fully when demonstrating against the President. When stating that ministers were 'corrupt', Bouterse also publicly announced that Wijdenbosch had to resign.[82] The latter could not do otherwise, as the NDP quickly lost its support.

Bouterse's criticism had nonetheless placed him in an odd position. After all, he himself had been the architect of the coalition. Having taken office as President, Wijdenbosch was regarded as Bouterse's frontman. During the 1980s, Wijdenbosch, a political scientist educated at the University of Amsterdam, had provided the as yet militarily dominated NDP (as well as its predecessor: the 25 February Movement) with a 'civil' appearance. However, once inaugurated as president, he took an increasingly independent stance by appointing his personal 'royal household' and loosening members of Bouterse's circle, including the (former) soldiers Graanoogst, Mijnals and Linscheer. Bouterse's aforementioned dismissal as state advisor had therefore become inevitable.

Wijdenbosch's political fate was apparently sealed after the vote was held in the National Assembly. Nevertheless a political impasse unexpectedly arose. For, in the midst of persistent rumours linked to bribery and intimidation, two parliamentarians had defected again. The opposition hereby lost the majority in order to force a vote on both an incoming president and vice president. The aforementioned Structured Cooperation required an interim government, which should be allowed at least 12 months to restore the politico-economic order. Subsequently, early elections would take place. For the positions of president and vice president André Telting, former head of the Suriname's Central Bank and Eddy Jharap, director of the state oil company Staatsolie, had been suggested. Their candidacy was no coincidence:

---

79   *NRC Handelsblad*, 25, 31 May and 1 June 1999.
80   Ibid., 7 June 1999.
81   According to Articles 74 and 83 of the Constitution, the National Assembly can 'have the President and Vice President resign prematurely' by means of a simple majority.
82   *NRC Handelsblad*, 31 May 1999.

they had become popular among common Surinamese thanks to a reputation-based on professional excellence and incorruptibility. However, the NDP and the other coalition parties wished the Wijdenbosch-led government to not only stay on but also to then call early elections. The opposition had little choice but to accept this. Finally, Wijdenbosch applied his constitutional powers to set the election date on May 25, 2000.[83] The desire to ceremoniously open the bridge across the Suriname River during the election campaign apparently prompted his decision. Lack of competence as well as vanity remained the mildest judgements which the people of Suriname delivered upon Wijdenbosch, who had embarked on his professional career as a civil servant in an Amsterdam district council.

Bouterse's future was far more complicated. He left the possibility of a further political career open after being sentenced by the court at The Hague. Reality probably left him with no other choice. Either a parliamentary seat or a presidency could possibly protect him against judicial investigations and/or prosecution in Suriname linked to the December murders. Moreover, interests of a material and criminal nature, pertaining to him personally and perhaps also to his 'relations' located in Colombia and Brazil seemingly forced him to remain in the centre of power. Despite Bouterse's re-election as the NDP's chairman a few months earlier, support for him had become much less self-evident even within his party, due to the economic crisis as well as the verdict of the court in The Hague. According to a survey by the Surinamese polling institute IDOS conducted a few days after the parliamentary motion had been forwarded against Wijdenbosch, only 14 per cent of the inhabitants of Paramaribo deemed Bouterse suited to serve as their future president. In fact, 70 per cent considered him inapt for this task.[84] According to IDOS, the government's administrative shortcomings had also translated into a sharp drop in support for the NDP.

After the coup of 25 February 1980, Bouterse had always managed to stay afloat as a charismatic *wakaman* (i.e., a hustler who can survive street life). As a humble sergeant and sports instructor who had laid hands on a nation state after an unbridled trade union conflict, as a Leader of the Revolution who would instil faith in the abilities of the people of Suriname and break through ethnic divisions and with the image of a successful businessman. Starting off as a Dutch soldier based in Germany while trading in second-hand cars as well as pornography, Bouterse succeeded in becoming a hero of the impoverished.[85] He has always slightly resembled the mythical spider named Anansi, a protagonist in Afro-Caribbean folktales, that always outsmarts everybody else. In Creole culture especially, this role generates both admiration and fear. By now, due to his conviction for drug-related crimes, Bouterse had become a prisoner in his own country. One could indeed legitimately now ask whether he did not need his party more than his party needed him.

---

83   Ibid., 16 July 1999.
84   The results of this opinion poll were broadcast on Dutch radio on 18 December 1999.
85   See: P. Reeser's in-depth biography, published in 2015, entitled *Desi Bouterse, een Surinaamse tragedie.*

15.6 Crisis after malpractice and corruption

Within a few months after President Wijdenbosch had taken office, the financial instability of a vulnerable and import-dependent economy once again became apparent. One of his first initiatives comprised discontinuing the structural adjustment programme. As early as March 1997, the IMF had warned that implementing the incoming government's plans would lead to an increasing government deficit, a weaker balance of payments and further inflation.[86] Successive increases in the salaries and pensions of civil servants, totalling as much as 50 per cent at the start of 1997, placed severe pressure on the budget. Construction of bridges across the Coppename and Suriname Rivers, with an estimated cost of Hfl 190 million, seized the scarce resources. In its 1998 annual report, *De Surinaamsche Bank*, the largest privately-owned bank active in Suriname, expressed its astonishment about the fact that the state budget 'does not even say a word about the most important commitment we as a nation have made for the coming years'.[87] According to a contract with a Dutch development and construction company named Ballast Nedam, monthly payments in cash had to take place during the construction phase. The introduction of a sales tax to increase revenue was watered down and further delayed for political reasons. Contributions from the bauxite sector to the government decreased from 40 million USD in 1997 to 29 million USD in 1998, a result of the falling profits Suralco and Billiton had experienced due to declining prices in the global market place.[88] Income tax revenues were disappointing, too, possibly the outcome of a forced departure of Dutch tax experts. Not insignificantly, Dutch financial aid, having risen to *c.*15 per cent of GDP in 1996, was reduced because of political issues between the Netherlands and Suriname.[89]

Despite a sharp decline in state revenues, the government maintained the level of expenditure. Thus, the small governmental surplus of 1996 turned into a double-digit deficit in 1998. Deficits were now financed by means of (a) reducing the reserves of Suriname's Central Bank, (b) borrowing from domestic as well as foreign banks and (c) accumulating arrears. Both the government and this bank consistently denied that public spending was monetarily financed. The IMF figures nonetheless revealed an increasing liquidity creation.[90] At the end of the 1990s the Surinamese guilder, equal to more than 0.50 USD prior to all these crises, was not even worth 0.001 USD.[91] Loans from domestic banks bore traits of monetary financing. For example, from the beginning of 1998, they granted loans to the government in excess of the legal lending ceiling.[92] Suriname's Central Bank now only partially reimbursed them for their advances or only after a very lengthy delay. The bank credit was in part converted into a long-term loan, implying that a future government had to solve debt problems. Indications existed that this bank was executing monetary transactions via a bypass route by means of providing deposits to government banks, which then passed the

---

86   *NRC Handelsblad,* 12 December 1997.
87   De Surinaamsche Bank, *Annual Report 1998,* 20.
88   Central Bank of Suriname, *Report 1997-2000,* 25-26.
89   *IMF Staff Report 1999* (unpubl.), 19; at the request of the Surinamese government only a *Public Information Notice (PIN), No. 99/80,* 19 August 1999 was published which included a summary.
90   *IMF Public Information Notice (PIN), No. 01/54,* 24 May 2001.
91   *IMF Working Paper, Suriname: A Case Study of High Inflation,* 1999 WP/99/157, 9.
92   Central Bank of Suriname, *Report 1997-2000,* 34.

money on to the government as a loan.[93] Part of the foreign loans also contributed to monetary financing, although this procedure was apparently concealed by means of tampering with this Central Bank's accounts. This practice implied that Suriname had to keep a certain number of dollar loans on deposit with those foreign banks involved, due to a lack of creditworthiness. Yet these amounts of dollars were added to the monetary reserves presented in the statistics. Surinamese guilders circulated on the basis of the equivalent.[94]

The external debt had increased significantly during this period, to wit, from 25 per cent of GDP in 1998 to almost 50 per cent of GDP in 2001.[95] These numbers were provided by the IMF. The Suriname's Central Bank's former President A. Telting, returning to his post in the third quarter of 2000, calculated an even higher level of external debt. This all brought the country close to debt levels encountered during the crisis which Central American countries experienced during the 1980s. According to Telting the government of Suriname had provided the IMF with an incomplete list of foreign loans.[96]

This expansionary fiscal and monetary policy had also boosted the demand for imported goods and services, and thus for dollars. At the same time, exports were disappointing. In 1999 and 2000, the economy shrank by *c.*10 per cent.[97] The rice sector had once again run into problems due to a poor macro-economic policy as well as a neglect of wet infrastructure. The cultivated areas of land had decreased by more than 32 per cent between 1996 and 2000, causing a sharp drop in export earnings.[98] Due to an unfavourable exchange rate regime a large gap between the official exchange rate and the parallel rate had developed as had been the case during the early 1990s, whereby net yields for rice farmers decreased. High interest rates of up to 35 per cent had not only caused many rice farmers to experience financial difficulties but also rendered investments almost unaffordable.[99] They were now forced to pay for their imported inputs with expensive US dollars purchased on the black market, while export earnings were settled at unfavourable official exchange rates via Suriname's central bank. A major cause of these high interest rates was a lack of trust in state policies, which kept inflation expectations high. In the government's view, this phenomenon was sufficient reason to meet the farmers' needs with subsidised loans, in turn, financed by means of foreign loans through this central bank. The IMF criticised this transaction.[100] The fall in numerous world market prices during 1998, brought about by the financial crisis in Asia, had affected the value of key Surinamese exports, to wit, alumina, aluminium, oil, gold, rice and shrimps. In addition, droughts resulting from the El Niño climate pattern led to a

---

93   Central Bank of Suriname, *Report 1997-2000*, 35. This bank mentions 'quasi-fiscal' activities which ceased after its incoming President, A. Telting, took office during the third quarter of 2000.
94   Ibid., 40.
95   *IMF Public Information Notice, No. 01/54*, 24 May 2001.
96   *NRC Handelsblad*, 22 July 1999.
97   *IMF Public Information Note No. 01/54*, 24 May 2001.
98   Central Bank of Suriname, *Report 1997-2000*, 30.
99   Ibid., 44.
100   *IMF Staff Report 1999* (unpubl.), 11; the IMF clarifies that the Central Bank of Suriname should not execute such on-lending practices and that these activities are not transparent because the subsidies are not reflected in the national budget.

lower agricultural production. On balance, in 1998, the small current account surplus dating to previous years had transformed into a substantial deficit amounting in access of 114.7 million USD.[101] Foreign loans stemming from the public and private sectors largely covered this deficit.

The collapse of the Surinamese guilder marked a deep economic crisis, which quickly turned into a political crisis (see p. 363ff.). On 14 May 1999, the Surinamese guilder lost 33 per cent of its value within a single day, dropping from 1,500 to 2,000 Sfl for a single USD. The Finance Minister Gobardhan's explanation was particularly noteworthy as he linked it to a seizure in the Netherlands of cocaine originating from Suriname, valued at tens of millions of US dollars, stating that 'these criminals are losing this and now urgently need currency'.[102] Suriname had not been able to borrow money abroad for several months due to a lack of creditworthiness. President Wijdenbosch even accused his fellow countrymen of having deterred foreign financiers when publishing negative information on the internet.[103] It thus became increasingly difficult for the government to meet its financial obligations. When monthly payments to Ballast Nedam associated with constructing those two aforementioned bridges proved to be at stake, too, Ballast Nedam provided an undisclosed loan to Paramaribo utilising export proceeds from the bauxite and oil sectors as a collateral.[104] Private banks were now hardly prepared to advance any payments. In July 1999, the government ran into acute liquidity problems whereby ministries could no longer obtain any credit for material expenditure. In Paramaribo, the exception made for the Ministry of Regional Development was considered a political manoeuvre. After all, this department mainly worked for Maroons and Indigenous peoples. The latter group formed a key part of the NDP electorate. [105] The government's need for money also caused a large number of private companies to suffer huge difficulties, as they now no longer received payments for supplies. This predicament led the employers' organisation VSB to threaten with the seizure of government property. This situation was especially difficult for private entrepreneurs. For, as a result of their huge claims pertaining to the government, banks could hardly create any financial space in order to provide loans to companies.

For a majority of Surinamese, this economic crisis was indeed disastrous as inflation rose rapidly. Although no official figures on local poverty exist, one may conclude that the inhabitants of Suriname by and large were impoverished. Apparently only a small minority benefited from either the unofficial or illegal economy, which included gold mining and drug trafficking. Physicians warned of an increase in malnutrition and diarrhoea among children. The elderly spoke of meals, which consisted only of bread and tea. Due to high costs, proper health care had become inaccessible to many. The state health insurance fund had no financial resources, because the insurance premiums forwarded by civil servants had

---

101 *IMF Public Information Notice, No. 99/80*, 19 August 1999.
102 *NRC Handelsblad*, 15 May 1999.
103 *De Ware Tijd*, 5 August 1999.
104 *NRC Handelsblad*, 3 August 1999.
105 Ibid., 21 and 22 July 1999.

disappeared into the state coffers. Hence hospitals and their medical doctors were forced to demand direct cash payments from patients.[106]

This economic crisis also imposed an increasingly heavy burden on the future. According to the IMF, the state's foreign debt obligations in 1999 and 2000 were already in excess of 50 million USD per annum, thus in access of 10 per cent of the annual export earnings and exceeding well over four times as much as in previous years.[107] The problem was in fact even more serious. For, due to the collapse of the Surinamese guilder, repayments and interest payments in dollars had become much more expensive. The nation's Central Bank's monetary stock of gold, comprising 61.4 million USD in 1996, had shrunk to a mere 4 million USD in 2000.[108]

---

106 Ibid., 2 August 1999.
107 *IMF Report on Article IV Consultation with Suriname*, 1999, 23 (unpubl.).
108 Central Bank of Suriname, *Report 1997-2000*, 55.

CHAPTER 16
Suriname in the 21ˢᵗ century

16.1 Introduction

Towards the end of the 20ᵗʰ century, Suriname was worse off if compared with 1975, the year it gained independence. The consequences of military coups, the war in the interior as well as corruption and mismanagement were painfully visible everywhere. For numerous households, parcels and financial support sent by family members residing in the Netherlands had become indispensable in order to survive. Due to high costs, adequate health care was hardly accessible to large numbers. Based on budget surveys referring to 1968/1969 and to 1999/2000, the General Bureau of Statistics calculated that the percentage of poverty-stricken inhabitants of Paramaribo and surroundings had more than tripled, to wit, from 21 to 65 per cent. They had 'insufficient resources to meet their basic needs'.[1] This large increase underscores the fact the middle classes were impoverished, too. Notably, the monthly salaries of school principals had dropped from (converted from Sfl) 860 Hfl in 1981 to 340 in Hfl 1999.[2] In fact, the average income of the people of Suriname had decreased almost continuously from 1978 until the turn of the 20ᵗʰ century. This development contrasted sharply when compared with events unfolding within the region (see Figure 16.1., p. 372). Official employment had not increased in all these years. On the contrary, the number of jobs had dropped. However, the public sector did witness the highest employment growth. Movements in bauxite prices, the suspension of Dutch aid as well as the temporary negative effects of the structural adjustment programme felt during the 1990s, combined with the turmoil caused by military coups and the Interior War, can only in part explain this decline.

According to an IDB's highly critical report, the government itself had 'hindered Suriname's development by inadequately executing the core tasks of government and by consuming a large share of national resources. A primary cause of the poor performance and high cost of government has been the over- ambitious role assigned to government'.[3] As early as in 1998, the World Bank and the IDB had in separately published reports reached staggering conclusions pertaining to the quality of education in Suriname. For, here these results were among the worst, despite having spent relatively more funds on education than most other nation states in the region, to wit, excess of 5 per cent of GDP.[4]

Only 40 per cent of the 12-19 year age group followed secondary education, thus establishing the lowest percentage in the Caribbean, with the exception of Haiti. As to primary education, 20 per cent of the pupils repeated a year of tuition, thus far more

---

1   Soedhwa 2005, 11.
2   Schalkwijk 2009, 45.
3   Martin, April 2001, xii.
4   See the World Bank publication entitled *Suriname. A Strategy for Sustainable Growth and Poverty Reduction. Country Economic Memorandum*, Washington, 31 March 1998, ix, 43-48; see also Inter-American Development Bank, *Suriname. Education sector study*, Washington, February 1998; the low level of education is confirmed in a later report by the Inter-American Development Bank, *Returns to Education in Suriname*, Washington, June 2013.

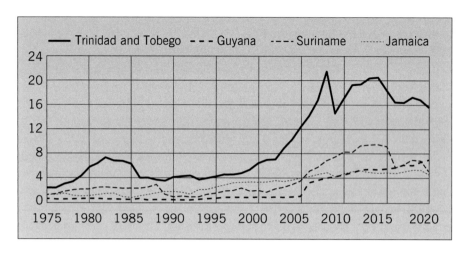

Figure 16.1. GDP per capita in thousands of current USD, 1975-2020. Source: The World Bank Open Data (data.worldbank.org).

	1975	1979	1987	1996	2000
Agriculture, livestock, fisheries [i]	17,100	17,100	14,360	12,472	11,646
Mining, bauxite processing (incl. hydro) [ii]	6,900	6,000	3,375	3,496	2,424
Industry	9,800	10,400	10,106	9,843	7,700
Gas, water, electricity (excl. hydro)	1,100	1,100	1,803	1,662	1,698
Construction	4,300	3,500	2,300	3,000	5,752
Commerce, restaurants, hotels	14,200	14,900	11,301	13,642	13,710
Transport, storage, communication	3,500	3,600	3,510	3,294	2,742
Financial institutions, commercial and housing services	1,700	2,200	2,359	2,703	2,716
Government (incl. defence)	29,400	39,600	37,531	33,031	34,206
Personal services	3,400	3,700	4,349	3,563	3,852
Total	**91,400**	**102,100**	**90,994**	**86,705**	**86,450**

Table 16.1. Indication of the number of jobs by sector. [i] From 1987 on, this category also includes forestry. [ii] From 1987, too, this category includes gold processing. Source: Algemeen Bureau voor Statistiek (ABS).

than the 5 per cent witnessed in Jamaica or the 4 per cent reported in Trinidad and Tobago. Youngsters populating the interior of Suriname were most disadvantaged. One of the causes of this non-performance which both the World Bank and the IDB mentioned was: for the majority of pupils attending school for the first time, the Dutch language was the second or third language spoken, while at home one conversed in Sranan Tongo or in another language. The Dutch education inspector W.H.M. d'Haens had already observed this shortcoming half a century earlier during a fact-finding mission to Paramaribo, after Suriname had delivered complaints concerning the inferior quality of education.[5] Further causes of this non-performance were: the

---

5   d'Haens, January 1947.

A History of Suriname

low quality and motivation among teachers as well as a lack of tutorial material. The IDB report not only referred to 'ghost teachers' but also stated that half the teaching staff, although never going to work, did receive salaries. Low participation levels encountered in secondary education was partly due to a lack of space. This situation led to the discouragement of pupils who wished to follow this level of tuition whereby numerous school-goers were referred to technical education, regardless of their suitability or interest.

The inadequacy of being capable of providing desired types of tuition was reflected in the inefficiency of Suriname's governmental apparatus, which was crippled by means of patronage, corruption, a lack of trained staff and poor management. Successive governments had displayed little ability as to solving any problems. Economic policies were as yet ethnically sensitive, rendering it difficult to find solutions, After all, a majority of Creoles continued to find employment within the state sector, while Hindustanis controlled agriculture. An excess of 50 per cent of the working population remained registered either as civil servants or as employees in one of the more than 100 (non-)commercial state-owned enterprises and institutions.[6] In addition, an excess of out-dated regulations as well as an interfering government severely thwarted economic developments (see p. 431-432). The small scale of the domestic market continued to form an obstacle, thus frustrating the growth of local private production. When Suriname acquired access to the Caribbean Community (Caricom) on 1 July 1995 the potential market increased. However, the majority of entrepreneurs were unable to compete due to a lack of expertise and/or experience.

A chronic weakness in government policy implied that revenues obtained both from natural resources and foreign aid were spent far more on consumption (i.e., paying civil servants' salaries, goods and services) when compared with other parts of the Caribbean.[7] Hence, investments in physical as well as in human capital lagged behind, causing sub-standard economic performances. It had already become clear that Dutch aid formed a substitute rather than an incentive for Surinamese investments (see p. 295). The World Bank, in its 1998 extensive report entitled *Suriname. A Strategy for Sustainable Growth and Poverty Reduction*, arrived at the damning conclusion that the economy of Suriname had remained 'one of the most disturbed' and 'also underperforming' in the region during the last 30 years.[8] Moreover, this economy still displayed the same one-sided structure, with its dominant bauxite sector and an extensive public sector, whereby the key new feature comprised a sharply increased size of the parallel or informal economy, in which gold mining and drug trafficking dominated.

16.2 The 'old' parties return to power

After the popular uprising against the Wijdenbosch-led government in May 1999, it was no longer surprising that the combined old parties returned to the heart of power. The only mutation in the *Nieuw Front* was replacing the Javanese KTPI with a party named *Pertjajah Luhur* (Full of Confidence).

---

6   Martin, April 2001, 40-41.
7   Ibid., 45.
8   The World Bank, 1998, vii.

	1972	2004
Maroon	35,838 (9.4 %)	72,553 (14.7 %)
Creole	119,009 (31.4 %)	87,202 (17.7 %)
Hindustani	142,917 (37.6 %)	135,117 (27.4 %)
Javanese	57,688 (15.2 %)	71,879 (14.6 %)
Mixed[i]	-	61,524 (12.5 %)
Other[i]	24,155 (6.4 %)	31,975 (6.5 %)
Unknown	-	32,579 (6.6 %)
Total	**379,607 (100 %)**	**492,829 (100 %)**

Table 16.2. Composition of the population according to ethnicity. [i]The figures of the groups presented here are not entirely comparable. For, in 1972, the category 'mixed' was classified under the category 'de rest' (i.e. 'other'). Source: Census 1972 and 2004, Algemeen Bureau voor Statistiek.

This change came with the same ethnic signature but had a more appealing leader called Paul Somohardjo. The elections held on 25 May 2000 reminded of the 1987 elections, when voters presented the NF's traditional ethnic parties with a landslide victory after suffering from years of dictatorship and mismanagement. The NF, in which the political veterans Venetiaan and Lachmon continued to play key roles, however, did not achieve an absolute majority with 47.6 per cent.[9] The fact the NF had obtained 33 of the 51 seats in the National Assembly was a result of Suriname's exceptional electoral system. The election results seemed to confirm a trend that had started in 1996, when the old ethnic parties, having obtained 41.8 per cent of the votes, took in a minority position for the first time. Remarkably, smaller parties (e.g., DOE, DA91, PVF) while seeking to foster issues such as good governance and party democracy, attracted more than 16 per cent of voters. The electoral system however did not see to it that this result was equally reflected in the number of seats.

A factor which explains such an electoral trend comprises the demographic evolution. For example, the 2004 Census discloses interesting shifts as to the numerical proportions of ethnic groups, when compared to the result of 1972. Noteworthy is the sharp drop from 31.4 to 17.7 per cent within the segment of Suriname's society that identified itself as being of Creole descent. Equally, if not even more, striking is: a strong rise in the number of Maroons from 9.4 to 14.7 per cent. This increase was mainly the result of a high birth rate. Perhaps the growing self-awareness among Maroons, as observed since the Internal War, had led them to describe themselves as Maroons more frequently. The decrease in the percentage of Hindustanis was less spectacular than when compared with Creoles. However, this phenomenon was not insignificant. In 1972, Creoles and Hindustanis combined made up more than two-thirds of the population, enabling the NPS and VHP to dominate politics. In 2004, their combined share of votes had dropped to less than 50 per cent. Introducing the category 'mixed' (in 1972 included in the category 'other') narrowed down the definition of Creole. This forms a key factor in explaining the sharp decline in the number of those who continued to identify themselves as Creole in the 2004 census.[10] A group that labels itself as 'mixed' is less inclined to vote for traditional ethnic parties. The size of the 'unknown' group is salient.

9   Schalkwijk 2000, 35.
10   Menke & Sno 2016, 91.

For, its members often refused to classify themselves as belonging to an ethnic group. Such a demographic fragmentation is not without consequences in a country where ethnic politics play key roles and whereby political decision-making will indeed prove to be more complex.

The *Millennium Combinatie* (MC), with the NDP of former army leader Bouterse as the largest partner by far, remained fixed at 15.1 per cent after the elections. This was partly due to the exit from the NDP of outgoing president Wijdenbosch. He together with his newly founded party named *DNP 2000* acquired almost 10 per cent of the votes, in spite of a disastrous governance.[11] A few days before the elections Wijdenbosch had presented the people of Suriname with a newly constructed bridge on the Suriname River. In his view, it had been built 'with the help of the Almighty'; he did nevertheless officially name it the Jules Wijdenbosch Bridge perhaps in order to enhance his own ego.[12] Bouterse had apparently limited the damage to his party by distancing himself from Wijdenbosch and his mismanagement, already during the latter's presidency. Important was also the fact that Bouterse had run for parliament for the first time. However, he did not deem the time ripe to run for president. A survey carried out by the Dutch national broadcasting company indicated that only 6 per cent of Surinamese voters considered Bouterse suitable to serve as president.[13] Once nominated for a parliamentary seat, however, he did seem to aim at re-establishing his grip on the NDP. Despite being re-elected as its chairman, Bouterse's NDP-leadership was not self-evident to all its members because of his drug conviction and the threat of a trial linked to the December murders. NDP members, including past confidants, businessmen and former soldiers, had followed Wijdenbosch upon his departure. They may well have assumed that a Bouterse-led NDP would not play a role as a potential governing party and thus no longer served their interests. 'The man is hurt, for the first time in twenty years', Minister Errol Alibux stated at the time, while personally siding with Wijdenbosch.[14]

With the help of several opposition members, Ronald Venetiaan was elected president for the second time, with the required two-thirds parliamentary majority. The 83-year-old VHP leader Jagernath Lachmon, who would pass away a year later, now presided over parliament. As had been the case during the early 1990s, the Venetiaan-led government was tasked with repairing its predecessor's bankrupt state finances. The government's budget was soon balanced. Guarantees provided by the Netherlands facilitated relieving the burden of foreign debt. Next, after 2 years of contraction, the economy grew again from 2001 on, in part the outcome of a skillful policy (see p. 418ff.). Nevertheless, the restructuring measures required in order to recover struck the population hard. For, subsidies on oil products were abolished, electricity and water tariffs rose sharply. In addition, at the beginning of the Venetiaan's tenure, the currency being strongly devalued led to a number of strikes.

The *Meerjaren Ontwikkelingsplan* (Multi-annual Development Plan), in which each and every Surinamese government has to present their plans for the coming 5 years

---

11   Schalkwijk 2000, 35.
12   *NRC Handelsblad*, 20 May 2000.
13   Ibid., 22 May 2000.
14   *De Volkskrant*, 13 April 2000.

to parliament, included themes (e.g., good governance, a public sector reform) to be executed between 2001 and 2005.[15] However, concrete objectives as well as a realistic timetable for the implementation hereof were lacking. Moreover, the achieved economic stability and growth could not conceal the stagnation as witnessed in many areas. These issues (e.g., poverty reduction, housing, education) did indeed directly affect citizens. Within the NF combination, the small social democratic SPA led by Fred Derby had often acted as a catalyst capable of countering the immobilism inherent in ethnic patronage politics. Here Derby's powerful personality played a key role for example, when in 1999 he had been able to organise massive protest actions leading to the collapse of the Wijdenbosch-led government. In the early 1990s, Derby had been the driving force in the power struggle between civilian government and the military ranks, which not only concluded the army's political role but also forced Bouterse to resign as army chief (see p. 335-337). In 2001, when Derby unexpectedly passed away, nobody within the coalition was able to break the deadlock.

Of all the politicians, Derby had also made the strongest efforts to bring the alleged perpetrators of the December murders to justice. His party had with this goal in mind deliberately laid claim occupying the department of justice in the Venetiaan-led cabinet. Moreover, as the sole survivor of the December murders, Derby was a key witness (see also p. 308). On 1 November 2000, the Court of Justice had ordered the Public Prosecutor's Office to commence a preliminary investigation, only weeks before the expiry of the limitation period. Such proceedings were the outcome of a complaints procedure initiated by the victims' families as well as human rights organisations. In the course of a press conference held a few days earlier, Bouterse had planned to disclose 'revelations', after having first refused to testify in court; apparently forced by circumstances he altered his earlier statements regarding the events on 8 December 1982 in Fort Zeelandia as forwarded in 1984, to wit, 'it was them or us, in time of emergency you act immediately'. Keeping to the narrative of an imminent coup, Bouterse declared he had not been present at this fort during the events, had not ordered what he now referred to as 'executions' but that he only was 'politically responsible'.[16] His accusation aimed at Derby was fresh. Without mentioning the latter's name, Bouterse spoke of a 'big-mouthed rat always fawning sweet talk' adding that this 'rat' may well have passed on information concerning an imminent coup to the intelligence services; Derby firmly rejected these accusations, which had no credibility whatsoever.[17] Bouterse's actions pertaining to the December murders always seemed to be fuelled by a mixture of anger, resentment and fear, which he usually concealed behind a mask of indifference and superiority. At an NDP meeting, shortly after the opening of a preliminary investigation by judicial authorities and his conviction for drug trafficking in the Netherlands, Bouterse voiced the suspicion that Dutch marines, dressed as civilians, were out to arrest him. This presumption was apparently partly intended to mobilise his supporters.[18] Six

---

15 Planbureau Suriname, *MOP, Meerjaren Ontwikkelingsplan 2001-2005* (Multi-annual Development Plan), Ch. 6 (studylibnl.com/doc/1053758).

16 *NRC Handelsblad*, 1 November 2000; on 10 December 1982 the official statement said that the victims had been 'shot on the run' (see p. 309).

17 Ibid., 21 October and 1 November 2000.

18 Ibid., 4 December 2000.

months later, after being heard by the examining magistrate during a preliminary investigation, Bouterse declared, seemingly unaffected, that he had experienced the interrogation 'as an expert witness'.[19] A few days earlier, in Paramaribo, Derby's posthumous testimony concerning the events in Fort Zeelandia, which had been taped for publication in the event of his untimely death, was disclosed in a newspaper publication:

> *'Three or four guys come in, you, you, you, they say, Daal, Rambocus, Sheombar, Kamperveen and Slagveer. They were dragged outside in a really heavy-handed manner and brought to Bouterse via that spiral staircase. Not much later we heard shots. Targeted fire, parraprrprrrprrr, at close range. [...] At a certain point I was in Bouterse's room. He stood up from behind his desk. The men signed off and Bouterse says, so Mr. Derby, come, sit down. Very formal. As he takes his first steps, I hear a man running up the stairs. With great tumult and cursing and ado, this man comes upstairs. Suddenly I see that it is [battalion commander] Bhagwandas. He rages against Bouterse. We had agreed, he says, that this mess should stop. Everyone has to die.'*[20]

Due to Suriname's limited judicial capacity, the pre-trial investigation continued until 2004, in the course of which several dozen witnesses were also heard in the Netherlands as a result of the mutual legal assistance treaty.

Bouterse was meanwhile given an opportunity to not only reorganise his party, which had been severely affected by the elections, but also to regain the trust of the population. The conditions favoured him as a result of the fact that the Venetiaan-led government, with the exception of its macro-economic policy, had made little progress. The inadequate fight against poverty formed the most poignant illustration of this administration's ineffectiveness. The IDB noted that the 'inefficient social safety net' provided free service to those 'who can afford to pay for themselves and fails to provide services to those at the base of the economic pyramid'.[21] Moreover, a largely manually executed administration hugely impeded the accurate tracking of expenditure on benefits. The fact that ministries were working at cross purposes contributed to the low effectiveness of the poverty policy. This in turn was the logical consequence of the on-going practice of politico-ethnic parcelling out the government apparatus.

Serious shortcomings in other areas were observed, too. For example, civil lawsuits forwarded by citizens as well as businesses remained unresolved for years due to a shortage of judges. Suriname had only eleven judges in 2007, less than half of the minimum needed for a functioning judiciary.[22] The low professional status, having eroded during the military dictatorship, also played a role here. Regular threats against judges as well as prosecutors also occurred. Training incoming judges, with technical support provided by the Netherlands, could only offer solace in the long term. Improving levels of education, which president Venetiaan had identified as a

---

19   Ibid., 27 June 2001.
20   Ibid., 21 June 2001.
21   IDB, *Country program evaluation: Suriname 2007-2010*, 5.
22   *De Volkskrant*, 26 September 2007.

'priority' in his government statement in 2000, witnessed little progress.[23] In 2004, the relevant ministry reported that the status of education 'had deteriorated in recent decades to a situation in which the sector's essential contribution to the development of the country has become almost impossible'.[24] In his government statement, Venetiaan also promised the 'reorganisation of the government apparatus', which would be 'aimed at increasing efficiency, effectiveness and personnel discipline'.[25] This was the first time that a public sector reform of this kind had been promised. Board member Michael Miskin of the *Centrale van Landsdienaren Organisaties* (Central Union of Civil Servants) explained in the Dutch press with remarkable frankness the reason why reforms did not work out:

> '*Politicians are afraid of unrest. It thus turns out that politicians use the state as a refuge, even for highly educated people. For, there are no social security benefits. This nepotism was the worst under Wijdenbosch.*'[26]

This trade union leader also explained how he had been able to find employment for his sister at the ministry of commerce by seeking the help of his father-in-law, who worked for a party included in the Wijdenbosch-led government:

> '*This is Suriname. People place a party flag in the garden and expect something in return. Should I condemn that? Is that not how the people wish it to be?*'

The Venetiaan-led government deemed the socio-political costs of reforming to be too high, not least due to a lack of alternative employment. The Dutch offer to utilise part of the aid funds in order to absorb the negative social effects of a public sector reform did not lead to any visible activity on Suriname's side. Its government did request the IDB to draw up a 'roadmap' aimed at reforms, which seemed to be a manoeuvre intended to postpone this issue. The promised investigation into and the punishment of corruption, having been announced as 'high on the list of priorities' in the government's declaration, was not implemented. Notably, the Wijdenbosch-led government's malpractices remained unpunished, too, in spite of the fact that a committee of inquiry, set up by the Venetiaan-led government, had revealed numerous concrete instances of misconduct in 2001. According to this committee, 'corrective measures were needed, especially within a legal system that takes itself seriously'.[27] Nevertheless, no action was taken in any of the cases pertaining to either the illegal use of state funds or the preferential treatment of friendly companies and individuals. The report disappeared into a drawer once it had clarified that the parliamentary group leader of the ruling NF might also have been guilty of an illegal foreign exchange transaction. In 2005, Suriname had fallen from the 49th to the 78th position on the 159 nations surveyed in Transparency International's Corruption Perceptions Index to be now ranked ex

---

23   Venetiaan, *Regeringsverklaring* (Government Statement), 15 November 2000.
24   Ministry of Education, *Educational Development in the Republic of Suriname* 2004, iii.
25   Venetiaan, *Regeringsverklaring* (Government Statement*)*, 15 November 2000.
26   *De Volkskrant*, 7 October 2004.
27   *Rapport van de Commissie Inventarisatie Staatsschuld* (Report by the Public Debt Inventory Committee), 23 March 2001, 79.

A History of Suriname

aequo with Morocco, Sri Lanka, Senegal and China.[28] Public services (e.g., public works, custom offices) were associated with corruption on a regular basis. Anti-corruption legislation was submitted to parliament, only to remain unprocessed. The Venetiaan-led government was nonetheless not entirely passive. In 2005, Dewanand Balesar (VHP), the then Minister of Public Works, was suspended for corruption and later sentenced to 2 years in prison. Two years earlier, the former NDP minister Errol Alibux had been imprisoned for 12 months for committing fraud against the state during his term of office resulting from a real estate transaction.

Due to increasing social tensions over an immigration flow that had already started during the early 1990s, circumstances had not become any easier for the government either. An influx of 'new' Chinese immigrants was particularly striking. Their arrival gave rise to negative sentiments, to which the media also contributed. President Venetiaan warned against such feelings when, in his annual address to parliament in 2006, he referred to 'a generalisation-based campaign against immigrants and tourists from a certain part of the world'.[29] Many visitors, having acquired tourist visa, were able to remain in Suriname as a result of a sub-standard immigration policy. During the 1980s, *c.* 200 migrants from the People's Republic of China (PRC) travelled to Suriname every year. In 1990 this number had suddenly risen to 4,800 and, in 1991, to more than 7,500, causing persistent rumours of corruption pertaining to Suriname's diplomats in Beijing. At the end of the 1990s, when a case of Chinese human trafficking via Suriname came to light in the USA, Paramaribo was forced to reinforce visa procedures. It remains unclear how many Chinese immigrants had been able to enter Suriname. Shortly after the turn of the century, according to official figures, in excess of 200 Chinese immigrants were registered each year. However, the number of passengers from the PRC who disembarked at Paramaribo-Johan Adolf Pengel International Airport often exceeded 1,000 individuals per annum. This renewed migration flow - once begun with contract workers in the 19th century - was part and parcel of the global migration of Chinese which had started as soon as restrictions were relaxed in the PRC. This migration was by and large sponsored, whereby one utilised networks interconnecting China-based companies seeking to expand their foreign markets.[30] The incoming Chinese became active not only in the retail trade, where they competed with the 'old' Chinese by not only establishing supermarkets (often rented or taken over from Hindustanis) but also by being employed in (import) trade, construction and the timber sector. Moreover, during the 1990s, Chinese labourers regularly stayed in Suriname on a temporary basis in order to work for China-based companies commissioned by the local government to asphalt roads and build houses.

Certain inhabitants of Suriname linked this immigration flow to criminality, economic exploitation and the deterioration of the local labour market. One could however also establish that these 'new' Chinese at least brought in affordable goods. It had also been suggested that the NPS and the NDP (both supported by often

---

28   See: transparency.org/en/cpi/2005
29   Tjon Sie Fat 2007, 61.
30   The above details originate from: Tjon Sie Fat 2007, 61-80 and Tjon Sie Fat 2009, 87-100, 457-467.

high-income Chinese businessmen) took an interest in immigration.[31] The negative stereotypes, frequently included in e-mails sent by readers to then be published in the local press, were apparently mainly motivated by a general dissent with the social circumstances. Of course, the multi-million USD investments and loans China provided were welcomed in Suriname. Nevertheless, at the same time, as was the case across the globe, scepticism arose concerning the intentions of the Chinese, all the more if one considers not only their interest in raw materials but also the attempts to expand their sphere of influence. It remains unclear how many Chinese populated Suriname during the first decade of the 21st century. According to the 2004 census, 3,664 Chinese nationals resided in Suriname that year. Between 2004 and 2012 the number of Chinese immigrants was considerably higher, to wit 6,377, to reach as many as 1,637 in 2008.[32] Needless to say, the number of inhabitants of Chinese descent was in fact much higher. In 2011, the PRC's Ambassador to Suriname mentioned the presence of 40,000 ethnic Chinese, without substantiating this statement.[33]

From the second half of the 1990s on, the number of Brazilian migrants had also grown significantly. They were attracted by the lucrative gold mines located in the Surinamese interior. Now and again the arrival of Brazilian gold miners (*garimpeiros*) caused dissent among Maroons, especially if their traditional territories were invaded. On the other hand, this ethnic group often collaborated with these miners (see p. 383-384ff.). Based on the official census of 2004, in which the General Bureau of Statistics relied on Brazilian informants, 20,000 Brazilians resided in Suriname, but several unofficial estimates were higher; according to this bureau, no more than 5,000 Brazilians resided in Paramaribo, many of their activities indirectly linked to gold mining.[34] Certain quarters of northern Paramaribo have been referred to as Little Belém, a slightly exaggerated observation as it merely consists of a few streets. The category 'others' also displayed an increasing number of immigrants and of Haitians in particular.[35]

16.3 Political emancipation of Maroons

It was only until 1963 that inhabitants of the interior (i.e., Maroons and the Indigenous peoples) were granted universal suffrage to then be included in the civil registry for the first time. This initiative originated from Jopie Pengel, the then NPS leader.[36] His party comprising 'city creoles' opined that the Maroons' votes would be easily won because of their ethnic proximity. The term 'bushland creoles' was introduced in order to underline this point of view. For years, a large number of Maroons' votes had fallen to the NPS. Nonetheless, the relationship between 'city' and 'bush' remained

---

31   Schalkwijk spoke of a 'political strategic goal', see: *De Ware Tijd*, 21 January 2012.
32   Lambert, Schalkwijk & Ritfeld 2016, 101-103.
33   The Chinese ambassador's estimate, as stated in *The New York Times* on 10 April 2011, of 40,000 ethnic Chinese residing in Suriname is much higher than the 7,885 mentioned in the 2012 census (Algemeen Bureau voor de Statistiek, *Suriname Census 2012*, 76). The former estimate seems more plausible. For, experts have pointed out that many Chinese in Suriname live together in the same house, e.g., 20 or 30 inhabitants per dwelling. Moreover, those executing the 2012 census did not ask sufficient follow-up questions, as they were usually non-Chinese speakers.
34   De Theije, 2007, 81-83;
35   Lambert, Schalkwijk & Ritfeld 2016, 101.
36   Breeveld 2000, 265-266; Scholtens 1994, 103-104.

extremely arduous. The seed of conflict resulting from interests pertaining to logging, gold mining and mining was also present. For example, promises regarding granting land rights to the Maroons and the Indigenous peoples were never fulfilled. During the 1960s, a forced transmigration of thousands of Saramakas, after the construction of the Afobaka Dam, had also traumatised the Maroons.

Until the end of the 19th century, the interior of Suriname had been the exclusive domain of the Indigenous peoples and Maroons. Logging, a key factor as to building houses in Paramaribo, lay largely in the hands of Maroons. After the first major gold finds and with the increasing importance of the extraction of balata gum, this situation changed when the colonial government began to issue gold as well as logging concessions to private entrepreneurs. As early as 1904, a number of high-ranking colonial officials had concluded that:

> 'The sooner the whole bushnegritude disappears and is included among the ordinary inhabitants of the colony, the better [...] these gentlemen have been in charge in our upper rivers all too long.'[37]

The same notion arose, remarkably, after the military coup in 1980 under Bouterse's leadership. We read in a 1982 policy paper published by the Ministry of the Interior and Justice:

> 'It will be necessary to work steadily on dismantling existing structures in order to introduce new ones at the same time, with great caution.'[38],

The traditional structures of authority in the Maroon society, according to this advice, impede the path of development and would only be of interest to research carried out by anthropologists. A remarkable reasoning, as successive governments, with the exception of donations (e.g., generators, outboard engines) presented during elections to the local population, had hardly resulted in developing the interior. From the year 2000 on, the relation between 'bush' and 'city' has changed dramatically, causing the political balance of power in Paramaribo to be affected. Here the Interior War between the Jungle Command and the National Army plays a major role. The Maroon population had to rely even more on itself. During the war years (1986-1992), the eastern part of Suriname had become isolated. Moreover, the currency reform of November 1986 had rendered worthless the money owned by the population residing in the interior. Bouterse's regime imposed this measure deliberately, implying that these Maroons could not travel to Paramaribo in order to exchange their cash for newly printed banknotes within the required 3 days. Such circumstances triggered an impulse as to small-scale gold mining. The Jungle Command not only seized pontoons from the government but also recruited *garimpeiros* equipped with the necessary technical expertise pertaining to, for example, hydraulic extraction methods. Gold revenues in part financed the Jungle Command's armed struggle. Moreover, gold was a stable means of payment by way of which Maroons could travel to French Guiana.

---

37   Scholtens 1994, 58.
38   Pakosie 2009, 22.

Figure 16.2. A small-scale gold mining site located near the Saramaka village named Nieuw Koffiekamp, 1996. Photo by Vincent Mentzel.

Many young Maroons, including schoolchildren, who were not able to return to Paramaribo after their holidays due to hostilities, now found employment in gold mines. Due to military violence, the educational system across the interior, which did not include any secondary schooling, had largely collapsed. Hence even more Maroon youngsters ended up as gold miners.

After the peace agreement of 1992, which brought a conclusion to the Interior War, small-scale gold mining evolved into the most important economic activity for the Maroon population. Between *c.*10,000 and 15,000 Maroons, the majority of whom were Ndyuka, populated goldfields located in eastern and central Suriname whereas *c.*300 Wayana Indians resided in the Lawa area.[39] Their living conditions were not without health risks. For, toxic mercury is applied in small-scale gold mining and malaria mosquitoes could thrive in newly-created, stagnant ponds. At the end of 2011, a medical report on two Wayana communities revealed that 60 per cent of those surveyed possessed a mercury level exceeding the international health standards; the fish consumed by the Indigenous peoples contained mercury (see also p. 438).[40] The Wayana were not only confronted with concessionaires within their traditional habitat, they themselves worked either for gold companies or as individual miners. At the same time, in the Tapanahoni area, ecotourism is important to the Wayana as a source of income, especially in the villages of Paloemeu (where the Trio and Akurio ethnic groups also resided) and Apetina.[41] In 2009, between 800 and 1200 surface

---

39   Heemskerk 2009, 19.
40   *De Ware Tijd*, 6 December 2011.
41   Boven 2006, 225 ff.

gold mines existed.[42] Maroon youngsters hailing from Paramaribo were employed in the informal gold sector too. Due to a lack of tuition as well as a negative image, this group (which is over-represented in crime statistics), had little chance of finding city jobs. In the interior, they can fall back on tribal and family relationships, from which they could acquire gold mining rights.

In addition, work as a prospector offered a certain freedom and independence, which fits in with Maroon culture. Many Maroons commuted regularly between 'city' and 'bush'. Their activities were not limited to only gold mining around which a service economy had developed comprising transport, machine shops, restaurants, shops, beauty parlours as well as brothels (*cabaré*). Based on a conservative estimate, *c.*14.000 prospectors and service providers worked at gold mining sites fields during 2009, between 70 and 80 per cent of whom were Brazilians.[43] The remaining percentage consisted of Maroons. Approximately between 5 and 10 per cent of those toiling in gold fields were female.[44] Many Maroon women also provided other services. A small number were sex workers. Urban women were also employed as machine owners, gold mine operators or supervise mining, while others ran restaurants, hotels or shops. The police was virtually absent from the interior. Nonetheless the number of conflicts remained limited here. If necessary, private security services stepped in to maintain order.

The distribution of earnings within small-scale gold mining - the utilisation of machines makes it more justifiable to speak of medium-sized mining - was carried out according to unwritten rules. Any experience obtained elsewhere indicated that such informal rules were effective because no one would benefit from any conflicts. Economists apply the term 'gold digging law' first introduced by Hernan de Soto, an expert in informal economy. Brazilian *garimpeiro*s at work in the interior of Suriname paid 10 per cent of their proceeds either to local landowners or to concessionaires, a number of whom were based in Paramaribo. Informal rules regarding the distribution of production within a team of gold miners came into play when excavation and/or hydraulic machines are utilised.[45]

The attitude of the Maroon population towards Brazilians was ambivalent. The latter command admiration for their knowledge of mechanical techniques, which put an end to classical gold mining whereby iron bowls (*baté*) were used. Collaboration was often encountered here, if only because Maroons benefit from it. One learned each other's language and amorous relationships flourished. Friction also occurred. The presence of brothels, accommodating mainly Brazilian and Dominican women, located near residential areas now and again gave rise to alarm among locals. Cases of theft were recorded in and around goldfields, too. A tragic form of violence was witnessed in Albina at the end of 2009 when a Brazilian, in a money-related conflict, stabbed a young Maroon to death. This murder led to reprisals during which Brazilian women were raped. Chinese and Brazilians were molested, too. Shops were

---

42   Heemskerk 2009, 13.

43   Ibid., 2010, 13.

44   Heemskerk 2009, 21.

45   Ibid., 21-22; the Surinamese anthropologist Chris Healy informed the present author on this subject during an interview held on 11 July 2009.

ransacked and set on fire.[46] These incidents led to a renewed call for regulating the informal as well as the illegal gold sector. This outcry was reiterated less than a year later when seven illegal workers were killed when a gold mine located at *Gowtu Berg* (Gold Mountain) in eastern Suriname collapsed. It had employed *c.*800 illegal gold miners, both Maroons and Brazilians.[47] At the end of 2008, the army and the police had registered illegal immigrants in parts of the interior. In addition, material was confiscated in the course of an action called 'Clean Sweep'. Its effect however was limited. Next, after the Brazilian government expressed its 'concern' regarding this initiative, Paramaribo could not ignore this response considering the importance of good bilateral relations.[48] In 2011, a fresh attempt was made in order to regulate the gold mining industry of Suriname (see p. 424).

This expanding industry has put pressure on communities of Maroons and Indigenous peoples. For, their traditional habitats were rapidly invaded by thousands of foreigners and others. Moreover, large financial interests could fuel dissent within both their communities. On occasion Maroon dignitaries allowed personal financial interests to prevail, thus provoking protest among their own people. In the Tapanahoni region this dissent sparked the following remarkable event. In 2009, Gazon Matodja, a widely respected Ndyuka *granman*, was urged to punish six captains in the traditional way. Without informing this *granman*, one captain had signed a contract with a French prospector in exchange for a monthly fee in gold worth many thousands of US dollars. This metal had been mined at a site sacred to the Ndyuka people. Ritualists honouring the Agedeonsu (the tutelary deity of Man and Nature) therefore played a key role here (see also p. 150). After a special meeting (*krutu*) attended by all tribal representatives, a fine was imposed on these captains comprising a large boat, 750 pieces of firewood, seven crates of alcohol and seven pieces of white cloth. The French gold operator was forced to discontinue his activities. In addition, Brazilians no longer showed up for work across the region.[49]

Small-scale gold mining did lead to tensions in Maroon communities. At the same time a rapidly growing economic activity boosted self-confidence. The migration from 'bush' to 'city' was no longer a foregone conclusion. However, traditional Maroon dignitaries witnessed a weakening of their authority. For, they had not played a role in the Interior War, when young people arose under the rebel leader Ronnie Brunswijk's leadership, nor in the realization of a national reconciliation and development agreement reached at Lelydorp in 1992 (see also p. 343). This agreement dealt with economically developing the interior as well as a statutory regulation of land rights. With an expanding gold sector, the urgency concerning the land issue had increased, especially after foreign multinationals had received gold concessions. In the course of the 1990s problems had already risen amidst the local population residing at the Saramaka village of Nieuw Koffiekamp, when the American company Golden Star acquired a gold mining concession in this region. Tensions rekindled, in 2004, as soon as the Canadian IAMGOLD Corporation, the employer of many

46   *NRC Handelsblad,* 29 December 2009.
47   *Starnieuws,* 21 November 2010.
48   *De Ware Tijd,* 18 March 2009.
49   Ibid., 1 April 2009.

hundreds of Maroons, obtained this concession. During the 1990s, the Saramakas were also confronted with timber concessions acquired by Asian companies. This resulted not only in the destruction of their land that had been cultivated in order to produce crops but also in the closure of hunting areas. Moreover, the local Maroon population still lived with the memory of a forced transmigration to Nieuw Koffiekamp as a result of the construction of a reservoir (see p. 286-287).

In 2000, the Saramakas felt prompted to lodge a complaint with the Inter-American Commission on Human Rights, an autonomous organ linked to the Organization of American States (OAS). On 28 November 2007, Suriname was finally condemned by the Inter-American Court of Human Rights (IACHR), when it confirmed the rights of the Saramakas to their territory.[50] Such a verdict is binding for affiliated nations, including Suriname, which had recognized the American Convention on Human Rights of 1969. This ruling could have far-reaching consequences for the granting of mining and logging concessions by the Surinamese government. The authorities should also take this verdict into account when further developing plans for the Initiative for the Integration of the Regional Infrastructure of South America (IIRSA), which deals with roads, hydropower and energy transport (see p. 434). Indigenous peoples increasingly argued for land rights, too, especially through the *Vereniging van Inheemse Dorpshoofden in Suriname* (VIDS; Association of Indigenous Village Chiefs in Suriname). Suriname was the only nation state in both North and South America which, even after the year 2000, had not introduced a single legal regulation with regard to the land rights of Indigenous and tribal peoples. Rules and regulations related to land ownership in Suriname were based on military decrees dating back to the early 1980s. They stipulated that 'all land is the domain of the State, insofar as no special persons (natural or legal persons) can prove their rights to it'.[51] In other words: the entire interior, including the habitats of Maroons as well as Indigenous peoples, is state-owned.

The IACHR, however, ordered Suriname in a verdict dated 28 November 2007 to execute the following:

'The State shall delimit, demarcate, and grant collective title over the territory of the members of the Saramaka people, in accordance with their customary laws [...] The State shall remove or amend the legal provisions that impede protection of the right to property of the members of the Saramaka people [...] and adopt, in its domestic legislation, and through prior, effective and fully informed consultations with the Saramaka people, legislative, administrative, and other measures as may

---

50   Inter-American Court of Human Rights Case of the Saramaka People *v.* Suriname, Judgment of November 28, 2007; see also: Price, *Rainforest Warriors: Human Rights on Trial* (2011) which contains an overview placed in a broader perspective of the struggle of Saramakas for their land rights. Acting as an expert witness for the IACHR, Price rightly speaks of a 'landmark judgment'. This sentence received worldwide attention and also proved significant to other Indigenous people across Central and South America.

51   Heemskerk 2009, 31; in Kambel & MacKay 2003, 80 ff; it is noted that, at the end of the 19th century, legislation on gold concessions continued to include provisions concerning the protection of the residential areas and farmland populated by Indigenous peoples and Maroons (including a reference to earlier peace treaties with Maroons). However, the Mining Decree of 1986 does not go quite that far in this respect.

be required to recognize, protect, guarantee and give legal effect to the right of the members of the Saramaka people to hold collective title of the territory they have traditionally used and occupied [...] The State shall adopt legislative, administrative and other measures necessary to recognize and ensure the right of the Saramaka people to be effectively consulted, in accordance with their traditions and customs, or when necessary, the right to give or withhold their free, informed and prior consent, with regards to development or investment projects that may affect their territory, and to reasonably share the benefits of such projects with the members of the Saramaka people, should these be ultimately carried out.[...].'[52]

Important additional findings by the IACHR were: (a) the Saramakas should be considered a 'tribal' people and (b) it should possess rights the Indigenous and tribal peoples enjoy under international law.[53] Suriname had just claimed the opposite. According to this court, however, the Saramakas were tribal as 'they are asserting their rights as alleged tribal peoples, that is, not indigenous to the region, but that share similar characteristics with Indigenous peoples, such as having social, cultural and economic traditions different from other sections of the national community, identifying themselves with their ancestral territories, and regulating themselves, at least partially, by their own norms, customs, and traditions'.[54] A reference was then made pertaining to the self-organisation in matrilineal clans as well as to the fact that 'the lands and resources of the Saramakas are part of their social, ancestral and spiritual essence'.[55]

This judgment once again clarified that policies executed by successive governments of Suriname sharply contrasted with the growing international consensus on the rights of Indigenous and tribal peoples. Also revealing within this context is the fact that the government had to be forced in 2005 by yet another ruling by the IACHR to pay compensation to relatives as well as survivors of the massacre perpetrated by the army at the Ndyuka village named Moiwana during the Interior War (see also p. 325 and 329). The IACHR had also ordered Suriname to start a judicial investigation into these murders. Even after a number of years however no action had been taken. The same idleness was observed with regard to the issue of land rights.

For the purpose of the IACHR proceedings, various Saramaka clans (*lo's*) had joined forces in the *Vereniging van Saramakaanse Gezagsdragers* (Association of Saramaka Authorities). The non-governmental organisation called Forest Peoples Programme, which works for tribal peoples worldwide, supported this association. This initiative was perhaps a first step in renewing the traditional authority for which Maroons in Suriname were now voicing ever louder arguments. André Pakosie, a prominent Ndyuka dignitary, then served as the highest representative of the traditional authority for the Ndyuka in the Netherlands. He advocated that

---

52   IACHR, Judgement of 28 November 2007, 61-62; in a similar ruling, the IACHR condemned Suriname in 2015 for violating the American Convention on Human Rights (Article 21 on the Right to communal property) in the case of the Indigenous peoples Lokono (Caribs) and Kaliña (Arawak) vs. the state, see: IACHR, Judgement of 25 November 2015.
53   IACHR, Judgement of 28 November 2007, 23.
54   Ibid., 23-24.
55   Ibid., 24.

A History of Suriname

(a) appointments of Maroon authorities should no longer only take into account the traditional matrilineal relations of kinship and (b) 'in addition to their knowledge of the Maroon culture and society, candidates should also be well educated'.[56] Subsequently Maroons would be able to defend their interests more effectively.

In keeping with the transforming relationship between 'city' and 'bush', Maroons began to manifest themselves much more emphatically in the arena of national politics. Within the context of Suriname, this phenomenon can be considered a minor revolution. For the first time, Maroons now obtained seats in parliament through their own initiatives. This outcome was a direct consequence of the decision the Maroon parties ABOP and BEP had made to join forces in the 2005 elections. Shortly afterwards, a splinter party named *Seeka* (a Ndyuka term meaning: renewal) also joined. With its five seats (7.3 per cent of votes), this *A-Combinatie* (A-C) proved to be indispensable to the formation of the incoming government.[57] President Venetiaan's NF, which had fallen from 33 to 23 parliamentary seats, was forced to form a coalition with the A-C in order to remain at the centre of power.

The Maroons' electoral success also started Ronnie Brunswijk's political career. As a result of trading in gold as well as timber, and presumably through drug trafficking, this former rebel leader had become a wealthy businessman. After serving as chairman of the *Algemene Bevrijdings- en Ontwikkelingspartij* (ABOP; General Liberation and Development Party), founded in 1990, Brunswijk now became a member of parliament. As a businessman, he had acquired sufficient means to finance political campaigns and to tie voters to him. Having not only commissioned the building of a football stadium (named Ronnie Brunswijk Stadion), he also invested in social housing projects located in his constituency of Marowijne and furthermore provided employment in his gold and timber concession areas. His sponsorship resulted in a soccer club named Inter Moengotapoe defending its national title on a number of occasions. Brunswijk was, however, personally reproached by Maroons, too, due to the fear his intimidating behaviour caused. Executions in the criminal drug scene were also alleged.[58]

The collaborating Maroon parties within the A-C express a characteristic emancipatory nature. Their first and foremost aim was to improve the lives of their supporters, who had been lagging behind in socio-economic aspects. One such priority, of course, was to legally establish the Maroons' rights pertaining to the lands they have lived on for centuries. During the 2005 election campaign, when assessing all parties involved, the A-C responded most clearly to ethnic sentiments. This can be explained by the efforts the ABOP undertook in order to emancipate members of its own ethnic group. The latter party's political leaders turned against the so-called 'city creoles' in particular. During an election meeting held in Brokopondo, for example, Brunswijk mentioned that 'city creoles' had taken 'the place of the Dutch'.[59] Another speaker remarked:

---

56   Pakosie 2009, 20.
57   See: nl.wikipedia.org/wiki/Surinaamse_parlementsverkiezingen_2005
58   Hoogbergen & Kruijt 2005, 273-274; these authors cite detailed accusations regarding such crimes by the Roman-Catholic clergy man named Toon te Dorsthorst.
59   Blanksma 2006a, 155.

'When someone comes to me [after the elections] *to complain and moan that those city negroes have fooled them again, I'm going to knock that person over with my elbow.'*[60]

Antagonisms between Maroon tribes had nonetheless risen, too. For instance, many Saramaka people were suspicious of Brunswijk, after all he was a Ndyuka. It thus had to be clarified to Maroon voters that the A-C was not merely to serve the Ndyuka, but all Maroons. This stance caused the host of the election event to ask:

'As the presidents of the A-Combinatie are not Saramaka people, will your votes go to the PL? Well then, who is Somo[hardjo] *to you? Is he a Saramaka? Do you look like people from the BVD or VVV or NDP? Or do you resemble Venetiaan?'*[61]

16.4 Desi Bouterse, President

Four years before the 2010 elections, the US Ambassador Marsha E. Barnes reported to Washington, D.C., that she questioned if President Ronald Venetiaan and Vice President Ramdien Sardjoe as 'aging political veterans, can develop the public relations savvy to convince the nation that their current course is the best course'.[62] While the government coalition all too often dealt with internal problems, Bouterse's NDP delivered strong opposition from the very outset. The decline observed in the 2005 elections had formed no incentive for the leaders of the NPS and the VHP to pursue a more targeted social policy or to rejuvenate their own party. Venetiaan's detached style of government made it easy for the NDP to present itself as an advocate of the people's interests, for example, by supporting the protesting street vendors in Paramaribo when, 6 months after taking office, the government ordered the police to remove all unauthorised peddlers. This initiative enraged working class neighbourhoods and the media reported on it for days. Venetiaan was referred to as a president with 'ten clean fingers' i.e., incorrupt and of irreproachable behaviour. In Paramaribo however the joke also went round that his fingers remained clean because he failed to address several real problems.

Especially the policy pursued by Michael Jong Tjien Fa, the Minister of Spatial Planning, Land and Forestry Management, caused wide-spread bad blood. This PL-member was responsible for issuing public land, an initiative which resulted in great anger because many had, often for years on end, unsuccessfully attempted to obtain plots of land to build houses on. Each and every Surinamese citizen can indeed claim free agricultural or building land from the government. Ample indications of malpractice benefitting their own Javanese political party supporters were nevertheless reported. Towards the end of Jong Tjien Fa's term of office, President Venetiaan announced that decisions had to pass through him, but in practice little changed.[63] Incoming regulations imposed in order to render the issuing of land more

---

60   Ibid., 156.
61   Ibid., 156.
62   Quoted from a diplomatic cable, leaked by WikiLeaks, entitled *President Venetiaan's government facing low approval ratings*, and dated 15 February 2006.
63   See: waterkant.net/suriname/2008/05/22

transparent only came into force at the end of the PL's tenure. These measures had been weakened in parliament by means of this party's pressure. Venetiaan on occasion fiercely criticised ministers and party leaders behind closed doors. In public, however, he was apparently only capable of cautiously preserving peace within the coalition, hereby giving voters an impression of lacking strength. The government's image was further tarnished when Alice Amafo, the Minister of Transport, Communications and Tourism (2005-2007) and A-C member resigned. For, it was reported she had paid for her 30th birthday celebrations with taxpayers' money.[64] Siegfried Gilds, the Minister of Trade and Industry (2005-2006) and an SPA-member, stepped down after being accused of assisting his next of kin with money laundering.[65]

As emancipatory parties, the A-C and the PL represented constituencies with the largest socio-economic disadvantages. This explains why they were most openly engaged in ethnic politics. Both parties were indispensable to the coalition majority. When serving as a minister, the PL-leader Paul Somohardjo (b. 1943) described how he would act when allocating social housing, thus:

'If someone was to apply for the same social housing as a local chairman of my own party, I would give priority to the local chairman. For, it was thanks to him that I became a minister.'[66]

In Somohardjo's opinion, patronage and clientelism formed a means of policy-making which did not require any secrecy. Serious integrity problems involving leaders of the PL and of the A-C had not impeded the 2005 coalition formation. Five years earlier, the Amsterdam-based Court of Appeal had convicted Chairman Ronnie Brunswijk of ABOP (part of the A-C) in absentia to a 6-year jail term for trafficking cocaine.[67] In 2003, Somohardjo had resigned as minister of social affairs and housing after being imposed with a suspended sentence comprising 2 months imprisonment for 'violating the honour' of young women participating in a beauty pageant.[68] Although now forced to give up his ambition to serve as vice president, this sentence did not prevent him from being elected to preside over parliament. Somohardjo was to be further discredited in 2007 after an altercation during a parliamentary session which had involved both Brunswijk and a NDP parliamentarian named Rashied Doekhi.[69]

Such events played a role in undermining the confidence of the people of Suriname in politics to which a lack of tangible improvement of the livelihoods of large groups continued to contribute. The UN Human Development Index with its indicators referring to health, education and income reveals that Suriname now fell well behind averages pertaining to Latin America and the Caribbean region, particularly in the fields of education and income. In 2011, Suriname was ranked no. 104 (out of 187 nations) and, in 2005, no. 86 (out of 177 nations).[70] The shortage

---

64   *De Volkskrant*, 13 March 2007.
65   In 2009 Gilds was sentenced to 12 months imprisonment: *de Volkskrant*, 4,May 2009.
66   As mentioned in an interview with the present author held on 10 July 2009.
67   *Trouw*, 11 October 2000.
68   *NRC Handelsblad*, 15 August 2003.
69   See: youtube.com/watch?v=7INOlwQ1jtQ
70   See: hdr.undp.org

of affordable housing formed a long-standing problem, too, thus posing an electoral risk to any coalition. Hence, young married couples with children often lived with their parents and grandparents.

The NDP chairman Bouterse had clarified prior to the 2005 parliamentary elections that his ambition was to officiate as president. The NDP had therefore entered these elections applying the campaign slogan 'Des for Pres'. Shortly before the incoming parliament was to elect its president, Bouterse dropped his candidacy due to a lack of support. Moreover, 2 months before the 2005 elections, the US Embassy in Paramaribo had firmly expressed its dissent with the NDP leader's possible presidency as follows:

> 'The U.S. and numerous other countries have difficulties maintaining ties with a government led by a convicted drug dealer. We hope the people of Suriname will elect a leader proven to be committed to democracy and democratic principles and who can drive the nation forward.'[71]

During a NDP meeting an enraged Desi Bouterse spoke of an attempt to 'intimidate' voters. The embassy's statement was, according to him, aimed at keeping the government formed by the NF members in the saddle, deeming them 'puppets of Dutch interest'.[72] A few days earlier, Jennifer Geerlings-Simons, the parliamentary group's chairperson, had reacted in a more neutral manner.[73] Apparently several NDP members tacitly welcomed the US pressure, as they were not expecting anything good from elections if Bouterse was to be their presidential candidate. Six months earlier, Bouterse had put an end to objections the KTPI and the DA (two small parties whose members feared their nation's isolation) had forwarded against his candidacy. Moreover, he terminated cooperating with these two parties in the *Millennium Combinatie*. Within NDP ranks, certain members referred to Geerlings-Simons, a physician, as a potential party leader. Her extensive social involvement and non-polarizing stance even created sympathy outside her party. However, at the beginning of 2006, she chose to resign as parliamentary group's chairwoman because the 'conditions' were no longer in place to fulfil her task 'in good conscience and to the best of my ability'.[74] Within the NDP, a conflict had risen after a coalition majority had excluded Bouterse from serving as a member of the parliamentary committee for defence. Hence, hawks within the NDP now wished to boycott all parliamentary committees. However, Geerlings-Simons refused to take such a far-reaching measure. The NDP leadership at that time still partly comprised veterans from the 'revolutionary years' after the 1980 coup, although their number was reduced once a group including former president Wijdenbosch had left the party in 2000. Bouterse was nevertheless able to reinforce his position again in 2008 after Wijdenbosch and others had reconciled with him. At the same time Rashied Doekhi, a confidant of Bouterse and a member of parliament, ended Wijdenbosch's possible ambitions by

---

71   *De Volkskrant*, 8 March 2005.
72   *De Ware Tijd*, 12 March 2005.
73   *De Ware Tijd*, 8 March 2005.
74   *De Ware Tijd*, 22 February 2006.

declaring on behalf of his NDP-section (Nickerie district) the latter could not become president.[75] Bouterse had no doubt approved this stance. The NDP had meanwhile presented the *Mega Combinatie* (MC), a partnership including small political parties named PALU, KTPI and NS.

At least as important were Bouterse's links to the *Nieuwe Generatie Gemeente Gods Bazuin* (New Generation Congregation of God's Trumpet), to which this Roman Catholic-educated NDP-leader had converted during the late 1990s. Religion continued to play a key societal role. Thus, electing a non-religious politician as the head of state was unthinkable. Churches mainly drew support from the poorer Creole neighbourhoods, but Christian Javanese attended services here, too. The rise of the *Volle Evangelie Gemeente* (Full-Gospel Congregation), which is to be considered part of the Pentecostal Church, can be compared to developments observed in many Protestant churches across Latin America. Lively, swinging revival services attracted not only the young; many no longer felt at home in the ageing and more formal *Evangelische Broedergemeente* (Moravian Brethren) which traditionally includes many NPS adherents or the traditional Roman Catholic Church. The aforementioned congregation's chief pastor, a self-proclaimed bishop named Steve Meye, did not conceal the fact he had personally given advice to Bouterse. In addition, this congregation frequently utilised the NDP venue to organise large gatherings.

From its founding in 1987 on, the NDP had profiled itself as multi-ethnic, hereby sharply taking distance from old ethnic politics. In this party's view, these politics not only aimed at maintaining the power of ethnic elites, synonymous with corruption and nepotism, but at the same time impeded Suriname developing. The revised NDP statutes of 2004 (and of 2019) still referred to the 'Revolution of 1980'.[76] The NDP did not differ hugely as to programmatic terms if compared with most other political parties, all of them striving for the construction of more houses, the improvement of education, the introduction of a general health insurance, a prominent role for the state in mining production, an increase in old-age benefits, the improvement of the infrastructure, a plot of land for every inhabitant and solving the land rights issues which the Indigenous peoples and Maroons had to deal with. After all, party politics were often not very ideologically coloured. The NDP's most striking programme feature was: to elect the president directly. Such a strong leader with a direct mandate should break with ethnic politics.

As observed during elections held in the district of Commewijne, certain ethnicity-based sentiments remained a key factor in voting behaviour, even amidst those who opted for political parties or alliances that could be deemed 'multi-ethnic'. In this district, according to the 2004 census, 48 per cent of the population was of Javanese stock. During the 2005 parliamentary elections, the Javanese PL acquired 22 per cent of the votes. An analysis carried out by the polling station indicated that the 'missing' 26 per cent of these votes went to Javanese candidates belonging to other parties. Across the Latour district of Paramaribo, once a NPS stronghold, ballot box

---

75   *De Waterkant*, 15 August 2008 (waterkant.net/suriname/2008/08/15).

76   See: ndpsuriname.com/media/publicaties

results revealed a correlation with the altered demography.[77] To both a greater or lesser extent, all parties and alliances took ethnicity-based sentiments into account with regard to their election strategies. In the NF with its multi-ethnic alliance, such sentiments often resulted in tensions which not only pertained to the number of eligible places each participating party had obtained on the joint list of candidates. During the 2005 elections, VHP-supporters deemed the time was right for a Hindustani to serve as president. Needless to say, this was not a foregone conclusion in the view of the Creole NPS. One therefore decided to wait and see which of these two parties could acquire a majority in parliament. In the course of a VHP-meeting held at Commewijne, a pandit stated in support of the VHP Hindustani candidate:

> 'Thanks to the party, the culture is maintained. You do not have all the say within the combination, but you must protect religion and culture.'[78]

The NDP-leadership ensured that each and every district had created a balanced ethnicity-based representation when nominating candidates for parliament, for district councils and for local councils. Moreover, elements linked to the cultures of various ethnic groups were always included in the well-orchestrated campaign rallies. The NPS, having for ever presented itself as a national party, traditionally contained a small minority including Chinese as well as Christian and Muslim Hindustanis. It can nonetheless not be denied that NDP meetings, attended by its active members and officials, were obviously more multi-coloured when compared with the gatherings of other parties. The NDP's multi-ethnic character rendered it an attractive alternative, especially for younger voters. This party also presented opportunities to those with political ambitions, who were hardly addressed elsewhere as a result of ossified relations and vested positions of power. A key principle in the NDP statutes comprises a 'nationalist ideology based on national independence, national solidarity and national awareness and unity'.[79] Nevertheless, the electoral programme as presented by the *Mega Combinatie* (2010-2020) also states:

> 'Our country is blessed with various ethnic groups, all with their cultural riches (languages, norms and values, cuisine, religion, typical talents, etc.). However, thanks to the mutual influence, our cultural richness is more than a sum of the individual cultures. So far, however, this wealth has hardly been exploited. Cultural policy must be placed within the context of collective responsibility, also as a guiding principle for national development. This means that in addition to expanding and improving the existing facilities for artistic and cultural education, the cultural policy to be pursued will have to be aimed at strongly stimulating cultural expression related to the cultural values of the Surinamese people and making use of all the positive elements in the various individual cultures.'[80]

---

77   Robert Ameerali, the future Vice President of Suriname (2010-2015), held a lecture on this subject at the US embassy. The US Ambassador quoted from it in a cable sent to Washington, D.C., from Paramaribo on 2 October 2009 under the heading *Suriname elections: voting by ethnicity remains commonplace.*
78   Blanksma 2006b, 41.
79   See: ndpsuriname.com/media/publicaties
80   *Verkiezingsprogramma* (Electoral program) *Mega Combinatie 2010-2020*, 21.

The NDP had hereby distanced itself from the 'revolutionary' stance on ethnicity after the 1980 coup. For, the Bouterse-led regime, supported by left-wing parties, then preferred to completely ignore their issue of ethnic diversity. Thus, at that time, the national census did not record the ethnic backgrounds of respondents. The NDP's renewed approach resembled the 'unity in diversity' which the Hindustani leadership had already propagated during the 1950s. The core concept was: all ethnic groups should 'preserve their own traditions and customs, but at the same time possess a largest common denominator, which forms the basis for national unity'.[81] This stance, launched by the VHP- politician Jnan H. Adhin (1927-2002) in 1957, formed a reaction to the strong Creole-tinted nationalism, a prelude to Suriname's independence. During the 1950s, Creoles deemed this viewpoint to express a lack of loyalty towards Suriname.

Since its founding in 1987, the NDP had remained outside the centre of power, be it with the exception of a short time after the 1990 coup, and between 1996 and 2000. The majority of the other political parties refused to cooperate with those whose chairman was held responsible for the December murders. The NDP leader's criminal drug record presented a more complicated issue for the NF. For, it had previously seen no obstacle in joining forces with Brunswijk, who had also been convicted of drug-related offences in the Netherlands. This political isolation reinforced the NDP's profile: an anti-elite party with traits of populist movements encountered across Latin America. Bouterse spoke admiringly of Venezuela and Bolivia, both governed by the populist leaders Hugo Chávez and Evo Morales. During a 2008 NDP-meeting he declared it was Suriname's turn 'to colour South America even more red'. Bouterse felt most affinity with Chávez.[82] Like the latter he had also initiated a military coup, although his views on socio-economic policies were far more moderate than those held by Venezuela's president. Both were flamboyant and charismatic, while voicing an anti-colonial rhetoric. Bouterse had often turned against the Netherlands, the former coloniser. According to a diplomatic report originating from the US Embassy in Paramaribo which was exposed through WikiLeaks and based on a 'consistently honest and factual' NDP informant, Bouterse while officiating as opposition leader had received financial aid from Venezuela.[83] Considering the mutual political sympathy, this form of assistance is indeed plausible. According to the same informant, Bouterse did visit Venezuela on various occasions, despite an international arrest warrant for a drug-related conviction. In public, Bouterse had personally reported he 'still travels regularly' to both Brazil and Guyana.[84] Moreover, officials serving at the Venezuelan embassy frequently attended NDP meetings. For president Venetiaan, such activities were reason to complain to Chávez during an inter-American summit in 2009. He objected against this embassy interfering in internal affairs, upon which Chávez recalled his ambassador for the sake of upholding bilateral relations.[85]

---

81   Jnan Adhin 1957, 38.
82   *De Ware Tijd*, 7 July 2008.
83   See: (a) the diplomatic cable, leaked by WikiLeaks, sent by the US Ambassador entitled *Possible Venezuelan meddling* on 7 November 2005 and (b) a cable entitled *Increased Venezuelan activism in Suriname has mixed success* which the US Ambassador sent on 9 June 2006..
84   Jurna 2007, 121.
85   *De Ware Tijd*, 24 April 2009.

Bouterse primarily engaged in extra-parliamentary opposition. Having been excluded from parliamentary committees, as previously mentioned, he never entered parliament again and therefore in due course had to abandon his seat, in accordance with regulations. While the December murder trial approached to finally begin on 30 November 2007, his verbal attacks on government politicians intensified. At the end of 2006, when he was re-elected as NDP president, he had accused the NPS of seeking to render him 'politically dead' through this process and thus split the NDP; Bouterse was calling for a truth and reconciliation commission; at the same time he warned: 'But if they want a war, they may come.'[86] A few months later, during a meeting of young people at the NDP-headquarters, Bouterse delivered his first public 'apologies' to those bereaved and referred to a 'dark page', adding at the same time that he would never let himself be locked up.[87] As to the 15 victims, Bouterse had, off the record, previously informed a Dutch television journalist as follows: 'In fact, there should have been many more of them'.[88] His alternatingly reconciliatory and defiant statements reflected growing uncertainty as to the outcome of the process. When his party launched a last-minute amnesty proposal in parliament, support from other parties was not forthcoming.[89] Bouterse focussed his sharpest attacks at Chandrikapersad Santokhi (b. 1959), the VHP Minister of Justice and Police (2005-2010). Their relationship grew tense once the latter had in the course of the 1990s acquired a reputation within the police hierarchy as a stronghold in the war on drugs, especially after the brutal assassination of his colleague Herman Gooding (see p. 329). While serving as a minister, Santokhi was heavily engaged in preparing the December murder trial. A few days prior hereto, Bouterse threw wild accusations at Santokhi during a NDP meeting implying that the 'sheriff' would not only see to it Bouterse was 'eliminated' but had also been involved in cocaine smuggling and had worked for foreign intelligence services.[90] It was all apparently yet another attempt to mobilize Bouterse's own supporters as well as to intimidate his opponents. Bob Marley & The Wailers' recording titled 'I Shot the Sheriff' became a classic at NDP rallies, while Bouterse swung his hips. Santokhi, in turn, delivered a warning that Bouterse in order to create a 'chaos' was working on 'attack plans' aimed at individuals who played key roles in law enforcement and crime-fighting.[91] The question now rose among NDP supporters: why, if true, had no measures been taken against their leader? Tensions ran so high that both the Minister and the attorney general of Suriname requested the USA as well as the Ambassador of the Netherlands for 'advice and assistance' from their home countries, should the government of Suriname be in danger.[92] A judge eventually forced Bouterse to retract his accusations against Santokhi.[93]

---

86   Ibid., 11 December 2006.
87   *NRC Handelsblad*, 12 March 2007.
88   Jurna 2007, 122.
89   *De Ware Tijd*, 3 April 2007.
90   *NRC Handelsblad*, 27 November 2007; *de Volkskrant*, 27 November 2007.
91   *NRC Handelsblad*, 29 November 2007; *de Volkskrant*, 29 November 2007.
92   As mentioned in a diplomatic cable, leaked by WikiLeaks and dispatched by the US Ambassador, entitled *Justice Minister talks privately about strikes, threats, politics, and the December murder trial in Suriname*, on 4 December 2007.
93   *De Ware Tijd*, 20 December 2008.

More than 3 years later, after US diplomatic cable exchanges had been exposed through WikiLeaks, the basis on which Santokhi had forwarded his accusations against Bouterse seemed to become apparent. These messages contained detailed information on a North American-Guyanese businessman named Shaheed 'Roger' Khan (b. 1972), considered the most powerful drug lord in the region. His arrest on 15 June 2006 in Paramaribo was carried out with the help of advanced US communications technology and formed the remarkable outcome of a fruitful bilateral cooperation. According to cables dispatched from embassies at Paramaribo, Georgetown (Guyana) and Port of Spain (Trinidad and Tobago), Bouterse had cooperated with Khan, who was referred to as the 'Pablo Escobar of Guyana'.[94] Based on several sources, the US authorities had already concluded prior to Khan's arrest that he upheld 'social and operational links to Desi Bouterse'.[95] Through Khan, Bouterse received 'the means to supplement his income through narcotics trafficking'. In exchange, Bouterse allegedly provided Khan with access to 'Surinamese criminal elements and structures, eased access to regular shipping to Europe in order to transport narcotics, and protection while in Suriname'.[96] Khan allegedly also finalised arms-for-drugs deals with the Revolutionary Armed Forces of Colombia (FARC) via Suriname and French Guiana. A location where Bouterse met Khan, as a US diplomatic cable mentions, would have been the parliamentarian Rashied Doekhi's residence located in Nieuw Nickerie.[97] The latter had been the NDP's presidential candidate in 2000. After this information was published in the press, Doekhi denied ever having seen Khan.[98] Bouterse allegedly also involved Khan with executing plans aimed at political liquidations whereby for example Santokhi and S. Punwasi, the attorney general of Suriname (2005-2014), would be targeted by hit men in order to create as much unrest as possible.[99] Two weeks after being detained, Khan was deported to Trinidad and Tobago.[100] Next, he was immediately extradited to the US and then sentenced to 40 years imprisonment for trafficking narcotics and committing other crimes.[101] According to the Public Prosecutor's Office serving the aforementioned attorney general, Khan had been deported because he was residing illegally in Suriname and 'posed a threat to public order, peace and security'.[102] The severe crackdown on crime carried out by the Venetiaan-led government not only

---

94   Examples of detailed information on the Bouterse-Khan relationship is largely derived from US diplomatic mail, see: wikileaks.org/cablegate. They are entitled (a) *Shaheed 'Roger' Khan, Guyana's own Escobar?* (Georgetown, 1 February 2006), (b) *Requests for evaluation of security information* (Georgetown, 24 February 2006), (c) *Interagency effort to apprehend Guyanese narco-crimina'* (Georgetown, 11 May 2006), (d) *Guyana response: Desi Bouterse and Shaheed Roger Khan activities* (Georgetown, 29 June 2006,) (e) *Desi Bouterse and Shaheed Roger Khan activities* (Paramaribo, 23 June 2006) and (f) *Extraordinary cooperation from T&T on moving narcotrafficker to the US* (Port of Spain, 6 July 2006).
95   See the US diplomatic cable (c) referred to in note above.
96   See the US diplomatic cable (e) referred to in note above.
97   Ibid.
98   *De Ware Tijd*, 9 September 2011.
99   See the US diplomatic cable (b) referred to in note above.
100 See the US diplomatic cable (f) referred to in note above.
101 The effective 15-year penalty was based on two of the three sentences, to wit, 10 years for illegal possession of firearms and 15 years for witness tampering. Both verdicts ran concurrent with this 15-year jail term. On 6 September 2019, Khan returned to Guyana, see: *Kaieteur News*, 6 September 2019.
102 *De Ware Tijd*, 30 June 2006.

enabled the police to dismantle huge drug networks but also caused the source of supplies to partly move to French Guiana. This crackdown hit Bouterse financially, forcing him 'to reach out to new partners such as Khan'.[103]

All this clearly indicated that Bouterse was still involved in drug-related crimes until at least 2006, while active as a parlementarian as well as the opposition leader. Evidence brought in against him apparently did not suffice to warrant any judicial action.[104] This issue again raised serious questions as to the effect of informal power, the role of illegal or criminal money in business and politics and the relation between the legitimate society and the criminal underworld.

The VHP politician Santokhi, while serving as a minister, was highly regarded for taking vigorous initiatives within and outside his party. He hereby utilised individuals in a rather unconventional way, to wit, based on their expertise and not on party loyalty. Measured in terms of the number of murder cases per 100,000 inhabitants, Suriname was the safest Caribbean country in 2010. With four murders per 100,000 inhabitants, Suriname did much better than Jamaica (53 murders), Belize (42 murders), Saint Kitts and Nevis (40 murders) and Trinidad and Tobago (36 murders).[105] Suriname's judiciary, although struggling with a shortage of capacity, was expanded to 19 judges, almost twice as much if compared to the situation during the previous government (see p. 377).[106] Santokhi was therefore widely deemed a suitable presidential candidate for the NF, which could, after all, score electoral gains thanks to successful results in the fight against crime. However, senior VHP politicians ignored the wishes expressed by a strong renewal movement. The unpopular VHP-leader and Vice President Ramdien Sardjoe (aged 74) aspired to officiate as president. The incumbent president Venetiaan (aged 73) had already stated he did not wish to stand for another term of office, though he did continue to lead the NPS list of candidates for parliament. The NF-campaign was again aimed at confronting the people of Suriname with the dark period of military dictatorship. Once again, their leaders stressed they had introduced economic stability. However, this in itself correct observation did little to further impress the less wealthy. President Venetiaan's lack of political feeling became apparent again when announcing, during the election campaign, that he had no intention of increasing child benefits or old-age allowances only 'for the sake of populist considerations'.[107] Many voters had hoped for just that. On the other hand, the government did increase civil servants' salaries, despite the IMF's warning as to the negative financial consequences concerning the treasury. The fact that ministers and parliamentarians (often simultaneously officiating as civil servants) also benefited from this pay rise only enhanced resentment among the less affluent. The VHP and NPS lacked a sophisticated electoral strategy, their elderly leaders campaigning on auto-pilot. Moreover, within a closed and hierarchical

---

103   See the US diplomatic cable (e) referred to in note above.
104   In the course of an investigation in 2013 executed by *NRC Handelsblad* the present author was given access to printouts of the contacts Khan had established through his satellite telephone. They indicated that he had called Desi Bouterse on several occasions between the end of 2005 and the time of his arrest, see: *NRC Handelsblad*, 21 September 2013; see also: *Kaieteur News*, 22 September 2013.
105   *The Economist*, 'Crime in the Caribbean', 10 February 2011.
106   *De Ware Tijd*, 25 April 2009.
107   Ibid., 17 April 2010.

culture, especially observed amidst old parties, not much room existed for either any internal criticism or open debates.

Bouterse's promise was as clear as it was powerful. He spoke of a 'social contract' with the Surinamese, improving the position of mothers, students, workers, entrepreneurs, Indigenous peoples and Maroons, for instance. In addition, despite his 64 years, he presented himself as a political innovator, heralding 'a new Suriname'.[108] Similar to Hugo Chávez in Venezuela, Bouterse also mingled with the public during non-election periods. At meetings he swung along smoothly to both traditional and modern music. Meanwhile, at least among poorer and younger voters, the December murder trial apparently damaged Bouterse only slightly. Despite his status of being the prime suspect, he was not obliged to appear in court and thus spared humiliating procedures during monthly hearings. To avoid any controversy, Bouterse waited until after the parliamentary elections to announce his presidential candidacy. The NDP, the main party within the *Mega Combinatie* (MC), also had attractive candidates in place as to mobilising the dissent of voters. In Paramaribo, André Misiekaba (b. 1976) was included in the list of candidates. This popular young member of parliament and pastor of the aforementioned Pentecostal Church not only appealed to Maroon voters because of his Maroon stock, but could also mobilise many others thanks to his oratorical talent. In the inland district of Sipaliwini, a Maroon called Hugo Jabini (b. 1964) became a frontrunner in the race against Brunswijk's A-C. Jabini had gained support among Maroons as the driving force behind the court trial of the Saramaka people vs. the State of Suriname regarding land rights, an initiative for which Jabini received international awards (see p. 385-386).[109]

The MC (with the NDP as dominant party) in spite of winning the parliamentary elections with 40.22 per cent of the votes, did not achieve the desired absolute majority, occupying only 23 of the 51 parliamentary seats. The NF acquired 14 seats with 31.65 per cent of the votes.[110] This poor result was mainly caused by a decision made by the Javanese partner, the PL, to participate independently during the elections. The NPS's sharply declined popularity did contribute to this loss. Changes were not very significant, but the MC was able to grasp the political initiative thanks to obtaining a larger number of seats.[111] Bouterse announced his candidacy for the presidency a few days after the parliamentary elections had taken place. However, a two-thirds majority in parliament was required before being elected. Hence the MC had to seek coalition partners. Otherwise, Bouterse would have to depend on the *Verenigde Volksvergadering* (United People's Assembly), which now comprised as many as 919 parliamentarians, district council members and local council members, where an absolute majority would suffice. Partly as a result of the electoral system's traits, the MC had a narrow majority in this assembly. Voting in the assembly had nevertheless often proved risky. Parties were capable of winning votes from rivals either by relying on ethnic sentiments or by means of bribery, as was presumably the

---

108 *Starnieuws*, 24 May 2010.

109 In 2015, Jabini was no longer a candidate for the NDP after he criticised his party for failing to deliver on promises of land rights for Indigenous people and Maroons, see: *Starnieuws*, 8 April 2015.

110 See: wikipedia.org/wiki/Surinaamse_parlementsverkiezingen_2010

111 The MC took advantage of the fact that a split-off, led by ex-President Wijdenbosch and having acquired 14.5 per cent of the votes in 2005, re-joined the NDP in 2010. He was one of the returnees.

Figure 16.3. The
NDP-chairman
Desi Bouterse (l.)
and the ABOP-
chairman Ronnie
Brunswijk
embrace at the
Best Western Hotel
(Paramaribo) after
agreeing upon
a governmental
coalition
on 3 June 2010.
Photo by Edward
Troon.

case in 1996 (see p. 350). The VHP and the NPS had already announced their refusal to cooperate with the MC in the case of Bouterse's candidacy, as according to them the people of Suriname did not support it. Santokhi had been forwarded as their candidate. His chances however had hugely diminished after his party's defeat in the course of the parliamentary elections.

The amazement was widespread when former army leader Bouterse and former rebel leader Brunswijk laughingly not only reached out to each other before the eyes of the media but also started to negotiate a cooperation. After a few days they raised champagne glasses at the Best Western hotel in Paramaribo to celebrate a coalition agreement between the MC and the A-C.[112]

The Javanese PL, while partnering with small parties within the so-called *Volksalliantie* (People's Alliance), joined the MC and the A-C with the intent to form a government. The MC, the A-C and the PL nevertheless soon went each their own way when their demands on cabinet posts were not immediately met with. The A-C as well as the PL then knocked on the door of the NF, their former coalition partner. However, this rapprochement was abruptly cut off after several weeks. Now, as a result of 'betrayal' during the secret ballot held in parliament: not the PL-leader Paul Somohardjo but the MC's candidate Jennifer Geerlings-Simons was elected to preside over parliament.[113] For Somohardjo this painful defeat was reason to opt for a coalition with the MC. The A-C followed suit, hereby providing Bouterse with the two-thirds parliamentary majority required. He was elected president on 19 July 2010. Filled with emotion, this former seditionist of semi-Indigenous stock declared that history had been written. For, 'that little Indian boy from Cassewinica will be President'.[114]

The alliance of the former arch-enemies Bouterse and Brunswijk is less surprising than it seems to be at first sight. Their pact fitted into the political culture comprising patronage and clientelism. After all, party leaders who do not participate

---

112   *Starnieuws*, 3 June 2010.
113   Ibid., 30 June 2010.
114   Ibid., 19 July 2010.

in a government can do little for their supporters. For, less chance exists as to acquiring social housing, plots of land to build a home on or even government jobs. The allocation of ministerial posts indicated how much the presidency was worth to Bouterse. Never before had a coalition partner been so generously rewarded for its loyalty as the A-C. Little wonder Bouterse was forced to quickly abandon his plan aimed at reducing the number of ministries from seventeen to ten. The A-C's seven parliamentary seats had yielded just as many cabinet posts, including the vice presidency. Prior to these elections, the A-C had feared the worst once the alliance of the Maroon political parties was excluded from participating in the constituencies of Paramaribo, Wanica and Para. In fact, the lists of candidates had been submitted too late due to dissent between the partnering ABOP and BEP. However, the electoral system worked strongly in the A-C's favour. For, in the interior constituencies with their large Maroon population far fewer votes per seat are required when compared with elsewhere. The relationship between the ABOP and the BEP remained strenuous, whereby the latter complained about Brunswijk's autocratic actions. Moreover, the BEP felt less than happy with the incoming government coalition, It would eventually lead to a split between these two parties. This outcome, however, remained without any consequences for the stability of the Bouterse-led government. The Javanese PL, having obtained six seats in parliament, had to content itself with three cabinet posts. In the previous legislature, the NDP had always fiercely criticised the PL for its shady practices regarding land allocation for which it apparently was now paying the price.

The Dutch government reacted bitterly to Bouterse's election. Minister of Foreign Affairs Maxim Verhagen (2007-2010), stated that the president of Suriname was not welcome in the Netherlands 'other than serving his prison sentence'. According to Verhagen, it could 'not be brushed aside that Bouterse was sentenced here to eleven years for drug trafficking'. The Hague would only maintain contact with Bouterse 'on the basis of functional necessity'.[115] Verhagen's future colleague Winston G. Lackin (1954-2019) reacted by stating that the ambassador of the Netherlands was 'not welcome' at the incoming president's inauguration. This Dutch diplomat nonetheless did attend this event after already having received a formal invitation from the outgoing government.[116] A courtesy visit to president Bouterse took place a few months later. Uri Rosenthal having succeeded Verhagen as the Dutch Minister of Foreign Affairs described the Netherlands-Suriname relationship in a letter addressed to the house of representatives in 2011 as 'business-like and engaged', a qualification the Dutch government had already applied in 2004.[117] Moreover, a shared history, common language and social networks formed the foundation for a 'continued strong interdependence' between both societies (see also p. 454).[118] The termination of Dutch development aid, based on the treaty funds, had already been announced. The lump sum of € 1.6 billion pledged on the occasion of Suriname's independence had almost been spent. In addition, from a global perspective, Suriname was no

---

115 *NRC Handelsblad*, 20 July 2010.
116 *Starnieuws*, 11 August 2010.
117 Kamerstuk 20361, nr. 147, 26 August 2011 (zoek.officielebekendmakingen.nl/kst-20361-147.html).
118 See the memorandum issued by the Dutch government entitled *Een rijke relatie, Suriname en Nederland: heden en toekomst* (A rich relationship, Suriname and the Netherlands: present and future), 4 June 2004: Kamerstuk 20361 nr. 116 (zoek.officielebekendmakingen.nl/kst-20361-116.html).

longer deemed poor. In The Hague's view, cooperation in the fields of justice and the police remained a Dutch interest because of the fight against crime (including drug trafficking) and illegality, although it remained unclear to what extent any confidential information could still be exchanged with Paramaribo. Now relations between both governments proved extremely difficult. For example, the ambassador of the Netherlands was not invited to attend the Independence Celebration, after the president of Suriname had previously not been invited to the Queen's Day celebrations Due to the tensions between these two governments, Bouterse's inaugural address, on 12 August 2010, deliberately mentioned a pursuit of the best possible relations between the 'Surinamese and Dutch people'; these words implied specifically: an 'intensive cooperation' between 'Surinamese in the Netherlands and Surinamese at home', whereby 'business ties' had to be reinforced.[119]

Not a single head of state attended the inauguration ceremony held at the Anthony Nesty Sports Hall, where the outgoing President Venetiaan had refused to personally hand the Presidential Chain of Honour to his successor. However, no real boycott or form of isolation was imposed on Suriname, measures for which the opposition had warned. Caribbean countries continued both their diplomatic and economic relations along the same lines. Suriname continued to participate in the rotating presidency of the Caricom. For Brazil, the relationship with the neighbouring country remained of significance, if only because of the presence here of c.30,000 fellow nationals. Collaboration in all areas, especially agriculture, was either continued or intensified. Nevertheless, during a candid interview, the Brazilian ambassador in Paramaribo had stated he was 'no friend of Bouterse', adding he had been instructed by Brasilia 'not to hug and kiss him after the inauguration'.[120] Suriname's relationship with Venezuela was less important from a political and economic point of view. At the end of 2010, President Chávez was nonetheless the first head of state to visit his 'big brother' Bouterse.[121] Framework agreements were signed concerning, for instance, rice cultivation and the supply of oil and fertiliser. By establishing an embassy in Paris, the Bouterse-led government intended to reinforce ties with the Republic of France. For, the overseas department of French Guiana is a direct neighbour of Suriname. This initiative complied with Suriname's desire to focus more closely on its part of the world, although it was also deemed a signal to the Netherlands. Suriname now placed economic interests at the forefront of foreign relations. The Bouterse-led government emphasized this stance even further than its predecessor had, all the more because the Dutch assistance treaty was expiring. The People's Republic of China, with whom intensive relations had existed for decades, now became an even more important partner (see also p. 379-380). President Bouterse referred to China as an 'interesting alternative for developing countries that want to discontinue their dependence on a limited number of donors'.[122] Paramaribo hoped the Chinese would fund large projects.

---

119 Quote from Bouterse's inaugural address held on 12 August 2010 in Paramaribo.
120 *NRC Handelsblad*, 14 August 2010.
121 *Starnieuws*, 27 November 2010.
122 Quote from Bouterse's speech held on July 26, 2011 at the swearing-in of the incoming Surinamese ambassador in Beijing, see: *Starnieuws*, 26 July 2011.

Washington had praised Suriname, and specifically Minister of Justice Santokhi, as a 'consistent counternarcotics ally of the United States' during the Venetiaan-led government.[123] In addition, the USA was allowed to utilise facilities located in Suriname to test military vehicles exposed to tropical conditions. The Americans expressed their great appreciation in 2007 when Robert M. Gates, the US Secretary of Defence, travelled to Paramaribo. He was the first US minister to visit independent Suriname. Its incoming government was keen to continue these good relations as proven most evident when president Bouterse successfully supported efforts by his key political opponent, the former minister Santokhi, directed at acquiring the post of President of the Inter-American Anti-Drug Abuse Control Commission (CICAD), an agency of the Organisation of American States (OAS).[124] The US-Suriname cooperation was continued across the board. In 2011, the US Secretary of State Hillary R. Clinton congratulated Suriname not only with the 36th anniversary of its independence but also for being a 'valued' partner when mentioning for instance a security initiative concerning the Caribbean region.[125] Earlier, John R. Nay, the US ambassador to Suriname (2009-2012), had warned the incoming president of Suriname on his inauguration day, when speaking to The Associated Press, thus: 'We have a deep interest in the rule of law and that there is an independent judiciary', adding that 'any interference in the trial would be a concern'.[126]

This statement formed an outright reference to the December murder trial. A few weeks before the presidential inauguration ceremony, taking place in August 2010, another court session had taken place, as reported in the court's Communique no. 38:

'At around 10.25 a.m. the hearing opens, and the case of the accused D.B. is called. The accused is not present at the hearing, his counsel is. The President of the Court Martial states it has been established that, for various reasons, the accused has not appeared since the beginning of the trial. Questioned about the reason why the accused is not present at the hearing today, counsel states he has understood he is in the process of settling protocol cases in connection with his inauguration as President of the Republic.'[127]

This was the final communiqué as the incoming government had now dismissed the court-martial's spokeswoman in charge of informing on the trial. Nonetheless Desi Bouterse, the main suspect and now president, assured to the local press he would 'not interfere in the progress of this criminal trial' which, in his view, was 'political'.[128]

Immediately after taking office, Bouterse placed non-partisan technocrats at the key financial-economic policy posts. Gillmore Hoefdraad (b. 1962), a former IMF

---

123 WikiLeaks, the diplomatic cable entitled *Bouterse retracts slanderous statements against Justice Minister, but will appeal court decision*, as dispatched by the US Ambassador in Paramaribo on 24 September 2008,.
124 *Starnieuws*, 1 September 2010.
125 Statement made on 23 November 2011 (2009-2017.state.gov/secretary/20092013clinton/rm/2011/11/177696.htm).
126 See: foxnews.com/world/suriname-ex-dictator-bouterse-a-convicted-smuggler-sworn-in-with-other-heads-of-state-absent
127 This communique was later removed from Ministry of Justice's website.
128 *De Ware Tijd*, 21 July 2010.

employee, began his term of office as the president (governor) of Suriname's Central Bank. Wonnie Boedhoe, a respected former president of the Surinamese Economists' Association, was appointed Minister of Finance (2010-2011). By doing so, Bouterse gave the impression he now not only valued a solid financial policy but also that he had drawn lessons from his personal mistakes. The parliament's approval of Robert Ameerali as Vice President having officiated as chairman of the Chamber of Commerce and Industry, instilled widespread confidence, too. The Maroon parties had put forward this entrepreneur of non-Maroon origin, because they did not agree on a candidate belonging to their own ethnic group.

When the government's deficit increased, it opted for rapid remediation measures. Hence, the promise of improving the lives of the disadvantaged was not kept for the time being. This shortfall was largely the outcome of a sharp increase in civil servants' salaries caused by the previous government and its arrears (see also p. 428). Such an increase in expenditure immediately put pressure on the national currency of Suriname's open economy due to the increased import demand, allowing the black currency market to revive. A devaluation was now inevitable: in the course of January 2011, the Central Bank decided to lower with 20 per cent the official exchange rate of the Surinamese dollar (SRD) which had been introduced in 2004; the exchange rate rose from 2.80 SRD to 3.35 SRD for 1 USD. At the same time, the government increased the fuel tax with 70 per cent as part of a Structural Improvement Programme. The population of Suriname was faced with an inflation rate of *c.*20 per cent, implying that the increases in old-age and child benefits evaporated.[129]

Bouterse's presidency seemed to be more than merely a stylistic break with the immediate past. This incoming president profiled himself as a can-do manager, who launched ambitious plans with fervour. He intended to operate as an 'executive' president and, if compared with his predecessor, leave far less initiatives to the council of ministers and to parliament. Shortly after taking office, Bouterse appointed a number of committees to not only prepare plans for key areas but to also report directly to him on issues such as housing, rice cultivation, health care, education and regulation of the informal gold sector. These committees eroded the role of ministers and their departments, which particularly angered coalition partners who saw their power undermined. Moreover, the National Assembly, where president Bouterse often failed to appear, had less sight on government plans. His approach revealed impatience, which on occasion turned into frustration. For example, merely 10 months after taking office, he lashed out sharply at the coalition partners at a meeting with district administrators held in New Nickerie opining:

'*Neither Volksalliantie nor A-Combinatie has a single notion of development. It is all about them: I have to be in the alliance, I have to be in the centre of power and I have to be able to accommodate people.*'[130]

Bouterse, too, ran up against the immobilism inherent in ethnic politics and patronage – a system he claimed he had already tried to put an end to with the 1980 military coup.

---

129   IMF *Country Report 12/281: Suriname 2012 Article IV Consultation*, 5.
130   *Starnieuws*, 17 June 2011.

A History of Suriname

For the time being, nothing came of either the intention to reform the government apparatus or to strive for the 'optimal occupation of positions based on competence and utility', as formulated in the coalition agreement.[131] In practice, party political appointments continued to occur in all departments whereby incumbent civil servants belonging to the undesired political persuasion were dismissed with full salaries because of - as it was usually phrased by governments in Suriname - the 'changed policy views'. During the budget debate in parliament, the minister of home affairs reported that, in the course of his first 11 months of tenure, the government had recruited 2,285 workers thus increasing the 40,000 already employed.[132] This number included the president's wife. Much to the amazement of many, she received compensation in order to fulfil her role as First Lady.[133] The president's spiritual advisor, pastor Steve Meye of *God's Bazuin* (God's Trumpet) received an official allowance, too. Bouterse's party fully participated in the traditional job carousel whereby civil servants were replaced even at lower levels. The well-informed magazine *Parbode* reported that at a ministry, which the A-C (Maroon alliance) managed, a lady of Maroon descent had replaced a Javanese waitress.[134] Events at the Department of Spatial Planning, Land Management and Forestry Policy demonstrated how difficult it was to overcome patronage. This department's minister Martinus Sastroredjo (KTPI) had to resign after a few months for trying too hard to deal with abuses pertaining to the issuance of public land as reported in the course of his predecessor Michael Jong Tjien Fa's (PL) tenure (2005-2010).[135] The leaders of both Javanese parties, Willy Soemita (KTPI) and Paul Somohardjo (PL), had requested President Bouterse to dismiss Sastroredjo. Several months later, a committee set up by Bouterse concluded that Jong Tjien Fa's employees had carried out orders 'even though it was known that this was against the law'.[136] Cronyism existed on a large scale. For the time being, the above findings did not lead to disciplinary or judicial actions against those involved. No wonder that in 2011 Suriname was ranked no. 100 in the Transparency Corruption Perceptions Index, quite low when compared with previous years (see also p. 378).[137]

The most ambitious initiative Bouterse announced comprised constructing 18,000 homes within 5 years.[138] During the previous government, according to its own assessment, *c.*4,000 homes had been 'built or renovated' by means of the Low Income Shelter Programme whereby private housing construction was stimulated with interest subsidies.[139] The Bouterse government's plan revealed an unusual vigour, which could score political points, but also entailed great uncertainties. All these 18,000 houses were to be owner-occupied dwellings. Their financing thus

---

131 *Regeerakkoord* (Coalition Agreement) *2010-2015*, 21 August 2010, 4.
132 *Starnieuws*, 8 July 2011.
133 Ibid., 14 January 2011; Bouterse also wished to retroactively award the allowance to the previous First Lady, Liesbeth Venetiaan-Vanenburg, but she refused the money.
134 *Parbode*, May 2011.
135 *Starnieuws*, 15 December 2010.
136 For a summary of the report entitled *'Domeingrond voor alle Surinamers'*, published in Paramaribo on 1 March 2011, see: *Parbode*, 1 June 2011.
137 See: transparency.org
138 Bouterse, *Regeringsverklaring* (Government Statement) *2010-2015*, 1 October 2010, 19
139 NPS, *Verkiezingsmanifest* (Electoral Manifest) *2010*, 12.

relied upon the citizens themselves.[140] Hence, much depended upon the willingness of local banks to provide mortgage loans on reasonable terms. In addition, a lack of domestic construction capacity implied that foreign partners and labourers were required. During the first year, the government signed a letter of intent with the China Dalian International Economic & Technical Cooperation Group, already active in Suriname for several years, as to the construction of 5,000 dwellings meant to house lower income groups, but a great deal remained unclear with regard to this proposal being implemented.[141] Major uncertainties concerning the financing and realisation of plans for large infrastructural projects arose, too. After taking office, Bouterse had announced a 'substantial upgrading' of Greater Paramaribo's road network in the coming decade. He also discussed new roads to be constructed inland between Apoera and Stoelmans Island, bridges across the Marowijne and Corantijn Rivers in order to promote economic integration in the region, and a deep-sea port at the estuary of the Suriname River (Puert' America) annex airport; in addition, Suriname was to become 'the food barn for the Caribbean' by means of, for instance, a large-scale expansion of rice acreages.[142] However, such projects (partly only feasible in the long run) could not be carried out without huge foreign and multilateral investments.

Bouterse's hopeful plans fitted in with a more broadly supported and nationalistic conviction of self-belief, as already expressed during the 1970s by politicians such as Frank Essed in his publication entitled *De mobilisatie van het eigene* (The mobilisation of one's own capacities) (see p. 291). Nonetheless, the volume of mega-plans Bouterse had promised while in office simultaneously raised the question: where does realism cease and bravura begin? After the first year, Bouterse had already become more cautious when pointing to the global crisis, mentioning a 'slowing down' of the implementation of certain projects.[143]

As a young man, Bouterse had hugely admired the very influential Johan A. Pengel (1916-1970), the Creole politician, for whom the former's father had worked as a propagandist. Once, shortly after the 1980 coup, Bouterse had mentioned within a small circle that he also wished to be such a leader, although he did not share Pengel's political views. When speeching Bouterse often expressed the desire to be accepted as a leader by the entire community. During his inauguration he promised, while invoking the 'Almighty Creator', that 'only servitude and sacrifice to all of you and to the nation, will be the guiding principles of my actions'; he further added that the opposition was 'not our adversary' but a 'cooperation partner to make and implement our policies, in order to achieve the widest possible support'.[144] During the 35th anniversary of Suriname's independence, Bouterse referred to a 'pride and warmth' that arose from 'the observation of the great commonality that characterizes the current state of development in our society'.[145] The below quote from this

---

140 *Starnieuws*, 6 October 2010.
141 *Starnieuws*, 21 September 2010.
142 Bouterse, *Regeringsverklaring* (Government Statement) *2010-2015*, 1 October 2010, 8, 21; .Bouterse's Inauguration Speech was held on 12 August 2010.
143 Bouterse, *Annual Address to Parliament*, 29 September 2011, 3.
144 Bouterse, *Inauguration Speech*, 12 August 2010., 3.
145 Bouterse, Speech on the occasion of the 35th anniversary of independence, 25 November 2010, 1.

A History of Suriname

statement indicates that the incoming president was nonetheless not unaware of the fact he did not find everyone on his side,

'*Those who do not yet feel called to share in this commonality are not yet on the right side of history, that characterises our country. [...] We should understand and respect them, because by doing so we increase the chance that the scales will fall from their eyes sooner, and they will come to grasp that the majority whom they do not want to join yet, aspire to the same thing they do. That aspiration is: all public efforts will lead to a happy existence on this land for all who belong to it and live on it.*'[146]

The final phrase of the above citation alluded to the National Anthem: 'No matter how we came together here, we are pledged to its soil.' Bouterse now fell in line with a sentiment already much earlier widely shared across Suriname. His vision can therefore be described as 'territorial nationalism'. In 1983 the distinguished historical sociologist Anthony D. Smith (1939-2016) introduced this characterization as a means of distinction from 'ethnic nationalism'. With regard to Suriname the term territorial nationalism was applied by the (Dutch) Caribbeanist Peter Meel.[147] This form of nationalism which aims at integrating ethnic groups into a new political community after achieving independence resembles the 'unity in diversity' as advocated amidst Hindustani circles (see p. 393).

Coalition and opposition did not differ fundamentally as to the correct direction of development: the consensus concerning the desirability of a stable macro-policy and economic diversification was broad. Whereas the NDP was most profiled pertaining to the representation of the interests of the less affluent, the need to combat poverty, however, was widely recognised. In addition, as the result of ethnicity-based loyalties, class conflicts in Suriname played a slightly less prominent role than elsewhere in Latin America. Patronage and clientelism mitigated class differences, too. In the eyes of many, however, president Bouterse lacked the credibility required in order to represent the 'commonality' he allegedly wished to advocate. For this reason he apparently felt aggrieved. Shortly after his conciliatory words spoken on Independence Day, he stated that 'coalition and opposition' no longer existed in Suriname, adding that 'unfortunately coalition and enemies' did.[148]

Bouterse's tainted history had rendered the chasm between him and at least part of the population insurmountable. Having been elected president by a two-thirds majority in parliament, Bouterse had not acquired a direct electoral mandate, unlike numerous other rulers residing in the region. The Institute for Development Oriented Studies (IDOS), which later correctly predicted the *Mega Combinatie*'s victory in 2010, revealed that at the end of 2008 in Paramaribo, Wanica, Nickerie and Commewijne only 29.9 per cent responded favourably to the question: should Bouterse become president? As much as 55.4 per cent stated he should not.[149]

---

146   Ibid.
147   Meel 1998, 257-281.
148   As stated in a speech held on 4 December 2010 and published in *Starnieuws* on 5 December 2010.
149   *De Ware Tijd*, 3 October 2008.

Human rights organisations had in vain put forward legal arguments questioning the legitimacy of Bouterse's presidency. In a letter addressed to parliament, the *Organisatie Gerechtigheid en Vrede* (Organization for Justice and Peace) and the *Stichting 8 December* (Foundation 8 December) had requested refraining from Bouterse's nomination based on Article 92 of the constitution. According to this article, a presidential candidate may not 'have performed any act contrary to the Constitution'.[150] Both organisations reported this had been the case. For, Bouterse had violated the 'right to life' as enshrined in Article 14 of the constitution. He had, after all, called himself 'politically responsible' (see p. 376) for the December murders. Moreover, the Inter-American Commission on Human Rights had designated Bouterse, the then army chief as the 'the author' behind the 1986 massacre among Maroons in the village of Moiwana.[151] The 1980 coup led by Bouterse was also a violation of the constitution, according to these two human rights organisations, as power had been acquired in an unconstitutional manner. According to the constitution, the Constitutional Court had the authorisation to judge the 'compatibility' of parliamentary decisions by means of fundamental rights, including the right to life.[152] Nonetheless successive governments had never set up this court because one feared it would be an impediment rather than an advantage.

Certain statements and actions, whereby president Bouterse added to doubts concerning his intentions, even stirred up dissent. In 2011, for example, he awarded the Golden Star of the Revolution medal to the nine surviving fellow putschists in appreciation of 'what they have done for the country and its people'.[153] This official act performed by the head of state was all the more controversial because the former putschists were all suspects in the December murder trial in which Bouterse himself was the prime suspect. Bouterse's creating a special security force, the Counter Terrorist Unit (CTU), without informing parliament was controversial too. The police chief mentioned he had not been notified, neither could the minister of justice and police provide any details. The CTU had appeared in public on the 35th Anniversary of Independence. Six months later, the national security chief Melvin Linscheer and a staff member of Bouterse's personal office, explained to the press the reason for establishing the elite corps which consisted of police officers, penitentiary officials, military personnel and members of the intelligence service. According to Linscheer, the CTU, being placed under Bouterse's direct responsibility, was responsible not only for safely removing the president in threatening situations but also for assisting the police when fighting crimes. Moreover, this unit could serve whenever the 'general security of the nation' was at risk or in the event of 'political disruption'.[154] This vague mandate raised questions, especially because the police had already provided for an anti-terrorist unit. Since the Interior War, the security chief Linscheer's reputation was dubious, having been linked to extreme acts of violence and disappearances as well as to a possible involvement in weapons-for-drugs deals, while officiating as the

---

150 *Starnieuws*, 19 July 2010; for the text of the constitution, see: the parliament's website of (dna.sr/wetgeving).
151 Inter-American Court of Human Rights, *Case of the Moiwana Community v. Suriname., Judgment of 15 June, 2005 (Preliminary objections, merits, reparations and costs)* , 77.
152 As mentioned in Article 144 of Suriname's constitution.
153 *Starnieuws*, 24 February 2011.
154 Ibid., 29 July 2011.

commander of the interior districts (see also p. 354-355). The appointment of Dino Bouterse (b. 1972), President Bouterse's son, to be in charge of 'logistics matters' at the CTU was very remarkable, too.[155] In 2005, this son had been sentenced to 8 years in prison for cocaine trafficking and arms smuggling to be released in 2008 as a result of good behaviour. Creating the CTU gave the impression Desi Bouterse did not trust the army nor the police, whose commanders had been replaced shortly after he had taken office. In addition, the outcome of the December murder trial remained uncertain. Taken together, it remained unclear how a possible conviction of the prime suspect Desi Bouterse would affect his presidency and possibly his political party. All this fuelled the speculation the CTU could then be deployed, albeit no more than speculation.

The opposition deemed it important to be prepared for elections. In any case, the VHP was prompted to elect a new leader. A year after being defeated in the parliamentary elections, the former Minister Santokhi was elected party leader with the support of a renewal movement. He was Bouterse's undisputed political rival. Developments were much slower within the NPS led by the former President Venetiaan. Apparently the traditional Creole party, one of the driving forces behind Suriname's independence in 1975, needed to be concerned about its political future for the first time.

In April 2012, the December murder trial led to growing unrest as Bouterse attempted to halt this legal procedure permanently, despite his earlier promise not to interfere. Shortly before the prosecutor was to deliver his indictment, parliament passed, with 28 against 12 votes, an amendment to the 1992 amnesty law initiated by the NDP in order to shield Bouterse from further prosecution.[156] Critics stated this amendment violated Article 131 (3) of the constitution that forbids 'any interference' in cases 'pending before the court'. The court martial suspended the trial and requested the prosecutor to answer the 'constitutional question' of interference.[157] The several thousand Surinamese who protested against the amnesty law in a silent march were, according to Bouterse, 'enemies of the people' and their protest was 'destabilising and criminal'.[158] This court's decision was a miscalculation by the president, who had hoped to put the *hebi* (heavy burden) that had haunted him since 1982 behind him for good.

Yet the issue regarding the December murders still had little electoral impact. Many NDP voters had pinned their hopes on the 'social contract' Bouterse had promised.[159] Firstly, civil servants' salaries were raised by 10 per cent. Child benefits and pension payments were also increased.[160] Towards the end of his term of office, a basic health insurance came into being, whereby the government covered the premiums for children under 16 years of age, students under 25 and everyone older than 60.[161] During the first few years, the surge in public spending was covered by

155   Ibid.
156   *NRC Handelsblad*, 5 April 2012.
157   *Starnieuws*, 11 and 16 May 2012.
158   Ibid., 6 May 2012.
159   Bouterse, *Regeringsverklaring* (Government Statement) *2010-2015*, 1 October 2010, 28.
160   IMF, *Suriname, Staff Report for the 2014 Article IV Consultation* (*Country Report no. 14/316)*, 6.
161   *Starnieuws*, 18 September, 1 October and 12 November 2014.

rising contributions from the oil and gold sectors, which benefited from higher world market prices. Next, however, in 2015 the public deficit rose to almost 10 per cent of GDP, which was partly covered by monetary financing.[162] In a sense Bouterse 'bought' his re-election as president by concealing the economic downturn for as long as possible. Two weeks before the 25 May 2015 elections, he was still speaking of 'good performance and positive prospects' in 'a challenging external environment'.[163] Less than a year later, the government negotiated a support package with the IMF, which was abandoned after paying the first tranche, due to the conditions (see p. 435).

As was the case during the Wijdenbosch era, at the end of the 1990s, inflation as well as the government debt rose rapidly. Now once again, gross corruption and drug-related crime thrived. In fact the president seemed to have no interest in seriously tackling these issues. The US State Department reported in its *2016 International Narcotics Control Strategy Report*:

> 'The Government of Suriname is officially opposed to narcotics trafficking, but little political will has been demonstrated to pursue vigorous enforcement. Corruption pervades many government offices in Suriname and may also play a role. Local criminal investigations of allegedly corrupt acts are rare and local prosecutions even rarer.'[164]

Symptomatic was Bouterse's appointment of the former public works minister Ramon Abrahams to lead his election campaign, shortly after the latter had resigned in June 2013 when media reports concerning corruption surfaced.[165] According to research published in the periodical *Parbode* in a coverstory under the heading 'The Abrahams affair. Stealing in politics pays', Abrahams allowed himself to receive millions of Surinamese dollars in bribes from contractors when awarding contracts privately. One of them declared he had to deliver a total of almost 1 million SRD 'in envelopes' to this ministry pertaining to seven contracts and that he also once visited the NDP's office 'for the party treasury'.[166] Once Bouterse took office in 2010, Suriname had again taken on traits of a kleptocracy, and his own party was not forgotten. The dozens of gold mining concessions presented to private individuals were extremely lucrative. These so-called areas of interest would eventually be exploited by the state together with the multinationals IAMGOLD and Newmont. Following questions asked by the opposition in parliament, even by Bouterse's party NDP, the government sent a list of concessions granted to the National Assembly in 2013.[167] An opposition-led investigation into these concessionaires revealed a list resembling a catalogue of favouritism. Beneficiaries included Bouterse's lawyer, his businessmen friends, the director of the Ministry of Natural Resources and an NDP activist.[168] Dino Bouterse also held interests in the mining sector, as he had personally

162   IMF Statement: *IMF concludes 2016 Article IV Consultation with Suriname*, 24 January 2017.
163   *Starnieuws*, 8 May 2015.
164   State Department, *2016 International Narcotics Control Strategy Report*, vol. 1, March 2017, 254.
165   *Starnieuws*, 11 June and 9 August 2013.
166   *Parbode*, August 2013.
167   *NRC Handelsblad*, 23 February 2018.
168   Ibid.

confirmed earlier, when describing himself as a 'manager in a gold mine' during an interview.[169] Ex-Jungle Commando and parliamentarian Ronnie Brunswijk, then still member of the government coalition, also obtained a handful of concessions.

A foster son and a family friend of Bouterse apparently owned one such company named Tranquillo. In a shady deal, the concession eventually went to IAMGOLD. In exchange, Tranquillo not only obtained another concession but also secretly received millions of euros from the state as compensation. In an equally shadowy way, the well-known tourist resort named Blanche Marie fell into the hands of a convicted drug criminal.[170] Such affairs raged on and on. At the EBS, an energy company, its supervisory board dismissed the director (a former minister) 'entirely in line with the government's policy of fighting corruption'.[171] Not much later Bouterse reinstated this director (a fellow party member) to that post, subsequently sending the board members home. A multi-million fraud regarding the provision of meals to after-school childcare institutions had, according to an unpublished report by the National Audit Office, involved 'possibly provable criminal acts' carried out by 'political figures'.[172] A 'crusade against corruption' promised by the president at his inauguration did not materialize.[173] The NDP parliamentary leader André Misiekaba had even called on parliamentarians to 'stop pointing the finger at each other'.[174] Bouterse was equally clear, stating '[...] let's put a lid on it'.[175] The fact that trafficking in cocaine was also growing is proven by the number of large seizures, often exceeding 1,000 kg. The most spectacular hereof was, in March 2018, the discovery of a submarine in the Saramacca district, intended for transporting cocaine.[176] Significant was Dino Bouterse's arrest in Panama, in 2013, during a DEA undercover operation, after which he was sentenced to 16 years in prison in the USA.[177]

The full extent of the economic crisis became apparent soon after the elections. Everyone experienced this downturn due to a number of painful measures, to wit, the devaluation of the SRD, an additional levy on fuel prices and a healthcare system that threatened to grind to a halt due to a lack of funds; inflation had risen to over 50 per cent.[178] According to a poll conducted by NGO Nikos in July 2016, the number of NDP followers in Paramaribo had shrunk to a mere 17.5 per cent, the NDP having acquired 49.3 per cent of the votes cast during the elections held just over a year earlier, which resulted in an absolute majority of 26 seats in the National Assembly.[179] Needless to say, not only the economic crisis triggered this downturn. Bouters's magic as a leader had worn off, even amidst the many less affluent Surinamese. His incompetence was now becoming obvious to everyone. During the

---

169 *Parbode*, June 2012.
170 *NRC Handelsblad*, 23 Februar 2018.
171 Ibid.
172 Ibid.
173 Ibid., 13 August 2010.
174 *Starnieuws*, 24 August 2017.
175 Ibid., 30 April 2018.
176 Ibid., 2 March 2018.
177 *NRC Handelsblad*, 1 March 2015..
178 IMF, *Suriname 2018 Article IV Consultation (Country Report 18/376)*, 27; for more information on devaluation and fuel prices, see: *Starnieuws*, 21 November 2015, 30 July 2015 and 1 December 2015.
179 *Dagblad Suriname*, 8 July 2016.

late 1990s, the anger voiced by demonstrators pertaining to mismanagement was directed at president Wijdenbosch, although Bouterse had personally backed him in order to occupy the highest post in the land.

Eight months after the elections, president Bouterse acknowledged for the first time that mistakes had been made when he remarked: 'The revenues were not monitored, and the expenses exceeded the revenues'. His appeal to the entire population of Suriname 'to adopt a national stance because it is now sink or swim' did not have a great deal of credibility.[180] For, he had dismissed well-founded advice year after year, including suggestions provided by the economists' association VES. Such appeals did indeed contribute to the further erosion of Bouterse's authority. One day after the devaluation of the SRD was announced, a small group of protestors gathered at the Onafhankelijkheidsplein (Independence Square). One of their cardboard signs read *"p'a moni de?"* (where is the money?).[181] An action group named *Wij zijn moe* (We are tired) grew into a broad protest movement. Unlike in the late 1990s, the initiators were not established organizations but well-educated young men and women including Stephano 'Pakittow' Biervliet, Curtis Hofwijks and Maisha Neus who increasingly manifested themselves as part of a political movement. Trade unions, business organizations and political parties later joined them. Discontent was not only expressed on the streets by the several thousand protesters but especially across the social media, where the now 70-year-old Bouterse was often creatively mocked as being an anachronism dating to the 20th century. This phenomenon provided protesters with fresh dynamism.

Though the December murder trial had brought about little electoral impact, this all changed when the Court of Justice ruled in late 2015 that adjourning this trial should be lifted.[182] That ruling followed a complaint which relatives of the victims had forwarded. They now invoked the constitutional article which contains guarantees to interested parties implying that a case should be heard within 'reasonable time'. Bouterse responded with a wild accusation: the judiciary is 'part of forces controlled by foreign countries'.[183] Tensions mounted even further when, in June 2016, the Court Martial effectively lifted the adjournment, not only citing the Inter-American Human Rights Treaty but also referring to the fact that, after 4 years, a constitutional court had still not been established to review the amnesty law.[184] Not entirely unexpectedly, he came up with a presidential resolution, which the full Council of Ministers accepted. It aimed at forcing the attorney general (the head of the Public Prosecution Office) to end the prosecution immediately. In so doing, he invoked Article 148 of the Constitution on state security.[185] However, the Court Martial ruled that a decision on the continuation of the trial was a matter for this court itself.[186] The reason why it took another 12 months before the military prosecutor Roy Elgin delivered his indictment pertaining to Bouterse comprised the fact the public prosecutor did not

---

180   *De West*, 22 January 2016.
181   *Starnieuws*, 22 November 2015.
182   Ibid., 1 December 2015; *NRC Handelsblad*, 3 December 2015.
183   *Starnieuws*, 22 January 2016.
184   Ibid., 9 and 10 June 2016.
185   Ibid., 29 and 30 June 2016, 1 and 2 July 2016.
186   Ibid., 30 January 2017.

wish to give the impression it was simply disregarding Bouterse's order. Their request to suspend the trial permanently finally met with the Court of Justice's declaration of inadmissibility.[187] On 28 June 2017, Elgin demanded a 20-year prison term as a sentence for Bouterse, the prime suspect. The latter had 'after calm deliberation and quiet consultation' with others 'assumed the capacities of judge and executioner'.[188] President Bouterse then wished to rescind confidence in the attorney-general by means of a resolution, thus forcing him to resign. Nevertheless, Bouterse refrained from doing so after sharp protests were voiced, for example, by trade unions and members of the business community.[189]

On 29 November 2019, the sentence followed in accordance with the demand. Now this military court, comprising female judges Cynthia Valstein-Montnor, Suzanne Chu and Rewita Chatterpal delivered a 116-page verdict. It stated that Bouterse, 'in association with' two other members of the military leadership, had been guilty of the assassination of 15 opponents of his regime.[190] Bouterse became the first head of state in the world to be convicted of murder while in office. At the time of this verdict he was on a state visit to China. One week later, after returning to Paramaribo, while standing before several thousands of supporters gathered at the NDP headquarters, the president spoke of a 'political sentence'.[191] He then utilized a special appeal procedure concerning those convicted in absentia. As a result, this sentence could not be executed for the time being allowing him to start preparations for the parliamentary elections to be held on 25 May 2020. This verdict however hugely influenced the prospects for electoral success. According to a poll taken shortly before and shortly after this verdict, the NDP support in the Paramaribo and Wanica districts had shrunk from one-third to one-quarter.[192]

Of probably even greater impact was a major scandal unfolding at the same time. It involved the *Centrale Bank van Suriname* (CBvS) and caused a shock throughout society. On 30 January 2020, the Suriname Bankers Association announced in a written statement that 100 million USD of the cash reserves, i.e. savings of citizens, deposited by the banks at the CBvS had disappeared. According to the bankers' statement, they had been 'misled for months' by the latter bank.[193] Later it turned out that as much as 197 million USD had vanished. These cash reserves should have been invested abroad, an arrangement not unusual in the banking world. The popular fury was best expressed through Steven Coutinho, director of *De Surinaamsche Bank*, when declaring on local radio: 'We have been played a game, money has been stolen from the people.' Hundreds of people gathered in front of the bank to demonstrate their support for the managing director following the rumour he would have to resign under government pressure because of his fierce statements.[194] Vice President

---

187   Ibid., 11 May 2017.
188   Ibid., 28 and 29 June 2017.
189   Ibid., 9, 10, 11, 12, 13 July 2017.
190   For the full text of this verdict (KRG-2019-46), see: rechtspraak.sr
191   *Starnieuws*, 6 December 2019.
192   Ibid., 16 December 2019.
193   Ibid., 30 January 2020.
194   *NRC Handelsblad*, 2 February 2020; see also: *The New York Times*, 'A Philosopher-Banker Who's Shaking Up a Nation', 8 May 2020.

Ashwin Adhin elicited jeers from many when acknowledging that the money had been used for 'importing onions and potatoes' as well as for currency interventions.[195]

This affair illustrated the government's panic with regard to an impending economic bankruptcy, only a few months prior to the elections. Shortly before that, the CBvS president, Robert-Gray van Trikt, had resigned.[196] A few weeks later, he was arrested, suspected of fraud when purchasing cars, and of entering into rigged contracts, which his own consultancy firm had allegedly been involved in, too.[197] His detention led the Public Prosecutor's Office to also seek to open an investigation into Minister of Finance Gillmore Hoefdraad. One of the eleven accusations concerned selling government property to the Central Bank in order to use the proceeds to close gaps in the government's budget, which the Banking Act does not permit. He was also allegedly guilty of aiding and abetting embezzlement.[198] The NDP majority in the National Assembly did not allow this investigation - permission for which is required if pertaining to suspected political office-holders.[199] A threat of criminal prosecution nonetheless remained, as the political balance of power could hugely differ after the elections.

At the beginning of 2020, Suriname was both economically and morally bankrupt, although the rule of law was still in place. On occasion of the 44th Anniversary of Independence, the Committee Christian Churches (CCK) compared Suriname's journey to Moses and his people when travelling to the Promised Land. Bad governance and corruption were harshly denounced thus:

> 'The government must act justly (see Psalm 72; Ezekiel 45.9; Isaiah 56.1) and that includes rewarding the good and punishing the bad. This is a simple task, but one that requires leaders who do not themselves transgress by, for example, enriching themselves and their immediate family and friends. It is often cited that the citizen must obey the government, but that is only on the condition that the government then adheres to the divine instructions and indeed rewards good and punishes evil.'[200]

Five months before the elections, President Bouterse was still able to announce an event one had been hoping for all these years: a major oil discovery off the coast.[201] A second such find followed not much later. He called on the people of Suriname to now put 'all negativity' behind them.[202] These oil finds however had the opposite effect. After all, who would dare to entrust the managing of astronomical sums of money acquired by means of future oil revenues to an incoming government led by Bouterse?

---

195 *Starnieuws*, 1 February 2020.
196 Ibid., 18 January 2020.
197 Ibid., 6 February and 3 May 2020.
198 Ibid., 24, 30 April, 3 May, 8 June and 17 June 2020.
199 Ibid., 8 June 2020.
200 *Omhoog*, November 2019.
201 *Starnieuws*, 7 January 2020.
202 Ibid., 2 April 2020.

A History of Suriname

16.5 From sheriff to President

The NDP's defeat during the parliamentary elections held on 25 May 2020 was thus no surprise. The VHP's victory, led by 61-year-old Chan Santokhi, was no surprise too - but its size was. With 108,240 votes, the VHP won almost 40 per cent of the voters and thus 20 seats in the National Assembly. In doing so, this party on its own now amply surpassed the result achieved 5 years earlier with the V7 combination (which included the NPS); the NDP saw its number of votes almost halved to 65,660 (24 per cent), a decline from 26 to 16 seats.[203] By means of its 'vote smart' campaign, the VHP had successfully attempted to as much as possible create a duel with the NDP. Group leader André Misiekaba's departure from the NDP was a telling step, highlighting the party's decline.[204] The Maroon party ABOP, led by Ronnie Brunswijk, obtained eight seats, three more than in 2015 (when the ABOP was named A-C); The ABOP benefited from the electoral system, requiring relatively few votes per seat in the interior, and a cooperation with the Javanese PL, that was weakened by internal quarrels; for the NPS, the three seats (in Paramaribo) were a setback.[205] The reform party DOE paid the price for its controversial participation in the Bouterse-led government, even though it had discontinued cooperating when the rule of law was threatened.[206]

Within a week after the elections, in fact before the official results were announced, the VHP, ABOP, NPS and PL had already formed a coalition.[207] Assisted by the Maroon party BEP, which had participated in the Bouterse-led government, Santokhi and Brunswijk were elected with the required two-third parliamentary majority to serve as President and Vice President respectively.[208] Brunswijk had personally seen to it he was elected as the parliament's President, because he wished to be the first Maroon to occupy that post too; he stepped down after being elected Vice President.[209] The fact he was openly speculating about becoming a future president did raise questions among critics as to the durability of this collaboration - after all, the ex-Jungle commando had already exercised power with the NDP in the past.

For many Surinamese, the originally Hindustani VHP had evolved into a credible alternative. Its metamorphosis had become first clearly visible during a large manifestation held on 18 January 2019 at its headquarters named *De Olifant*. Never before had the speakers and audience been so varied. A respected columnist wrote in the newspaper *De Ware Tijd*: 'If you had told someone ten years ago that a VHP mass

---

203 Ibid., 4 June 2020.
204 Ibid., 30 July 2020.
205 Ibid., 4 June 2020; the result in absolute numbers of votes once again clearly revealed perverse effects included in the electoral system. The NPS had attracted one-third more votes (32,394) than the ABOP (24,900), but nevertheless acquired five fewer seats. It is significant to note here that, on 9 April 2022, the Constitutional Court decided to consider an application for a review of the electoral system in relation to the Constitution hereby embracing the principle of non-discrimination, see: *Starnieuws*, 18 February and 9 April 2022. A few months later, the Constitutional Court ruled that the electoral regulation does not express 'one person one vote'. Hence, the principle of equality as well as various articles included in the constitution and in international treaties were violated. This ruling could indeed imply far-reaching consequences for Suriname's balance of political forces after elections; see: *Starnieuws*, 5 August 2022.
206 Ibid., 9 July 2016.
207 Ibid., 30 May 2020.
208 Ibid., 13 July 2020.
209 Ibid., 29 June 2020.

Figure 16.4. Chan Santokhi's inauguration on 16 July 2020 which the outgoing president Desi Bouterse (r.) attended. C/o Communicatie Dienst Suriname.

meeting would unfold like this, you would certainly have been branded crazy.'[210] The second and fourth positions on the list of candidates eligible in the district of Paramaribo were reserved for Creoles.

Immediately after the 2015 elections, Santokhi had already personally drawn the conclusion: the only way the VHP was able to conquer the centre of power was by going into the elections on its own. The formation of a front of parties, each with its own ethnic basis, was a dead end. This view was held by Santokhi and by a large part of the population. The emancipation process of the individual ethnic groups was mostly completed, with the small exception of the Maroons and Indigenous peoples. This outcome implied that the VHP had to considerably expand its number of supporters. Demography also rendered such a change to be imperative. For, those with 'mixed race' formed a rapidly growing population group, as the censuses had shown. Moreover, after the catastrophic decade of Bouterse's presidency, many desired genuine innovation: good, transparent governance and real action against corruption.

The transformation within the VHP, which occurred in relatively short time, cannot be seen as being separate from Santokhi's leadership. Serving as a police commissioner and minister of justice, he had gained a reputation as a fearless fighter against drug-related crimes, hereby never avoiding confrontation with Bouterse. This stance made him a natural leader of the opposition, even outside his own party. The derogatory nickname 'sheriff' with which Bouterse had labeled him became a badge of honour for Santokhi (see p. 394). The door-to-door campaign promising to 'save the country' and 'recover the stolen money' had already started in 2016.[211] VHP branches were established as far away as in the villages inhabited by Maroons and Indigenous peoples. Though this initiative was unlikely to win any seats, it did contribute to the party's multi-coloured image. Reality had long overtaken an attempt by the NDP launched in 2019 to reverse the political tide by means of an amendment to the electoral law which aimed at banning party combinations. Moreover, parties when placing candidates on each other's electoral lists circumvented this law.

On 16 July 2020, Bouterse handed over the presidential ribbon to the newly-elected president. This ceremony took place a month earlier than usual - to the relief of the outgoing government, it seemed. For, no money remained to pay the salaries

---

210 *De Ware Tijd*, 21 January 2019.
211 As stated during a speech held in the district of Para, see: *Starnieuws*, 6 May 2019.

A History of Suriname

of civil servants. As a result of mass appointments, their number had increased with 5,535 to reach 51,528 in the months before the transfer of power.[212] Moreover, the Covid-19 pandemic had struck Suriname. In his inauguration speech President Santokhi stated: 'The state treasury is empty, there is a scarcity of foreign currency and there is a sky-high debt hanging over our heads.'[213] When taking office, he had literally found the state apparatus ransacked. Computers had vanished. Ministers had purchased cars at bargain prices. A few months after the transfer of power, former Vice President Ashwin Adhin was arrested. He was allegedly guilty of the 'unlawful appropriation and destruction' of government equipment.[214] In the meantime the former Finance Minister Hoefdraad was added to Interpol's international list of wanted persons.

The recently installed government could only pay the civil servants' salaries with loans provided by local banks. Social measures funded in this way included increases in pensions and child allowances.[215] Hence, restructuring measures became slightly more bearable. The value of the SRD had halved after a devaluation, resulting in a rising inflation as well as a declining purchasing power. Moreover, fuel prices rose after a tax increase. A majority of the population uncomplainingly submitted to these harsh measures, realizing they were inevitable. Moreover, the incoming government fulfilled its promise to fight corruption by establishing a special anti-corruption unit inside the Public Prosecutor's Office. It additionally employed 13 prosecution officers who worked energetically on major cases.[216]

However, the government's support base soon risked being undermined as a result of appointments, which again resembled nepotism. Vice President Brunswijk nominated his brother Leo Brunswijk to serve as chairman of the Staatsolie's supervisory board, claiming that this company was 'teeming with members of the previous government'.[217] Other members of their family were presented with public posts, too. Many Surinamese were further shocked when president Santokhi saw to it that his wife, the lawyer Mellisa Seenacherry, was appointed to Staatsolie's supervisory board.[218] This move also incited criticism from within the party. After consistently accusing the previous government of favouring 'family and friends', it had indeed not been expected that Santokhi would take such a step.

In the coalition agreement, the first 9 months were designated the 'urgency phase', after which the 'stabilisation phase' spanning 2 years was to begin, followed by the 'growth phase'.[219] The main priority was to restructure the national debt (which had meanwhile risen to almost a factor 1.5 of GDP). For, only such restructuring

---

212 Ministry of Finance and Planning, *Budget 2020. Wijzigingsnota* (Letter of Amendment), Paramaribo, 17 November 2020; see: *Starnieuws*, 18 November 2020.

213 Santokhi, *Inauguration Speech*, 16 July 2020.

214 *Starnieuws*, 16 November, 1 and 2 December 2020.

215 Ministry of Finance and Planning, *Budget 2020. Wijzigingsnota* (Letter of Amendment), Paramaribo, 17 November 2020; see :*Starnieuws*, 18 November 2020.

216 *Starnieuws*, 3 October 2020.

217 *NRC Handelsblad*, 21 August 2020.

218 *Starnieuws*, 21 August 2020. Only 2 years later, President Santokhi, under public pressure, announced that his wife as well as the Vice President's brother would give up their positions on Staatsolie's supervisory board. They were replaced by technocrats; *Starnieuws*, 31 August 2022.

219 Ibid., 15 July 2020.

could provide a prospect of financial and socio-economic stabilization in 2021.[220] The Santokhi-led government, incapable of meeting its debt obligations, therefore immediately turned to the IMF for support.

Improved relations with the USA, France and the Netherlands undoubtedly proved helpful. Of particular significance was Mike Pompeo's visit to Paramaribo. He was the first US secretary of state ever to do so, even preceding his Dutch colleague Stef Blok. This visit had not only to do with oil finds off the coast, but also with geopolitical interests, especially China's growing influence in the region. Pompeo made no secret of his mission. At Paramaribo, during a press conference, he condemned the way how 'the Chinese Communist Party invests in countries', which ultimately has 'political costs'.[221] The enraged Chinese ambassador to Suriname then spoke of 'provocative statements'.[222] The Sino-American rivalry witnessed across the Caribbean will not do the government of Suriname any harm, because it could help president Santokhi to keep his promise to the Surinamese, to wit, present them with 'a beautiful Suriname' in exchange for their trust.[223]

The fulfilment of that promise was hampered by the virtually non-existent financial leeway given the disastrous legacy of the previous government and the spreading corona pandemic. Initially, as noted above, a majority of the people of Suriname resignedly accepted the inevitable financial and economic measures, of which the phasing out of energy subsidies, as agreed with the IMF in 2021, hit the hardest. With inflation rising to c.60 per cent, the population's impatience increased.[224] Moreover, frictions persisted as to the cooperation of Santokhi's VHP with the ABOP, a Maroon party. This phenomenon manifested itself, for example, when its Vice President Brunswijk forced the ABOP Minister Diana Pokie of Land and Forest Management to resign. Officially, Pokie stated she 'no longer had the support of the party leadership'.[225] A few months later, however, she revealed in a newspaper interview that she had refused to assist in transferring a building plot to one of the Vice President's brothers, as it had already been assigned to another citizen: 'I refused because there was no basis for doing so'.[226] Hence this minister had simply not colluded in a corrupt act which had subsequently resulted in her having to give up her post. President Santokhi apparently had little power to react which affected his position and credibility, and of his party.[227] For some time, discontent had been observed amidst the coalition partner NPS, which only held a few ministerial posts.

---

220 IMF, *World Economic and Financial Surveys, Regional Economic Outlook (Western Hemisphere)*, October 2020, 32.
221 Report published by US State Department, 17 September 2020 (2017-2021.state.gov/index.html).
222 *De Ware Tijd*, 18 September 2020.
223 *NRC Handelsblad*, 24 July 2020.
224 IMF, *Suriname. Request for an extended arrangement under the extended fund facility. Staff Report*, 9 December 2021, 4-10; an agreement with the IMF on an Extended Fund Facility comprising 690 million USD for three years was reached on 29 April 2021, with Suriname continuing to implement a recovery program, see also: IMF press releases on 29 April and 29 July 2021. The IMF Executive Board finally officially approved this agreement with Suriname in December 2021.
225 *Starnieuws*, 14 July 2021.
226 *De Ware Tijd*, 15 November 2021.
227 President Santokhi did intervene 2 years later, after much public outcry, when he not only postponed a construction project involving land grants, which in particular benefited the Vice President's political party colleagues, but also commissioned further investigations; *Starnieuws*, 7 August 2022.

A History of Suriname

This predominantly Creole party, which had been a driving force behind Suriname's independence in 1975 and which included many highly educated members, felt it was being treated as a junior partner in this coalition.

These entanglements fueled the ever-dormant ethnic sentiments within the society. In addition, it undermined the VHP's renewed image as a multi-ethnic, no longer purely Hindustani, organization. Its party leader Santokhi had successfully presented the revitalized VHP after internal reforms put in place prior to the 2020 elections (see p. 413). He was apparently aware of all this when, in a remarkable speech addressed to the Surinamese Economists' Association (VES), he asked aloud why, during the 46 years since its independence, Suriname had not succeeded, bar a few short periods, in providing a good living standard for its people. He next pointed to (a) the 'absence of unity and solidarity in thought and action', (b) an 'overly politicised administrative system', (c) the 'absence of exemplary and strong leadership' and (d) of 'a willingness to listen to expert advice'.[228] These words prompted critics to respond that the president was thereby implicating himself. Nonetheless, criticism of the government coalition's appointments policy persisted, with the ABOP going the furthest in appointing 'family and friends' to government posts.

A significant development for public acceptance was: on 24 November 2021, not coincidentally the day before the independence anniversary, the Santokhi-led government had succeeded in reaching a so-called Tripartite Agreement with the trade union movement and the business community.[229] This was the first time such an event occurred in Suriname, where trade unions traditionally take a tough stance. This agreement reflected the societal awareness of the need to tackle the economic crisis together. However, at the same time, it also illustrated the government's awareness of the need to constantly seek support in order to overcome any broad felt skepticism. This agreement included a social safety net, an increase in social benefits, wage adjustments as well as tax measures (see p. 439). Nevertheless, despite compensatory measures, especially in support of the poor, it was inevitable that almost everyone would lose out in terms of prosperity, given also the decrease as to Suriname's GDP to wit by 15.9 per cent in 2020 and 3.5 per cent in 2021.[230]

Further reinforcing the judiciary could also contribute to supporting the government. By 2021, for example, the number of judges serving the Court of Justice was increased to 30, while the long-desired financial independence of Suriname's judiciary was also realized for the first time.[231] New appointments in both the police and security apparatus were to further conduce to reducing crime, with drug trafficking still playing a key role.[232] The sentences of former Finance Minister Gillmore Hoefdraad (in absentia) to 12 years' imprisonment in December 2021 and, a month later, of former Central Bank's Governor Robert van Trikt to 8 years' imprisonment

---

228 *Starnieuws,* 25 January 2022.

229 Ibid., 24 November 2021.

230 IMF, *Suriname. Request for an extended arrangement under the extended fund facility. Staff Report),* 9 December 2021, 4.

231 *Starnieuws,* 9 October and 30 December 2021; in 2020 the Court of Justice had already been reinforced by means of six additional judges, see: *Starnieuws,* 19 December 2020.

232 Ibid., 2 September 2021 and 4 January 2022; in September 2021, for example, in excess of 4,000 kg cocaine originating from Suriname was intercepted at the port of Rotterdam, see: *Starnieuws,* 17 September 2021.

pertaining to the aforementioned fraud cases perhaps illustrates a more resolute anti-corruption approach as promised.[233] However, it remained to be seen whether possible new cases of corruption would be tackled effectively. The promised 'recovery of stolen money' was apparently indeed far more complicated for the time being. The activities of the Constitutional Court, established in 2020 under the previous government, also inspired confidence. This Court declared the 2012 amnesty law (which should have protected the then President Bouterse from further criminal prosecution stemming from the December murders) to be contradictory with Suriname's constitution and international human rights treaties.[234]

The most important asset providing the people of Suriname with any perspectives comprised the aforementioned off-coast oil and gas discoveries which drew the attention of international investors. Thus, in January 2022, during visits by the presidents of Brazil and Guyana to Paramaribo, contours of a new South American energy alliance between Suriname and these two nations became visible.[235]

This promising economic partnership had geopolitical significance, too. For, President Santokhi had already announced in August 2021 that Suriname was to access the Forum for the Progress and Integration of South America (PROSUR), which had been established in 2019 after the UNASUR's break-up.[236] In doing so, he clearly distanced himself from the line of his predecessor Bouterse, who had maintained close ties with the internationally isolated autocratic regime in Venezuela.[237] A few months earlier, Santokhi had stated before an international forum that 'Suriname and the USA share internationally accepted norms of inter-state relations and conduct based on democratic governance, rule of law and protection of human and political rights'. He further spoke of a 'geopolitical and strategic partnership' with the USA, referring also to oil and gas exploitation in the region.[238] The fact that Santokhi, at the dawn of the Year of the Tiger, presented various representatives of the Chinese community in Suriname with a national decoration, only illustrated that each and every president of Suriname must also continue long-standing relations with China.[239]

According to the coalition agreement of July 2020, the financial-economic 'stabilisation phase' was to be reached after only 9 months, a time frame which soon proved insufficient. The IMF predicted that Suriname could only count on modest economic growth starting in 2022, thus further testing the patience of the people of Suriname, despite the promising prospects based on oil and gas discoveries (see next paragraph).

16.6 Economy in transition

The Hermitage Mall, designed in a contemporary Caribbean-American style, was built in Paramaribo during the first decade of the 21ˢᵗ century. With its global product

---

233   Ibid., 17 December 2021 and 31 January 2022.
234   Ibid., 22 July 2021.
235   See: oilnow.gy (21 January 2022).
236   *Starnieuws*, 22 August 2021.
237   The crisis within the UNASUR was related to the developments in Venezuela, see Burgess 2018.
238   *Starnieuws*, 19 March 2021. Santokhi delivered these statements during the annual Horasis Global Meeting for Latin America and the United States.
239   Ibid., 2 February 2022.

	2000	2010
Total	**513 USD**	**2,034 USD**
Alumina	66.7%	24.5%
Gold	11.7%	57.5%
Oil	5.4%	12.9%
Agriculture, fishery et al.	16.2%	5.1%

Table 16.3. Exports of raw materials and goods in million USD and percentages per sector. Source: IMF, *Suriname 2005 Article IV Consultation -Staff Report* (Statistical Appendix) and IMF, *Suriname 2011 Article IV Consultation - Staff Report 2011*, 9, 21 and CBvS, *Annual Report 2010*, 9.

assortment, this vast shopping centre not only attracted large numbers of customers but also reflected confidence in a renewed economic perspective. As a result of the liberalization of the telecom sector, the market for mobile services in Suriname made a giant leap forward, too. In 2010, the internet capacity was hugely improved by means of an additional submarine communication cable connecting to the outside world. From 2011 on, container ships entering the port of Paramaribo had been handled faster than anywhere else across the Caribbean thanks to a multi-million investment, hereby offering opportunities to serve as a regional transport hub. Suriname's interior became more accessible after the route to the South was asphalted. The access to French Guiana had improved after a bridge across the Suriname River opened in 2000. Its construction was controversial due to the questionable financing provided during the Wijdenbosch-led government (see p. 366). However, positive effects were soon noticeable, too, thanks to improving the road linking Paramaribo with Albina (Marowijne district). The number of visitors from French Guiana who spent their euros in Paramaribo increased. Moreover, housing projects located on old plantation lands were realised in the backward district of Commewijne, located on the other side of the Suriname River. Meanwhile, hotel chains (e.g., Best Western International Inc., Marriott International Inc.) became established in Paramaribo. An urban dynamism discernible in and around this capital during the first decade of the 21st century was the result of continuous economic growth which compared favourably with numerous other Caribbean nations states.

The economic growth of 5 per cent per annum on average was largely the outcome of exporting raw materials.[240] Thanks to an increasing importance of gold and oil, Suriname was no longer primarily dependent on alumina (a semi-finished product of bauxite). The export value of alumina, gold and oil rose from 429.6 million USD in 2000 to 1,932 million USD in 2010 (see Table 16.3). Now able to benefit from higher commodity prices in a fast growing global economy, Suriname's GDP in 2010, according to the then applicable fixed exchange USD rate, amounted to 4,368 million USD. This sum tallies with 8,256 USD per capita and thus renders Suriname a middle-income nation.[241]

The exact size of Suriname's economy is not easy to determine because of a large informal sector. Between 2003 and 2007, according to the General Bureau of Statistics of Suriname (ABS), the informal economy comprised between 16 and 19 per cent of the official economy.[242] Furthermore, 51 per cent of those at work outside the agricultural

---

240 IMF *Suriname, Article IV Consultations, Staff Report* (the reports from 2007 till 2011).
241 The World Bank Open Data (data.worldbank.org).
242 Keenswijk-Fung A Loi, Nankoe & Sobhie 2016, 253.

sector could be considered informal. As the ABS reported, Suriname thus occupied a position in the middle.[243] A great deal of informal labour took place either at small-scale gold mines (see also p. 382-383) or in thousands of one-man businesses (e.g., petty traders, repairmen, caterers, transporters) and *hosselaars*: individuals who survive by means of casual labour or begging. Over-regulating the economy as well as a low degree of official employment stimulated this informal sector. Those with official jobs often profited from a *hossel*, too. It was difficult to estimate the volumes of incomes amassed from criminal activities, especially trafficking narcotics. In banking circles the impression existed that the relevance of drug money obtained through cocaine transit had diminished as a result of effective crime-fighting when compared to the 1990s.[244] Nevertheless, in 2010, major shipments of cocaine hailing from Suriname were discovered as far away as in South Africa and Pakistan, suggesting the drug-related economy was still substantial.[245] Around 20 casinos, by and large licensed under the Wijdenbosch-led government, reflected a level of informal, illegal and criminal activities which should not be underestimated.[246] Several casinos were allegedly engaged in money laundering. Their licensees were Surinamese, who had often leased the exploitation to Asians, Turks or Eastern Europeans.

The considerable significance of this informal sector complicated an assessment of the degree of poverty, which is not very visible in Suriname. The mitigating effect of private money remittances which exceeds several tens of millions of euros per annum and which stems from the Netherlands has been ascertained.[247] However, the 'very unequal' distribution of income, as the ABS had determined, indicated the poverty issue continued to be sizable.[248] Research based on the 2012 Census reports that 16.3 per cent of Suriname's households should be deemed 'poor', whereas 52.8 per cent are 'at risk'; only 28.8 per cent should be considered 'non-poor'.[249]

The growing gold sector formed a key factor in the prosperous economic development (see Table 16.3). Production had been boosted when, in 2004, the Canadian Cambior Inc. (taken over by IAMGOLD in 2006) began large-scale gold mining in the mineral-rich Brokopondo district. Suriname's economy remained sensitive to fluctuating global commodity prices, but proved slightly less vulnerable thanks to an increased gold production. This became apparent when Suriname weathered the Great Recession of 2009 relatively well. Alumina and oil prices did

---

243 ABS, *Suriname in cijfers*, nr. 251/2008-10, Paramaribo 2008..

244 *NRC Handelsblad*, 10 September 2009.

245 *Starnieuws*, 17 December 2010, 18 February and 5 March 2011.

246 A list of licenses issued had been revealed in 2016 by a member of parliament, see: *Starnieuws*, 6 July 2016.

247 Unger & Siegel 2006, 20; between 2004 and 2006, according to estimates, based on their personal research and on that of others, the amount ranged between 58 and 145 million euros per annum; the Dutch Ministry of Development Cooperation came to an estimate of 100 million euros, see p. 4 of a policy memorandum: Ministry of Development Cooperation, *Een rijke relatie. Suriname en Nederland: heden en toekomst*, 4 June 2004.

248 In 2004 Suriname's Gini coefficient (i.e., an international measure of income inequality) was 0.5488, indicating a 'highly unequal distribution', see: ABS (General Bureau of Statistics), *Suriname in Cijfers, Inkomensongelijkheid en inkomensverdeling in Suriname*, nr. 236/2007/06, 16.

249 Sobhie, De Abreu-Kisoensingh & Dekkers 2016, 263-282; on the basis of a sample from the census, the internationally accepted method of material deprivation was used, whereby a household is called poor if it does not have essential material possessions to function adequately (e.g. tap water, electricity, cooker, medical insurance, mobile phone, refrigerator).

indeed drop, but gold prices rose because investors viewed gold as a 'safe haven' in times of a crisis.

Resulting from its sensitivity to external influences, a sound macro-economic management is even more relevant to Suriname if compared to many other countries. A decrease in value of the exported alumina, oil or gold has an immediate negative impact on the government's income as it receives less funds from taxes and dividends. In 2008, the three aforementioned sectors together accounted for 95 per cent of goods exports, hereby amassing more than 50 per cent of Suriname's GDP and more than 33 per cent of the state revenues.[250] Any negative developments at play within the global market must be counterbalanced by means of a rapid adjustment of monetary and budgetary policies. Otherwise, foreign exchange shortages, currency problems, increases in interest rates and inflation will follow. Rendering Suriname's economy truly resilient in the long run required structural reforms, further diversification and more value being added to raw products. The excessively large civil service continued to weigh heavily upon the national public budget. For, between 2000 and 2002, 13 per cent of GDP was spent each year on civil servants' salaries, much more than encountered in the rest of Latin America and the Caribbean, where the average was 5 per cent of GDP.[251]

After Suriname's public finances had completely derailed during the late 1990s, the Venetiaan-led government initially focused on restoring a balanced budget. Prior hereto civil servants and pensioners were compensated for the impoverishment witnessed in the course of previous years, resulting in higher inflation and currency depreciation. However, in 2003, a small budget surplus was achieved, for example, thanks to an improved tax collection and tax increases. A flawless introduction of the Surinamese dollar marked the year 2004, whereby as many as three zeros of the heavily devalued Surinamese guilder were removed. Opting for a new currency with such a renowned name aimed at symbolizing the restoration of both stability and self-confidence. The introduction of a debt ceiling for government expenditures was also significant in this respect. This measure comprised, as in the eurozone, up to 60 per cent of GDP in domestic and foreign loans. According to the amended Banking Act, officials employed by Suriname's Central Bank could be imprisoned for breach of duty. This bank's President A. Telting had personally written the text of this act in order to prevent successors from allowing money presses to print bills again.[252] Another key priority of the government was to pay all overdue foreign debts owed to Brazil, Germany and the USA. This undesired financial legacy had been handed down by the military regime during the 1980s as well as by the Wijdenbosch-led government. Public external debts fell sharply between 2000 and 2010, to wit,

---

250 IMF, *Suriname: 2009, Article IV Consultation; IMF Country Report No. 10/44*, February 2010, 5.
251 IMF, *Suriname: Selected Issues and Statistical Appendix, IMF Country Report No. 03/357*, November 2003, 3.
252 As stated in an interview the present author held with André Telting on 9 July 2009, see: *NRC Handelsblad*, 10 September 2009.

from 44.3 per cent of GDP to less than 10 per cent.[253] At the end of 2009, Suriname had acquired one of the region's lowest debt ratios. The goal now was to seek to restore the state creditworthiness, which had been severely affected by bad payment behaviour and accumulated debt. Reducing debts was partly achieved with the help of Dutch guarantees extracted from treaty funds. As a result, Standard & Poor's and Fitch Ratings increased their credit ratings for Suriname.[254]

The Venetiaan-led government consciously anticipated the termination of aid provided by the Netherlands since Suriname's independence in 1975. At the start of 2005, Paramaribo and The Hague had agreed upon 'phasing out of the current broad development cooperation relationship' within 5 years.[255] However, due to Suriname's limited absorption capacity, it would take a few more years to spend all the money. Agnes van Ardenne, the Minister of Development Cooperation (2003-2007), acknowledged that the Dutch aid (€ 1.6 billion) forwarded in 1975 had 'insufficiently' contributed to Suriname's development.[256] Numerous experts had previously noted that this 'free' aid had mainly stimulated consumer spending (see p. 295). The government of Suriname's policy which aimed at international creditworthiness reflected a growing confidence in its economy. Rick van Ravenswaay, the Minister of Planning and Development Co-operation, having held a final consultation with The Hague in 2008, described the Dutch aid being terminated as 'good', stating: 'We must now determine our own path. If you know you have to pay back, you have to choose well.'[257] Between 2000 and 2010, donations from Dutch treaty funds amounted to a mere 1.75 per cent of GDP per annum on average.[258] By way of comparison, private remittances from the Netherlands were probably five times as large. Losing the assistance provided by the Netherlands was therefore no longer insurmountable, also given the increased revenue from raw materials for instance.

A large debt reduction and increased foreign exchange reserves laid a basis for further economic development. Foreign credits became accessible to Suriname-based companies. Moreover, the government now acquired a better access to both the international capital market and to loans which multilateral institutions provided. These two factors enabled Suriname to not only finance infrastructural projects, but to also acquire a share in the exploitation of raw materials. The Venetiaan-led government advocated its participation in the gold and bauxite sector in order to increase its revenues. Oil extraction had already been placed

---

253 IMF, *Suriname: 2003 Article IV Consultation, IMF Country Report No. 03/356*, 21; *Public Information Notice: IMF Executive Board Concludes 2011 Article IV Consultation with Suriname*, 4 May 2011; André Telting informed the present author, in an interview on 9 July 2009, that the public external debt was as high as 55 per cent of GDP in 2000; according to Telting, this debt had been under-reported by his predecessor. Telting also revealed he had shared this information with the IMF during a presentation held in June 2009. As early as in 1999, he had publicly reported that the IMF underestimated the size of Suriname's foreign public debt, see: *NRC Handelsblad*, 22 July 1999.

254 See: countryeconomy.com/ratings/suriname

255 As mentioned in a letter sent by Minister Agnes van Ardenne to the Dutch Parliament on 4 February 2005: Kamerstuk 20361, nr.120 (zoek.officielebekendmakingen.nl/kst-20361-120.html).

256 Ministry of Development Cooperation, *Een rijke relatie. Suriname en Nederland: heden en toekomst*, 4 June 2004, 3. Here Minister Van Ardenne also referred to the relatively high per capita income as a valid argument for terminating the existing development aid relationship.

257 *NRC Handelsblad*, 10 September 2009.

258 IMF, *Suriname: 2011 Article IV Consultation, IMF Country Report No. 11/256*, August 2011, 10.

A History of Suriname

	2007	2008
Bauxite sector (alumina)	USD 83.0	USD 47.5
Gold	USD 16.1	USD 53.5
Oil	USD 97.1	USD 178.3
Total	USD 196.2	USD 279.3
In percentage of government revenue	28.3	36.3

Table 16.4. Government revenue acquired by mining in indicated million USD and as a percentage of the total government revenue. Source: IMF, *Suriname: 2009 Article IV Consultation – Staff Report*, 5.

in the government's hands by means of Staatsolie, a fully integrated oil company entirely owned by the Republic of Suriname. Desi Bouterse, who took office as President in 2010, continued discussions with all parties concerned. Prospects for the three aforementioned sectors were deemed excellent towards the end of 2009, as major investment plans demonstrated.

Gold mining had become more important to Suriname than the bauxite sector, even if small-scale and mainly informal operations are left out of the equation. The Canadian IAMGOLD Corp. was by far the largest mining company. In 2010 it produced a record volume of 395,000 troy ounces (11,198 kg) thanks to its Rosebel gold mine located in the Brokopondo district.[259] This opencast site provided work for c.1,500 labourers, more than the 922 employed by Suralco.[260] IAMGOLD's annual contribution to the government of Suriname, the owner of a 5 per cent share in this corporation, had exceeded Suralco's contribution from 2008 on.

In 2011, the Bouterse-led government began negotiations pertaining to an investment of 800 million USD provided by the IAMGOLD Corp. in order to expand its activities. This initiative should lead to a higher financial benefit for Suriname. Government participation was also discussed with the Suriname Gold Company (Surgold), a joint venture created by the Alcoa Corporation and the Newmont Mining Corporation. The latter two US-based multinationals had developed ambitious plans for gold mining in the proximity of the Nassau Mountains (East Suriname) where Alcoa had obtained a concession linked to bauxite mining. Of the almost 30,000 kg gold Suriname exported in 2010, 17,000 kg originated from small-scale, informal operations.[261] According to the IMF, this sector exported between 600 and 700 million USD worth of gold in 2010, however yielding the government of Suriname a mere 1 million USD in royalties.[262] A positive spending effect of the informal gold sector comprised the many thousands who found employment here.[263]

Initially, Suriname's Central Bank acted as the sole purchaser and exporter of the by and large illegally produced gold with the aim of putting this sector in good order. Nonetheless, the maximum quantity of just about 6,000 kg per annum this bank purchased during the late 1990s was no more than 25 to 30 per cent of the total, whereas c.15 per cent reached local jewellers; the rest disappeared across the border,

---

259 IAMGOLD, *Annual Report 2010*, 12.
260 Hakrin Bank, *Annual Report 2010*, 23-24 and the Bauxiet Instituut Suriname.
261 Information presented by the Gold Regulation Committee's chairman, see: *Starnieuws*, 13 October 2011.
262 IMF, *Suriname: Article IV Consultation, IMF Country Report No. 11/256*, August 2011, 8.
263 The highest estimate of 30,000 employees stems from the Gold Sector Ordering Committee's chairman, see: *De Ware Tijd*, 7 July 2011; this number has been estimated far lower by others, to wit at 14,000, see: Heemskerk 2010, 13 (see also p. 382-383).

Figure 16.5. Illegal gold mining site (2012) inside the Brownsberg Nature Park, located on the edge of the Brokopondo Reservoir. Photo by Erlan Sleur.

mainly into French Guiana; in 2002, purchases and exports of gold were delegated to a small number of Paramaribo-based licensees; the 6 per cent bank fee which the aforementioned bank received was limited to a royalty of only 1 per cent; from then on, almost all these exports passed through official channels.[264]

The government however continued to have little control over the gold mining itself. Next, just months after his inauguration, President Bouterse instated the Gold Sector Regulation Committee. The state wished to have 'its authority clearly and actively present across all lines of the gold sector.'[265] This measure included the registration of all individuals involved. This committee's task was to enable an effective taxation, to wit, a flat-rate levy for all operators of excavators utilised when extracting gold.[266] Applying mercury also needed to be addressed more effectively in order to not only minimise its harmfulness to human beings and the environment but to also deal with its inefficiency resulting from the loss of substantial quantities of gold. Whereas previous governments had made hardly any efforts to regulate the informal gold mining sectors, the plans forwarded by the Bouterse-led government could potentially have an impact. Nevertheless corruption and incompetence proved a major obstacle (see p. 408-409 and 433-434). In 2011, an agreement was reached with the Dubai-based gold refinery Kaloti Precious Metals to establish the Kaloti Suriname Mint House in order to add more value to the gold mining industry in

264 Due to a lack of sufficient foreign exchange, Suriname's Central Bank could not purchase more gold, see: Heemskerk 2010, 20-22.

265 *Starnieuws*, 20 December 2010.

266 IMF, *Suriname: Article IV Consultation, IMF Country Report No. 11/256*, August 2011, 8.

A History of Suriname

Suriname itself.[267] This refinery was later linked, in its Arab home base, to suspect (money laundering) practices.[268]

The dwindling importance of the bauxite sector, having accounted for 75 per cent of all exports for decades, was reflected in a declining employment, too. This sector had employed 6,200 workers during 1975. In 1998, their number had dropped to 2,343.[269] The companies named Suralco and Billiton carried out research into procedures as to securing the supply of raw bauxite, revisiting the Bakhuys Mountains (West Suriname). In 1999, a setback was witnessed when Suralco closed its aluminium smelter in the town of Paranam (Para district), hereby reducing the number of jobs in the bauxite sector by a further 500.[270] This shortfall brought an end to aluminium production, which had started more than 30 years earlier. The smelter at Paranam was loss-making due to the low aluminium prices noted on the London Metal Exchange. Moreover, the Wijdenbosch-led government's unfavourable exchange rate policy had already undermined this smelter's competitiveness. Its subsequent shutting down further illustrated the sensitivity of Suriname's economy concerning external forces. During 2003, in a more favourable climate, Suralco and BHP Billiton (a merger of Billiton and Australian BHP) decided to combine their Suriname-based activities. BHP Billiton now took a 45 per cent stake in the alumina plant located at Paranam, thereby increasing its capacity. By taking this step, they reacted upon the Venetiaan-led government's desire to realise an integrated aluminium industry with state participation based on the bauxite as well as the hydropower potential encountered in Western Suriname. Plans pertaining to this ambitious project had already been made during the 1970s. A railway line had been constructed with Dutch development aid, too (see p. 293).

A Memorandum of Understanding included arrangements concerning the continuity of the bauxite sector. In 2009, however, Suralco and BHP Billiton terminated their collaboration after disputing the future strategy regarding the West Suriname project. Having decided to cease its activities in Suriname after almost 70 years, BHP Billiton sold its share of the alumina production to Alcoa.[271] Negotiations with the government on a state participation in this alumina plant proved tough. However, Alcoa continued to prepare for the mining of bauxite in the Nassau Mountains in order to ensure future supplies. Plans for Western Suriname were put on hold, not least because of the global crisis. Nevertheless the Bouterse-led government increased pressure by hinting, as its predecessor had, at Chinese and other foreign interests. As new economies (e.g., China, Brazil) emerged, Alcoa was no longer the only potential partner.

This US-based multinational had in the meantime not only become the only bauxite company active in Suriname, it was now also the largest supplier of electricity as well as a potential gold producer. After the aluminium smelter located at Paranam had closed down, all the electricity the Brokopondo hydro-power dam provided now entered into the national grid. This fact led to tensions between Alcoa and Suriname.

267 *Starnieuws*, 6 December 2011.
268 *The Guardian*, 25 February 2014.
269 Centrale Bank van Suriname, *Jaarverslag 1975*, 79; *Jaarverslag 1997-2000*, 24.
270 Ibid., *1997-2000*, 24.
271 *Waterkant*, 29 October 2008 and 1 May 2009.

For example, by linking the price of electricity to the price of oil, as officially agreed upon by the Wijdenbosch-led government in 1999, the government of Suriname had to forward ever more payments to Alcoa's subsidiary Suralco. The latter company was thus effectively subsidised by the state. Successive governments had requested adjusting this deal, but in vain. Hence politicians from all parties raised the question: should the 1958 Brokopondo agreement, which had obliged Alcoa to construct a smelter, not be simultaneously amended? In addition, the government had long-standing plans to expand hydropower capacity for new gold mines, but these intentions were hampered by the Brokopondo Agreement. A key factor comprised diverting water from the Tapanahoni River Basin, thus allowing this waterway to be increased towards the Afobaka Dam located at Lake Van Blommestein, over which precisely Alcoa had been allowed to control for 75 years.[272] As a result of the sometimes abundant water quantities (which led to inland floods in 2006), the export of fresh water (to the Caribbean) could also become a possibility. Opposition voiced by inhabitants of the interior eventually resulted in the temporarily shelving an inititiave aimed at generating any additional electricity.

Staatsolie, while already generating electricity through a subsidiary, would have been the key investor in the TapaJai Hydro Project which includes several smaller power plants (e.g., at Tapanahoni and Jaikreek). This state-owned company was founded in 1980 and had developed into a modest exporter during the 1990s. In 2010 it produced almost 6 million barrels of crude oil. As of 1997, having opened a refinery located near Paramaribo (largely financed by means of a loan guaranteed by the Dutch government in cooperation with the ABN AMRO (a bank based in the Netherlands), Staatsolie produced diesel, fuel oil, asphalt and semi-finished products in addition to crude oil.[273] As much as 50 per cent of its production was sold to Suralco in order to meet the alumina plant's energy needs. From 2015 on, its refinery capacity would more than double, facilitating lighter products such as petrol.[274] The fact that Staatsolie financed 70 per cent of its investment programme comprising 1 billion USD between 2008 and 2012 hereby utilising its own resources was indicative of its strength and ambition.[275] As an entirely state-owned enterprise, Staatsolie was the largest contributor to Suriname's state coffers. Its prospects being excellent, it played an exemplary role based on a skillful management. Between 2010 and 2014, the proven oil reserve had grown from 72 to 100 million barrels thanks to a multi-year onshore exploration programme.[276] Expectations had also been pinned on discovering oil off the coast of Suriname, all the more when, from 2015 on, large quantities of oil were found off the coast of Guyana. Staatsolie's foreign partners therefore continued to express a wish to invest in exploration at sea, despite previous unsuccessful efforts.

Resulting from major investments in the gold, bauxite and oil sectors, the growth rate of Suriname's economy could potentially continue at a relatively high level in the medium term, though a sensitivity to volatile commodity prices remained, as would turn out to be the case in due course. During 2011, the IMF even predicted

---

272   For more information to expand the hydropower capacity, see: Boksteen 2011.
273   Staatsolie, *Annual Report* 2010, 9-11.
274   *Starnieuws*, 13 December 2014.
275   Staatsolie *Annual Report 2010*, 9.
276   Ibid., 15; Staatsolie, *Annual Report 2014*, 10.

A History of Suriname

a growth of 7.7 per cent in 2014, when investment activities were to peak.[277] This outcome is indeed comparable with the Brokopondo push of the 1960s (see p. 289). Export growth, especially in the gold and bauxite sectors, could further increase foreign exchange reserves. In addition, the government's income could also rise sharply if the state was to acquire shareholdings in these sectors. The Inter-American Development Bank (IDB) expressed its confidence by providing 300 million USD in loans to Suriname as is stated in the Country Strategy 2011-2015. This is a much larger amount when compared with the 103 million USD forwarded during the previous period.[278] Based on its *Meerjaren Ontwikkelingsplan* (Multi-annual Development Plan) as to 2012-2016, the Bouterse-led government thus assumed a high investment level comprising 23 billion Surinamese dollars (equal to 6,890 million USD) whereby 47 per cent was to be provided by the private sector and 53 per cent by the public sector.[279] More than half hereof had to be forwarded to mining and energy supplies. This high share in investments (during the previous multi-year development plan the government had accounted for only 17 per cent) was partly a result of the state's ambition to participate in the gold and bauxite sectors. Moreover, in the multi-year development plan as to 2012-2016, entitled *Suriname in transformatie*, the total investment was significantly larger than stated in the previous plan, to wit, 50 per cent more if expressed in USD.[280]

The latter plan not only illustrates the incoming government's huge ambitions, it also raised doubts on its realism. In order to increase lending capacities, President Bouterse had suggested in parliament that raw, not yet mined, materials could serve as collateral by means of 'creative financing modalities'.[281] However, not only the opposition deemed this a risky course of action. Bouterse appeared equally realistic when, a few months later, he did not rule out a short interruption as to their realization.[282] The IMF had warned Suriname's authorities to 'pace government projects in line with the country's implementation capacity, and seek to finance them through affordable foreign loans or grants, so as not to unduly burden the country's debt service capacity'.[283] Not only Suriname's financial strength was at stake. For, the number of specialized labourers capable of carrying out mega-projects did not suffice. The government had already assumed that migrant workers were required in order to execute, for example, its ambitious housing programme.[284] The expected growth impulse however also offered opportunities for economic diversification over time, hereby not only creating new productive jobs but also reducing cyclical fluctuations.

The gold, bauxite and oil sectors were key contributors to the extensive economic growth. Nevertheless, because of their capital intensity, these sectors were of limited significance to employment numbers, whereby the informal gold sector is not taken

---

277   IMF, *Suriname: Article IV Consultation, IMF Country Report No. 11/256*, August 2011, 29.
278   IDB, *Country Strategy with the Republic of Suriname 2011-2015*, November 2011, Executive Summary.
279   Planbureau Suriname, *MOP, Meerjaren Ontwikkelingsplan 2012-2016* (Multi-annual Development Plan), 229; see also: *Starnieuws*, 29 August 2011.
280   Planbureau Suriname, *MOP Meerjaren Ontwikkelingsplan 2006-2011* (Multi-annual Development Plan), 206.
281   *Starnieuws* 8 June 2011.
282   Bouterse, *Speech at the opening of the parliamentary year*, 29 September 2011, 3.
283   IMF, *Mission for the 2011 Article IV Consultation with Suriname - Concluding Statement*, 17 February, 2011.
284   *Starnieuws*, 19 October 2011.

into the account. Employment growth was highest in the public sector and the construction sector, which had hugely benefited from the growth spurt immediately after the turn of the century.[285]

Including the more than 100 commercial and non-commercial state-owned companies the IMF estimated that the public sector accounted for *c.*60 per cent of the formal sector employment in the period 2000-2005.[286] In 1998, according to an IDB-report, 8.9 per cent of the total population was employed in the public sector, three times more than in the rest of Latin America and the Caribbean.[287] Towards the end of 2009, the expenditure on civil servants' salaries had further increased after a general revaluation of functions within the civil service, whereby senior civil servants were paid the most. The Venetiaan-led government had launched a wage reform operation aimed at enhancing its appeal to trained and specialised staff. However, the intended improvement in quality was hardly achieved. For, accommodating political friends employed both at ministries and at state-owned companies had become even more attractive thanks to those substantially higher salaries. As early as 1998 the World Bank had concluded that public services in Suriname were found to be amongst the 'weakest' across the Caribbean region, impeding a development of the market sector.[288] A decade later, hardly any reasons to alter this assessment existed.

Suriname faced the typical challenge experienced by commodity producing nations, to wit, not to consume the extra income by increasing the government spending, but to apply it productively in order to allow job growth in the market sector. One would then finally be able to start downsizing the civil service, which had taken on the character of a social security provision. In 2008, the IMF had advocated establishing a 'natural resource fund' as soon as new mining projects had commenced and public debt arrears had been cleared.[289] Norway and Chile set examples for such a sovereign wealth fund. At the beginning of 2012, Bouterse announced the payment of USD 20 million in seed capital.[290] With a reserve fund, into which part of the proceeds acquired from exploiting commodities is forwarded, the government would not only be able to absorb any financial setbacks, but to also finance productive investments. This initiative could also provide incentives for the market sector including tax cuts, whereby labour becomes less expensive while supportive policies for departing civil servants are created, too. For the time being, this fund would not become a reality.

The best opportunities for economic diversification across Suriname are encountered in agriculture, fisheries, forestry, tourism and services. Notably the banana cultivation recovered, even after the state-owned company and sole exporter Surland had almost collapsed due to poor management, the lack of investment resources and plant diseases. Within a few years, thanks to financial as well as technical

---

285 IMF, *Suriname: Statistical Appendix, IMF Country Report No. 07/179*, May 2007, 12.

286 IMF, *Suriname: Towards Stability and Growth*, 3 March 2009; an overview of commercial and non-commercial state enterprises can be found in: IMF, *Suriname: Statistical Appendix, IMF Country Report No. 07/179*, May 2007, 47-53..

287 Martin 2001, 40-41.

288 The World Bank, *Suriname. A Strategy for Sustainable Growth and Poverty Reduction. Country Economic Memorandum*, Washington, 31 March 1998, vii.

289 IMF, *Suriname: Article IV Consultation - Staff Report, IMF Country Report No. 08/293*, August 2008, 18.

290 *Starnieuws*, 1 January 2012.

support from the European Union (EU) and the Inter-American Development Bank, the *Stichting Behoud Bananen Sector* (Foundation for the Preservation of the Bananas Sector) was able to double its body of employees reaching 2,500 in 2010.[291] This foundation now proved profitable for the first time, implying that privatization on favourable terms had become a possibility. This outcome was desirable as the sector was facing fierce competition as a result of the international trade liberalisation and the phasing out of EU trade benefits. In addition, involving a private party could create room to invest in further expansion. In 2010, the export value amounted to 35 million USD.[292]

Due to a growing global demand for food, the rice sector, almost entirely concentrated at a district in West Suriname named Nickerie, was presented with opportunities to increase production. From 2010 on, Surinamese rice, of which *c.*33 per cent was exported, was granted duty-free and quota-free access to the EU, under the Economic Partnership Agreement with this part of South America. Related favourable transitional arrangements were imposed as early as 2008. Moreover, Suriname's access to the Caricom, available from 1995 on, implied the Caribbean market was opened. Now Jamaica and Haiti became key purchasers. As a result of the insufficient production capacity, Suriname was not even able to meet export demands. Around the year 2000, the rice sector first had to recover from heavy blows caused by government mismanagement, rendering credits as well as imports of inputs unaffordable (see p. 367). After years of divestment and neglect of plant breeding, recovery set in thanks to rising world market prices, government aid and help from the EU. In *c.*2000, the rice sector, with its *c.*1,400 farmers, provided employment for approximately 8,000 families.[293] Export proceeds amounted to almost 40 million USD in 2010; the size of the rice fields had increased from 42,000 ha in 2000 to *c.*55,000 ha in 2010, be it less large than the *c.*60,000 ha measured during the mid-1990s.[294] More than half of these fields formed part of large-scale farms.[295] The Bouterse-led government's ambition was to expand these fields to 150,000 ha by 2020. This goal fitted in with a desire to turn Suriname, as Bouterse stated, into the 'food barn' of the Caribbean.[296] This ambition, already expressed by the Venetiaan-led government, would require major investments in, for example, 'wet' infrastructure. Any spin-off effects could create extra jobs in the processing and transport sectors. At the same time, expanding rice cultivation is expected to reinforce the large scale, not only for reasons of efficiency, but also because interest in agricultural work in Suriname remains insufficient. The livestock sector, which applies residual products from rice cultivation for animal feed, could also develop further by means of large-scale investments. However, an absence of a certification system continued to impede exports. Similar problems occurred in horticulture. In accordance with

---

291   Ibid., 26 April 2011.
292   Centrale Bank van Suriname, *Jaarverslag 2011*, 11.
293   Ministry of Agriculture, Livestock and Fisheries, *Beleidsnota (Policy Note), LVV 2010-2015*, 20.
294   Ministry of Agriculture, Livestock and Fisheries, *Beleidswitboek Rijst (Policy White Paper Rice)*, September 2011, 18.
295   Ibid., 11.
296   Bouterse, *Regeringsverklaring* (Government Statement) *2010-2015*, 1 October 2010, 9 and 16.

its predecessor, the Bouterse-led government also wished to revitalise palm oil production, for which foreign investors were sought.

The fishery sector, its export revenue having reached almost 100 million USD for the first time in 2007, does not merely form a major source of foreign exchange.[297] As it provides in more than 6,000 jobs, this sector is indeed hugely significant to employment.[298] Japanese, South Korean and Chinese companies dominate industrial fishing with large boats, whereas the Surinamese are either active in fish processing and (in cooperation with Guyanese) in small fisheries. Exporting shrimp especially to the US is of key relevance. The state-owned enterprise named Suriname American Industries Ltd. (SAIL) purchases and processes catches brought in by fishermen. Other fish processors export their produce to the EU. However, an inadequate supervision of Suriname's coastal waters implied that illegal fishing could pose a threat to this sector. Solid opportunities for developing aquaculture, in which certain local entrepreneurs invested, apparently existed.

As 93 per cent of its land area is covered by forest, Suriname is ranked at the very top of the list of the world's most-forested nation states.[299] The largest part of this forestation does not qualify for timber exploitation because of the inaccessibility, extensive tree species diversity and high transport costs. Two million of the more than 15,000,000 ha have been issued based on a franchise.[300] According to the *Stichting Bosbeheer en Bostoezicht* (Foundation for Forest Management and Forest Supervision), as much as 1,000,000 cubic metres of timber could be produced sustainably per annum, much more than the 250,000 cubic metres acquired in 2010.[301] Timber exploitation had received a boost with the arrival in 2007 of the Hong Kong-based Greenheart Group Ltd. It took over the role as the largest timber producer and processor in Suriname, hereby replacing the bankrupt state-owned Bruynzeel. With international climate change negotiations underway, however, fresh opportunities arose for Suriname to generate substantial sources of income by protecting tropical rainforest and biodiversity within the context of the global reduction of carbon emissions and trade in emission rights. After actively contributing to the aforementioned talks, in part due to its own vulnerability to sea-level rise, Suriname will have to contain deforestation pertaining to logging, gold mining, agriculture, livestock farming and infrastructural measures. In 1998, Suriname had already gained international recognition by designating 1.6 million ha of tropical forest in order to create the *Centraal Suriname Natuurreservaat* (Central Suriname Nature Reserve). The World Bank's Global Environment Facility (GEF) and the UN provided Suriname with funding for this project aimed at forest management as well as the promotion of ecotourism. Funding for many other projects followed.[302] A few years earlier, issuing large-scale concessions to Asian timber companies had been

---

297 IMF, *Suriname: Statistical Appendix, IMF Country Report No. 08/294*, 26 August 2008, 27.

298 Ministry of Agriculture, Livestock and Fisheries, *Beleidsnota* (Policy Note) *2010-2015*, 78-79.

299 See: REDD+ Suriname (surinameredd.org/en/reddplus-suriname); the UN program named REDD+ [Reducing emissions from deforestation and forest degradation] is a UN program is meant to limit the effects of climate change.

300 Hardner & Rice, 2001, 250.

301 *De Ware Tijd*, 7 October 2011.

302 For detailed information, see: thegef.org/country/suriname

cancelled as a result of great concern, encountered inside and outside Suriname, regarding not only environmental consequences but also the inadequate control capacity of Suriname's government. Suriname benefited for the first time from the World Bank's mechanism entitled REDD+ (Reducing Emissions from Deforestation and Forest Degradation), when in 2013 the sum of 3.8 million USD was assigned in order to prepare for a REDD+ project.[303]

A notable development in the services sector concerns the emergence of offshoring facilitated by fast Internet connections. This innovation involves companies based in the Netherlands which outsource activities to Suriname, including call centres, administration and software development.[304] A shared language and relatively low costs form an important incentive for these Dutch companies. For a long time, tourism had almost entirely depended upon family visits by Dutch citizens with Surinamese roots. From 2008 on, more tourists travelling from outside the Netherlands visited Suriname: their total numbers had increased with 33 per cent to exceed 200,000 in 2010.[305] In a publication entitled *Best in Travel*, the travel guide book publisher Lonely Planet listed Suriname as one of its Top 10 destinations for 2010 describing it as presenting 'the best of both worlds'.[306] Suriname's appeal lay in Paramaribo, a vibrant capital with a unique wooden town centre included in the UNESCO's World Heritage List, as well as in entertainment venues such as casinos. The pristine tropical rain forest fulfils the desire for ecotourism. Relaxing visa regulations in 2011 provided a further incentive. Nevertheless expensive flight connections due to a Surinam Airways/KLM Royal Dutch Airlines monopoly and a lack of infrastructure continued to frustrate tourism.

Even after the turn of the century, Suriname continued the struggle to realise its economic potential: the country had lagged far behind in creating an environment conducive to business. Numerous suffocating rules and regulations, in part a legacy dating from colonial times, still existed. Establishing public limited companies required the president's signature, formerly the governor's. According to a 2011 World Bank report entitled *Doing Business 2012*, acquiring this signature took 500 days, implying that the entire procedure went on for 694 days.[307] Entrepreneurs could start with a 'company in formation', which would render them personally liable. Robert Ameerali, Suriname's Vice President (2010-2015), accelerated this procedure considerably. According to *Doing Business 2014*, the time needed in order to obtain the president's signature was now reduced to 14 days. However, the entire process continued to require 208 days, thus placing Suriname amidst the rear guard of nation states. This disadvantage was also the case as to the registration of ownership, which took 107 days in 2014 compared to 197 days in 2012.[308] Other obstacles concerning business transactions were numerous too. For example, current laws and regulations as well as efficient procedures to facilitate business were inadequate,

---

303 As published by REDD+ Suriname; see: surinameredd.org/nl/reddplus-suriname/readiness-preparation-voorstel
304 *NRC Handelsblad*, 10 September 2009.
305 Figures published by Stichting Toerisme Suriname (STS), see: *Starnieuws*, 4 January 2012.
306 See: traveller.com.au/lonely-planet-names-top-10-destinations-for-2010-hupk
307 The World Bank, *Doing Business* Report 2012, 128.
308 Ibid. 2012, 128; ibid., 2014, 27 and 226.

which had an inhibiting effect on domestic and foreign investors. Whereas a new investment law of 2002 contained fiscal incentives, any form of investor protection was seriously lacking due to the absence of dispute and arbitration procedures. Moreover, contracts were difficult to enforce due to capacity constraints within the judiciary hereby enabling legal proceedings to take 5 years and almost three times as long as elsewhere in the Caribbean region. Companies were exposed to high financial risks in the event of a counterparty failing as a result of the non-existence of any appropriate insolvency laws and a lack of judiciary capacity. Moreover, the absence of an adequate credit registration and rating system held back any lending. No wonder Suriname had dropped on the Ease of Doing Business index from rank no. 158 (of 183 nations) in 2012 to rank no. 161 (out of 189 nations) in 2014.[309]

Suriname's financial market had been dominated by the Hakrinbank (51 per cent government-owned), De Surinaamsche Bank (10 per cent government-owned) and the Republic Bank of Trinidad and Tobago. Interest rates on loans were therefore relatively high. Moreover, banks traditionally provided mainly short-term trade credit because of the limited risk. During the early 1990s an inadequate supervision and cartel-like practices maintained by the established banks had even led to the emergence of 'underground' banks which then developed into pyramid schemes to collapse after several years. It was only in the course of 2011 that banking supervision was improved, when parliament approved the previous government's proposal to entrust Suriname's Central Bank with this task. In 1991, the banking landscape had changed slightly with the arrival of the newly founded and privately-owned Finabank N.V. The long-awaited merger of the *Landbouwbank Suriname* (focussing on agricultural credits) and the *Surinaamse Volkskredietbank*, both relatively small and state-owned, was finalised in 2014.

Suriname's slow adaptation to economic internationalization stemmed from several obvious causes. Partly a result of selecting civil servants based on political loyalties, ministries lacked the expertise to quickly adapt legislation and/or regulations to the modern requirements of the market economy. In addition, society and certainly its political scene had been inward-looking for a long time. Receiving free development aid from the Netherlands and having close relations with its former coloniser presented no incentives for change either. In fact Suriname, a South American Dutch-speaking nation, was rather isolated. Moreover, the state traditionally played a key role in the economy, which reached far beyond macro-economic management. Almost 50 by and large loss-making state-owned companies were active within the private sector, covering nearly all areas of economic activity.[310] The small-scale domestic market had always impeded private initiatives, causing the public authorities to establish their own production companies. In his publication entitled *De toekomst van ons verleden* (The future of our past) Jules Sedney, a former prime minister (1969-1973) and former President of the Central Bank, aptly concluded that Suriname suffered from 'economic navel-gazing'. [311]

---

309   Ibid. 2012, 6; ibid., 2014,3.
310   Martin 2001, 40-41.
311   A revised edition of the 1997 publication presents a more optimistic view, see: Sedney 2017, 17.

'The world is moving towards larger entities. Those who do not participate become lonely and those who look the other way are left behind. This is not a plea for selling out values, but a warning against Quixote economic and political pedantry under the alias of nationalism. [...] The romantic nationalism of the 1950s stimulated creative achievements in the cultural field and provided a positive impulse to the pursuit of independence. In other areas, it plunged us into isolation, obscured our world view and led to spiritual inbreeding.'[312]

From 2000 on, however, successive governments altered their policies. The efforts the two Venetiaan-led cabinets had made in order to increase Suriname's international credit standing, thus establish access to foreign credit facilities, were significant. The (Creole) nationalistic sentiment, to wit, that public enterprises should not fall into foreign hands became less and less relevant. The Venetiaan-led government carried out its initially unsuccessful attempts to privatise Bruynzeel (timber company), *Stichting Behoud Bananen Sector* (Foundation for the Preservation of the Banana Sector) in Suriname and the Patamacca Project (palm oil), hereby appealing to foreign investors. In 2015 at the latest, the Bouterse-led government wished to privatise a dozen state-owned enterprises in the agricultural sector and elsewhere. The newly established Investment & Development Corporation Suriname (IDCS) was charged with implementing this policy which sought to create joint ventures between Surinamese companies and foreign partners. The opposition expressed the fear that state-owned enterprises, of which many had acquired large areas of land, would fall into the hands of the government's 'friendly relations'.[313] That danger was not inconceivable, especially if foreign investors stayed away. After all, a small group of 'new rich' with questionable entrepreneurial qualities and large assets, often acquired through corruption and (drug-related) crimes, would be capable of taking over public enterprises. Partly for this reason, at the end of the 1990s, the World Bank had already argued in favour of presenting foreign investors with a controlling stake.[314] According to this Bank privatisation could also serve to develop a local capital market. Indeed, if compared to the rest of the region, a backlog existed here too. The opposition's fears soon materialised when, during the Bouterse-led government, the Bruynzeel company's extensive concession was obtained by a deputy minister in 2012 while IDCS had already delivered an application.[315] In 2018, the Stichting Machinale Landbouw (SML; Mechanized Agriculture Foundation) established at the rice growing centre named Wageningen, positioned on the Nickerie River, was dubiously acquired by an entrepreneur affiliated to the government party NDP.[316] The IDCS died a slow death and was succeeded in 2017 by a newly created institute named Investsur.[317]

---

312 Sedney 1997, 158.
313 *De Ware Tijd*, 28 October 2011.
314 The World Bank, *Suriname. A Strategy for Sustainable Growth and Poverty Reduction. Country Economic Memorandum*, Washington, 31 March 1998, 57-71.
315 *Starnieuws* 21, 22, 28 December 2012 and 17 January 2021.
316 Ibid., 17, 18, 19, 21, 22 and 23 October 2018.
317 Ibid., 18 April 2017.

A stronger orientation towards the outside world resulted from the general awareness that globalisation compelled Suriname to act accordingly in order to reap the benefits. In 1995, entering the Caribbean Community (CARICOM) had already been a key step. Now economic reforms became inevitable. Imports from the Caribbean region rose sharply, forcing certain Suriname-based firms to close down. However, the CARICOM also offered access to a market of 15 million consumers, allowing the rice sector, for example, to benefit. Another key development was Suriname's membership, as from 2008 onwards, of the Union of South American Nations (UNASUR). However, attempts to turn the latter union along EU lines into a single market of *c*.400 million consumers stalled on political and ideological grounds.[318] Establishing a solid infrastructure forms an indispensable element of regional integration. From the very start, in September 2000, Suriname participated in the Initiative for Regional Infrastructure Integration in South America (IIRSA), whereby Brazil and the IDB took the lead.[319] Part of this initiative consisted of constructing and improving roads, waterways, ports, energy transport systems, airports and telecommunications. Suriname's plans aimed at upgrading the East-West connection by way of building bridges across the Marowijne and Corantijn Rivers, thus establishing links with Brazil's regional road infrastructure. These initiatives fit in with the IIRSA's goals as does the increase in hydropower capacity, including the aforementioned TapaJai project. Over time, Suriname could develop into an energy exporter by means of expanding high-voltage power lines to, for example, French Guiana. Suffering from an energy shortage, this neighbour state had shown great interest in this project.

Regional integration undoubtedly offers Suriname the best opportunities for economic growth. On more than one occasion, its politicians have referred to an alternative ranking presented by the World Bank in 1995, on the basis of which Suriname was ranked no. 17 in the list of potentially most affluent nations in the world by virtue of its large amount of natural resources per capita.[320] Less attention was paid to the fact Suriname took in a far lower position as to its human capital due to an inferior education system. All experts agree that investing in human beings is an important key to development.

In the decade leading up to 2020, once again an opportunity was wasted as to transforming the economic potential into prosperity and thus allow the majority of Surinamese people to benefit. In fact, their state had been knocked back for years due to mismanagement and corruption (see also p. 408-409 and 433). In October 2020 the IMF estimated that Suriname's national debt at the end of that year would amount to 145.3 per cent of GDP; by far the largest part hereof comprised foreign debt, the remainder was domestic debt, but even that portion was largely denominated in US dollars.[321] The debt was thus eight times higher than in 2010 (18.5 per cent).[322] Between 2010 and 2019, GDP per capita dropped from 8,256 USD to 6,854 USD (see

---

318 Burges, 3 May 2018.

319 The IDB noted that the IIRSA was hampered by, for instance, 'a weakening of regional consensuses about the role and contents of the regional integration movement', see: IDB 2008, 30.

320 Chernela 1997, 42-49.

321 IMF, *World Economic and Financial Surveys, Regional Economic Outlook (Western Hemisphere)*, October 2020, 32.

322 *Public Information Notice, IMF Article IV Consultations with Suriname 2012*.

p. 372, Figure 16.1).[323] This implied that the billions borrowed were scarcely applied towards increasing productive capacity.

In 2016, the government of Suriname entered the international bond market for the first time. In October, through an investment firm named Oppenheimer Funds, an expensive bond loan of 550 million USD was arranged at an interest rate of 9.25 per cent. It was to be redeemed in 2026.[324] With the 300 million USD included in this bond, Staatsolie, which acquired lower revenues due to low oil prices, was able to pay off its short-term loans in order to continue investing in oil exploration. This financially healthy state oil company returned the amount to the state treasury after only 2 years. However, the Surinamese government did not utilise the expensive money it had borrowed to redeem the Oppenheimer bonds. This would have been possible under favourable conditions as the value had already fallen sharply as a result of Suriname's diminished creditworthiness. Instead, the choice was made to pay off a large number of cheaper debts and arrears.[325] This policy marked the disastrous state of public finances: the public deficit had risen to almost 10 per cent of GDP in these years; moreover, expenditures had continued to rise while revenues fell due to lower oil and gold prices.[326]

In addition, Suriname's reputation suffered greatly when its cooperation with the IMF was concluded after only a few months. This termination followed a loan agreement of 478 million USD in May 2016, the first tranche of which had already been collected.[327] The government had in fact abused this agreement in order to realise the loan provided by the Oppenheimer Funds. At the end of 2016, Suriname also secured a 350 million USD loan with the Chinese-owned Eximbank of which 235 million was earmarked for improving the road network, a task to be carried out by a Chinese company named Dalian, which had been active in Suriname for some time.[328] Its contribution to Suriname's productive assets was unclear. In 2019 as a result of other loans, too, through an amendment to the Public Debt Act, the loan ceiling was raised from 60 to 95 per cent of GDP, a necessary initiative intended to prevent the criminal prosecution of Minister of Finance Gillmore Hoefdraad.[329] That same year widespread outrage arose when Glenn Gersie, the Governor of Suriname's Central Bank (2016-2019), resigned. The reason for this was not, as Hoefdraad claimed, that 'irregularities' had been discovered, but Gersie's refusal to cooperate with monetary financing.[330] The latter revealed 12 months later during an interview aired by a local radio station that Hoefdraad, with President Bouterse's support, had vetoed him to publish the legally required annual reports.[331] Only after the 2020 elections was the annual report of 2015 published. The Central Bank's reputation was also damaged earlier on in 2020 when the Federal Reserve System (The Fed), the US central bank,

---

323   The World Bank Open Data (data.worldbank.org).
324   *Starnieuws*, 19 October 2016.
325   Ministry of Finance and Planning, *Budget 2020 Wijzigingsnota* (Note of Amendment), 17 November 2020.
326   IMF, *Staff report for the Article IV Consultation with Suriname*, 2019, 6 and 31.
327   *Starnieuws*, 17 May and 21 May 2016, 24 January 2017.
328   Ibid., 30 November 2016.
329   Ibid., 1 November 2019.
330   Ibid., 21 February 2019.
331   *ABC Radio*, 24 August 2020.

cancelled the Banknote Trading Agreement, causing a serious shortage of USD notes.[332] According to this agreement, the Central Bank of Suriname (CBvS) received cash dollars in exchange for book transfers to The Fed, but the latter feared money laundering when the dollars ended up in private cambios. A supermarket owner and NDP affiliate who sold basic necessities at extremely low prices owned one of these cambios. The banking sector's image had, in 2017, already been tarnished when *De Surinaamsche Bank* (DSB), the nation's largest, threatened to collapse. What caused this mishap? This bank had borrowed sizable sums of money from the CBvS to then on-lent it to the state thus creating a form of indirect monetary financing. However, the state did not return this money.[333] Two years later, a scandal broke out pertaining to *De Surinaamse Postspaarbank* (SPSB) whereby millions had allegedly been misappropriated by means of loans provided to befriended relations. Though the SPSB's director was suspended pending an investigation, President Bouterse subsequently reinstated his party colleague. In August 2020, this director was nevertheless arrested.[334] The fact Suriname now dropped from position no. 161 to no. 162 on the Ease of Doing Business index was no huge surprise.[335]

Meanwhile, after 99 years of activity in Suriname, Alcoa had ceased its operations in 2015 due to a lack of prospects for a profitable continuation. Now around 2,000 workers became redundant.[336] That same year, after negotiations, a presidential commission had signed a memorandum of understanding with Alcoa, agreeing to terminate the 1958 Brokopondo Agreement on 31 December 2019. The Afobaka Dam would then pass into the state's hands. This outcome may indeed be considered very remarkable. For, according to the Brokopondo Agreement, the dam was to be simultaneously handed over to Suriname free of charge as soon as Alcoa terminated its activities. Now Suriname was forced to continue to pay for 4 years of power supplies provided by Alcoa, thus allowing this US-based multinational to easily cover expenditures related to a mandatory environmental clean-up. Moreover, with an exclusion of competitors, Alcoa had been presented with the option of exploiting bauxite deposits located in the Bakhuys Mountains for several more years. The presidential commission was widely distrusted because of its chairman Dilip Sardjoe, a businessman whom the media had for years associated with improper practices as well as kickbacks. In 2017, despite a request from parliament to forward a revised proposal, president Bouterse presented it with the same memorandum of understanding, much to the surprise of many. According to Bouterse, 'hard ball' or arbitration was no option as it would have been too time-consuming.[337] Eventually, on 30 August 2019, the coalition parties in the National Assembly agreed to close this deal, despite a damning report by external lawyers called upon by parliament itself.[338] In order to pay 111 million USD in arrears, Suriname was now forced to issue

---

332 *Starnieuws*, 27 February 2020.
333 As mentioned in an interview with former DSB board member H. Moison as published in *Trouw* on 11 November 2017.
334 *Starnieuws,* 3 May and 13 August 2020.
335 For this index in its entirety, see: doingbusiness.org
336 *Starnieuws*, 30 October and 18 November 2015.
337 Ibid., 18 and 19 July 2017.
338 For the full report dated 30 July 2019, see: *Starnieuws*, 7 August 2019.

A History of Suriname

yet another bond loan through OppenheimerFunds. This loan pertained to supplying power by Alcoa, for which gold as well as oil revenues served as collaterals.[339]

The impact of Alcoa's departure would have been much more difficult to digest a decade earlier, but the oil and gold sectors had long since eclipsed the bauxite sector. Staatsolie had also reinforced its position by taking stakes in the activities of the multinationals IAMGOLD and Newmont (formerly Surgold). It gained control of the Afobaka Dam, too, thus significantly expanding its activity as an electricity supplier. This diversification allowed Staatsolie to be less vulnerable to price fluctuations and to boost its strength. In early 2020, it launched a plan to invest more than 1 billion USD in oil, gold and power generation, of which over 900 million USD would originate from this company's resources. Another 195 million USD (i.e. 45 million more than the target of 150 million) was raised by means of an international bond issue.[340] The oil which the US-based company Apache and the French company Total discovered off the coast of Suriname, as had been announced in early 2020, did undoubtedly boost investor confidence (see also p. 412). Managing director Rudolf Elias stated in the Staatsolie's annual report: 'The company and the country will never be the same again.'[341] President Santokhi, in office since July 2020, even believed that constructing a bridge across the Corantijn River hereby providing access to neighbouring Guyana, where the first oil revenues had already flowed into the state coffers, could be realised during his term of office.[342]

Oil and gas extracted from the sea floor would not reach dry land until 2025 at the earliest, according to experts. Under the agreements, Staatsolie could acquire a 20 per cent stake in the exploitation of an Apache/Total oil field, for which it would have to seek between 1 and 2 billion USD in the international capital market.[343] However, the expected revenues for the state of Suriname were estimated to be much higher, especially after two more large oil fields were discovered in the same off shore area. Staatsolie's top executive Elias, mentioned a sum of between 20 and 60 billion USD, depending on the international oil price.[344] Moreover, spin-offs were to be expected. Staatsolie composed an overview of the 200 Suriname-based companies considered potential suppliers of goods and services.[345] Malaysia's state-owned firm Petroliam Nasional Berhad (Petronas) with investment partner Exxon Mobil Corporation discovered a fourth oil field in December 2020.[346] Staatsolie's strong financial position was partly the result of its 25 per cent stake in the Newmont-operated Merian gold mine, which had opened in late 2016. In 2019, this mine (with operating rights until 2039) contributed almost 25 per cent of the state oil company's gross earnings. In 2020, Staatsolie expanded its interest in the gold sector by acquiring a 30 per cent stake in the Pikin Saramacca mine which IAMGOLD had recently

---

339   *Starnieuws,* 19 December 2019.
340   Staatsolie, *Annual Report 2019,* 11.
341   Ibid, 7.
342   *Starnieuws*, 4 October 2020.
343   Staatsolie, *Annual Report 2019,* 7 and 12.
344   *Starnieuws*, 2 August and 30 October 2020.
345   Ibid., 2 August 2020.
346   Ibid., 11 December 2020.

commissioned.[347] In 2019, Newmont Suriname (1,100 employees) produced 14,855 kg gold.[348] In 2019, too, production at IAMGOLD's Rosebel mine (1,400 employees) had reached 7,116 kg.[349] In 2020, Vice President Brunswijk reported that the volume of small-scale gold mining was 'almost as large' as the volume which the multinationals garnered.[350] This same year, the recently chosen government installed a new commission tasked with regulating the small-scale gold sector. Preparations were also made as to establishing an independent authority with enforcement as well as regulatory powers: the *Delfstoffen Instituut Suriname* (Minerals Institute Suriname).[351] The problems remained the same: mercury pollution, uncontrolled deforestation and the even more pressing issue related to the land rights for those populating the interior (see also p. 385-386). A damaging form of gold mining comprised floating pontoons. Moreover, illegal Chinese gold diggers applied chemicals containing cyanide particles.[352] In September 2020, Suriname and France, both signatories to the Minamata Convention on Mercury, agreed on a joint response to environmental issues encountered in the border region.[353]

Various NGOs, including Conservation International Suriname, warned that, after 2025, Suriname's forest coverage, to wit, 93 per cent of its territory was in danger of falling below 90 per cent.[354] According to an international study on gold and timber concessions, 'corruption up to the highest level' existed (see also p. 408-409).[355] From 2015 on, the exports of the small-scale gold sector had been handled through Mint House Kaloti and the Central Bank of Suriname. Contributions to the treasury in that year, despite a royalty increase from 1 to 2.5 per cent, reached only 5.4 million USD whereas the export was valued at almost 370 million USD.[356] In 2017, the entire gold sector exported a total of *c.*40,000 kg. Its export value reached 1.5 billion USD equaling 74 per cent of Suriname's total goods and commodities exports.[357] Due to the volatility of commodity revenues, the economy remained very vulnerable. In fact, the government budget continued to depend on it for *c.*25 per cent of revenues.[358] The *Spaar- en Stabilisatiefonds* (Savings and Stabilisation Fund) which had been established in 2017, following an Norwegian example, was nevertheless not provided with money.

---

347   Staatsolie, *Annual Report 2019*, 6 and 11.
348   Newmont, *Annual Report 2019*, 39.
349   IAMGOLD, Annual Report 2019, 16.
350   *Starnieuws*, 7 September 2020.
351   Ibid., 8 September 2020; see also: Conservation International Suriname, *Natuurpublicatie CIS*, 5th ed., 2020.
352   *De Ware Tijd*, 29 October 2020; see also: WWF, *Healthy Rivers, Healthy People, addressing the mercury crisis in the Amazon*, 2018.
353   *Starnieuws*, 5 September 2020. The Office of the Prosecutor announced in October 2022 that a dozen pontoons had been seized and dismantled across the border area in an attempt to combat environmental crime; *Starnieuws*, 1 October 2022.
354   Conservation International Suriname, *Natuurpublicatie CIS*, 5th ed., 2020.
355   Ibid.
356   Central Bank of Suriname, *Annual Report 2015*, 51.
357   Conservation International Suriname, *Natuurpublicatie CIS*, 5th ed., 2020; Suriname's total merchandise exports amounted to 2,034 million USD in 2017: IMF, *Suriname, Staff Report for the 2018 Article IV Consultation*, 2018, 31.
358   IMF, *Suriname, Staff Report for the 2019 Article IV Consultation with Suriname 2019*, 30-31.

Meanwhile, the agricultural sector was in decline whereby the rice sector experienced a decrease in its exports to the EU. This outcome was due to an increasing competition from poverty stricken countries which had been granted a tariff-free as well as a quota-free access to the European marketplace. Due to the depreciation of the Suriname dollar, this sector also had to deal with higher costs when importing inputs such as fertilizers.[359] The banana production had run into serious problems caused by the Moko disease. In 2014, Suriname had sold the company which owned acreage in Nickerie and in Jarikaba to a Belgian firm called Univeg. At the end of 2020, this banana company, having changed its name to Food and Agriculture Industries, returned to state hands with a debt of 7 million USD.[360] In a detailed report dated 2017, the World Bank continued to observe great potential in agriculture thanks to 'abundant land and water and a favorable growing environment'.[361] Aside from rice, it mentions fruits, vegetables and animal feed. Nevertheless, in order to increase exports to the neighbouring regions and to Europe, and to attract foreign investment, efforts were still required in the domains of quality and certification.

However, the first priority on the threshold of a new decade was to restore Suriname's creditworthiness and thus its macro-economic stability. This outcome was not only important for a company such as Staatsolie (which had to meet its capital needs on the international capital market) but also for desired potential investors, including those forming part of the Surinamese diaspora. International credit rating agencies had downgraded Suriname to the junk status.[362] Shortly after taking office, the Santokhi-led government had suspended all interest payments and repayments regarding the Oppenheimer loans. The same occurred with other loans. It had therefore not only quickly opened negotiations with creditors concerning debt rescheduling but also communicated with the IMF on a support package. These initiatives aimed at providing further financial breathing space.

The *Crisis- en Herstelplan 2020-2022* (Crisis and Recovery Plan 2020-2022) was presented to the IMF and the creditors. It included measures in order to increase revenues, reduce expenditure and soften the impact on the less affluent section of the population, to wit: (a) a 10 per cent solidarity levy on all higher incomes, (b) an increase in import taxes, (c) an increase in land revenue as well as royalties in the small-scale gold sector, (d) a production fund serving entrepreneurs, (e) a reduction in electricity subsidies with support only for lower income groups (f) an increase in civil servants' salaries and in old-age and child allowances, and (g) financial aid for the most needy.[363] Moreover, in 2022 the value added tax had to be introduced (in order to replace the turnover tax), whereby direct taxes would be reduced by means of a compensation.[364] The aforementioned plan reflected the deep fall of the economy. The GDP per capita at the end of 2020 had dropped to 4,917 USD, below the

---

359 *EPA Monitoring*, 'Trends in the EU Rice Market', 21 March 2019 (epamonitoring.net).
360 *Starnieuws*, 24 September and 7 November 2020, and 14 January 2021.
361 The World Bank, *Suriname sector competitiveness analysis, identifying opportunities to investment and diversification in the agribusiness and extractive sectors*, 2017, Executive Summary, xvi.
362 For an overview of the credit status of Suriname, see: countryeconomy.com/ratings/suriname
363 Ministry of Finance and Planning, *Crisis- en Herstelplan 2020-2022*, Paramaribo, 10 May 2021, 18.
364 Ibid., 57.

level reached as early as 2006 (see Figure 16.1. p. 372).[365] A key cause hereof was the devaluation of the SRD from 7.52 to 14.29 for 1 USD.

In spite of all the international goodwill presented to the incoming government, the people of Suriname were obviously facing difficult times. Only later would they be able to observe part of their nation's potential wealth. On 29 September 2020, President Santokhi had stated in his annual address to parliament: 'What I can already tell you is that, both bilaterally and multilaterally, the confidence in this government is extremely high, and with it the willingness to support Suriname.'[366]

The conclusion of an agreement with the IMF on an Extended Fund Facility comprising USD 690 million for 3 years provided the clearest proof of this. In April 2021, a staff level agreement was reached.[367] The fact it took till December of that year for the IMF Board to give the green light was mainly due to China, which wanted certainty as to the arrears on Suriname's bilateral debt.[368] This IMF arrangement was designed to support Suriname's national plans aimed at restoring fiscal sustainability, while at the same time protecting the vulnerable by means of a social safety net. Essential was reducing the huge public debt - the result of long-term fiscal imbalances and the large depreciations of the exchange rate - to a sustainable level. The IMF estimated public debt at nearly 129 per cent of GDP at the end of 2021, of which 88.2 per cent was external and 40.6 domestic. A year earlier, according to the IMF, the total public debt was 147.7 per cent.[369] Particularly with regard to domestic debts, the government of Suriname had been able to eliminate several arrears. The IMF spoke of a 'constructive dialogue' between Suriname and its foreign creditors 'to secure a reasonably timely and orderly agreement to restructure the country's debt'. The IMF assumed in its projections that Suriname's total public debt would have declined to 101.9 per cent of GDP by 2026.[370] In June 2021 the Central Bank of Suriname unified the official and parallel exchange rate, while introducing a market-determined rate. The SRD traded at c.20.96 to the USD and remained fairly stable.[371] The market-determined exchange rate should help the economy in adjusting to external shocks and rebuilding foreign reserves, which could also grow with financing inflows provided by international institutions. The IDB thus approved the 'Suriname country strategy 2021-2025' which mentioned as much as 450 million USD in loans for projects regarding institutional strengthening, macro-fiscal

---

365 The World Bank Open Data (data.worldbank.org); Suriname's total GDP at the end of 2020 had reached 2,884 million USD, according to World Bank data.

366 Santokhi, Jaarrede in het parlement (Annual Address in parliament), 29 September 2020, 10.

367 *IMF Staff-Level Agreement with the Republic of Suriname on a $690 million Three-Year Program Under the Extended Fund Facility*; source: press release, 29 April 2021.

368 IMF, *Suriname. Request for an extended arrangement under the extended fund facility. Staff Report*, 9 December 2021, 4; it may be added here that two well-informed sources confirmed to the present author that the issue of bilateral debt to China had caused delay. It had amounted to 537 million USD, see also: *Starnieuws*, 2 February 2022.

369 IMF, *Suriname. Request for an extended arrangement under the extended fund facility. Staff Report*, 9 December 2021, 33.

370 Ibid., 14, 33; the IMF assumed that 10 per cent of GDP in new debt was needed in order to recapitalize the Central Bank as well as commercial banks, see: ibid., 15; see also: West 2022.

371 Ibid., 16-18; this fact implied that the USD/SRD rate had depreciated with 180 per cent since January 2020, see: ibid., 7.

A History of Suriname

performance, digital transformation, supporting local content, regional connectivity, education and infrastructure.[372]

The Santokhi-led government faced a herculean task: rebalancing a debt-laden economy while unleashing growth potential in the private sector. The government deficit stood at no less than 19 per cent of GDP at the end of 2019, not coincidentally a pre-election year. According to the IMF this was 'due to ballooning expenditures on civil servant compensation and an expansion of untargeted electricity subsidies'. Although the incoming government succeeded in reducing the public deficit to 9.7 per cent by the end of 2020, the program agreed with the IMF called for a slight surplus to be created during the following years.[373] This should be achieved inter alia by limiting the nominal increase of the wage bill, which had grown due to wage increases and the previous government recruiting of thousands of new civil servants during the last months before the elections (see p. 415). The wage bill had risen to *c.*10.5 per cent of GDP, not only well above the historical average of 8.3 per cent but also exceeding the historical average of 8 per cent observed across Latin America and the Caribbean. In the program agreed upon with the IMF, the wage bill was to reach 7 per cent of GDP by the year 2024.[374] Such a reform would cause a minor revolution for a country that still suffered from restraints based on clientelism and ethno-political issues.[375] It is true that the government had concluded a tripartite agreement with trade unions and employers, hereby agreeing on a social safety net, benefits, wage adjustments and taxes. (see p. 417). Needless to say, that did not guarantee any social peace, given the sensitive measures needed to get Suriname's economy back on track. In 2024, too, electricity tariffs had to be fully cost-effective. Considering a tariff of 0.04 USD per KWH, i.e., 30 per cent of costs, Suriname's tariffs were among the lowest in the world. Next, in a first step, electricity tariffs went up by 103 per cent in July 2021. Lump sums were paid to the smallest users, who generally are also most vulnerable, in order to mitigate the effects.[376]

At least equally important as the aforementioned program created to restore fiscal sustainability, was thus the *Meerjaren Ontwikkelingsplan* (Multi-annual Development Plan) 2022-2026. It had been prepared in consultation with numerous interest groups, experts and businesses to be approved by parliament at the end of 2021.[377] With its implementation, Suriname's growth potential was to be effectively harnessed. The government estimated the total expenditure at 'less than USD 1.3 billion'.[378] This amount was considerably more modest and realistic than the 6,890 million USD the

---

372 *IDB Group approves 2021-2025 Suriname country strategy*, source: news release, 16 December 2021 (iadb. org/en/news).

373 IMF, *Suriname. Request for an extended arrangement under the extended fund facility. Staff Report*, 9 December 2021, 8, 33.

374 Ibid., 9-10; for the average size of the public wage bill in Latin American and the Caribbean (2002-2018) see: Worldwide Bureaucracy Indicators Dashboard (worldbank.org/en/data/interactive/2019/05/21/ worldwide-bureaucracy-indicators-dashboard).

375 The Minister of Internal Affairs Bronto Somohardjo estimated in 2022 that, out of 53,000 civil servants, as many as 30,000 were superfluous, see: *Starnieuws*, 26 May 2022.

376 IMF, *Suriname. Request for an extended arrangement under the extended fund facility. Staff Report*, 9 December 2021., 10.

377 *Starnieuws*, 20 December 2021.

378 Planbureau Suriname, *MOP, Meerjaren Ontwikkelingsplan 2022-2026 (Multi-annual Development Plan)*, 2021, 157-158.

Bouterse-led government wished to spend by means of the *Multi-annual Development Plan 2012-2016*, of which 53 per cent was to be funded by the government itself (see p. 427). The Santokhi-led government hereby underlined that this document was 'not an unrealistic wish list of eye-catching mega-projects'.[379]

This development plan included a number of key elements such as business environment, offshore oil and gas, education, nature and environment, public administration, social protection, electricity supply, gold sector and agriculture.[380] These key elements have been worked out into a large series of measures, often presented with timetables. For instance, in order to finally cause Suriname to rise on the Ease of Doing Business Index, measures mentioned include amending bankruptcy legislation (e.g., improving the rights of creditors), the construction law, reducing the waiting period for a business license, establishing an independent complaints office, amending tax laws, establishing a credit registration office, creating a greater role for the National Development Bank with, for example, a participation fund for start-ups and a fund for technical assistance.[381] This catalogue of measures alone shows the huge task facing the government, whose capacity for implementation (due to a lack of knowledge, management personnel and patronage), as mentioned earlier, has always been seriously lacking. In its development plan, the government itself refers to a 'deep-rooted incapacity to diversify the economy and thus make it more resilient'.[382]

Even more will be required from the government of Suriname when managing the expected boom in the oil and gas sector. At least, it clearly recognized (a) the risks of 'more income inequality, corruption, loss of other economic sectors' and (b) examples hereof observed in other nation states 'from which lessons should be learned'.[383] The spearhead of the Multi-annual Development Plan 2022-2026 is local content, which should contribute to the highly desired economic diversification. Suriname-based companies were to obtain 'a significant share' in the supply chain. In addition, a Local Content Development Office, in which Staatsolie was to play a role, should map out the opportunities and monitor any progress. By means of training (also in partnership with foreign offshore training institutes), education and standards, companies should be raised to the required level in order to acquire the status of an 'approved vendor'. In 2017, while following foreign examples, Suriname had been able to establish a so-called savings and stabilization fund. It was to be stocked with revenue from mining and oil and gas extraction, which according to this development plan should also play a role in bolstering the economy.[384]

After the offshore oil discoveries in 2020, the initial investment activities or related preparations also took off. For instance, DP World (already active in Suriname as a container terminal operator through a subsidiary) announced in 2021 an investment comprising USD 100 million for the construction of an Offshore Support Base located

---

379   Ibid., 3.
380   Ibid., XII-XIII.
381   Ibid., 29-35.
382   Ibid., 2.
383   Ibid., 2.
384   Ibid., 23-25.

A History of Suriname

at the estuary of the Suriname River.[385] In addition, Staatsolie was actively looking for co-investors to set up port facilities in Nickerie and develop local content together with Suriname-based companies. Ambitious plans also existed for processing and distributing gas from the offshore fields, including the production of hydrogen fuel by means of natural gas.[386]

The development of the oil and gas sector as well as related spin-off activities were apparently enhanced through Suriname's cooperation with neighbouring Guyana (where exploitation of the off-shore energy sector was already underway) and Brazil. During the 2022 International Energy Conference in Guyana, President Santokhi underlined that: 'The sustainable benefits go beyond our borders'.[387] The desire for this far-reaching interregional cooperation had also been expressed a month earlier at Paramaribo when the presidents of Suriname, Guyana and Brazil met (see p. 418). According to these three nations, this cooperation should not only include oil and gas, but also technical expertise, local content, electrical interconnection (also with French Guiana) as well as road and port infrastructure.[388] This interaction also brought the objectives for this region created by the Initiative for the Integration of the Regional Infrastructure of South America (IIRSA), supported by the IDB, a step closer to reality after many years of delay. In other words: integrating the Guiana Shield and linking it to Northern Brazil.

In addition, Suriname was still faced with the task of capitalizing on the conservation of its forests within the framework of the international climate objectives. This goal was not achieved, despite subsidies provided by the World Bank's REDD+ mechanism (see p. 431). Suriname took a remarkable and potentially significant step during the 26th UN Climate Change Conference of the Parties (COP26) held in Glasgow (31 October-13 November 2021). Here Suriname formed an alliance with Bhutan and Panama by signing a declaration. As the only three carbon negative nations in the world, all three now chose to protect their carbon absorbing forests. In this declaration they called for (a) international finance, (b) preferential trade, (c) carbon pricing and (d) further support for their economies as well as for other carbon-negative nations yet to emerge.[389] In the Multi-annual Development Plan 2022-2026, the government of Suriname referred to the sale of carbon credits to western countries with high greenhouse gas emissions as one of the

---

385 *Starnieuws*. 16 August 2021.
386 Ibid., 2 June 2021. Noteworthy was an agreement the government of Suriname signed in March 2021 with an unknown Danish company called Hybrid Power System Group (HPSG) in order to produce hydrogen by means of solar and wind energy in the eastern district of Commewijne. Florian Elabdi, a Copenhagen-based journalist, revealed this project to be a fraudulent initiative set up by businessmen with dubious antecedents. His investigation clearly proved the risks Suriname runs when negotiating with foreign investors because of its lack of technical and legal expertise. Its government subsequently declared the agreement null and void as HPSG had misrepresented matters, see: *Starnieuws*, 10 February 2022, and F. Elabdi, 'Danish businessmen behind 'dodgy' green energy project in Suriname', in: *Danwatch*, 10 November 2021 (danwatch.dk/en).
387 *Starnieuws*, 16 February 2022.
388 Ibid., 21 January 2022; oilnow.gy (21 January 2022).
389 See: reuters.com/business/cop/forget-net-zero-meet-small-nation-carbon-negative-club-2021-11-03; In a press statement, dated 29 March 2022, the Ministry of Finance also mentioned the possibility of using 'green instruments' in the debt negotiations with international creditors, with the option of repaying debt via a so-called Surinamese Green Fund (finance.gov.sr).

options.[390] This plan includes a long list of actions Suriname should carry out in order to at least maintain its climate-friendly status, in particular as to the rehabilitation of forest areas affected by illegal logging and small-scale gold mining (whereby the aforementioned long-standing problem of poisoned rivers and creeks when applying mercury was yet to be addressed) as well as adjusting legislation and strengthening its enforcement.[391] Suriname now adhered to recommendations forwarded by the IDB in a report on its climate policy and subsequent risks.[392]

In this context, legal recognition of the territorial rights of the Indigenous peoples and Maroons remained urgent. As stipulated in Suriname's development plan, these two ethnic groups could thus also be further involved in the production of non-timber forest products (e.g., care, medicines), which would contribute to preserving the forest and its biodiversity. In 2021, the government did accept a draft bill on land rights. However, the further approval procedure was slow, despite judgements delivered by the Inter-American Court of Human Rights in which Suriname had been condemned for many years prior hereto (see p. 385-386).[393]

The feasibility of Suriname's development plan was closely linked to any financial leeway the Santokhi-led government could create in its budget and thus to negotiations held with creditors on restructuring the public debt. After all, according to the IMF, this debt was unsustainable even 'under the maximum feasible fiscal adjustment in the next 15 years'.[394] However, the IMF also observed a 'meaningful upside risk to the country's payment capacity' in the promising oil discoveries located off the coast of Suriname. Nonetheless, the IMF could not take this fact into account as to its projections due to the absence as yet of 'clear private sector investment plans

---

390 Planbureau Suriname, *MOP, Meerjaren Ontwikkelingsplan 2022-2026* (Multi-annual Development Plan), 2021, 67.

391 Ibid., 65-68.

392 IDB, *State of the Climate Report, Suriname. Summary for policy makers*, July 2021, 51. This report not only highlights the degree Suriname was at risk due to the rising sea level. For, 87 per cent of its population as well as the majority of its economic activities are concentrated in lower coastal areas. It further points out the dangers pertaining to generating hydroelectric power by means of the Afobaka Dam. This assessment was based on the predicted less frequent but more intense periods of rainfall, see p. 16, 18, 44 and 45. During the first months of 2022, the water level of the adjacent Brokopondo Reservoir rose to such an extent that excess water had to be drained from the Afobaka Dam's scuppers, causing the severe flooding of nearby Maroon villages, see: *Starnieuws* 11, 20 April and 25 May 2022. See also: IDB, *Climate change impacts on hydropower and electricity demand in Suriname*, May 2022.

393 *Starnieuws*, 15 June 2021.

394 IMF, *Suriname. Request for an extended arrangement under the extended fund facility. Staff Report*, 9 December 2021, 47.

to extract these resources' to be noted among the oil companies involved.[395] In any case, reaching an agreement with creditors was merely one single step on a long road leading to creating a resilient economy of which the entire population could benefit. Suriname had cherished this ambition since acquiring independence in 1975.

---

395 Ibid., 28; in its negotiations with international creditors on debt restructuring, the Surinamese government was already leveraging the potential oil wealth with the use of the so-called 'value recovery mechanism', whereby bondholders are partially compensated for debt reduction afterwards with offshore oil revenues, see: press release Ministry of Finance, Paramaribo, 29 March 2022 (finance.gov.sr). The fact TotalEnergies decided in October 2022 to postpone until mid-2023 its Final Investment Decision (FID) as to exploiting the offshore reserves thus formed a setback for the government; *Starniews*, 7 October 2022. Moreover, Suriname felt compelled to request the IMF to renegotiate terms pertaining to the financial aid package because the 'social impact had become unbearable', while the currency depreciated, partly due to changed conditions in the global economy; *Starnieuws*, 16, 29 September and 7 October 2022. Kristalina Georgieva, Managing Director of the IMF, expressed a readiness for flexibility 'in light of high food and fuel prices' during a meeting with President Santhokhi; @KGeorgeva / Twitter. The IMF had meanwhile suspended the payment of two tranches as Suriname had fallen behind in implementing the economic program; *Starnieuws*, 27 June and 6 September 2022.

EPILOGUE

After being appointed Associate Professor of Sociology and Cultural Studies of Suriname and the Netherlands Antilles at the University of Leiden on 26 May 1950, R.A.J. van Lier described West Indian societies as having a minimum of 'expansive force', where very little is accomplished other than by authorities.[1] A few years earlier, J.S. Furnivall had stated that plural societies suffer from a lack of 'common social will'.[2] The renowned essayist-*cum*-novelist V.S. Naipaul, originally from Trinidad and Tobago, was equally pessimistic. For, in *The Overcrowded Barracoon and Other Articles* he referred to Caribbean nation states as follows:

> '*They are manufactured societies, labour camps, creations of empire; and for long they were dependent on empire for law, language, institutions, culture, even officials. Nothing was generated locally; dependence became a habit. How without empire, do such societies govern themselves? What is now the source of power? The ballot box, the mob, the regiment?*'[3]

G.J. Oostindie, Professor of Anthropology and Comparative Sociology of the Caribbean, stated on 18 January 1994 in his inaugural address delivered at the Rijksuniversiteit Utrecht (the Netherlands) that the post-war history of Guyana, Trinidad and Tobago, and Suriname 'seems to confirm much of the often as defeatist disparaged theory of plural society [...]'. He further deemed the situation of these three nation states as 'a constantly renegotiated and thus varying degree of mostly peaceful coexistence'.[4] Those observing the events unfolding in Suriname either after the return of democratic civilian rule in 1987 or from its independence acquired in 1975 on, should indeed make every effort to preserve optimism. Indeed, military dictatorship, drug mafia and informal power have impeded any desired further developments. In a way, they provided Suriname with the guise of a colony whereby merely the division of roles had changed and wherein a corrupt local elite had taken over the position occupied by colonists. Moreover, in 2010, the parliament of Suriname elected Desi Bouterse, a former seditionist, to serve as the nation's president. He had been convicted of cocaine trafficking and was also a prime suspect in a murder trial. Nevertheless, two strongly ethnically oriented party combinations representing Javanese and Maroons assisted Bouterse in achieving the required two-thirds parliamentary majority. Moral considerations did not play a role in their choice. In any case, a desire the political leaders expressed to co-govern within a coalition in order to 'accommodate' themselves as well as their socio-economically disadvantaged followers prevailed here.

The post-2000 events in Suriname disclosed a society in transition which did not always proceed at the same pace everywhere. The deep economic contraction

---

1   Van Lier 1950, 3-4.
2   Furnivall 1945, 168.
3   Naipaul 1972, 254.
4   Oostindie 1994, 20.

that struck in *c*.1990 was a societal crisis, too. This phenomenon not only reflected a dubious colonial legacy but also illustrated the deadlock witnessed within an ethno-political culture causing immobilism, a clear trait of segmented societies. The special aid relationship with the Netherlands, to wit, a 'free' development funding, had reinforced political and economic inertia. The economic globalisation nonetheless rendered reform measures, on occasion of a revolutionary nature, inevitable in numerous areas. Such necessary reforms should certainly include: halving the civil service, increasing the quality of education, modernising laws and regulations in order to facilitate business, and privatising many parastatal companies. Otherwise, integrating Suriname into the Caribbean and the Latin American regions, as all politicians advocated, would not be feasible. Such reforms require a different way of political management and, even more so, a different political culture. After all, the state, i. e., the political elite of Suriname, had always largely derived its legitimacy from a possibility of keeping patronage alive. During the 1950s and 1960s, for example, a so-called fraternization policy flourished thanks to a growth in prosperity, thus enabling ethnic parties to not only generously serve but also emancipate their supporters. The mutual distribution of government jobs as well as of plots of land and permits was not only instrumental in achieving political consensus, it also enabled politicians to maintain ethnic peace.

Ethnicity-based sentiments have not led to uncontrollable eruptions in Suriname. This fortunate outcome is in part thanks to moderate actions undertaken by key political leaders, in particular by Jagernath Lachmon, a Hindustani. Moreover, through the combination of proportionality and regionalisation, the electoral system as introduced in 1987 forces the political parties to either recruit their candidates from various ethnic groups or to participate in elections by means of a multi-ethnic combination. The desire expressed by established parties to adapt this system can lead to conflict. For, in the interior districts, relatively few votes per parliamentary seat are required which is hugely advantageous to the local population, to wit, Maroons and Indigenous peoples (see p. 413, note 205).

Ethnic sentiments can reignite especially during an economic crisis. For instance Hindustanis, when active as independent entrepreneurs within the agriculture and trade sectors, are by and large economically more resilient than most Creoles, who rather depend on either public sector jobs or 'hustling'. Socio-geographical research executed around the end of the 1990s, for example, proved that Creole residential neighbourhoods located in Paramaribo did not develop further in a socio-economic sense, whereas residential areas housing predominantly Hindustanis did.[5] With the influx of mainly uneducated Maroons into an urban environment of Paramaribo – partly as a result of the Interior War – this discrepancy became an even more serious issue. Surinamese with Asian roots focussed strongly on labour, education and family values and thus take a hard-to-bridge lead on the lower-class Creoles especially. It is no coincidence that the number of students of Asian descent enrolled at the Anton de Kom University of Suriname is disproportionately large. Hans Breeveld, the Creole former minister, chairman of a university think tank, university lecturer and poet lamented thus:

---

5   Schalkwijk & De Bruijne 1997, 127.

A History of Suriname

'Let's dance on days when the farmer plants peanuts, harvests vegetables, guards his herd, [...] but don't be angry with others who have bigger houses, more land, possess more wealth than you.'[6]

The various ethnic groups have always created a rather stereotypical image of each other. In 1992, scholars from Suriname as well as the Netherlands carried out relevant research which included the same questions as asked in the course of well-known studies executed during the early 1960s by both J. D. Speckman and H. C. van Renselaar (see p. 273).[7] Again, Hindustanis attributed negative traits (e.g., not being future-oriented, laziness and criminal conduct) to Creoles. On the other hand, the Creoles continued to deem Hindustanis as being avaricious, unreliable and discriminating. And again Creoles felt less positive about themselves than Hindustanis and Javanese did. Yet another interesting conclusion was: the higher educated have a more positive attitude towards their own ethnic group and a less negative attitude towards other groups. Good education apparently contributes to reducing ethnic dissent. However, the fact that the higher educated are more inclined to provide socially desirable answers may have played a role here. Extreme ethnic polarization, as witnessed across neighbouring Guyana, did not occur in Suriname. Notable, within this context, is the fact that the ethnically mixed quarters of Paramaribo became increasingly intermingled between 1980 and 1992. Although ethnically more homogeneous residential areas developed additional traits of segregation, Paramaribo itself did not experience any strict types of distinction along ethnic lines.[8] During the late 1990s, more than 50 per cent of the Hindustanis, Creoles and Javanese opined that the race factor no longer played a role as to social mobility, thus suggesting a further progress as to the emancipation of the various ethnic groups home to Suriname.[9] Nevertheless, in 2000, election results were highly ethnicity-based whereby votes were cast in support of those 'who look like me'.

Can all this indeed be different? In any case, the question may be raised if, in the course of the 21st century, such a highly negative viewpoint should still be attributed to plurality, as Furnivall and Van Lier suggested.[10] After all, it has gradually become clear that everything we now consider to be diversity can exert a positive influence on both economic development and intercultural exchange. In 1939, when Furnivall first utilised the term 'plural society', he referred to Southeast Asia.[11] However, decades later precisely in for instance Malaysia and Indonesia a flourishing economy developed, partly thanks to a solid inter-ethnic cooperation.

In 2008 the sociologist Jack Menke introduced the concept of 'nation creation' pertaining to Suriname.[12] Based on a more positive approach, it forms the pendant of 'nation building', whereby the (colonial) state organises society from above by means of striving for a uniform culture. Nation creation however is based on (cultural)

---

6   Breeveld 1992, 30.
7   Verberk, Scheepers & Hassankhan 1997, 133-146.
8   Schalkwijk & De Bruijne 1997, 126-127.
9   Schalkwijk 1996, 38.
10   Van Lier 1971, 9-16.
11   Furnivall 1939, 446-471.
12   Menke 2008, 11-59.

societal groups that develop, through collective efforts, a 'nation' built on 'solidarity, mutual respect and harmonious coordination between the ethnic groups and their cultures'.[13] Menke rightly observes that Suriname has a 'complex' but 'harmonious cultural diversity' which had evolved in a 'fairly natural way'.[14]

This phenomenon can be observed, for example in music when styles on occasion blend.[15] Moreover, this can be defined as a form of creolization, i.e., a mutual cultural influence and intermingling, as has been going on across the Caribbean and elsewhere for a much longer time.[16] When independence was achieved in 1975, the popular music of Suriname was as yet largely linked to Creole culture. Next, 'Hindipop' bands entered the scene in order to mix Afro-Caribbean styles as well as *kaseko* with South Asian and Bollywood dance music.[17] Now young Creole musicians started collaborating with Maroon musicians who had migrated to Paramaribo. Being open to fresh influences, including those from abroad, apparently benefitted local musical traditions. A 'harmonious diversity' can further be observed within the religious sphere. Followers from each religious tradition now celebrate Divali, the Hindu festival of lights. The conclusion of the holy month of Ramadan is a national holiday.

It does remain to be seen if 'nation creation', being a bottom-up process initiated by socio-cultural groups, leads to any far-reaching political changes. As early as during the 1970s a progressive politico-cultural movement named *Volkspartij* (People's Party) had opposed ethnic politics and gleaned a large following among the progressive young population of Suriname. The theatre-maker Henk Tjon (1948-2009) founded the broadly acclaimed *Ala Kondre Dron Ensemble* (All Countries Drum Ensemble) which included members from all ethnic groups.[18] Bea Vianen (1935-2019) became the most widely read author. In her novels entitled *Sarnami, hai* (1969) and *Strafhok* (1971), the protagonists revolt against ethno-religious prejudices. However, socio-political traditions proved too strong in the long run.

And 4 decades later? Politicians in Suriname continued to be strongly inclined to fulfil the 'broker'-role for the supporters in their ethnic groups. In addition, delivering open criticism was soon interpreted, in accordance with the nation's political tradition, as a lack of loyalty to one's specific group. The political leadership and its traits of personalism as well as a hierarchical culture were hardly conducive to any critical self-reflection and/or open debate. An extensive survey conducted in 2003 among the 25 key political parties disclosed the fact they as yet 'have no tradition of formulating and elaborating strategic national goals or development issues [...] generally speaking, parties have a strong focus on internal issues'.[19]

In Furnivall's rigid 'plural society'-concept (as first applied by Van Lier) the existence of a far-reaching social segregation between ethnic groups is assumed.

---

13   Ibid., 54.
14   Menke 2009, 2.
15   Bilby 2001, 296-329.
16   Oostindie 2006, 215-230.
17   This genre of merry dance music, originating from traditional Surinamese-Creole *kawina* music, has been influenced by calypso and pop music. *Kaseko* has adopted two *kawina* elements: (a) singing according to a call and response pattern and (b) the use of percussion instruments.
18   Menke 2008, 51-52.
19   Menke 2004, 30-31.

         A History of Suriname

In the course of the 21st century, developments within the socio-economic and cultural spheres of Suriname have, to say the least, blurred the lines between the various population groups to a certain degree. Here an active and partly multi-ethnic civil society has developed, which has also become more visible. In 2008, an estimated 5,000 non-commercial private organizations (e.g., churches, associations, cooperatives, foundations, political parties) existed.[20] Apparently the influence of civil society on the nation's politics and society was on the rise. Notably, certain politicians were not very enthusiastic when the Netherlands wished to utilise a modest segment of the aid funds for projects planned by non-governmental organisations. These politicians may well have deemed such initiatives as a prime threat to their own powerful positions. Notable, too, was the relative success as witnessed during the 2005 and 2010 elections of several newly founded, non-ethnic parties which opted for 'good governance' to be a top priority. An example hereof is the party which emerged from the civil society named *Democratie en Ontwikkeling in Eenheid* (Democracy and Development in Unity). A growing support among young people for the multi-ethnic NDP also pointed towards social changes.

Equally remarkable was the renewal of politics as desired by young VHP members once one had succeeded in putting an end to more than 50 years of autocratic leadership in 2011. Electing this renewal movement's candidate Chandrikapersad Santokhi (b. 1959) as the VHP's leader, this party's leadership had caused a head-on confrontation. For that reason alone this event formed a breakthrough (see also p. 413-414). Choosing Santokhi, a former Minister of Justice and Police (2005-2010), as its leader probably does herald a broader reform of old politics. The VHP may indeed appeal to non-Hindustanis if it succeeds in raising its profile by means of issues regarding 'good governance' and 'security'. The Hindustani population had completed its emancipation process, although a strong group identity did remain. Opting for a more modern and transparent VHP leadership was a logical consequence. The NPS, with its largest following among the Creole middle class, faced the same challenge.

In Suriname, autocratic leadership (in part a colonial legacy) had been acceptable to voters for decades because emancipating one's own ethnic group was the first priority. The sociologist-*cum*-former politician Marten Schalkwijk speaks aptly of a 'constant field of tension between emancipation processes and the type of leadership'.[21] This description may partly explain the reason why both the Javanese leader Paul Somohardjo and the Maroon leader Ronnie Brunswijk, in spite of criminal convictions, hardly experienced any dissent from within their specific ethnic groups. The considerable support for the NDP leader, Desi Bouterse, especially among lower class Creoles, is also partly the result of their socio-economic disadvantage.

Nevertheless, the failure to combat poverty experienced under previous governments delivers an unsatisfactory explanation for Bouterse's election as President. Indeed, Suriname was the first nation whose serving head of state was tried (and convicted) by the courts on account of multiple murders.[22] The accompanying trial had by no means impeded his election as president in 2010.

---

20   Schalkwijk 2009, 16.
21   Lotens 2000, 44.
22   See also: Reeser 2015, 223-241.

Bouterse's inconceivable walk through life is often compared with that of the spider named Anansi, a protagonist encountered in Caribbean and African folktales. A pure survivor, admired especially in Creole culture, this insect is always able to outwit its opponents (see also p. 365). Therefore, Bouterse's conviction for drug trafficking is considered acceptable. The fact this verdict was read in Suriname's former coloniser, the Netherlands, reinforces that sentiment. Gloria Wekker, the Dutch (now emeritus) professor (of Surinamese descent), who has focused on gender studies and sexuality in the Afro-Caribbean region and diaspora, describes Bouterse, in a 'cultural-critical interpretation' of his presidency, as a *wakaman koni* (smart *wakaman*). This term stems from the Colonial Era, when being clever for lack of any further alternatives was the best survival strategy and the best achievable outcome:[23]

> '*Bouterse in particular appeals to the feeling that he, with the carrot but probably with the stick, will ensure that all needy Surinamese households will be given a helping hand and he is a living poster child of the fact that wakaman behaviour will get you further than a good education.*'[24]

Wekker's interpretation is related to an earlier analysis presented by the British sociologist Peter J. Wilson regarding the role of 'respectability' and 'reputation' among the relatively wealthier and less affluent groups residing across the British Caribbean. In his view, respectability involves cultural values derived from traditional European/American, colonial and Christian influences, with which the well-educated Creole middle and upper classes in particular identify. Reputation is based more on recognition within one's own group. This expression of counterculture is observed in particular among the less affluent Creole class in which hedonism and machismo both play a role.[25] Wilson makes it clear at the same time that the phenomenon he describes 'is not bounded by race or geography, or culture for that matter'.[26]

The fact that Bouterse's criminal record did not stand in the way of being elected as president may also pertain to a cultural context in which shame (Sranan: *tapu yu shén*, meaning: to cover one's shame) plays a non-negligible role within large parts of the population. Avoiding a 'loss of face' does indeed weigh more heavily than a sense of sin and guilt. The politician, playwright and poet Albert Helman (1903-1996) referred to this specific cultural phenomenon in a publication entitled *Facetten van de Surinaamse samenleving* (Facets of the Surinamese society).[27] This society's small scale is apparently of influence here, too. Former Prime Minister Jules Sedney attempted to explain the lukewarm reactions to Bouterse's election thus: 'Marriages have made recent enemies into mutual parents-in-law and have brought mutual families closer together through ties of blood and affinity.'[28] In other words: this small scale may well obscure notions such as guilt and penance. Maybe that is the reason

---

23 Wekker 2010, 169-173.
24 Ibid., 172.
25 Wilson 1969, 70-84; Wilson´s 1973 thesis, a case study on the conflict between reputation and respectability, is based on fieldwork in Providencia, a Columbian isle located off the coast of Nicaragua.
26 Wilson, 1969, 81-82.
27 Helman 1977, 130-131.
28 Personal communication forwarded to the present author by means of an e-mail dated 26 July 2010.

A History of Suriname

why the accomplished author Astrid Roemer's attempt to capture Suriname's reality in a trilogy was such a success. Based on a poignant family history, this trilogy titled *Onmogelijk moederland* (Impossible motherland), features the December murders, drug trafficking, ethnic preoccupations, corruption and patronage.[29]

The continuation of the December murder trial with Bouterse as the main suspect apparently indicated, at least for the time being, that the government he led would respect the course of justice, although pressure from the USA as well as a number of regional countries played a role here. However, while international economic integration received broad societal support, Suriname had fallen short as to complying with universal legal norms and standards to which it was committed after joining the Inter American Convention on Human Rights in 1987. This step had not been randomly taken in the very year military despotism came to an end. Whereas, in several Latin American countries, crimes committed in the course of dictatorships were prosecuted, it remained remarkably silent in Suriname for a very long time.

All this formed the consequence of both an inward-looking political culture and political opportunism. The December murder trial could only commence as a result of pressure exerted by the families of the victims. Key cases pertaining to drug trafficking allegedly orchestrated by former military as well as assassinations of police officers and disappearances remained untouched. The Inter-American Court of Human Rights attempted to persuade Suriname to react upon the 1986 massacre in Moiwana as well as on the land rights of Indigenous people and Maroons. Nevertheless, the Surinamese authorities did not take much notice of this Court's stance for the time being. In 2007, Hans Lim A Po, the director of the FHR Lim A Po Institute for Social Studies (Paramaribo), delivered the Fred Derby Lecture. This prominent lawyer aptly stated that as to Suriname's political culture 'the awareness of the interwovenness of national norms with international ones has unfortunately not yet broken through'.[30] On the significance of a well-functioning rule of law for Suriname, we read:

> 'This is more important in multicultural societies such as ours, where the values of the rule of law and the resulting rules of conduct form the minimum bond between the population groups with their various value patterns.'[31]

After the 1980 coup, the people of Suriname have had to uphold continuous efforts to restore both democracy and prosperity. This effort proved to be not always successful. Net migration to the Netherlands, for example, following the earlier exodus of *c.*1975, the year of independence, increased from more than 1,574 souls in 1981 to 7,076 in 1993, when stricter Dutch admission rules caused a sharp decline.[32] Such an exodus, a phenomenon familiar to the Caribbean, had seriously weakened Suriname not only economically but also in the administrative sector. Moreover, those who stayed behind experienced a negative psychological effect. Within this

---

29   Roemer 2016.

30   Lim A Po 2007.

31   Ibid.

32   Algemeen Bureau voor de Statistiek, *Suriname in cijfers, No. 185-99/01*, 1999, 54.

context, the exodus of prominent writers and musicians to the Netherlands was not without significance.

Now and again a striking civic vitality manifested itself, as observed with the broad, massive resistance witnessed during the deep economic crisis which took place when the Wijdenbosch-led government was in power. From 2000 on, the undercurrent in the society of Suriname that craves for true renovations has gained momentum, whereby economic globalisation, further regional integration and an increasing usage of social media among the young are stimulating forces.[33] Strong economic growth along with an improved distribution of wealth, for which an economic potential exists, can create favourable conditions. Targeted poverty policies aimed at disadvantaged groups, including the Maroons and the Javanese, can reduce a tendency towards patronage. A start can also be made as to decreasing the size of the government apparatus, while utilising an adequate social safety net. Such a step is definitely feasible, but does require courageous political decision-makers. In certain parts of the English-speaking Caribbean, for example, appointing civil servants was entrusted to an independent committee, positioned as distant as possible from any political influence.[34]

The fact that Dutch treaty aid came to an end almost 40 years after the 1975 independence is an advantage rather than a disadvantage. These funds had clearly not contributed to the economic resilience as had been intended in the development treaty concluded between both nations. Instead it reinforced the level of inertia in Suriname. As a result of this treaty, the Dutch government was in fact jointly responsible for Suriname's economic policy, which often stirred up mutual resentment. A report entitled *Een belaste relatie* (A burdened relation) dealt with aid forwarded between 1975 and 2000. In it we read that hence a serious dialogue 'on the commonality of the relations and the adequacy of the aid provided [had] not or hardly taken place' between the Netherlands and its former colony.[35] It must be added here that in recent years useful projects (e.g., dyke construction, other forms of infrastructure, debt relief aid) were financed, too. Ending the treaty assistance can create room for sound relations, in which the governments involved play less prominent roles. The more than 300,000 people with Surinamese roots residing in the Netherlands, with a shared language and history, form a solid basis. In 2009, according to figures provided by the Royal Dutch Embassy, already more than 500 private partnerships existed between both countries, for example, in the education and culture sectors.[36] Apparently a reinforcement of relations established by the two civil societies which The Hague was striving for, was thus already taking place. Moreover, from 2000 on, a shared history had become a larger part of the collective Dutch

---

33   The Dutch Caribbeanist Peter Meel rightly notes in this context that 'transparency, accountability, sustainability and inclusiveness are well-received concepts that energize civil society, but fail to appeal to the governing elite. Political leaders wishing to enhance nation building and social justice creation would do well to suit their actions to their words, collaborate with civil society actors and terminate clientelist practices'. See: Meel 2022, 211.

34   Oostindie 2008, 59-69.

35   Kruijt & Maks 2003, 65; this report contains an evaluation of the aid relationship between the Netherlands and Suriname, commissioned by the governments of both countries.

36   As stated in a letter sent by the Minister of Foreign Affairs to Parliament, 26 August 2011, Kamerstuk 20631, nr. 147 (zoek.officielebekendmakingen.nl/kst-20361-147.html).

memory. This is evidenced, for example, by including the history of slavery and slave trade in the historical canon, creating a monument on slavery and the 'deep regret' for the role of the Netherlands in slavery which the Dutch government expressed during the 2001 UN-Conference against Racism, Racial Discrimination, Xenophobia and Related Intolerance, held in Durban (South Africa).[37]

Suriname's genuine development can ultimately only be the result of an effort on the part of its population. From 2000 on, the opinion is apparently shared that economic internationalization is more of an opportunity than a risk. Suriname's efforts in connecting the often praised 'unity in diversity' with the promotion of the public cause will form a key issue. That endeavor calls for an unorthodox approach, certainly within Suriname's social context. Steven Coutinho, the banker-*cum*-philosopher who in the early 2020s had voiced, as previously mentioned, the anger Surinamese people felt regarding the disappearance of savings kept at the CBvS, had published a book in 2018 with the telling title *Breaking rank, how to lead change when yesterday's stories limit today's choices*. Drawing on his personal experiences as an international banker and leadership coach, Coutinho analyses the cultural and psychological factors which impede the modernization of small-scale post-colonial Caribbean societies, to wit, (a) low risk tolerance, (b) helplessness, deference and victimization, (c) low levels of altruism, (d) demotivation and disengagement, (e) low trust levels and (f) short term focus.[38] A publication by the sociologist Herman Vuijsje is entitled *God zij met ons Suriname. Religie als vloek en zegen* (God be with us Suriname. Religion as a curse and a blessing). In this worth reading journalistic report Vuijsje refers to what he describes as a 'renewed discovery trip to multi-religious Suriname'. More than 90 per cent of Suriname's population belongs to religious communities. A large number of their members deeply believes in the spirit world. Vuijsje inquires, without wishing to answer, after the relationship between this religious world and 'the feelings of fear and distrust that are widespread in Suriname and contribute to the stagnation in the country'.[39]

Prior to Coutinho and Vuijsje, many authors asked the same questions and delivered similar analyses. Yet signs indicating that Suriname is liberating itself from obstacles do exist. As of 2019, Suriname is the only nation in the world where a sitting president was convicted of (multiple) murder. The rule of law proved to be strong in the face of a populist leader who, like no other, was able to harvest the favour of the people, in spite of his felonies, corruption and incompetence. After his conviction, having been absent from each and every court hearing, Bouterse made

---

37   *NRC Handelsblad*, 3 September 2001. In 2022, a majority of Dutch parliamentarians for the first time proclaimed that the Kingdom of the Netherlands should officially make good for its colonial-era role in the slave trade and slavery. *NRC Handelsblad*, 19 October and 4 November 2022. On 19 December 2022, Prime Minister Mark Rutte condemned slavery as a 'crime against humanity'. He also formally and posthumously apologised to the enslaved as well as all their descendants on behalf of the government of the Netherlands 'for the actions taken by the Dutch state in the past', to then pledge to create a fund aimed at for instance establishing socio-cultural initiatives related to awareness and healing. Rutte further announced that Willem-Alexander, King of the Netherlands, would attend the commemoration of the abolition to be held on 1 July 2023 in Amsterdam, hereby fuelling expectations he would deliver Royal apologies. *NRC Handelsblad*, 20 December 2022.

38   Coutinho 2018, 19-26.

39   Introduction on the author's website (hermanvuijsje.nl).

a statement for the first time on appeal. Speaking before the Court Martial he again alleged, pertaining to the 15 victims of the December murders, that 'a dangerous military invasion of the former colonizer' had been prevented.[40] In a speech to his supporters, he claimed that his successor was 'throwing the country back fifty years [...] You are only going to be able to remove this kind of thing with weapons'.[41] To a majority of Surinamese, his words sounded like the powerless echo of a bygone era.

After the prosecution's plea in June 2017, Bouterse informed his supporters that 'God has put me here, no judge will take me away' ('*Gado pot' mi dja*').[42] Nonetheless, ultimately the people of Suriname removed Bouterse, an outcome of fresh social dynamics. The fact that young people led protests not only in the streets but also on social media sparked broad resistance. The heavy mortgage on further development after a decade of decline will however once again test the tensile strength of Suriname's society.

---

40   *Starnieuws*, 30 November 2020.
41   *De Ware Tijd*, 1 December 2020.
42   *Starnieuws*, 3 July 2017.

BIBLIOGRAPHY

Abbenhuis, M.F., 1943a, *Volksplanting*, Paramaribo.

Abbenhuis, M.F., 1943b, 1944, 1946, *Verhalen en schetsen uit de Surinaamse geschiedenis. 1683-1783*, 3 vols., Paramaribo.

Adhin, J.H., 1973, *Honderd jaar onderwijsontwikkeling in vogelvlucht*, Paramaribo.

Adhin, J.H., 1975, 'Afgoderij als delictum sui generis. Strafbepalingen inzake 'Baljaaren'', in: *Surinaams Juristenblad*, vol. 20/21, 15-21.

Adhin, J.H., 1998, 'Eenheid in verscheidenheid' in: H.R. Neijhorst (ed.), *Cultuur en Maatschappij. Veertig artikelen van Jnan H. Adhin*, Paramaribo, 34-38 (dbnl.org/tekst/adhi001eenh01_01/).

Ahlbrinck, W., 1956, *Op zoek naar de Indianen* [...], Amsterdam.

Amersfoort, J.M.M. van, 1987, 'Van William Kegge tot Ruud Gullit: de Surinaamse migratie naar Nederland: realiteit, beeldvorming en beleid', in: *Tijdschrift voor Geschiedenis*, 100/3, 475-490 (vijfeeuwenmigratie.nl).

Amersfoort, J.M.M. van, 2011, *How the Dutch Government stimulated the unwanted Immigration from Suriname*, paper 47, International Migration Institute/University of Oxford (migrationinstitute.org).

Arbell, M., 2002, *The Jewish Nation of the Caribbean. The Spanish-Portuguese Jewish Settlements in the Caribbean and the Guianas*, New York.

Azimullah, E., 1986, *Jagernath Lachmon. Een politieke biografie*, Paramaribo.

Balai, L.W., 2011, *Het slavenschip Leusden. Slavenschepen en de West-Indische Compagnie, 1720-1738*, Zutphen.

Ball, E., 1998, *Slaves in the family*, New York.

Bartelink, E.J., 1916, *Hoe de tijden veranderen. Herinneringen van een ouden planter*, Paramaribo (digitalcollections.universiteitleiden.nl).

Beek, R. ter, 1996, *Manoeuvreren. Herinneringen aan Plein 4*, Amsterdam.

Beeldsnijder, R.O., 1994, *'Om werk van jullie te hebben'. Plantageslaven in Suriname 1730-1750*, PhD thesis Leiden University, Utrecht.

Beet, C. de, 1981, Introduction to and translation of Johannes King, *Berichten uit het Bosland (1864-1870)*, Utrecht.

Beet, C. de, 1984, *De eerste Boni-oorlog 1765-1778*, Utrecht.

Beet, C. de & R. Price, 1982, *De Saramakaanse vrede van 1762,* selected documents introduced by the authors, Utrecht.

Beet, C. de & M. Sterman, 1981, *People in between: the Matawai Maroons of Suriname*, PhD thesis Utrecht University, Meppel (dbnl.org).

Benoit, P.J., 1839, *Voyage à Surinam*, Brussels.

Benoit, P.J., 1980, *Reis door Suriname*, Zutphen (Dutch transl. of the 1839 ed., with 99 coloured drawings).

Bijlsma, R., 1924, 'De Brieven van gouverneur Van Aerssen van Sommelsdijck aan de directeuren der Sociëteit van Suriname uit het jaar 1684', in: *New West Indian Guide/Nieuwe West-Indische Gids*, vol. 5(1), 424-437 (brill.com).

Bijlsma, R., 1925, 'De Brieven van gouverneur Van Aerssen van Sommelsdijck aan de directeuren der Sociëteit van Suriname uit het jaar 1684 II en III', in: *New West Indian Guide/Nieuwe West-Indische Gids*, vol. 6 (1), 41-48, 593-602 (brill.com).

Bilby, K., 2001, 'New Sounds from a New Nation. Processes of Globalisation and Indigenisation in Surinamese Popular Music', in: R. Hoefte & P. Meel, *20th century Suriname. Continuities and Discontinuities in a New World Society*, Leiden/Kingston, 296-329.

Blanksma, A., 2006a, 'Etniciteit en nationalisme tijdens de Surinaamse verkiezingscampagne in mei 2005', in: *OSO, Tijdschrift voor Surinamistiek en het Caraïbisch gebied*, vol. 25(1), 149-165 (dbnl.org).

Blanksma, A., 2006b, *De koek en de kruimels. Etnische en nationalistische mobilisatie tijdens de Surinaamse verkiezingscampagne 2005*, Amsterdam (adoc.pub/de-koek-en-de-kruimels.html).

Blom, A., 1787, *Verhandeling van den landbouw in de Colonie Suriname*, Amsterdam (delpher.nl).

Boerboom, H. & J. Oranje, 1992, *De 8-decembermoorden. Slagschaduw over Suriname*, Den Haag.

Boers, A.E., 1911, *Over de beweging in deze dagen*, Paramaribo (delpher.nl).

Boksteen, L., 2011, *Deelstudie impact van vergroting beschikbare hoeveelheid water in het bestaande Brokopondo stuwmeer. Project strategische analyse en participatief actieplan voor Zuidoost Suriname*, Paramaribo (parbode.com/wp-content/uploads/2011/12/Lothar-Boksteen.pdf).

Boom, H., 1982, *Staatsgreep in Suriname*, Utrecht.

Boots, A. & R.Woortman, 2009, *Anton de Kom. Biografie*, Amsterdam/Antwerpen.

Bos, D., 1911, *De economische en financiële toestand der kolonie Suriname. Rapport aan de minister van koloniën*, Den Haag (archive.org/stream/deeconomischeenf00neth/deeconomischeenf00neth_djvu.txt).

Bos, D., 1913, *Nader rapport van de Suriname-commissie*, Den Haag.

Bosch, G.B., 1843, *Reizen in West-Indië*, Utrecht (dbnl.org).

Bosch Reitz, G.J.A., et. al., 1868, *Algemeene toelichting tot een plan van immigratie naar Suriname*, Paramaribo (books.google.com).

Bosman, H.W.J., 1948, 'De betalingsbalans en het geldwezen van Suriname tijdens de Tweede Wereldoorlog', in: *New West Indian Guide/Nieuwe West-Indische Gids*, vol. 29(1), 48-54 (brill.com).

Boven, K., 1992, 'De Wayana', in: *SWI Forum*, vol. 9(1-2), Paramaribo, 145-161.

Boven, K., 2006, *Overleven in een grensgebied. Veranderingsprocessen bij de Wayana*, PhD thesis Utrecht University (dspace.library.uu.nl).

Boxer, C.R., 1957, *The Dutch in Brazil*, Oxford.

Brakel, S. van, 1914, 'Een Amsterdamse factorij te Paramaribo in 1613', in: *Bijdragen en Mededeelingen van het Historisch Genootschap*, vol. 35, 83-86 (dbnl.org).

Brana-Shute, G., 1979, *On the corner. Male social life in a Paramaribo Creole neighborhood*, Assen.

Brana-Shute, G. (ed.), 1990, *Resistance and Rebellion in Suriname. Old and New*, Williamsburg.

Brana-Shute, R., 1985, *The manumission of slaves in Suriname 1760-1828*, PhD thesis University of Florida (ufdc.ufl.edu).

Brana-Shute, R. & R.J. Sparks (eds.), 2009, *Paths to Freedom: Manumission in the Atlantic World*, Columbia, SC.

Brandon, P., & U. Bosma, 2019, 'De betekenis van de Atlantische slavernij voor de Nederlandse economie in de tweede helft van de achttiende eeuw', in: *TSEG - The Low Countries Journal of Social and Economic History*, vol. 16(2), 5-46 (tseg.nl/articles).

Brave, I., & R.D. van den Berg, 1998, *Nederland en Suriname. Ontwikkelingssamenwerking van 1975 t/m 1996*, Ministry of Foreign Affairs, The Hague.

Breeveld, H., 1992, *Wissele Mammie*, Paramaribo.

Breeveld, H., 2000, *Jopie Pengel 1916-1970. Leven en werk van een Surinaams Politicus*, PhD thesis Anton de Kom Universiteit Suriname, Schoorl.

Breugel, G.P.C. van, 1842, *Dagverhaal van eene reis naar Paramaribo en verdere omstreken in de kolonie Suriname*, Amsterdam (dbnl.org).

Bruijne, G.A. de, 1976, *Paramaribo, stadsgeografische studies van een Ontwikkelingsland*, Bussum.

Bruijne, G.A. de, 2006, *Libanezen in Suriname. Van Bcharre naar Paramaribo 1890-2006*, Leiden.

Bruijne, A. de, 2007, 'De eigenlijke bevolking van Suriname', in: *OSO, Tijdschrift voor Surinamistiek en het Caraïbisch gebied*, vol. 26(1), 12-26 (dbnl.org).

Bruijning, C.F.A. & J. Voorhoeve (eds.), 1977, *Encyclopedie van Suriname*, Amsterdam/Brussel.

Bubberman, F.C., 1974, 'Uit Suriname's prehistorie; archeologie de basis onzer kennis', in: *Suralco Magazine*, nr. 1, 1-9.

Buddingh', H., 2010, 'Een uitgelezen plek voor nieuwsgierige reporters', in: J. Leerdam & N. Beyer, *Suriname en ik. Persoonlijke verhalen van bekende Surinamers over hun vaderland*, Amsterdam, 76-80.

Buddingh', H., 2021 (1995), *De geschiedenis van Suriname*, Amsterdam.

Burges, Sean, 2018, 'UNASUR's dangerous decline: the risks of a growing left-right split in South America', in: *Americas Quarterly*, May 3, 2018 (americasquarterly.org).

Buschkens, W.F.L., 1974, *The family system of the Paramaribo Creoles*, Den Haag (brill.com).

Campbell, M. C., 1988, *The Maroons of Jamaica 1655-1796. A History of Resistance, Collaboration & Betrayal*, Granby, Mass.

Capitein, J.E.J., 1742, *Staatkundig-Godgeleerd onderzoekschrift over De Slaverny, als niet strydig tegen de Christelijke Vryheid*, PhD thesis Leiden University, Leiden.

Cardenas, O., 1988, *De revolutie van de sergeanten*, Nijmegen.

Chernela, J.M., 1997, 'The Wealth of Nations', in: *Hemisphere*, vol. 8(1), 42-49 (academia.edu/7803471).

Chin, H.E., 1971, 'Suriname. Ontwikkelingshulp en economische ontwikkeling', in: *Internationale Spectator*, vol. 25, issue 15, 1441-1459.

Chin, H. E. & H. Buddingh', 1987, *Surinam. Politics, Economics and Society*, London/New York.

Choenni, C.E.S., 1992, *Hindostanen in de politiek. Een vergelijkende studie van hun positie in Trinidad, Guyana en Suriname*, Rotterdam.

Cock Buning, W. de, 1926, *Rapport over Suriname in opdracht van de Vereniging van Kamers van Koophandel en Fabrieken in Nederland*, Den Haag.

Cohen, R., 1991, *Jews in another environment. Surinam in the second half of the eighteenth century*, Leiden.

Comvalius, Th.A.C., 1936, 'Het Surinaamsch negerlied: De banja en de doe', in: *New West Indian Guide/Nieuwe West-Indische Gids*, vol. 17(1), 213-220 (brill.com).

Coutinho, S.W., 2018, *Breaking Rank. How to lead change when yesterday's stories limit today's choices*.

Dalhuisen, L., M. Hassankhan & F. Steegh (eds.), 2007, *Geschiedenis van Suriname*, Zutphen.

Da Costa, I., 1823, *Bezwaren tegen den Geest der Eeuw*, Leiden (dbnl.org).

Dale Scott, P. & J. Marshall, 1998 (1992) *Cocaine Politics: Drugs, Armies, and the CIA in Central America*, University of California.

Derveld, F.E.R., 1981, *Politieke mobilisatie en integratie van de Javanen in Suriname*, PhD thesis Leiden University, Bedum.

Dew, E., 1972, 'Surinam. The test of consociationalism', in: *Plural Societies*, vol. 3(4), 35-56.

Dew, E., 1996 (1978), *The Difficult Flowering of Surinam. Ethnicity and Politics in a Plural Society*, Den Haag/Paramaribo.

Dew, E., 1994, *The Trouble in Suriname, 1975-1993*, New York.

Dorsthorst, A. te, 2022, *De tragiek van de Binnenlandse Oorlog, Suriname 1986-1992*, Paramaribo.

Dragtenstein, F., 2004, *'Trouw aan de blanken'. Quassie van Nieuw Timotibo, twist en strijd in de 18de eeuw in Suriname*, Amsterdam.

Dragtenstein, F., 2009, *Alles voor de vrede. de brieven van Boston Band tussen 1757 en 1763*, Den Haag.

Drescher, S., 1995, 'The long Goodbye. Dutch Capitalism and Antislavery in Comparative Perspective', in: G. Oostindie (ed.), *Fifty Years Later. Capitalism and Antislavery in the Dutch World*, Leiden.

Elabdi, F., 2021, 'Danish businessmen behind 'dodgy' green energy project in Suriname', in: *Danwatch*, 10 November 2021 (danwatch.dk/en).

Elkins, S., 1959, *Slavery. A Problem in American Institutional and Intellectual Life*, Chicago.

Elout van Soeterwoude, W., 1884, *Onze West*, Den Haag (books.google.com).

Eltis, D., P.C. Emmer & F.D. Lewis, 2016, 'More than profits? The contribution of the slave trade to the Dutch economy: assessing Fatah-Black and Van Rossum', in: *Slavery and Abolition*, vol. 37(4), 724-735 (researchgate.net).

Emmer, P.C., 1981, 'The West India Company, Dutch or Atlantic?', in: L. Blussé & F. Gaastra, *Companies and Trade*, Den Haag, 71-97.

Emmer, P.C., 1989, 'Anti-slavery and the Dutch. Abolition without reform', in: C. Bolt & S. Drescher (eds.), *Anti-Slavery, Religion and Reform. Essays in Memory of Roger Anstey*, Folkestone, 80-98.

Emmer, P.C., 2019, *De geschiedenis van de Nederlandse slavenhandel, 1500-1850*, Amsterdam (3rd rev. ed.).

Equiano, O., 1995 (1798) *The Interesting Narrative of the Life of Olaudah Equiano, or Gustavus Vassa, The African*, London.

Essed, F.E., 1973, *Een volk op weg naar zelfstandigheid*, Paramaribo.

Essed, F.E., 1975, *De mobilisatie van het eigene. Een ruimtelijk fysieke bijdrage aan de integrale planning*, Paramaribo.

Evers, I. & P. van Maele, 2012, *Bouterse aan de macht*, Amsterdam.

Fatah-Black, K., 2013a, *Suriname and the Atlantic World, 1650-1800*, PhD thesis Leiden University, Leiden (scholarlypublications.universiteitleiden.nl).

Fatah-Black, K., 2013b, 'Orangism, Patriotism and Slavery in Curaçao', in: C. Anderson, et al. (eds.), *Mutiny and Maritime Radicalism in the Age of Revolution: A Global Survey*, Cambridge, 35-60.

Fatah-Black, K. & M. van Rossum, 2015, 'Beyond Profitability: The Dutch Transatlantic Slave Trade and its Economic Impact', in: *Slavery & Abolition*, vol. 36 (1), 63-83 (pure.knaw.nl).

Fatah-Black, K., 2015, *White Lies and Black Markets, Evading Metropolitan Authority in Colonial Suriname 1650-1800*, Leiden.

Fatah-Black, K., 2017, 'The usurpation of legal roles by Suriname's Governing Council, 1669-1816', in: *Comparative Legal History*, vol. 5(2), 243-261 (scholarlypublications. universiteitleiden.nl).

Fatah-Black, K., 2018, *Eigendomsstrijd. De Geschiedenis van slavernij en emancipatie in Suriname*, Amsterdam.

Fatah-Black, K., L. Lauret & J. van den Tol, 2022, *Dienstbaar aan de keten? De Nederlandsche Bank en de laatste decennia van de slavernij, 1814-1863*, Leiden (dnb.nl/media/osjhordo/dienstbaar-aan-de-keten-dnb-en-de-laatste-decennia-van-de-slavernij-1814-1863-2.pdf). English summary: dnb.nl/media/ilvjlw4q/serving-the-chain.pdf.

Fermin, P., 1770, *Nieuwe algemeene beschryving van de colonie van Suriname*, (vols. 1, 2), Harlingen (dbnl.org). French ed. 1769.

Fernandes Mendes, H.K., 1989, *Onafhankelijkheid en parlementair stelsel in Suriname. Hoofdlijnen van een nieuw en democratisch staatsbestel*, Zwolle.

Fogel, R.W. & S.L.Engerman, 1974, *Time on the cross. The Economics of American Negro Slavery*, New York.

Fogel, R.W., 1991, *Without consent or contract*, New York/London.

French, H.W., 2021, *Born in Blackness; Africa, Africans, and the Making of the Modern World, 1471 to the Second World War*, New York.

Furnivall, J.S., 1939, *Netherlands India. A Study of Plural Economy*, London.

Furnivall, J.S., 1945, 'Some Problems of Tropical Economy', in: R. Hinden (ed.), *Fabian Colonial Essays*, London.

Gelder, R. van, 2018, *Dichter in de Jungle, John Gabriel Stedman 1744-1797*, Amsterdam.

Genovese, E. D., 1972, *Roll, Jordan, Roll. The World the Slaves Made*, New York.

Gobardhan-Rambocus, L., 2001, *Onderwijs als sleutel tot maatschappelijke vooruitgang. Een taal- en onderwijsgeschiedenis van Suriname, 1651-1975*, PhD thesis Leiden University, Zutphen.

Gobardhan-Rambocus, L., 2008, 'Spiegel van een verdeelde samenleving. De pers in jaren van sociale onrust, 1863-1937', in: M. de Koninck & A. Sumter et al. (eds.), *K'ranti! De Surinaamse pers 1774-2008*, 55-88, Amsterdam.

Goeje, C.H. de, 1941, 'De Oyana-Indianen', in: *Bijdragen tot de Taal-, Land- en Volkenkunde*, vol. 1(2), 71-125 (brill.com).

Goslinga, C., 1971, *The Dutch in the Caribbean and on the Wild Coast, 1580-1680*, Assen.

Gowricharn, R.S., 1990, *Economische transformatie en de staat. Over agrarische modernisering en economische ontwikkeling in Suriname, 1930-1960*, PhD thesis Utrecht University, Den Haag.

Graaff, B. de & C. Wiebes. 1998, *Villa Maarheze. De geschiedenis van de inlichtingendienst buitenland*, Den Haag.

Groenfelt, E. & J. Menke, 1996, 'Statistisch overzicht verkiezingsuitslagen', in: J. Menke (ed.), *Politiek in Suriname. Politieke ontwikkelingen en verkiezingen voor en na 23 mei 1996*, Paramaribo, 68-76.

Groot, S.W. de, 1982, 'Marrons versus kolonisten', in: *OSO, Tijdschrift voor Surinamistiek en het Caraïbisch gebied*, vol. 1(2), 63-73 (dbnl.org).

Groot, S.W., 1984, 'A comparison between the history of maroon communities in Surinam and Jamaica: An introduction', in: *OSO, Tijdschrift voorSurinamistiek en het Caraïbisch gebied*, vol. 3, 73-82 (dbnl.org).

Groot, S.W. de, 1989, 'Het Korps Zwarte Jagers in Suriname. Collaboratie en Opstand', in: *OSO, Tijdschrift voor Surinamistiek en het Caraïbisch gebied*, vol. 7(2), 147-160 and vol. 8(1), 7-20 (dbnl.org).

Haakmat, A., 1987, *De revolutie uitgegleden*, Amsterdam.

Haenen, M. & H. Buddingh', 1994, *De Danser. Hoe de drugshandel Nederland veroverde*, Amsterdam.

Haenen, M., 1999, *Baas Bouterse. De krankzinnige klopjacht op het Surinaamse drugskartel*, Amsterdam.

Haens, W.H.M. d', 1947, *Rapport i.z. de reorganisatie van het onderwijs in Suriname*, Paramaribo.

Hardner, J. & R. Rice, 2001, 'Economic Opportunities for Forest Resource Use', in: P. van Dijck, *Suriname. The economy, prospects for sustainable development*, Kingston, 247-275.

Harlow, V.T., (ed.), 1971, *Ralegh's Last Voyage* [...], Amsterdam/New York (repr. of 1932).

Hartsinck, J.J., 1770, *Beschryving van Guiana, of de Wilde kust, in Zuid-America*, 2 vols., Amsterdam (dbnl.org).

Hassankhan, M.S., 1993, 'Immigratie en integratie van contractarbeiders. Hindostanen en Javanen in Suriname', in: L. Gobardhan-Rambocus & M.S. Hassankhan, *Immigratie en Ontwikkeling. Emancipatie van contractanten*, Paramaribo, 69-117.

Heemskerk, M., 2009, *Kleinschalige goudwinning in Suriname, een overzicht van sociaaleconomische, politieke en milieu-aspecten*, Amsterdam (adoc.pub/kleinschalige-goudwinning-in-suriname-een-overzicht-van-soci.html).

Heemskerk, M., 2010, *The Gold Marketing Chain in Suriname* (Report for WWF Guianas), Paramaribo (respect.international/the-gold-marketing-chain-in-suriname).

Heijer, H. den, 2013 (1994) *De geschiedenis van de WIC*, Zutphen.

Heilbron, W., 1982, *Kleine boeren in de schaduw van de plantage. De politieke economie van de na-slavernijperiode in Suriname*, PhD thesis Erasmus Universiteit Rotterdam, Paramaribo.

Heilbron, W. & G. Willemsen, 1980, 'Goud- en balata-exploitatie in Suriname', in: *Caraïbisch Forum*, vol. 1(1), 66-84; vol. 1(2), 87-101.

Heldring, A., 2011, *Het Saramacca Project. Een plan van joodse kolonisatie in Suriname 1946-1956*, Hilversum.

Helman, A., 1926, *Zuid-Zuid-West*, Utrecht (dbnl.org).

Helman, A., 1977a, *Cultureel Mozaïek van Suriname*, Zutphen (dbnl.org).

Helman, A., 1977b, *Facetten van de Surinaamse samenleving*, Zutphen (dbnl.org).

Helman, A., 1983, *De foltering van Eldorado. Een ecologische geschiedenis van de vijf Guyana's*, The Hague (dbnl.org).

Herlein, J.D., 1718, *Beschryvinge van de volksplantinge Zuriname*, Leeuwarden (dbnl.org).

Hengel, G. van, 2017, 'Zwarte dinsdag. Het bloedige einde van een volksopstand', in: *Historisch Nieuwsblad*, vol. 26(12), 23-27.

Heuvel, J. van den, 1999, *De jacht op Desi Bouterse. Hoe het Suri-kartel de Nederlandse drugsmarkt veroverde*, Den Haag.

Higman, B.W., 1995 (1984) *Slave Populations of the British Caribbean, 1807-1834*, University of the West Indies.

Hira, S., 1982, *Van Priary tot en met De Kom, de geschiedenis van het verzet in Suriname, 1630-1940*, Rotterdam.

Hirschland, F., 1993, *Dossier Moengo 290 uur*, Den Haag.

Hoefte, R., 1987a, 'Het politiek bewustzijn van Hindostaanse en Javaanse contractarbeiders, 1910-1940' in: *OSO, Tijdschrift voor Surinamistiek en het Caraïbisch gebied*, vol. 6(1), 25-35 (dbnl.org).

Hoefte, R., 1987b, *Plantation labor after the abolition of slavery. The case of plantation Mariënburg (Suriname), 1880-1940*, PhD thesis University of Florida, Gainesville.

Hoefte, R., 1990a, *De betovering verbroken. De immigratie van Javanen naar Suriname en het rapport Van Vleuten (1909)*, Dordrecht.

Hoefte, R., 1990b,'De beeldvorming omtrent de Javaanse cultuur in Suriname', in: *OSO, Tijdschrift voor Surinamistiek en het Caraïbisch gebied*, vol. 9(2), 7-19 (dbnl.org).

Hoogbergen, W.S.M., 1984, *De Boni's in Frans-Guyana en de Tweede Boni-oorlog 1776-1793*, Utrecht.

Hoogbergen, W., 1985, *De Boni-oorlogen, 1757-1869: marronage en guerilla in Oost-Suriname*, PhD thesis Utrecht University, Utrecht.

Hoogbergen, W., 1989, 'Aluku', in: *New West Indian Guide/Nieuwe West-Indische Gids*, vol. 63 (3/4), 175-198 (brill.com).

Hoogbergen, W., 1990, *The Boni Maroon Wars in Suriname*, Leiden.

Hoogbergen, W., 1996, *Het kamp van Broos en Kaliko. De geschiedenis van een Afro-Surinaamse familie*, Amsterdam.

Hoogbergen, W. & O. Ten Hove, 2001, 'De vrije gekleurde en zwarte bevolking van Paramaribo, 1762-1863', in: *OSO, Tijdschrift voor Surinamistiek en het Caraïbisch gebied*, vol. 20(2), 306-320 (dbnl.org).

Hoogbergen, W. & Kruijt, D., 2005, *De oorlog van de sergeanten. Surinaamse militairen in de politiek*, Amsterdam.

Hoppe, R., 1975, 'Het politiek systeem van Suriname. Elite-karteldemocratie', in: *Acta politica*, vol. 11, 145-177.

Hurault, J., 1960, 'Histoire des Noirs Refugiés Boni de la Guyana Française', in: *Revue Française d'Histoire d'Outre-Mer*, vol. 47, 76-137 (persee.fr/collection/outre).

Ismael, J., 1949, *De immigratie van Indonesiërs in Suriname*, PhD thesis Leiden University, Leiden.

Jabini, F.S., 2012, *Christianity in Suriname. An overview of its history, theologians and sources*, Carlisle.

James, C.L.R., 1963, *The black Jacobins. Toussaint L'Ouverture and the San Domingo Revolution*, New York.

Jansen van Galen, J., 1995, *Kapotte Plantage. Suriname, een Hollandse erfenis*, Amsterdam.

Jansen van Galen, J., 2000, *Hetenachtsdroom. Suriname, erfenis van de slavernij*, Amsterdam.

Jansen van Galen, J., 2005, *Laatste gouverneur, eerste president. De eeuw van Johan Ferrier, Surinamer*, Leiden.

Janssen, J.J., 1974, 'Uit Suriname's prehistorie, De Surinaamse Indianen, wie zijn zij en waar kwamen zij vandaan', in: *Suralco Magazine*, nr. 1, Paramaribo, 10-20.

Janssen, R., 2011, *In search of a path. An analysis of the foreign policy of Suriname from 1975 to 1991*, Leiden (brill.com/view/title/23063).

Jong, L. de, 1979, *Het Koninkrijk der Nederlanden in de Tweede Wereldoorlog*, vol. 9, part 1, Amsterdam (niod.nl).

Jurna, N., 2007, *Van onze correspondent. Standplaats Paramaribo*, Amsterdam.

Kagie, R., 1980, *Een gewezen wingewest. Suriname voor en na de staatsgreep*, Bussum.

Kagie, R, 2012, *Bikkel. Het verhaal van de eerste politieke moord van het Bouterse-Regime*, Amsterdam.

Kambel, E.R. & F. MacKay, 2003, *De rechten van inheemse volken en marrons in Suriname*, Leiden.

Kappler, A., 1854, *Zes jaren in Suriname. Schetsen en tafereelen uit het maatschappelijk en militair leven in deze kolonie*, Utrecht (dbnl.org).

Kars, M., 2020, *Blood on the River. A Chronicle of Mutiny and Freedom on the Wild Coast*, New York.

Keenswijk-Fung A Loi, J.A.D., M. Nankoe & R. Sobhie, 2016, 'Werkgelegenheid in Suriname van 2004 tot 2012', in: J. Menke (ed.), *Mozaïek van het Surinaamse volk: volkstellingen in demografisch, economisch en sociaal perspectief*, Paramaribo, 241-262 (statistics-suriname.org).

Kempen, M. van, 2002, *Een geschiedenis van de Surinaamse literatuur* (5 vols.), PhD thesis University of Amsterdam, Paramaribo (dbnl.org).

Kempen, M. van, 2016, *Rusteloos en overal. Het leven van Albert Helman*, Haarlem.

Kesler, C.K., 1930, 'Duistere bladzijden uit de geschiedenis van Suriname', in: *New West Indian Guide/Nieuwe West-Indische Gids*, vol. 11(1), 113-141 (brill.com).

Khemradj, R., 2002, *Jagernath Lachmon. Een politiek testament*, Amsterdam.

Klerk, C.J.M. de, 1953 (1999), *De immigratie van Hindostanen in Suriname*, Amsterdam, Den Haag (ufdc.ufl.edu).

Klinkers, E., 1997, *Op Hoop Van Vrijheid. Van Slavensamenleving naar Creoolse Gemeenschap in Suriname, 1830-1880*, PhD thesis Leiden University, Utrecht.

Kloos, P., 1971, *The Maroni River Caribs of Surinam*, Assen.

Köbben, A.J.F., 1979, *In vrijheid en gebondenheid: samenleving en cultuur van de Djoeka aan de Cottica*, Utrecht.

Kolfin, E., 1997, *Van de Slavenzweep & de Muze. Twee eeuwen verbeelding van slavernij in Suriname*, Leiden.

Koeman, C. (ed.), 1973, *Schakels met het verleden. De geschiedenis van de kartografie van Suriname 1500-1971*, Amsterdam.

Kom, A. de, 1981 (1934, 2020), *Wij slaven van Suriname*, Amsterdam (dbnl.org).

Kruijt, D. & M. Maks, 2003, *Een belaste relatie. 25 jaar ontwikkelingssamenwerking Nederland-Suriname, 1975-2000*, 17 December 2003. (Kamerstuk, 20361, nr. 113 (zoek. officielebekendmakingen.nl/kst-20361-113.html).

Kruijt, D., 2020, 'Suriname: The National Army in Politics', in: *Oxford Research Encyclopedia of Politics*, December 2020 (oxfordre.com/ politics).

Kuhn, F.A., 1828, *Beschouwing van den toestand der Surinaamsche plantagieslaven*, Amsterdam (books.google.com).

Lambert, F.K., M. Schalkwijk & E. Ritfeld, 2016, 'Binnenlandse en buitenlandse migratiepatronen 2004-2012', in: J. Menke (ed.), *Mozaïek van het Surinaamse volk: volkstellingen in demografisch, economisch en sociaal perspectief*, Paramaribo, 95-111 (statistics-suriname.org).

Lammens, A.F., 1982, *Bijdragen tot de kennis van de kolonie Suriname, tijdvak 1816-1822* (ed. G.A. de Bruijne), Amsterdam.

Lamur, C., 1983, *The American take-over. Industrial emergence and Alcoa's expansion in Guyana and Suriname (with special reference to Suriname 1919-1921)*, PhD thesis Anton de Kom University Suriname (rev. ed. Dordrecht, 1985).

Lamur, H.E., 1977, 'Demography of Surinam plantation slaves in the last decade before Emancipation: the case of Catharina Sophia', in: V. Rubin & A. Tuden, *Comparative Perspectives on Slavery in New World Plantation Societies*, New York, 161-173.

Lamur, H. E., 1981, 'Demographic Performance of Two Slave Populations of the Dutch Speaking Caribbean', in: *Boletin de Estudios Latino Americanas y del Caribe*, 30, 87-102 (dare.uva.nl).

Lamur, H. E., 1985, *De Kerstening van slaven van de Surinaamse plantage Vossenburg 1847-1878*, Amsterdam.

Lamur, H. E., 1987, *The production of sugar and the reproduction of slaves at Vossenburg, Suriname 1705-1863*, Amsterdam.

Lans, W.H., 1842, *Bijdrage tot de kennis der kolonie Suriname*, Den Haag (books.google.com).

Lenders, M., 1996, *Strijders voor het Lam. Leven en werk van Hernhutterbroeders en -zusters in Suriname, 1735-1900*, PhD thesis University of Amsterdam, Leiden.

Lichtveld, U.M. & J. Voorhoeve, 1980, *Suriname: Spiegel der vaderlandse kooplieden. Een historisch leesboek*, Den Haag (dbnl.org).

Lier, R.A.J. van, 1950, *The development and nature of society in the West Indies*, Amsterdam.

Lier, R.A.J. van, 1971, *Frontier Society: A Social Analysis of the History of Surinam*, The Hague (transl. from Dutch).

Lier, R.A.J. van, 1977 (1949), *Samenleving in een grensgebied: een sociaal-historische studie van Suriname*, Amsterdam (3rd rev. ed.).

Lijphart, A., 1969, 'Consociational Democracy', in: *World Politics*, vol. 21(2), 207-225 (cambridge.org/core/journals).

Lijphart, A., 1971, 'Cultural Diversity and theories of Political Integration', in: *Canadian Journal of Political Science*, vol. 4 (1), 1-14 (cambridge.org/ core/journals).

Lim A Po, H., 2007, *Van de 'rule of political law' naar de 'rule of professional law'. Onze rechtsstaat onder druk van globalisatie en devaluatie*, 6th Fred Derby Lecture, Paramaribo, 18 May 2007 (unpubl. ms.).

Linde, J.M. van der, 1963, *Heren, slaven, broeders: momenten uit de geschiedenis der Slavernij*, Nijkerk.

Linde, J.M. van der, 1966, *Surinaamse suikerheren en hun kerk. Plantagekolonie en handelskerk ten tijde van Johannes Basseliers, predikant en planter in Suriname, 1667-1689*, Wageningen.

Linde, J.M. van der, 1987, *Jan Willem Kals. Leraar der Hervormden. Advocaat van Indiaan en Neger*, Kampen.

Lohnstein, M.J., 1987, 'De werving van de militie in Suriname in de 18e eeuw', in: *OSO, Tijdschrift voor Surinamistiek en het Caraïbisch gebied*, vol. 6, 67-84 (dbnl.org).

Loor, A.H., 1992, *Gedenkboek van de Centrale Bank van Suriname*, Paramaribo.

Loor, A.H. & E.W. van Brussel, 1995, *150 jaar boerenkolonisatie in Suriname, 1845-1995*, Paramaribo.

Lotens, W., 2000, *Gesprekken aan de Waterkant*, Paramaribo.

Marshall, E., 2003, *Ontstaan en ontwikkeling van het Surinaams nationalisme. Natievorming als opgave*, Delft.

Marshall, E., 2010, *De arbeiders zijn me heilig. Fred Derby vakbondsleider en politicus*, Amsterdam.

Martin, D., 2001, *Governance in Suriname*, Inter-American Development Bank, April 2001 (publications.iadb.org).

Mbeki, L. & M. van Rossum, 2017, 'Private slave trade in the Dutch Indian Ocean world: a study into the networks and backgrounds of the slavers and the enslaved in South Asia and South Africa', in: *Slavery & Abolition*, vol. 38 (1), 95-116 (doi.org/10.1080/0144 039X.2016.1159004).

McKee, H., 2018, 'From violence to alliance: Maroons and white settlers in Jamaica, 1739-1795', in: *Slavery & Abolition*, vol. 39 (1), 27-52 (tandfonline.com).

McLeod, C., 1993, *Elizabeth Samson. Een vrije, zwarte vrouw in het 18e-eeuwse Suriname*, Utrecht.

Meel, P., 1990, 'A reluctant embrace. Suriname's idle quest for independence', in: G. Brana-Shute (ed.), *Resistance and rebellion in Suriname. Old and new*, Williamsburg, 259-290.

Meel, P., 1998, 'Towards a typology of Suriname nationalism', in: *New West Indian Guide/ Nieuwe West-Indische Gids*, vol. 72(3-4), 257-281 (brill.com).

Meel, P., 1999, *Tussen autonomie en onafhankelijkheid. Nederlands-Surinaamse betrekkingen 1954-1961*, PhD thesis Utrecht University, Leiden.

Meel, P., 2009, 'Anton de Kom and the Formative Phase of Surinamese Decolonisation', in: *New West Indian Guide/Nieuwe West-Indische Gids*, vol. 83(3-4), 249-280 (brill.com).

Meel, P., 2011, 'Diverging Directions: Race, Culture and Class in the Works of Anton de Kom and Caribbean Contemporaries', in: B. Meeks (ed.), *Caribbean Reasonings - M.G. Smith: Social Theory and Anthropology in the Caribbean and Beyond*, Kingston/ Miami, 221-243.

Meel, P., 2014, *Man van het moment. Een politieke biografie van Henck Arron*, Amsterdam.

Meel, P., 2022, 'Power Sharing, Nation Building and Social Justice', in: H. Henke & F. Reno (eds.), *New political culture in the Caribbean*, UWI Press, 195-214.

Meiden, G.W. van der, 1987 (2008) *Betwist Bestuur. Een eeuw strijd om de macht in Suriname, 1651-1753*, PhD thesis Leiden University, Amsterdam.

Meijvogel, M., 2017, *Nederlandse abolitionisten en Surinaamse slaven. De Nederlandse abolitionistische beweging en de vrijkoping van slaven 1856-1863*, Bachelor thesis Leiden University, Leiden.

Menke, J. (ed.), 1996, *Politiek in Suriname. Politieke ontwikkelingen en verkiezingen voor en na 23 mei 1996*, Paramaribo.

Menke, J., 1998, *Restructuring Urban Employment and Poverty. The Case of Suriname*, PhD thesis University of Amsterdam, Paramaribo.

Menke, J. (ed.), 2004, *Beleidsontwikkeling bij politieke partijen in Suriname*, Paramaribo.

Menke, J. (ed.), 2008, *Natievorming en natiecreatie in Suriname*, Paramaribo.

Menke, J., 2009, *Het spanningsveld tussen methodologie en diversiteit in de samenleving*, Paramaribo.

Menke, J. & I. Sno, 2016, 'Ras en etniciteit in volkstellingen in Suriname', in: J. Menke (ed.), *Mozaïek van het Surinaamse volk, volkstellingen in demografisch economisch en sociaal perspectief*, Paramaribo, 76-94 (statistics-suriname.org/wp-content/uploads/2019/02/mozaiek-van-het-surinaamse-volk-versie-5.pdf).

Mijs, A.A., 1973, *Onderwijs en Ontwikkeling in Suriname*, Amsterdam.

Mintz, S.W. & R. Price, 1992, *The Birth of African-American Culture. An anthropological perspective*, Boston (former 1976 title: *An anthropological approach to the Afro-American past. A Caribbean perspective*, Philadelphia).

Mitrasing, F.E.M., 1959, *Tien jaar Suriname: van afhankelijkheid tot gelijkgerechtigheid: bijdrage tot de kennis van de staatkundige ontwikkeling van Suriname van 1945-1955*, PhD thesis Leiden University, Leiden.

Moerland, J., 1984, *Suriname. Landendocumentatie*, Zutphen.

Molendijk-Dijk, E.F., 1992, *Indianen in Zeeuwse bronnen. Brieven over Indianen in Suriname tijdens het Zeeuwse bewind gedurende de periode 1667-1682*, Paramaribo.

Multatuli, 1987, *Max Havelaar, or, The Coffee Auctions of the Dutch Trading Company*, London.

Naipaul, V.S., 1962, *The Middle Passage. Impressions of five colonial societies, British, French and Dutch, in the West Indies and South America.* London.

Naipaul, V.S., 1972, 'Power?', in: *The Overcrowded Barracoon and Other Articles*, London, 246-254.

Nassy, D. C., et al., 1788, *Essai historique sur la colonie de Surinam avec l'histoire de la nation Juive Portugaise & Allemande y etablie*, Paramaribo (delpher.nl).

Neslo, E., 2015, 'The formation of a free non-white elite in Paramaribo, 1800-1863', in: *Caribbean Studies*, vol. 43(2), 177-210 (semanticscholar.org/ paper).

Neslo, E., 2016, *Een ongekende elite. De opkomst van een gekleurde elite in koloniaal Suriname 1800-1863*, PhD thesis Utrecht University, Utrecht (dspace.library.uu.nl).

Oomens, M., 1983, *De positie van plantageslaven in Suriname 1808-1863*, Amsterdam.

Oostindie, G., 1989, *Roosenburg en Mon Bijou. Twee Surinaamse plantages, 1720-1870*, PhD thesis Leiden University, Dordrecht (pure.knaw.nl).

Oostindie, G., 1992, 'The Enlightenment, Christianity and the Suriname Slave', in: *The Journal of Caribbean History*, vol. 26(2), 147-170 (pure.knaw.nl).

Oostindie, G., 1993, 'Voltaire, Stedman and Suriname Slavery', in: *Slavery and Abolition*, vol. 14(2), 1-34 (pure.knaw.nl).

Oostindie, G., 1994, *Caraïbische dilemma's in een 'stagnerend' dekolonisatieproces*, Leiden (pure.knaw.nl).

Oostindie, G., 2006, 'The Study of Ethnicity in the Dutch Caribbean. Full Circle to Furnivall?', in: *Latin American and Caribbean Ethnic Studies*, vol. 1(2), 215-230.

Oostindie, G., 2008, *Democratie en deugdzaamheid* (lecture series), Willemstad.

Oostindie, G., 2012, 'History Brought Home: Postcolonial Migrations and the Dutch Rediscovery of Slavery', in: U. Bosma (ed.), *Postcolonialism in the Netherlands*, Amsterdam, 155-173 (pure.knaw.nl).

Oostindie, G. & I. Klinkers, 2001, *Het Koninkrijk in de Caraïben. Een korte geschiedenis van het Nederlandse kolonisatiebeleid 1940-2000*, Amsterdam.

Oudschans Dentz, F., 1927, *De kolonisatie der Portugees Joodsche Natie in Suriname en de geschiedenis van Joden Savanne*, Amsterdam (delpher.nl).

Oudschans Dentz, F., 1938, *Cornelis van Aerssen van Sommelsdijck, een belangwekkende figuur uit de geschiedenis van Suriname*, Amsterdam (delpher.nl).

Oudschans Dentz, F., 1955, 'Grepen uit de geschiedenis van het onderwijs in Suriname in de 17e en 18e eeuw', in: *New West Indian Guide/Nieuwe West-Indische Gids*, vol. 36(1), 174-182 (brill.com).

Paasman, A.N., 1984, *Reinhart. Nederlandse literatuur en slavernij ten tijde van de Verlichting*, PhD thesis Universiteit van Amsterdam, Leiden (dbnl.org).

Pakosie, A., 2009, 'Gaanman en Asantahene, Kabiten en Omanhene. Een vergelijking van twee traditionele gezagsstructuren: Ndyuka en Asante', in: *Siboga*, vol. 19(2), 3-29.

Palthe Wesenhagen, J.C., 1849, *Beschouwingen betreffende de vrijverklaring der slaven in de kolonie Suriname*, Amsterdam (books.google.com).

Panday, R.M.N., 1959, *Agriculture in Surinam 1650-1950, an inquiry into the causes of its decline*, PhD thesis University of Amsterdam, Amsterdam/Paris.

Parker, M., 2015, *Willoughbyland. England's Lost Colony*, London.

Paula, A.F., 1993, *'Vrije' slaven. Een sociaal-historische studie over de dualistische slavenemancipatie op Nederlands Sint Maarten 1816-1863*, PhD thesis Utrecht University, Zutphen.

Penard F.P. & A.P. Penard, 1907/08, *De menschetende aanbidders der zonneslang*, vols. 1-3, Paramaribo (dbnl.org).

Penta, K., 2002, *A mercenary's tale. Hijacking, kidnapping and assassination*, London.

Pijl, Y. van der, 2007, *Levende-doden. Afrikaans-Surinaamse percepties, praktijken en rituelen rondom dood en rouw*, PhD thesis Utrecht University, Amsterdam (dspace. library.uu.nl).

Pistorius, Th., 1763, *Korte en zakelyke beschryvinge van de colonie van Zuriname*, Amsterdam (dbnl.org).

Postma, J., 1990, *The Dutch in the Atlantic slave trade, 1600-1815*, Cambridge.

Postma, J., 2003a, 'A Reassessment of the Dutch Altlantic Slave Trade', in: J. Postma & V. Enthoven (eds.), *Riches from Atlantic Commerce. Dutch transatlantic trade and shipping*, Leiden, 115-139.

Postma, J., 2003b, 'Suriname and its Atlantic Connections, 1667-1795', in: J. Postma & V. Enthoven (eds.), *Riches from Atlantic Commerce. Dutch transatlantic trade and shipping 1585-1817*, Leiden, 287-322.

Price, R., 1976, *The Guiana Maroon Wars: A Historical and Bibliographical Introduction*, Baltimore.

Price, R., 1983, *First time. The historical vision of an Afro-American people*, Baltimore/London.

Price, R., 1990, *Alabi's world*, Baltimore/London.

Price, R., 2001, 'The miracle of creolization, a retrospective', in: *New West Indian Guide/ Nieuwe West-Indische Gids*, vol. 75(1-2), 35-64 (brill.com).

Price, R., 2011, *Rainforest Warriors. Human Rights on Trial*, Philadelphia.

Price, R., 2013 (1973), *Maroon Societies: Rebel Slave Communities in the Americas*, New York.

Pronk, J., 2020, *Van wingewest tot natiestaat*, Volendam.

Quintus Bos, A.J.A., 1964, 'De Ontwikkeling van de Rechtspositie van de vroegere Plantageslaven in Suriname', in: Surinaamse Historische Kring, *Emancipatie 1863-1963. Biografieën*, Paramaribo (dbnl.org).

Ramcharan, N., 2008, 'Het donkerste tijdperk voor de persvrijheid. De pers tijdens de militaire dictatuur, 1980-1987', in: M. de Koninck & A. Sumter (eds.) *K'ranti! De Surinaamse pers 1774-2008*, Amsterdam, 173-190.

Ramsoedh, H., 1990, *Suriname 1933-1944. Koloniale politiek en beleid onder gouverneur Kielstra*, PhD thesis Utrecht University, Delft.

Ramsoedh, H., 1993, 'De geforceerde onafhankelijkheid', in: *OSO, Tijdschrift voor Surinamistiek en het Caraïbisch gebied*, vol. 12, 43-62 (dbnl.org).

Ramsoedh, H., 1995, 'Helmans politieke kruistochten', in: *OSO, Tijdschrift voor Surinamistiek en het Caraïbisch gebied*, vol. 14(1), 22-36 (dbnl.org).

Ramsoedh, H., 1997, 'Klassenstrijd versus verbroederingspolitiek. Het politiek leiderschap van Jagan en Lachmon', in*: OSO, Tijdschrift voor Surinamistiek en het Caraïbisch gebied*, vol.16(1), 155-170 (dbnl.org).

Ramsoedh, H., 2018, *Surinaams onbehagen. Een sociale en politieke geschiedenis van Suriname,1865-2015*, Hilversum.

Reagan, R., 2007, *The Reagan Diaries*, New York.

Reeder, A., J. Rijssen & R. Wijks, 2019, *Op zoek naar Papa Koenders*, Volendam.

Reeser, P., 2015, *Desi Bouterse, een Surinaamse tragedie*, Amsterdam.

Reesse, J.J., 1908, *De suikerhandel van Amsterdam van het begin der 17e eeuw tot 1813.* [...], Haarlem (delpher.nl).

Reesse, J.J., 1911, *De suikerhandel van Amsterdam van 1813 tot 1894. Een bijdrage tot de handelsgeschiedenis des vaderlands, hoofdzakelijk uit de archieven verzameld en samengesteld*, Den Haag.

Renselaar, H.C. van, 1963, 'De houding van de Creoolse bevolkingsgroep in Suriname ten opzichte van andere bevolkingsgroepen (in het bijzonder ten opzichte van de Hindostanen)', in: *Bijdragen tot de Taal-, Land-, en Volkenkunde*, vol. 119(1), 93-105 (brill.com).

Rijsdijk, H.E., 1975, *Programma voor de sociaal-economische ontwikkeling van Suriname*, Paramaribo.

Roemer, A., 2016, *Onmogelijk moederland*, Amsterdam.

Samson, Ph., 1947, 'Kiesvereenigingen in Suriname', in: *New West Indian Guide/Nieuwe West-Indische Gids*, vol. 28(1), 161-174 (brill.com).

Samuels, J., 1946, *Schetsen en typen uit Suriname*, Paramaribo (dbnl.org).

Schaaijk, M. & J. van der Straaten, 1984, 'Suriname's economie en de ontwikkelingssamenwerking Nederland-Suriname', in: *Economisch Statistische Berichten*, 7 november 1984, 1040-1047 (researchgate.net/profile/M-Schaaijk).

Schalkwijk, A. & A. de Bruijne, 1997, *Van Mon Plaisir tot Ephraïmszegen; welstand, etniciteit en woonpatronen in Paramaribo*, Amsterdam.

Schalkwijk, M., 1969, 'De etnische stem in de Surinaamse politiek', in: J.

Menke, *Politiek in Suriname. Politieke ontwikkelingen en verkiezingen voor en na 23 mei 1996*, Paramaribo, 32-49.

Schalkwijk, M., 2000, 'Een analyse van de gevoerde campagne en uitslag van de verkiezingen van mei 2000', in: J. Menke (ed.), *Politiek Suriname. Traditie en verandering rond het jaar 2000*, Paramaribo.

Schalkwijk, M., 2009, *Ontwikkeling als blijvende uitdaging*, Paramaribo (nikos.sr/publications).

Schalkwijk, M., 2011, *The Colonial State in the Caribbean. Structural Analysis and Changing Elite Networks in Suriname 1650-1920*, Amsterdam.

Scheer, P., 1995, 'Voor Koningin en Moederland', in: *OSO, Tijdschrift voor Surinamistiek en het Caraïbisch gebied*, vol. 14(2), 188-194 (dbnl.org).

Schiltkamp, J.A. & J.Th. de Smidt (eds.), 1973, *West Indisch Plakaatboek. Plakaten, ordonnantiën en andere wetten uitgevaardigd in Suriname, 1667-1816*, 2 vols., Amsterdam.

Scholtens, B., 1985, *Suriname tijdens de Tweede Wereldoorlog*, Paramaribo.

Scholtens, B., 1986, *Opkomende arbeidersbeweging in Suriname. Doedel, Liesdek, De Sanders, De Kom en de werklozenonrust 1931-1933*, Nijmegen.

Scholtens, B., 1987, *Louis Doedel, Surinaams vakbondsleider van het eerste uur. Een bronnenpublikatie*, Paramaribo.

Scholtens, B., 1994, *Bosnegers en overheid in Suriname. De ontwikkeling van de politieke verhouding, 1651-1992*, PhD thesis Radboud University, Nijmegen (repository.ubn.ru.nl).

Schwartz, S.B., 1985, *Sugar Plantations in the Formation of Brazilian Society. Bahia, 1550-1835*, Cambridge.

Sedney, J., 2017 (1997). *De toekomst van ons verleden. Democratie, etniciteit en politieke machtsvorming in Suriname*, Paramaribo.

Sedoc-Dahlberg, B. (ed.), 1990, *The Dutch Caribbean. Prospects for Democracy*, New York.

Siwpersad, J.P., 1979, *De Nederlandse regering en de afschaffing van de Surinaamse slavernij (1833-1863)*, PhD thesis Rijksuniversiteit Groningen, Groningen.

Shultz, G., 1993, *Turmoil and Triumph*, Washington.

Simons, G., 1996, *Cuba: From Conquistador to Castro*, London.

Smit, A.L., 1947, *Surinaamse Bauxiet Maskerade*, Paramaribo.

Sobhie, R., A.D. Abreu-Kisoensingh, & G. Dekkers, 2016, 'Materiële welvaart en armoede onder huishoudens', in: J. Menke, *Mozaïek van het Surinaamse volk: volkstellingen in demografisch, economisch en sociaal perspectief*, Paramaribo, 263-284 (statistics-suriname.org).

Soedhwa, B., 2005, *Longitudinal analysis of possible links between poverty and mortality in Suriname* (General Bureau of Statistics), Paramaribo (cicred.org/Eng/Seminars/Details/Seminars/Trivandrum2005/Trivandrum0205.htm).

Speckman, J.D., 1963, 'De houding van de Hindostaanse bevolkingsgroep ten opzichte van de Creolen', in: *Bijdragen tot de Taal-, Land- en Volkenkunde*, vol. 119 (1), 76-92 (brill.com).

Staal, G.J., 1928, *Nederlandsch Guyana. Een kort begrip van Suriname*, Amsterdam (dbnl.org).

Stedman, J.G., 2010 (1988), *Narrative of a Five Years Expedition against the Revolted Negroes of Surinam* (first transcription of the original 1790 ms.; edited, introduced and annotated by R. Price & S. Price), Baltimore.

Stedman, J.G., 1987 (1799, 1806) *Reize naar Surinamen*, Zutphen.

Stipriaan, A. van, 1990, 'What's in a name? Slavernij en naamgeving in Suriname tijdens de 18e en 19e eeuw', in: *OSO, Tijdschrift voor Surinamistiek en het Caraïbisch gebied*, vol. 9(1), 25-46 (dbnl.org).

Stipriaan, A. van, 1993, *Surinaams Contrast. Roofbouw en overleven in een Caraïbische plantagekolonie, 1750-1863*, PhD thesis Vrije Universiteit Amsterdam, Leiden (alexvanstipriaan.com).

Stipriaan, A. van, 2006, 'Slavery in the Dutch Caribbean: The Books No One Has Read', in: J. De Barros et al. (eds.), *Beyond Fragmentation: Perspectives on Caribbean History*, Princeton, 69-92 (researchgate.net).

Suparlan, P., 1995 (1976), *The Javanese in Surinam. Ethnicity in an ethnically plural society*, PhD thesis University of Illinois, Urbana Champaign.

Teenstra, M.D., 1835, *De landbouw in de kolonie Suriname voorafgegaan door eene geschied- en natuurkundige beschouwing dier kolonie*, vols. 1-2, Groningen (library.wur.nl).

Teenstra, M.D., 1842, *De Negerslaven in de Kolonie Suriname, en de uitbreiding van het christendom onder de heidensche bevolking*, Dordrecht (dbnl.org).

Theije, M. de, 2007, 'De Brazilianen stelen al ons goud!'; Braziliaanse migranten in stad en binnenland', in: *OSO, Tijdschrift voor Surinamistiek en het Caraïbisch gebied*, vol. 26(1), 81-99 (dbnl.org).

Thoden van Velzen, H.U.E. & W. van Wetering, 1988, *The great father and the danger: Religious cults, material forces and collective fantasies in the world of the Surinamese Maroons*, Leiden.

Thoden van Velzen, H.U.E., 1990, 'Hekserijgeloof', in: *Skeptische Notities*, vol. 5, 1-13 (skepsis.nl/hekserijgeloof).

Thoden van Velzen, H.U.E., 2003, *Een koloniaal drama. De grote staking van de Marron vrachtvaarders, 1921*, Utrecht.

Thoden van Velzen, H.U.E. & W. van Wetering, 2004, *In the Shadow of the Oracle, Religion as Politics in a Suriname Maroon Society*, Long Grove.

Thoden van Velzen, H.U.E. & W. Hoogbergen, 2011, *Een zwarte vrijstaat in Suriname. De Okaanse samenleving in de 18e eeuw*, Leiden.

Thomson, J.R., 1911, *Waar gaat 't heen*, Paramaribo (delpher.nl).

Tjon Sie Fat, P.B., 2007, "Immigratie van Chinezen schijnt de laatste jaren toe te nemen': het anti-Chinese discours in Suriname', in: *OSO, Tijdschrift voor Surinamistiek en het Caraïbisch gebied*, vol. 26 (1), 61-80 (dbnl.org).

Tjon Sie Fat, P.B., 2009, *Chinese New Migrants in Suriname. The Inevibility of Ethnic Performing*, PhD thesis University of Amsterdam, Amsterdam (books.google.com).

Toes, J., 1992, *Wanklanken rond een wingewest in de nadagen van de Surinaamse slavernij*, PhD thesis Vrije Universiteit Amsterdam, Hoorn. Torfs, J., 1969, *Evaluation of the educational system and plans of Surinam*, Unesco-report, Paris (unesdoc.unesco.org).

Traa, A. van, 1946, *Suriname, 1900-1940*, Deventer.

Udemans, G., 1655, *'t Geestelyk roer van 't coopmans schip*, Dordrecht. (books.google.com).

Unger, B. & M. Siegel, 2006, *The Netherlands-Suriname corridor for workers remittances, prospects for remittances when migration ties loosen*, Utrecht (brigitteunger.nl/projects-working-papers).

Valentine, D., 2016, *The CIA as organized crime: How illegal operations corrupt America and the World*, Atlanta.

Verberk, G., P. Scheepers & M. Hassankhan, 1997, 'Etnocentrisme in Suriname', in: *OSO, Tijdschrift voor Surinamistiek en het Caraïbisch gebied*, vol. 16(2), 133-146 (dbnl.org).

Verhey, E. & G. van Westerloo, G. van, 1983, *Het legergroene Suriname*, Amsterdam.

Verkade-Cartier van Dissel, E.F., 1937, *De mogelijkheid van landbouw-kolonisatie voor blanken in Suriname*, PhD thesis Utrecht University, Amsterdam (delpher.nl).

Vianen, B., 1997 (1971) *Strafhok*, Schoorl.

Vianen, B., 1988 (1969) *Sarnami, hai*, Haarlem (dbnl.org).

Vlier, N.G., 1840, 'Redevoering over den invloed van de beoefening der menschlievendheid op het wezenlijk geluk' (speech to the Society for the Common Good, 15 april 1839), in: *Surinaamsche Almanak* 1840, 161-186 (dbnl.org).

Vink, S., 1997, *Suriname door het oog van Julius Muller. Fotografie 1882-1902*, Amsterdam.

Vink, W., 2010, *Creole Jews. Negotiating community in colonial Suriname*, PhD Leiden University, Leiden.

Voorhoeve, J. & H.C. van Renselaar, 1962, 'Messianism and Nationalism in Surinam', in: *Bijdragen tot de Taal-, Land-, en Volkenkunde*, vol. 118(2), 193-216 (brill.com).

Voorhoeve, J. & U.M. Lichtveld, 1975, *Creole Drum. An Anthology of Creole Literature in Surinam*, New Haven/London (dbnl.org).

Voort, J.P. van de, 1973, *De Westindische plantages van 1720 tot 1795. Financiën en handel*, PhD thesis Katholieke Universiteit Nijmegen, Eindhoven (repository.ubn.ru.nl).

Vries, E. de, 2005, *Suriname na de binnenlandse oorlog*, Amsterdam.

Vries, E. de, 2021, *Hans Valk. Over een Nederlandse kolonel en een coup in Suriname (1980)*, Zutphen.

Vrijman, L.C., 1937, *Slavenhalers en Slavenhandel*, Amsterdam (delpher.nl).

Vuijsje, H., 2019, *God zij met ons Suriname. Religie als vloek en zegen*, Amsterdam.

Waal Malefijt, A.M. de, 1963, *The Javanese of Surinam. Segment of a plural society*, Assen.

Waesberge, R. van, 1976, *Suriname, een stukje Derde Wereld*, Den Haag.

Walle, J. van de, 1946, *Rapport over de sociale structuur van Suriname en Curaçao*, Paramaribo.

Ward, J.R., 1988, *British West Indian Slavery 1750-1834. The process of amelioration*, Oxford.

Warnsinck, J.C.M., 1936, *Abraham Crijnssen, De verovering van Suriname en de aanslag op Virginie*, Amsterdam.

Warren, G., 1667, *An Impartial Description of Surinam Upon The Continent of Guiana in America*, London, (books.google.com).

Watson, A, 1989 (2012), *Slave Law in the Americas*, Athens, GA.

Wekker, G., 2010, 'Bouterse for president. Een cultuurkritische interpretatie', in: Leerdam, J. & N. Beyer (eds.), *Suriname en ik. Persoonlijke verhalen van bekende Surinamers over hun vaderland*, Amsterdam.

Wekker, J., 1990, 'Indiaanse geografische namen in Suriname en de overige Guyana's', in: *OSO, Tijdschrift voor Surinamistiek en het Caraïbisch gebied*, vol. 9(1), 7-24 (dbnl.org).

Wekker, J., 1992, 'Archiefdocumenten verhalen over indianen', in: *SWI Forum*, vol. 9 (1-2), 99-127.

Wekker, J., 1993, 'Indianen en Pacificatie', in: *OSO, Tijdschrift voor Surinamistiek en het Caraïbisch gebied*, vol. 12(2), 174-186 (dbnl.org).

Welten, A, 1998, 'Geen bakra's maar boeroes. Nederlandse boerenkolonisten en hun Surinaamse nakomelingen', in: *OSO, Tijdschrift voor Surinamistiek en het Caraïbisch gebied*, vol. 17(2) 181-193. (dbnl.org).

West, O., 2022, 'Suriname to offer creditors oil-linked bonds, sees 'unique' ESG opportunity in restructuring', in: *GlobalCapital*, 8 February 2022 (globalcapital.com).

Westerloo, G. van, 1993, *De laatste dagen van een kolonel. Surinaamse notities*, Amsterdam.

Wetering, W. van & H.U.E. Thoden van Velzen, 2013, *Een zwarte vrijstaat. De Okaanse samenleving in de 19e en 20e eeuw*, Leiden.

Willemsen, G.F.W., 1980, *Koloniale Politiek en Transformatieprocessen in een Plantage-economie, 1873-1940*, PhD thesis Erasmus Universiteit Rotterdam, Rotterdam.

Williams, E., *Capitalism and Slavery*, Chapel Hill, 1944.

Wilson, P.J., 1969, 'Reputation and respectability: a suggestion for Caribbean ethnology', in: *Man*, New Series, vol. 4, no. 1, 70-84 (ur.booksc.org/book/47271381/20813e).

Wilson, P.J., 1973, *Crab antics. The social anthropology of English-speaking Negro societies of the Caribbean*, New Haven.

Winter, J.M. van, 1952, 'De openbare mening in Nederland over de afschaffing der slavernij', in: *New West Indian Guide/Nieuwe West-Indische Gids*, vol. 34(1), 61-90 (brill.com).

Wiznitzer, A., 1954, 'The number of Jews in Brazil', in: *Jewish Social Studies*, vol. 16(2), 107-114 (penelope.uchicago.edu).

Wolbers, J., 1861, *Geschiedenis van Suriname*, Amsterdam (dbnl.org).

Wooding, C.J. , 1972, *Winti, Een Afro-Amerikaanse godsdienst in Suriname. Een cultureel historische analyse van de religieuze verschijnselen in de Para*, PhD thesis University of Amsterdam, Meppel.

Wooding, C.J., 1981, *Evolving culture. A cross-cultural study of Suriname, West-Africa and the Caribbean*, Washington.

Woodly-Sobhie, R., 2012, *Armoedemetingen in Suriname*, Paramaribo.

Woodward, B., 1987, *Veil: The secret wars of the CIA, 1981-1987*, New York.

Zamuel, H.S., 1994, *Johannes King. Profeet en apostel in het Surinaamse Bosland*, PhD thesis Utrecht University, Zoetermeer.

Zee, H. van der, 2000, *'s Heeren slaaf. Het dramatische leven van Jacobus Capitein*, Amsterdam.

Zeefuik, K.A., 1973, *Hernhutter zending en Haagsche maatschappij. Een hoofdstuk uit de geschiedenis van zending en emancipatie in Suriname*, PhD thesis Utrecht University, Utrecht.

Ziel, H.F. (ed.), 1973, *Life at Maripaston* (incl. ms. in Sranantongo written by Johannes King). Den Haag (library.oapen.org).

Zijlstra, S., 2015, *Anglo-Dutch Suriname: Ethnic interaction and colonial transition in the Caribbean, 1651-1682*, PhD thesis University of Amsterdam, Amsterdam.

Zunder, A., 2010, *Herstelbetalingen. De 'Wiedergutmachung' voor de schade die Suriname en haar bevolking hebben geleden onder het Nederlands kolonialisme*, Den Haag.

Sourced Documents

Algemeen Bureau voor de Statistiek (ABS; General Bureau of Statistics), *Suriname in cijfers*, No. 185-99-01, Paramaribo, 1999.

Algemeen Bureau voor de Statistiek (ABS; General Bureau of Statistics), *Suriname in cijfers. Inkomensongelijkheid en Inkomensverdeling in Suriname*, nr. 236/2007-06, Paramaribo, 2007.

Algemeen Bureau voor de Statistiek (ABS; General Bureau of Statistics), *Suriname in cijfers*, nr. 251/2008-10, Paramaribo, 2008.

Algemeen Bureau voor de Statistiek (ABS; General Bureau of Statistics), *Suriname Census 2012*, vol. 1, September 2013 (statistics-suriname.org/wp-content/uploads/2019/05).

Algemene Rekenkamer (Dutch General Bureau of Audit), *Verslag 1982*, The Hague (zoek. officielebekendmakingen.nl/uitgebreidzoeken/historisch).

Amnesty International, *Suriname, violations of human rights*, 1987 (decembermoorden.com).

Bouterse, D., president, *Inauguration speech*, Paramaribo 12 August 2010 (caribbeanelections.com).

Bouterse, D., president, *Regeringsverklaring 2010-2015* (*Government Statement*), Paramaribo, 1 October 2010 (dna.sr/media/89565/jaarrede_president.pdf).

Bouterse, D., president, *Speech on the occasion of the 35th anniversary of independence*, 25 November 2010.

Bouterse, D., president, *Speech at the opening of the parliamentary year*, Paramaribo, 29 September 2011 (dna.sr/media/89488/jaarrede_2012.pdf).

Centrale Bank van Suriname, *Jaarrapporten* (Annual Reports). (cbvs.sr/publicaties/cbvs-rapporten/jaarrapporten).

Chin A Sen, H., *Regeringsverklaring 1980 en urgentieprogramma van het kabinet Chin A Sen* (Government declaration 1980), 1 May 1980.

Comité Christelijke Kerken (Committee Christian Churches). *Commentaar op concept basisuitgangspunten en hoofdlijnenprogramma van de 25 Februari Beweging* (Comments on draft basic principles and outline programme of the February 25 Movement), Paramaribo, 25 November 1983.

Comité Christelijke Kerken (Committee Christian Churches), *Waarachtigheid, Behoorlijk Bestuur en Welzijn* (Truthfulness, Good Governance and Well-being), memorandum, Paramaribo, 21 February 1998.

Commissie van onderzoek (Commission of Enquiry), *Onderzoek naar de rol van de Nederlandse militaire missie in Suriname voor, tijdens en na de staatsgreep van 25 februari 1980* (Investigation into the role of the Dutch military mission in Suriname before, during and after the coup d'état of 25 February 1980), The Hague 1984.

Conservation International Suriname, *Natuurpublicatie CIS*, 5th edition, 2020 (conservation.org/suriname/news-publication).

Coopers & Lybrand Deloitte, *A programme for adjustment and structural adaptation in Suriname*, Paramaribo, 1990.

Court-martial (Krijgsraad), *KRG-2019-46*, verdict against Desi Bouterse Paramaribo, 29 November 2019 (rechtspraak.sr).

De Surinaamsche Bank, *Annual Report 1998*, Paramaribo.

EPA Monitoring, *Trends in the EU Rice Market 2019*.
epamonitoring.net. *Gedenkboek 50 jaar Vooruitstrevende Hervormings-Partij VHP*, (Memorial book 50 years VHP), Paramaribo 1999.

Grondwet (Constitution) Suriname (dna.sr/wetgeving).

Hakrinbank, *Annual Report 2010*.

Handelingen van het parlement (M*inutes of Parliament*) and other parliamentary documents, various years (zoek.officielebekendmakingen.nl/uitgebreidzoeken/historisch).

Human Rights Watch, World Report 1992 (hrw.org/reports/1992/WR92/index.htm).

IAMGOLD, *Annual Report*s (iamgold.com/English/investors/financials).

IMF, *Various Reports on Suriname* (imf.org).

Inter-American Commission on Human Rights (IACHR), OAS, *Report on the human rights situation in Suriname*, Washington, 5 October 1983 (cidh.org/countryrep/Suriname83eng/TOC.htm).

Inter-American Commission on Human Rights (IACHR), *Second report on the human rights situation in Suriname*, Washington, 2 October 1985 (cidh.org/countryrep/Suriname85eng/chap.7.htm).

Inter-American Commission on Human Rights (IACHR), Annual Report 1986-1987, ch. IV, Suriname (cidh.oas.org/annual.eng.htm).

Inter-American Commission on Human Rights (IACHR), Annual Report 1990-1991, ch. IV, Suriname (cidh.oas.org/annual.eng.htm).

Inter-American Commission on Human Rights (IACHR), Annual Report 1991, ch. IV, Suriname (cidh.oas.org/annual.eng.htm).

Inter-American Court of Human Rights, *Case of the Moiwana Community v. Suriname, Judgement of June 15, 2005 (Preliminary Objections, Merits, Reparations and Costs)* (corteidh.or.cr/docs/casos/articulos/seriec_124_ing.pdf).

Inter-American Court of Human Rights, *Case of the Moiwana Community v. Suriname, Judgement of February 8 2006 (Interpretation of the Judgement of Merits, Reparations and Costs)* (corteidh.or.cr/docs/casos/articulos/seriec_145_ing.pdf).

Inter-American Court of Human Rights, *Case of the Saramaka People v. Suriname, Judgment of November 28, 2007* (corteidh.or.cr/docs/casos/articulos/seriec_172_ing.pdf).

Inter-American Court of Human Rights, *Case of the Kaliña and Lokono Peoples v. Suriname, Judgement of November25, 2015 (Merits, Reparations and Costs)* (corteidh.or.cr/docs/casos/articulos/seriec_309_ing.pdf).

Inter-American Development Bank, *Suriname: Education Sector Study*, Washington, 1998.

Inter-American Development Bank, *Suriname: country strategy with the IDB 2007-2010*, Washington, June 2007 (issuu.com/idb_publications/docs/policiestra_en_16198).

Inter-American Development Bank, *Evaluation of IDB Action in the Initiative for Integration of Regional Infrastructure in South America (IIRSA)*, April 2008 (publications.iadb.org).

Inter-American Development Bank, *IDB Country Strategy with the Republic of Suriname 2011-2015*, Washington 2011 (dbdocs.iadb.org/wsdocs/getdocument.aspx?docnum=36533868).

Inter-American Development Bank, *Returns to education in Suriname*, Washington, June 2013 (publications.iadb.org).

Inter-American Development Bank, *Estimating the size of the informal economy in Caribbean States*, Washington, 2017 (publications.iadb.org).

Inter-American Development Bank, *State of the Climate Report, Suriname. Summary for Policy Makers*, July 2021 (publications.iadb.org).

Inter-American Development Bank, *Climate change impacts on hydropower and electricity demand in Suriname*, May 2022 (publications.iadb.org).

Koloniale Verslagen (Colonial Reports), various years (zoek.officielebekendmakingen.nl/ uitgebreidzoeken/historisch).

List of allocated gold concessions in the Areas of Interest of IAMGOLD and Newmont, appendix of a letter sent by President Desi Bouterse to Parliament, Paramaribo, 7 June 2013 (surinamenieuwscentrale.com/ overzicht-uitgegeven-concessies-de-areas-interestvan-iamgold-en-newmont).

Manifest van de Revolutie (Manifesto of the Revolution), Paramaribo, 1 May 1981 (kennisaanval.blogspot.com/2011/01/manifest-van-de-revolutie-in-suriname.html).

Ministry of Development Cooperation, *Een rijke relatie: Nederland en Suriname, heden en toekomst* (policy memorandum), The Hague, 4 June 2004, Kamerstuk (Parliamentary Document) 20361, no. 116 (zoek.officielebekendmakingen.nl/kst-20361-116.html).

Ministry of Agriculture, Livestock and Fisheries, *Beleidsnota LVV 2010-2015* (Policy Note LVV 2010-2015), Paramaribo, 2010 (lvv.gov.sr/media/1177/lvv-beleidsnota-2010-2015.pdf).

Ministry of Agriculture, Livestock and Fisheries, *Beleidswitboek Rijst* (Policy White Paper Rice), prepared for FAO, Paramaribo, September 2011 (docplayer.nl/90531663-Preparation-of-sub-sector-white-papers-fao-project-tcp-sur-3301-1-ministerie-van-landbouw-veeteelt-en-visserij-beleidswitboek-rijst.html).

Ministry of Education, *Suriname voorwaarts!* (literacy campaign Alpha '84) Paramaribo, 1984.

Ministry of Education and Community Development in Suriname, *Educational development in the Republic of Suriname* (report prepared for UNESCO, and presented at the 47th session of the International Conference on Education), Paramaribo 2004 (kennisbanksu.com/onderwijs).

Ministry of Finance and Planning, *Budget 2020 Wijzigingsnota* (Note of Amendment), Paramaribo, 17 November 2020.

Ministry of Finance and Planning, *Crisis- en Herstelplan 2020-2022* (Crisis and Recovery Plan), Paramaribo, 10 May 2021 (dna.sr/media-en-documentatie/ overige-documenten).

Minutes of deliberations of the Den Uyl government in the years 1973 and 1974, Nationaal Archief (National Archives), inv. nr. 2.02.05.02.

Moiwana '86 (Human Rights Bureau), *In memoriam Herman Gooding*, Paramaribo, 1990.

Moiwana '86 (Human Rights Bureau), *Mensenrechten 1991 Suriname* (*Human Rights 1991 Suriname*), Paramaribo, 1992.

Moiwana '86 (Human Rights Bureau), *Memre Moiwana*, Paramaribo 1992.

Newmont, *Annual Report 2019* (newmont.com).

NIKOS (NGO), *Opinion Poll in Paramaribo, June-July 2016* (nikos.sr).

NPS, *Verkiezingsmanifest 2010* (Electoral Manifest 2010) (sites.google.com/site/2010nps/ Downloads/documenten).

Pamphlet on Dutch investment funds and planters in Suriname, *Brief van eenen Utrechtsen heer* [...] *aan zynen vriend te Utrecht*[...] (Letter from an Utrecht gentleman [...] to his friend in Utrecht), Utrecht, 1777 (google.books.com).

Planbureau Suriname, *MOP, Meerjaren Ontwikkelingsplan 2001-2005* (Multi-annual Development Plan), Paramaribo 2001.

Planbureau Suriname, *MOP, Meerjaren Ontwikkelingsplan 2006-2011* (Multi-annual Development Plan), Paramaribo 2006 (swris.sr/wp-content/uploads/2017/ 12/ Meerjaren-ontwikkelingsplan.pdf).

Planbureau Suriname. *MOP, Meerjaren Ontwikkelingsplan 2012-2016* (Multi-annual Development Plan), *Suriname in transformatie,* Paramaribo 2012 (adoc.pub_ ontwikkelingsplan-suriname-in-transformatie.pdf).

Planbureau Suriname, *MOP, Meerjaren Ontwikkelingsplan 2022-2026* (Multi-annual Development Plan), *Omdenken, Verbinden, Doen* (Re-thinking, Connecting, Doing), Paramaribo 2021 (dna.sr/media-en-documentatie/overige-documenten).

Programma en Statuten van de 25 Februari Beweging (VFB), Paramaribo, 12 May 1984.

Raamverdrag inzake vriendschap en nauwere samenwerking tussen het Koninkrijk der Nederlanden en de Republiek Suriname (Framework Agreement on friendship and closer cooperation between the Kingdom of the Netherlands and the Republic of Suriname), The Hague, 18 June 1992 (wetten.overheid.nl/BWBV0001175/1995-05-01).

Radio address by Queen Wilhelmina, 7 December 1942 (houseofdavid.ca/queen.htm).

Rapport van de commissie inventarisatie staatsschuld (Report by the Public Debt Inventory Committee), Paramaribo, 23 March 2001.

Reagan, R., president, *Address at the U.N. General Assembly*, New York, 26 September 1983 (reaganlibrary.gov/archives).

Regeerakkoord 2010-2015 (Coalition Agreement 2010-2015), Paramaribo, 21 August 2010 (gov.sr/media/1033/1_regeerakkoord_2010-15.pdf).

Rekenkamer van Suriname (Court of Audit of Suriname), *Report 1980-1987, Annual Report1992, Annual Report 1997*, Paramaribo.

Santokhi, Ch., president, *Inauguration speech*, 16 July 2020 (hindorama.com/inaugurele-rede-president-van-suriname-en-acceptatie-speech-chandrikapersad-santokhi).

Santokhi, Ch., *Jaarrede 2020 in het parlement* (Annual Address 2020 in Parliament), Paramaribo, 29 September 2020. (dna.sr/media-en-documentatie/jaarrede-president).

Speciale onderzoekscommissie (Special enquiry committee) *Domeingrond voor alle Surinamers* (Land of the state domain for all Surinamese), 1 March 2011; unpublished; see: *Parbode*, 1 June 2011 (parbode.com).

Staatsolie, Annual Report, various years (staatsolie.com).

State Department, *2017 International Narcotics Control Strategy Report, vol. 1*, Washington, March 2, 2017 (state.gov).

Suriname Studie Syndicaat, *Rapport der studiecommissie naar aanleiding van haar bezoek aan Suriname*, Den Haag, 1919 (delpher.nl).

The World Bank, *Suriname. A Strategy for Sustainable Growth and Poverty Reduction. Country Economic Memorandum*, Washington, 31 March, 1998.

The World Bank, *Doing Business Report*, various years (doingbusiness.org/en/reports/ global-reports/doing-business-yyyy).

The World Bank, *Suriname sector competitiveness analysis, identifying opportunities to investment and diversification in the agribusiness and extractive sectors*, Washington, 2017 (openknowledge.worldbank.org).

Treaty on development cooperation Netherlands-Suriname (*Overeenkomst Nederland-Suriname betreffende ontwikkelingsamenwerking*), *25 November 1975* (wetten. overheid.nl/BWBV0003908/1975-11-25).

Venetiaan, R., president, *Regeringsverklaring 2000-2005* (Government Statement), Paramaribo, 15 November 2000.

Verkiezingsprogramma (Electoral Program) *Mega Combinatie 2010-2020* (caribbeanelections.com).

Wako, A., *Report by the Special Rapporteur on summary or arbitrary executions*, Annex 5, Visit by the Special Rapporteur to Suriname, United Nations Commission on Human Rights, 12 February 1985 (decembermoorden.com).

Wako, A, *Report by the Special Rapporteur on summary or arbitrary executions,* UN Commission on Human Rights, 44th session, 19 January 1988 (digitallibrary.un.org/record/154840?ln=en).

Warwick Research Institute, *A programme for structural adjustment*, Paramaribo,1992.

Wijdenbosch, J., president, *Regeringsverklaring 1996-2001* (Government Statement 1996-2001), Paramaribo, 1 October 1996.

WikiLeaks, diplomatic cables sent by the US embassy in Paramaribo during the Venetiaan-led government: *Possible Venezuelan meddling*, 07-11-2005 (wikileaks. dic.at/tag/NS_0.html); *President Venetiaan's government facing low approval ratings*, 15-02-2006 (wikileaks.org/cablegate); *Increased Venezuelan activism in Suriname has mixed success*, 9-06-2006 (wikileaks.org/cablegate); *Justice Minister talks privately about strikes, threats, politics, and the December Murder trial in Suriname*, 4-12-2007 (wikileaks.org/cablegate); *Bouterse retracts slanderous statements against Justice Minister, but will appeal court decision*, 24-09-2008 (wikileaks.org/cablegate); *Suriname elections: voting by ethnicity remains commonplace*, 2-10-2009 (wikileaks. org/cablegate).

WikiLeaks, several diplomatic cables sent by US embassies located in the Caribbean on the Guyanese drug trafficker Shaheed 'Roger' Khan and his relationship with Desi Bouterse (wikileaks.org/cablegate); sent from Georgetown: *Shaheed 'Roger' Khan: Guyana's own Escobar*, 1-02-2006; *Request for evaluation of security information*, 24-02-2006; *Interagency effort to apprehend Guyanese narco-criminals*, 11-05-2006; Guyana response: *Desi Bouterse and Shaheed Roger Khan activities*, 29-06-2006; sent from Paramaribo: *Desi Bouterse and Shaheed Roger Khan activities*, 23-06-2006; sent from Port of Spain: *Extraordinary cooperation from T&T on moving narcotrafficker to the U.S.*, 6-07-2006.

WWF, *Healthy Rivers, Healthy People, addressing the mercury crisis in the Amazon*, Report, 2018 (wwfint.awsassets.panda.org/downloads/healthy_rivers_healthy_people.pdf).

Zeeuws Archief (Zeeland Archives), letters sent by governors of Suriname et al., GIDS 102 Gids Staten van Zeeland en Suriname, 1667-1684 (1692): *Governor Philip Julius Lichtenberg to the States of Zeeland*, 18-03-1669 (ZA, 2.1., 2035-124); *Governor Pieter Versterre to the States of Zeeland*, 25-03-1675 (ZA, 2.1., 2035-249/250/251); *Governor Pieter Versterre to an unknown*, 4-07-1675 (ZA, 2.1., 2035-260/261/262);

*Governor Pieter Versterre to the States of Zeeland,*16-12-1675 (ZA, 2.1., 2035-271); *Governor Johannes Heinsius to the States of Zeeland,* 3-05-1679 (ZA, 2.1., 2035-328); *Commander Abel Thisso to incoming Governor Heinsius,* 18-12-1678 (ZA 2.1., 2035-282/307/308/309); *Governor Jonathan Atkins of Barbados to Johannes Heinsius,* 28-05-1679 (ZA, 2.1., 2035-331). Digital access: archieven.nl/nl/zoeken? mivast=0&mizig=210&miadt=239&miaet=1&micode=GIDS102&minr=2721419& miview=inv2&milang=nl

Sourced newspapers and (news)websites
ABC Radio (abcsuriname.com).
Conservation International Suriname (conservation.org/suriname).
Dagblad Suriname (dbsuriname.com).
De Volkskrant (delpher.nl - 1919-1995; volkskrant.nl from 1996 on).
De Ware Tijd (dwtonline.com).
De West (dagbladdewest.com/yyyy/mm/dd).
EPA Monitoring (epamonitoring.net).
Global Environment Facility, GEF (thegef.org/country/suriname).
Inter-American Development Bank (publications.iadb.org).
International Monetary Fund (imf.org).
Kaieteur News (kaieteurnewsonline.com).
De Leidse Courant (leiden.courant.nu).
NRC Handelsblad (nrc.nl/handelsblad).
Parbode (parbode.com).
Omhoog (omhoog.org).
REDD+ Suriname (surinameredd.org/en/reddplus-suriname).
Staatscourant (staatscourant.nl).
Starnieuws (starnieuws.com).
State Department (state.gov).
Surinaamsche Courant. Gouvernements Advertentie Blad (delpher.nl).
Surinaamsche Almanach (dbnl.org).
The Economist (economist.com).
The Guardian (theguardian.com).
The New York Times (nyt.com).
The World Bank (openknowledge.worldbank.org).
The World Bank Open Data (data.worldbank.org).
Trouw (trouw.nl).
Vrij Nederland (vn.nl).
Waterkant (waterkant.net).

Index of persons

Morales, Evo   393

Mungra, Alwin   275, 344

Mungra, Atta   345-346, 349, 351, 362

Naarendorp, Harvey   302-303, 313

Naipaul, V.S.   7, 447

Nassy, David C. (17th century)   48, 109

Nassy, David C. (18th century)   49

Nay, John   401

Neijhorst, Henry   305

Noriega Manuel   331-332

Oemrawsingh, Sugrim   308

Ojeda, Alonso de   9

Ommeren, H.C. van   261

Ommeren, H.J. van   215

Oostindie, G.J.   447

Ormskerk, Fred   299

Pahlad, George   346, 352

Pakosie, André   386

Palthe Wesenhagen, J.C.   100-102, 165

Pengel, Johan Adolf (Jopie)   260-263, 265-269, 276, 287, 292 380, 404

Persad, Sital   218

Pichot, Samuel   38-39

Pitt, William   159

Playfair, Frank   335

Plessis, Salomon du   38-44

Pokie, Diana   416

Pompeo, Mike   416

Prade, Hans   356

Present   105

Priary   18

Price R.   84, 110, 112, 141, 385

Price S.   84

Pronk, J.   279, 293, 333, 358, 362

Punwasi, S.   395

Quassie   125

Quay, Jan de   267

Radakishun, Pertab   315, 346, 349, 350, 352

Rahman, Lesly   308

Raleigh, sir Walter   9

Rambocus, Soerendre   297, 304, 308, 377

Rame, Maurits de   15

Raveles, Robin (alias Dobru)   266

Ravenswaay, Rick van   422

Raye, Joan   34-35, 37, 62

Reagan, Ronald   309-311, 332

Rensch, Stanley   329

LIST OF ABBREVIATIONS

ABOP	Algemene Bevrijdings- en Ontwikkelingspartij
ABS	Algemeen Bureau voor de Statistiek
AC	A-Combinatie
ARP	Anti Revolutionaire Partij
ASFA	Associatie van Surinaamse Fabrikanten
BEP	Broederschap en Eenheid in de Politiek
BVD	Basispartij voor Vernieuwing en Democratie
CARICOM	Caribbean Community
CBvS	Centrale Bank van Suriname
CCK	Comité van Christelijke Kerken
CHU	Christelijk Historische Unie
CIA	Central Intelligence Agency
CIS	Conservation International Suriname
CLO	Centrale Landsdienaren Organisatie
CPH	Communistische Partij Holland
C47	Centrale 47
DA91	Democratisch Alternatief 91
DEA	Drugs Enforcement Administration
DNP	Democratisch Nationaal Platform
DOE	Partij voor Democratie en Ontwikkeling door Eenheid
EBG	Evangelische Broedergemeente
EBS	Energiebedrijf Suriname
EEC	European Economic Community
EF	Eenheidsfront
EU	European Union
FAI	Food and Agriculture Industries
FAL	Federatie van Arme Landbouwers
FAO	Food and Agriculture Organisation
GDP	Gross Domestic Product
GEF	Global Environment Facility
H-JPP	Hindostaans-Javaanse Politieke Partij
HPP	Hindostaanse Progressieve Partij
HPP	Hernieuwde Progressieve Partij
HVA	Handels Vereniging Amsterdam
IACHR	Inter-American Commission on Human Rights
	Inter-American Court of Human Rights
IDB	Inter American Development Bank
IDOS	Institute for Development Oriented Studies
IMF	Internationaal Monetair Fonds
IIRSA	Initiative for the Integration of the Regional Infrastructure of South America
KTPI	Kaum Tani Persatuan Indonesia (Indonesian Farmers Party)
KVP	Katholieke Volkspartij

MC	Mega Combinatie (before: Millennium Combinatie)
MOP	Meerjaren Ontwikkelingsplan
NACO	Norwegian Aluminium Company
NBS	Nationalistische Beweging Suriname
NDP	Nationale Democratische Partij
NF	Nieuw Front
NHM	Nederlandsche Handel-Maatschappij
NMR	Nationale Militaire Raad
NPK	Nationale Partij Kombinatie
NPS	Nationale Partij Suriname
OAS	Organization of American States
OSAV	Organisatie van Samenwerkende Autonome Vakbonden
PALU	Progressieve Arbeiders- en Landbouwers Unie
PNP	Progressieve Nationale Partij
PNR	Partij Nationalistische Republiek
PL	Pertjajah Luhur (Full of Confidence)
PROSUR	Forum for the Progress and Integration of South America
PSV	Progressieve Surinaamse Volkspartij
PvdA	Partij van de Arbeid
PVF	Politieke Vleugel van de FAL
PWI-Bank	Particuliere Westindische Bank
REDD+	Reducing Emissions from Deforestation and Forest Degradation
RTC	Ronde Tafel Conferentie
RVP	Revolutionaire Volkspartij
SAWO	Surinaamsche Algemeene Werkers Organisatie
SBM	Surinaamsche Bauxiet Maatschappij
SDAP	Sociaal Democratische Arbeiders Partij
	Surinaamsche Democratische Arbeiders Partij
SDP	Surinaamse Democratische Partij
SNA	Suriname News Agency
SPA	Surinaamse Partij van de Arbeid
SRD	Surinamese dollar
SRI	Sarekat Rakjat Indonesia (People's Association Indonesia)
SVB	Surinaamsche Volksbond
SWC	Surinaamsch Werkloozen Comité
UNASUR	Union of South American Nations
VES	Vereniging van Economisten in Suriname
VFB	25-Februaribeweging
VHP	Verenigde Hindostaanse Partij, Vatan Hitkari Partij (from 1966), Vooruitstrevende Hervormingspartij (from 1973)
VIDS	Vereniging van Inheemse Dorpshoofden in Suriname
VOC	Verenigde Oost-Indische Compagnie
VSB	Vereniging Surinaams Bedrijfsleven
VVD	Volkspartij voor Vrijheid en Democratie
WIC	West-Indische Compagnie
WWF	World Wide Fund for Nature

A History of Suriname